P9-CAO-324

RABBIT, JETTA & SCIROSCO.
THE COMPLEXITIES THEREOF.

HOW TO KEEP YOUR VOLKSWAGEN ALIVE

·OR·

POOR RICHARD'S RABBIT BOOK

·BEING·
A MANUAL OF
STEP BY STEP PROCEDURES FOR THE COMPLEAT IDIOT

BY
RICHARD SEALEY

ILLUSTRATED BY
PETER ASCHWANDEN

JOHN MUIR PUBLICATIONS
SANTA FE NEW MEXICO

Copyright © 1980, 1986 by John Muir Publications
All rights reserved

Published by   John Muir Publications, Inc.
                P.O. Box 613
                Santa Fe, New Mexico 87504

Library of Congress Catalogue Card No. 79-91278
ISBN 0-912528-47-8

First Edition May 1980
Second Printing November 1980
Revised Edition May 1982
Revised Edition February 1986

Tune Up Your Rabbit Book

Changes and Additions to the 1986 edition

Kindly turn to page 398 and take a few moments to read and follow the instructions given in **Procedure 00** on updating this edition with the latest changes and additions covering all models through 1985.

PLEASE NOTE:

The repair and maintenance procedures in this book are based on the training, personal experiences and research of the author, and on recommendations of responsible automotive professionals. If you follow all the directions specifically, you should be able to complete the procedures in this book successfully and safely.

Please understand that the recommendations and warnings herein cannot cover all conceivable ways in which service procedures may be done, or every possible hazard and risk involved. The author, illustrator and publisher are not responsible for any adverse consequences that may occur in connection with the procedures explained in this book. Please do not use the book unless you are willing to assume the risk of adverse consequences. We urge you to consult with a qualified mechanic before using any procedure where these is any question as to its completeness or appropriateness.

We especially advise you to heed all WARNINGS and CAUTIONS, to use all recommended safety precautions called for throughout the book—and to use common sense.

table of Contents

Introduction

BY EVE MUIR

This book, like its predecessor "How To Keep Your Volkswagen Alive" by John Muir, helps bridge the communications gap between us and our machines. In this case the new, water-cooled generation of Volkswagens: Rabbits, Sciroccos and Jettas.

Cars are designed, built and used by humans like us, and it's up to us to get on *their* wavelength. We cannot expect them, or any other machine, to get on ours. However, communication is sometimes hampered by our lack of attention, fear of the unknown lurking beneath the hood, and a phenomenon Rolf Cahn calls "calculated incompetence." If, upon being asked to cook, a person burns the rice, you can imagine how often they're asked to cook. When I knew nothing about cars I never had to change the oil, much less haul the engine out and in. On the other hand, the freedom I feel because I've learned to carry a spare V-belt and can change a broken one (when no one else is around) makes me feel more competent and less paranoid when the dreadful break happens.

Having this book in the car along with some tools and spare parts will help *any* Rabbit or Scirocco owner feel less helpless. It's a case of, "If I, the original idiot, can do it, anyone can."

Driving a hassle-free car includes not only listening to it when it's well so you can tell by changes in sounds when it's ailing, but also using your nose to smell changes, especially heat; your eyes—warning lights; touch for changes in shifting, steering, braking; your brain and feeling antennae for awareness of the road. Watch the odometer and do the maintenance on time. Become in tune, in other words, with the beast that transports you.

John and I met Richard Sealey, a man of many talents including race car mechanic-ing, in England. We fell in love with the whole family immediately, so a year later when Alice, Richard, Amber and Jade decided to settle on this side of the Atlantic, Richard and John thought to continue the "How To Keep Your VW Alive" series by collaborating on the Rabbit book. It was wonderful to have Richard's fresh energy and enthusiasm to go with.

John died in November, 1977, and the project became Richard's, with the help of Peter Aschwanden whose sketches, diagrams and cartoons make the work easier and more fun. And as John used to say, "We gotta learn to have fun with everything we do."

Richard has also had the help of everyone here at JMP, Inc. For example, we bought an old beat up Rabbit and proceeded to take turns driving it around the ruts of Santa Fe. Almost daily a "dreadful" happened: the muffler fell off, the steering went haywire, the handbrake cable broke, and on and on. The cry was, "Richard, the Rabbit is stuck on the corner of Monte Sol and Old Santa Fe Trail. HELP!" . . . Poor Richard.

We also offered unlimited editorial advice which often had Richard tearing out his abundant hair, but we were there to try Procedures and generally encourage as well.

So here it is, "Poor Richard's Rabbit Book," and to paraphrase John, "COME TO KINDLY TERMS WITH YOUR RABBIT FOR IT BEARS YOU."

Eve Muir

Acknowledgements

Here's where I thank everybody who has helped me put this book together. It's been a long road, but here it is, for all of you:

Eddie Arguello, Peter and Jeannie Aschwanden, Walter Bird, Vincent and Judy Boccalini, John Bott, Melody Brooks, Rolf Cahn, Brad Chisolme, Norlyn Coar, Virena Cordell, Joe Corriz, Anna Diaz, Fred Feibel, Steve Fox, Armando Garcia, Karen Ginsberg, Tosh Gregg, George Le Grice, Pete Ham, Bob Hoy, Larry Hays, Dick Hughes, Jean Hull, Keith Hunt, Gary Jester, Bob Lee, Ernie Lopez, Richard Lopez, Eugene Law, Maggie Maestas, Phil Martinez, Gene Mauldin, Daniel Mayer, Tom Murphy, Marty Ortiz, Bob Richardson, Ray Robinson, Rocky Mountain VW, Joe Roybal, Ron Le Salle, Rufus, Mike Schmid, Andrew, Edward, Nance and Nicholas Sealey, William Stabler, Dolores Sturgis, Harry Thomas, Elmer Townsley, Rosemary Trujillo, Anthony Vigil, Nancy Waite, Carl Weinmeister, Will White and Jerry Wright. There are many more wonderful people who helped and encouraged me along the way; if I neglected to mention you, please forgive me.

Extra thanx to Glen Strock for graphic assistance, Johnny Stick for gluing it all together, Jeanne Flannery for all those run-arounds, Judy Burch for the index, and Bill Conant for things mechanical. More thanks are due to Paul Abrams (Turtle) who appreciates a good pun, Carl Franz, Lorena Havens, Ken Luboff, Eve Muir, and my father Leonard Sealey for editorial advice and salvation. Merci, Barbara (Babs, Toots) Luboff for those dancin' fingers.

This book is dedicated to my family,
Alice, Amber Rose and Jade Blossom,
with love.

Author's PREFACE

Hello chums. Are you browsing through this book in your bookstore or have you purchased it already? Whatever, let me first tell you a few things about Volkswagen's Rabbit (Golf, Caribe and Scirocco). I'm going to use the word Rabbit to describe all the models. It makes things much simpler.

VW designed and manufactured a water-cooled engine to power the "new generation" of Volkswagens and decided to follow the trend to small, light, front wheel drive vehicles. The advantages of this type of design are many. Fuel economy and compliance with U.S. emissions laws are just two.

The Rabbit is an excellent vehicle. It is well constructed, responsive to all controls, easy to drive and safe. It is not, however, an off road car. If you live down a very stony, bumpy track, you should be aware of the low ground clearance. Why not leave the car at the beginning of the track and walk the last 100 yards as a physical fitness measure?

I find the Rabbit very easy to work on. The engine compartment is large and well laid out, so lumbago won't strike and routine maintenance procedures are simple and quickly performed. Lots of American automotive parts manufacturers are making stuff for the Rabbit now, so the cost of replacements is becoming lower.

Since John Muir's original Volkswagen Idiot book was published, there have been thousands of letters and telephone calls from people giving thanks and encouragement. These communiques from around the world have given me the energy to write this second "Idiot" book which follows the format of the first.

VW in their wisdom have installed the water-cooled engine into the Vanagon. The tune-up, maintenance, fuel injection and diesel chapters may be helpful to owners of water-cooled Vanagons, but the chapters weren't specifically written for them: so improvise. For anything other than engine work consult John's How To Keep Your VW Alive.

The instructions have been tried by people with no prior mechanical expertise. All you need to do is follow them slowly and carefully. Many people who never had a wrench in their hands before were given a chapter of this book and some tools. They all successfully performed the procedures and everyone of them said the same thing: a friend to help and give encouragement was the biggest, single factor in completing a project; and having the correct tools was another plus. One un-initiated person tried a difficult procedure with Friend helping, the correct tools, the appropriate chapter and lots of time. She did wonderfully and decided to pursue car mechanics further.

Take some time to learn about your Volkswagen. It makes many different sounds—many peculiar to your car—which you will come to recognize. A change in one of these announces that it's time to lift the hood and examine things carefully. Just keep tuned in and you'll know when changes occur. Listen.

Enjoy your car and enjoy the book. I'm sure that by working together we can cure almost all ills—even the dreaded stripped nut syndrome.

Poor Richard

CHAPTER 1

HOW TO USE THIS BOOK

The internal combustion engine is a relatively simple affair; basically the same now as it was when first invented by Mr. Otto. Indeed, he would probably be disappointed in the direction automobile designers have taken. They seem to have opted for ''high tech'' complexity instead of efficient simplicity. Despite the Rabbit's complexities, this book's step-by-step approach takes the myth and mystery out of repair and maintenance. All you need is to add common sense and self confidence.

Consider yourself a student as far as things mechanical are concerned. Don't skip steps. Seemingly useless steps will often save you time and frustration. Although it may be handy to have a shop-trained VW mechanic around to help, Ivor Bigwrench next door may not be the person to advise you if his experience is limited to '67 Fords. So read and digest the book, then systematically, step-by-step, follow the procedures.

Each car has idiosyncracies and a personality of its own. For example, the steering wheel vibrates when the speedometer hits 50 mph or the radio suddenly crackles maniacally. The radio problem is one you either can learn to live with or fix later. The wheel difficulty is one requiring attention right away! The idea is to keep a sense of priorities. Get what's important together as soon as possible but keep cool about idiosyncracies.

There are three types of Procedures in this book: Maintenance, Diagnostic and Repair.

Maintenance Procedures tell how to keep your Rabbit or Scirocco in top working order by doing the periodic tasks in Chapter 10.

Diagnostic Procedures help you determine *what's* wrong with the car when it tells you something is wrong. For example, *The Rabbit Won't Start*, Chapter 7, tells why and what to do to get it going. It also tells how to deal with minor repairs like broken wires or ones which have fallen off.

You'll be referred to the proper Repair Procedure when you've found out what's wrong and what needs to be done. They tell you *how* to carry out repairs. A troubleshooting guide follows Chapter 21 for those who have some mechanical knowledge.

All Procedures are classified by Phase number according to degree of difficulty and apply to both Rabbits and Sciroccos although I often refer only to Rabbits; it's those ears that get me. Differences between the two models are noted in the steps of any Procedure.

PROCEDURE 00: CHANGES FOR THE 1982 EDITION:

Turn to page 398 and follow **Procedure 00** to update your book.

PROCEDURE 0:   HOW TO RUN PROCEDURES, Phase 1

Condition: You are here to learn how to perform your own diagnosis, maintenance and/or repair.

Tools and Materials: Ability to read English and follow directions fully and accurately, and a Friend.

Remarks: Procedures are designed to give step-by-step instructions which require a minimum of independent thought, proficiency and ingenuity on the part of the person performing them.

Step 1. Analysis

Read the Procedure from beginning to end before you start work. That way you'll familiarize yourself with the full scope of the problem.

Step 2. Preparation

Gather all the tools and materials needed for the Procedure. Prepare your work area by taking beer cans to the recycling center, sweeping up the potting soil and aardvark clippings.

Before starting work move the car into position and gather wheel chocks, jack and blocks in case it needs to be in the air (see *SAFETY FIRST!*). Make sure there's hand soap, rags and a cap for your hair. Wear clothing suitable for grimy work. If the Procedure requires new parts, call the VW dealer or foreign car parts supplier to make sure they have what you need. Either do your parts shopping first or arrange transportation to the parts store before your car is in a thousand pieces in the driveway.

Step 3. Proceed

Read all the steps in the relevant Procedures before starting work. Then, as you do the work, the very best thing is to have 'Friend' reading the words to you as you proceed. The worst thing is to be lying under the car trying to turn pages with mucky fingers as dirt is falling into your eyes. Soon you'll be in a raging mood that will keep you from correctly doing anything. Your knuckles might even get skinned because you're frustrated.

When you've finished a Procedure, read through it again to be sure you've done *all* the steps and put back all the pieces.

Step 4. The Final Straw

When you strip a thread, twist off a stud, or drop a bolt into the engine innards, don't cut your throat. Turn to Chapter 20 where ye shall find salvation.

Step 5. Cleanliness

Organization is vital to your sanity! Keep everything clean as you go along. Ask Friend to clean parts as you take them off the car and in return do something nice later. Make sure you've got Baggies, tape and an indelible pen at hand. After a part is off and shiny bright clean put it into a Baggie and mark it immediately. Don't let the kids play with your carefully identified Baggies even if they want to make a car of their own. Also, if you take the engine out, don't leave the car out in the rain with all the wires and tubes beautifully marked, identified and exposed.

When you've finished, clean your tools thoroughly and put them away before you take your overalls off and roll one.

Step 6. Standard Instructions.

When you see the word **FRONT** throughout the book it means the front of the car. This makes **left** the driver's side except for in a few scattered Isles. **Front** of the **engine** is closest to the inside of the right fender. The **rear** of the **engine** bolts to the transmission and the rear of the transmission ends up mounted on the inside of the left fender. This makes the **right** of the **engine** point toward the rear of the car. Here's a sketch:

The words 'turn key to *ON*' mean turn the key one notch so the dash warning lights blaze but the engine doesn't start. 'Turn the engine on' means just that, so turn the key all the way and start it.

Step 7. The Karmic Law of Return or Getting Back What You Put Out

If you approach a broken down vehicle with frustration and anger, fixing it will be all the more difficult. Consider the problem with a clear head, a positive attitude and plenty of time. As you get into it, you'll be more relaxed and might even find yourself having fun. The *fact* facing you is that something is wrong and it has to be fixed, so make it as easy on yourself as possible and try to feel good about the whole thing.

All measurements are given using the metric system since that's the one the car was designed around. American equivalents follow in parentheses. Here's a quick guide:

10 millimeters (mm) = 1 centimeter (cm)	1 cm = .39 in
100 cm = 1 meter (m)	1 meter = about 39 in
1000 mm = 1 m	1 in = 2.54 cm
1 mm = .04 inch (in)	1 foot (ft) = 30.48 cm

SAFETY FIRST!

Throughout the book I give repeated reminders about safety for you and anyone helping. Don't ignore them. A mistake could cost a hand or even a life.

Don't attempt to lift a car with anything but a proper jack in good condition. If it's a hydraulic type, check that the raising and lowering mechanism is operating correctly and that the fluid level is OK.

Never work under your car unless it's chocked, jacked and blocked on LEVEL, FIRM ground. "Chock, Jack and Block" is not the name of an auto parts store but rather an instruction to: chock the wheels with a couple of wedges back and front, jack up the car using the jack points (to the front of the rear wheels and the rear of the front wheels), and block the car by supporting it with *solid* wooden, reinforced concrete or metal blocks. Jack stands under the rear axle or front wheel bearing housings, etc., are even better. Don't jack or block the car by the front or rear bumpers and please don't use a hollow concrete or pumice block because it will crumble.

Keep children, pets and curious onlookers at a safe distance. A person to *help* is invaluable, but a distractor is not what you need. Have them take the dog for a walk, clean parts or supply you with vittles.

WEAR SAFETY GLASSES AT ALL TIMES AND KEEP THEM CLEAN. Use a painter's mask to prevent stuff like brake dust from coating the insides of your lungs.

If you are partial to rings, jewelry and assorted baubles, please remove them before starting work. Stuff long hair under a cap or tie it behind your head. Scarves, neckties or any flowing garments should be removed. Wear comfortable clothing with the sleeves either rolled up or properly buttoned. Substitute tattered jeans or coveralls for dresses or new slacks.

DO NOT SMOKE ANYTHING while working on your car. I once watched a $75,000 race car go rapidly up in smoke because a mechanic worked on the fuel system with a lit cigarette in his mouth. The paint on one side of my car in the next bay was ruined. The mechanic? He survived . . . and was fired.

When working on your car, keep a modern fire extinguisher *handy*. Be sure it will put out gasoline fires and check its workings regularly. Keep helpers informed of its whereabouts.

DO NOT run the engine in a garage unless the garage doors and windows are wide open. Carbon monoxide in the exhaust gasses of a gasoline engine will make you sleepy and careless. It can also kill you. Diesel fumes, while they don't directly kill, are poisonous, so don't inhale them either.

If you require a light, make sure the bulb is surrounded by a metal or plastic safety cage. Approved lights can be found in any parts store. **Never** use a household type of standing lamp. If it's knocked over, the bulb can shatter, exposing the metal filament. If any combustible fuels contact the filament, hope that your insurance is up to date.

Drain oil, coolant and other fluids into a catch pan and transfer them into a sealed plastic container marked POISON. Dispose of waste materials properly—not down the drain.

Store gasoline in a container designed expressly for that purpose. Keep the container away from sources of heat.

Screw the cap on any container tightly to keep the curious out.

Always disconnect the ground strap from the battery when working on the fuel or electrical system. Tuck the strap away from the battery so it doesn't accidently reconnect itself.

If you spill gasoline, wipe it up with rags and allow the soiled rags to air dry before using them again.

Wipe up oil spills immediately. It's best to sprinkle sawdust or sand onto the spill. Then when all the oil has been soaked up by the sand, shovel it up, put it into garbage bags, and dispose of it properly.

Don't keep a pile of oily rags in the corner of your garage. They have this weird ability to build up heat and ignite themselves. Lay out oil soaked rags to air dry somewhat; then wash or discard them. I wash my rags in a strong organic cleaning solution and reuse them. There are also companies which supply rags in bundles which you can rent or buy.

Work at your own speed. Don't rush a job. And do EVERYTHING it says to do in the Procedures. Check your work carefully and tidy up afterward, ready for the next time.

Remember, you can successfully do all the Procedures in this book.

Be careful and good luck!

What is wrong with this picture?

CHAPTER 2

～ HOW A RABBIT RUNS ～

A book on how an automobile works probably wasn't required reading in high school, so I hope these few pages will clarify the myths surrounding the workings thereof. However, you don't need to understand this chapter in order to work on your car!

Your Rabbit/Scirocco is a relatively simple beast consisting of Herr Otto's engine, the wheels, transmission, brakes and other pieces to get you around. This running gear is topped off by two or four door body.

There are two types of Rabbit engines: gas and diesel. Early gas engine models were equipped with a Zenith carburetor, but in 1977, VW changed to a more efficient Bosch fuel injection system. The diesel Rabbit arrived in the U.S. in late 1977: as yet there are no diesel Sciroccos. In an attempt to produce an 'economy' model, the Bronze Edition Rabbit was produced in small numbers in 1978. It was fitted with a small Solex carburetor and given its name because that was the only color you could buy.

Nikolaus Otto

Layout

The engine has the transmission bolted to its back, tilts backward at about a 30° angle, and sits transversely (sideways) in the engine compartment at the front of the car.

The 30° tilt allows a lower, more streamlined hood profile, unlike those chrome flying ladies and clipper ship hood ornaments which created a lot of drag that increased fuel consumption. It's not much of an increase, but considering the way prices at the pumps are headed, every little saving over the lifetime of your car counts. But I do miss that bit of flash.

The laid back effect of the engine and transmission arrangement puts more weight directly over the front wheels. When you're out in mud or snow, the weight improves traction and helps the front wheels pull you along. The tilt also makes things easier to work on, because the spark plugs, distributor and other important stuff are a cinch to get at. Ferrari owners—eat your hearts out.

Why it Works

The power that moves your car is created by controlled burning of fuel inside the cylinders. In order to get this combustion, we need a proper mixture of compressed fuel and air plus, in a gas engine, an electrical spark to get things cooking.

When you turn the ignition key all the way over, current is sent from the **battery** to the **ignition system** (for the spark) and to the **solenoid** on the **starter motor.** Let's first follow the current through the solenoid.

The solenoid is an electromagnet. When it's energized by juice from the battery, it pushes the starter gear into teeth on the outside of the **flywheel.** It also closes a contact that sends current directly to the starter motor. The starter motor turns the flywheel and the flywheel turns the **crankshaft.** And the ankle bone is connected to the shin bone, and the shin bone is… There are four **connecting rods** which push the **pistons** up and down inside the **cylinders** when the crankshaft turns. Life has begun.

When the compressed fuel-air mixture in the cylinder ignites and burns, hot rapidly expanding gasses thrust the pistons downward. The pistons and their connecting rods take over from the starter motor and keep the crankshaft turning. The engine is now running on its own and the starter motor mechanism automatically disengages.

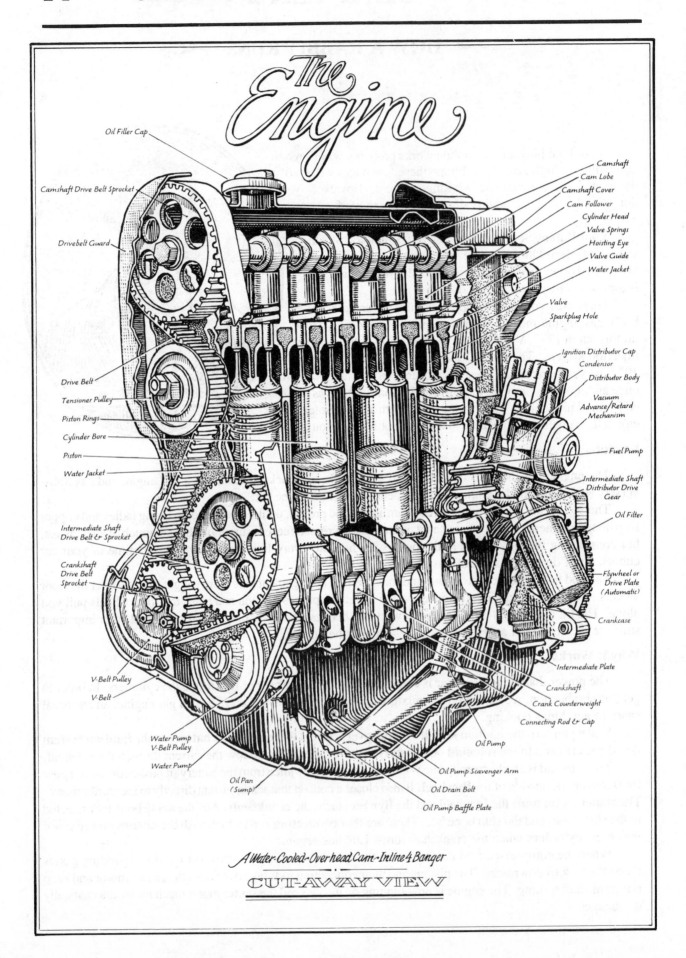

The Engine

Oil Filler Cap

Camshaft Drive Belt Sprocket

Drivebelt Guard

Drive Belt

Tensioner Pulley

Piston Rings

Cylinder Bore

Piston

Water Jacket

Intermediate Shaft
Drive Belt & Sprocket

Crankshaft
Drive Belt
Sprocket

V-Belt Pulley

V-Belt

Water Pump
V-Belt Pulley

Water Pump

Oil Pan
(Sump)

Camshaft

Cam Lobe

Camshaft Cover

Cam Follower

Cylinder Head

Valve Springs

Hoisting Eye

Valve Guide

Water Jacket

Valve

Sparkplug Hole

Ignition Distributor Cap

Condensor

Distributor Body

Vacuum
Advance/Retard
Mechanism

Fuel Pump

Intermediate Shaft
Distributor Drive
Gear

Oil Filter

Flywheel or
Drive Plate
(Automatic)

Crankcase

Intermediate Plate

Crankshaft

Crank Counterweight

Connecting Rod & Cap

Oil Pump

Oil Pump Scavenger Arm

Oil Drain Bolt

Oil Pump Baffle Plate

A Water-Cooled-Overhead Cam-Inline 4 Banger

CUT-AWAY VIEW

Fuel and Air Mixture

Carbureted Engines:

Here's how the fuel-air mixture gets to the cylinders. **Gasoline** in the **fuel tank** is sucked into the **fuel pump** by the action of wafer valves in the pump. These valves are moved by a lever riding on an elliptical lobe on the **intermediate shaft** inside the **crankcase** (engine block).

Well, anyway, gas is pumped into a reservoir in the **carburetor** called the **bowl.** A float inside the bowl shuts off the fuel supply when the bowl is full. Gasoline then flows from the bowl to calibrated holes (called **jets**) through which gas is sucked into the carburetor **throat** and mixed with air. From the carburetor throat the fuel-air mixture is drawn into the engine's cylinders to be burned.

There is a **butterfly valve** at each end of the carburetor throat. The top valve is called the **choke.** When it closes, it literally chokes off some of the air, making the fuel-air mixture *richer* in gasoline. The choke is automatically controlled by the temperature of the engine **coolant** (water-antifreeze mixture). When the engine is cold, the choke is closed, making the engine easier to start. When the engine is warm the choke opens, making the fuel-air mixture *leaner* in gasoline.

The butterfly valve at the bottom of the carburetor throat (called the **throttle valve**) controls the amount of fuel-air mixture allowed into the cylinders. This lower valve is attached by a cable to the accelerator pedal inside the car. The pressure of your foot on the pedal also controls the **accelerator pump** inside the carburetor. As logic would have it, more gasoline sprays into the carburetor throat when the pedal is pushed down for more power.

Fuel Injection:

This is another method designed to get gas into the cylinders. The type used in the Rabbit is the Bosch Continuous Injection System (C.I.S.). This accurate and efficient system produces more engine power and uses less fuel and emits a cleaner exhaust while doing so.

The *volume* of air drawn in through the **intake mouth** of the **mixture control unit** is measured by an **air flow sensor plate.** The faster the car moves along, the more air that is drawn in. On the other side of this fuel-air partnership, the **fuel distributor** sends gas to four **injection nozzles**, each pushed into a **manifold tube** in the intake air distributor on the right side of the cylinder head. Like a marriage made in car heaven, the proper amount of gas is matched to the appropriate amount of air coming in to produce the correct mixture. A fine mist of this gas mixture is sprayed in front of each **intake valve** in the cylinder head directly above the cylinders.

Ignition-Spark Circuit—Gasoline Engines

Let's go back to the key. When the key is turned all the way on, some of the juice from the battery goes through the solenoid to the starter motor, while the rest goes to the **coil** and the **ignition system.**

The coil has a soft iron **core**, surrounded by thousands of turns of thin wire, called the **secondary winding.** Outside this winding is another coil of thicker wire called the **primary winding.** It has relatively few turns of wire compared to the secondary winding. There are thus two circuits in the ignition system, the primary and secondary.

Primary Circuit

In the primary circuit, current enters the coil and travels through the primary winding, through the closed **contact points** in the **distributor** and back to ground. This current flow inside the coil creates a magnetic field which is concentrated by the soft iron core.

Meanwhile back at the distributor, the distributor shaft turns and the points open, breaking the circuit and stopping the flow of current through the primary winding. The magnetic field collapses. But alas, there's still a tendency for the current to jump across the open points. So a small cylinder called the **condenser** prevents this. Rather than try to explain how the condenser accomplishes this feat, I'll just call it magic.

Secondary Circuit

When the magnetic field in the primary winding collapses, it actually generates an electrical current inside the secondary winding. This current speeds through thousands of turns in the secondary winding, increasing the voltage along the way from the original 12 volts to a staggering 30,000 volts! The change from the primary circuit to the secondary circuit happens thousands of times a minute as the points open and close.

These 30,000 volts leave the top of the coil through a heavy **high tension** wire, go to the center of the distributor cap, head down to the **rotor** and out the end of the rotor arm. As the rotor is turned by the distributor shaft, the current jumps from the arm to a metal pin in the distributor cap, and by means of another heavy wire goes to a **spark plug.** A hefty spark jumps across the central electrode to the spark plug body. Zap!

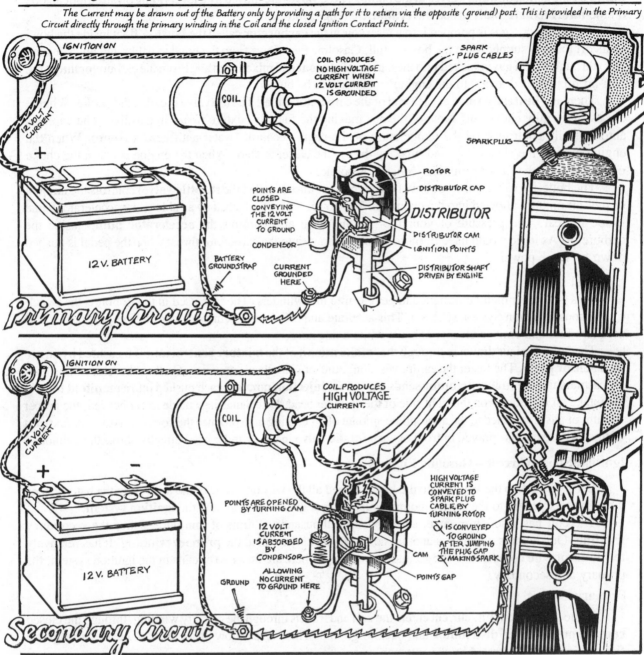

The Current may be drawn out of the Battery only by providing a path for it to return via the opposite (ground) post. This is provided in the Primary Circuit directly through the primary winding in the Coil and the closed Ignition Contact Points.

When the Points are open however the Primary Circuit is interrupted and the current seeks ground in the Condenser where it is dead-ended, sending a sort of backsurge to the Coil. In the Coil the magnetic field surrounding the primary and secondary windings collapses under the strain. The secondary winding, through a process called Induction, picks up the pieces (so to speak), converts the collapsed current into a burst of several thousand volts and shoots it out to be distributed to the appropriate spark plug where, after making a spark (the point of all this), it is finally grounded, completing the secondary circuit. Got it? OK, now picture it happening a few thousand times a minute.

Cylinders and Pistons

Three springy metal **piston rings** fit into three **ring grooves** in the **pistons** which make an airtight seal between the piston and the cylinder wall. The connecting rods on the crankshaft pull the pistons down inside the cylinders. An intake valve opens and sucks the fuel-air mixture into a cylinder.

The intake valve closes. The crankshaft continues to turn and the piston rises compressing the fuel-air mixture up into the **combustion chamber**, the space between the top of the piston and the dome-shaped cylinder head. Just after the piston reaches the top of its stroke, the spark jumping across the spark plug electrodes ignites the compressed gasoline in the presence of the air.

Energy liberated by this burning forces the piston back down, providing the power to move your Rabbit. Powered by energy liberated in another cylinder, the piston rises again, the exhaust valve opens and the burnt gasses are pushed down the exhaust pipe into the outside air.

The ending of this cycle is the beginning of the next. And so it goes. Sorta like life.

OK, back in the cylinder, as the fuel burns, the pistons are forced down, moving the connecting rods and crankshaft. When the speed of the flywheel that's bolted to the back of the crankshaft exceeds the rotation speed of the starter, the starter motor disengages itself.

The Rabbit has what's termed a four cycle engine. One complete cycle means the crankshaft has made two revolutions and the pistons have gone up and down two times. During every two revolutions (one cycle) of the crankshaft, the plugs in the cylinders fire once. Things are designed so that each of the four pistons is at a different point in the cycle at any one time, and only one piston is on the power stroke. If they all fired at the same time, you'd have a hell of a mess.

In both carbureted and fuel injected engines four piston strokes make up a complete cycle. They are:

Intake stroke: The intake valve opens as the downward stroke of the piston sucks in a mixture of gas and air.

Compression stroke: The intake valve closes. The piston changing direction, makes an upward stroke, compressing the gas-air mixture in a ratio of about 8 to 1.

Power stroke: Just after the piston reaches the top of its compression stroke, the spark plug fires, igniting the fuel. The energy liberated forces the piston back down.

Exhaust stroke: Changing direction yet again, the piston rises, the exhaust valve opens and burnt gasses are pushed out past the valve through the exhaust system into the outside air.

The burn first happens in cylinder number 1, then in numbers 3, 4 and 2. This never changing progression is called the **firing order.**

The **crankcase** holds the seat of power. It's carefully machined to form the cylinders in which the pistons and connecting rods go through their ups and downs. It surrounds the intermediate shaft and the crankshaft.

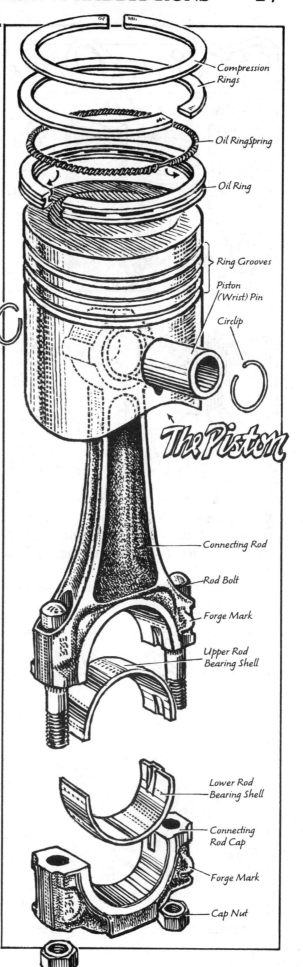

Compression Rings

Oil Ring Spring

Oil Ring

Ring Grooves

Piston (Wrist) Pin

Circlip

The Piston

Connecting Rod

Rod Bolt

Forge Mark

Upper Rod Bearing Shell

Lower Rod Bearing Shell

Connecting Rod Cap

Forge Mark

Cap Nut

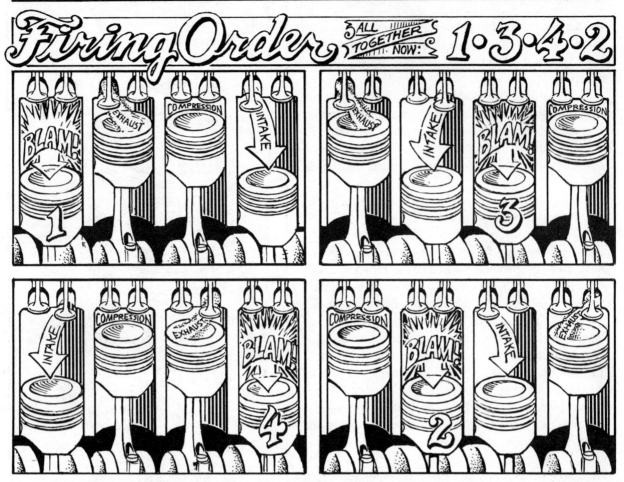

The **crankshaft** is the central source of power. It's a heavy steel forging that's been machined in certain places. It turns inside five **main bearings** which rest on five supports inside the crankshaft called **bearing saddles**. Five **main bearing caps**, each with two bolts, secure the crankshaft to these bearing saddles.

The **connecting rods** bolt around the **cranks** (also called **throws**) on the crankshaft. These throws convert the up and down motion of the pistons into the round and round movement of the crankshaft.

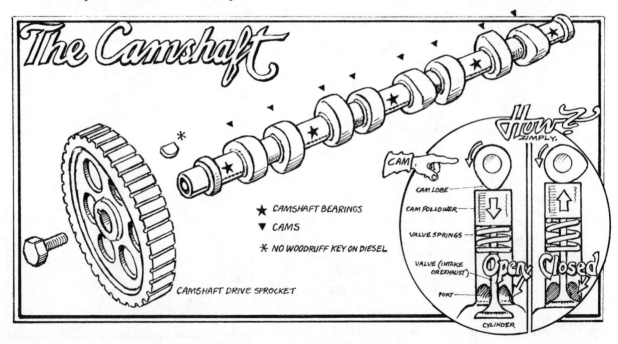

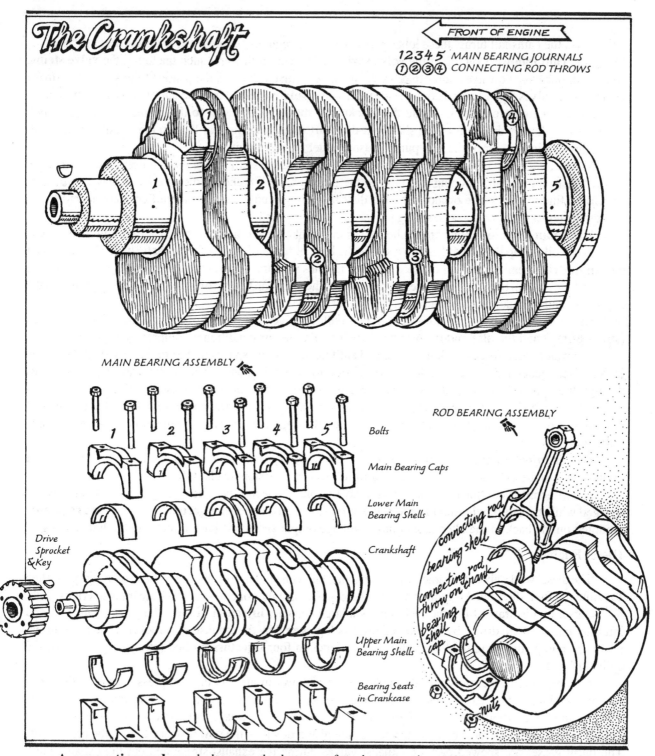

The Crankshaft

FRONT OF ENGINE

1 2 3 4 5 MAIN BEARING JOURNALS
①②③④ CONNECTING ROD THROWS

MAIN BEARING ASSEMBLY

ROD BEARING ASSEMBLY

Bolts

Main Bearing Caps

Lower Main
Bearing Shells

Crankshaft

Drive
Sprocket
& Key

Upper Main
Bearing Shells

Bearing Seats
in Crankcase

connecting rod
bearing shell
connecting rod
throw on crank
bearing
shell
cap
nuts

A **connecting rod cap** bolts onto the bottom of each connecting rod securing it to the crankshaft. Connecting rod **bearings (rod inserts)** fit between the rod and the crankshaft.

Both main and rod bearings are thin steel shells which are replaced when worn. Doing so protects the machined surfaces of the crankshaft. All the bearings are lubricated by the engine oil.

The clutch assembly and flywheel (or torque converter drive plate on automatics) are bolted to the rear of the crankshaft and the drive belt sprocket to the front.

The **camshaft** sits inside the **cylinder head** bolted on top of the crankcase. The camshaft has a drive belt sprocket bolted to the front and is driven by the toothed flexible **drive belt (timing** or **spur belt)** powered by the crankshaft.

The Rabbit's camshaft sits above the **valves** which is why it's called an overhead cam. The camshaft revolves in five non-replaceable bearings and has eight lobes which determine the up and down action of the valves. As the camshaft turns, these lobes periodically and regularly depress **valve adjustment discs** in the top of the **cam followers** on top of the **valve springs.** The cam followers touch the top of the **valve stems.** Each cylinder has two valves; an **intake** valve and an **exhaust** valve. As the pistons follow the four stroke cycle, these valves move up and down inside steel **valve guides** pressed into the aluminum cylinder head.

The **intermediate shaft** is inside the crankcase, above and parallel to the crankshaft. A drive belt sprocket is bolted to the front of the shaft. As the shaft turns, an elliptical lobe in the middle of the shaft moves an arm in the rear of the fuel pump, pushing fuel to the carburetor.

At the same time, a drive gear on the end of the intermediate shaft meshes with a gear on the end of the vertical distributor shaft, opening and closing the points. Late '78 and on diesel engines have a **vacuum amplifier** fitted in the place occupied by the distributor in gas engines. This amplifier is connected to the brake booster to give you more stopping power.

An **oil pan** (or **sump**) bolted to the bottom of the crankcase acts as a reservoir for the engine oil. In gas engines the **oil pump** driveshaft fits into a slot in the base of the vertical distributor shaft. In diesel engines an **oil pump drive gear** on the end of the driveshaft meshes with the gear on the intermediate shaft. Thus the intermediate shaft in both gas and diesel engines drives the oil pump to send oil through the passages inside the crankcase and cylinder head to keep everything lubricated.

The V-belt (driven by the crankshaft V-belt pulley) drives the **water pump**, the **air injection pump (smog pump)** and the **alternator.** Another V-belt works the air conditioner compressor if you have one.

The water pump forces **coolant** (water and antifreeze) through spaces in the crankcase called the **water jacket.** Heat generated in the cylinders is transferred to the coolant and carried to the **radiator.** Air rushes through the radiator and cools the water/antifreeze mixture as the car moves forward. The coolant is then pumped back into the water jacket and begins its journey anon. An electric **cooling fan** bolted to the back of the radiator pulls extra air through the radiator when the engine exceeds a set temperature—like in heavy traffic or hot weather.

The **air injection pump** is part of the emission control system and is found in carbureted cars only. It pumps air into the cylinders to help lower harmful exhaust emission levels. OK so far?

The **alternator** continually produces around 14 volts of electricity. The battery gets 2 volts to keep it charged while the radio, windshield wipers and other electrical components get the rest. A **voltage regulator** mounted on the back of the alternator controls voltage output and sends juice directly to the lights at night.

Diesel Engines

The diesel works about the same as the gas engine, but with one basic difference. Instead of using spark plugs to ignite the fuel, diesel fuel is ignited by air. There's no distributor or coil to complicate things. Tricky, huh?

Diesel fuel is drawn from the fuel tank by a large capacity **injection pump.** The pump, camshaft and intermediate shaft are driven by the toothed drive belt powered by the crankshaft sprocket, which also turns. From the pump, fuel is pushed through injection pipes to four **injectors** pushed into the right side of the cylinder head.

As the piston moves down on its intake stroke it draws in air. On the compression stroke the air is compressed into a space 23.5 times smaller than the space it originally occupied. As it's compressed, it heats up to about 900°C (1650°F). When the piston reaches the top of its stroke, fuel is injected into the hot air and ignites. The energy liberated by this burn forces the piston down on the power stroke to turn the crankshaft. The burnt gasses are spewed past the exhaust valves during the exhaust stroke and out the exhaust pipe.

Four **electric heaters** are screwed into the left side of the cylinder head to improve starting on cold mornings. These automatically operating heaters raise the temperature at the top of the cylinders (the combustion chambers) making it easier for the fuel to ignite. The heaters work only when the key is on and cut off when the engine starts.

A control pull knob to the left of the steering wheel is used to advance the timing of fuel delivery to the cylinders about 2.5°, also helping the engine to start in cold weather. Chapter 21 tells the whole story.

The Drive Train—All Models

Power produced by the engine is transferred to the front wheels via the **drive train**, a term used to collectively describe the flywheel, clutch (torque converter on automatics), transmission and drive shafts.

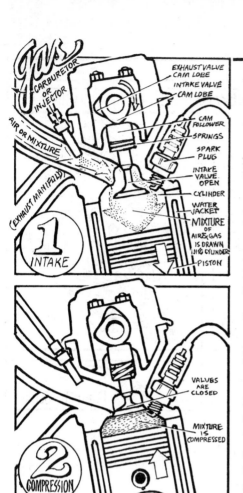

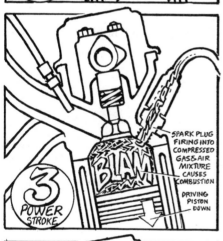

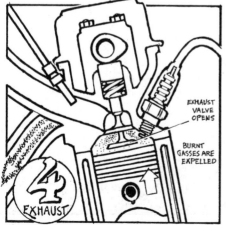

Remember the flywheel bolted to the back of the crankshaft? Well, the flat machined face of that useful item acts as part of the clutch, and the teeth around its circumference engage the starter assembly to turn the engine over for starting. Because it's very heavy, it 'stores' energy to maintain the revolving motion of the crankshaft as the engine goes through its cycles.

The flywheel transmits its energy to the transmission via the **clutch assembly.** A two-surfaced **clutch disc** is sandwiched between the smooth flat surfaces of the flywheel and the spring loaded **pressure plate.** When your foot presses down the clutch pedal, a linkage pushes a pin onto a **release plate** which in turn presses onto the pressure plate allowing the clutch disc to run free. This effectively disconnects the engine from the transmission for starting, idling, and shifting gears.

Although the engine is most efficient when running at moderately high speeds, we often want to slow down or even stop. The transmission helps make that possible.

By means of a complex gearing device the transmission matches the speed of the engine to the speed of the wheels. For example, when climbing a steep hill the engine will be running fast while the wheels are actually turning slowly. Going downhill, the car wheels move faster without much help from the engine. The transmission determines which gear is best for each driving situation.

Without your help an automatic transmission determines which gear should be engaged to match engine output. The automatic transmission is designed to operate best at certain revolutions and changes gear accordingly. A fluid-filled **torque converter** is bolted onto a kind of flywheel called a **torque converter drive plate.** This drive plate has teeth all around its circumference and acts generally just like a flywheel.

Two **drive shafts** going to the front wheels (the drive wheels) are connected to the transmission by **constant velocity** (CV) joints. These allow the drive shafts not only to turn the wheels, but also to move up and down with road bumps. Shock absorbers surrounded by coil springs take the jolt out of your journey. Each wheel has its own suspension system called a **MacPherson strut.** The front wheels are suspended while the rear wheels are bolted onto an **axle beam** which ties them together.

Now there's one big problem: when going around a curve the inside drive wheel travels a shorter distance that the outside drive wheel. If the axle were one piece, the inside tire would drag slightly (known as 'scrubbing'). The car would handle poorly and the front tires would wear out before their time.

To avoid this problem we have the **differential**, a ring and pinion gear device that allows both wheels to rotate at different speeds while maintaining their driving power.

The **steering wheel** points the Rabbit in the direction you want to go. Turning the wheel turns the steering column, which is connected by two universal joints to the **steering rack.** The steering rack connects the **tie rods** to the steering arms on the **wheel**

The Diesel does it differently ∼ See Diesel Chapter.

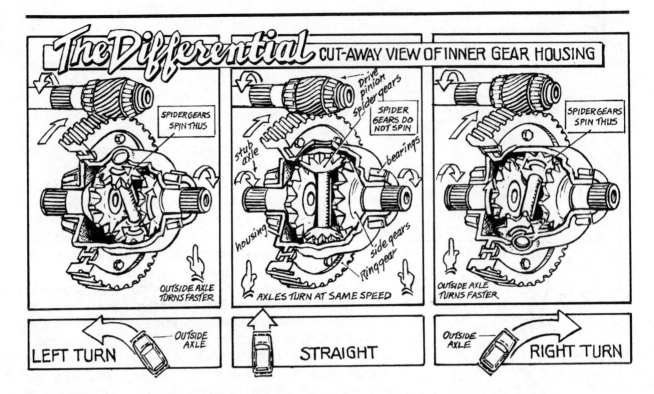

bearing housings (steering knuckle), and last, but not least, the wheels.

The Exhaust Gas Recirculation System (EGR).

This EGR System is responsible for most of the hoses and plastic pipes criss-crossing your engine. The 'how it all works' description is in Chapter 13, so let's leave it for now.

There are various other devices, such as brakes and lights, fitted onto your Rabbit. If you want information on how they work, please turn to the appropriate chapter.

That, ladies and gentlemen, is the end of the tour. Tenkyu.

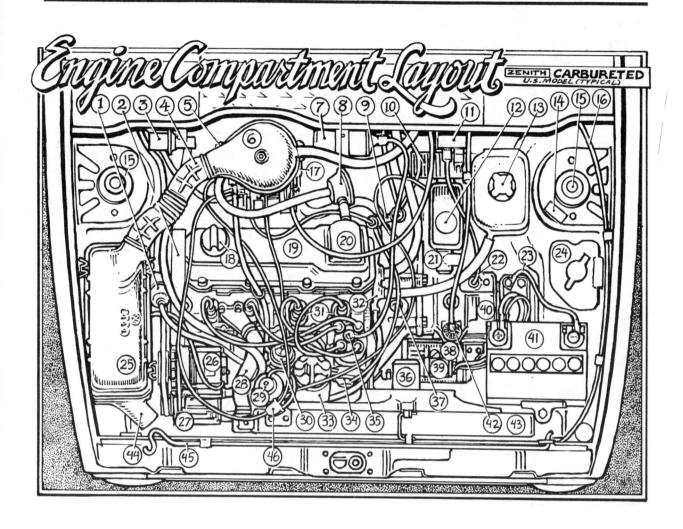

Engine Compartment Layout — ZENITH CARBURETED U.S. MODEL (TYPICAL)

1 Fuel Filter

2 Drive Belt Cover

3 Anti-Backfire Valve

4 Air Intake Elbow

5 Automatic Choke Unit

6 Air Duct

7 Ignition Coil

8 PCV Valve

9 Temperature Valves

10 Brake Vacuum Booster (Servo)

11 EGR Counter Box

12 Brake Fluid Reservoir

13 Coolant Expansion Bottle

14 VW's Computer Hook-Up Box

15 Suspension Strut Top Mount Box

16 Hood Release Cable

17 Carburetor

18 Oil Filler Cap

19 Valve Cover

20 Accelerator Cable

21 Brake Master Cylinder

22 Speedometer Cable

23 Battery Ground Strap

24 Windshield Washer Fluid Tank

25 Air Cleaner Box

26 Alternator

27 Air Injection (Smog) Pump

28 Coolant Hose from Radiator

29 Diverter Valve

30 Fuel Pump

31 Spark Plug

32 Coolant Manifold

33 Oil Filter

34 Distributor Vacuum Advance Unit

35 Ignition Distributor

36 Cooling Fan

37 Timing Hole

38 Starter

39 Solenoid

40 Transmission

41 Battery

42 Clutch Cable

43 Radiator

44 Air Intake

45 Hood Prop Rod

46 2nd Stage Diverter (Two-Way) Valve

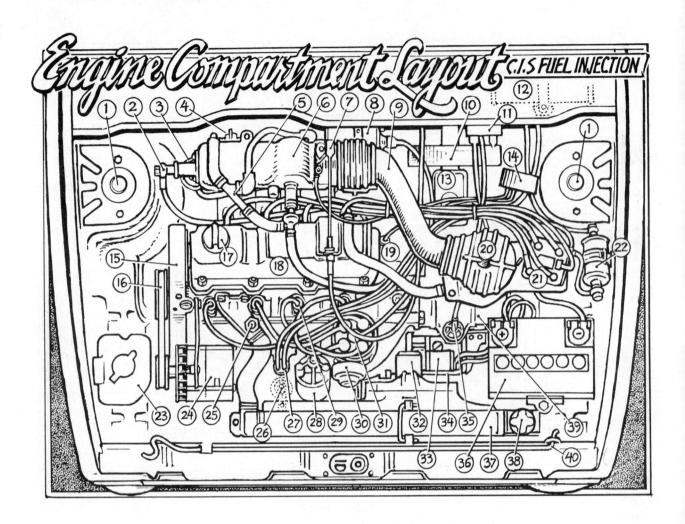

Engine Compartment Layout C.I.S FUEL INJECTION

1 Suspension Strut Top Mounting
2 Cold Start Valve (Fifth Injector)
3 EGR Valve
4 Auxiliary Air Regulator
5 Vacuum Hose Manifold
6 Common Intake (Air) Manifold
7 Throttle Cable
8 Ignition Coil
9 Intake Air Elbow
10 Brake Vacuum Booster (Servo)
11 EGR Counter Box
12 Charcoal Filter Canister (Some Models)
13 Brake Fluid Reservoir
14 Vacuum Amplifier

15 Drive Belt (Timing Belt) Cover
16 V-Belt
17 Oil Filler Cap
18 Cam Cover
19 EGR Temperature Valve
20 Intake Air Funnel
21 Fuel Distributor
22 Fuel Filter
23 Windshield Washer Fluid Tank
24 Alternator
25 Thermo-Time Switch
26 Barometric Cell (Some Models)
27 Control Pressure Regulator

28 Oil Filter
29 Spark Plug
30 Distributor Vacuum
   Advance Unit
31 Ignition Distributor
32 Cooling Fan
33 Solenoid
34 Starter
35 Clutch Cable
36 Battery
37 Radiator
38 Coolant Filler Cap
39 Transmission
40 Hood Prop Rod

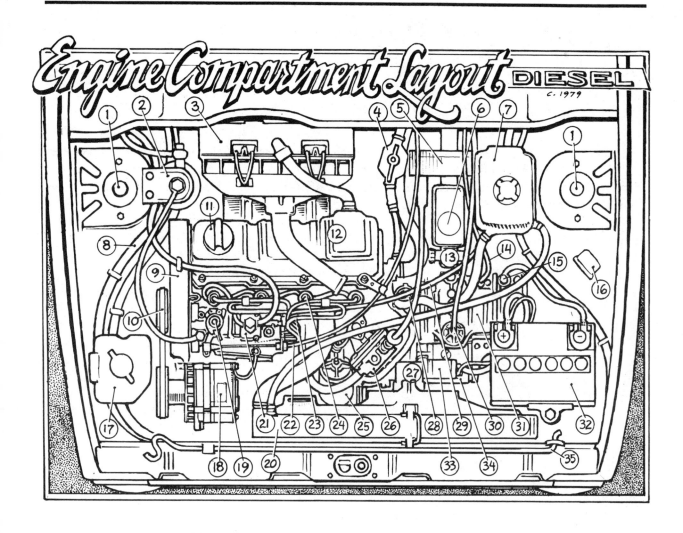

Engine Compartment Layout DIESEL c.1979

1 Suspension Strut Top Mounting
2 Fuel Filter
3 Air Cleaner Box
4 Heater Valve
5 Brake Vacuum Booster (Servo)
6 Brake Fluid Reservoir
7 Coolant Expansion Tank
8 Air Conditioner Hoses
9 Drive Belt (Timing Belt) Cover
10 V-Belt
11 Oil Filler Cap
12 Cam Cover

13 Brake Master Cylinder
14 Speedometer Cable
15 Battery Ground Strap
16 Air Conditioner Relay
17 Windshield Washer Fluid Tank
18 Alternator
19 Throttle Lever
20 Radiator
21 Injection Pump
22 Throttle Cable
23 Injection Tubes
24 Injector

25 Oil Filter
26 Vacuum Pump
27 Radiator Cooling Fan
28 Timing Hole
29 Cold Start Cable
30 Clutch Cable
31 Transmission
32 Battery
33 Solenoid
34 Starter
35 Hood Prop Rod

CHAPTER 3

➤ BUYING A BUNNY ➤

Before embarking on a Rabbit hunt, please read this chapter. It was written to help you buy a cherry instead of a lemon. I'll show you how to avoid getting ripped off or conned. Buying any car—new or used—is a traumatic experience, but we can learn to make it tolerable and perhaps fun. This is the time. This chapter is also for those of you who want to check out the car you already own.

If you're hot to drop $6,000 or so for a new one, there's no need to inspect things like brake linings or the clutch because hopefully (?) they won't be worn at all. But I heartily recommend a compression check on any car before you buy it, as assurance that the engine is healthy. It's possible that the person who put it together installed their Thermos in place of a piston, so spend what time is needed to scrutinize.

Dealers put every new car through a multi-point check—'dealer prep' it's called in the trade—but sometimes the mechanic misses something that may cause trouble as soon as the car is off the lot. Is there anything more irritating than to have to return a new car for diddly repairs under warranty that should have been caught in the first place? This chapter will help you catch 'em in front.

Rabbit or Pick-up?

The first step is to decide if a Rabbit is actually what you need. For carrying livestock and loveseats, the Rabbit pick-up might be the thing for you. Although the Rabbit has a remarkable load carrying capacity when the rear seat is lowered, it's primarily designed as a people carrier. Ground clearance is fairly low, so consider what rocks and ruts can do to the underside.

First check out a brand new one. The VW dealer has a few lying around. Take a test drive and get a feel for the way the car handles and looks when new. You'll keep this in mind when checking used cars to see how far they've fallen from their former glory. Listen to the new engine run and examine the interior and underside just to gather information. Thank the salesperson politely, then check out the used Rabbits on the dealer's lot.

Make a note of model, year and price, along with any factory options or accessories that are included on a car you fancy. Ask what they'll take for the car if you pay cash. (Write the figure down.) These days it often doesn't make much difference. The dealer would rather finance the deal and make the interest too!

Once you find a car that interests you on a lot, at a VW dealer or privately owned, it's time to examine it. 1975 was the worst year for Rabbits. Avoid a 1975 automatic unless it's *perfect* or a gift.

PROCEDURE 1: VISUAL PRE-PURCHASE CHECK. Phase 1.

Condition: You are thinking about buying a Rabbit or Scirocco and have found one which arouses yearning.

Tools and materials: Time and money.

Remarks: Don't feel pressured by the owner. If they don't want you to run these checks, say goodbye. It's your money. This careful examination must be done in daylight. Small dents, dings, scratches, ripples and oil leaks are very difficult to see at night, even with a flashlight. Take a fast look and return in the morning with your fine-toothed comb. This Procedure will take about an hour, so reserve enough time to do it properly.

Step 1. First Impressions

Walk all the way around the car and see if the tires have been painted black. Open the doors—have the floor mats been painted and have the pedal covers been painted/replaced?

Lift the hood. Engine too clean to be true? Be cautious, but not paranoid as you proceed with the checks. A good car doesn't need 'dressing up'. Get on your knees and look underneath the car. Start at the front and work your way to the back, looking carefully at everything as you go. What kind of condition is the oil pan in? If it's dented or badly scraped, the car has been driven over rough ground. There may be heavy wear on the engine/transmission mounts as well as on the steering gear and suspension.

Check the tie rods (the things that actually steer the car). Are they bent? Do they have hammer marks from being straightened? How are the rubber boots on the ball joints at the ends of the tie rods? Look at the constant velocity (CV) joints—the cylinders at each end of front drive shaft. They'll probably be dirty, but there shouldn't be any oil dripping from the joints. The CV joints should be packed with grease, but an unscrupulous person may have squirted oil into the joints to make them run quietly.

Check for rust beneath the crud inside of the front wheel well. If there is rust, continue to pry. If you find a spot of rust anywhere, examine the rest of the car for further evidence of the dreaded scourge. If the car is rusty you'd better get it cheap!

Lift the hatchback and see if the hydraulic piston holds it up. Open the doors and check for rust at the very bottom of the door and on the inside sill. Look at the door hinges. Do the windows roll up and down easily.

Lift up the floor mats and scrape away the dirt. Any holes? Do the same check in the rear passenger compartment and the trunk. Lift out the spare tire from beneath the carpet in the trunk and check the floor underneath.

Is there any rust around the points where the shock absorbers are mounted at the side of the trunk? Lift the hood and check the shock mounts in the engine compartment. Any rust around the front, rear or side lights?

Open the rear hatchback again and look around the trunk. If you see dents in the metal or deep scratches in the paintwork, heavy loads have been carried—meaning wear on rear shocks and axle beam.

Prop the hood and have a good look around the engine compartment. Is the engine filthy? **Gas Models:** Check the base of the spark plugs to see if they're bright and shiny—or rusty. Rusty plugs means they've been in the cylinder head for a long time.

Pry the two spring clips away from the distributor cap with a screwdriver. The distributor cap, by the way, is the brown plastic thing with 5 thick wires coming from it. Cars built during 1979 and on have a metal shield around the cap. Either pull the braided wire off a connector on the shield or remove the screw holding the wire in place (1980).

When the cap is off, check it for cracks and carbon tracks up on the inside. The four brass contacts should be crud free. Now pull the rotor off the vertical distributor shaft and remove the opaque plastic dust cover. Look inside the distributor. There shouldn't be any oil or grease hanging around.

Conventional ignition systems: push open the little arm of the ignition points and examine the round contact on the end. That arm closes onto another contact and both contacts should be kept clean. A careful car owner keeps the ignition system in top condition. Even if the points and distributor cap are in terrible condition, don't stop. They're easily replaced. Chapter 10 tells how. Put the dust cover and rotor back on and replace the cap. Be sure the spring clips are in proper position to keep the cap on tight. **1979-on:** Screw or re-connect the braided wire onto the distributor body. **Electronic Ignition:** There are no points inside the distributor for you, so just check that everything is neat and clean.

All Models: Get down on one knee by the right front wheel and peer past the inner wheel well at the crankshaft V-belt pulley. Look behind the pulley for signs of oil on the crankcase. If the amount of dirty oil is significant, the front main seal has probably blown, allowing oil to escape. There will be a few drops on the ground by now if the seal is shot. Have a look. The engine has to be removed to replace this seal.

Now look underneath the engine. Any more drips of oil falling to the ground? If oil is dripping where the transmission connects to the engine, the rear oil seal is shot. The transmission has to be removed to fix that one. A broken rear oil seal will also cause the clutch to slip. Another problem you don't need.

Pull the dipstick from the left side of the engine and check the oil level. The oil should be on or just below the upper mark. Rub some of the oil from the dipstick between your thumb and forefinger. If it's very thick or gummy, STP or some other additive has probably been dumped in the oil to help seal the piston rings and generally quiet down a noisy engine. Does the oil feel gritty? If so, the former owner (perhaps I should say present owner) hasn't done the routine maintenance procedures required to keep the car alive. Wipe the dipstick clean and push it back into its hole without touching the engine and getting crud on the end of the stick.

Gritty oil is enough to turn me off, but continue the Procedure for a while. You'll get a view of how widely these cars can vary in health. Withdraw the dipstick again and check the oil for consistency. If it's thin, frothy, grey and watery, or has a greenish tinge, there's a strong possibility the coolant has become mixed with oil as the result of a blown cylinder head gasket. Bad news. Fresh oil is clear and amber colored, and a healthy grey/blue if it's been in the engine for awhile. Ask when the last oil change was done. (Diesel engines will turn new oil black in about 300 miles, so this oil color won't necessarily apply to them. Check the consistency of the oil, however, and do the 'between the fingers' test very carefully.)

Remove the oil filler cap from the top of the camshaft cover and examine the inside of the cap. You are looking for a milky/grey sludge, a dirty froth and evidence of rust. All are caused by water contamination due to neglect and failure to change the oil at regular intervals. A lot of sludge on the cap means an additive—probably moly-sulphide (sister of Polly) based—has been added to the oil. Find out why. Some people add all kinds of junk to temporarily quiet down a dying engine in the vain hope it will chug along forever. It will if it's never used.

Take the top off the plastic brake fluid reservoir on top of the master cylinder. Check the fluid level. It should be on, or just below, the line on the side of the reservoir. If it's low, part of the hydraulic brake system may be leaking. We'll check in a minute.

Have a close look at the radiator. Remove the radiator cap (engine *must* be cool) or the top from the white plastic expansion bottle. Look at the underside of the cap and the coolant inside the radiator/expansion bottle. If you see *any* oily deposits, coolant is definitely mixing with the oil somewhere in the engine's innards. Bad news. Antifreeze gives the coolant a greenish tinge. If it's clear or light brown, there's no antifreeze in the coolant. There should be.

Look at the hoses leading into the radiator. Use your hands to bend them a little to check for cracks and splits. Do all the hoses have a hose clamp at each end? Check the radiator for leaks. Is there any rust or severe dents anywhere on the radiator? Has it been repaired with 'Liquid Solder'? Liquid Solder stops leaks for a while without removing the radiator for a proper repair.

If the car has an automatic transmission, pull on the handbrake between the front seats, start the engine, and let it idle. Pull out the automatic transmission fluid (ATF) dipstick from the right side of the transmission. Rub a little between your fingers. It should be a clear red color and feel clean with no particles of dirt or grit floating about. Smell it: there should be no burnt odor. If the fluid is discolored and smells funny, the transmission has been overheating and breaking down the fluid and the inner seals. That's trouble. So unless you want to buy and install a rebuilt transmission, bid the owner a fond adieu.

Put the handbrake on; it should come up about three clicks if it's adjusted properly. How much play is in the foot pedals? They shouldn't move more than about 15mm (5/8 in) before you feel resistance. If the rubber covers on the pedals are very worn you have an indication of how much use the car has had. New covers? You'll have to determine if the car has been used a lot becase the rubbers may have been kicked off and replaced with new ones. Ask the owner while you look 'em straight in the eye.

Look at the odometer (the numbers in the speedometer) and see how many miles are recorded. As a rule of thumb, finger or foot, most people don't drive more than a thousand miles a month, so divide the mileage on the odometer by the age of the car in years. If the result is a multiple of 12,000 or thereabouts, the car has had 'normal' use. Of course, there is no way of checking that the mileage on the odometer is true. Sometimes the speedometer cable breaks and isn't replaced for awhile. Perhaps the cable has been disconnected on purpose. Shame!

The condition of the upholstery is a clue to the car's general condition. Fabric seats will probably have a few burn marks from fallen cigarette ashes or seeds, but the material should be basically sound. If the cloth is badly worn or frayed, the seats will need recovering before all the stuffing falls out. Is the driver's seat squashed out of shape? If so, the owner either ate too much or spent a lot of time in the car. Lots of time means lots of miles, despite what the odometer may say.

Rock the car at each corner by pushing down on the fenders one at a time. If the car wallows like a water-logged elephant on a trampoline after you release it, the shock absorbers are shot and need to be replaced. That's not a simple operation on Rabbits. Don't let the owner dismiss that with a 'it only needs shocks.'

Back on your knees. If nothing else, this inspection will give you a good workout. Look under the car again. If any oil spots have formed on the pavement during your inspection, find where they're coming from.

Kneel beside one of the front wheels, grab the top of the tire and pull it toward you. There should be no play. Now hold the tire at the nine and three o'clock positions and try to rock it from side to side. Any play in this direction means something is wrong with the ball joints, the front wheel bearings, or the wheel isn't on tight. If anything's loose, pry off the plastic lug nut covers and wheel cover or hub cap. Check that the large nut holding the wheel onto the drive shaft is tight. Check the other front wheel too. Loose nuts are every-where. Now push/pull the rear wheels. Any play in them can usually be corrected because the bearings are adjustable. The front wheel bearings, however, are not, and have to be replaced if faulty. Not the easiest or cheapest of jobs.

Carefully check the flexible brake hose behind the front wheels for cracks; any fluid leaking from either end of that hose? Check the other side too. There should be no evidence of leaks. There are? Don't drive the car—it's dangerous!

Roll down the driver's window, reach in and turn the key to ON but don't start the engine. Hold the steering wheel (you're outside the car) and turn it until you feel some resistance. There should be no more than 13mm (½ in) of play before resistance is felt. Watch the front wheel as you turn the steering wheel. It should begin to move smoothly through the entire wheel arc. There should be no clicks or sticky parts during the turn. You may hear a 'groaning' as you turn the wheel, but this problem is cured by lubricating the steering rack. (See Chapter 15.) The wheel is fairly difficult to turn because you have resistance from both tires. If it won't turn at all, you forgot to turn the ignition key to ON to release the steering lock. Don't reject the car if you have front end problems—the cure might be found in a low purchase price!

Step 2. The Light Show

Keep the key turned to ON and see if all the dash lights (except the little thermometer) come on. If any do not (except the thermometer), turn to Chapters 8 and 9. They must be working to get a clear picture of the engine's condition. If the car is a dealer's, ask them to fix the lights before you continue.

Try the light switches to make sure they work. Switch the headlights to both high and low beams. Do the emergency flashers work? Start the engine and see if the dash warning lights go out. They should.

Release the handbrake and its light on the dash should blink out. Turn the engine off.

Put the key in the ignition and turn it to ON. A diesel-engined car has a little red light to the left of the steering column or in the dash. It should light up for about 10 to 30 seconds, then go out. It's a visual reminder that the heaters in the cylinders are on. These heaters help the diesel start more easily.

Step 3. Time Out

It's time for some deep meditation. If the sales manager or owner is becoming agitated, just flash a winning smile and ask for a little time to think. You'll get it.

Walk around the car for a final once-over. Do you like the way it looks? It isn't going to rise up on its back legs and cry, ''I'm the one for you!'' You'll have to make the decision based on the information you've been gathering. But not just yet—if you like what you've seen so far, it's time to dig even deeper.

Telephone or go to your bank and ask for the blue book value for the make and year of the car you're interested in. Don't believe the figure that the seller gives you; you want to check independent sources of information. This blue book gives the wholesale and retail prices of all vehicles sold in the United States. Other countries have their own equivalent. Extras such as air conditioning and low mileage increase the value; while high mileage, poor body/interior condition, tire wear, etc., lower a car's value. Three values are given according to the condition: poor, good or excellent. If the *asking* price is within reason, it's back to work.

PROCEDURE 2: MECHANICAL PRE-PURCHASE CHECK. Phase 1.

Condition: You've found a car that merits further attention.

Tools and materials: Phase I tool kit, compression tester (not for diesel),   safety glasses, old clothes, paper and pencil, Friend, and something to lie on.

Remarks: This is where you put on your old clothes and get your hands dirty.

Step 1. Drivers, Start Your Engines

Don't start the car in a closed garage; exhaust fumes can kill you. As soon as the engine starts, all dash lights except the seat belt light and handbrake symbol should go out. If the oil light stays on, turn off the engine and check the oil level. If it's low, add some of the same type that was used before. If you don't know the type, use SAE 10W-30 detergent oil. If the alternator light remains on, there is probably some fault in the charging system. Don't drive with that light on.

Did the engine turn over quickly or was it dragging? A puny sounding starter motor usually means the battery is weak. Turn the engine off and start it again. Do the on/off routine about six times. If the battery is on its last legs, this test will drive it to its knees.

Rest the battery (and your right hand) for a moment and ask Friend or the seller to take your place behind the steering wheel. Have them start the engine while you keep a sharp eye on the exhaust pipe. A diesel will puff out a bit of black smoke, then settle to a faint blue haze. Gas engines shouldn't puff out anything but a little white smoke when the engine is cold. Wait a few moments for the white stuff to fade, then have Friend quickly depress the accelerator pedal. They call it 'blipping the throttle' where I come from. There should be no blue smoke coming from the tail pipe. The diesel version initially will puff out a little more smoke than it did at idle, but it shouldn't be excessive. Black smoke from a diesel means one or more faulty injectors or an improperly timed injection pump. (More on the diesel in Chapter 21.) If 'blipping' the gas engine sends blue/black smoke from the tailpipe, there's a problem with either the oil return system inside the crankcase or poor piston ring sealing inside the cylinders. Constant smoking indicates that the valve guides or piston rings are worn or the valves are not seating properly. Only a compression test can tell you more. You won't be able

to do a compression test on a diesel engine because the compression inside the cylinders is too high for regular testers to handle. Ask the dealer to do it. They'll charge for the test if the car isn't theirs, but it's well worth it.

Keep the engine running and try these little tricks. Hold your hand about six inches from the end of the tailpipe and see if any pieces of debris are deposited into your open palm. You should feel even pulses of gas. Now don't inhale. Is there any nasty black stuff on the inside of the tailpipe, or drops of gasoline falling to the ground? If so, the fuel-air mixture setting is wrong, the automatic choke isn't set correctly, or the valves aren't seating properly. It's usually the mixture that's wrong, especially on carbureted cars.

If the pulses of gas feel uneven on your palm, do this test. Hold a dollar, pound, yen or ruble note between the first finger and thumb of each hand. Hold the banknote about 25mm (1 in) from the end of the tailpipe. Watch carefully, please. (Don't let anyone see you doing this, they might call the folks in white jackets to take you away.) The bill should be forced away from the end of the pipe by the steady stream of exhaust. If it momentarily flutters or is drawn toward the pipe at regular intervals, one or more of the exhaust valves is not seating correctly, causing a slight pressure inversion inside the cylinder head. Do the dollar bill test until you're sure of the results. If you think you have a pressure inversion, a valve job is imminent. Valve jobs can be expensive if new parts are needed. Call a machine shop and find out how much.

Keep the engine running and get down on your knees again. Pass the palm of your hand along the exhaust pipe, about 25mm (1 in) *away* from the pipe. Are there holes in the muffler or catalytic converter (if there is one)? Carefully check the clamps holding the muffler and converter to the exhaust pipe. Don't burn yourself! If you feel an exhaust leak, it **must** be fixed.

While you're under there, check the rubber hangers holding the exhaust pipe, catalytic converter and muffler to the bottom of the car. On older cars, it's likely that part of the exhaust system will be held up by lengths of baling wire or string. These will do only as a temporary repair. The rubber hangers prevent the exhaust system from banging against the bottom of the car and driving you crazy.

Time to lift and prop the hood. Listen carefully for a hissing noise around the engine. You're listening for exhaust gases escaping between the exhaust manifold on the right side of the cylinder head and the head itself. Pass your hand all around, but not on, the engine, feeling for streams of exhaust being forced out. Don't touch the exhaust manifold. It's very hot.

Leave the engine running and get back inside the car. The coolant temperature light should still be off. The automatic cooling fan will probably have whirred for a minute or two while you're looking things over. If the water temperature light is on and the fan hasn't turned on yet, get out and check the connection into the rear of the fan motor. If you can't get the fan to turn on, there're three possible problems: the thermoswitch on the left side of the radiator is bad, the fan motor relay on the relay plate (fuse box) just above the driver's knees is broken, or the fan motor is shot. (See Chapter 17, Procedue 3.)

Now that the engine is good and warm you can do a few more tests. Turn the engine off. On gasoline engines on the top left of the camshaft cover (the black metal cover on the top of the engine) there's a plastic hose running to the Positive Crankcase Ventilation (PCV) valve. On diesels the hose runs into the intake manifold. Use a screwdriver to loosen the hose clamp holding the hose at the camshaft cover end and then pull the hose free. Start the engine again and watch for gas puffing out of the hole in the camshaft cover. All engines will have a *small* amount of gas escaping. It's called 'blow-by'. Lots of blow-by means lots of trouble. Have Friend rev the engine a few times. A strong steady stream of whitish gas coming out of the hole indicates worn piston rings. A puff! puff! puff! like an old time railway steam engine means you can bet your bottom guilder that the piston rings in one or more cylinders are not forming a good seal against the cylinder walls. A compression test should confirm your suspicions. Gas engine owners turn to Chapter 10, Procedure 20 and do the test. Diesel owners get the compression test done by a dealer. When you have the results, decide if you want to continue examing this particular car. If you're still hot, please continue.

Turn off the engine and replace the hose connection and tighten the hose clamp.

Sit in the driver's seat, start the engine, pull up the handbrake as hard as you can and put the car into Drive (D) or first gear. Slowly let out the clutch. Automatics: gently depress the accelerator a little way. The brake holding the rear wheels won't allow the car to move, and the engine will stall quickly if the handbrake system is in good working order. If the car moves forward, either the handbrake cables or the rear brake shoes need adjusting/replacing.

Step 2. Test Clutch (Not Automatics)

Depress the clutch pedal and put the shift lever into first gear. Keep the handbrake on. Put the heel of your right foot on the brake pedal and reach out to the accelerator pedal with your toes as you gently release the clutch with your left foot. Keep pressing down on the accelerator as you let out the clutch pedal. If the engine dies as soon as the clutch is engaged, the clutch is in good condition. The clutch is trying to transfer energy to move the wheels via the transmission but is prevented from doing so by the brakes. Do this test only once, and don't let the engine race. If the clutch is engaged you'll wear away what little clutch plate lining remains. If the engine continues to run after the clutch pedal is completely released, the clutch is worn out and needs to be replaced immediately. It's a time consuming job, but not expensive if you don't have to replace everything in the clutch mechanism.

Step 3. See How It Drives (All Models)

Have Friend read this to you or your test drive may end in disaster. Put on your seat belts. Drive a few miles to get the feel of the car. How does it compare to the new Rabbit you drove at the VW dealer?

Check the rearview mirror to see if anyone is behind you, then gently apply the brakes while keeping the accelerator partially depressed. The car should continue to drive in a straight line. If it pulls to one side, the brakes are wearing unevenly or there is brake fluid on the brake components on the side opposite to which the car pulls. Pull over and check the rear view mirror for cars. When the road is clear, start off again. Now try an emergency stop. Brace yourself and slam on the brakes while depressing the clutch at the same time. The car should remain pointed in a straight line and stop rapidly.

Shift to First gear and take off again. Change gears a number of times to see if they engage easily. If you have an automatic transmission, try keeping the transmission in First gear for awhile, then Second and then up to Drive. Don't change back from Drive to First. All models: Get up to 55 miles per hour and feel how the car drives. Does it vibrate? Does the steering wheel wobble? If so, the wheels are out of balance, the ball joints on the tie rod ends or control arms are worn, and/or the front wheel bearings are worn.

Check your rearview mirror carefully. While gently steering the car over to the right, let go of the steering wheel and see if the wheel returns to center. Do the same maneuver to the left.

Drive the car up a hill with the gas pedal pushed to the floor. Release the pedal and listen to the sound of the engine. If you hear a tick-tick-tick, the connecting rod bearings are worn. If you hear a deep knock-knock-knock, the main bearings are suspect. If you hear either sound (or both) the engine is in urgent need of a rebuild. Has the oil light on the dash come up? Stop and check the oil level if it has.

Diesel: diesel engines have an audible 'knock' at idle which should disappear when you speed up. If the knock persists, you probably have a faulty injector. If the knock increases while doing the hill test, the main bearings are probably shot.

Reject the car unless you want to get into Chapter 18 (Engine Rebuild).

Step 4. Check Transmission

Automatics: Is there any problem engaging the passing gear when you floor the gas pedal? If so, the cable running from the gas pedal to the transmission probably needs adjustment. This is easy to do. (Chapter 7, Procedure 1, Automatics Step 3).

Any other suspected problems should be investigated by a VW dealer or transmission specialist.

All Models: There are three basic clues to bad transmissions: difficulty engaging all gears; the gearshift lever popping out of gear; or an audible whine or nasty noise coming from the transmission itself. Automatic transmissions often have a *slight* noise coming from the final drive bearing. If there is a very noticeable whine, the final drive bearings may be worn. Get a specialist to listen. Repairing a transmission is costly.

If you have a standard transmission and find it difficult to get into one or two gears, the gear lever relay rods (the changing mechanism) are probably out of adjustment. (Chapter 16, Procedure 4).

Let's try the standard transmission pop test. Stop the car, put it into first gear and accelerate fairly hard until you're doing about 15 or 20 miles per hour. Quickly take your foot off the gas pedal. The car should stay in gear. If it pops out, try the test again. Now change into second gear until you're doing about 40 miles an hour. Take your foot off the gas again. Try third and fourth gears. If the lever pops out of any gear, the transmission needs to be overhauled.

Find a place where you can back up safely. Put the car into reverse and back up in a long straight line at about 15 mph. Is there a horrible noise coming from the engine or transmission? Try the pop test again. Stick the car in reverse and get up to about 10 mph. Quickly release your foot from the gas pedal. If it pops out of reverse, well . . .you know.

If you're *still* interested in the car at this stage, drive to the VW dealer or find someone who specializes in foreign car transmissions. Ask them how much a rebuilt transmission costs. You could either trade in the faulty transmission for a rebuilt one, or have the bad one rebuilt. When you have a dollar figure, add it to the asking price of the car and check the total against the blue book value. Overhauling a transmission—standard or automatic—requires specialized knowledge and tools. Add some money for the time and effort you'll need to remove the transmission and take it to the repair shop.

Step 5. Check Differential

The differential allows the two front wheels to turn at different speeds so you can corner smoothly, so it's nice to have a good one.

Chock, jack and block the left front of the car after putting it into gear (Chapter 1, Safety First).

Grab the wheel at the 9 and 3 o'clock positions and turn it gently. The play in the differential should be no more than 25-75mm (1-3 ins). If it's more than that, the differential is beginning to wear; repairing it will wear a considerable hole in your pocket. Install Friend in the car and get the engine started with the handbrake on and the gearshift in neutral.

Put it into Drive (D) or first gear and gently depress the gas pedal or release the clutch, depending on whether you have an automatic or stickshift. As the clutch begins to engage, the wheel will start to spin. The noise it makes should be very sweet; you shouldn't hear any rumbles or nasty, cracking and breaking noises like popcorn under a steam roller. Have Friend go through all four gears. The wheel will be rotating at fairly high speed when fourth gear is reached, so this test should be approached with a certain amount of caution. Not fear, just caution. If the wheel bounces around in third or fourth gear, it's probably out of balance. No big deal.

Turn off the engine, assist Friend out of the car and grasp the left front wheel at the 9 and 3 o'clock positions after it stops spinning. Gently rock it side to side, then holding it at the 12 and 6 o'clock positions, rock it up and down. This is another test for a bad bearing or slack in the ball joints. There should be little or no play. Replacing the front wheel bearings takes a considerable amount of work. (Chapter 15, Procedure 9).

Step 6. Brakes

If the brakes didn't seem too good on your test ride, take a closer look by pulling a rear wheel. (Chapter 14, Procedure 5).

Step 7. Become a Magician

You and Friend must now magically remove all traces of your visit. Gather all your tools, flashlight, etc., and put them in your tool bag. Clean off any greasy fingerprints and generally return the car to its original state. Ask what the car will go for in hard cash, then move back five paces and start thinking.

WELL, WHAT DO YOU THINK OF IT?

WHAT DO I THINK OF WHAT?

Step 8. Calculating Reality

Don't feel pressured! Because you have gone to a lot of trouble to evaluate the car, you may feel pressure to buy it because everyone has been so patient while you worked. Ignore any impatient signs or restless pacing as you think about what to do. Take a pencil and paper and jot down the blue book figure you got from the bank. Add or deduct dollars for accessories and/or damage. Write down the asking price of the car, and below that write the price asked by a VW dealer for a similar one. (Subtract about $200 for the price they charge for the guarantee.) Now note what you are prepared to pay. Carefully consider all the car's negative points and subtract money for what problems definitely exist or could occur in the near future. Even if this is the fourth car you've looked at and you really need wheels, don't rush! You don't want a car that will take all your free time to get into running order—or do you? Stay cool—the right car will turn up.

Find out the cost of repairs by calling your VW dealer and asking how much they charge to fix what's wrong. Most dealers will tell you what the labor charge would be, and how much the parts cost. You can do the repairs for just the price of the parts. Subtract this from the asking price. You have four figures: the blue book price, the asking price, the VW dealer price, and the amount of money you're prepared to part with. Phew!

Step 9. El Bargain

A comfortable way to negotiate a deal is on your home turf. So clean the kitchen, shine up the kids, put on a pot of tea and invite the owner in. If you're at a dealer's you might have to sit in cigarette smoke surrounded by nude-y posters unless you've stumbled across a New Wave establishment.

Remember, most people like to haggle. Even dealers fall on hard times, although they make money on every single car they sell, usually lots of it. I'm not able to give you an indication of a fair price for a fair car as this differs every day all over the world.

I like the African method of buying a car. Start out with an incredibly low offer, maybe $500 below what you'd actually consider paying. If the owner has hysterics and leaves, slamming the door, or boots you out (even though it's your house), you started a little too low. But stick close to your estimated top figure and try not to go over it. Don't be taken in by the old line, ''Well, I have someone else interested in the car; they're willing to give me a down payment but need a week to come up with the cash.'' I must have heard that one a thousand times. On the other hand, don't dilly-dally needlessly or a good car will be gone.

Some time ago a friend asked me to look around for a car. We checked the VW agency—too expensive—tried the used car lots—too funky—but one evening the following appeared in the local rag.

For Sale 1976 Rabbit, doesn't run, good body, low mileage. We rushed over to check out the car and asked why it wouldn't run. The owner said he'd heard a horrible grating noise in the engine, turned it off and never dared start it again. Good thinking. We looked at the car, good paint under a layer of dirt, nice upholstery, engine compartment relatively clean, good tires and an honest looking owner. I whipped out my bag of tools and took the cam cover off. The cam and valve adjusting discs seemed fine. The next place I looked for trouble was inside the oil pan since it had a huge dent in it. I pulled it off and found that the oil pump scavenger arm was broken. I replaced the pan and borrowed the phone to call the VW dealer. New pump $60.

I ran through as many of the pre-purchase checks as possible. The mileage was 34,000, which seemed about right, so I felt good about the car, and fixing an oil pump is no big deal. I wiped my hands and offered the owner $400 below his asking price. He accepted my next offer $250 below his price. Next day we towed the car home, bought a new pump and oil pan gasket, and installed the pump in about 30 minutes. We then poured 4 quarts of cheapo SAE 30 oil through the engine to flush out any junk, replaced the gasket, oil pan, and added good oil.

One good deal and two happy people.

I have an acquaintance who bought a '76 Rabbit cheap, drove it for one day, and rolled it over into an arroyo. Fortunately, he was wearing a seat belt and survived with narry a scratch. The car was a writeoff as far as the insurance company was concerned, so he bought it back from them and sold it piece by piece for parts. He came out ahead!

Step 10. Now What

The money has changed hands and you've got what you need. Great. Do yourself a favor and take it to VW to get the front wheel toe-in and camber checked. It's often called an alignment job. These suspension angles affect the way the car drives and steers and keeps the tires from wearing unevenly. Get all four wheels balanced while you're at it. VW doesn't align or balance the wheels on new cars anymore—terrible!

If you've bought a used car, it's equally important to get the alignment checked out. Change the engine oil and filter and install a new fuel filter if the car is fuel injected or has a diesel engine.

Step 11. Warranty

VW offers a 12 month, 20,000 mile guarantee on every new car. This applies to almost everything except the tires. An extended warranty is yours for the buying.

If anything goes bad on the car while it's covered by warranty, take it to VW. You could violate the warranty agreement if you attempt repairs yourself. Let them fix it!

A used car dealer may offer a short limited warranty. As my attorney says, get it in writing. Check the car very carefully, point out any defects on the car, and have them rectified (or subtract money) before you invest in it.

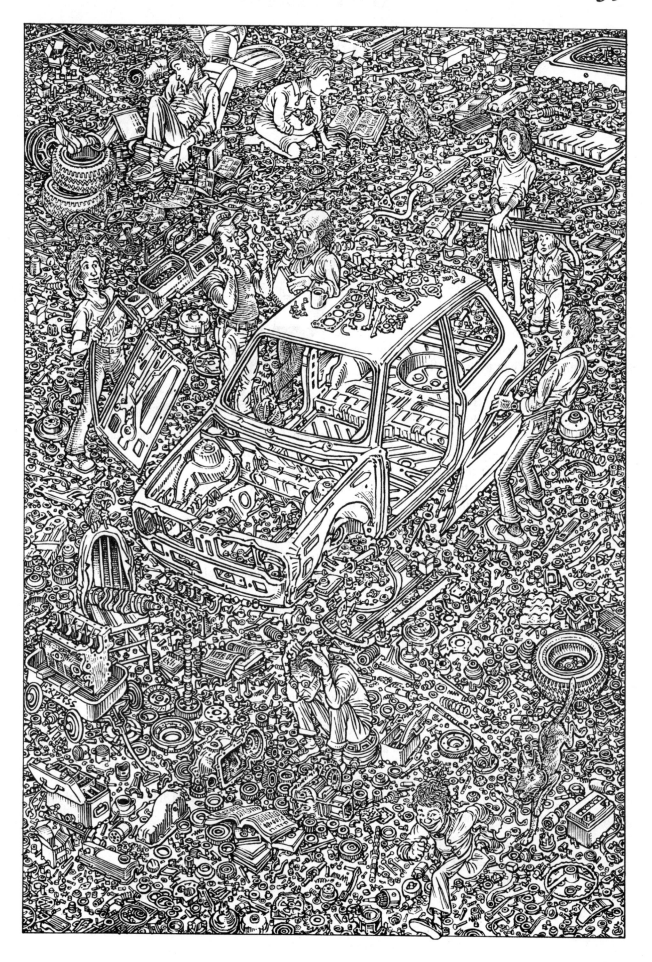

CHAPTER 4

⚊ TOOLS ⚊

If you followed my advice about how to buy a Rabbit, you probably have a few bucks left over. This money can go for tools.

The Rabbit uses the metric system and you must provide yourself with tools to match. On the following pages you'll find three lists of tools and odds and ends to help keep your Rabbit alive. There's a basic set that everyone should carry, even if you never intend to do anything, so the good Samaritans in the Mustang will have the right tools (and these directions, of course) when they stop to help you. Their tools won't fit.

OK, so you need a set of tools, at least enough to keep your Rabbit going. But what kind to buy, where to buy them, and how much to pay?

I prefer Snap-On tools (a brand name). They'll literally last forever, are easy to clean and feel terrific. Believe it or not, a finely crafted tool actually gives you extra confidence, especially if you're new to the world of machines and mechanics. Good tools are not cheap, but at the current rates for a mechanic's labor, you'll soon have your investment back. It's no exaggeration to say that a ten dollar tool can do a hundred dollar repair job, and more than once, if necessary.

There are many quality tool manufacturers other than Snap-On. Large department store chains carry a quite acceptable substitute for the very best. Sears, for example, offers a lifetime guarantee on their Craftsman tools. Be careful, however, when buying large sets of tools on sale. The quality is fine, but you may buy tools you won't actually use. Who needs twenty extra hacksaw blades?

If you're low on cash you can read the Procedure through first then buy only what you need for that work. It takes very little to get started and few bucks will set you up to do the maintenance. Then, with time, you'll build up the full Phase I kit. You might get hung up with a road emergency or two but this will just encourage you to increase your tool stash. On the other hand, if you equip for Phase I right away, you'll be ready. When that V belt breaks in the middle of a snowy Christmas Eve a couple of hours from home, you'll have a warm heart to go along with your cold fingers.

I've found tools in pawn shops, flea markets, surplus stores, and places like that. Antique tools are also popular these days. They're usually slightly bent or well worn after a hard life down on the farm. But what was made for a Model A Ford is not going to fit a VW Rabbit. Besides, you'll pay twice the price just because the seller says, "Well, you know, it's an antique."

Carefully inspect used tools for hairline cracks, especially around the squared inside surfaces of wrenches. Make sure load-bearing surfaces are not rounded off, as that makes the tool useless.

In case you have any U.S. tools on hand, some have direct metric equivalents. The wrench substitutions that can be used when up the proverbial creek are:

11mm = 7/16 in	17mm = 11/16 in
13mm = 1/2 in	19mm = 3/4 in
14mm = 9/16 in	21mm = 13/16 in
15mm = 5/8 in	22mm = 7/8 in

If you file an old 3/8 in open end just a little in the jaw, it will fit a 10mm nut beautifully.

Wrap a piece of adhesive tape around an American sized wrench and mark it with the equivalent mm size.

When you can't afford certain tools or will rarely need to use them, consider trading one of your skills (like fixing Rabbits) for the use of a friend's tools. I find, however, that friendships can be strained when someone borrows tools and then loses one, breaks another, doesn't get them back in time, or runs off to Florida with the loaned toolbox in the trunk. I lend mine, but I make it clear that they are part of my livelihood and I would really like to have them back.

Don't buy ripped off tools, their Karma is tragic.

The basic set of tools is called Phase 1 and will perform Procedures marked Phase I. The next degree of difficulty or whatever calls for Phase II tools. Phase III tools include just about everything you would ever need for a Rabbit.

The size of your tool collection will depend on just how independent you wish to become from your local VW dealer, shade tree mechanic, or anyone in between. In addition to the tool lists, I've included basic spare part kits which should be in the car at all times.

Some Procedures may call for more complicated tools. Tool rental places can supply pullers, reamers, drills, and even large socket sets—things you might need once in the lifetime of your Rabbit.

A few Procedures call for special tools not found in any of the tool lists. The required special tool will be listed under "Tools and materials" found at the beginning of the Procedure.

Once again, is it worth it? Well, consider this: a friend of mine was driving along happily in her Rabbit, listening to her favorite tape, when the engine suddenly crapped out. This is the kind of situation that can make the strong weep, especially when you're in the middle of the Arizona desert and late for Thanksgiving dinner at Mom's.

Up with the hood and out with the tools conveniently stored in an old lunchbox. A few quick checks came up with a broken rotor in the distributor. Into the spares kit (another old lunch box; this woman likes flea markets) for a replacement. Fifteen minutes later she was on her way again and got home in time to make the gravy. What would have been the cost of a tow truck and mechanic's time, not to mention the hassle? Let's not even think about it.

PHASE I, TOOLS

Some tools don't have to be the best to keep your Rabbit rolling. Whenever a discount store tool is adequate, I've noted it in the list. All other tools should be of the highest quality you can beg, borrow, or buy.

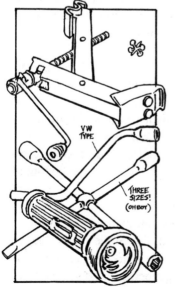

Jack   It should come with the car and either be fastened inside the left hand side of the trunk with a rubber strap or be underneath the spare wheel in the trunk. If it's not there, look under the seats. The jack fits in the ridge between the wheels on the underside of the Rabbit. If you have to buy one, check the junk yards for the proper Rabbit jack. No luck? Buy a scissor jack or 1-ton hydraulic jack from Sears, or a place like that. Avoid cheap, shoddy jacks.

Lug Wrench   The angled kind that should have come with the car is best. If you have to buy one, get a good one; it's essential. A 17mm socket will also work and, in a pinch, a 17mm box end wrench.

Flashlight   Get one with a magnet holder-on and check the batteries regularly.

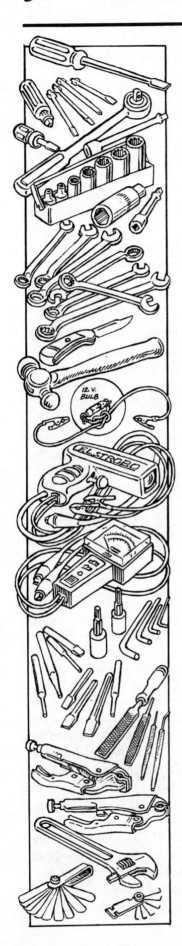

Big Screwdriver	46cm (18 in) or 60cm (24 in) with a plastic or wooden handle.
Screwdriver	The kind with a handle and several detachable blades, including a small blade or electrical work and a phillips type head. Discount store screwdrivers are not recommended.
3/8 in Drive Metric Socket Set	With socket sizes from 8mm to 19 or 22mm. Buy a spark plug socket, 21mm (13/16 in), and a universal drive. The set will have 2 in, and a 4 in or 6 in extensions for turning impossible-to-reach nuts or bolts. The word 'drive' applies to the size of the square hole in the bottom of the socket. The square drive part of the ratchet handle fits into this square hole.
Box of Combination (Box/Open End) Wrenches	8mm, 10mm, 13mm, 14mm, 15mm, 16mm, and 17mm. Two 13mm wrenches (one short and one long) are nice to have.
Pocket Knife	With a sharp blade.
Hammer	Light ball peen.
Test Light	Buy it at a discount store or make one like Peter's sketch.
Strobe Timing Light	Some mechanics used to consider this an unnecessary, new-fangled invention. The Rabbit requires fine tuning to keep it operating at maximum efficiency. To get the timing right, you must use a timing light! A cheap light from a discount store will do, but if you can afford it get something of better quality. Diesel Rabbit owners do not need a timing light.
Tach Dwell Meter	To set the points and engine idle RPM. Diesel Rabbits don't need this tool, either. Another discount store tool if you're short of money.
Allen Wrenches	5mm, 6mm, 7mm and 8mm. The socket type that fits onto a ratchet handle is best and easiest to use.
Chisel and Punch Set	For metal, not wood. Get a copper or brass drift and a medium 'diamond tip' chisel (a round punch with a flat end) to remove wheel bearing races, etc.
Files	A small flat point file, a 13mm (1/2 in) fine cut half-round and medium cut, medium-sized rattail file.
Vice Grip Pliers	The 20cm (8 in) size with a narrow flat jaw. If you can afford it, get a wide jaw, too.
Crescent Wrench	25cm (10 in). A handy tool to have when you can't find your 17mm wrench hidden at the bottom of your toolbox.
Feeler Gauges and Plug Gapper	Buy a *metric* set with blades. U.S. sizes are usually stamped beneath the metric sizes; discount store feeler gauges will do. Some feeler gauges have an arm to adjust the spark plug electrode. If yours doesn't, buy a gapper from a discount store.

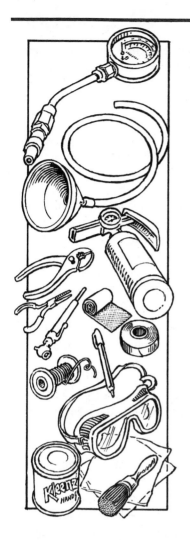

Compression Tester	Diesel owners don't bother; your engine requires a very expensive type.
Filler Hose (Automatics)	A flexible automatic transmission fluid filler hose with a funnel attached to one end. Buy it from a discount store.
Fire Extinguisher	One which will put out gasoline fires. Make sure it's U.L. listed and keep it in the car or around the work area.
Pliers	Two pairs, regular and needle-nosed.
Tire Gauge	To check the air pressure.
Odds n' Ends	60 cm (24 in) of 50mm (2 in) fine emery cloth, rolled up with a rubber band. A role of soft tie wire (baling wire). Masking tape. Safety glasses or goggles. An absolute must if you value your eyesight. Indelible pen. Plastic electrical insulating tape. Baggies.
Conveniences	Pair of coveralls, stocking cap for long hair, rags, cleaning pan, solvent and stiff brush, low stool to sit on while you work, a piece of cardboard or sheet of plastic to lie on, painter's mask and hand-cleaning solution. A cheap plastic dish pan to use when changing the oil. A good substitute is a cardboard box, about 45cm (18 in) square, lined with plastic, a garbage bag for example.

PHASE I, SPARE PARTS

This list is what I carry with me at all times. I don't even pick up the kids from school without this stuff. If you can afford to keep a stash of the first three items, please do. If not, do your periodic maintenance procedures on time (Chapter 10) and buy these parts when you take a long trip. Buy ignition parts and V-belts from a VW dealer; they fit better than copies.

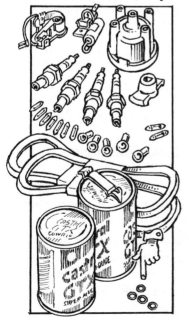

Ignition Points and Condenser Distributor Cap and Rotor Spark Plugs	
Fuses and Bulbs	Carry a package of fuses and two tail light and turn signal bulbs.
V–Belts	To fit the alternator and smog pump (if you have one). If your car has air conditioning, get the extra long belt to accommodate the air conditioner pulley, especially if you plan to travel during the summer.
Oil	Carry two quarts of the type you prefer. Read the beginning of Chapter 10 to find out what type you prefer.
O Rings	If you have fuel injection, buy four rubber O rings for the injection nozzles. The parts person at VW will give you the right ones.

After awhile you'll find yourself with a handy collection of nuts, bolts, washers, rings, studs and other miscellany. Keep this stuff in a can with a screw-on top and it'll become your best friend (especially after you drop your last 13mm nut into the dust). It's also something for the kids to rattle while you're under the car.

PHASE II, TOOLS AND EQUIPMENT

If you've enjoyed Phase I, you'll want to get into Phase II. It's a little more involved.

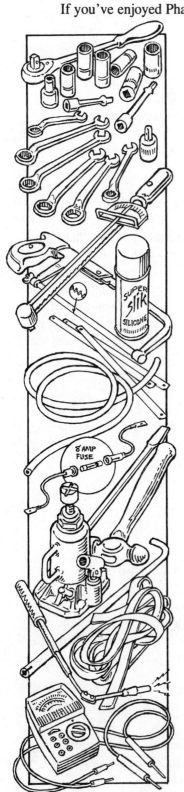

Ratchet Handle	A good 1/2 in drive
Sockets	1/2 in drive: 13mm, 15mm 17mm, and 19mm.
Extensions	1/2 in drive: 50mm (2 in) long and a 15cm (6 in) long. Buy two 15cm (6 in) extensions if you have an automatic transmission. You'll need them to remove the starter.
Adaptor	1/2 in to 3/8 in, so you can use the 1/2 in ratchet handle with the 3/8 in sockets.
Combination Wrenches	To complete your set: 9mm, 11mm, 12mm, 16mm, and 19mm. Don't buy an 18mm, you'll never use it.
Torque Wrench	1/2 in drive, 0 to 160 pounds, which is 0 to 20.74 meter kilograms (mkg). There's a front axle nut that has to be torqued to 167 lbs, but we can work that out later.
A Hacksaw and Blades	Course and fine.
Silicone Lubricant	Spray can, non-aerosol if you can find one.
Plastic Hose	A 1.20m (48 in) piece of 4mm (5/32 in) plastic hose (internal diameter) for draining brake fluid and bleeding the brakes. Brake fluid is poisonous. Never use this hose for siphoning gas or water once it's contaminated with brake fluid.
Electrical Wire	30cm (12 in) piece of $1.5mm^2$ (14 gauge) electrical wire with a small spade connector on each end and a replaceable 8 amp fuse in the middle. This is essential for fuel injection system tests and various electrical tests on the relay plate (fuse box).
Bar	A 45 cm (18 in) iron bar with a point on one end and a chisel on the other.
Ball Peen Hammer	A 1-1/2 lb or 2 lb ball peen hammer.
Scissor Jack	A scissor jack or one-ton hydraulic jack, in addition to the jack that came with the car. Get a good one.
Tow Rope	A nylon strap is best, check discount stores for a good one on sale.
A Magnet	The inspection type with a 13mm (1/2 in) magnet on an extendable handle. A smaller one is also nice.
A Volt/Ohm Meter	Radio Shack makes a good inexpensive one called a 'Micronta.' A meter is very handy for battery continuity and other electrical tests. It's needed for testing the electrical and fuel injection systems.

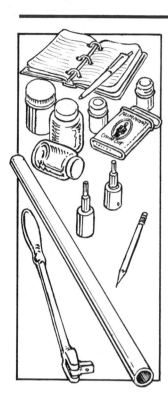

A Notebook	With oil resistant paper and something waterproof with which to write. A 'space pen' is great but expensive—buy one from a good camping store.
Containers	A couple of small plastic containers with close-fitting lids, a small can with a screw type lid. Ask your smoking friends for a tobacco can.
Allen Wrench	A 10mm, 3/8 in drive to fit on your ratchet handle. Cars '78 and on require a polygon type for removing the starter and cylinder head. (Mac or Snap-On have them.) (See Diagram.)
C.V. Joint Tool (Allen Head Socket)	It's an 8mm, 3/8 in drive, 12-pointed polygon allen wrench for removing the socket head bolts in the constant velocity joints. You can also buy this from your Snap-On or Mack tool dealer. (See Diagram.)
Flex Handle or Breaker Bar	1/2 in drive 60 cm (24 in) long.
Cheater	A 1 meter (3 ft) piece of 50mm (2 in) pipe to slip over the end of your breaker bar.

PHASE II, SPARE PARTS

A can of heavy-duty brake fluid meeting SAE recommendation J1703 and motor vehicle safety standard 116 DOT3.

Constant velocity joint grease from VW.

A collection of clamps, 13mm (½ in) to 50mm (2 in).

Lengths of electrical wire of various gauges.

Push-on electrical connectors of various types and sizes, and if you want, a pair of special electrician's pliers with connector sealing teeth and wire stripping notches.

If you have fuel injection, consider getting an injector and a spray can of chemical cleaner called Berryman Chemtool B-12^{tm}. This magic stuff will free up binding plungers and clean injectors (we'll get into this later). Your local auto parts store should have it. If not, ask them to get it for you. VW highly recommends it.

You don't have to stash these spare parts in your car unless you're off on a cross-country trip. It's good just to have them around and will save you from running out to the parts store early Sunday morning.

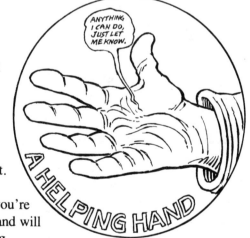

PHASE III, TOOLS AND SPARES

You need Phase III stuff only if you want to get serious about being a mechanic. It helps to be able to reach into your toolbox and pull out the correct tool for the correct job. But you don't always need Phase III tools for Phase III jobs. You've probably got them covered with Phase II tools, and the ones you don't have, you can borrow or rent.

I don't suggest a list of spares for Phase III. If you carry out preventive maintenance you'll be aware when something major is about to give up the ghost. If you think the clutch might have only a few thousand miles left on it and decide to drive cross-country to visit Aunt Ethel, it's a good idea to carry a spare clutch and the tools to change it; or do it before you go.

Phase III includes enough tools to rebuild the Rabbit's engine or just about any other metric car. OK, this is what you'll need:

PHASE III, TOOLS

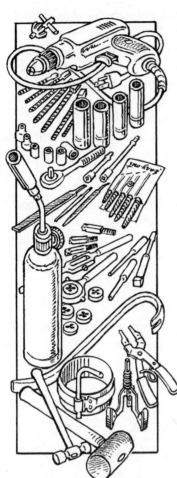

Electric Drill and High Speed Bits	Buy good brand name bits.
Deep Socket Set	8mm through 19mm. A 30mm or 1-3/8 in socket for removing the front driveshaft nuts.
1/4 in. Drive Socket Set	They're very nice for fiddly little stuff.
Files	Finer and coarser than the ones you already have.
A Set of Easy Outs	For removing broken studs or bolts. The Snap-On ones are the best I've ever seen.
A Big Tool Box with Drawers	Get one on sale.
Metric Tap and Die Set	To restore bad threads or make new ones. Include one to restore spark plug threads in the cylinder head.
Chisels and Punches	Different lengths and widths from the ones you have.
Bar	A 60cm (24 in) wrecking bar.
Butane Torch Set	With an extra tank and a couple of nozzles
Circlip Pliers	See Diagram.
Ring Compressor	For installing the pistons in the crankcase. Not vital, but it makes life easier when rebuilding the engine.
Ridge Reamer	Sometimes called a cylinder bore hone set. It fits into an electric (or hand) drill.
Hammers	A brass one and a rubber one.

Other sources of help and advice

Companions to this book are the **VW Owners Manual**, which should be in the glove compartment of your Rabbit, and the repair manual put out by VW for the Type 17 Rabbit and the Type 53 Scirocco. The second edition is the one for you. The first edition doesn't cover the smog control or fuel injection systems.

A fine book is the **Volkswagen Service Manual for Rabbit, Scirocco** published by Robert Bentley, Inc. Another good book is the **Haynes Workshop Manual**. Volkswagen also puts out some excellent technical manuals on the fuel injection system and certain other troubleshooting guides.

A really good source of information is your VW dealer. You'll find the service manager and mechanics can be very helpful when they have time, and will give all kinds of information and tips if you get stuck. The people here in Santa Fe are terrific and have helped me and my friends whenever they've been asked.

Safety

I told you in Chapter I that I'll refer constantly to safety measures. Use your head! Not as a substitute for a 10 lb hammer, but to select the correct tool for each job. Wear your safety glasses at all times to protect your eyes while working, and a painter's mask when dealing with dust, especially during brake jobs. That stuff is *very* nasty. I want you to make it through all the Procedures without so much as a scratch.

Take good care of yourself.

CHAPTER 5

❧ DRIVING IT ❧

I'm not going to try to teach you how to drive with this book. That's a job for a certified instructor or a friend with steel nerves. Your Rabbit, however, wants to be driven in a certain way; one that will prolong its life span to the maximum. With proper driving technique, you'll save yourself a lot of money and spend less time wearing greasy coveralls.

If you haven't driven a small import or subcompact American car before, you'll soon discover that your Rabbit likes to be driven with spirit. That doesn't mean you have to drag race every Corvette you see at traffic lights or take corners on two wheels, but it does like to zip around.

It's very important, therefore, to *never* lug the engine! Don't take off in second or third. That's the quickest way to burn out the clutch and give the engine a generally hard time.

On the other hand, don't wind the engine to maximum revs as you work your way through the gears. The car's engine sounds will tell you when to shift. You'll get used to it quickly.

If your engine has a carburetor and you like to drive hard, you'll notice the revs sometimes linger when shifting from first to second and second to third. This is caused by the smog control device designed to burn excess gas in the carburetor before the engine goes down to lower revolutions.

HOW TO DRIVE A WATER-COOLED VOLKSWAGEN

Step 1. Daily Checks

Turn to the first part of Chapter 10 and run through the daily maintenance stuff in Procedure 1.

Step 2. Check Dashboard Warning Lights

Put the key in the ignition, turn it to ON and see that all the red lights come on, except the little thermometer symbol. That's the coolant temperature warning and it comes on only when the engine is overheating. No lights? Turn to Chapter 8, Procedure 1 or Chapter 9, Procedure 2.

Step 3. Start It

All the lights functioned properly and the nagging buzzer has been de-buzzed by clicking your safety belt on. Turn the key off and back on again to start the engine. Diesel people, go through your starting routine: turn the key to the first postition, pull the glow plug knob to the left of the steering wheel and wait until the dash warning light goes out. Now turn the key to start the engine.

Don't pump the pedal or press it to the floor. If you're a compulsive pedal pumper, give it just one small tap and sit on your foot until the engine has started.

In sub-zero weather you might have to give it two or three tries. A well-tuned Rabbit, however, with correct viscosity oil in the crankcase should start immediately. Those of you who live in total sub-zero temperatures, like the North or South Pole, might consider a recirculating type water heater or an electric dipstick. They're sold in auto parts stores. A word or two of warning: if the car won't start, there's no need to hold the key in the start position for minutes at a time listening to the frantic whirr of the starter motor. You'll

quickly burn out the starter and drain the battery. Starters in two friends' Rabbits needed to be replaced because they were too lazy to do tune-ups. Their cars started only after many rotations of the starter accompanied by the usual oaths. Do tune-ups—before it costs you!

Step 4. To Shift or Not To Shift

Besides being unsafe, sloppy shifting of the gears is murder on your neck muscles, transmission linkage, clutch mechanism, and engine/drive train mounts.

The Rabbit engine works best at an even speed, between 2,000 and 4,000 rpms (revolutions per minute), and it's the transmission's job to keep the engine happy and well.

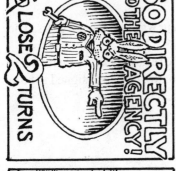

For a new or rebuilt Rabbit engine, I highly recommend a break-in period. The way you treat your engine during the first 600 miles will strongly influence its lifespan. Don't overstrain it; drive as though it were made of very expensive glass. Be careful not to lug it so that it shudders, and *never* take off from a standstill in second gear. Here are the break-in speeds:

With a standard transmission, don't take first gear beyond 18 mph, second beyond 33 mph, third beyond 50 mph, and fourth, well, Smokey says you can't do more than 55 so we'll say 55 mph.

If you have an automatic transmission, don't go above 25 mph in first, 39 mph in second, and 55 mph in Drive.

By the time the engine has been driven 600 miles you should have changed the oil once (at 300 miles). Do it again now at 600 miles (but don't use 'slippery' oil). Chapter 10, Procedure 9 tells how. When 600 miles are up, you can take first gear to 28 mph, second to between 12 and 50 mph, third between 19 and 55 mph, and fourth to between 25 and the legal speed limit of the day.

It REALLY PAYS to break in the engine properly.

Step 5. Driving Tips

The Rabbit drives very well; it holds the road and is very forgiving of driver error. Keep your eyes on the road and you'll never have to find out how forgiving. Avoid the temptation to lane hop. Weaving in and out may save 3 minutes in 40 miles, but you'll wear out not only the tires but your passenger's nerves. If you see crosswind warning notices, drop your speed by about 5 mph or so, more if you're pulling a trailer. The Rabbit sits well on the road and isn't easily blown around.

The aerodynamic shape of the Rabbit sometimes causes a strange sensation when a semi truck comes roaring by too closely. It tends to suck you up behind. Don't tailgate big trucks—or anyone else, for that matter. It's dangerous, especially if the driver ahead of you suddenly slams on the brakes

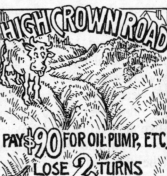

and doesn't have brake lights.

When you find yourself caught between two large vehicles, air turbulence will tend to pull your Rabbit in peculiar directions. Keep a firm grip on the wheel, but stay relaxed—it's a little like piloting an airplane. You'll soon be aware of any weird handling tendencies of your Rabbit and how to deal with them. Get a VW or front-end shop to align and balance your front wheels, if the steering wheel wobbles in your hands at any speed.

For driving on mud, snow or ice, snow tires or dual purpose radials are a must. Put snow tires on the front wheels, since the drive is from the front! Use radial snow tires—don't mix radial and bias ply tires. Dangerous! Remember that your car is low to the ground and won't go through heavy snow drifts or deep ruts.

Step 6. Safety.

Manufacturers are at last trying to build 'safety' into their cars. They now have roll bars, side beams, impact-resistant bumpers, telescopic steering, seat belts, air bags, etc. All this is fine and commendable, but it's up to you to drive safely and avoid crash-testing the safety equipment. It seems good sense to *always* wear your seat belts. Statistics show, etc., etc., etc.

VW designed the luxury edition Rabbits to be inoperable unless the safety belt is clicked into position on the door. Other Rabbits have buzzers and a dash warning light to remind you to fasten your belts before moving off. The first thing many people do after buying a Rabbit is remove the buzzer. Keep yours in place, even though it seems designed for annoyance rather than as a gentle reminder.

Trusty German engineers have also incorporated a brake fail-safe system so that the brakes, one front and one rear wheel, will work even if the hydraulic system is punctured.

Keep the car's vital systems alive—brakes, signals, lights, windshield wipers, etc.—and your chances of remaining safe will improve greatly.

Step 7. Skids.

It happens in every movie. The bad guys drive full blast into a corner, the car skids through a department store window and stops in a wonderful shower of plate glass. It's not just that crime doesn't pay—the car's tires were unable to maintain contact with the road surface and the car went out of control.

To be certain this never happens to you, keep your speed down to a safe level. Take it easy on curvy mountain roads; brake before you get to a curve, not when you're halfway through it.

However, if your car goes into a skid, the rear end will try to overtake the front, and you should know what to do. Let's say you daydream into a *right*

hand curve and suddenly lose it. Don't panic! Turn the steering wheel a little to the *left* (in the direction you're skidding) and keep your foot on the gas a little. The power at the front wheels will pull you out of the skid. If you lose control on a *left* hand curve, turn the steering wheel a little to the *right*.

Step 8. Panic Stops

Casting a lingering eye on the driver in the Alfa may rapidly initiate you into the art of panic stops.

When that time comes, push both the clutch and brake pedals down through the floor boards at the same time. Depressing the clutch pedal prevents the engine from pulling the car along while the brake system tries to stop the wheels.

If you're really barrelling along, 'pump' the brake pedal. This allows the wheels to retain their grip on the road. Lose grip and you lose direction. Lose direction and…

I've taken my Rabbit onto a state police skidpan (a big flat tarred area covered with a thin layer of water to make it slippery) and done all sorts of fancy sliding tricks. Not only was it lots of fun, but I was pleased to see how easily the car pulled out of the skids. So were the state police; they hate cleaning up.

Step 9. Conserve Gasoline

A car engine is a notorious energy waster; only about one quarter of the heat energy it produces is actually used. The rest is taken away by the cooling and exhaust systems, or just plain lost to friction. Wasted energy is wasted money and resources. There are many ways to conserve fuel, but keeping your car in excellent tune and driving gently are probably the best. So do the routine maintenance procedures on time.

Here are some other tips on stretching a tankful of fuel and keeping exhaust pollutants to a minimum. Don't pump the gas pedal twenty times before starting the engine. Move off smoothly in first gear and engage second gear as soon as the engine feels comfortable. When you get up to highway speed (55 mph) ease your foot off the gas pedal until the car maintains the speed you want.

Tire burning starts and squealing stops are very wasteful. Slow down smoothly before an obstruction so you don't have to come to a complete stop. Even a rolling speed of 5 miles per hour will save fuel as you gently accelerate away.

Let the engine idle when you come to a complete stop. Don't rev the engine impatiently like a cruiser outside the ice cream shoppe.

If you are stuck at a railway crossing or a ticker tape parade, turn off your engine until the procession passes.

When you have to climb a hill, shift down into a lower gear. Don't try to get up in high gear. It's bad for the engine and worse for the clutch.

Keep the fuel tank as full as possible but not so full that it slops out when you park on a slight hill. In winter, an almost empty tank will allow water vapor in the fuel system to freeze and shut off your fuel supply. Also the water vapor will condense and rust the tank, causing big problems, especially with the fuel injection system. In summer, park in the shade so the fuel doesn't vaporize.

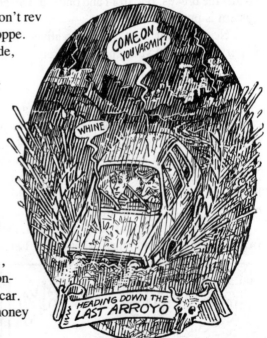

HEADING DOWN THE LAST ARROYO

If you use a roof rack to haul camping stuff, skis, etc., remove it when your holiday is over. A rack can increase gas consumption up to 6% by altering the aerodynamic shape of your car.

By following these economy tips you'll save yourself money and help stretch dwindling oil supplies.

CHAPTER 6

❧ TOWED AND PUNCTURED ❧

This chapter covers a few things that don't require much in the way of tools, time or energy; but is stuff you should know. The towing procedure following the flat tire information should be done with extreme care.

I don't want to insult any ace mechanics by telling you how to change a tire. But some people have never done it, so those who know how please skip ahead. Changing a flat tire is basically the same procedure you'll follow any time a wheel has to be removed.

PROCEDURE 1: CHANGING A TIRE. Phase 1.

Condition: You've got a flat tire or a busted wheel.

Tools and materials: A sturdy jack, a large screwdriver, a lugwrench and an inflated tire mounted on a wheel that fits your car. The spare tire should be in the trunk under the mat.

Step 1. Safety First

If the tire goes flat while you're driving, carefully pull over to the side and switch on the emergency flashers. Don't change a tire in the middle of the road, no matter how deserted it may seem. As soon as you get the car jacked up, someone will come belting along in a semi.

Ask your passengers to get out of the car and keep well away from the road. Safety! The shoulder on a busy highway is one of the most dangerous places on earth. Hold onto small children and keep pets in the car so they don't jump away and cause havoc.

Step 2. Chock, Jack and Block the Car

Put the car into gear or park and pull on the handbrake. Get your lugwrench. It's usually in the trunk, strapped to the left side of the inner body panel or under the spare tire below the trunk carpet. Find some big rocks or something to chock each tire on the side of the car opposite the one you are going to be changing. Got that?

Pry off the hubcap with your screwdriver. If you have those phoney black plastic lug nut covers instead of the genuine article, work them off with the screwdriver. I can never do this without breaking at least one.

OK, now put the lugwrench squarely on one of the lug nuts and loosen it by turning counterclockwise ↻. It won't move? The lug nuts were probably put on by someone who thought the air impact wrench was a machine gun, so you'll have to really throw your weight into it. Try this: put the lugwrench on the nut with the handle horizontal. Be sure the wrench is fully and firmly engaged onto the lug nut 'cause if it slips you'll have a nice fat bruise on your shin. Stand on the handle and use the car roof for balance. Now bounce (carefully) on the handle, lightly at first.

When all four nuts are loose—just loose, we'll take them off later—set the jack in the ridge under the triangular mark stamped in the lower body panel nearest to the burst tire. If the ground is soft, put a board or flat rock under the jack. Raise the car until the flat tire is about 13 cm (5 in) off the ground.

Block the car in case the jack slips or fails. It happens more often than you might think, so please be careful! If you don't have a block or large rock, put the spare wheel under the car. For a rear flat, put it under

the axle beam. Up front put the wheel under the suspension. If the jack lets loose, the block (or wheel) will prevent the car from falling all the way to the ground—or onto your hand or foot. If it does fall, you'll have a hell of a time getting it back up without room to put the jack. When it's safely jacked and blocked, rock the car to see if it really *is* safe.

Stuck out in the rain somewhere or in a hurry? Don't cut corners by leaving out the support block. That's the one time the jack will fail.

With the car jacked and blocked, remove all four lug nuts and pull off the wheel.

Step 3. Exchange Wheels

Roll your spare over to where you're working. If you used it for a safety block, drag it out from under the car and put the flat tire in its place. Rotate the wheel until the holes in the wheel line up with the holes in the hub. Now lift the spare into position on the wheel hub and screw on a lug nut. Now screw on the other three nuts. Spin them on with the lugwrench until they are just firm. If you try to tighten them down before the car has been lowered to the ground, the wheel will spin or you might force the car off the jack and onto your foot.

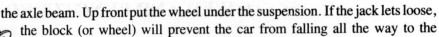

Remove the block or flat tire from under the car and lower the jack. Tighten all four lug nuts as firmly as you can. If you aren't very strong or have a bad back, try standing—carefully again—on the lugwrench handle. One bounce should do it. Snap on the black plastic lug nut covers or hubcap. Put your tools and the flat tire into the trunk and head for the nearest service station. Paranoia will lurk in your trunk in the strange shape of a flat tire, so get it fixed right away.

My Rabbit once became hard to steer, so I pulled over and checked the tires. The left front was going down fast. Out with the jack and off with the wheel. Five minutes later I'm on my merry way driving past all the gas stations and tire repair places. "Tomorrow, tomorrow I'll take it in."

One week later, beat and weary after rebuilding and installing an engine, I hauled myself into my car. You guessed it; this time the spare was flat, remember? The moral: Fix Flats Fast.

While they're fixing the flat, check the air pressure in your other tires. It should be 1.90 kg/cm^2 (27 pounds per spare inch). Add 3 psi if you have heavy friends or groceries in the back seat.

Check each tire for cuts and scrapes, both in the tread and sidewalls and replace any tire with poor tread or gashes. If you're not sure about a tire's condition, ask the service station attendant for advice. But try to buy your tires from a tire store; they're usually a lot cheaper. Call and compare prices.

If you need new tires, get good quality steel belted radials, not bias ply tires. Your car was designed to run on radials. Changing to bias ply tires will alter the handling characteristics so instead of moving like a Rabbit, it'll go around corners like a gorilla on a skateboard—heavily.

PROCEDURE 2: TOWING. Phase 1.

Condition: Break down!

Tools and materials: Tow car, good quality tow rope/chain, Friend.

Remarks: You're sitting on the side of the highway, no tools, too tired to think and not able to do anything but get the car towed to harbor. There are four towing eyes on the underside of the Rabbit and Scirocco—two in front and two in back. It's very important you don't lash your towing cable around either the front or rear bumper. A jerky tow driver may drag your bumper home and leave you and the rest of the Rabbit on the highway.

If your car has an automatic transmission, do not tow it more than thirty miles or faster than thirty miles per hour. The automatic transmission has an oil pump which pumps only when the engine is working. So, if the engine isn't turning over while the car is moving, the transmission isn't being lubricated. The 30 mile, 30 miles-per-hour towing limit is *ABSOLUTELY CRUCIAL*. The dollars you try to save by towing the car a few extra miles over the 30 mile limit will soon be in the hands of the transmission shop owner. A tow truck is needed to lift the front wheels off the ground if you have a long way to go, or you can remove the front drive shafts. See Chapter 16.

Cars with a standard transmission should also be held to the thirty miles-per-hour speed limit, but you can tow it almost any distance. Do the journey in 50-mile hops, then rest awhile to give everything a chance to cool down.

Step 1. Safety

Tape a sign in the rear window of the car to be towed, reading ''Car in Tow.'' Turn on your emergency flashers and the flashers of the vehicle doing the towing.

Step 2. Prepare to Tow

Attach the tow rope, chain, cable or strap through the towing eyes welded to the bottom of the car, and tie the other end to the vehicle doing the towing. Whatever you use, the length between the two vehicles should be no longer than 4.5 meters (15 feet). If it's longer, other drivers may not realize you're being towed and try to nip in between the two vehicles, with quite spectacular and alarming results! Tie a rag in the middle of the tow line to prevent this from happening.

Step 3. Tow Away

Get in the car and turn the ignition key to ON to free the steering wheel lock. If your car has

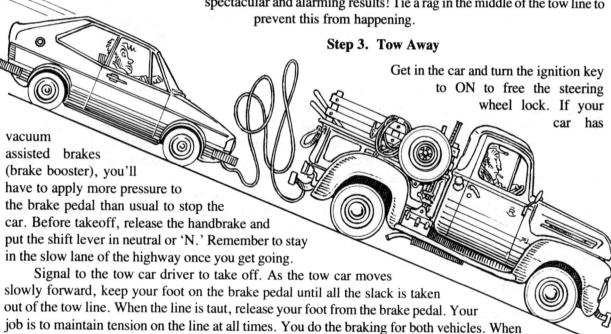

vacuum assisted brakes (brake booster), you'll have to apply more pressure to the brake pedal than usual to stop the car. Before takeoff, release the handbrake and put the shift lever in neutral or 'N.' Remember to stay in the slow lane of the highway once you get going.

Signal to the tow car driver to take off. As the tow car moves slowly forward, keep your foot on the brake pedal until all the slack is taken out of the tow line. When the line is taut, release your foot from the brake pedal. Your job is to maintain tension on the line at all times. You do the braking for both vehicles. When stopping for a traffic light or something, the towing vehicle should be put into neutral while you apply your brakes to eventually stop both cars.

Keep the tow line tight. If it goes slack and the tow driver takes off suddenly, the necksnapping jolt of your car may come as a little surprise. Tight, slow and smooth is the way it goes. If the tow line breaks as you are moving, just coast until you find a safe place to stop. Don't slam on the brakes, someone might be very close behind!

Tow your car to a VW dealer if it's still under warranty. If you attempt to repair any defect while it's still covered by warranty, you may end up paying.

CHAPTER 7

A TRIP INTO THE INTERIOR
ORIENTATION AND RABBIT WON'T START

If you've ever owned an air-cooled Volkswagen, you'll recall that the engine and running gear were in the back of the car. The new breed, however, is water-cooled and the engine and transmission are mounted transversely (sideways) in the front. Before we get into anything mechanical, let's take a guided tour inside the engine compartment to learn names and find out what does what.

Diesel owners have an engine compartment diagram in Chapter 21, but you'll be referred back here if you have to deal with the starter, solenoid, etc.

Deluxe Rabbits and all Sciroccos have a hood latch release lever to the left of the driver's legs, so if you've got it, pull it. Lovely . . . Lift and prop the hood, or bonnet as they say in the old country, and let's check what's under it.

All Models: The engine is capped by a black metal **camshaft cover**.
On the front of the cover is the **oil filler cap**, and on the back, a hose. This hose may incorporate a flattened plastic cylinder called the **positive crankcase ventilation (PCV) valve**. The aluminum casting to which the camshaft cover is attached is called the **cylinder head**. Four **spark plugs** screw into the left side of the cylinder head which is fastened to the top of the **crankcase (engine block)** by 10 big bolts. The bolts are hidden by the camshaft cover. Inside this cast iron crankcase are four **pistons**, the **crankshaft, intermediate shaft**, etc. The whole works is collectively termed the **engine**.

At the front of the engine, close to the right fender, is a steel **belt guard** which keeps stray fingers out of the **camshaft drive belt (timing belt** or **spur belt)**. This toothed belt is driven by a **sprocket** wheel bolted to the end of the crankshaft. It passes over two other sprockets to turn the intermediate shaft and camshaft. Chapter 2 explains what and why it all works. The oil **dipstick**, a thin metal rod curved at the top, lives halfway along the left side of the engine.

TRANSMISSION

The rear of the transmission is supported by a mount on the inside of the left fender. There's another mount (also partially supporting the engine) on the right side of the transmission which bolts to the underside of the car. A third mount at the left of the engine/transmission bolts to the **front crossmember**, just below the radiator. The **drive shafts**, one at each side, each have two **constant velocity (CV) joints** that run from the transmission to the center of the front wheels. Kneel down and find them.

Standard

The **clutch cable** runs from the **clutch release lever** on the left of the transmission, up and through the **firewall** (a wall between the engine and the driver), fastening to the driver's **clutch pedal**. Depressing the pedal moves the clutch release lever, freeing the **clutch disc**, allowing you to change gears. Peer over the top right side of the transmission and you'll see some rods and levers, the gear change **relay levers**.

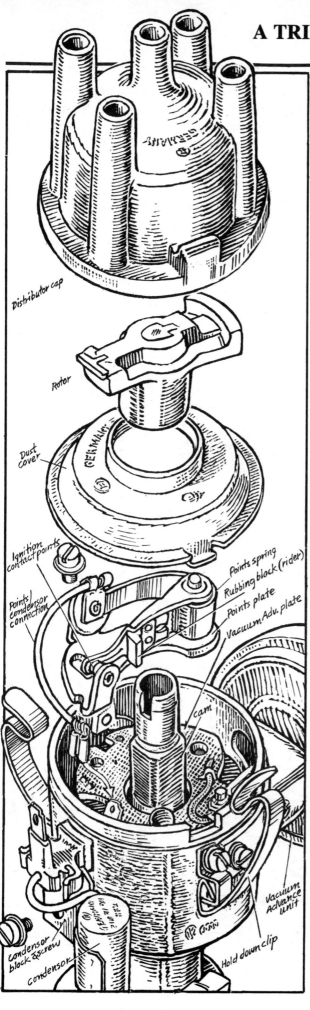

Distributor cap

Rotor

Dust Cover

Ignition contact points

Points/ condensor connection

Points spring

Rubbing block (rider)

Points plate

Vacuum Adv. plate

cam

Vacuum Advance unit

condensor block & screw

Condensor

Hold down clip

Automatic

There are three cables running from a bracket on the left rear of the transmission. One goes to the **accelerator pedal**, another to the **gear shift lever** (both inside the car) and the third to the **carburetor** or **throttle valve** (fuel injection) on the engine.

IGNITION SYSTEM

The **distributor**, on the left side of the engine toward the rear, has a dull red or black cap sprouting five thick black plastic **high tension (HT)** wires or leads. Bronze Edition and post-1978 cars have a bright metal shield around the distributor to cut out radio interference.

Beneath the distributor cap are the **rotor** and **points**. On the distributor body is a small metal cylinder as thick as your finger called the **condenser**. Opposite the condenser screwed onto the distributor body is the **vacuum advance/retard unit**, a metal flying saucer with one or two thin plastic hoses coming from it.

The center wire from the distributor cap snakes into the center of the **coil**, horizontally mounted on the firewall. On each side of that wire on the coil is a small terminal. One accepts a thin green wire from the side of the distributor, the other accepts wires from the **ignition switch** (the key), the electric idle jet and the automatic choke on carbureted cars. Fuel injected cars have wires which disappear into all that wiring harness spaghetti which we won't worry about.

Meanwhile, back at the distributor cap, four wires run to the spark plugs. **Spark plug connectors** on the ends of those wires push onto the metal threads on the protruding spark plug ends. Pull a connector and see.

FUEL SYSTEM

Carburetors

The **carburetor** is bolted to the **intake manifold** which is bolted to the right side of the cylinder head. The **accelerator cable** runs from the **accelerator** (or **gas**) **pedal** inside the car to the **throttle arm linkage** on the side of the carburetor. A black metal pear-shaped **air intake elbow** is bolted to the top of the carburetor. Its job is to direct air into the carb after the air's been cleaned by the paper element inside the **air filter housing** at the front of the right fender. Follow the hoses and locate the filter housing.

Bolted onto the left side of the engine, just below the third spark plug, is the **fuel pump** which has two hoses attached to it. This pump sucks fuel (gasoline) from the tank at the rear of the car through a small transparent **fuel filter** to the carburetor. When fuel reaches the carburetor, it's mixed with air, sucked into the cylinder head and ignited by the spark plugs. Remember the PCV valve? Well, a hose attached to it goes to the air intake elbow on top of the carb to recycle polluted air. OK?

Fuel Injection

Just behind the battery is the heart of the fuel injection system: the **mixture control unit.** It consists of a **fuel distributor**, **air flow sensor** (under the rubber elbow) and a replaceable **air filter element** (in the base of the control unit). The fuel distributor has seven braided metal hoses bolted to its top. Just to the left of the unit is the **fuel filter**, an aluminum cannister with a braided hose at both ends.

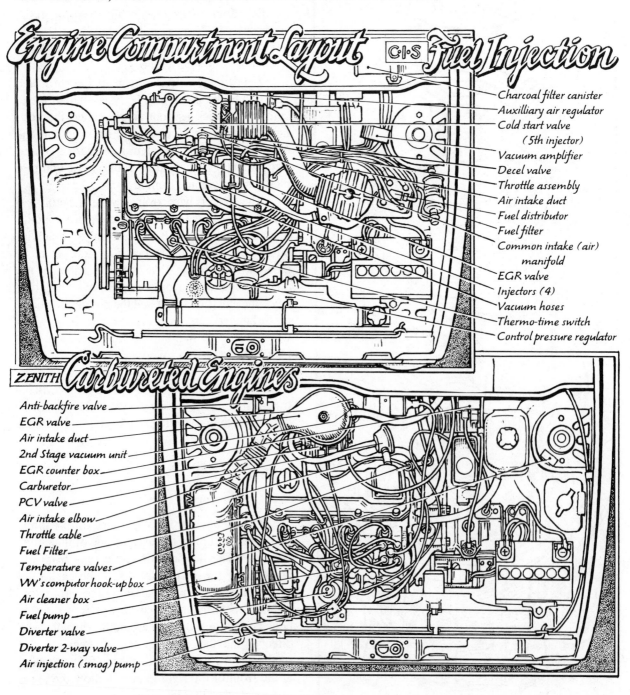

Engine Compartment Layout CIS *Fuel Injection*

- Charcoal filter canister
- Auxilliary air regulator
- Cold start valve
  (5th injector)
- Vacuum amplifier
- Decel valve
- Throttle assembly
- Air intake duct
- Fuel distributor
- Fuel filter
- Common intake (air)
  manifold
- EGR valve
- Injectors (4)
- Vacuum hoses
- Thermo-time switch
- Control pressure regulator

ZENITH *Carbureted Engines*

- Anti-backfire valve
- EGR valve
- Air intake duct
- 2nd Stage vacuum unit
- EGR counter box
- Carburetor
- PCV valve
- Air intake elbow
- Throttle cable
- Fuel Filter
- Temperature valves
- VW's computor hook-up box
- Air cleaner box
- Fuel pump
- Diverter valve
- Diverter 2-way valve
- Air injection (smog) pump

Gasoline is pumped from the gas tank by an electric fuel pump bolted just in front of the right rear wheel. The gas first passes through an **accumulator** behind the pump, then goes to the fuel filter and on to the fuel distributor.

From there it's sent via thin braided **fuel lines** to four **fuel injectors** pushed into **manifold tubes** in the intake air distributor on the right side of the cylinder head. Another small hose sends fuel from the fuel distributor to the **control pressure regulator** bolted to the engine just below the spark plugs. The regulator helps the car start in cold weather and sends any unused fuel from the regulator back to the fuel tank via the fuel distributor.

Bolted onto the right side of the cylinder head is the **intake manifold**. At one end of it, toward the right fender, you'll find the **cold start valve** which has both an electrical connection and fuel line attached. This valve sprays fuel received from the fuel distributor into the intake manifold to help the car start on those frosty mornings.

The **accelerator cable** runs from the **accelerator (gas) pedal** inside the car to the **throttle valve** inside the **throttle valve housing** which is part of the intake manifold.

Remember the hose beginning at the camshaft cover? Well, the other end of it attaches to the mixture control unit to recycle polluted air. This completes a cycle we'll talk more about in Chapter 12.

ELECTRICAL SYSTEM

All Models: Most people (including mechanics) are baffled when something goes wrong with their car's electrical system. Fortunately, most of the things which do go wrong are fixed easily.

Let's start with the **battery.** It has two **posts**, a negative (−) and a positive (+). Battery **terminals** on the ends of the two **battery cables** clamp onto the posts. The negative post is closest to the left fender and the wire from it grounds on the rear transmission mount.

The large, usually red, wire clamped to the positive battery post runs downward to the **starter.** The wire actually bolts to the large terminal on the **solenoid**, a cylinder mounted on top of the starter. The solenoid is a switch that controls the operation of the starter (more in Chapter 2). On automatic cars the starter is on the right side of the engine facing the firewall. It's hard to see from the top; feel for it or look from underneath. Follow the red (+) battery cable and you'll find it wherever it may be.

A major component of this system is the electricity-producing **alternator**, a round metal cylinder with a thick electrical wire plugged into its back. The alternator is hung on the left front of the engine and is driven by a V-belt via the crankshaft pulley.

If you have an air conditioner, the alternator is directly below the large silver **compressor** driven by its own V-belt on the left front of the engine. Getting at the alternator with the compressor in position will give you fits.

The alternator has some gizmos inside, which you can't see, called diodes. They convert alternating electrical current (AC) to direct current (DC) which is used by your electrical system.

Attached to the back of (or built inside) the alternator is the **voltage regulator** which keeps the current produced by the alternator at a usable level.

COOLING SYSTEM

At the front of the car beween the headlights is the **radiator** and **cooling fan. A microswitch** on the left side of the radiator switches the fan on when the coolant reaches a temperature of 95°C (203°F). The fan pulls air through the radiator to help lower the coolant temperature. The belt driven **water pump** bolted onto the left of the engine, toward the front, pumps coolant via hoses into the radiator and around the engine. Trace the big hose on the bottom right side of the radiator to the pump.

When working on the engine, snap apart the plastic connector in the cooling fan wire or pull the plug from the back of the fan motor. It'll save your fingers from a nasty cut.

On '75 and '76 gas model and all diesel models, you'll find a white plastic coolant expansion bottle by the left or right fender. There are two marks on the front of the plastic bottle; the upper shows the correct coolant level when the engine is hot and the lower the correct coolant level when the engine is cold.

Air Conditioner

The air conditioner compressor is the large belt driven aluminum cylinder above the alternator, toward the right front of the car. It's mounted on a metal plate and has a few large hoses coming from it. One goes to an extra radiator (the **condenser**) in front of the engine coolant radiator. It's not a brilliant move to loosen any air conditioner hoses because freon will spurt out and freeze your eyelashes together. Besides that, the air conditioner will force warm air into the passenger compartment instead of cold. If that happens, get VW or a gas station to recharge the air conditioning system with a can of freon.

EMISSION CONTROL SYSTEM, EXHAUST GAS RECIRCULATION SYSTEM (EGR)

This system is mostly responsible for the horde of hoses criss-crossing your engine. It reduces exhaust pollutants by sending exhaust gas into the intake manifold where it combines with the fuel-air mixture and is burned. Let's tour the EGR system.

Carbureted Engines

On top of the radiator you'll find the **diverter valve.** If you have an early car, it'll have just one hose coming from it. Later models have a **second stage diverter valve**, a cylindrical or square one-inch box toward the front of the first stage diverter valve with four hoses popping out. From the first stage diverter valve a 25mm (1 in) diameter black rubber hose goes to the **air injection pump (smog pump)**, a belt-driven cylinder bolted beneath the alternator. Another 25mm hose runs from the pump to the front part of the air filter. A smaller black hose crosses near the front of the engine and goes toward the firewall to the **anti-backfire valve.** From that valve a large hose runs to the intake manifold.

Feel behind the carburetor for a squashed aluminum cylinder with two connections. It's called the **EGR valve.** The upper connection should be plugged with a plastic cap, while the lower one may have a thin plastic pipe sprouting from it. If present, the pipe goes toward the rear of the engine into a connection on the **vacuum manifold.** Your pipe may be missing if the car has had the latest carb modifications (Chapter 11). This manifold is where all the small plastic pipes meet and Happy Hour is between 5-7 on Fridays. That flattened pancake thing on the back of the cylinder head is called the **temperature valve**; it's part of the vacuum advance operation. It's not on Canadian cars. The vacuum manifold sculpture with all the small plastic pipes going in and out has five temperature valves, three on top and two on the bottom. This controls vacuum spark advance operation, and other systems which require vacuum at a certain temperature.

Now look on top of the carburetor. The black metal air intake elbow has one braided hose going past the coil, through the firewall into the **activated charcoal filter.** Another hose goes to the PCV valve which we tagged already. Yet another black hose goes to a **check valve** between the diverter valve and a copper-colored pipe bolted across the cylinder head just below the spark plugs. It's part of the air injection system.

Fuel Injection

There are different systems for different years, one for air-conditioned cars and yet another for California. The idea is basically the same—to reduce exhaust pollutants. I'll identify the components common to all.

At the front of the intake manifold close to the right fender ye shall find the **EGR valve**. A metal pipe runs from its bottom into the exhaust pipe. A thin plastic pipe from the side of the valve crosses the engine compartment and ends up at the **EGR temperature valve** bolted to the rear of the cylinder head.

From that valve another thin pipe goes to the **EGR vacuum amplifier** bolted inside the left fender. Various hoses leave the amplifier. One heads to the **vacuum tank**, usually located beneath the battery, while another snakes back to the **throttle valve housing** in the intake manifold.

You may have a big **barometric cell** with two red pipes connected to it bolted on top of the radiator. That's part of the high altitude kit if you're into high living.

California cars may have a few extra pieces I haven't described. If you want a full explanation, turn to Chapter 13.

All carbureted and injected cars have a black **EGR counter.** It's a plastic box fastened behind the left side of the firewall with one speedometer cable in the front running to the transmission. Another speedometer cable runs from the rear of the EGR counter to the rear of the speedometer on the dash. This EGR box counts the number of miles the car travels and lights the EGR warning light on the dash when it's time to inspect the EGR system.

THE FUEL EVAPORATIVE CONTROL SYSTEM

This anti-pollution device prevents the release of fuel vapor into the outside atmosphere. Check the diagram to see how it works. The activated charcoal filter is located behind the firewall on the left side of the engine compartment. There's no maintenance to this system other than checking that the hose clamps are all tight and that the connecting hoses are in good condition.

EGR

SPEEDO CABLE HOOK-UP

EGR COUNTER BOX

THE BRAKE SYSTEM

Stuck to the left side of the firewall is the **master cylinder** and the white plastic **brake fluid reservoir** on top of it. If your car has 'power assisted' brakes, there is a large black pie-shaped cylinder bolted directly behind the master cylinder with one large hose running to the intake manifold. That's the vacuum powered **brake servo.** See Chapter 14 for a full description of the brake system.

WINDSHIELD WIPERS

On the inside of the left or right fender lies another plastic container with a small electric pump attached to it. This is the **windshield washing fluid container.** You'll notice a thin plastic pipe snaking from the top of the container to a nipple midway to the rear of the hood. Make sure this container is filled to the correct level with water. Maybe add a dirt and bug solvent, too. Don't use dishwashing liquid—it'll smear your windshield. The **windshield wiper motor** is up and behind the left side of the firewall. An arm connects it to the **wiper blades.**

That's the end of the introductory tour. If you would like to know more about a certain system, turn to the appropriate chapter.

ENGINE STOPS OR WON'T START

The mechanical, electrical and fuel systems need to be operating correctly for your Rabbit to start and keep on running. Look in the most obvious places first. Or, as my friend Murphy says, "You should look in the last place first because the last place you look is always the first place you find it." If you've already familiarized yourself with the engine compartment layout, you should spot anything broken or disconnected.

Remember that **FRONT** is the front of the car and **LEFT** is the driver's side. When loosening, turn the nut, bolt or screw counterclockwise ↺ as you're facing it; when tightening, turn it clockwise ↻ .

You're belting down a country lane when your engine suddenly loses power but continues to run at idle with the gas pedal flat to the floor. Coast along awhile and check your dashboard to see if any red lights come

REMEMBER:

FRONT OF ENGINE   FRONT OF RABBIT
① ② ③ ④

CYLINDER Nº'S:
① ② ③ ④
FIRING ORDER:
1-3-4-2

on. Nothing? Take a deep breath and count yourself lucky. Coast to the side of the road. Leave the engine on, get out and lift and prop the hood. The accelerator cable may have broken or the bolt securing the cable to the carburetor throttle arm may have fallen out, Procedure 1. If not, the accelerator cable mounting bracket may have come loose from the carburetor itself, Procedure 2.

If your car is fuel injected, check that the accelerator cable is still attached to the throttle valve on top of the intake manifold. All models slide the clip off from the center of the protective carpet (if you've got one) above the driver's knees and remove the carpet. Check the plastic gizmo on the pedal end of the accelerator cable. Is it still fastened to the pedal? If not, attach it! Now try the pedal. Better?

All Models: The water temperature red warning light lit up on your dashboard or the temperature gauge hit red in a fancy Rabbit? Your engine is hot, so the electric fan should be working overtime to cool things down. If the fan isn't running, see if it has died (Chapter 17, Procedure 3). If the red alternator light (the battery symbol) came on, go to Chapter 8. When the red oil light (the oil can symbol)blazes on, turn the engine off damn quick and get yourself to Chapter 9.

If your car won't start or just quits as you're driving along, there's a number of things to do. First lift and prop the hood and check beneath the drive belt guard at the front of the engine to see if the belt is still in one piece. Broken? Turn to Chapter 10, Procedure 23. Does the engine turn over slowly or not at all? Check the battery, starter, solenoid or ignition switch, Procedures 3-6. If the engine spins over quickly but won't catch, check the fuel and ignition systems, Procedure 7.

When you try to start the engine but hear nothing but a click and maybe the dash lights all die, either the battery cables are loose on the battery, Procedure 3, or the starter pinion gear is stuck to the outside toothed edge of the flywheel, Procedure 5.

If you have an automatic transmission and have to wiggle the shift lever to get it started, the starter cut-out switch on the base of the shift lever is out of line, Procedure 11.

If your battery is new or recently recharged but runs down after a few days driving, either you have a short or the alternator is kaput, Procedure 4 or Chapter 8.

Check all the fuses in the relay plate above the driver's knees. If any are blown, replace with one of the same color. Disconnect the battery ground strap (10mm wrench) before you do so. Don't wrap aluminum foil around a blown fuse. You may ruin the relay plate and that's expensive to replace.

Does the engine make funny noises when you try to start it? That's an indication of compression problems if you've had starting troubles for a while. A compression hassle doesn't happen overnight unless it's winter and the crankcase cracked because you forgot to check the concentration of antifreeze in the coolant, the head gasket sprung a leak or someone swiped your spark plugs. To check compression, see Chapter 10, Procedure 20.

PROCEDURE 1: ACCELERATOR CABLE BROKEN OR LOOSE (Gasoline Models Only). Phase 1

Condition: The engine loses power but continues to run at idle and/or the gas pedal lies flat on the floor. Diesels go to Chapter 21, Procedure 5 or 6.

Tools and materials: Phase 1 tool kit, new accelerator cable and/or mounting hardware.

Remarks: Before you get into the depths of this procedure, call VW and ask the service manager if a broken accelerator cable is included in a recall program. State the year of your car and the transmission type.

The accelerator cable can break at the throttle assembly, the pedal or anywhere else it feels like breaking. It usually happens in inclement weather.

On fuel injected cars the cable pops onto a ball atop the throttle valve housing; on other models, it fits on the throttle arm on the side of the carburetor. The other end hooks over a small arm on the gas pedal.

If you need to replace a broken cable, take the old one to the dealer for comparison or jot down your chassis number to give the parts person. There are lots of different cables so make sure to get the right one.

During installation, it's most important not to kink or bend the cable in any direction. A bent cable is next to useless and will prevent smooth acceleration action.

Step 1. Check Linkage—Standard Transmission

Begin by lifting and propping the hood. Has the cable broken or come loose from the throttle linkage? An 8mm nut holds the cable in a small barrel clamp fitted in the throttle arm on the side of the carburetor. No nut or barrel? Look around the engine compartment for them, and if they don't come to light, buy new ones from VW or go to Step 2.

Fuel Injection: Is the cable still popped onto the ball on the throttle valve? A thin metal U clip should be attached to the rubber block on the end of the cable. Maybe it slipped off and is lurking somewhere in the engine compartment. If you can't find it or it's broken, use a piece of wire to hold the block onto the linkage until you get a new one.

In both systems, if the cable is still attached to the linkage, pull on the end of the inner cable and see if the thing comes out of the outer sheath. It does? The cable is broken, Step 3.

If the cable doesn't come all the way out, it's still intact so open the driver's door and remove the clip from the center of the protective carpet (if present) above the driver's knees. Remove the carpet; don't lose the clip.

See how the end of the cable is attached to the top of the gas pedal? If it isn't, attach it. Now try the pedal unless the cable is broken. Unhook the cable from the pedal where it passes through the pedal arm if you're here to replace the accelerator cable.

Go to the front of the car and loosen the 8mm bolt holding the cable onto the carburetor throttle linkage. Don't lose that little barrel clamp. Completely unscrew the 10 or 13mm nut closest to the carb which holds the cable sheath onto the carburetor bracket. Pull the cable out of the bracket and remove the other nut. Baggie both. **Fuel Injection:** Loosen the 10 or 13mm nuts holding the cable onto the camshaft cover. Cut any plastic clips holding the cable against the wiring harness and remove the cable from the car.

Cable installers, go to Step 3.

Step 2. Make a Wire Nut—Carburetors Only

Use pliers to twist a 15cm (6 in) piece of baling wire onto the old cable. Now slip the wire through the hole where the cylinder used to be in the throttle linkage and twist the wire back onto itself. Keep the cable taut as you twist. Chubby Checker, where are you now? This makeshift repair will work until you stumble across a VW dealer and buy a new cable and/or clamp.

Step 3. Install New Accelerator Cable—All Models

Tools and materials: New cable, millimeter rule, Friend.

Push the end of the cable with the plastic slotted gizmo attached through the hole in the firewall. Have Friend work from inside the car and hook the gizmo onto the gas pedal. Push the rubber grommet into the firewall and make sure it's snug. You may need to employ a small screwdriver to work the grommet into position. Their wages are low so take your time.

Screw one of the two 10 or 13mm nuts three quarters of the way onto the threads on the cable sheath and push the sheath through the bracket on the carburetor or camshaft cover. Screw on the other nut. Keep the cable lying as it wants to—don't try to force it because it will bind up and won't work smoothly. **Carburetors:** Push the inner part of the cable into the barrel clamp in the carb linkage and pull the inner cable through the barrel until the cable is taut. Tighten the 8mm bolt in the barrel clamp.

Step 3. (Cont'd.)

Fuel Injection: Pop the plastic cable end onto the ball on the throttle valve.

Get back inside the car or ask Friend if the cable is still properly hooked to the gas pedal arm.

Move the nuts on the sheath until you have slight tension on the cable sheath and then tighten the two nuts onto the carb bracket.

Install Friend in the car with foot holding the gas pedal to the floor, or put a brick on it. See how the cable pulls open the throttle linkage lever? We want 1mm of clearance between the lever and the 'full open' stop on the carburetor or throttle valve housing. Pull on the cable and watch the throttle arm almost touch the metal stop. Play with the nuts on the cable sheath until the clearance is correct, then give the nuts an extra cinch to keep the cable from moving.

Automatic Transmission

To confuse the issue, there are two accelerator cables on automatic transmissions. One, the *pedal cable*, runs from the gas pedal to a lever on the side of the transmission while a second, the *throttle cable*, goes from another transmission lever to the carburetor or throttle valve. The diagram shows it.

If your gas pedal is flat to the floor, remove the protective carpet from above the driver's knees and see if the pedal cable is still attached to the pedal. Now check that the other end of the cable is hooked over the horizontal transmission lever. Pull on the cable to see if it's broken. If so, Step 6.

Step 4. Check Throttle Linkage—Carburetor (Fuel Injection, Step 5)

The cable sheath is held by two nuts to a bracket on the side of the carburetor. The inner cable extends out of the sheath, through the throttle linkage into a spring. A small circlip holds the cable secure. No spring or circlip? Hunt around for it. A piece of wire twisted around the cable will hold things until you can get to VW. Pull on the cable to find out if it's broken.

If the carb linkage is fine, look at the bracket on the transmission and see if the cable end has popped off its ball mount on the end of the transmission lever. First pull on the cable to see if it's broken. Looks good? Repop it onto the transmission lever. Broken cable? Go to Step 7.

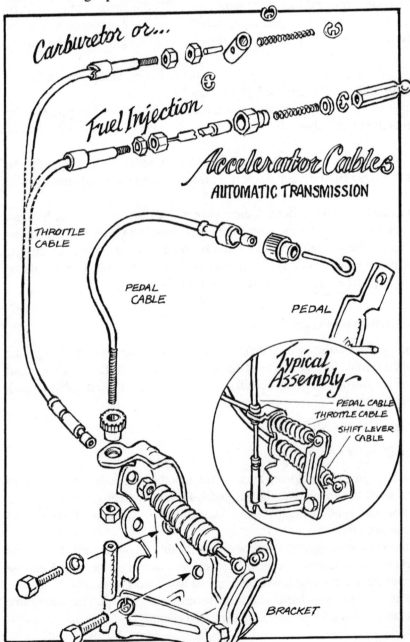

Carburetor or...

Fuel Injection

Accelerator Cables

AUTOMATIC TRANSMISSION

THROTTLE CABLE

PEDAL CABLE

PEDAL

Typical Assembly

PEDAL CABLE
THROTTLE CABLE
SHIFT LEVER CABLE

BRACKET

Step 5. Check Throttle Linkage—Fuel Injection

The end of the cable has a nut and a metal bar with a 'pop' connector on the end. Has the cable end popped off or has the metal end slipped off the cable? Check the diagram to see what the cable end arrangement should look like. If any of your parts are missing, VW sells a cable linkage kit. Buy one and install it. Cinch the circlips closed with pliers if they don't fit well.

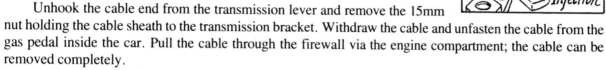

Step 6. Remove/Install Pedal Cable

Unhook the cable end from the transmission lever and remove the 15mm nut holding the cable sheath to the transmission bracket. Withdraw the cable and unfasten the cable from the gas pedal inside the car. Pull the cable through the firewall via the engine compartment; the cable can be removed completely.

Be very careful not to kink the new cable as you push the end through the hole in the firewall and insert the wire end into the gas pedal. Get the rubber grommet firmly into the firewall. Slip the other end through the transmission bracket and install the 15mm nut. Hook the cable end over the transmission lever. Have Friend hold the gas pedal down or put a gold brick on the pedal as you screw the locknut at the transmission against the bracket by hand. Pull down on the lever to check for free play in the cable. If there's any, turn the knurled plastic adjusting nut up or down the cable to eliminate it. When it's right, tighten the 15mm nut and try the pedal with your foot. Smooth and easy is the effect you want.

Take a test drive. If the automatic transmission won't 'kick down' into a lower gear when you stomp on the gas pedal, adjust the knurled plastic knob to take up slack in the cable. Try again. OK this time?

Step 7. Remove/Install Throttle Cable

Remove the end of the cable from the carburetor linkage or throttle valve. Loosen (or remove) the locknuts holding the cable sheath onto the carburetor or camshaft cover.

Pop the other end of the cable off the transmission lever. Roll back the rubber accordian boot and loosen the 15 or 17mm nut holding the cable against the transmission bracket. Slip the cable out of the bracket (there's a little slot in the bracket probably covered with crud) and withdraw the cable from the car.

When you get the new cable, screw one of the locknuts from the old cable onto the carburetor end of the cable sheath. Remove the throttle linkage cable end from your old cable and install it on the new one. Check that the fuel injection or carburetor throttle valve linkage is in the closed position. If you have a carburetor be sure the choke valve on the right side of the carb (closest to the right fender) is open fully. Pull open the throttle valve assembly and get the throttle off the fast idle cam on the right side of the carburetor. See the diagram in Chapter 11.

Push the end of the cable through the carburetor bracket or camshaft cover bracket. Screw on the other locknut and pop the cable onto the throttle valve (fuel injection); or push it through the throttle linkage, slip on the spring and secure the cable end with the tiny circlip (carburetors). Squeeze the ends of the circlip together if it's loose.

Now, go back to the transmission and push the transmission lever back as far as it will go. Then, without kinking the cable, push it into the transmission bracket, roll back the rubber accordian and finger tighten the 15 or 17mm nut. Pop the end onto the ball on the transmission lever.

Adjust the locknuts on the carb bracket or camshaft cover until all free play is eliminated from the cable. Make sure the transmission lever stays all the way back. Tighten all the locknuts and take a test drive.

PROCEDURE 2: FIX LOOSE ACCELERATOR CABLE MOUNTING BRACKET—CARBURE-TORS ONLY. Phase 1.

Condition: The engine loses power and continues to run at idle, but the accelerator cable is OK.

Tools and materials: Screwdriver, new screws?

Step 1. Find Screws

The accelerator cable mounting bracket is held to the side of the carburetor by two or three screws. Any missing? Look in the engine compartment. You should find at least one. If not, dig into your screw stash box or start thumbing.

Step 2. Install Screws

Position the bracket on the side of the carb, install and tighten the screws.

PROCEDURE 3: CHECK BATTERY AND CABLE CONNECTIONS. Phase 1.

Condition: The engine will not turn over, won't turn over fast enough to start, dash lights go dead or nothing happens at all when you turn on the key. Remember to click your door-mounted safety belt into position (if you've got one) or else nothing will ever start!

Tools and materials: Phase 1 tool kit, perhaps a new battery.

Remarks: Check the connections at both ends of the little green wire running from the distributor to the coil. If either end is disconnected, the engine won't start. Also check the thick center wire between the coil and distributor.

Step 1. Check Battery

Turn the key to ON and flip on the headlight switch. If the lights are good and bright and you can toot the horn as well, the battery is OK; so turn the lights and key off and go to Step 3. Low headlights and dim dash warning lights point to a dying battery or bad connections. First check that the water level in your battery is 13mm (½ in) below the battery cap or 3mm (⅛ in) above the plates inside the battery. If it's low, adding water (distilled, if possible or boiled water which has cooled) may revive the battery at least temporarily. If you're stuck out in the middle of nowhere, try to get a push start or a jump because the alternator will power the electrical system for a short time. Go to a gas station and have someone check the battery charge for you. They'll tell you if you have a dead cell. If not, have the gas station 'trickle charge' your battery to bring it up to snuff.

If the battery is shot (like a dead cell or two) buy a new one at Sears or Montgomery Ward or other such large guarantee places. Before parting with your old battery, check the date on the top. You may still have some warranty time left, which means money back. Wouldn't that be nice?

When you turn the key all the way over to START, if all that happens is a click and the dash lights go out, the connections are bad. You may even be able to hear a sizzling sound from the battery. See if the terminals and the posts on the battery are covered with nasty white crud. If so, put on your safety glasses or sunglasses from the glove compartment, loosen them, scrape them shiny clean with a pocket knife, retighten and try starting your car again. When you get home, do Chapter 9, Procedure 2, Step 1.

Battery connection OK, continue.

Step 2. Check Starter Action

With a good battery and clean terminals, put the car in neutral (N) and try to start it. If all you hear is a click, the starter is stuck and has to be freed. Procedure 5.

PROCEDURE 4: QUICK 'N EASY CHECK FOR SHORTS. Phase 1

Condition: If your new or recently charged battery runs down after a day or two of driving, you have a short or a bad alternator. A short means a break or worn spot in the insulation on a wire that allows the electrical current to drain from that wire to ground, thereby running down the battery.

Tools and materials: Phase 1 tool kit, Friend

Remarks: This test won't work if you keep the car door open!! Remove fuse S7 from the relay plate if you've got an electric clock.

Step 1. Does You Car Have a Short?

Turn off everything electrical: ignition, radio, heater, lights, turn signals, everything! Disconnect the battery ground strap (10mm) and clean the end of the cable. Shine the battery post too. Now hold the cable close to the post. If you see a small spark jumping between the cable and the post, you have a short. Tuck the battery ground strap out of the way.

Step 2. Find the Short

Remove the clip from the protective carpet above the driver's legs and locate the relay plate with the fuses on the base. Flip open the hinged cover and pull out fuse S1 on the far left. Do the ground cable-to-battery post test again. If it still sparks, you haven't found the short yet. Off with the battery ground strap and put the first fuse back in and try the second. Go through them all until you stop the spark from jumping when you touch the cable to the battery ground post.

When you do locate the circuit with the short, either take the car to an electric shop, proudly tell them where to look for the short and have them repair it, or find it yourself with a VOM. Isolate the faulty wire, wrap damaged insulation with electrical tape or replace it entirely. Chapter 20 tells you how to use a VOM. Try the ground cable again. When you get no more sparks, reattach the ground cable and tighten the clamp.

PROCEDURE 5: LOOSEN STUCK STARTER. Phase 1

Condition: You turn the key to the START position and hear nothing but a click. Battery and terminals OK.

Tools and materials: Hammer, Friend or a strong back.

Remarks: The starter (on a standard transmission) is a black cylinder on the left side of the transmission with a small cylinder on top called the solenoid. Electrical wires run into the rear of the solenoid. Automatic transmission starters are on the right side of the engine/transmission.

Step 1. Tap It Loose (Standard Transmission Only)

The starter pinion gear is probably stuck to the flywheel teeth. Turn off the key and tap the starter a few times (*not* the solenoid) with your hammer. Try to start the car. No go? Try this:

Step 2. Rock it Loose (All Models)

Put the car in third gear and release the handbrake. (Automatics put the shift lever in Drive—D.) Go to the front of the car and with your *back against* the front of the car put your hands under the bumper. Have Friend do the same. If you have a weak back, don't do this—get someone to do it for you. Plant your heels firmly on the ground and straighten your legs. Get the car into a rocking motion. Do this about five or six times. Try the key again. It should work.

Step 3. Why Did It Stick?

Check the starter mounting bolts. If they're loose, the starter will bind up and the pinion gear inside won't return to its original position. Automatics have the starter in a very inaccessible place. See Procedure 9.

PROCEDURE 6: CHECK STARTER, SOLENOID AND SWITCH. Phase 1.

Condition: The battery and terminals are OK but the starter doesn't turn over. You've done Procedure 5.

Tools and materials: Phase 1 tool kit.

Remarks: Automatic owners: Procedure 9, Step 5.

Step 1. Examine Starter—Standard Transmission

First put the shift lever in neutral, ignition off, handbrake on. Get out, lift and prop the hood and look directly down into the engine compartment. You'll see the starter on the left side of the transmission.

First check the large black plastic covered cable leading to the threaded bolt on the rear of the solenoid. If the nut holding the cable on is loose, tighten it (13mm wrench). This may solve your problem. Next check that the electrical connectors on the two thinner wires going to the small connections on each side of the solenoid are pushed on tightly, and that the metal spade terminals they fit onto are clean, bright and shiny.

Put your plastic handled pliers or screwdriver across the two large bolts (terminals) on the solenoid. The wire from one terminal goes to the battery, the wire from the other to the starter motor. What you're doing is directly connecting the battery to the starter motor. The starter should whirr into action but not turn the engine over.

If the starter doesn't whirr, it's shot. You'll have to replace it or get it overhauled. It's easier and quicker to replace it, Procedure 8. If the starter whirrs sweetly, let's check the solenoid.

Step 2. Check Solenoid

Keep the handbrake on and the ignition off and put your plastic handled pliers/screwdriver across the terminal on the solenoid which accepts the big wire coming from the battery and the small right side terminal. The wire on this terminal is red with a black stripe. The starter motor whirrs? You have troubles with the solenoid or ignition switch. It's probably the solenoid.

Gently tap the solenoid with a small hammer all around the outside, except where the electrical wires connect. Try to start the car with the key. If it starts, the guts of the solenoid are rusty, dirty or binding up. You can live with this for a while as long as you carry your hammer (Maxwell), but replace it as soon as possible (Procedure 8).

If shorting the wires and tapping the solenoid doesn't improve matters, you have ignition switch troubles.

Step 3. Check Ignition Switch Connections

Turn off the key and remove the two Phillips screws holding the plastic molding under the steering column. You may have to squeeze the sides of the plastic to get it off.

Lie across the driver's seat and look at the underside of the column. You'll see a cluster of wires (perhaps inside a black plastic sheath) running to a black plastic connector at the bottom of the ignition switch. Pull the connector off the switch (don't pull by the wires). Are all the wires firmly inserted into the connector? Push all of them on to be sure they're tight. Install the connector back on the ignition switch and try to start the car again. No luck? Remove the connector again and hold the ignition key all the way over in the START position with one hand while you wiggle the wires to the connector with the other. When the starter motor springs into life, find the loose wire and push a wooden matchstick or toothpick into the connector beside the loose wire to keep it tight. Start the car again. That'll fix it.

If by chance a loose wire isn't your curse, do the short cut ignition switch trick in Procedure 10. If that won't fix it, come back here.

Step 4. Check Wiring

Find the wires from terminals #30 and #50 in the ignition switch connector and trace them down the steering column into the wiring harness and to the solenoid. Check that the wire is definitely bad (Chapter 20, Procedure 10).

Step 4. (Cont'd.)

If it's shot, run a new length of wire of the same gauge or thickness from the ignition switch connector to the solenoid and connect the stripped ends onto the proper terminals.

Reconnect the connector and try the ignition key. Voila! The starter will engage and start the car. There's no point in ripping out the bad wire. Leave it in, but cut off the ends, tape them up and then tape your new wire securely to the wiring harness with plastic electrical tape.

If you've checked the battery, starter, solenoid and ignition switch and the car still won't start, we must check the fuel and ignition systems.

PROCEDURE 7: CHECK FUEL AND IGNITION SYSTEMS. Phase 1.

Condition: Car will not start and you've checked the battery, starter, solenoid and ignition switch.

Tools and materials: Phase 1 tool kit, Friend, VOM.

Remarks: Fuel injection owners, go through all the steps that apply to your system. If the car still won't start, turn to Chapter 12.

Step 1. Check Fuel

Although your gas gauge may read full, your tank may be as empty as my pockets. Remove the gas cap and rock the car up and down. Do you hear miniature waves at the bottom of the tank? You don't? Get some gas, pour it in and try again. It'll take a few turns of the starter to pump the gas through the lines into the carburetor or fuel distributor. While you're at it, check the fuel filter (Chapter 10, Procedure 11, Carburetors; and Chapter 12, Procedure 2, Fuel Injection).

Step 2. Check Coil and Choke Connections

Find the coil; it's the cylindrical thing hanging horizontally on the firewall with one thick wire and other smaller wires going to it. Push on the big center wire. If it's loose, pull it out and check the end of it for grunge. Clean it with emery paper. Now use steel wool wrapped around a screwdriver tip to clean the inside of the socket on the coil which accepts the wire. Push the wire back in and try to start the car. Still won't start? Trace the same wire to the center of the distributor and push it firmly into the distributor cap after pulling the wire and checking that the end connection is bright and shiny. While you're here check the thin green wire running from the coil to the side of the distributor. Also check that the other wires on the coil are clean and tightly connected.

Check the brown plastic automatic choke connection on the left side of the carburetor. Sometimes it comes loose and grounds on the engine, stealing juice from the coil. Repairing loose wires or bad contacts may have solved the problem. Try starting the car. If it won't go, don't kill the battery by continual attempts—move to the next step.

Step 3. Check Coil

Warning! Make sure there's no loose gas or disconnected gas lines lying idle in the engine compartment when you do this and the following step. Don't smoke either. You might lose more than your eyebrows. If any gas has spilled, wipe it up and wait for the engine to dry before proceeding. Keep your fire extinguisher handy.

Pull the thick wire from the center of the distributor cap. Turn the key to ON, and hold the wire with something insulated like a rag, chopsticks, insulated pliers, etc. Hold it 3mm (⅛ in) from any bare metal part of the engine. Except, of course, the carb or fuel pump. A good strong coil will give you a nasty burn, so beware! Ask Friend to turn the engine over with the key or short the solenoid as per Procedure 6 if your car has a standard transmission.

You should have a bright blue-white or pure white spark. If the spark is yellow but still strong, the coil is OK for now but you'll soon need a new one. A weak orange spark or nothing at all means it's time to replace the coil. Chapter 10, Procedure 17, Step 2.

Checking SPARK

ABOUT 3MM 1/8"

ZZAT!

A STRONG BLUE SPARK →

Step 4. Check Spark and Spark Plugs

Turn off the key and install Friend (no Friend and standard transmission? See Chapter 20, Procedure 16) in the car while you remove a plug and do the test like in Peter's diagram. No tools? Pull any spark plug connector from a spark plug. Push a wood or plastic-handled screwdriver into the end of the connector. Hold the screwdriver by the handle and touch the shaft to any bare metal part of the engine. Now lift the screwdriver so the shaft is 3mm (⅛ in) from the bare metal. Keep your fingers off the metal part of the screwdriver. Ask Friend to turn the engine over. Be sure the shift is in neutral because it might start. A spark should jump the gap between the screwdriver shaft and the engine. Turn the key off, and put the connector back on the plug. Remove all four spark plugs; examine, clean and gap them. Chapter 10, Procedure 14, Step 12. Reinstall the cleaned plugs and continue. Make a note to buy new plugs if they're needed.

If you didn't get a spark out the end of the spark plug wire, your points might be maladjusted. Not psychotic, just maladjusted. Although getting a spark from the plug wire indicates juice is flowing to the plug, it might be getting there at the wrong time. Or the spark may be too weak to do its job. Perhaps the distributor has jiggled out from the gear on the intermediate shaft. Let's check.

Step 5. Distributor in Right?

Hold the distributor by the body and pull it up. Did it move? Movement indicates that the U-shaped clip holding the distributor to the crankcase is loose or missing. Check. If it's missing, buy a new one along with the retaining bolt (head size 13mm, thread size 10mm). If all is tight, go to Step 6.

Remove the distributor cap (Chapter 10, Procedure 14, Step 1)), the vacuum lines and bolt holding the U-shaped clip. Remove the clip and pull the distributor out of the crankcase. Take a look at the slot in the base of the distributor shaft. Is it full of junk? Clean it with a thin screwdriver and rag. How's the rubber O ring which fits around the shaft and the paper gasket? The gasket may have been left in the crankcase. Buy new ones if they're worn or missing.

Before installing the distributor, turn to Chapter 10, Procedure 16 and do Steps 1 and 2. Then return here. Thoroughly clean out the hole in the crankcase where the distributor fits.

Hold the distributor in your hand, remove the rotor, pull off the plastic dust cap and put the rotor back on. Now turn the distributor shaft by twisting the rotor until the little line on the sparking end of the rotor lines up with a small line on the distributor rim. Gently lower the distributor into the hole in the crankcase and wiggle it around until it's fully seated. When the distributor's in right, the rotor shouldn't move more than 4mm (5/32 in) in either direction ⟲ ⟳ . Install the clip, 13mm bolt and the vacuum lines but don't tighten the bolt yet. If you've got all your tools with you, turn back to Chapter 10 and do the remaining steps of Procedure 16.

If you're stuck on the road somewhere, you can time the engine 'by ear.' Have Friend turn the key and try to start the engine while you keep your fingers out of the V belts. Turn the *body* of the distributor (don't hold onto the spark plug wires) until the engine starts. Ask Friend to step on the gas to increase the engine revs to about 3000 rpm, but don't race the engine, just get it to a healthy speed. If the engine coughs and sputters, turn the distributor either clockwise ⟳ or otherwise until things smooth out. Now release the gas pedal and idle the engine again to see if it continues to run. OK? Tighten the 13mm bolt and drive on. Do Chapter 10, Procedure 12, when you get home. Check and perhaps change the ignition points too.

Step 6. Check Ignition Components

Remove the distributor cap (Chapter 10, Procedure 14, Step 1, if you don't know how) and look at the points. Get Friend to turn the engine over with the key. The points should open and close as the shaft in the center of the distributor turns. If they don't touch at all or don't even open, adjust the gap per Chapter 10,

Step 6. (Cont'd.)

Procedure 9. If the points have a nasty white deposit on them, clean them off with a small file and adjust the gap (Chapter 10, Procedure 9). Install new points if possible.

The sparking end of the rotor should also be clean. Use emery paper if cleaning is required. Flip the distributor cap over and examine the four contacts inside the roof. They too should be clean. Use your scout knife to get any deposits off and leave them shining. Buy a new cap if the contacts are deeply scored or burned away. When all that stuff is reinstalled, let's check the condenser. Leave the cap off the distributor.

Remove the thin green wire running from the coil to the distributor at the coil end, terminal #1. Put a piece of thin cardboard between the point contacts and turn the ignition key to ON. Connect one end of your test light (or VOM switched to 15 volts DC) to coil terminal #1. Touch the other end of the test light or VOM to the coil end of the thin green wire. What you've got is a circuit with a 'bulb' between the distributor and the coil. If the test light goes on or you get a 12 volt reading on your VOM, the condenser is shot. Chapter 10, Procedure 25, tells how to replace it.

Step 7. Check Fuel Pump, Filter and Gas Lines (NOT for Fuel Injected Cars—see your tests beginning with Procedure 1 in Chapter 12)

If you got a nice juicy spark from the end of the coil and the spark plug wires and the ignition components checked out OK, the fuel system must be at fault. Find a small container and pull the hose running from the fuel pump to the carburetor at the carb end. Dangle the hose into the container. Have Friend turn the engine over with the key (or do it yourself with a screwdriver across the solenoid). Make sure there's no gas anywhere near the solenoid when shorting it; the spark could ignite the works. Keep the fire extinguisher handy.

As the engine turns over, gas should pump out of the hose by the action of the fuel pump. If you get a strong stream of gas, reconnect the hose to the carburetor. Make sure it's a good tight connection. Wait until any spilled gasoline has dried, then start the engine. If it doesn't start, you have troubles with the compression, carburetor or ignition/valve timing. Follow along.

Little or no gas being pumped means you've found the trouble. If the fuel filter has any dirt in it, it probably hasn't been changed recently so replace it now. Dirt may have clogged the fuel lines and the jets inside the carburetor. If the car runs poorly after you've replaced the filter, reserve a day for Chapter 11.

Step 8. Clean Fuel Pump Screen (Not Fuel Injection)

Remove the screw and washer from the top of the fuel pump and stash them safely. Lift off the top of the pump and turn it upside down. A conical plastic screen held in place by a rubber gasket inside the pump filters the fuel. Buy a new screen and gasket or blow the crap out of the old screen and rinse it and the gasket in clean gasoline. Install the screen carefully. Put the top on the pump (get the notch over the projection on the pump body) and replace the washer and screw. Pull the gas hose from the carburetor and check the flow again. If you still don't have a good stream of gas, disconnect the fuel line running from the gas tank to the fuel pump at the pump end. Put the line in your mouth and blow; don't suck. If the line is crud-free, you will hear bubbling in the tank if the neighborhood dogs aren't barking.

If blowing the tube doesn't make you hear bubbles or increase the flow of gas, find a coil of baling wire and fold the end back on itself with pliers and wrap the first 25mm (1 in) with plastic tape so you don't puncture the gas line. Work the wire through the gas line until you're sure the line is clear and that gas is coming to the pump. Reconnect the line to the fuel pump and tighten the hose clamp. Now turn the engine over a few times until the pump fills with gas and pushes some into the carburetor. Still no stream of gas? The pump needs further checking and possible replacing. Gas supply OK? Go to Step 11.

Step 9. Check Fuel Pump

Find a clean empty coffee can and fill it three quarters full with clean gasoline. Pull the gas line running from the fuel tank to the pump from the top of the pump. Search in your garage for a length of hose and fit it on the top fuel pump intake. Dangle the other end into the gasoline in the coffee can. Now remove the gas line

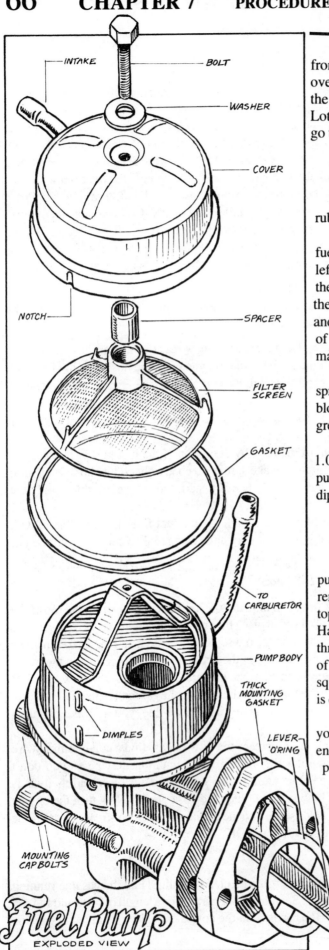

INTAKE

BOLT

WASHER

COVER

NOTCH

SPACER

FILTER SCREEN

GASKET

TO CARBURETOR

PUMP BODY

THICK MOUNTING GASKET

DIMPLES

LEVER 'O'RING

MOUNTING CAP BOLTS

Fuel Pump
EXPLODED VIEW

from the carburetor and have Friend turn the engine over with the key while you check the gas flow from the end of the carburetor hose. No gas—pump shot. Lotsa gas—pump OK. Reconnect the gas lines and go to Step 11.

Step 10. Replace Fuel Pump (Not Fuel Injection)

When you go to VW for the pump also get a new rubber O ring.

First remove the oil dipstick, then pull the two fuel lines from the fuel pump and mark them "FP left" and "FP right." Use a piece of wire to hang them out of the way. Remove the two bolts holding the fuel pump to the crankcase (6mm allen wrench) and pull the pump and thick plastic gasket block clear of the crankcase. Now remove the rubber O ring remaining inside that orifice (hole) in the crankcase.

Install the new O ring (give it a shot of silicone spray if you've got some), then install the plastic block and then the fuel pump. Put a small blob of grease on the end of the fuel pump lever.

Replace the two allen bolts and torque them to 1.0 mkg (7 ft lbs). Push the two fuel lines onto the pump and tighten the hose clamps. Replace the dipstick.

Step 11. Check Carburetor (Not Fuel Injection)

You've already checked the gas flow to the pump and from the pump to the carburetor. Now remove the 10mm nut holding the air cleaner to the top of the carburetor. Look into the carburetor throat. Have Friend press the accelerator pedal or move the throttle lever on the side of the carburetor a number of times. A thin stream of vaporized gas should squirt into the throat each time the accelerator pedal is depressed or the throttle lever is moved.

If not, check the electric idle cutoff valve facing you at the base of the carburetor as you look into the engine compartment (see illustration on the next page). Turn the key to ON and pull the electrical spade connection from the valve. Clean the valve terminal, then touch the wire several times to the terminal. Each touch should produce a fairly distinct click. If not, buy a new valve and install it— simple job: turn the key off and pull the wire from the terminal at the front of the valve. Remove the cutoff valve via the machined nut just behind the cylindrical part of the valve (17mm wrench). Plug the hole in the carburetor with a piece of rag until you install a new valve.

Remember to reconnect the electrical spade connection when the new valve is in.

Step 12. Think About It . . .

By now you've spent lots of time and energy trying to start your Rabbit. Hopefully you will have succeeded. Turn to Chapter 10 and do the entire tune-up procedure including the compression test. If it still won't run properly, turn to Chapter 13 and read on.

There's the faint possibility you have crud in the gas tank. Sometimes the stuff moves about and only blocks the fuel supply when you're driving. When you start looking for the blockage, the crud sinks to the bottom of the tank (or the carburetor float bowl) and pretends it isn't there. Procedure 2, Steps 3 and 4, in Chapter 12 tells how to check the inside of the tank and, if necessary, how to remove it.

PROCEDURE 8: STARTER AND SOLENOID REPLACEMENT/REPAIR, Phase 2.

(Standard Transmission Only—Automatics go to Procedure 9)

Condition: Starter or solenoid doesn't work.

Tools and materials: Phase 1 tool kit, Liquid Wrench^{tm}, starter and/or solenoid, Permatex No. 2^{tm} or Volkswagen Special Starter/Solenoid Assembly Sealer. 1979 and on with manual transmission need the polygon head allen wrench.

Remarks: If your solenoid is bad and you decide to replace it, order one from VW and find lots of time and a clean place to work. If just the starter is bad, t.s. (tough situation) – I've never been able to buy one without a solenoid.

More Remarks: In these days of replacement technology, if there's anything wrong with the starter or solenoid, most mechanics at VW automatically put in a new starter. They don't repair starters, no matter what. Come to think of it, neither do I. Starters are not only tough to work on but parts are scarce. Call your local auto electric shop and ask what they charge to rebuild or repair a VW starter. It may be cheaper than buying a new one. (If you decide to tackle starter work, the official VW repair manual has very nice exploded views which show you how.) I'd replace the starter and solenoid as a unit. Less time, less hassle and you can get $$ back when you exchange the old starter for a new one—it's called a 'core charge.'

Step 1. Remove Starter and Solenoid—Engine in Car (Standard Transmission only)

Disconnect the battery ground strap (10mm wrench) and tuck it away from the battery so it can't spring back and restore the circuit with a zap. Disconnect the black plastic covered cable running to the threaded stud on the solenoid (13mm). Pull off the cable and finger tighten the lockwasher and nut back on the stud for safe-keeping. Now pull the two thin wires going to each side of the solenoid. They have different type connectors so you can't go wrong when reconnecting them.

Look at the way the starter is bolted to the engine. There are two methods. One uses two 15mm bolts or polygon socket head bolts passing through the flywheel housing (that's the transmission case), one of which screws into a nut welded to the top arm of the front engine/transmission mount. The lower bolt just has a regular nut. The alternative method uses three 13mm nuts to hold the starter against the flywheel housing and a rear support bracket attached to the starter and the transmission. Remove the appropriate bolts and put them into a marked Baggie.

Stay on your feet and grab the starter with one hand and pull it gently toward the left fender. If it doesn't come easily, pull harder and give it a slight twist when it starts to move. Lift the starter out of the engine compartment. Careful, it's heavy.

Step 2. Examine Starter for Wear

It should be clean (mud is OK) and the toothed pinion gear on a shaft going into a sealed bearing should have a full set of teeth. I wish I did. The bearing shouldn't squeak when the shaft is rotated. Half way up the

Step 2. (Cont'd.)

shaft is another small sealed bearing which also should turn easily. Do not oil these bearings. You can pack the small one with high temperature bearing grease if you want, but be sure to wipe off any excess. Leave the large bearing alone.

If the shaft squeaks or makes nasty noises as you turn it, you need a new Bendix mechanism. This rarely happens. If the pinion gear is covered with black powder and sticky dust, at the very least the brushes are shot. Clean the starter and trade it in or take it to a starter repair shop. Replacing starter? Go to Step 5.

Step 3. Solenoid Replacers: Remove Solenoid from Starter

Phone VW before starting work to make sure they have a solenoid or can get one without too much delay. There are two types of solenoid mountings: two screws and three screws. Order the right one.

Remove the nut and lockwasher holding the wire running from the starter body to the solenoid (13mm wrench). Remove the wire, then replace the lockwasher and nut on the stud for safekeeping. Remove the screws holding the solenoid to the starter. They're at the front of the solenoid opposite the 13mm nut you just removed. They should come out fairly easily. If not, squirt on a few drops of Liquid Wrench and let it soak in. If they still won't turn, put a wrench onto the screwdriver shaft near the handle (or clamp on a pair of vice grips). Have Friend hold the starter or put it in a vice while you turn the vice grips and the screwdriver handle counterclockwise ⟲. When the screws are removed, the solenoid will slide out, leaving behind a cylinder attached to a spring. Unhook the cylinder and remove it.

Step 4. Attach New Solenoid to Starter

If your new solenoid has a slot on the end of the cylinder, hook it on the end of the lever inside the starter body. No slot—no worry.

Now rub a fingerful of Permatex No. 2 or special VW sealer around the edge of the solenoid where it fits into the starter. Replace the two or three screws through the starter body into the solenoid. Push the solenoid into position and tighten the screws. Put the wire with the metal tab onto the lower stud on the rear of the solenoid. Screw on and tighten the 13mm nut and lockwasher and repeat the screwdriver-vice grip trick on the screws going into the front of the solenoid. Get them tight.

You've just replaced the solenoid!

Step 5. Test New Starter

It's a good idea to see if your new or rebuilt starter really works before you install it. Just reconnect the wires and get someone to turn on the key. Keep your fingers away from the gear end.

Step 6. Install Starter in Car

Starters that mount with two large 15mm or polygon head bolts are easy. Push the starter back into the flywheel housing, making sure the long shaft fits into its hole inside. Slide in one of the bolts and finger tighten it into the welded nut on the motor mount. Do the other bolt, too. When you're sure the bolts aren't cross-threaded, torque them to 3.0 mkg (21 ft lbs).

If you have the other type mounting, fit the starter into the transmission housing and push it home. Screw in the three 13mm bolts securing the front part of the starter and tighten 'em. Install the rear support bracket onto the starter and replace the two 10mm nuts—fingertight, no more. Push the 13mm bolt through the hole into the starter mounting bracket and screw it into the threaded hole in the transmission case.

When you tighten the front 13mm bolts and the rear 13mm bolt, the bracket should fit snugly against the transmission. You don't want to strain the mounting bracket. If there's strain on the starter, it will continually bind on the flywheel and you'll have to do the whole Procedure again. So be sure you've got it right. If things are somewhat strained, remove the 10mm nuts from the starter rear, the 13mm bolts from the transmission and pull off the bracket. Use a file to enlarge the two 10mm holes of the starter mount. Now everything should fit fine. Try it and see. OK? Torque the 13mm bolts to 1.6 mkg (11 ft lbs) and the two 10mm nuts to 0.6 mkg (4 ft lbs). Left your torque wrench by the side of the road in Tucumcari? Just tighten the nut and watch your wrist. You've hit the correct torque when the center wrist tendons stand up through the skin as you gently pull on the wrench.

In both cases install the black plastic-covered cable on the solenoid and tighten the lockwasher and 13mm nut. Now push the two plastic connectors onto their connections on the solenoid.

Install the battery ground strap (10mm wrench) and be sure the battery terminals are bright and shiny. Clean them now and save pulling all your tools out later.

PROCEDURE 9: CHECK AND REMOVE STARTER (AUTOMATICS ONLY). Phase 2.

Condition: Starter or Solenoid doesn't work.

Tools and materials: Phase 1 tool kit and at least a 30cm (12 in) extension for your socket set, safety goggles.

Remarks: This is a difficult and time consuming job that shouldn't be attempted on the side of the highway or in the middle of the night.

Step 1. Get Ready

Remove the battery ground strap (10mm) and tuck it out of the way.

Step 2. Chock, Jack and Block

Chock the rear wheels and jack up the front of the car as high as you can and support it very well with blocks, or better yet, jack stands.

Step 3. Get Under

Put on safety goggles and have in hand a screwdriver with a longish shaft and a 13mm socket wrench with a swivel head and your 12 in extension.

Crawl under the car on your back carrying your tools.

The starter is on the right side of the engine (running parallel to it). There's a tin cover over the starter's body and solenoid. You can't see the solenoid but it's there, believe me. Use a screwdriver to loosen the hose clamp around the tin cover and slide the clamp off. Remove the two 10mm nuts on the rear of the starter and pull off the cover.

Step 4. Check Solenoid/Starter

Reconnect the battery ground strap and turn back to Procedure 6 and do the starter checks in Steps 1 and 2. Bad starter or solenoid? Carry on.

Step 5. Remove Bolts and Loosen Rear Support Mount

Remove the two 13mm bolts from the front of the starter flange where it bolts to the transmission. You can see them easily. A third bolt at the top of the flange is very difficult to get to, hence, the long extension. Feel for and remove it. Now *loosen* the 13mm nut holding the starter rear support mount to the transmission, and swing the mount away from the starter. No need to remove the support mount, it's just something else to lose track of. Put all those bolts in a safe place.

Step 6. Remove Starter and Solenoid

Remove the 13mm nut holding the large wire to the solenoid. Take off the wire and screw on the lockwasher and nut for safekeeping. Pull off the other two small wires going to the solenoid. Mark the thin red wire on the right terminal "Right."

Pull the starter toward the right and when it starts to come, give it a slight turn to the left or right, depending on which way works. Carefully lower the starter/solenoid assembly out of the engine compartment. Don't forget to bring the tin cover with it.

Step 7. Examine Starter

Procedure 8, Step 2. Go to Step 10 in this Procedure if you're installing a new starter/solenoid unit.

Step 8. Separate Solenoid and Starter

Procedure 8, Step 3.

Step 9. Install New Solenoid

Procedure 8, Step 4.

Step 10. Test New Starter

Engine out of the car (referred here from Chapter 18): install the starter and test it (Procedure 6, Step 2).

Engine in place: reinstall the battery ground strap (10mm) and get under the car with your 13mm wrench. Attach the big wire to the stud on the solenoid. Make a good ground connection by holding the starter firmly against something metal, then short your plastic-handled pliers or screwdriver across the two main terminals. If it works, great. If it doesn't, check that you have a good ground. If it still doesn't go, hook up the little solenoid wires and get Friend to turn the key all the way over. Double check everything you've done. If it still doesn't work, 25 years in a Zen monastery might possibly calm you. You don't like the monastic life? Well, check the cable connections on the battery and remember to click door-mounted seat belts into position. Maybe you've got the little solenoid wires on the wrong terminals. Switch 'em.

Step 11. Install Starter

Disconnect the battery ground strap again (10mm wrench). With the car still chocked, jacked and carefully blocked, safety glasses on, lie on your back, grab the starter (with the big hose clamp around it) and attach it to its mount. Reconnect the large wire to the threaded stud on the solenoid (if it's off) and tighten the 13mm nut. Attach the two thin wires on the connections on each side of that nut. The red one goes to the right terminal.

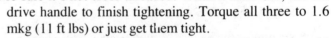

Fit the starter into the flywheel housing. Put one 13mm bolt through the starter into the transmission and make it finger tight. Now install the other two bolts, finger tight too. The top one is tough so you may have to put it into your socket, then attach the extension to the socket (leave the drive handle off for now) and start the bolt into its hole with your fingers. Tighten with your hands until you're sure it's not cross-threaded. When it feels OK, use the drive handle to finish tightening. Torque all three to 1.6 mkg (11 ft lbs) or just get them tight.

Install the rear starter support mount (13mm wrench) and torque it similarly. With the hose clamp in place on the starter, slide the tin cover over the starter until the two threaded studs fit into their holes. Install and tighten the two 10mm nuts. Tighten the hose clamp around the tin cover.

Hook up the battery ground strap (10mm).

Check that battery terminals are bright and shiny. You're on your way.

When H. Turtle replaced his starter he did not get on his way immediately for he found that the front transmission mount had moved about an inch from its alignment. It required Friend, large screwdriver and brute strength to pry the mount into place and hold it there while H.T. replaced the starter mounting bolts. It could happen to you I guess.

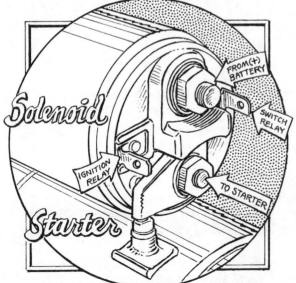
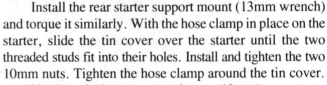

PROCEDURE 10: REPLACE IGNITION STARTER SWITCH. Phase 2

Tools and materials: Phase 1 tool kit, a 24mm or 15/16th socket and a 6mm or 7/32nd allen wrench, new switch.

This is a tedious job, so be sure you have half a day and a full measure of patience. However, a friend is still driving around with the short cut repair I'm about to show you.

Short Cut Ignition Switch Trick

Put the car in neutral (N) with the handbrake on.

Remove the lower plastic panel under the steering column (phillips screwdriver) if it's still in place and put it away. The plastic MPC connector for the ignition starter switch is directly below the key. Pull this plastic connector and examine it carefully. You'll see five slots with electrical contacts nestled inside.

This is how to get the car started: check the diagram and compare it to your connector. Strip the ends on a 15cm (6 in) piece of insulated wire and stick one end of the wire into the slot marked A, terminal 30. Stick the other end into the slot marked B, terminal 50. The starter motor will whirr madly and try to start the engine. As soon as it 'starts,' pull the wire from slot B and stick it into slot C, terminal 15. Your engine will continue to run and the dashboard lights and turn signals will work. If you want the headlights, wipers and windshield washer to operate, jump another piece of wire from slot C to slot D.

To stop the engine, just pull the jumper wire from slot A. This little setup can keep you going for months. Just don't forget to insert the key into the steering lock and turn it to the right. If you neglect this maneuver, the steering column will be locked and you'll quickly drive yourself into the nearest wall.

If all the wire pulling and slotting gets a bit much after a particularly fine model airplane club outing, you may feel the urge to buy and install a new ignition switch. On the other hand, you may not.

Step 1. Preliminaries

Disconnect the battery ground strap (10mm wrench).

Rabbits—Turn the steering wheel until the front wheels are facing straight ahead. Pull off the central steering wheel cover (the thing you press to beep the horn) by grabbing it with both hands, thumbs at the bottom and fingers at the top, and giving it a good hard tug. If it won't come off, insert a butter knife under the plastic cover half way between the center coat of arms and the outside of the cover. Find one of the springs that holds the cover in position. There's one at the right side and one at the left. With the screwdriver in the spring, gently pry the cover upward. If you hear a nasty cracking noise, you sat on the eggs you just bought or you've broken the plastic plate beneath the cover. Don't worry if it's the plate. It's easily repaired with plastic cement.

Step 1. (Cont'd.)

Disconnect the small ground wire from the connection in the middle of the plastic cover.

Sciroccos—Turn the steering wheel until the front wheels are facing straight ahead. Draw a pencil line from the edge of the rubber steering wheel center (the horn ring) to one of the metal spokes. Now peel the edge of the rubber away from the wheel. Use your fingers, not a screwdriver or other metal object—you'll rip the rubber. When it's off, stash it.

Step 2. Remove Steering Wheel—All Models

The nut holding the steering wheel to the steering column (24mm socket) is tight! Hold the wheel with one hand and turn the socket counterclockwise ⟲ with the other. Put the nut and the spring washer into a marked Baggie. Now scratch a mark from the steering column to the inside of the steering wheel or put a punch mark on the face of the steering column and another down on the inside of the steering wheel. Be doubly sure you get the steering wheel in the right place when it's time to reinstall it. (**Sciroccos**—pull the horn wire connection.)

Pull off the steering wheel. Don't tug at it with all your might, you may end up with the wheel neatly fastened to your nose. Gently rock it side to side and work it off the column.

Step 3. Free Column Hardware

Remove the bolt from the left underside of the steering column ignition switch housing (6mm allen wrench or socket). On some Rabbits the steering column switch housing is held together by a phillips screw—remove it. The steering column wiper/turn signal switch is facing you with two arms sticking out—one for the lights and the other for the windshield washer and wipers.

Step 4. Remove Multi-Point Connector(s)

Pull off the plastic MPC's with bunches of wires running into them. Mark them Left, Right and Center. The right one fastens to the base of the ignition switch. They're hard to get mixed up, but you never know. Some models just have one MPC, so pull that.

Step 5. Remove Column Hardware

Let's remove the entire steering column turn signal and wiper arm switch assembly. Unscrew the three or four screws from the steering column wiper/turn signal switch. Mark and Baggie them. Pull the switch mechanism toward you to free it from the steering column. Put it somewhere safe!

Now lever the plastic spacer sleeve off the column. Use a medium screwdriver and be careful not to burr the ends of the sleeve. Baggie it.

Put the key into the ignition switch, grasp the ignition switch housing and gently lever it off the steering column. Too stubborn? Tap it lightly on the metal part of the base with a rubber or brass hammer. Lift the housing off the steering column.

Step 6. Remove Switch

Turn the housing upside down so the ignition starter switch terminals are facing you. Remove the phillips head screw holding the switch in its housing. The screw is about half an inch inside the part of the housing which slid over the steering column. Hold the switch by the terminals and pull it out. If it won't come easily, grab one of the terminals with a pair of pliers and tug while gently moving it side to side.

Presto, it's out. When you go to buy a new switch, compare the new to the old to make sure they're the same.

Step 7. Install New Switch

Line up the slot in the switch with the slot in the base of the ignition lock. Turn the key if necessary. Slide in your new switch and install the phillips screw to hold it in place. Try the key again to see if everything feels right.

Step 8. Reinstall Column Hardware

Reinstall the housing containing the new ignition/starter switch onto the steering column. Make sure it's in the original position and install the allen or phillips head screw. Slide on the column spacer sleeve and knock it down until it's equal to the dimension in the diagram. If you damaged the spacer and it's loose, buy a new one. Reposition the turn signal/wiper switch mechanism and its three or four screws.

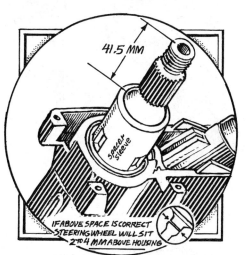

Step 9. Install Multi-Point Connectors

Slide on the single or three plastic MPC's, left, right and center.

Step 10. Install Steering Wheel, etc.

Line up the scratch or punch marks. Install the spring washer and the nut and tighten it to 5 mkg (36 ft lbs) and reconnect the small electrical horn wire to the steering wheel cover.

   Rabbits—Repair any damage to the steering wheel cover with plastic cement—the type used to stick those model car kits together. Snap the cover onto the steering wheel. Be sure it's not upside down.

   Sciroccos—Find and line up the pencil marks on the rubber wheel center and the steering wheel. Roll the edge of the rubber cover onto the wheel center and work the thing on securely. Don't use a screwdriver to get that cover on. Fingers will suffice.

   Put back the lower plastic steering column protector. Install and tighten up the phillips head screws. Now clean up and you're finished!

PROCEDURE 11: FIX SHIFT LEVER CONTACT PLATE AND/OR CONSOLE LIGHT (AUTO-MATICS). Phase 1.

Condition: The console light has blown or you have to wiggle the shift lever to get the car to start. Battery, solenoid and starter OK. Door mounted seat belt fastened?

Tools and materials: Phase 1 tool kit, butter or grapefruit knife, new bulb.

Remarks: If the shift lever isn't engaging all the gears properly, the selection lever cable is probably out of adjustment. Fix it (Chapter 16, Procedure 3).

   The contact plate is basically a switch that allows current to flow to the starter only when the shift lever is in Park (P) or Neutral (N). The plate can break, come loose and therefore be out of alignment, or the wires running to it can fall off. It's a simple thing to fix.

Step 1. Remove Shift Knob

Put the shift lever into Neutral (N). Handbrake on? Good. Remove the allen screw from the left side of the shift knob (2mm—5/64 in—allen wrench or tiny screwdriver and pull off the knob).

Step 2. Remove Indicator Plate

The plastic gear indicator plate tells you what gear you're in. Use a butter or grapefruit knife blade to carefully lever the plate from the console. The red plastic propeller that TWA gives away with cocktails is a great tool also.

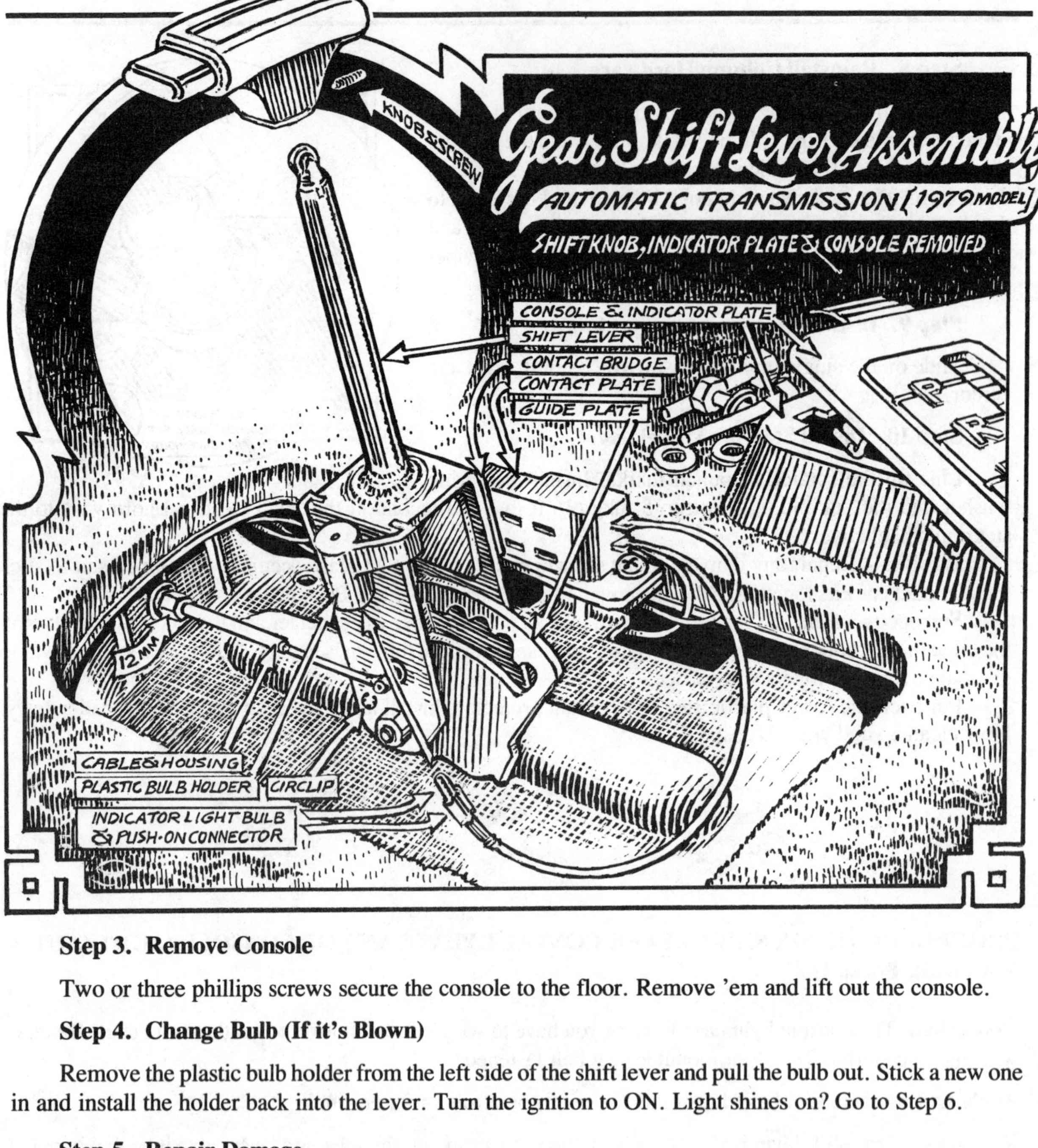

Gear Shift Lever Assembly
AUTOMATIC TRANSMISSION [1979 MODEL]
SHIFT KNOB, INDICATOR PLATE & CONSOLE REMOVED

KNOB & SCREW

CONSOLE & INDICATOR PLATE
SHIFT LEVER
CONTACT BRIDGE
CONTACT PLATE
GUIDE PLATE

12 MM

CABLE & HOUSING
PLASTIC BULB HOLDER   CIRCLIP
INDICATOR LIGHT BULB
& PUSH-ON CONNECTOR

Step 3. Remove Console

Two or three phillips screws secure the console to the floor. Remove 'em and lift out the console.

Step 4. Change Bulb (If it's Blown)

Remove the plastic bulb holder from the left side of the shift lever and pull the bulb out. Stick a new one in and install the holder back into the lever. Turn the ignition to ON. Light shines on? Go to Step 6.

Step 5. Repair Damage

You can now see the contact plate on the right of the shift lever. A contact bridge on the right of the shift lever touches the plate when the lever is in N or P. Check that all the wires are connected to the plate and/or bridge. If the plate and bridge aren't lined up, juice can't get to the starter. Loosen the one or two phillips screws on the contact plate and move it until things line up. Keep the lever in Neutral (N). The car will now start with nary a wiggle of the shift lever if the door type seat belts are fastened. If the metal contacts on the plate or bridge are dirty, clean them with alcohol or tape player head cleaner.

If the plate or contact bridge is broken, install a new one. The contact bridge just pushes into the shift lever.

Step 6. Install What You Took Off

Check that all the wires are pushed into position on the contact plate and bulb holder. Install the console and screw it to the floor with the phillips screws. Slip the indicator plate over the shift lever and snap it into the console. Finally, put the shift knob on and tighten the allen screw. Finito.

CHAPTER 8

ALTERNATOR RED LIGHT ON!

The alternator and voltage regulator work in harmony to provide a constant supply of healthy electricity to charge the battery, light the headlights and power other things electrical. This chapter covers these electrical goodies and the systems which depend on them.

The crankshaft turns, rotating the V-belt, which turns the alternator pulley and the rotor inside the alternator. The alternator generates an alternating current (AC) of electricity that is converted to direct current (DC) by six little gizmos inside the alternator called silicone diodes.

The amount of electricity produced by the alternator depends on the revolutions per minute (rpm) of the engine. Because the engine doesn't always turn at the same speed, the alternator's output varies. For example when the engine is idling, the alternator might put out 14 volts at 20 amps. But at 2000 rpm it might be 50 volts at 18 amps. If this higher voltage were to reach the electrical circuit, it could burn it out and the battery would overcharge, causing it to boil and blow to pieces. A voltage regulator prevents this from happening by diverting voltage over 14 volts to ground. Twelve volts supply the Rabbit's operating needs and two extra volts keep a gentle charge going into the battery.

On models through 1976, the voltage regulator is attached to the back of the alternator and is replaceable. Later model alternators have the regulator inside the alternator and it's impossible to repair or replace, so the whole alternator has to be replaced if the regulator goes out. Modern transistorized voltage regulators, however, have no internal moving parts so they rarely go bad.

Two types of alternators are used: the U.S. made Motorola and the German Bosch. The following Procedures apply to both types, although you may have to use different size wrenches for the Motorola. Replace a faulty alternator with the same type fitted to your car.

If the alternator red light on the dash comes on, something is wrong in the electrical system. In addition to the simple red light, your deluxe Rabbit or Scirocco may have a more sensitive ammeter on the dash with a C (charge) on one side of the scale and a D (discharge) on the other. If the battery is receiving the right amount of current from the alternator, the needle in the ammeter will hover around the center mark, slightly to the C side. If the needle moves just a little in the D scale, the V-belt is probably loose and the alternator is not turning enough to 'generate' sufficient electricity. If the needle is all the way over to the D side, it's the same as the red alternator light on the dash lighting up. Something is wrong.

To have this warning system in the first place, the red light itself must work. Procedure 1 deals with the circuit repairs necessary to get the red light ablaze when the key is turned to ON.

When the red light stays on after the engine has started or comes on as you are driving, turn to Procedure 2.

If the red dash light ever stays on after the ignition key has been shut off, action is needed **immediately.** There are two possible problems. The voltage regulator is shot and draining the battery, or there is a poor ground connection somewhere. Procedure 2.

Don't try to save time by not disconnecting the battery ground strap when I ask you to. You may end up spending a lot more time and money than you bargained for by damaging something you didn't want to damage. Please make sure there's no loose gas lying around the engine. Electricity and gas don't mix—they **Explode!**

It's very difficult to troubleshoot the charging system without special tools. There are a number of techniques which point to answers but won't prove them. For example: if you need to add water to the battery every day or two, it indicates the alternator is overcharging, which points to a faulty voltage regulator.

If the battery is dead all the time, even after a long journey, insufficient voltage is getting to the battery to keep it fully charged. The alternator or voltage regulator is faulty, unless you have a short in a main wire somewhere. That's unlikely. It's usually a bad alternator.

If you're stuck on the road you can do a 'shade tree test' which will tell you if the alternator's putting out current. Here's how: start the engine and loosen the battery positive cable (10mm wrench). Rev the engine to about 2000 rpm and lift the positive cable off the battery. Don't keep the cable off for more than a few seconds. If the engine immediately dies, the alternator isn't putting out any current. You need a new one. Procedure 2, Step 3, explains how to install it.

If the engine continues to run when the positive cable is disconnected, enough current is being 'generated' to supply the engine's needs. Reconnect the battery cable and tighten the bolt. However, it may be that the alternator is only supplying a small amount of current, not enough to keep the battery charged and supply the rest of the electrical components with their needs. Ask VW or an auto electric shop to test it.

When you buy a rebuilt alternator, remember that electrical items are usually *not* returnable unless they prove to be faulty. Be sure your alternator is kaput before you shell out the cash for a replacement.

If none of your dash lights comes on when the key is turned to ON, make sure your battery is alive (try to start the car). If it isn't, get it charged before you begin these procedures. Also, check battery connections, Chapter 9, Procedure 2. If that doesn't fix the lights, the ignition switch must be kaput. Turn to Chapter 7, Procedure 6, Step 3, and check the switch.

PROCEDURE 1:   CHECK AND REPAIR THE RED LIGHT (ALTERNATOR) CIRCUIT. Phase 1.

Condition: The red dash warning light *does not* come on when the ignition key is turned to ON. You may have been referred here from Chapter 3 or Chapter 17.

Tools and materials: Phase 1 tool kit, 6mm allen wrench, test light or VOM (Volt-Ohmmeter), maybe a new bulb or bulb holder.

Remarks: If all the dash lights come on except the alternator light when you turn the key to ON, a little investigation is needed. The wiring could be defective (Steps 1 and 2), the bulb blown (Steps 3-7), or the circuit is faulty inside the alternator or voltage regulator.

Check the fuses in the relay plate above the driver's knees. Replace any which are blown.

Step 1. Check Bulb Circuit

To disconnect the large plug from the rear of the alternator, loosen but don't remove the 8mm nut holding the clip which secures the plug. Twist the clip to one side and pull the plug. Running into the back of the plug are three wires protected by a black plastic sheath. Pull the sheath slightly away from the plug and you'll see a blue wire. Insert your test light or red (positive) VOM probe (switched to 15 DCV) into the socket of the plug opposite the blue wire. Turn the ignition switch to ON and ground the end of the test light or meter on a clean unpainted metal surface. If the test light and the dash warning light come on or the meter reads 12 volts, the problem lies in the wiring or with the alternator or voltage regulator. If they don't come on, go to Step 3.

Sometimes the blue wire gets loose from the metal socket inside the plug. To check, stick the plug back into the alternator, turn the ignition key to ON and wiggle the blue wire. Any light on the dash? If not, stick a thin screwdriver or a toothpick into the back of the plug alongside the blue wire. Does the dash bulb now light? Great. We can do a simple repair.

Step 2. Fixing Blue Wire in Plug

Turn off the ignition and disconnect the battery ground strap (10mm). Pull the plug out from the rear of the alternator. Use needle nose pliers to pull the metal connector attached to the blue wire from the front of the plug. If the connector comes out leaving the blue wire behind, you have just found your problem. (Rich and foolish purists might be tempted to buy a new plug. Don't bother, it's too much work to install. A new plug comes equipped with millions of wires and you'll have to connect them all.) Dig inside the front of the plug for the blue wire and pull it through. Reconnect the metal connector to the blue wire and push it back into the plug.

If you can't find the blue wire from the front of the plug, pull it out from the rear. Splice a 10cm (4 in) piece of insulated electrical wire of the same gauge (or slightly heavier) onto the blue wire with an insulated connector (Chapter 20, Procedure 14).

The hole from which you pulled the wire has probably closed up, so the easiest thing to do is drill a new one all the way through the plastic plug. Make the hole big enough to take your new piece of spliced-on-wire. Push the new wire through the back of the plug until it sticks out the front. Strip the end of the wire (remove plastic covering) and pry open the end of the connector which was attached to the blue wire. Squeeze it onto the new wire with a pair of pliers. Get the new wire into the plug by pulling it from the back. Be sure the connector fits snugly into the front of the plug. Push the plug back onto the alternator, reconnect the battery ground strap and try the ignition. It works? Great.

If the bulb doesn't light up when the plug is installed in the rear of the alternator, but works when you ground the blue wire, the alternator or voltage regulator is bad. The procedure for testing either is beyond you. So go to VW or the electric shop to have them checked. If they tell you that yours is shot, a rebuilt one will be cheaper than a new one. In fact, you can have the one from my car that Peter so kindly customized when he rolled the car over La Bajada Hill.

If you couldn't get the dash light to work when you grounded the blue wire, maybe it's the bulb. Let's check.

Step 3. Test Bulb and Bulb Holder

This takes five minutes or an hour depending on the size of your hands. The Procedure for checking the alternator warning light bulb is the same as for any other bulb in the dash. The other bulbs are just in different places.

Buy two spare bulbs from VW if you discover that yours is blown because it's likely you'll either break or lose one while trying to replace the thing. I'm going to deal with small handed people first. Huge hands see Step 5.

Step 4. Locate and Remove Bulb—Small Hands (Deluxe or Scirocco, go to Step 5).

Put a cap on if you have long or curly hair. Remove any bracelets, wristwatches, or rings. Disconnect the battery ground strap (10mm). If the floor around the clutch and brake pedals is dirty, clean it up a bit. Put the gear shift lever into third or Park (P) and thread yourself into the driver's space with your shoulders on the floor and your legs draped over the back of the seat. Comfortable? I doubt it. Slide your hand up inside the rear of the dash past all the wires. The bulb is in a tiny plastic holder clipped into the printed circuit behind the dash. Be careful! Don't claw the printed circuit; it's delicate and next-

It IS POSSIBLE TO REMOVE AND REPLACE THE WARNING LIGHT BULBS WITHOUT REMOVING THE RADIO.

Step 4. (Cont'd.)

to-impossible to repair and difficult to replace.

Hold the bulb holder between your first finger and thumb and twist the holder counterclockwise ⟲. Gently pull it out of the printed circuit. Moving carefully, thread yourself out of the car. Didn't wear a cap? It hurts when your hair gets caught on the steering column lever, doesn't it?

Now that you have the bulb and holder in your fragile grasp, go to Step 6 and test while I deal with huge-handed people.

Step 5. Locate and Remove Bulb—Huge Hands and Deluxe and Scirocco

The radio has to come out of the dash. If you don't have a radio, just pull the plastic box or plate from the dash and disregard all the radio instructions.

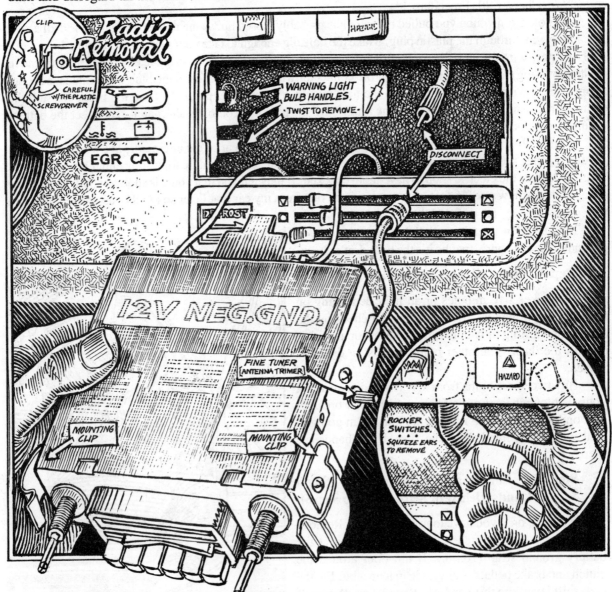

The radio is removed by first pulling the control knobs off. There's a small one with a larger one underneath on each side. They'll come off easily, leaving two metal stems with a thread at the bottom. These are the radio controls and stick out of a plastic plate that is held onto the radio by two nuts. Remove the nuts and washers and gently pull off the plastic plate.

You are left with the radio clipped in place on the dash (see diagram). Lever those spring metal clips with a screwdriver, using the heel of your hand as shown in Peter's drawing. Don't use the fragile plastic around

Step 5. (Cont'd.)

the radio as a leverage point. Pull the radio clear and let it hang down. As you pulled it forward, you probably disconnected the antenna. If you didn't, pull the antenna plug from the rear of the radio.

Standard model owners now can get easily at the alternator or warning light bulb. It's the one behind the battery symbol on the dash. Grasp the bulb *holder* between your thumb and forefinger and turn the bulb holder ¼ turn counterclockwise ◯ . Got it? Good, go to Step 6, please.

Deluxe Rabbit and Scirocco owners have a bit more work to do. The bulb is located between the headlight high beam indicator and the turn signal lights. You'll have to loosen part of the dash to get to the bulb.

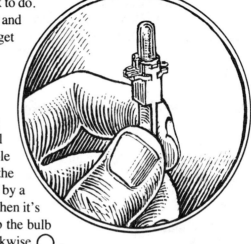

After removing the radio, remove the heater control levers. These just pull off as does the round knob from the heater fan speed control. Gently pry out the plastic panel in which the heat control levers slide. Toward the left rear of that gaping orifice (hole) is a phillips screw. Remove it and carefully pull the dash insert forward about six inches. Now you should be able to reach the alternator warning light. If you can't, remove the speedometer cable from the back of the speedometer. It's held by a round silver captive nut. Undo the nut with your fingers and when it's loose, pull the cable free. Now grasp the bulb holder and twist it ¼ turn counterclockwise ◯ .

Step 6. Check Bulb and Holder

The holder has two little nipples. Is there evidence of corrosion on them? If so, clean them with emery paper until they're bright. Also clean the place where the holder fits into the printed circuit. Use a Q-Tip dipped in alcohol or tape recorder head cleaner. *DO NOT* use sandpaper or anything coarse (or vulgar).

To test the bulb and holder switch your VOM to RX1K (to measure continuity) and touch the probes to the two nipples on the holder. If the needle swings over to zero ohms, the bulb and holder are OK. The holder was probably loose in the printed circuit, preventing the bulb from lighting when the ignition was turned ON. Pull the two nipples down a bit with your fingernail so they form a better contact with the printed circuit. Clean both bulb holder contacts with a piece of fine emery paper and Q-Tip the printed circuit with head cleaner.

If the needle on your VOM stayed still, check the bulb. Hold the bulb up to the light. Is the filament inside the glass intact? If it's broken, that's your trouble. Even if the filament looks OK, test it by touching the probes of your VOM (RX1K) to the two tiny wires sticking out from the base of the bulb. A reading of zero ohms indicates the bulb is fine. Check the wires on the base of the bulb. If one of the wires is broken, you need a new bulb. Depending on what you find, put the old bulb back in its holder or replace it with a new one.

Insert the bulb holder into the hole in the printed circuit behind the dashboard and turn it ¼ turn clockwise ◯ . You will feel the holder click into place. Reconnect the battery ground strap, turn the ignition key to ON and bask in the warm glow of the alternator warning light. It still isn't on? Merde, the trouble is in the printed circuit on the rear of the dash, or the relay panel (fuse box) above the driver's legs; something that can't be fixed. Usually a bad relay plate will make other electrical functions weird. For example, the handbrake warning light comes on at odd times, the headlights work only on high beam, the dash lights don't work at the correct times, etc.

Ask VW or an electric shop to test things for you. If the plate is beyond resurrection, you'll have to replace it. See the end of Step 5 in Procedure 2.

Step 7. Install Radio

Successful troubleshooters must disconnect the battery ground strap again. Deluxe Rabbit and Scirocco owners reconnect the speedometer cable if you disconnected it. Push the end of the cable into the back of the speedometer before tightening the captive nut with your fingers. Push the plastic dash insert into the dash and screw in the phillips screw. Don't use the screw to lever the insert into position or you'll crack the plastic.

Push on the heater panel and controls. Plug the antenna into the rear of the radio before you put it back into the dash. (If you don't, you'll soon be wondering why the radio won't work). Now install the radio. As you slip the radio into the dash, make sure the two metal clips on its side fit properly into the plastic dash. Careful of the plastic and your fingers; the clips are strong. Install the plastic plate, the two washers, two nuts and the tuning, volume and tone control knobs. You're finished.

PROCEDURE 2: CHECK AND REPAIR RED LIGHT (ALTERNATOR) CIRCUIT. Phase 1. ALSO PROCEDURE TO REMOVE/INSTALL ALTERNATOR. Phase 1.

Condition 1: The red alternator warning light stays on *all* the time, even when the engine is running. If the light comes on as you're driving, see Step 3.

Condition 2: The red alternator warning light stays on when the key is turned off (Step 5).

Tools and materials: Phase 1 tool kit, 6mm allen wrench, test light or VOM, ruler, metal pipe or hammer handle.

Step 1. Check Grounds

Weird things happen even to Rabbits. A poor ground can cause the red alternator warning light to stay on all the time. Check the braided metal ground strap which runs between the alternator and the engine. The connections at both ends should be clean and tight. If not, remove the 8mm nut from the back of the alternator and pull off the strap. Clean the end until it shines and do the same with the little threaded stud on the alternator. Examine the strap very carefully. If it's frayed or broken, buy a new one. Now remove the bolt holding the strap to the engine crankcase (13mm wrench). Clean both the end of the strap and the mounting point on the crankcase. Install the strap and tighten the belt.

Check that one end of the battery ground strap is properly fastened on the battery post and the other tightly bolted onto the rear of the transmission. I've found some cars without the tranny bolt. If you've got one, remove it (13mm wrench) and clean the end of the strap. If it isn't there, buy one and install it. Clean the place on the transmission where the strap fastens. Do these simple measures stop the light from continually shining? I hope so. If not, continue on.

Step 2. Check V-Belt

Examine the alternator V-belt. If there is too much movement (deflection) in the belt, it won't turn the rotor inside the alternator. No electric charge will go to the battery and the red light will stay on. The belt should be in perfect condition. If it's at all frayed or cracked, replace it right away. You should have a spare belt in the trunk. If not, take your old belt to VW to check for size.

If your belt looks great and is not slipping, go to Step 4.

Step 3. Change or Tighten Alternator V-Belt and/or Remove Alternator

Pull the plug from the rear of the alternator and remove the braided ground strap if you're replacing the alternator (8mm wrench). The bottom of the alternator is attached by a long 6mm allen head pivot bolt to a bracket on the engine, and the top is attached by a curved metal bracket. Air-conditioned cars may have a slightly different arrangement. In some cases the alternator is best reached from under the car.

Begin by loosening the top 13mm nut holding the alternator to the curved slotted metal bracket. You may need two wrenches, one to hold the bolt head steady as you turn the nut with the other. (Remove the nut and bolt if you are replacing the alternator.) Now slip your 6mm allen wrench through the hole in the drive belt guard (if necessary) and put it into the socket head bolt at the bottom of the alternator. Put a 13mm wrench on the other end of the bolt and loosen the nut. (Remove it to replace the alternator.) If you are replacing the belt, push the alternator towards the engine and slip the old belt off the V-belt pulleys. Put on the new belt and check the tension as described further on in this Step.

If you are replacing the alternator, slide the socket head bolt sideways and free the alternator. To install a new/rebuilt alternator, first swap the multi-blade fan from the old onto the new, if it's missing, and position the new alternator on the engine, and slip the socket head bolt through the two bottom ears. Install the 13mm nut. Put the top 13mm nut and bolt into the top ear and onto the metal bracket. Position the V-belt on the crankshaft and alternator pulleys and check the tension.

If the belt is just loose, pull the alternator toward you and tighten the 13mm nut and bolt on the curved metal bracket until the bolt is snug—but not tight. Stick a two-foot metal pipe or wooden axe handle between the alternator and the crankcase and use it to lever the alternator away from the crankcase. Tighten the 13mm bolt.

The belt should have between 10-15mm (3/8-9/16 in) of belt deflection. Check by placing a ruler across the belt loop halfway between the two pulleys, and another at a right angle to the first. Press the top of the belt with your thumb and measure how far in it deflects. If the belt is too tight, loosen the 13mm bolt a little while keeping the pipe or handle behind the alternator, and ease the tension on the belt a little.

When the belt tension is correct, tighten the socket head bolt at the bottom of the alternator (13mm). Put back the plug in the back and secure it with the clip (8mm). Install the braided ground strap. Get all your tools out of the engine compartment and start the engine; make sure the battery ground strap is on and fixed.

V·BELT DEFLECTION 10 TO 15MM 3/8" TO 9/16"

There shouldn't be any mechanical noises coming from the alternator. A high pitched whine or shriek means the V-belt is too tight. Run it like that for long and you'll be needing a new alternator rather quickly. Adjust the V-belt deflection until it's correct (10mm-15mm) and the gremlins will yell no more.

Sometimes a rebuilt alternator fails to perform as it should. It's possible that the person rebuilding it left out an essential ingredient to make it work. It's a bit like trying to make leavened bread without yeast. I've installed four different rebuilt alternators in one car before finding a good one. Talk about doubting one's diagnosis!

The next time you go out for a sandwich, drive to VW and buy a spare belt to stash in the trunk. If the red light still stays on, proceed.

Step 4. Investigate Further

If the damn light continues to shine as the engine speed increases, there's a short either in the alternator, the wiring between the alternator and the bulb, or between the bulb holder and the printed circuit on the rear of the dash. Or the relay plate is screwed up.

Loosen the 8mm nut on the clip holding the plug in the rear of the alternator and pull out the plug. Turn on the engine. If the red light comes on, you have a short between terminal D+ on the alternator and relay plate terminal C2. Disconnect the battery ground strap (10mm wrench) and remove the protective carpet (if you have one) from the driver's knees. The relay plate is the thing with the plastic cover and all the fuses. Take out the phillips screw from the edge of the relay plate and pull the plate away from the little metal retaining ears. Be careful with all the wires. Hold the relay plate gingerly in your hands and turn it around. See all those big colored plastic plugs? The one you're interested in is clear and fits into the socket marked C. Pull it out. Reconnect the battery ground strap and turn on the engine. If the dash alternator light comes on, the wiring between the relay plate and the alternator is shorted. Take the car to an auto electric shop and tell them what troubleshooting you've done already.

If the warning light doesn't go on, there's a problem between plug D in the relay plate and the printed circuit behind the dash. Let's find the trouble.

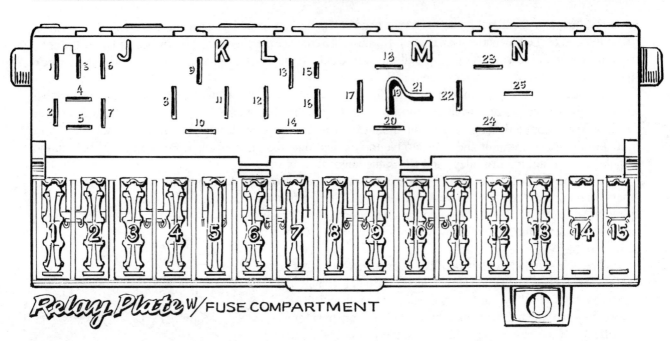

Relay Plate W/FUSE COMPARTMENT

Put plug C back into its socket and pull blue-colored plug D from the relay plate. Make sure the battery ground strap is connected. Turn on the engine. If the warning light comes on, the printed circuit behind the dash is bad or wire D+ at the alternator is grounded. Off to the electric shop to get it fixed. If the light doesn't come on, the relay plate is grounded and must be replaced. Buy one from VW.

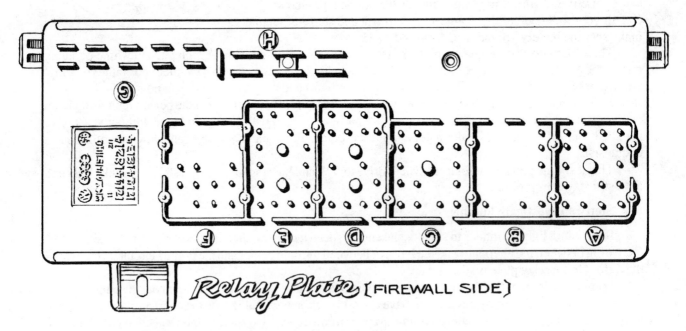

Relay Plate [FIREWALL SIDE]

Step 5. Replace Relay Plate

Remove the battery ground strap (10mm). With your new relay plate in hand, pull the left plastic plug from the bad relay plate and put it in its corresponding place on the new one. Do all the plugs one at a time so you don't mix them up. When all the connectors have been moved, disconnect the brass colored spade connectors one at a time and replace them on the new plate in the same positions as on the old plate. Do this job slowly and carefully; you know how much a new relay plate costs!

Reconnect the battery ground strap and your light will shine!

Step 6. Red Light On, Ignition Key Off

Pull the plug from the rear of the alternator. Light goes out? (Battery ground strap must be connected.) The alternator/voltage regulator needs repair. Remove the alternator (Step 3) and either buy a new/rebuilt unit or take it to an electric shop or VW for repair.

If the light doesn't go out when the plug's pulled there's a short somewhere. The electric shop beckons.

Relay Plate, Fuse Compartment Side

Socket J: Headlight dimmer relay (vacant from 1977 on)
Socket K: Rear Window defogger relay (Load reduction relay 1978 on)
Socket L: Fuel pump relay on fuel injection cars
Socket M: Windshield wiper intermittent relay, Scirocco only
Socket N: Turn signal/emergency flasher relay

Fuse Positions In A Typical (?) Rabbit

1. Low beam, left (driver's) side
2. Low beam, right side
3. High beam, left side, & high beam warning light
4. High beam, right side
5. Rear window defogger (if installed)
6. Stop lights & emergency flasher system
7. Cigarette lighter, interior light, clock
8. Turn signals & indicator light
9. Diverter valve (fuel inj.), automatic choke, horn, back-up light
10. Fresh air fan (1979), rear window defogger warning light (1976, if installed)
11. Fresh air fan (1976), windshield wiper/washer, rear window washer pump (if installed)
12. License plate light
13. Right side parking, tail & marker lights
14. Left side parking, tail and marker lights
15. Radiator cooling fan

Relay Plate, Firewall Side

Socket A: Front left harness
Socket B: System wiring analysis
                 (vacant from 1978 on)
Socket C: Front right harness
Socket D: Dashboard wiring
Socket E: Dashboard wiring
Socket F: Rear Harness
G & H: Terminal Connections

CHAPTER 9

☞ RED OIL LIGHT ON! ☜

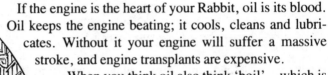

If the engine is the heart of your Rabbit, oil is its blood. Oil keeps the engine beating; it cools, cleans and lubricates. Without it your engine will suffer a massive stroke, and engine transplants are expensive.

When you think oil also think 'boil'—which is what will happen to your engine's guts if you neglect to keep the oil level up to scratch inside the crankcase.

If there's not enough oil in the engine, whatever oil there is has to work that much harder to keep things cool and lubricated. Being just a pint low will put a heavy strain on bearings and the oil pump. If the coolant level is also low, the engine will overheat very quickly. Your poor Rabbit will be heading for an appointment with Chapter 18, Engine Overhaul, quicker than you'd like.

You check the oil level on the dipstick every morning, don't you? No? Well, you should. OK, let's do a trial run.

PROCEDURE 1: CHECK OIL. Phase 1.

Condition: The beginning of a new day.

Tools and materials: Something to wipe the dipstick on.

Step 1. Check Level

Lift and prop the hood; don't start the engine. Remove the dipstick from the left side of the engine and wipe it clean on a paper towel, blade of grass, or your sock. Slip it back into its hole. Wait a few seconds, then pull the dipstick out again. Check the level of the oil on the stick; it should be on or just below the uppermost mark. If it's on the lower mark, you need a quart of oil RIGHT AWAY.

Step 2. Add More Oil

I carry a quart of oil in a plastic bottle and add a little whenever the level is noticeably lower than the top mark. (See Chapter 10, Procedure 9, Step 6 for a 'how not to spill oil' tip.) Your engine will appreciate it if you don't wait until it's an entire quart low before adding more. You can buy a very inexpensive plastic quart bottle complete with pouring spout and cap.

NEVER ADD TOO MUCH OIL. Overfilling the crankcase will eventually cause the front or rear main crankshaft seals to blow out. If you accidentally add too much oil (a 1/2 quart or more—the oil level on the dipstick will be higher than the top line), remove the oil pan drain plug (Chapter 10) and drain the excess into a catch pan.

Don't let the gas station attendant check the oil for you (these days it would seem like a miracle if they even offered). Wait until the gas tank is full, the windows washed (you'll probably have to do this, too), and the tire pressure checked. This gives the oil inside the engine plenty of time to run down through the passages into the oil pan on the bottom of the crankcase. Your dipstick measures the amount of oil in this pan, so if the level is checked before it's all down, you risk adding too much oil and blowing a seal.

Oil Light

The red oil pressure light (Sciroccos may also have an oil pressure gauge) not only warns the absent-minded when the oil level is too low but also indicates potential engine problems caused by low oil pressure. It's the 'idiot light' on the dashboard with the picture of an old fashioned railroad oil can.

    Please get into the habit of checking that the red oil light comes on when you turn the key to ON and goes off IMMEDIATELY after the engine has started. This shows that the oil pressure is at the proper operating level. If the light doesn't come on at all, something is wrong. (Procedure 2.)

    If the oil light comes on as you're driving, turn off the engine and pull over to the side of the road to evaluate the condition of your engine. The light will come on only if the oil level is very low, the oil pressure drops or the light or oil pressure sensor is malfunctioning. The more miles you drive with the light on, the more money it will cost you. It's like throwing fistfuls of dollar bills out the window. Should the red EGR or CAT light come on, turn to Chapter 13.

PROCEDURE 2: CHECK RED OIL PRESSURE IDIOT LIGHT, Phases 1 and 2.

Condition: One fateful morning you turn the ignition key to ON and the red oil light doesn't come on.

Tools and materials: Phase 1 tool kit, box of baking soda and a small brush, Vaseline.

Remarks: If your dash lights all work *except* the oil pressure light, go to Step 2.

Step 1.   Check Battery Connections

    If none of the dash lights comes on, or you hear a 'tick' and the starter won't turn the engine over—or nothing works at all—try this. If the oil light is the only one that doesn't work, go to Step 2.

    Lift and prop the hood. How do the battery terminals look? They should be clean, not covered with white crud. Tap the terminals with a light hammer. Do the dash lights come on or wink at you? If so, you have a lousy battery connection. *Battery corrosion is acid*: wear safety glasses and don't get any of that crud on your best suit or you'll be needing a new one before the day is over. Make sure that metal tools don't cause a short between the positive and negative posts. Remove rings and bracelets—they could cause a nasty burn or shock.

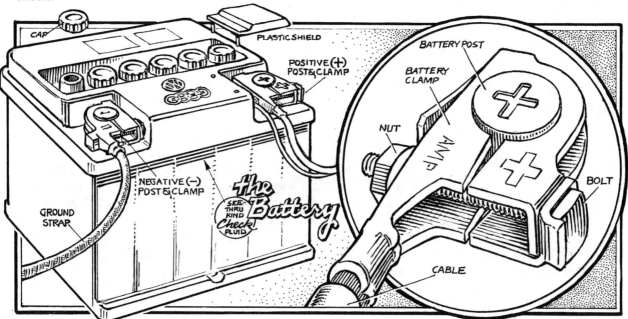

The battery terminals and posts can be cleaned with the battery in the car, but if you have time, remove it. Keep onlookers away; battery acid is dangerous stuff.

Mix a heaping tablespoon full of baking soda with two cups of water and paint the battery terminals with the solution. Wire brush the foaming crud off the terminals. Stroke the wire brush *away* from you only. Keep on with the soda solution until all the white crud has been dissolved, then flush things clean with plain water.

Loosen the nut from the positive terminal (10mm wrench). You may have to put vise grips on the head of the bolt to loosen the nut. If the nut is stripped, use vise grips on the bolt head and the nut to loosen it. If the whole thing is severely corroded, you'll probably break the bolt before the nut comes loose. Don't worry, you would've had to replace the whole thing anyway.

Pry the terminal away from the battery post. Push a screwdriver or small chisel blade between the two sections of the terminal and spread it. If it's really stuck, spread the jaws of the terminal and carefully tap one side of the terminal with a small hammer to get it off. Try not to damage the battery post. Resist the temptation to use your biggest hammer to knock the whole thing off; you'd undoubtedly break the battery post off, too. Now remove the negative (ground) terminal. If you're a gadget freak, parts stores sell a special battery post/cable terminal cleaning tool. Clean the posts and terminals with the wire brush and soda until they are scalpel clean. It's possible to buy a spray can of special corrosion inhibitor which works very well, but your medicine cabinet probably has an acceptable substitute. Install the terminals onto the battery and tighten the 10mm bolts. Smear the posts and terminals with a thin coat of vaseline, and then clean up. That'll take care of things for a while. Keep an eye on the battery and do the soda Procedure when the white stuff starts to build up again. If you allow the corrosion to advance unchecked, it will eat through the cable terminals and you will have to buy and install new ones. Also check the battery ground strap. If it's eaten through, buy and install a new one.

Battery connections OK? Go on.

Step 2. Check Oil Pressure Sensor Wiring

Lift and prop the hood. Find the oil pressure sensor. It looks like this on all cars but Sciroccos built after 1978. The sensor is screwed onto the rear of the cylinder head, or (Sciroccos 1978 and on) on top or in front of the aluminum manifold onto which the oil filter attaches. Be sure not to mix it up with the coolant temperature connection that's screwed into the small water manifold on the rear of the cylinder head; it's the one above that.

OIL PRESSURE SENSOR

CONNECTOR

Cylinder head (Rear)

Check the wire and spade connector on the back of the sensor. If it isn't connected, clean it up and connect it. If the wire has broken off the connector, buy a new connector, attach it to the wire and push it onto the oil sensor.

Turn the key to ON. Still won't light up? Check the oil sensor wire for breaks in the insulation. It may be shorting out against something metal. If the wire and connector look OK but the light still won't come on, go to the next step.

Step 3. Check Light Bulb and Wiring

Pull off the connector from the back of the oil sensor (or, 1978 and later Sciroccos, from the top of the oil filter manifold). Hold it against the crankcase or an unpainted part of the body to make a good ground. Turn the key to ON and ask someone to check the dash lights. If the oil light comes on when you ground the wire, the bulb is OK. Advance to Step 6.

If the light doesn't go on, the wire is broken or the bulb is blown. Let's check the wiring first. The wire (blue with a black stripe) runs into the main wiring harness and then into a plug in the back of the relay plate.

Disconnect the battery ground strap (10mm wrench). The relay plate is just above the driver's knees. There may be a protective carpet hiding it. If so, take out the small plastic clip holding the center of the carpet in place and pull it down and out.

To free the relay plate, first remove the Phillips screw from the bottom right side of the plate. Now lift the plate up from the two metal retaining ears. Twist the plate around to expose the colored plastic plugs with all the wires running into them.

Step 3. (Cont'd.)

Find the blue/black wire going into the clear plug at position C and check to see if it is firmly inserted in the plug. Wiggle the wire a bit, reconnect the battery ground strap and push on the connection to the oil sensor switch. Turn the key to ON. If the bulb lights up, the connection in the clear plastic plug was bad.

You can stick a thin piece of wood matchstick or a toothpick in the back of the plug to hold the wire tight. This repair will last forever. Don't try to solder it yourself; it's a job for an expert. If you insist on a solder job, take it to VW or an electric shop.

If wiggling the wire doesn't make the light work, you'll need a Volt Ohm Meter (VOM) to check things. Disconnect the battery ground strap again and pull the connector from the back of the oil sensor switch. Turn the VOM to RX1K. Put the red probe onto the metal connector on the end of the oil sensor wire connector and ground the other probe on a clean unpainted part of the crankcase. If you get a reading of 0 (zero) OHMS, go to Step 5.

If the needle stays at ∞, you either have a short or the wire isn't properly connected in the clear plastic plug. If wiggling and jiggling the wire doesn't get a zero reading, replace the wire with a new one (Step 4).

Step 4. Replace Wire

Tools and materials: Roll of 1.5mm^2 (16 gauge) electrical wire; female spade connector.

You can do this simple job yourself if you feel confident. If you prefer help, go to an auto electric shop. They'll do the job cheaply, especially if you tell 'em what to do.

Disconnect the battery ground strap (10mm). Now loosen the relay plate from the metal ears and turn the plate around; then pull the clear plastic plug from position C on the back of the plate. Look at the *front* of the plug for terminal 12. That's the one to which the blue/black oil pressure sensor switch wire connects. Run a new piece of wire from the plug through the wiring harness to the engine compartment. Put a new female spade connector onto the stripped end of the wire (Chapter 20, Procedure 14), and push it onto the oil sensor switch. Keep the wire fairly taut; you don't want it to catch on anything.

Cut the wire close to the clear plastic plug and strip and twist the end. Push it into the rear of terminal 12 on the plug, but leave the blue/black wire in place. Force a toothpick into the hole to make sure all stays put. Hook up the battery ground strap and turn the key to ON. The light will work. Remove the battery ground strap again and reinstall the relay plate. Put the protective carpet back (if you've got one) and re-connect the battery ground strap. Finished.

Step 5. Replace Bulb

If the wire checked out OK with the VOM (a 0 reading), the bulb must be blown. Find the bulb holder. It's on the printed circuit board just behind the oil can symbol on the dashboard. Turn to Chapter 8, Procedure 1, Step 4 (for skinny hands) or Step 5 (for huge hands) for instructions on how to check the bulb and holder. When the bulb or its holder is repaired or replaced, come back here.

Step 6. Check Oil Pressure Sensor

If the bulb still won't light, the oil pressure sensor is bad. Buy a new one from VW.

Remove the old sensor with a crescent wrench and carefully replace it with the new one. The sensor has tapered threads which seal as they are screwed in. Do not screw the sensor in too tightly. You'll feel when it's time to stop.

Connect the wire and battery ground strap. Turn the ignition key to ON. If for some remarkable reason the light still doesn't come on, don't be discouraged. The new sensor must be bad, too. Maybe it's just not your day. It happens. Exchange your defective sensor and install the new one.

Step 7. Beyond the Pale

If you haven't fixed it by now the problem lies within the relay plate or printed circuit behind the dash. Get VW to fix it—they made it.

PROCEDURE 3: CHECK OIL SYSTEM, Phase 1.

Condition: Red oil light comes on when you're driving.

Tools: Phase 1 tool kit.

Like a shot in the dark or a stab in the back, the dash oil can symbol suddenly lights up before your very eyes. Time for teeth gnashing and despair? NO! Pull to the side of the road and shut off the engine right away! Take a few deep breaths and cross your fingers; you may need only a quart of oil.

I hope it's not raining.

Step 1. Check Engine and Oil

Lift and prop the hood. If everything is hot, it'll smell hot and the radiator fan will whirr like a banshee. Diesels and older Rabbits have a plastic expansion bottle by the left fender. Check the coolant level in the bottle.

DO NOT REMOVE THE SCREW TOP or you'll get a boiling hot water/antifreeze bath. Just look through the translucent sides of the bottle. If it's empty, that's Clue #1. People with no expansion bottles read on and check the radiator coolant level when 10 minutes have elapsed.

Clue #2: Check the oil. Remove the dipstick; if it's too hot to handle, wrap something around it. Is there any oil at all showing on the dipstick? If not, lay something on the ground and crawl under the car. Check the oil pan drain bolt. If it's not there or if lots of oil is leaking around it, that's your problem.

The drain bolt fell out on us once. Luckily, my companion noticed the red light winking at her. She immediately shut off the engine and pulled over. Good thinking Alice, the engine was saved!

If the oil pan bolt is missing, hitch into town and get another one, along with a new copper washer. Don't forget to buy oil. And while you're at it, I'd change the oil filter too, because the heat may have dislodged some crud inside the engine. Chapter 10, Procedure 9, Steps 3 and 4.

Install the new drain plug and copper washer. If you have your torque wrench along, torque the bolt to 3 mkg (22 ft lbs). If you don't, just get it tight. Change the oil filter and pour in 3.7 quarts of new oil. You're on your way.

What if you dove under the car and found the oil pan plug safe and sound, but the level on the dipstick way below the lowest mark? Check very carefully around the engine for signs of a severe oil leak. Take a close look at the front part of the crankshaft where the V-belt pulleys bolt on. A steady drip-drip-drip of oil from there means a blown front seal. You need a new one quick. You can't replace it right now on the side of Interstate 5, but add oil and do it within a few days. (Chapter 18 tells how—the engine has to come out, I'm sorry to say.) If oil drips from the rear of the engine or out of the transmission, the rear oil seal is shot. That too needs to be replaced. So add oil, drive home, and turn to and do the replacement (Chapter 16, Procedure 6).

Coolant level OK? No leaks? Drain plug in?

Add enough oil to bring the level up to the top mark on the dipstick. How long has it been since you checked or changed the oil and filter? Gingerly start your engine and listen for abnormal noises, described in gruesome detail in the beginning of Chapter 18.

If a noise tells you something is definitely wrong, or if you're unsure about the sounds you're hearing, DON'T DRIVE THE CAR. Call a friend and ask for a tow, either all the way home or to the nearest safe parking spot or garage. Even if the car can move on its own power, a few extra miles of driving may cause a great deal of damage and a hefty increase in the repair bill. A connecting rod bearing crying for help can easily turn into the last gasps of the crankshaft. (Chapter 6, Procedure 2).

It takes a second or two for the oil to circulate throughout the engine block, so a tapping sound at first is nothing to panic over.

Step 1 (Con't.)

If the engine sounds normal, please check the red dash light. With the oil back in the engine and no expensive noises, the red oil light will go out. Phew...Drive on with the resolution to check the oil level daily. You've been lucky.

If you added oil, then heard unpleasant sounds after starting the engine (and the oil light stayed on), well . . .you've got trouble.

If your engine didn't need oil, but the light is still on and the engine is hot and/or making nasty noises . . . you've got trouble too. Let it cool for an hour before trying to start it. Your engine was so hot that the oil became too thin to lubricate all the bearing surfaces. When the engine has cooled, check the oil level and start it, but *don't rev it!*

The red light may go out after the car has idled a few moments. If it does, rev the engine and listen for damage sounds. Sound normal? Drive on but think about what caused the problem. Have you done this month's maintenance? Is the car loaded to the gills? Is there a strong headwind? Is the radiator blocked by aardvark clippings? Do you have a low tire causing drag? Are you pulling a trailer? All these—and more—can lead to engine overheating. Check the coolant level in the radiator. If it's low, start the engine and add water *slowly* until it's on the mark.

Does the electric radiator fan work properly? If not, turn to Chapter 17, Procedure 3. Check the electrical connection on the back of the fan.

Check the water hoses, especially the main hoses from the radiator to the water pump and to the manifold on the left side of the cylinder head.

Check the heater hoses from the small manifold on the rear of the cylinder head. Replace any broken hoses.

For those of you whose engine sounds normal but who can't get the red light to turn off, please go to the next Procedure.

PROCEDURE 4: CHECK OIL PUMP

Condition: Red light stays on—engine OK, oil and coolant levels up to scratch.

Tools and materials: Phase 1 tool kit, Lubriplate, 3M Weatherstrip adhesive.

Step 1. Does Pump Pump?

Take your crescent wrench and remove the oil pressure sensor from the rear of the cylinder head or from the oil filter manifold. Is the hole in the manifold or cylinder head clogged with crud? If so, clean it out with a piece of wire, being careful that the stuff doesn't fall further into the engine. Install Friend in the car. Put your finger over the hole in the head or oil filter manifold and have Friend start the car with the gear shift lever in neutral. Do you feel pressure on your finger? If not, keep the engine running and move your finger away from the hole a little and see if any oil is squirting out. Have Friend step on the gas a little. Any oil?

Step 2. Now What?

If you get oil out of the hole, the pump is working. However, we have no way of telling if the pump is working efficiently unless you have an oil pressure gauge. A lot of crud in the cylinder head/oil filter manifold means that there's a lot of junk inside the crankcase. Complete this Procedure, then fill the crankcase with cheap oil. Run the engine half an hour, change the oil filter, drain the oil, and refill it with good oil this time (Chapter 10, Procedure 9).

If you didn't get any oil squirting out of the hole, the pump isn't working. You can now do one of two things: pull the oil pan and examine the pump or take the car to VW for an oil pressure check.

I would check the oil pump myself rather than take it to VW (see the following Procedure) but you might be fed up with the whole thing by now.

Step 2. (Cont'd.)

If the oil pump works OK but the light still won't go out, you have a problem with bad grounds, with the printed circuit on the rear of the dashboard, or the relay panel itself is messed up and shorting out. Rather than tearing out your hair or messing up the electrical system, go to VW or an auto electric shop and let them take care of it.

PROCEDURE 5: REPLACE OIL PUMP, Phase 1.

Condition: No oil pressure

Tools and materials: Phase 1 tool kit; receptacle for draining oil; another oil pump, if necessary, oil and new filter.

Remarks: Retime the engine at the end of this procedure, Chapter 10, Procedures 15 and 16.

Step 1. Drain Oil

Loosen and remove the 19mm oil drain bolt and let all the oil run into some kind of receptacle. (Chapter 10, Procedure 9, Step 2.)

Step 2. Chock, Jack and Block

Put the transmission in neutral and pull the handbrake tight. Put chocks behind the rear wheels and jack up the front of the car as high as you can. Block it well for safety.

Step 3. Remove Oil Pan

Remove the twenty bolts holding the oil pan to the bottom of the crankcase (5mm allen wrench or 10mm socket). The socket headed bolts have a washer and a square metal spacer between the bolt head and the oil pan. Put all the bolts, etc. into a marked Baggie. Pull off the oil pan and gasket.

Step 4. Remove Oil Pump

The oil pump is held inside the crankcase by two 13mm bolts. The shiny metal arm sticking out of the oil pump is the oil scavenger arm (it may be broken off). Remove the two 13mm bolts and pull the pump free.

Step 5. Inspect Pump Shaft—Gas Engines

The pump has a long shaft that goes up to engage with the base of the distributor drive shaft. Check the end of the oil pump shaft. If it's broken, it will probably be stuck inside the base of the distributor. Remove the metal fork holding the distributor in place (13mm wrench) and pull the distributor free. Check the slot in the base to see if the broken piece of oil pump shaft is in there. If so, pull it out and reinstall the distributor. You need a new oil pump! If the oil pump shaft is OK, we have to inspect the inside workings of the pump.

Step 6. Inspect Pump Shaft—Diesel Engines

Your oil pump is not connected to the base of the distributor since you don't have one, but to the oil pump drive gear into which the shaft on the oil pump fits. This drive gear is driven by the intermediate shaft. If your pump checked out OK, you will have to remove the 13mm bolt that holds the clip where there is normally a distributor (behind the rear injector #4). Beneath that is a washer and the oil pump drive gear. If that drive gear is stripped or broken, get a new one from VW. Slip it into the hole in the crankcase and replace the washer and cap. Put on the 13mm bolt and clip.

Late model diesels have a secondary vacuum pump in place of a clip. To remove it, first loosen the 12mm captive nuts on both ends of the spiral tube. Remove the tube. Now remove the 13mm nut holding the

Step 6. (Cont'd.)

U-shaped clip around the base of the vacuum pump and pull it upward to get the pump off. The oil pump drive system is the same as for gas engines.

Step 7. Examine Pump

The base of the pump is held onto the main pump body by two 10mm bolts. Remove these and pull off the bottom half of the pump. Any major problem should be obvious. Turn the main shaft to see if the two gears inside the pump turn freely. If everything is all mashed and mangled in there, you'll need a new oil pump. Mashed gears also mean particles of metal are lurking inside the engine oil. Remove the oil filter (see Chapter 10, Procedure 9) and run a couple of quarts of cheapo oil through the engine to flush out any pieces of metal. Consider getting intimate with Chapter 18 (Engine Rebuild) and stripping the engine if you find little bits of metal anywhere. Let the oil drain into your receptacle. Even if the gears *look* fine, continue . . .

Step 8. Check Backlash

Clean out the inside of the pump with solvent and let it drain a minute. Break out your feeler gauge and stick a 0.20mm (.008 in) blade between the pump gears as shown in the diagram. If the blade's too thick and won't fit, don't fret—all is well so far. Should there be too much play between the gears and the blade, the pump gears are worn and need to be replaced. See if VW has any in stock. If so, have them install the new gears in your pump.

Find a metal straight edge and lay it across the top of the pump

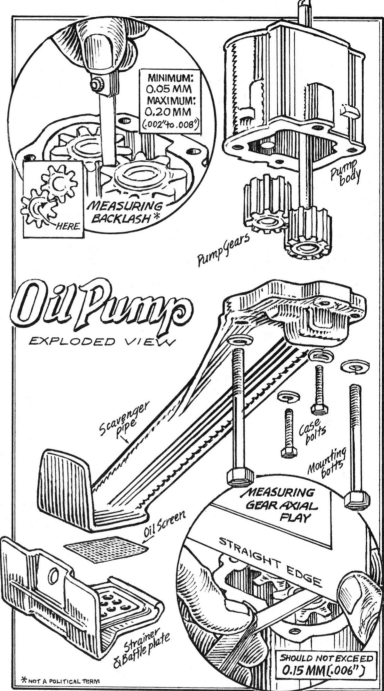

directly over the gears. Push the gears down into the pump and measure the clearance between the top of the gears and the bottom of the straight edge. If the clearance is greater than 0.15mm (.006 in) you need a new pump.

New oil pumps don't come with a new strainer or strainer housing, so you'll have to pry off the strainer and housing from your old pump with a screwdriver and install them onto your new one. Clean the strainer and the housing thoroughly with kerosene, gasoline or solvent. Make sure the strainer and housing seat properly—important. As an added precaution, let's brush the crankshaft and the connecting rods with solvent or kerosene.

Step 8. (Cont'd.)

Put a 19mm socket onto the main drive belt sprocket bolt on the end of the crankshaft and turn the crankshaft pulley one full revolution (360°). Clean any traces of oil from the crankshaft with solvent. You'll be looking up at it through the hole left by the departed oil pump.

Step 9. Install Oil Pump

If you have Lubriplate handy (an engine assembly lubricant) put a small amount on the end of the oil pump drive shaft where it fits into the end of the distributor. If not, use a blob of grease. Install the oil pump and torque the two 13mm bolts to 2 mkg (14 ft lbs). Make a final check that the strainer housing (with its strainer screen inside) is properly seated on the end of the oil pump scavenger arm. Use your vise grips to pinch the edges of the strainer housing tightly together. Clean off the base of the crankcase and remove any traces of oil from inside the oil pan. Reinstall the oil pan drain bolt along with the copper washer and torque it to 3.0 mkg (22 ft lbs). Squeeze a line of 3M Weatherstrip adhesive on the bottom of the crankcase and the top of the oil pan. Fit a new oil pan gasket atop the oil pan and mate it with the bottom surface of the crankcase. Screw a bolt into each of the four corners of the oil pan. When you have the pan correctly positioned, screw in the remaining 16 bolts. Socket-headed bolts should be torqued to 1 mkg (7 ft lbs) and regular hex bolts to 2.0 mkg (14 ft lbs). Torque the corner bolts first, then the rest.

Step 10. Install New Oil Filter

Fill your new oil filter ¾ full with the same oil you will be adding to the crankcase and smear a fingerful of oil on the rubber gasket on top of this new filter. Screw the filter on until it touches the engine and then screw it three-quarters of a turn or more. (Diesels, turn the filter 1½ turns after you touch bottom.) Fill your engine with 3.7 quarts of your favorite oil and you're on your way! (Chapter 10, Procedure 9).

If the oil pump checked out OK but you still have no oil pressure, proceed.

Step 11. Your Chance in a Million—The Intermediate Shaft

The intermediate shaft drives the oil pump. If this shaft breaks, the car will not run at all. When it dies, it makes very expensive noises. Another possibility is that the two bolts holding the intermediate shaft retaining plate and seal onto the front of the crankcase have come loose. In that case, the intermediate shaft will move forward slightly and no longer drive the oil pump. The drive belt will still turn the intermediate shaft, so you will have to look at the front of the engine to see if the drive belt sprocket has come loose or if the intermediate shaft has moved forward. That rarely happens. If it does, you have my sympathy. To fix it, you must lift the engine and transmission high enough out of the engine compartment to withdraw the intermediate shaft. Turn to Chapter 10, Procedure 23 to see how to remove the drive belt shield. If the chance in a million is yours; then turn to Chapter 18. You'll have to go through all the engine electrical and vacuum disconnects before you can lift the engine.

CHAPTER 10

TUNE-UP, LUBRICATION ⤐ AND MAINTENANCE ⤐

Welcome to the most important part of the book. This is where you'll really learn how to keep your VW Rabbit alive! Regular maintenance is the key to Rabbit longevity, and doing it yourself ensures not only that it's done right, but puts you in rapport with your transportation.

This Chapter is also where you get your money back: the cash you laid out for this book and tools.

We'll cover all the nagging little problems you may have been experiencing since you bought the car, as well as routine maintenance to keep it in tip-top shape. You'll be amazed what an hour of work with this chapter and a few parts will do.

VW agencies charge big bucks for a simple tune-up, and the cost of a major one will make you wince. Labor charges are at least $20.00 per hour, or more. Do you make that much? I sure don't. And just as important as the money saved is the satisfaction you'll feel by having done it yourself.

Remarks: If your car is still covered by warranty, take advantage of it. A warranty is included in the price of the car, just like a radio or air conditioner. Any problems which show up during the warranty period should be noted down and discussed with your VW service manager and fixed! A recurring problem may not be dealt with to your satisfaction during the term of the warranty, but don't wait until the warranty runs out to complain! Later, if something major goes on your car as a result of not having that problem fixed properly by the agency, the written record will help your case to get it fixed by VW for no charge.

Buy a folder (or use the back of this book) to keep all notes, maintenance records, parts receipts, etc., neatly together. It's the Virgo in me.

BODY CARE

I don't know about you, but I'm very lax when it comes to taking care of my body. My car's body, I mean.

Whether you plan to keep your Rabbit forever or trade it in every year, its cash value is judged mainly by the appearance of the body work. Keep it clean and free from rust; it will last longer and maintain its "blue book" value.

I suggest washing the car as part of your weekly maintenance schedule, but you probably won't get around to it. Some car wash places recycle dirty wash water. Don't use them if your winter roads are salted. The water retains the salt and salt causes corrosion.

A coat of good wax every three months or so will preserve the paint. Should you have a fender bender accident, get it fixed quickly so water won't seep under the paint and cause rust. Small chips in the paint should be touched up with paint available from your VW dealer.

VW recommend that you perform their routine maintenance schedules at 1,000, 7,500, 15,000 and every 7,500 miles ad infinitum. I think 7,500 miles is too long, so do yours daily, weekly, monthly, and at 3,000, 5,000, 15,000 and 30,000 mile intervals. If your car develops engine problems, run through the Procedures in this chapter before doing anything else.

Do you drive at high speed? If so, do the 5,000 mile procedures every 3,000 miles. If you drive very little, say a few times a week or month, just do your maintenance at regularly scheduled times, and don't forget to change the oil every 3,000 miles.

Oil

The Rabbit engine was designed to operate efficiently using any type of *fresh* multigrade *detergent* oil. NON-DETERGENT OIL MUST NOT BE USED.

Oil is important! It coats all the moving parts inside your engine with an unyielding, very slippery film. This film is constantly circulated around the engine by the oil pump, keeping heat buildup (a by-product of friction) to a minimum. The oil temperature is held fairly constant by the coolant (water/antifreeze mixture) flowing inside the walls of the crankcase.

There must be sufficient space between two moving surfaces for oil to get in so it can lubricate and carry away heat. Unlubricated surfaces (such as bearings) get very hot, very fast. Heat causes metal distortion, parts failures, and sickening repair bills.

Use a quality brand name oil with which you are familiar; one you can find anywhere.

Whichever brand you use, be sure the blurb on top of the can includes the words "Service API/SE" or "Service SE-SD-CC (MS-DM)". These terms indicate that various agencies, including the military, have tested and verified the manufacturer's claims.

The initials H.D. (Heavy Duty) mean very little these days and may or may not be on the can.

Diesel engine Rabbits should use oil labeled "Service API-CC" or "MIL-L-46152". Change the oil in your diesel every 3,000 miles under normal conditions, no matter what anyone else tells you.

Avoid any oil labeled "Recycled," "Remanufactured," or "New oil blended with 100% recycled oil." The ecological ideal is sound, but in reality oil molecules wear out, especially when subjected to high engine temperatures. Recycling or blending can never restore an oil molecule's lost ability to lubricate properly.

OK, let's talk about viscosity, the ease with which a liquid flows. Oil with low viscosity is labeled with a low number, such as S.A.E. 10W. It's thin and pours easily, even at low temperatures. High viscosity oil (S.A.E. 50) is thick and doesn't pour easily. It is so thick, in fact, that in cold weather it will prevent the starter from turning over the engine fast enough to start.

When oil warms up it gets thinner and loses some of its lubricating ability. You want an oil that's thick enough to lubricate at high temperatures but thin enough, when cold, to enable you to start your engine easily. This problem has been solved by blending a low viscosity oil with petroleum derivatives to create multigrade oil (like S.A.E. 10W-30) which will lubricate effectively over a wide range of temperatures. Refer to Peter's charts to determine which oil you need.

During its trip around your engine, lubricating the camshaft, crankshaft, connecting rod bearings, pistons, and other moving parts, the sticky oil becomes contaminated with bits of sludge, crud and grit. Most of this gets filtered out by the replaceable oil filter. Big chunks are stopped by a strainer in the arm of the oil pump.

Condensation (water) is another oil contaminator. When condensed water accumulates it causes corrosion, and corrosion eats engines.

A HIGH VISCOSITY OIL.

The Rabbit engine runs at quite a high temperature, thanks to all the smog control stuff they've attached to it. If you drive five continuous miles at least every other day, any water in your oil will boil off, eliminating condensation and damaging corrosion. If you drive only a few miles a week, change the oil more often because short laps around the block to buy a quart of milk won't raise the engine temperature high enough to boil off water in the oil. Changing the oil every month will avoid corrosion problems.

Synthetic Oils

I don't know too much about them except that they cost a lot. And I can't see how any oil can be left inside an engine for 15,000 miles and not get contaminated with water and acids. If you decide to switch to a synthetic oil, first drain *all* the regular type oil from the engine. Also, *please* don't use synthetic oil immediately after an engine rebuild— the rings won't seat properly.

Slippery Oils

Some companies have a new type of oil containing graphite which they claim will reduce engine wear. These oils are more expensive than regular oils and are still subject to condensation buildup and dirt contamination. I guess if you abuse your car's engine it needs all the help it can get, and slippery oil may be helpful. Again, don't use a slippery oil just after an engine rebuild.

Transmission Oil (Standard Transmission)

Transmission oil is thick and heavy and isn't subjected to the same rigors as engine oil. All it has to do is coat gears and shafts with a good lubricating film. There's no problem with contamination unless a seal breaks and allows junk in. Use S.A.E. 80W-90 all year 'round. Look for MIL-L-2105 API/GL4 on the label. Change it every 30,000 miles.

Additives

There are a number of additives, conditioners, supplements, extenders, augmenters, and other such types advertised by companies looking to make a fat living around the fringes of the automotive world. These additives don't do ONE THING to extend the life of a healthy engine. A can of Miracle Shytte will not give you twenty thousand miles between oil changes unless you want to change engines at the same time. Stick the company decals on your back window, but keep their junk out of your engine.

In very cold weather it's OK to put some gasoline de-icer (with methanol as the major ingredient) into the gas tank to keep the fuel lines from freezing. Not diesel.

Grease

In these modern times grease isn't what it used to be—it's better. Use a lithium base grease for everything except the constant velocity joints. These require a lithium grease with some molybedenum disulphide added. VW sells special C.V. joint grease —use it. Keep dirt and grit away from your grease supply. These particles play havoc with all moving parts.

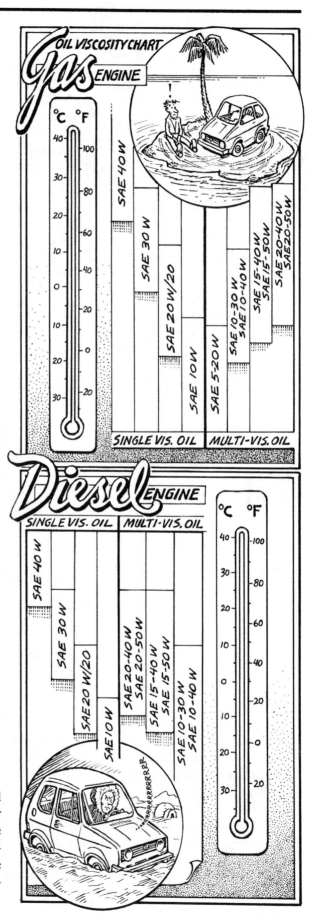

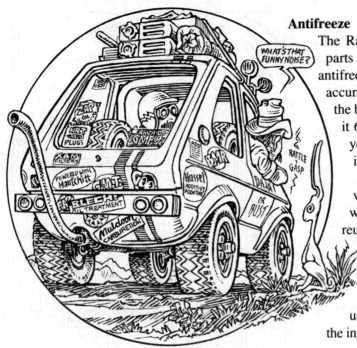

Antifreeze

The Rabbit keeps it cool by wrapping the moving parts of the engine in a jacket containing a water/antifreeze mixture. The term antifreeze isn't totally accurate because the stuff (ethylene glycol) raises the boiling point of water. Ideally you should mix it 60% antifreeze and 40% water and use it all year 'round. It's an excellent rust and corrosion inhibitor as well, but **do not** add it to the oil!

Keep a screw top container full of a 50% water 50% antifreeze mix, to top the radiator when the coolant level gets low. Antifreeze is reusable if you need to drain it from the engine for any reason. It must remain clean, however. Contaminated antifreeze can eventually damage the engine. Change it every year. (September is a good time to do it), and use only a *phosphorous free* antifreeze. Read the ingredients and mixing instructions on the bottle.

Routine Maintenance Schedules

Diesel owners: do the following checks, also special checks for diesel in Chapter 21.

PROCEDURE 1: DAILY MAINTENANCE, Phase 1.

Step 1. Check the oil level

Step 2. Check the coolant level

Step 3. Check the battery

Step 4. Check the tires

Step 5. Check the lights

Step 6. Check A.T.F. level (Automatic transmission)

Step 1. Check Oil Level

The car should be on level ground with the engine off for five minutes. Pull out the dipstick located halfway down on the left side of the engine. Wipe the oil off the bottom of the dipstick and replace it in its little hole. Don't brush the dipstick against anything dirty, or you will pick up crud that your engine doesn't need.

Pull the stick out again. The oil level should touch the **top** line on the stick. If the oil level is on the lower line add about one U.S. quart (0.95 liters) of oil. (The same type and SAE rating that you already have inside your engine.) If the oil level is halfway between the two marks on the dipstick add about ½ quart or just enough to bring the level up to the top mark. Pour any remaining oil into a plastic screw top container and stash it in the trunk. If you absentmindedly add too much oil, you'll have to drain the excess through the oil pan drain plug before driving the car. Adding more oil than is needed (over the top mark) will cause an oil seal to blow somewhere, as well as cause foaming as the crankshaft churns it up.

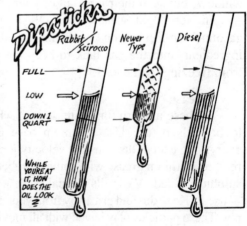

Step 2. Check Coolant Level

Unscrew the radiator cap (engine must be cool) and look down the hole to check the level of the water/antifreeze mixture, or check the level against the marks on the white plastic expansion bottle. When it's low, add clean water/antifreeze mixture to bring the level up. If the radiator needs constant topping up, you have a leak. Examine the radiator hoses, the joint at the bottom of the water pump and the condition of the radiator or expansion bottle. If the engine gets very hot, see Chapter 17, Procedure 2.

Step 3. Check Battery

Put on your safety glasses and unscrew the plugs in the top of the battery or pop the plastic cover. The fluid (electrolyte) level should be about 6mm (¼ in) above the metal plates inside the battery. If it isn't, carefully add distilled water, keeping your eyes well away from the top of the battery as you pour. You can buy distilled water from a drugstore or any auto parts store. It's cheap. If none is available, use boiled (allow it to cool) or clean tap water, but don't make a habit of it. **Do not add acid** or any type of additive to your battery. It's dangerous and unnecessary.

Step 4. Check Tires

Walk around the car and examine each tire for cuts and buried objects such as nails, chunks of glass and boy scouts. Check the inner and outer sides of the tire very carefully. If you find any cuts or deep abrasions, change the tire **RIGHT NOW.** Blow outs, especially at high speeds, are somewhat harrowing.

Examine the tread pattern on the front tires for uneven wear. If one part of the tread is worn more than another, have the wheel alignment checked by a specialist.

Now check the air pressure inside all four tires. Remove the dust cap from the inflation valve and press your pressure gauge firmly over the end of the valve. The gauge should read 27 pounds per square inch (1.90 kg/cm^2). If any need air, stop and fill 'em. If you drive fully loaded or on the freeway all the time, add 3 psi (0.21 kg/cm^2) to the rear tires.

A loss of about 6 psi (0.42 kg/cm^2) of pressure during a week means you have a slow leak that may turn into a fast one rather suddenly, so get it fixed.

Step 5. Check Lights

Turn the key to ON. Switch on the headlights, then walk around the car and see if all your lights are on. Switch the headlights from high to low beam and check that they work in both positions. Turn off the lights and key, and switch on the emergency flashers. All four turn signal lights will flash. If one isn't working, make a note to buy a replacement bulb. See Chapter 19, Procedure 2.

Ask Friend or passerby to check the rear brake lights when you press the brake pedal. Brake lights are important; fix any problems right away. Always check all the lights before driving at night. You don't even have to get out of the driver's seat.

Turn the key to ON. Check the dashboard idiot lights. They should all be on—with the exception of the water temperature symbol which comes on only when the coolant temperature is above normal.

Start the engine. The idiot lights—except the handbrake-on light—should all go out. While you wait for the engine to warm up, try the windshield wipers and the horn. The neighbors will love you! If the EGR or CAT lights stays on, release the handbrake. Still on? Turn to Chapter 13.

Step 6. Check A.T.F. Level (Automatics)

Keep the engine running, put the gear lever in neutral (N) and be sure the handbrake is on. Lift and prop the hood. The ATF dipstick sticks out of a tube in the rear of the transmission, up by the left fender. The level of the fluid should be on the topmost line of the dipstick. If it's low, add enough fluid to bring the level up to

Step 6. (Cont'd.)

. the mark. If you need to add only a pint or so, pour any left over fluid into a plastic screw top container. Label the jar ''Automatic Transmission Fluid—POISON'', and store it in a safe place away from the inquisitive.

Check's over, you're on your way.

PROCEDURE 2: WEEKLY MAINTENANCE, Phase 1.

Step 1. Do daily maintenance procedures	**Step 7. Clean engine compartment**
Step 2. Check brake fluid level	**Step 8. Check windshield wiper blades**
Step 3. Check coolant hoses for cracks	**Step 9. Check spare tire air pressure**
Step 4. Check windshield washer fluid level	**Step 10. Clean car inside**
Step 5. Check V belts	**Step 11. Wash windows and lights**
Step 6. Check battery terminal connections	**Step 12. Bathe car if it's filthy**

That's what you've got to do, so let's do it.

Step 1. Run through the Daily Maintenance Procedures

Step 2. Check brake fluid level

Lift and prop the hood. Wipe clean the plastic brake fluid container on top of the master cylinder and see if the fluid level matches the line on the fluid reservoir. If it's low, turn to Chapter 14 and read the first few pages.

Step 3. Check Radiator and Coolant Hoses for Cracks

Start the engine and bend the hoses to bring any small cracks to light. Watch your fingers! Replace damaged hose(s), with the engine off. Use the water/antifreeze mixture to bring the coolant level up to the top mark if necessary.

Step 4. Check Windshield Washer Fluid Level

The fluid container is hung on the inside of the right or left fender. Fill it with water and a little windshield cleaner fluid. If you are of organic sympathies, add a drop or two of any bio-degradable household cleaning liquid instead of cleaner fluid. Don't use detergent, soap or spot remover. Screw on the cap. Check the hose from the washer to the jet on the hood and if it's worn or cracked, replace it. If the jet shoots water over the top of the car or into the faces of people in line at the bus stop, change the aim with a pin.

Step 5. Check V-Belts

Carefully examine all the V-belts at the front of the engine. Any nicked belts should be replaced. The belt that turns the alternator seems more prone to wear than the others, so give it a good look. The alternator belt should be tight, with about 10mm-15mm (5/8 in) of deflection. Deflection means the belt can be moved toward center a certain distance by pressing in on it with your thumb. There's a deflection diagram in Chapter 8, Procedure 2.

Step 6. Check Battery Connections

If there's any corrosion, put on your safety glasses and turn to Chapter 9, Procedure 2; or, turn to the chapter, and then put on your safety glasses.

Step 7. Check the Engine Compartment for Dirt and Debris

Dirt and debris are not famous outlaws, but clean out leaves or junk caught around the engine. Clean in front of the radiator and behind the firewall. Wipe away oil spills and look for oil leaks around the engine and transmission. Check all the vacuum lines and connections and the PCV valve and hoses on top of the camshaft cover.

Step 8. Check Windshield Wiper Blades

'Statistics' show that poor vision from bad wiper blades causes a lot of accidents, especially in winter. Don't forget the rear window wiper if you've got one.

Step 9. Check Air Pressure in Spare Tire

It's in the trunk, underneath the mat. It should be 31 lbs psi (2.18 kg/cm^2).

Step 10. Clean Trash from Inside Car

Rotten onions, soda bottles, beer cans, and other junk rolling around the driver's feet are hazardous (and smelly).

Step 11. Wash all Windows and Lights

In winter also clean chrome surfaces with a soapy rag. Rinse with water, then wipe the chrome with a clean, lightly oiled rag.

Step 12. Wash the Car

Wash the car if it's filthy; especially if you drive on salted roads.

PROCEDURE 3: MONTHLY MAINTENANCE. Phase 2.

Step 1. Do daily and weekly maintenance	**Step 6. Check steering mechanism**
Step 2. Check muffler and exhaust system	**Step 7. Check clutch free pay**
Step 3. Check brake hoses and pipes	**Step 8. Check accelerator and clutch cables**
Step 4. Clean car's underbody	**Step 9. Check ignition system**
Step 5. Check brake linings, adjust hand-brake and rear brakes.	

Pull on the handbrake and put the shift lever in 1st gear or park (P). Put chocks around the two right wheels, jack up and block the car safely. Look at the muffler and the pipe running to it for rips and holes. Check the clamps, rubber hangers and welds on the entire exhaust system. Put the gear lever in neutral (N) and start the engine. Reach underneath and run one hand along (but not on) the length of the system to feel for exhaust leaks. Lower the car to the ground. Chapter 13 tells how to change exhaust system components.

Step 3.　Check Brake Hoses and Pipes

Check the rubber brake hoses which run to the front disc or drum brakes for signs of rubbing and corrosion. Examine the metal hydraulic brake pipes and their connections for cracks, leaks and damage at front and rear. Replace any worn brake components. Chapter 14.

Step 4.　Clean Car's Underbody

Remove any accumulated mud from the car's underbody and check that the protective coating is in good condition. Look for rust and damage. Wash away any crud from inside the wheel wells, especially behind the front wheels where engine heat will speed corrosion. Buy a can of underbody coating and paint it on any bare patches, but keep it off the rubber brake hoses and the exhaust system. It smells like scorched kippers when hot.

Step 5.　Check Front and Rear Brake Linings or Pads for Wear (and adjust if necessary)

Chapter 14. Also, check that the handbrake works OK (comes up three notches—no more). Brush the dust off your knees and continue.

Step 6.　Check Steering Mechanism

Chapter 15, Procedure 1, tells how.

Step 8.　Check Accelerator and Clutch Cables

If the clutch free play didn't bring any defects to light, have another look just to be sure. Examine the accelerator cable and sheath for cracks, especially where it attaches to the carburetor or throttle plate (fuel injection).

Automatic transmission people, check all three cables to the bracket on the side of the transmission for tightness and condition.

Step 9.　Check Ignition System

Remove and compare the spark plugs to the condition chart in Procedure 14, Step 12. Examine the spark plug cables, the connections at the distributor cap and the plugs; and remove and inspect the distributor cap, Procedure 14, Step 1. Check the point dwell, Procedure 15, Steps 1 and 2, and adjust the point gap if necessary, Procedure 14, Step 9.

PROCEDURE 4:　EVERY 1500 MILES, Phase 1.

Step 1.　Do Daily, Weekly and Monthly Maintenance

Step 2.　Change Engine Oil and Filter

If you drive in very dusty areas, do Procedure 9. The rest of you can wait 'til 3,000 miles go by.

Step 3.　Examine and Clean Air Filter

Procedure 10 tells how.

Step 4.　Clean the Heads on your Tape Player

PROCEDURE 5: EVERY 3000 MILES, Phase 1.

Step 1. Do Daily, Weekly, Monthly and 1500 Mile Maintenance

Step 2. Check Engine and Transmission Mounts

Look at the rubber and metal components of the mounts on the insides of the right and left fenders, the lower front crossmember, and the one bolted to the underbody. Are all the nuts/bolts tight? Clean the mounts free from dirt and oil.

Step 3. Change Oil and Filter

Go onward to Procedure 9.

PROCEDURE 6: EVERY 5000 MILES, Phase 1.

Step 1. Do Daily, Weekly, Monthly, 1500 and 3000 Mile Maintenance

Step 2. Do Tune-Up Procedures 14-18
           Points and Plugs, 14
           Point Gap, 15
           Timing, 16
           Coil, 17
           Idle, 18

Step 3. Check Air Filter

Procedure 10.

Step 4. Check Fuel Filter (Carbureted Models)

Procedure 11.

Step 5. 1975 Cars Only—Check Air Injection Pump Air Filter

Procedure 12.

Step 6. Check Transmission Oil Level

Procedure 13.

Step 7. Check Seats and Interior, etc.

Clean/replace floor mats, pedal rubbers, interior trim, etc. Clean and lubricate the door hinges and door and hood locks with WD-40.

Step 8. Check and Clean/Replace Positive Crankcase Ventilation (PCV) Valve and Hoses

If you have a PCV valve (a small flattened plastic cylinder) installed in the hose running from the camshaft cover to the carburetor, loosen the clamps securing it to the hose, and clean it in solvent. Do the same with the hose. Replace the valve and tighten the hose clamps.

Buy a new PCV valve if it's crudded up to the gills and install it in the hose. Replace the hose if it is split or soaked in grease.

Cars built after 1975 sometimes don't have a PCV valve, but have a deflection plate installed in the air intake elbow on top of the carburetor. With a long brush dipped in solvent, clean the inside of the hose coming from the elbow to the camshaft cover.

PROCEDURE 7: EVERY 15,000 MILES, Phase 2.

Step 1. Do Daily, Weekly, Monthly, 1500, 3000 and 5000 Mile Maintenance

Step 2. Check Ignition Timing/Components

Replace plugs, points, rotor, maybe the distributor cap and condenser, Procedures 14, 15, 16, 17, 18 and maybe 25.

Step 3. Check Compression

Procedure 20.

Step 4. Check Valve Clearance and Valve Timing

Procedures 22 and 23 or 25.

Step 5. Grease Constant Velocity Joints

Procedure 19.

Step 6. Replace Fuel Filter (Carbureted see Procedure 11, Fuel Injection, Procedure 21)

Step 7. Replace Automatic Transmission Fluid

Only if you drive in mountainous country or frequently tow a trailer. Otherwise do this at 30,000 miles, Procedure 25.

Step 8. Check Wheel Lug Nuts

Use the lug wrench in the trunk and make sure they're tight.

Step 9. Check Camber and Toe-in

Have a front end shop align the front wheels.

Step 10. Check Headlight Alignment

Chapter 19, Procedure 1, Step 4.

Step 11. Check Exhaust Gas Recirculation System

The EGR dash light comes on at 15,000 mile intervals. Chapter 13, Procedure 1 or 2 shows how to turn it off. Examine the exhaust system for cracks and leaks in the pipes.

PROCEDURE 8: EVERY 30,000 MILES (OR EVERY TWO YEARS), Phase 2.

Step 1. Do Daily, Weekly, Montly, 1500, 3000, 5000 and 15,000 Mile Maintenance

Step 2. Change Brake Fluid

Don't neglect to change this fluid. It's important for both your safety and the health of the brake system. (See Chapter 14, Procedure 3.)

Step 3. Replace the Condenser

See Procedure 24.

Step 4. Replace Automatic Transmission Fluid

See Procedure 25.

Step 5. Replace Catalytic Converter (California only)

Chapter 13, Procedure 6.

Step 6. Change Drive Belt (Timing Belt)

See Procedure 23.

PROCEDURE 9: OIL CHANGE, Phase 1.

Condition: You've put 300 or 600 miles on a new or rebuilt engine or you've driven 1500 dusty miles or 3000 regular miles.

Tools and materials: Phase 1 tool kit, new oil filter, 3.7 U.S. quarts (3.1 Imperial qts or 3.5 liters) of new oil (read about oil at the beginning of this chapter), new copper compression ring for oil drain plug and a pan to catch oil—a cardboard box lined with a plastic garbage bag makes a good catch pan. Cut the box down so that it easily slides under the oil pan; something to lie on.

Step 1. Get Ready

Warm up the car and park it on level ground. Gather your tools, oil filter around you.

Step 2. Drain Oil

The oil will drain a lot better if the engine is hot. Don't bother to try draining the oil from a cold engine in the depths of winter, it'll be thick as glue. If you can, let the oil continue to drip out overnight. Scotch tape a note on the inside of the windshield to remind you space cases there's no oil in the crankcase!

Slide under the front of the car with your 19mm socket or box end wrench in hand. Find the engine oil drain plug in the bottom of the oil pan. Don't put your head under the plug—hot engine oil is not recommended as a face pack.

Loosen the drain plug counterclockwise ◯ with your wrench. Make sure the catch pan is directly below the plug and remove it with your fingers. You may not be in Saudi Arabia, but you'll experience an oil gusher. Let it drain. Crawl out from under the car, bringing the drain plug with you. Does the oil sticking to the threads on the plug have a silvery tinge or is it just plain dirty? If there are small slivers of metal in the oil, something's wrong in the engine's innards, so continue with this Procedure, then turn to Chapter 18 and read the first few pages. OK, clean the oil drain plug with a rag and put it somewhere safe.

Step 3. Remove Oil Filter

Slide the catch pan under the filter. It's a soup can sized cylinder screwed onto an aluminum bracket on the left of the engine; facing down and toward the radiator. Remove the filter using your oil filter removal wrench by looping the wrench around the filter, and turning clockwise from the top.

Gas Engines:

If you don't have an oil filter removal wrench or yours won't fit in that small space, perhaps you can screw the filter off with your (and Friend's) hands? No? Here's a little trick. Find a big screwdriver and stick the blade through—yes through—the right side of the filter and out the other side. This destroys the filter but you're here to install a new one. You may need to hammer on the handle end of the screwdriver to get it through the filter. Use the screwdriver handle as a lever to unscrew the filter. You may have to make two thrusts through the filter before you can unscrew it by hand.

Diesel Engines:

Dealers install some oil filters with a special tool which fits into a slot in the filter base. If you can't get the thing off with the filter wrench or the above screwdriver method, try this. Find a thick washer about 25mm (1 in) in diameter and cut it in half. Clamp both halves, with the cut straight edges facing up into a pair of vise grips. Put the edges of the washer into the oil filter base and unscrew it. Use this tool to tighten your new filter.

Note: Not all replacement filters for the diesel engine have a slot in the base. Use the filter wrench or two strong pairs of hands to get the filter right against the engine. See next step.

Step 4. Install New Oil Filter

Remove the protective plastic cap from the new filter if it has one. Open a new can of oil (see Step 6 if you don't know how) and smear some with your finger on the rubber gasket on top of your new filter. Wipe any old oil from the aluminum filter bracket. Fill the filter with fresh oil and screw it onto the mounting bracket with your hands. When the top of the filter meets the bracket, give it only another **three quarters** turn. Use your hands for this, not the removal tool.

Diesel: Tighten the filter 1¼ turns after you touch bottom. **This is very important.** Most diesel engine bearing failures are due to poorly installed filters that allow the oil to escape from between the filter and the mounting bracket. No oil, no bearings.

Step 5. Replace Oil Drain Plug

Wait until the oil flow is about one drop per minute, then remove the oil catch pan. Slip the new copper ring onto the drain plug and screw the plug into the oil pan. Torque the plug to 3.0 mkg (22 ft lbs). If you don't have a torque wrench, just get the plug fairly tight with a box end wrench. If it's too loose, the plug will seep oil when the crankcase is refilled. Don't overtighten or you'll never get it out next time.

Step 6. Refill Crankcase with New Oil

Pull out the dipstick, wipe it clean and stick it back in its little hole. Wipe the can tops clean and open 3 quarts of oil. Use a church key or screwdriver to make two holes opposite each other on the can top. Are you absolutely certain you replaced the oil drain plug? Wipe the oil filler cap clean, remove it and put a rag around the filler hole on top of the camshaft cover and pour in 3 quarts. You can put a thumb over one hole of the top of the can, position the can over the filler hole and then remove your thumb, thus preventing spillage. Install the cap and start the engine. Let it run for one minute, then stop the engine, wait a minute and check the dipstick. If the oil level is low, slowly add about a half quart more. Remember the rag. Give it a minute to drain down into the oil pan before checking the dipstick again. Add a bit more if necessary but don't overfill it. Install the filler cap. Check the drain plug and oil filter with the engine running to be sure there are no leaks. Pour any extra oil into a plastic screw top container and stash it in the trunk.

Step 7. Clean Up

Pour the old oil into a suitable container like a plastic milk, water, tropical punch or antifreeze bottle. If you used the cardboard box and garbage bag set-up, flatten the box and throw it into the oil bag, along with the oil cans and filter. Dump it into another plastic bag and throw them away. Do *not* pour used oil down the drain. If there is a recycling station nearby, dispose of old oil there.

The next morning, or after a short drive, look under the car for oil leaks. If you didn't tighten the oil drain plug or the oil filter enough, there will be a little oil around these fittings. Tighten them if need be.

PROCEDURE 10: CHECK AIR FILTER. Phase 1.

Condition: 5,000 miles or you've been in a dust storm, or you've rebuilt your carburetor.

Tools and materials: Screwdriver, maybe a new filter element.

Remarks: Some carbureted Sciroccos have a different setup—see Step 4. Fuel Injected Models, see Step 5, Diesel, see Step 6.

Step 1. Remove Filter Element (Carbureted Rabbits)

The air filter is inside a plastic housing at the front of the right fender inside the engine compartment. Snap open the four clips holding the top of the filter housing to the bottom. Remove the filter element.

Step 2. Check and Clean Filter

Tap the filter element gently against the front tire to remove any trapped dirt particles. Do not dunk this pleated paper filter into any type of solvent. It will dissolve before your very eyes!

Hold the filter up to the sunshine (or the light emitted during a reactor meltdown) and if there are any holes or cracks in the pleats, get a new one.

Before the filter is installed, wipe the inside of the filter housing with a clean, lightly oiled, lint-free cloth. Don't use a paper towel; they tend to shed.

Look carefully at the filter element. The word UP may be printed in large letters on the side. When you install the filter, UP must be up, if you see what I mean. If there's no UP, remember the pleats face down. This applies to new filters too, though it is especially important that you reinstall your old filter properly. If it's upside down, any dirt remaining in the old filter will be sucked into the carburetor. Nasty.

Step 3. Install Filter

Slip in the filter element (pleats down) and replace the cover. Snap the four clips closed and check that the body of the filter housing is properly fitted into the fender.

Step 4. Remove and Replace Air Filter Element (Some Carbureted Sciroccos)

Most Sciroccos have the same setup as described for the Rabbit. However, some have the air filter sitting on top of the carburetor.

Snap open the four clips holding the front and rear parts of the air cleaner housing together. Remove the filter element, go back and do Step 2, and then come back here.

Replace the filter element and put the front and back together. Snap the clips closed and check that the filter housing is properly fitted onto the carburetor.

Step 5. Remove and Replace Air Filter Element (All Fuel Injected Models)

You'll find the air filter element in the base of the mixture control unit. That's the thing close by the left fender with all the braided metal fuel lines sprouting from the top. The top is held onto the base by four metal spring clips.

Snap open the clips (you may need to use a screwdriver) and carefully lift up the top of the mixture control unit by holding it at the right front corner. Don't try to remove the top of the unit completely. It's held tight.

Grasp the front of the filter and slide it out of the bottom of the control unit. See and do Step 2, then return here.

Replace the filter in the bottom of the control unit, pleats down. Press back the top of the mixture control unit until it all fits snugly. Snap closed the spring metal clips.

Step 6. Remove and Replace Air Filter Element (Diesel)

The air cleaner housing is that big plastic box to the right of the cylinder head.

Snap open the wire clips holding the rear part of the air cleaner housing to the front part. Remove the filter element, and check it as per Step 2.

Install the new (or old) filter into the housing the same way it came out and snap closed the clips.

PROCEDURE 11: CHECK FUEL FILTER (CARBURETED MODELS). Phase 1.

Condition: 15,000 mile maintenance, carburetor/engine rebuild.

Tools and materials: Phase 1 tool kit, new filter.

Step 1. Check the Filter in the Fuel Line

If there are *any* traces of dirt in the filter, replace it. Loosen the two clamps holding the filter in the gas line, take out the old filter and push. Make sure that the arrow on the new filter body points forward towards the headlights. Tighten the two clamps.

PROCEDURE 12: CHECK AIR INJECTION PUMP AIR FILTER (EARLY CARBURETED CARS ONLY). Phase 1.

Step 1. Remove Air Pump Filter

You'll find this cannister type filter inside a housing on the left side of the engine. A large hose runs from the top of the filter to the air injection pump at the front of the engine.

Take off the wingnut and washer at the bottom of the housing and pull out the paper filter cartridge.

Step 2. Check and Clean Filter

Tap the filter against the tire to remove particles of dirt. Hold it up to the light. If the paper is torn anywhere, old or soaked with oil, replace it.

Wipe the inside of the housing with a lightly oiled, lint-free rag.

Step 3. Install Filter

Install the filter into the cannister housing, then screw on the washer and wingnut. Tighten the wingnut by hand.

PROCEDURE 13: CHECK TRANSMISSION OIL. Phase 1.

Condition: 5,000 mile maintenance.

Tools and materials: Phase 1 tool kit, S.A.E.80W-90 oil.

Step 1. Check the Level

The car *must* be on level ground. The transmission oil filler plug is a 17mm allen bolt on the rear of the transmission, just in front of the left drive shaft. When you remove the plug (17mm allen wrench) a tiny amount of oil may seep out. That's fine; it means the transmission is full. Replace the plug.

If there's no seepage, stick your litle finger into the oil filler hole and delicately feel for the oil. The oil level should be just a hair below the bottom of the oil fill hole. Low?

Step 2. Add More Oil

If it's more than 3mm (⅛ in) below the hole, add SAE80W-90 transmission oil until it's level with the bottom of the fill hole. (Read "Transmission Oil" in the first part of this chapter for the type of oil to use.)

Replace the plug and wipe up any spills.

  TUNE-UP

The big day has arrived. 5,000 miles have long passed beneath the radials or you've just bought your Rabbit, so it's time to break out the tools and parts and have some fun. Turn you faded memory back to Latin class. Remember the immortal lines:*Nova Sparkum Plugum Pointa et Condensera, Hassle Fria Est.*

I like to do my tune-up procedures in a monkey suit and white gloves with everything at my fingertips ready to slip into the engine. A regular 5,000 mile tune-up will take anywhere from one to five hours if you've never done one before. If this will be a major tune-up, with say the 15,000 or 30,000 mile routine maintenance thrown in too, you'd better reserve the best part of a day the first time out.

Don't be a slave to the 5,000 mile interval. If your car feels a little sluggish in the morning and 5,000 miles aren't up, run this Procedure. Likewise, if I hit the 5,000 mile mark in a rainstorm, you won't find me out there with water running down my neck. A leeway of a few hundred miles is fine. A few hundred, mind you, not a few thousand.

PROCEDURE FOR TUNE-UP: POINTS, PLUGS, TIMING, COIL AND IDLE ADJUSTMENT. Phases 1 and 2.

Condition: Tune-up time.

Tools and materials: Phase 2 tool kit, including Tach Dwell meter to set the distributor point gap, a stroboscopic timing light to set the ignition timing, Q-Tips and alcohol. If required: new spark plugs, distributor cap, rotor, points, condenser and possibly a coil. Wear your hat, long hairs!

Remarks: People here from Engine Rebuild, Chapter 18, shouldn't have to replace any ignition system parts. Just clean up the plugs, Step 12.

PROCEDURE 14: POINTS AND PLUGS. Phase 1.

Step 1. Remove Distributor Cap

If you are not sure what points are, please turn to Chapter 2 and be illuminated.

Models up to 1979: Use a screwdriver to pry free the two spring clips holding on the distributor cap. Remove the cap, let it hang free and pull off the rotor from the vertical distributor shaft and then take off the opaque plastic dust cover. Clean the dust cover.

Models 1979 and on: These new types require you to pull off the spade connector on the end of the braided ground wire from the plastic gizmo on the side of the distributor. Some cars have the braided wire screwed to the body of the distributor. Remove the screw, free the strap, then reinstall the screw in the distributor for safekeeping. Then pry the two spring clips free from the distributor cap. Pull off the metal distributor shield along with the distributor cap. Remove the rotor from the top of the vertical distributor shaft and then take off the opaque plastic dust cover. Wipe the dust cover clean with a rag.

Models 1980 and on: Most 1980 and newer models are equipped with electronic ignition. This means that the innards of the distributor don't have points or anything else that needs adjusting.

If you pop the distributor cap you'll see a regular looking rotor. Beneath the rotor is a device called the Hall generator. It's a simple piece of electronics with a trigger wheel at its base.

The main advantage of electronic ignition (besides the absence of moving parts) is that all the energy contained in the ignition coil is available to the spark plugs. Very little is lost inside the distributor. In fact, the electronic ignition system is about 40% more efficient than the regular point type ignition.

I won't get into the workings thereof, but all you really need to do is keep the sparking end of the rotor clean and keep the inside of the distributor free from dirt and grime. It's also important to maintain the distributor cap as explained in Procedure 14. Go to Step 3.

Step 2. Check the Points

Using a screwdriver as a lever between the long arm of the points and the vertical distributor shaft, spread the points and have a look at the two small round contact surfaces on the end of the point arms. They should be flat and smooth. Do either of the two surfaces have pits or small white deposits on them? Look closely. If so, they must be replaced. Once upon a time, during the Middle Ages of motoring, folks would file away deposits on their points. In this disposable generation, we go to the parts store and buy new ones because the material used in new ones is impossible and impractical to clean.

Check the condition of the point rubbing block (point rider) for wear. That's that little brown ear on the arm of the points that rubs against the cam on the base of the distributor shaft. If it's off square or worn down almost to the metal arm, you need new points.

Step 3. Remove Spark Plugs

If you are here from other regions of the book, your plugs are out already. Put a rag over the exposed distributor and use masking tape to mark the four spark plug wires: 1, 2, 3 and 4. Number 1 is at the front of the engine closest to the right fender. Pull the metal or rubber caps (fastened to the end of the wires) off the spark plugs. Don't tug on the wires. Carefully turn your spark plug wrench counterclockwise $\bigcirc$ and remove all four plugs. Lay them down in numerical order so you know which cylinder each came from. Points OK people go to Step 6.

Step 4. Liberate Distributor Cap

There's a wire from the center of the distributor cap to the coil on the firewall. Pull it out of the distributor cap and tuck it out of the way. Push the distributor cap and the 4 spark plug wires sticking out of its top to one side.

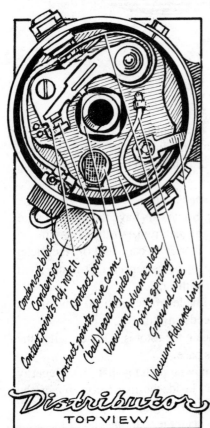

Step 5. Remove Old Points

Look into the distributor. You can see that the points are held in the distributor by just one screw.

Find the short wire that runs from the points to a connection on the inside of the distributor. The connection is a simple spade type terminal. Pull the wire off.

Now loosen the screw holding the points in position with a screwdriver. Grip the points with your fingers and pull gently upward as you continue to loosen the screw. When the screw is free, pull the points and the screw away out from the distributor.

Did the screw fall into the distributor? If so, use your small magnet to retrieve it. If the screw head is mangled, buy another; it makes life much simpler when it's time to replace the points. The screw has a metric thread. Or should.

Step 6. Clean Inside of Distributor

Clean it out with a clean lint-free rag or a Q-Tip. Dip the cotton into alcohol or a non-petroleum base cleanser (don't use tequila or other sticky booze). Points OK people go to Step 8.

Step 7. Install Points

Get your new points out of the package and compare them to your old ones. Do they match? If not, take your old ones to the store and exchange 'em for the real thing.

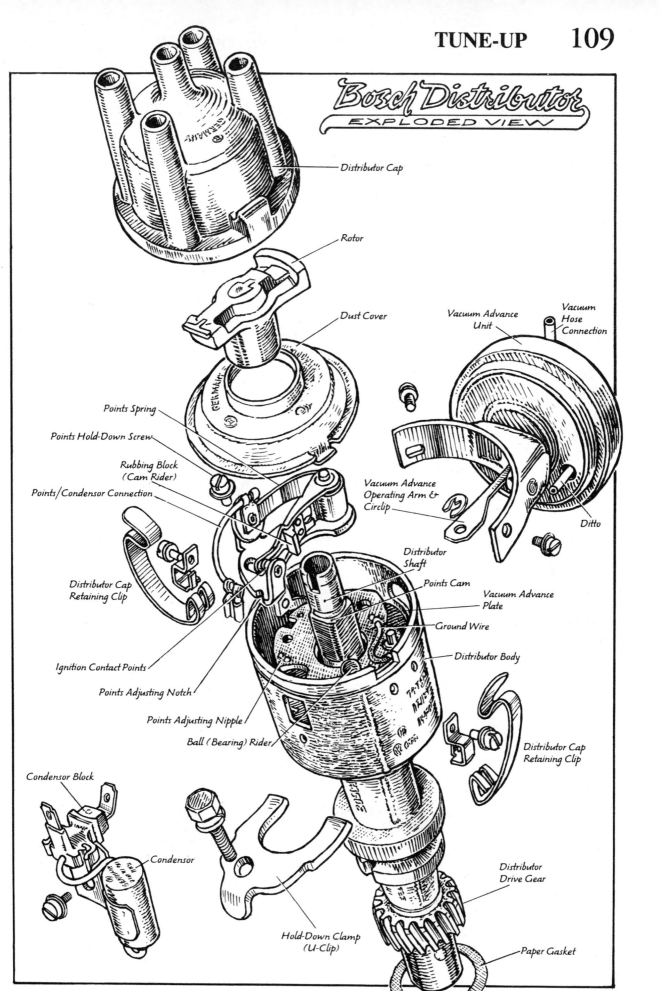

Bosch Distributor
EXPLODED VIEW

Distributor Cap

Rotor

Dust Cover

Vacuum Advance Unit

Vacuum Hose Connection

Points Spring

Points Hold-Down Screw

Rubbing Block (Cam Rider)

Points/Condensor Connection

Vacuum Advance Operating Arm & Circlip

Distributor Cap Retaining Clip

Ditto

Distributor Shaft

Points Cam

Vacuum Advance Plate

Ground Wire

Distributor Body

Ignition Contact Points

Points Adjusting Notch

Points Adjusting Nipple

Ball (Bearing) Rider

Distributor Cap Retaining Clip

Condensor Block

Condensor

Hold-Down Clamp (U-Clip)

Distributor Drive Gear

Paper Gasket

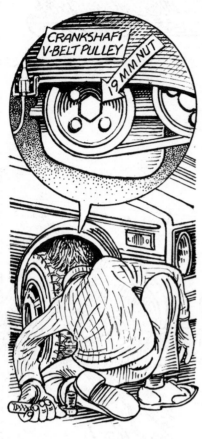

Put the small screw that held your old points in place into the hole in your new points. Gently lower the points into the distributor, lining up the screw with the hole as you go. Fit the base of the point pivot arm into the small hole in the distributor and tighten the screw—slowly now—don't get the threads crossed. The points will 'seat' when they're in right. The screw should be tight, but there's no need to snap the screwdriver blade in half.

30,000 mile maintenance folks, replace the condenser (Procedure 24, this Chapter).

Step 8. Lubricate Distributor

Squirt four drops of any oil on the felt wick in the top of the vertical distributor shaft. Your new points probably had a small capsule of grease included with them. Break it open, hold it under your nose and sniff delicately. Ahhh, grease! Put a small dab of it on the distributor cam and behind the point rubbing block. No grease? Use a drop of wheel bearing grease or engine assembly lubricant. Got nothing? Use nothing. Peter's drawing shows all. Clean up any spills so oil won't foul the point contacts.

Step 9. Adjust Points

Dig around your tool box, find your feeler gauge and a 19mm socket. Pull out the 0.40mm (0.016 in) blade. Friend: Turn the steering wheel to the right, then look behind the right front wheel—put the 19mm socket on the nut holding the V-belt pulley onto the crankshaft and turn it clockwise ⟳ . You, meanwhile, should watch the points open and close as the point rubbing block makes constant contact with the cam on the base of the vertical distributor shaft. The hissing and sighing you hear as the crankshaft is turned is the sound of air being forced out through the spark plug holes. If your plugs are still in the cylinder head, you won't hear the sound. Ask Friend to stop turning when the point rubbing block is *exactly* on one of the corners of the distributor cam. The points are now open.

OK, slide the 0.40mm feeler gauge blade between the two contacts on the points. It should just slip in nicely. The point arm shouldn't be forced wider open as you insert the blade, nor should there be enough room to rattle the blade or tap dance. A good snug fit is what's called for. Try a thicker and thinner blade to test how they feel.

If the point gap is not 0.40mm, loosen the screw holding the points in the distributor—just slightly. Insert a medium-sized screwdriver blade between the two nipples near the contacts on the points. The edge of the screwdriver blade will fit into a little notch in the points. Turn the screwdriver slightly clockwise ⟳ to open the gap and counterclockwise ⟲ to close it. If you can't make the point arm move, loosen the holding screw a bit more. Try moving the point arm now. Test the gap again with the 0.40mm blade.

Now tighten the point holding screw. Keep the feeler blade between the contacts, and hold one screwdriver between the nipples and the adjusting notch and use another screwdriver to tighten the screw holding the points in place. Maintain *light* pressure clockwise ⟳ on

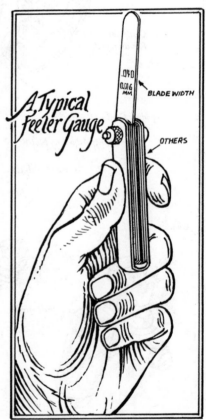

A Typical Feeler Gauge

Step 9. (Cont'd.)

the screwdriver in the adjusting notch. This counters the tendency of the point arm to move slightly counterclockwise and close the gap as you tighten the screw. Give the point holding screw a final tightening.

Measure the gap again. If the points tightened up or the gap is too wide, readjust them. When the gap is perfect, remove the 19mm socket from the crankshaft nut. Connect the little wire that goes from the condenser to the outside of the distributor onto the spade connector. If you're going to change the condenser (30,000 miles) go to Procedure 24, then return here.

Step 10. Install Dust Cover and Rotor

Clean any trace of dirt or grease from the plastic dust cover. Pop it on top of the distributor, making sure the tab on the underside fits properly into the notch in the distributor rim. Twist the dust cover around until it lies flat.

If you're using your old rotor, lightly clean the sparking end with a *fine* file. Then rub the cleaned part against the side of a tire. Carbon in the tire will add a final polish to the metal tip. Dust off the rest of the rotor. Line up the slot in distributor shaft with the protruding lug in the bottom of your old or new rotor, and push the rotor firmly down. It only fits one way. Twist it from side to side to be sure it's all the way down.

Step 11. Install Distributor Cap

If you're reinstalling the old cap, first scrape any deposits off the four brass contacts inside the cap with a knife blade or small file. Wipe the cap completely clean. If you can't get the contacts clean, buy a new cap. Install the cap on top of the distributor and pop the two metal spring arms into position.

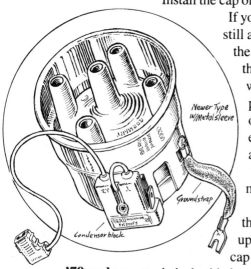

If you're installing a new cap, compare it with the old one (spark plug wires still attached). **'79 and on**, remove the old one from the metal shield. Turn the new cap around so it's in the same position as the old one. Pull one of the plug wires out of the old cap and examine the metal end. Clean it with a small wire brush or soapless scouring pad if it's cruddy. Now plug it into the corresponding hole in the new one. Do 'em all one by one. This way you can't get them mixed up. Not the time to be distracted by questions or wisecracks. Give the wires a light tug to be sure they are fully home.

Place the cap on top of the distributor ('79 and on—install the metal shield).

The distributor cap will fit only in one position. If you can't fasten the spring metal clips—don't beat on them—you haven't lined the cap up properly. There's a slot on the distributor rim into which an ear on the cap fits. Fasten the spring clips.

'79 and on attach the braided ground wire to the connection on the plastic gizmo or, in some models, to a screw on the side of the distributor.

Step 12. Check, Clean, Gap and Install Spark Plugs

Don't install the plugs yet if you're going to do a compression test (Procedure 20) or valve clearance measurement (Procedure 22). Do these now and then come back here.

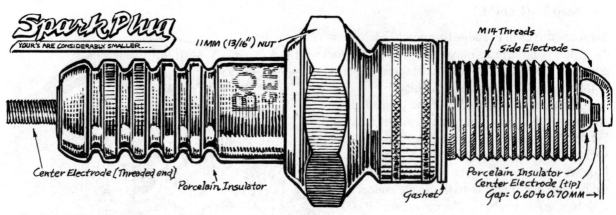

Step 12. (Cont'd.)

Carefully compare your plugs to the ones in Peter's chart (page 113) to see if they're reusable. The electrode (the part which screws into the cylinder head and protrudes into the combustion chamber) should be free from nasty deposits. The condition of the plugs tells you a lot about what's going on inside the engine. A well tuned engine will put a tan or light grey deposit on the electrode. This is easily cleaned off with a light wire brush.

If the end of the plug is covered with oil, either oil is escaping past the piston rings, a valve isn't seating properly, or a valve guide seal is kaput. I'd do a compression check on all cylinders (Procedure 20).

Electrodes that are burnt away, with black or grey spots on the central insulator, indicate the engine is overheating—usually caused by incorrect ignition timing. We can soon fix that—Procedure 16.

If the electrode or the central insulator is worn away, change the plugs. They've been in the head too long. Just like the chap with dysentery.

Plug electrodes covered with a glaze are probably the wrong type. Check that they are Bosch W 200 T30 (carbureted engines) or Bosch W 175 T30 (fuel injection) or suitable equivalents. If you have removed the catalytic converter, use Bosch W 175 T30 plugs in carbureted engines if the old plugs were fouled with soot.

Black flaky deposits on the plug end indicate the fuel/air mixture is too rich in gas (Chapter 11 or 12), the ignition timing is wrong or you have incorrect plugs.

Lots of white/grey flakes on the electrode indicate poor quality gasoline, use of fuel and/or oil additives (how could you!) or the plug wasn't screwed into the cylinder head tightly.

Are the electrodes all bashed in? The plug is too long and has been mangled by the piston, or there's a foreign object inside the cylinder. Have Friend turn the engine over with a 19mm socket on the crankshaft bolt while you shine a light into the plug hole and watch the piston rise to the top of its stroke (TDC). See anything? If you spot a UFO (Unfriendly Foreign Object), stick a magnet or piece of wire into the hole and get it out. Do a compression check (Procedure 20) to find out if the UFO cracked a piston, ring or something.

I once had an earring fall into a cylinder of a very expensive race car engine five minutes before the race started. Using a piece of wire and a flashlight I got it out before anybody realized what I was really

doing. I said, "I want a sample of carbon from the top of the piston." No wonder they thought I was weird, but despite my klutziness, we won the race.

Before installing new or cleaned plugs, you must adjust the electrode gap; called 'gapping the plugs.' The gap should be 0.60mm to 0.70mm (0.024 to 0.028 in). To measure the gap use a 0.60mm feeler gauge blade or, in an emergency, lay the front and back covers of this book together. Use a plug gapper or needle nose pliers to bend the *side* electrode and increase the gap. Do not bend the center insulator. You will

damage the porcelain insulation and ruin the plug. Decrease the gap by using the gapper or tap the electrode end of the plug lightly on a wrench handle or other clean metal surface. Not too hard now.

When all four plugs are gapped, smear a little multipurpose grease on the threads. A drop of clean engine oil from the dipstick will do if you have no grease. Don't get oil or grease anywhere near the electrodes. Carefully screw the plugs into the cylinder head *by*

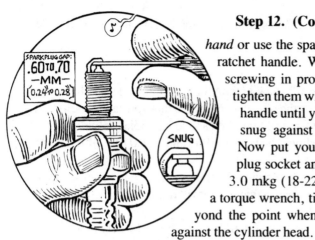

Step 12. (Cont'd.)

hand or use the spark plug socket without the ratchet handle. When you're sure they are screwing in properly, not cross-threaded, tighten them with the socket on the ratchet handle until you feel the base of the plug snug against the cylinder head. Stop. Now put your torque wrench onto the plug socket and tighten the plugs to 2.5-3.0 mkg (18-22 ft lbs). If you don't have a torque wrench, tighten just ⅛ to ¼ turn beyond the point when you have the plug snug against the cylinder head.

A cross-threaded plug will destroy the threads in the cylinder head if you continue to tighten it. If the plug doesn't go in easily, check the threads on the plug. If they are messed up, toss it and get a new one. Try to start the new one correctly.

If you can't get the plug in right, you'll have to clean the threads inside the cylinder head with a tool called a thread chaser. Your VW dealer may lend you one (if you do the job in the parking lot) or at least tell you where you can get the job done. Actually, the chaser isn't an expensive item, so you might consider buying one. Compare the chaser threads to the spark plug threads so you know you've got the right tool.

If your plugs are very difficult to remove and install, there is corrosion on the cylinder head threads which must be removed with the thread chaser. If the threads are completely ruined, the VW agency or machine shop will have to insert a helicoil into the plug hole. See Chapter 20, Procedure 6.

Install the spark plug wires onto the plugs in correct order. If any wire insulation is worn, replace it. Make sure the wires fit tightly in the distributor cap and into the connectors which snap onto the spark plugs. If a connector comes off the plug wire, clean the inside of the connector with a knife or thin screwdriver. Now peel the rubber part down the wire, screw the connector onto the wire and then peel the rubber bit back over the connector. All tight?

Install the coil wire into the center of the distributor cap if it's out. Take the 19mm socket off the crankshaft bolt if it's still on.

PROCEDURE 15: CHECK AND ADJUST DISTRIBUTOR POINT GAP (DWELL). Phase 1. (Up to 1980)

Condition: You've adjusted the ignition point gap.

Tools and materials: Phase 2 tool kit.

Remarks: 'Experienced' mechanics might like to go to Chapter 20, Procedure 18, if you've used a dwell meter before.

Step 1. Connect Tach-Dwell Meter

Is this the first time you've ever faced a Tach-Dwell Meter? Have no fear, it won't bite.

Take the meter out of its box and read the enclosed instructions or the ones on the side of the box. Connect the red (positive) lead to the *metal* part of the terminal on the coil from which a small wire runs to the distributor. This is #1 coil terminal. Connect the black (negative) lead onto the negative battery post.

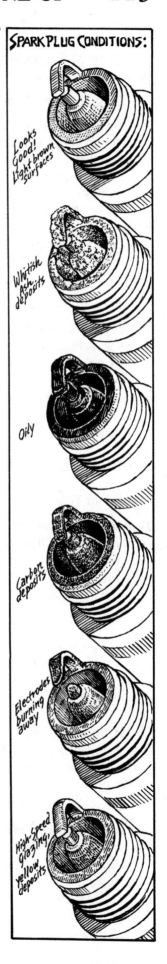

SPARK PLUG CONDITIONS:

Looks Good! Light brown surfaces

Whitish Ash deposits

Oily

Carbon deposits

Electrodes burning away

High-Speed Glazing, yellow deposits

Some meters hook up another way: the red and black leads connect to the battery and a small (often green) lead attached to coil terminal #1.

Step 2. Check Reading

Switch the meter to Tach. Be sure the meter leads aren't stuck in the V-belts or fan blades. Pull the plug from the cooling fan (or snap apart the plastic connector). If the plug is so corroded that you cannot pull it off, be aware that the fan might switch on, so careful with the fingers! Start the car and let it idle for two minutes. Read engine revolutions on the RPM scale. The reading should be between 900 and 1,000 rpm. If it's below 900 or above 1,000, adjust the idle now—Procedure 18.

Switch the meter over to Dwell. If there is a two-position switch on the meter, one for eight cylinder engines and the other for four, switch it to four. (Some meters have no switch on them and read eight cylinders only, so divide the reading you get in half.)

With the engine still running, note the dwell angle on the 4 cylinder scale. It should be between 44° and 50° if you installed new points, and 42° to 58° if you left in your old ones.

Step 3. Readjust Points?

If you are not within dwell tolerance, it's back to adjustment. A low dwell reading means the point gap is too wide. A high dwell reading means the gap is too small. Adjust the points accordingly (Procedure 14, Step 7). When the gap is right, replace the distributor components (Procedure 14, Steps 8 and 9).

All Models: Check the dwell again. Rev the engine to about 2,000 rpm by either pulling on the accelerator cable lever or asking Friend to step on the gas. The dwell reading should not vary by more than one degree, plus or minus, from your initial reading at 900 or 1,000 rpm. A greater variation indicates a worn distributor (see Procedure 26). Turn the engine off.

PROCEDURE 16: ADJUST IGNITION TIMING. Phase 1.

Condition: Tune-up.

Tools and materials: Friend, Phase 1 tool kit, including stroboscopic timing light and Tach-Dwell meter. (This is where you'll pay yourself back.) If you don't have a stroboscopic timing light, rent/borrow one or ask a mechanic to time your engine. It cannot be done accurately without one. You may also need a drop of white or yellow paint and a thin brush.

The point gap (dwell) must be correct (Procedure 15) before you time the engine.

Step 1. Get Ready

The cooling fan may turn on at any second, so pull out the plug from the back of the fan motor to save your fingers. If you leave it connected, be careful.

Early cars with manual transmissions have a Top Dead Center (TDC) sensor (wire) running from the inspection hole on top of the transmission to a computer box on the top inside of the left fender. Pull the plug on the transmission and tuck it out of the way.

Remove the metal or plastic pop top from the TDC plug on top of the transmission. Use an old-fashioned box type spark plug wrench, needle nose pliers, or a pair of vice grips to unscrew the plug counterclockwise. Cars with automatic transmissions have the timing hole on the left side of the transmission, a little to the left of the distributor. There's no plug in the hole.

Step 2. Find and Identify Timing Mark

Put the shift lever in neutral (N), the hand brake on, turn the steering wheel to the right, and then turn the key off. Put your 19mm socket on the bolt in the center of the crankshaft V belt pulley.

Have Friend turn the crankshaft nut clockwise with the socket as you watch the TDC hole in the transmission. You are looking for the 3° notch in the flywheel. This notch is three degrees after top dead center (ATDC) and is just past the 0° TDC mark. In the automatic transmission, the 3° mark is a line on the drive plate which may or may not be stamped 3°. Whichever type of transmission you have, the 3° mark has to be aligned with a pointer just inside the transmission. See the diagram on next page. You can check that the pointer is aligned properly by taking off the distributor cap. Is the mark on the sparking end of the rotor lined up (or close to) the little line on the distributor rim? Lift up the dust cover to check. Have Friend turn the crankshaft a few times while you watch and check that you've got the right mark. When you have positively identified the 3° mark and it is aligned with the pointer, clean it or carefully paint it white or yellow. Paint the TDC pointer as well. Have Friend remove the socket from crankshaft bolt, while you plug the coil wire back in.

Step 3. Connect Strobe Timing Light and Tach-Dwell Meter

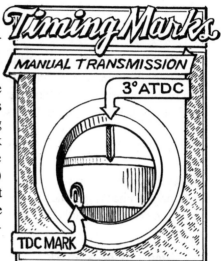

With the shift lever still in neutral (N), connect the meter (Procedure 15, Step 1) and switch it to Tach. Now connect the timing light according to the instructions in its box. Your dog ate them? OK, connect the positive (red) lead to the positive battery post and the negative (black) lead to the battery ground post. These days most lights have an inductive pick-up connection which clips onto #1 spark plug wire. Make sure the arrow on the connection points *toward* the spark plug and keep the leads well away from belts and sprockets. Start the engine (handbrake firmly on and all the wires away from V belts, etc.) and let it warm up. The revs should be between 900 and 1,000. Don't adjust the idle just yet; have Friend step on the gas pedal or pull on the cable yourself to get the revs up. If the revs are too high, adjust the idle—Procedure 18.

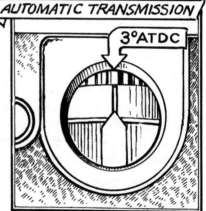

Point the strobe light towards TDC hole in the transmission. When you pull the trigger, a pulse of high intensity light shoots from the business end, making it possible to see the paint marks on the flywheel drive plate. The light only fires when an electric current is sent from the distributor down the plug wire to #1 spark plug.

If your engine is timed correctly and the revs are OK, the light will show that the pointer inside the TDC hole is lined up with the 3° ATDC mark on the flywheel or drive plate. If things are not lined up, go to Step 4 and rotate the distributor to advance or retard the moment when current is sent to the plugs. Everything lines up? Adjust the idle (Procedure 18) if need be and then check the timing again.

Step 4. Adjust Timing

Turn off the engine. Loosen the 13mm bolt holding the U-shaped clip around the bottom of the distributor. Start the engine and fire the light at the TDC hole again. Gently turn the distributor back and forth with your hand (don't hold the wires) and watch the TDC hole until the pointer and the 3° ATDC mark line up.

The idle may increase or decrease when you turn the distributor to line up the notch with the pointer. Check the RPM scale on the Tach Dwell meter to see if the idle is still between 900 and 1,000 rpm's. If it's not, turn to Procedure 18 and adjust the idle. When it's correct, continue with the timing procedure.

Stop the engine and tighten the 13mm bolt. Start the engine and check the timing once again. Everything still lines up? Fab. Keep the engine running.

Step 5. Check Distributor Advance

Carbureted engines: Check that the throttle valve closes. Pull the vacuum retard hose from the *rear* connection on the vacuum cannister attached to the distributor. The timing mark should *advance* toward the rear of the car. No? Go to Procedure 18 and do Step 3. Then retime the engine. Advance OK? Return the vacuum hose and continue.

All models: Keep the engine running and the light pointed at the TDC hole. Pull on the accelerator cable (or have Friend depress the gas pedal) and watch the 3° line move before your very eyes. It should move toward the rear of the car as the spark is automatically advanced by the distributor. If it doesn't, check the condition of the plastic vacuum lines (hoses) to the cannister on the side of the distributor. That's the vacuum advance mechanism. If the hoses are OK, the advance mechanism isn't working. Check the distributor (Procedure 26).

Keep the light connected and point it at the rear of the *camshaft* sprocket. The light should show a dot on the rear of the sprocket lining up with the base of the left side of the camshaft cover. Look carefully—you'll see it. Stop the engine, have Friend turn the crankshaft (19mm socket) and hit the camshaft dot with some white paint, if needed. If the dot doesn't line up when the engine's running, turn to Procedure 23.

Step 6. Finish Up

If things are OK, turn off the engine and carefully put away the timing light in its box, screw back the plug in the transmission and reconnect the cooling fan wire. Watch your fingers, the fan is likely to go back on! Put the TDC sensor back on, if you have one.

PROCEDURE 17: CHECK COIL. Phase 1.

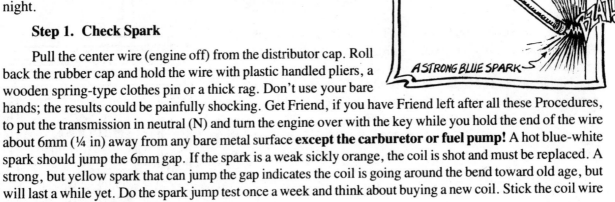

Condition: Engine misses, quits in mid-flight, sometimes won't start or just checking. The small effort required to check the coil will be more than repaid if it's plotting to crap out some dark rainy night.

Step 1. Check Spark

Pull the center wire (engine off) from the distributor cap. Roll back the rubber cap and hold the wire with plastic handled pliers, a wooden spring-type clothes pin or a thick rag. Don't use your bare hands; the results could be painfully shocking. Get Friend, if you have Friend left after all these Procedures, to put the transmission in neutral (N) and turn the engine over with the key while you hold the end of the wire about 6mm (¼ in) away from any bare metal surface **except the carburetor or fuel pump!** A hot blue-white spark should jump the 6mm gap. If the spark is a weak sickly orange, the coil is shot and must be replaced. A strong, but yellow spark that can jump the gap indicates the coil is going around the bend toward old age, but will last a while yet. Do the spark jump test once a week and think about buying a new coil. Stick the coil wire back into the distributor cap.

Step 2. Replace Coil

Condition: Old coil is shot.

Transfer the connections from the old coil onto the new one before you remove the old coil from the bracket on the firewall. Then loosen the 8mm nut holding the coil inside its bracket. Withdraw the old coil and slide in the new one. Tighten the nut. Do the spark test again to see what a good spark looks like. Still with me? Great. We're almost finished. But you may have to adjust the engine idle.

PROCEDURE 18: IDLE ADJUSTMENT. Phase 1.

Condition: Tune-up: engine idles poorly.

Tools and materials: Small screwdriver, Tach-Dwell Meter unless you have a tachometer in the dash.

Remarks: If the car idles well, *don't* do this Procedure.

Step 1. Check Idle (Carbureted Engine)—Fuel Injection go to Step 5.

If you took a lunch break, put the shift lever in neutral (N), hand brake on, and warm up the car before you continue. Hook up the Tach-Dwell meter (Procedure 15, Step 1) and turn the switch to Tach. The meter should read between 850 and 1,000 rpm's. If it doesn't, find the idle speed screw at the bottom of the carburetor on the *right* side below the automatic choke mechanism.

Step 2. Adjust Idle (Carburetors)

To increase idle speed, turn the screw counterclockwise ◯. To decrease the idle, turn the screw clockwise ◯. Adjust idle, turn engine off and put everything away—**Automatics,** hold it—put your foot down hard on the brake pedal and shift into Drive (D). Does the engine still idle well? If not, shift back to N and adjust the idle up to 1,000 rpm. Put it in Drive again. Better? Wonderful.

If adjusting the idle screw doesn't alter your idle one iota, either the carbon monoxide (CO) content of the exhaust is wrong or someone has been messing with your carburetor, so go to the next Step.

Step 3. Adjust Throttle Valve Gap (Carbureted)

The throttle valve adjusting screw is on the left side of the carburetor. The screw should have a plastic cap to discourage idle adjusters (I guess).

Remove the 10mm nut from the metal air intake elbow on top of the carburetor and remove the elbow. Move the choke butterfly (the gold colored hinge-like thing facing you as you peer into the top of the carburetor mouth) to the fully open position (the vertical, up-and-down position). Hold it there if it won't stay by itself. Remove the plastic cap and unscrew the throttle valve adjusting screw until the tip of the screw no longer touches the throttle valve lever. Now screw it back in again until the tip just touches the lever. Turn it in an additional ¼ turn. Put back the plastic cap and the metal air intake elbow. Readjust the idle (Step 2). Check ignition timing if you're here from Procedure 16, Step 5.

Step 4. Have Exhaust Gas CO Content Measured and Adjusted

You will now have to get the CO content of your exhaust gas analyzed and adjusted by a VW dealer because it is altered when you mess with the idle. You can get in *big* trouble with the Feds ($$) if your exhaust gas CO content is too high. Also, the car runs better when it's correct.

Step 5. Check the Idle (Fuel Injection)

Warm up the engine for 5 minutes if it's cold. Put the shift lever in neutral (N). Shut off the engine. Hook up your Tach-Dwell Meter (Procedure 15, Step 1) and switch it to Tach. Start the car again and read the RPM scale. The needle should be between 850 and 1,000 rpm's.

Step 6. Adjust Idle (Fuel Injection)

If adjustment is required, put a 7mm wrench on the *brass* colored idle screw on the back of the throttle valve housing, just behind where the accelerator cable attaches to its linkage. Turn it clockwise ◯ to decrease idle speed or counterclockwise ◯ to increase it. If you have an automatic, hold the brake down hard and put the shift lever into drive (D). Does the car still idle well? If not, shift to N and adjust the idle to 1,000 rpm. Put it into Drive again. Better?

Step 7. Have Exhaust Gas CO Content Measured and Adjusted (Fuel Injection)

See Step 4.

If you are here as part of the 15,000 mile maintenance, it's time to press on with the Procedures and grease the constant velocity joints (Procedure 19). The 5,000 mile tune-up people can clean up and relax for another 5,000 miles. If the engine still doesn't run right, turn to Chapter 12 or 13.

PROCEDURE 19: LUBRICATE CONSTANT VELOCITY JOINTS. Phase 1.

Condition: 15,000 mile maintenance

Tools and materials: CV Joint Grease (buy it from VW), grease gun with a pointed fitting to get behind the rubber boots protecting the CV joints.

Remarks: There are two CV joints on each front driveshaft; an inner, close to the transmission, and an outer, close to the wheel. This makes a total of four CV joints.

Step 1. Read Chapter 20, Procedure 15, to learn how to pry open the VW clamp holding the rubber boot over the outer CV joint closest to the right front wheel. Stick your grease gun under the rubber boot into the CV joint and pump the gun five times to fill the joint with grease. Don't overdo it and split the rubber because the entire driveshaft has to be removed to replace a rubber boot. Pull the end of the boot back over the cast ridge on the driveshaft and secure it with the VW clamp. If you can't fasten the VW clamp onto the driveshaft,

use regular hose clamps. Now do the same thing to the inner CV joint on the transmission end of the same driveshaft. Continue with the two joints on the other driveshaft. If you feel your driveshafts are having troubles, turn to Chapter 16, Procedure 8.

PROCEDURE 20: COMPRESSION CHECK.
Phase 1. (Not for Diesel)

Condition: 15,000 mile maintenance, prepurchase check, engine condition check.

Tools and materials: Spark plug wrench, compression tester safety glasses, masking tape, paper and pencil, Friend, 4 teaspoons of S.A.E.80W-90 oil, cap for long hair. A disposable 50cc syringe (without the needle) is a great tool for Step 6.

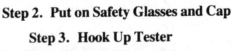

Remarks: The engine should be warm and the battery, starter and solenoid in good operating condition. A weak batttery won't turn the engine over fast enough to give you an accurate compression reading. Also, deduct $0.14/cm^2$ (2 psi) of pressure for each 1,000 ft above sea level. This Procedure is *not* for diesel.

Step 1. Remove Spark Plugs

Write the numbers 1, 2, 3 and 4 on four separate pieces of masking tape. Stick #1 on the spark plug wire going to No. 1 plug; it's at the front of the engine, closest to the right fender and drive belt. Stick the other pieces on the other 3 spark plug wires in numerical sequence. Remove all four spark plugs and lay them down in numerical order so you can reinstall them in the same holes. Pull the big center wire out of the coil. Later on you can compare the plugs to Peter's chart in Procedure 14, Step 12. Write numbers 1, 2, 3 and 4 on the top of your paper, dividing it into four columns.

Step 2. Put on Safety Glasses and Cap

Step 3. Hook Up Tester

Push or screw the threaded (or rubber) end of your compression tester into #1 spark plug hole.

With the gear lever in Neutral (N), have Friend turn the engine over using the key, while pressing the gas pedal to the floor. The engine can't start—the coil wire and plugs are out. Watch the dial of the tester. Make a mental note of the first position the needle reaches as the engine turns over the first time. Have Friend continuously turn the engine over for 5 seconds. The needle on the gauge will rise in spurts. Underneath #1 on your paper, write the number the needle first jumped to, then the number reached on the last engine revolution.

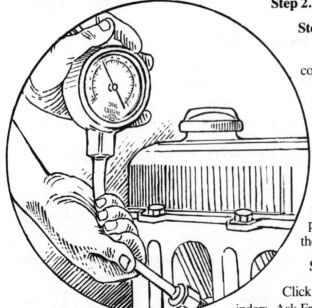

Step 4. Test Other Three Cylinders

Click the tester back to zero and do Step 3 on the other three cylinders. Ask Friend to keep a foot down on the gas pedal during the test.

Step 5. Evaluation

Look at your figures. If you have one figure substantially lower than the others, repeat the compression test for that particular cylinder. Be sure you pushed or threaded the tester fully into the spark plug hole.

At sea level, a reading of 10-13 kg/cm^2 (142-184 psi) is normal. Remember to deduct 0.14 kg/cm^2 (2 psi) for each 1,000 feet of altitude. Here at 7,000 feet in Santa Fe, I deduct 0.98 kg/cm^2 (14 psi).

If the reading for all the cylinders is around 7.49 kg/cm^2 (107 psi), things are just about OK for the moment, but you should do a compression check every 1,000 miles from now on.

If there's a difference of more than 3.0 kg/cm^2 (42 psi) between any cylinders, the wear limit has been reached and an overhaul is required. We need to find out what's wrong. Any cylinder with a very low reading likely has a valve or piston ring problem. If the readings for two adjacent cylinders are around 1.5-3.0 kg/cm^2 (21-42 psi) lower than the readings for the other two cylinders, your cylinder head gasket is probably blown. It needs to be changed (Chapter 18).

Look at your first figure for the low cylinder. If it's also lower than the first reading for the others, let's do some more tests. Also do the following step if your compression is around the 7.49 kg/cm^2 (107 psi) mark.

Step 6. Find Cause of Low Reading

Squirt a small amount (about a teaspoon) of S.A.E.80W-90 oil into the spark plug hole of the cylinder with the low reading. S.A.E.50 will do if you don't have S.A.E.80W-90. Insert the compression tester into the cylinder and have Friend turn the engine over for 5 seconds.

If there's about a 10% increase in compression, chances are your piston rings are worn or the cylinder wall has been scored by a damaged or broken piston ring, allowing compression to escape.

If you don't get an increase in compression by adding oil, one of the valves is not seating properly. You'll need a valve job in the not too distant future, so think about it before taking a long trip. A reading below 6.3 kg/cm^2 (90 psi) in any cylinder means a stuck valve, broken piston or piston rings, or your compression gauge has given up the ghost. Let's hope it's the gauge. If not, it's engine rebuild time. Sorry, that's the breaks.

If you want a second expert opinion on the internal condition of your engine, go to any well-equipped garage for a "Leak-down" test. This checks for leakage between the valves and their seats, the piston rings and the cylinder wall sides or the cylinder head and the crankcase. The test isn't expensive. It's a worthwhile investment, especially if your compression readings are on the 107 psi borderline. Clean the plugs (Procedure 14, Step 12) and screw them back into the cylinder head. Push on the coil and spark plug wires. Finally, put your tools away and clean up.

PROCEDURE 21: REPLACE FUEL INJECTION FUEL FILTER. Phase 1.

Condition: 15,000 miles, dirt in the fuel system, you just bought a used fuel injected car.

Tools and materials: Phase 1 tool kit, new fuel filter.

Remarks: The filter is a silver canister fitted into the fuel line held inside the left fender by a bracket. There are different styles of filters, so use your chassis number to get the correct replacement. Keep your fire extinguisher close by.

Step 1. Disconnect Battery Ground Strap

Use your 10mm wrench.

Step 2. Remove Filter

Place a clean rag under the filter fuel line connections to mop up dripping gasoline. Loosen and free the brass colored captive nuts from the fuel lines on the ends of the filter (15mm or 17mm wrench). Next loosen the 10mm nut holding the filter into its clamp. Slide the filter out. If it won't come loose, remove the nut from the clamp and pry open the clamp enough to let the filter slide free.

Step 3. Install New Filter

Install your new filter with the arrow pointing forward toward the headlights. Reinstall the clamp and the 10mm nut. Hook up the fuel lines, and tighten the captive nuts. Reconnect the battery ground strap. Voila, fini!

PROCEDURE 22: VALVE CLEARANCE MEASUREMENT. Phase 1.

Condition: 15,000 mile routine maintenance, noisy valves, 1,000 mile interval after engine rebuild, or 300 mile interval after a valve job.

Tools and materials: Phase 1 tool kit, new camshaft cover gasket, new cylinder head end plug and front seal strip, paper and pencil.

Remarks: No matter what anyone has written, sworn, claimed or sent by carrier pigeon, **THE ENGINE MUST BE COLD TO MEASURE VALVE CLEARANCE!** Cold means between 5°C - 30°C (40°F - 85°F). Do this Procedure carefully.

Step 1. Free Positive Crankcase Ventilation (PCV) Valve or Hose

Loosen the hose clamp holding the PCV valve to the top right of the camshaft cover. Pull off the hose.

Step 2. Remove Accelerator Cable (Fuel Injection and Automatic)

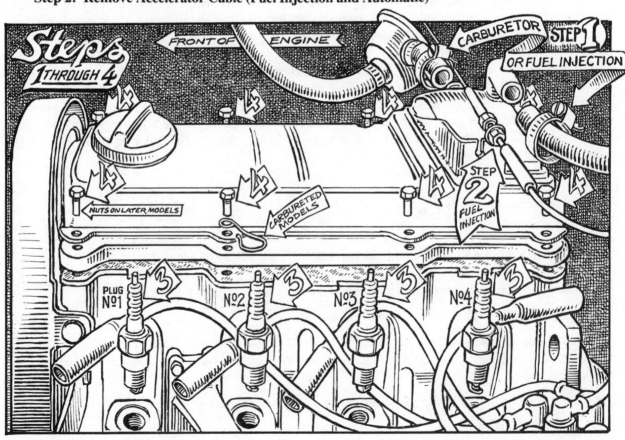

Fuel Injection: Pop the end of the cable off the mount at the throttle assembly. Just pull it upward; it'll come off. Loosen the rearmost nut on the accelerator sheath. Use two 10mm or 17mm wrenches, one to hold and the other to turn. The sheath is held onto a bracket on top of the cam cover. Move the cable out of the way.

Automatic: You have a similar attaching method (as above) on top of the cam cover but it takes two 15mm wrenches to loosen the rearmost nut. Don't disconnect the cable from the carburetor; it's too much trouble.

Step 3. Remove Spark Plugs (All Models)

Write the numbers 1, 2, 3 and 4 on four pieces of masking tape and stick them on the four spark plug wires. #1 plug is closest to the V-belts by the right fender. Pull off all four wires and use your spark plug wrench to unscrew the four spark plugs. Lay them down in the same order as they came out.

Step 4. Remove Camshaft Cover

Remove the eight nuts or bolts holding the camshaft cover to the top of the cylinder head (10mm socket). Put the nuts or bolts in a marked Baggie.

Now remove the long metal spacer from each side of the cover. If you have a carbureted model, don't lose the thin wire which holds the fuel line. This wire should be attached to the second from the right camshaft cover bolt. Pull off the camshaft cover along with its cork gasket. Leave the gasket on the cylinder head if it's stuck. Broke it? Buy a new one.

1980 and on: See Procedure 23, Step 4.

Step 5. Align Camshaft Lobes

First we'll measure the valve clearance on cylinder #1. Put a 19mm socket on the bolt in the center of the *crankshaft* belt pulley. The bolt is most easily reached through the right fender well, so turn the steering wheel all the way to the right. Don't put the socket on the *camshaft* drive belt sprocket by mistake; turning it will stretch the belt. Have Friend turn the crankshaft bolt clockwise ⟳ until you see that the lobes on the camshaft are pointing upward. See the diagram.

If you look carefully at the bottom of the lobes you'll see they are no longer resting on the adjusting discs (at least they shouldn't be). This indicates the intake and exhaust valves for No. 1 cylinder are in the closed position. And closed they must be to measure the clearance between the top of the valve adjusting disc and the bottom of the camshaft lobes. If you don't think you've got the lobes pointing upward, have Friend turn the socket on the crankshaft sprocket 'round and 'round until you're sure the lobes are pointing up.

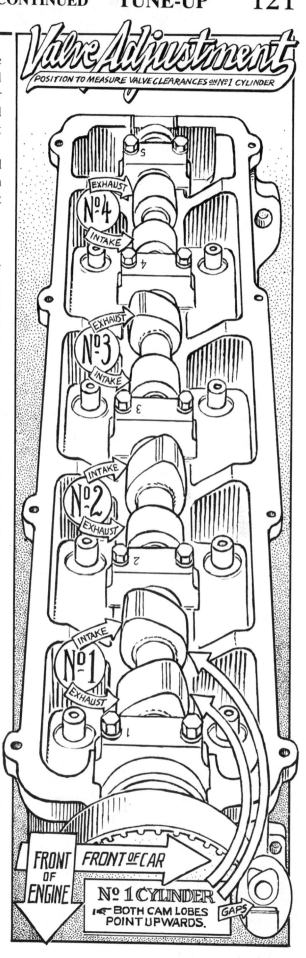

Valve Adjustment
POSITION TO MEASURE VALVE CLEARANCES ON Nº1 CYLINDER

EXHAUST · Nº4 · INTAKE

EXHAUST · Nº3 · INTAKE

INTAKE · Nº2 · EXHAUST

INTAKE · Nº1 · EXHAUST

FRONT OF ENGINE · FRONT OF CAR

Nº1 CYLINDER
BOTH CAM LOBES POINT UPWARDS. · GAPS

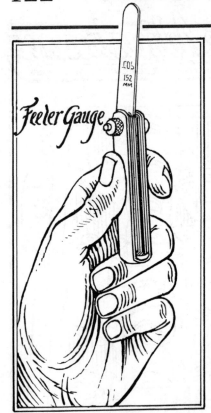

Feeler Gauge

Step 6. Measure Intake and Exhaust Valve Clearance in #1 Cylinder

The clearance for the *exhaust* valve should be between 0.35 and 0.45mm. Find the 0.35mm blade on your feeler gauge. All the valve adjusting discs are marked in millimeters, so unless you want to do mind-boggling calculations on the kitchen table, use a metric feeler gauge.

Make sure the gauge blade is clean because dirt will alter the measurement. Take your time.

Slip the 0.35mm blade between the first lobe on the camshaft and the valve adjusting disc. We're measuring the *exhaust* valve clearance. Push the blade all the way under the camshaft lobe. If the blade rattles around in the gap or won't go in at all, try other sizes until you get a snug fit.

When you've got a blade that fits correctly, write the size of the blade (the clearance) down on a piece of paper or use the chart provided. Now measure the *intake* valve clearance for No. 1 cylinder in the same way. It should be between 0.15 and 0.25mm, so start with the 0.15mm feeler blade. That is, the gap below the *second* lobe on the camshaft and its adjusting disc. Write the clearance down.

Step 7. Measure Valve Clearances for #3 Cylinder

Turn the socket on the bolt in the center of the crankshaft 180° (½ turn) clockwise. The camshaft lobes for No. 3 cylinder will now point upward. Measure the *exhaust* valve clearance first. In this cylinder the exhaust is the valve *closest* to the #4 cylinder. Write down the measurement under #3 exhaust on the chart provided. Now measure the intake, the valve closest to cylinder #2. Write that measurement under #3 intake.

Step 8. Measure Clearance in Cylinder #4

Turn the crankshaft sprocket clockwise another 180° (½ turn) and measure the valve clearances of #4 cylinder. The exhaust for #4 is the valve closest to the *rear* of the cylinder head. The intake is the valve *closest* to cylinder #3. Write down your measurements.

#1 CYLINDER		#2 CYLINDER		#3 CYLINDER		#4 CYLINDER	
Exhaust	Intake	Exhaust	Intake	Intake	Exhaust	Intake	Exhaust

Step 9. Measure Valve Clearances for Cylinder #2

Turn the crankshaft sprocket clockwise another 180° (½ turn) and measure the valve clearances of #2 cylinder. First measure the exhaust valve clearance (closest to cylinder #1), then the intake valve clearance.

Step 10. Do It All Again

Do steps 6, 7, 8 and 9 once again. Write this second set of clearances underneath the first ones. If they don't agree, measure the clearances again and again and . . . until you get a set of numbers that do!

Step 11. Your Calculations, Please

Let's start with the *intake* valves. If your measurements are between .15mm and .25mm, your intake valve clearances are OK. If your measurements are outside these figures, you'll need to adjust the clearance.

To *increase* clearance, you need to *reduce* the thickness of the valve adjusting disc.

To *reduce* clearance, you need to *increase* the thickness of the valve adjusting disc.

Now the *exhaust* valve clearances. If your figures are between .35mm and .45mm all is fine. If greater or less, the disc has to be changed.

If you don't have a selection of discs or tools to change them, it's time to put things back together (Steps 12-16) and drive the car to the dealer. VW mechanics will depress the cam followers with a special tool #VW546, remove the disc with another special tool (it can be done with a small screwdriver) and reinstall a disc of a different thickness to get the valve clearances correct. If you decide to buy a set of discs and the special tools, turn to Procedure 22A.

Give the mechanic the clearances you measured for all the valves, so s/he just has to determine what size disc to install. Make an appointment for a specific time so that you can be around when the discs are replaced. Watch the mechanic go through the measuring procedure after s/he's finished changing the discs.

Change the discs when the engine is cold! Tell the mechanic that you've just installed a new cam cover gasket and head seals.

Step 12. Clean Cylinder Head

Use a dull knife or paint scraper to remove all traces of the old cork gasket from the top of the cylinder head. Don't let pieces of cork fall inside the head. If the gasket is stubborn, soak it with a shot of gasket remover for awhile, then wipe off any deposits. Clean the camshaft cover in solvent until it shines.

Step 13. Install Camshaft Cover

Fit a new cork gasket into the groove on the underside of the cleaned camshaft cover. Install a new rubber cylinder head end plug and front seal strip. Put the cam cover on top of the cylinder head. Install the two long metal spacers and the eight nuts or bolts that go through the spacer and cam cover into the cylinder head. **Carbureted engines:** reinstall the wire gas line support onto the front, second-from-the-right camshaft cover bolt. Tighten the nuts or bolts in diagonal fashion (see Chapter 20, Procedure 7) to 1.0 mkg (7 ft lbs).

Models 1980 and on: Reposition the belt guard and screw the allen bolt up tight.

Step 14. Install Accelerator Cable (All Models)

Automatics: Slide the cable sheath onto the bracket on top of the camshaft cover. Use two wrenches to tighten the 10mm or 15mm rearmost nut so that the two nuts clamp the cable on the bracket. **Fuel Injection:** Pop the accelerator cable onto the throttle assembly pivot and tighten the nuts on the bracket.

Step 15. Install PCV Valve/Hose

Slide the PCV valve hose (or the plain hose) onto the connection on top of the camshaft cover and tighten the hose clamp.

Step 16. Install Spark Plugs

Go back to Procedure 14, Step 12 and do it.

PROCEDURE 22A: VALVE ADJUSTMENT. Phase 2.

Condition: You have done Procedure 22 and found that the valve clearances are outside specified tolerances.

Tools and materials: You must have the special tool needed to depress the cam followers. The official VW version is termed the VW 546, but other manufacturers make an identical tool (VW 10-208 or US 4476) which is used to remove the clearance discs from the top of the cam followers. This tool is very handy, but a thin blade electrician's type screwdriver is a reasonable alternative. The special tools can be purchased from the VW dealer or a foreign car parts house. It may not, however, be possible to just buy either special tool separately.

Remarks: A selection of clearance (adjusting) discs must be available. The dealer has them in profusion, and you may be able to simply swap your old disc for the size you need. The most commonly used sizes are between 3.55mm to 3.80mm. You can buy the discs for around two dollars a shot.

The discs run from 3.00mm to 4.25mm in 0.05mm increments. Please don't attempt to grind down your discs in an effort to get the needed size. You won't even get close, and worse, the camshaft will be badly damaged in no time at all.

Please read this Procedure all the way through before you begin work. I'll run through the steps for the exhaust and intake valves in cylinder number one. The work is identical for the remaining six valves in the other three cylinders. Number one cylinder is closest to right fender. The valve order from the front of the engine is : exhaust intake; exhaust intake; intake exhaust; intake exhaust.

Diesel: Make sure the piston in the cylinder on which you are working isn't at top dead center (TDC). Turn the crankshaft bolt about ¼ turn past TDC. This will prevent the valves from hitting the top of the piston when you depress the cam followers.

Step 1. Align Camshaft Lobes

Turn back to Chapter 10, Procedure 22 and do Step 5.

Step 2. Use Your New Tool

Insert the cam tool VW 546 between the two cam lobes in No. 1 cylinder making sure that the two ridges on the base of the tool slide onto the edges of the two cam followers. Press down the tool handle and the cam followers will sink into the cylinder head. Keep pressing and position the disc tool (or screwdriver) in the two small slots in the top of the exhaust cam follower. Don't press the followers too far into the head or else the disc will be impossible to grasp. Gently ease the disc out from the follower, and when it's free, release pressure on the depressing tool.

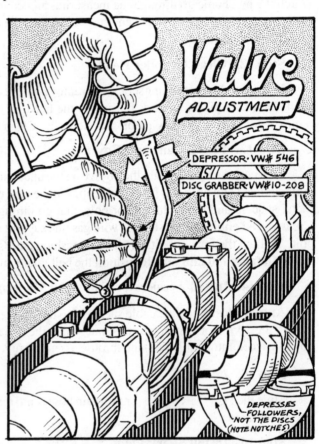

Valve ADJUSTMENT

DEPRESSOR· VW# 546

DISC GRABBER·VW#10-208

DEPRESSES FOLLOWERS, NOT THE DISCS (NOTE NOTCHES)

Step 3. Examine Disc

The disc has a number etched on the down side facing the valve. If the numbers have worn away, you'll need to measure the disc with a micrometer. A measuring tape won't do.

Step 4. Mathematics 101

Let's say that the clearance you measured in Step 6 of Procedure 22 (Chapter 10) was 0.3mm bigger than required. All you have to do is replace your disc with one 0.3mm thicker. That will make the clearance between the heel of the camshaft and the top of the disc smaller when the new disc is installed. Right? Right. Likewise, if the disc you took out was 3.50mm thick, then in order to *decrease* the gap by 0.3mm, then you need a 3.80mm disc. The new disc is thus 0.3mm thicker than the one originally installed. Confused? Here's another explanation.

If your measured clearance between the cam and the disc was *less* than the specified maximum (exhaust 0.45mm), subtract *your* measured clearance from the maximum specified. Now subtract the number you just calculated from the thickness of the disc you just removed from the cam follower. This gives you your new disc size.If the disc you require is thinner than any disc in the selection, you'll need to install the next thicker disc. OK.

Now, if your measured clearance was *more* than specified (exhaust 0.45mm), subtract the maximum specified clearance from the clearance you measured. Now *add* the figure to the thickness of the disc you just removed from the cam follower. This gives you the new disc size needed. If the disc required is thinner than any disc in the selection, you'll need the next thicker disc.

This method works for intake valves too. Just remember that maximum intake clearance is 0.25mm.

Step 5. Install New Size Disc

Lightly oil the clean disc with clean engine oil. Depress the cam followers with the tool and use your fingers to slip the disc into the top of the cam follower with the etched number facing *down*. If the disc goes in at an angle, align it correctly with a small screwdriver. Is it level? Release the tool and check again to see that the disc is in nice and flat.

Now do the intake valve clearance adjustment and swap the disc if you need to.

Step 6. Adjust Clearances in Remaining Cylinders

Use the above Steps to change the discs in the other three cylinders to bring valve clearance within tolerance. See Chapter 10, Procedure 22, Steps 7-9.

Step 7. Check Your Work

Turn the crankshaft over twice and measure clearance in all eight valves. All measurements should now be within tolerance (intake 0.15mm-0.25mm; exhaust 0.35mm-0.45mm). Make written note of the disc sizes in all the cam followers. That way you won't have to remove the discs to determine their thickness when it's valve clearance measurement time again.

Turn back to Procedure 22 and complete Steps 12-16.

PROCEDURE 23: CHECK VALVE TIMING (15,000 MILES) AND/OR CHANGE CAMSHAFT DRIVE BELT (TIMING OR SPUR BELT) (30,000). Phase 2. (Not Diesel)

Condition: 15,000 or 30,000 mile maintenance, your timing belt needs to be replaced, referral from Chapter 18.

Tools and materials: Phase 1 tool kit, strobe light, piece of white chalk or white paint and small brush.

Remarks: If you are here to change your drive belt, do Step 5 then jump to Step 14.

Step 1. Clear the Way

This is an awkward job that takes a certain amount of patience. If your car has a carburetor, remove all the air cleaner ducts and the metal elbow on top of the carburetor (10mm wrench). This stuff just gets in the way, and you'll need all the space you can get.

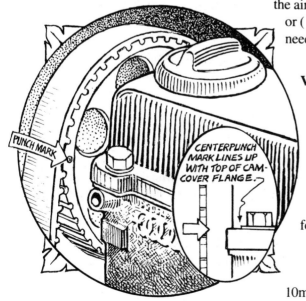

PUNCH MARK

CENTERPUNCH MARK LINES UP WITH TOP OF CAM-COVER FLANGE.

Step 2. Remove Air Injection Pump (Smog Pump) V-Belt (if your model has one)

The pump is suspended on a bracket beneath the alternator. Loosen the long 13mm bolt which holds it in place. Now push the pump toward the engine and slip off the V-belt.

Step 3. Remove Alternator V-Belt

If you have never removed or adjusted this V-belt before, turn to Chapter 8, Procedure 2, Step 3.

Step 4. Remove Belt Guard

The belt guard is on the front of the engine. It's got four 10mm bolts holding it in place which go through four rubber grommets with metal spacers and washers to absorb vibration. The two 10mm bolts facing you as you look into the engine compartment are easily removed. The other two 10mm bolts are 'round the back, and take a fair bit of arm manipulation to get at. Take all four nuts off the bolts. Cars with air conditioning should leave the bolt passing through the water pump housing in position. Just remove the nut. Put the other three bolts and nuts in a marked Baggie.

If I were to give full instructions on how to get the guard out this book would be longer than the Bible. It's tricky, but it will come. Don't force it or bend the thing to look like a crushed beer can. If it won't come easily, remove the three 10mm bolts from the water pump V-belt pulley. Slide off the pulley and stash it with the bolts. Now thread the drive belt guard out of the engine compartment. Clean it with solvent.

The top part of the belt guard is held by a 6mm allen bolt on the front of the guard. When the top's off two 10mm nuts hold the plastic bottom part onto the crankcase.

Step 5. Align Timing Marks

Turn the steering wheel all the way to the right. Then turn the *crankshaft* sprocket bolt clockwise   (19mm) until the dot on the rear of the camshaft sprocket lines up with the edge of the left side of the camshaft cover. A notch in the crankshaft V-belt should be in line with a dot on the front face of the intermediate shaft sprocket. See the diagram. If you can't see the notch or the dots, clean the sprockets or pulley with solvent until you can. Put a drop of paint or chalk on all three marks. If everything lines up properly, your valves are probably in time. But let's check. Belt changers jump to Step 14.

PUNCH MARK

NOTCH IN PULLEY

WATER PUMP PULLEY

CRANKSHAFT V-BELT PULLEY

INTERMEDIATE SHAFT DRIVE SPROCKET

Step 6. Install Alternator V-Belt (Everybody)

Reinstall the V-belt pulley onto the crankshaft sprocket and torque the allen bolts to 2 mkg (14 ft lbs). Then see Chapter 8, Procedure 2, Step 3, to install the alternator V-belt.

Step 7. Timing

Remove the socket from the crankshaft sprocket bolt. Hook the positive and negative leads of your timing light to the corresponding battery posts. Put the other lead onto the #1 spark plug wire. Make sure the car is in neutral (N), handbrake on, pull the cooling fan plug and start the engine. (Don't get your light leads caught in the V-belts.) Point the end of the light at the notch on the crankshaft pulley and the dot on the intermediate shaft sprocket. The white paint should show the two lining up. If they don't, adjustment is required. Now shine the light at the dot on the rear of the camshaft sprocket. That should line up with the edge of the camshaft cover. We want all three marks to line up. If they don't, turn off the engine and put your 19mm socket back onto the crankshaft bolt.

Step 8. Line 'Em Up

First remove the TDC sensor plug (if you've got one) from the top of the transmission and then unscrew the plastic plug from the TDC hole (Procedure 16, Step 1). Automatics have no plug. Turn the crankshaft bolt (19mm) until the TDC mark (a O stamped on the flywheel or drive plate) lines up with the pointer in the TDC hole. Pull off the distributor cap, remove the rotor and plastic dust cover, then reinstall the rotor.

Step 9. Line 'Em Up Again

When the O mark on the flywheel is aligned with the pointer in the transmission TDC hole, the mark on the sparking end of the rotor should be aligned with the thin line in the top edge of the distributor. It may not be. Likewise, the intermediate shaft, crankshaft pulley and camshaft pulley dots and notches should line up. They don't? They soon will.

If the V-belt is in position, loosen the lock nut (15mm or 17mm) on the drive belt tensioner (the untoothed wheel around which the belt runs). The tensioner will move 'round to slacken the drive belt. Use your hands to pull the belt off the camshaft pulley. Line up the notch and the two dots. It's most important to keep the TDC mark right on the pointer in the transmission. Make sure the camshaft sprocket dot is aligned with the left edge of the camshaft cover. Get the rotor mark lined up with the line on the distributor. If the rotor mark won't quite line up with the distributor line, don't worry. The ignition timing is a bit off and you can correct it later when the valve timing is right.

If you've had the camshaft sprocket off for any reason, be sure you reinstalled it the right way. Remove the oil filler cap and see if the first two lobes on the camshaft are pointing up. If the sprocket is installed backward, the lobes will be pointing down, depressing the cam followers. Get 'em up.

Step 10. Tighten Drive Belt

Hold the top of the belt with both hands and pull it up hard toward the camshaft sprocket. Don't move the notch or dot. If either the crankshaft V-belt pulley (notch) or the intermediate shaft sprocket (dot) moves, let go of the belt and reposition them. Slip the belt around the belt tensioner, then lever it with your fingers onto the camshaft sprocket. Everything line up OK?

Put a crescent wrench on the belt tensioner and a 15mm or 17mm wrench on the tensioner lock nut. Turn the crescent wrench clockwise to put some tension on the drive belt. Hold the belt halfway between the intermediate shaft sprocket and the camshaft sprocket with your finger and thumb. Give the belt a 90° twist (¼ turn). You don't have to be Charles Atlas, but if you can twist it more than 90°, it's too loose (Lautrec). If it's difficult, turn the crescent wrench counterclockwise a bit for more slack. When you can twist it 90° without too much difficulty, the belt tension is right. Tighten the lock nut on the tensioner and torque it to 4.5 mkg (32 ft lbs).

OFFSET IDLER

TENSION ADJUST.

Check DRIVE BELT TENSION. SHOULD TWIST TO 90° BETWEEN SPROCKETS

Step 11. Check Valve Timing Again

Install the distributor dust cover, rotor and cap. Start the engine again and use your timing light to see if all the marks line up properly. They don't? Do the whole thing again. Wait—my friend Joe Corriz showed me a fast way to do this. His method requires very strong fingers or two pairs of hands, and is described in Procedure 17 of Chapter 20.

If everything lined up OK, check the drive belt tension (90° twist) and start the engine again. An engine with a too-tight belt will sound like a coyote with a sore tooth. If you hear the coyote, shut off the engine and slightly loosen the belt tensioner lock nut as you keep a crescent wrench on the tensioner to keep it from moving too far. Let the tensioner move a fraction, then tighten the lock nut. Check the 90° twist and then start the engine and listen. Noise gone?

Step 12. Tidy Up

Remove the alternator V-belt, replace the drive belt guard and reinstall the alternator and smog pump V-belts. Both V-belts need a deflection of 10mm-15mm (3/8-9/16 in). Install the carburetor air cleaner ducts and metal elbow if you removed them.

Sometimes the belt will rub on the drive belt guard if the belt isn't installed straight. Loosen the 4 bolts and get the guard away from the belt. Tighten the bolts. Better?

Step 13. Check Ignition Timing

Go to Procedure 16 and check the ignition timing. It's important if you want the car to run properly.

Step 14. Belt Changers Welcome

Remove the three 6mm allen bolts which hold the V-belt pulley onto the crankshaft. Slide the pulley off and clean it. Now loosen the lock nut (15mm or 17mm) on the drive belt tensioner—that's the untoothed wheel on which the drive belt rides. The tensioner will move around as you loosen the nut to allow you to remove the drive belt. Pull the belt off, check that the marks line up (Step 5), then install a new belt.

Now do Steps 7 through 13 and complete the belt installation, OK?

PROCEDURE 24: REPLACE CONDENSER (30,000 MILES). Phase 1.

Step 1. Pre-1979 Models (1979 and on, Step 2)

The condenser is the small silver cylinder attached vertically to the side of the distributor. Remove the distributor cap, rotor and dust cover and pull the little wire off the condenser terminal inside the distributor body. To get the condenser off, remove the screw holding the condenser to the distributor body. There is a long, thin wire (usually green) from the coil to a spade connection next to the condenser. Pull the spade connection from the condenser terminal and tuck the wire out of the way.

Work the condenser out from the distributor. The plastic part which presses through a hole in the distributor may be stuck, so pull a little harder.

Position your new condenser on the side of the distributor, and reinstall the screw. Attach the long thin wire from the coil onto the spade terminal next to the condenser, then attach the little wire from the points onto the condenser terminal inside the distributor. Everything attached?

Step 2. 1979 Models and On

The condenser is the small cylinder attached to the back of the distributor. Pull the thin white wire running from the plastic gizmo on the side of the distributor. Pull the thin green wire from the gizmo which goes to the coil. Use the side of a thin screwdriver blade, or a right-angle screwdriver to remove the screw holding the condenser in place. Pull the condenser away from the distributor.

You may find it impossible to replace the condenser with the distributor in place. This is especially true with U.S. Rabbits. Scratch, draw or paint a line from the base of the distributor to the crankcase. When you reinstall the distributor just line up the lines. No hassle.

Position your new condenser on the distributor and carefully replace the securing screw. Install the distributor if you removed it (see Procedure 26, Step 6). Connect the spade connctor on the end of the white wire back onto the plastic gizmo on the distributor. Now, stick the green wire from the coil onto that gizmo.

Look inside the distributor again. Push the spade connector on the end of the small wire attached to the points onto the condenser terminal sticking through the distributor. Everything attached? If you did this procedure as part of your 30,000 mile tune-up, go back to Procedure 14, Step 8 and continue. Check your ignition timing if you removed the distributor, Procedure 16.

PROCEDURE 25: CHANGE AUTOMATIC TRANSMISSION FLUID. Phase 1.

Condition: 30,000 mile maintenance, the automatic transmission has been overworked (towing a trailer, lots of driving in the mountains, etc.) or fluid has leaked out after engine/transmission work.

Tools and materials: Phase 1 tool kit, solvent, lint-free rags, 3.0 liters (3.2 U.S. quarts, 2.6 Imperial quarts) automatic transmission fluid labeled DEXRON^R, catch pan, new transmission pan gasket, flexible filler hose with funnel—buy one from a discount store.

Remarks: Drive the car a few miles to warm up the transmission fluid before draining it.

Step 1. Drain Fluid

Slide your catch pan under the automatic transmission fluid (ATF) pan.

Some transmissions have drain plugs, others don't. If you are fortunate enough to have a plug, remove it and drain the fluid (17mm wrench).

If you don't have a drain plug, remove the two *rear* 13mm bolts holding the ATF pan to the bottom of the transmission. Now *loosen*—but don't completely remove—the two *front* 13mm bolts. Carefully lower the back of the ATF pan and drain the fluid into the catch pan.

In both cases, twiddle your thumbs until the drips have almost stopped. Then remove the two front bolts, the ATF pan and its gasket.

Step 2. Examine Strainer and Replace or Clean It

Early filter type strainers cannot be cleaned. Check the filter and replace it if you find any dirt or crud. Later models have a removable screen type strainer that can be cleaned with solvent. For cleaning or replacement, remove the center screw holding either type of filter in position. Be sure to install the screw before reinstalling the ATF pan.

Step 3. Clean ATF Pan

Use solvent to scrub the pan inside and out. Dry it with lint-free rags or let it air dry.

Step 4. Replace Gasket

Install the new gasket on top of the ATF pan without gasket cement.

Step 5. Install ATF Pan

Carefully reinstall ATF pan onto the bottom of the transmission and screw in the four 13mm bolts. Make sure the gasket stays in position. Tighten the bolts by hand, then diagonally torque them (Chapter 20, Procedure 7) to 2.0 mkg (14 ft lbs). If your transmission has a drain plug, reinstall the plug in the base of the pan. Torque it to 2.0 mkg (14 ft lbs). Tightening the bolts to more than 2.0 mkg (14 ft lbs) will warp the pan and make a fluid-tight seal impossible.

Step 6. Refill Transmission Fluid

Remove the dipstick from its tube on the right side of the transmission and wipe it clean. Stick the fluid filler hose into the dipstick/filler tube on the right rear of the transmission and pour in 3.0 liters (3.2 U.S. qts) of automatic transmission fluid. Reinstall the dipstick, start the engine and let it idle in neutral with the handbrake on. Remove the ATF dipstick and check the level of the fluid. If necessary, add small amounts until the level is up to the mark.

When the level is correct, keep the engine running and kneel to check the transmission pan for leaks. If there's a leak, either you forgot to replace the gasket, you put your new gasket in wrong, or the pan bolts aren't tight.

In order to fix a leak you'll have to go through the whole procedure again if you find that the pan bolts are tight. Clean the catch pan carefully, so that when you drain the ATF, it can be reused. If the fluid becomes contaminated in any way, toss it out and replace with fresh stuff.

Step 7. Clean Up

Pour your used ATF into a plastic screw-top bottle and properly discard it. If it has to lie around until trash day, label the container **POISON** and put it in a safe place, not on the kitchen table.

PROCEDURE 26: CHECK DISTRIBUTOR. Phase 2.

Condition: The advance/retard mechanism doesn't work—the distributor shaft is broken/worn or you've removed it for some reason; distributor springs are shot (mechanical) or advance/retard mechanism is faulty (vacuum).

Tools and materials: Phase 1 tool kit, new advance/retard canister, paper distributor gasket if required.

Remarks: A faulty advance/retard canister or worn/loose springs will cause the car to backfire like hell or make it difficult to start and idle. Check it by doing Procedure 16, Step 5. If you know that the plastic vacuum lines are good, we have to check the internal workings.

Step 1. Check Springs

Remove the distributor cap, rotor and dust cover, then stick the rotor back on and turn it to the right. The shaft will turn slightly but should spring back to its original position as soon as you release the rotor. If it doesn't, either the springs in the depths of the distributor are shot, or there's junk down there. Continue with this Procedure and check if the circlip is loose and jamming the works. If it isn't, it's the springs and we can't fix them. They're set very carefully to comply with emission control standards. Get VW to check/replace the springs. If the distributor is shot, buy a new or used one the same as yours.

Step 2. Mark Vacuum Lines

Mark the one or two plastic vacuum advance/retard lines going to the vacuum canister with tape. Put a #1 on a piece of tape and stick it to one line, and another #1 on the corresponding connection on the vacuum canister. Likewise a #2, etc.

Step 3. Examine the Interior

Opposite the points you'll see an arm passing through a slot in the side of the distributor into the back of the vacuum advance/retard canister. There should be a small vertical pin on the strangely shaped metal plate to which the arm is secured by a small circlip. The points are also screwed onto this plate. When vacuum is present in the canister the plate moves, altering the position of the points to advance the spark.

If the circlip isn't in place, has the canister arm come off the pin? The circlip is probably inside the guts somewhere. Has the pin broken off the plate? If so, the circlip is probably still in place on the pin, but you'll have to get a new (or used) distributor. Should the circlip just be missing, the distributor has to be removed to find the clip. If all is in place, go to Step 7 and replace the vacuum canister.

If you are remarkably lucky, the arm is just off the pin and you found the circlip without removing the distributor, so put the arm back onto the pin. Examine the circlip; if it looks OK, put it back on and squeeze the ends together with needle-nosed pliers. Replace the dust cover, rotor and cap, and retime the engine (Procedure 16). If you weren't so lucky, continue.

Step 4. Remove Distributor

First remove the thin green wire from the plastic gizmo or condenser on the side of the distributor. Now paint, draw or scratch a line from the base of the distributor to the crankcase. Thus, when you reinstall the distributor, line up the marks. Reinstall the rotor and turn the engine over with a 19mm socket on the crankshaft pulley bolt. Line up the sparking end of the rotor with the line on the top edge of the distributor. Turn to Procedure 16 and do Step 2. Unscrew the 13mm bolt holding the metal clip around the distributor base. Pull off the clip and the distributor. Be careful with the thin paper gasket between the distributor and engine.

Step 5. Find Circlip

Turn the distributor upside down and shake. Anything rattling down there? If so, continue shaking until the clip falls out. Stick the clip (or a new one) onto the pin and close the ends with needle-nosed pliers.

Step 6. Install Distributor

Turn the rotor until its tip lines up with the mark on the top edge of the distributor. Check the TDC mark in the transmission hole and then examine the paper gasket and O ring around the distributor for tears. If either the ring or gasket is worn/broken, replace. Install the distributor onto the crankcase after lining up the scratch marks and making sure the rotor doesn't move. Install the metal clip with the 13mm bolt and tighten it.

CHAPTER 11

FUEL AND AIR DO MIX—PART 1

✒ The Carburetor ✒

The carburetor is no more than a container designed to store enough gasoline for the engine's immediate use. It mixes this gasoline with air and squirts it through tiny holes (jets). The piston then pulls the mixture through the carburetor and into the cylinders to be compressed and ignited.

Fuel injection, another method used to get fuel and air into the cylinder, is the subject of the next chapter.

Rabbits shipped to the U.S. in 1975 and '76 and Sciroccos shipped from 1975 to June of '76 are carbureted. These cars have a Zenith 2B2 carburetor which is what this chapter is all about. If your bunny is a Bronze Edition or "stripped" or "basic" version then it has a Solex carburetor which is not covered here. Sorry. Please read the rundown on chokes at the end of this chapter.

The carburetor, or carb for short, is a very delicate and sensitive instrument which gets lots of abuse. For example, a dirty air filter won't catch the crud from incoming air and these particles end up inside the carb. Likewise a dirty gas filter will cause the carb to clog up. Poor quality gasoline and a badly tuned engine also contribute to carburetor wear and tear.

To have a carburetor rebuilt by experts is expensive and not always satisfactory. You and I can do it with relaxed determination and attention to detail. It'll take at least a full day counting breaks for the restoration of sanity. Do not try to rebuild the thing the night before a trip along the Alcan Highway. Wait until you have peace and quiet . . . and time. The work is really more like fine watch repair than car repair, and you'll need an uncluttered, clean place in which to work.

If you're modifying the carb to the latest specs, then the catalytic converter needs to be removed (*not* California). That job takes about two hours. Refer to the exploded carburetor diagram to get an overview of the names and placement of the components. No need to become intimate, but some familiarity with the parts will be helpful when the thing's in pieces.

Before taking the extraordinary step of ripping the carb out by its roots, make sure the engine is in the best possible tune by running through the Tune-up Procedure in Chapter 10. If that doesn't make the engine run properly, come back here and we'll rebuild the carb.

PROCEDURE 1: CARBURETOR REMOVAL. Phase 1.

Condition: The engine refuses to run properly after a complete tune-up, you have crud in the gas tank and therefore also in the carburetor or you are modifying the carburetor to post-1975 VW specifications.

Tools and materials: Phase 1 tool kit, some rags, solvent, a stiff brush, an old tooth brush, notebook and pencil, indelible pen and masking tape.

Remarks: If you disassemble the carburetor and find it full of crud/water, examine the inside of the gas tank for rust, etc. Chapter 12, Procedure 2, Step 3. The Procedure for removing the tank is in the same Chapter.

You may decide to install a professionally rebuilt carburetor instead of doing the rebuild yourself. These are sometimes available from foreign auto parts stores. VW doesn't sell them—nor do they plan to. If you manage to find one, be sure the rebuilt carburetor carries the same part number as your old one. There's a metal tag with the carburetor part number stamped on it attached by one of the four bolts securing the top part of the carburetor to the middle part.

Before installing a rebuilt carburetor, do Procedure 4 to get the various adjustments correct. Install a new gas filter in your gas line when the carburetor is back on, and check the air filter, Chapter 10, Procedure 10, before you start the engine.

You'll spill a little gas during the removal Procedure so take note of the credo—**ALWAYS DISCONNECT THE BATTERY GROUND STRAP BEFORE STARTING CARBURETOR WORK.** Got it? Keep your fire extinguisher close by and keep smokers busy elsewhere making snacks. Read the tool and material list in Procedures 2 and 3 if you're doing the rebuild yourself.

The Procedure for removing the carburetor is the same for 1975 and 1976 models.

If your engine compartment is dirty, nasty, greasy and filthy, clean it all out. You don't want to get any junk into the carburetor or the intake manifold when the carburetor is off. I recommend a crud cleaner called Gunk, which you buy in concentrated form. Read the mixing instructions on the side of the bottle. Use a stiff brush to coat everything under the hood except the distributor and alternator. Let things soak in the juice for about 20 minutes.

Start the engine and then hose everything off with water. Try not to aim jets of water directly at the distributor cap or alternator. Let the engine run until it's all dry. You now have a spanking clean engine compartment. Before you begin, mark all the thin plastic vacuum hoses which go to and from the carburetor. Mark all of them with masking tape and an indelible pencil. Even better, draw yourself a diagram showing where everything goes. This is important! It's impossible for me to describe what goes where, but this is something you can (and must) do yourself. Refer to the hose layout diagram before removing anything to see if the hoses are connected correctly. Check the hose diagram on the underside of your hood. It's especially important to get the vacuum advance connection correct. This is the one that angles up next to the electric idle jet. Don't forget to mark the hose going from a connection on the rear of the carburetor to the anti-backfire valve close to the rear of the right fender. With everything tagged and marked; double, triple and quadruple checked so you're sure it's marked correctly, you can begin to remove the carburetor.

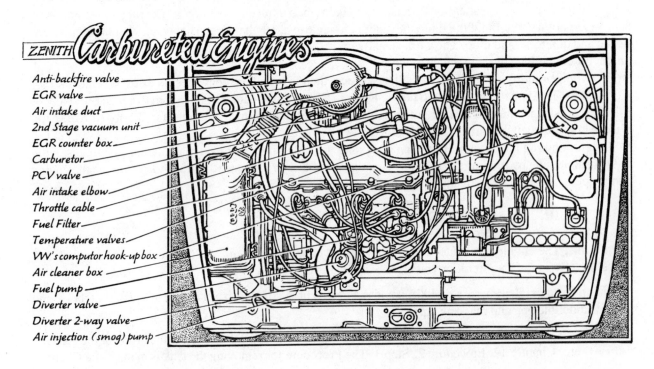

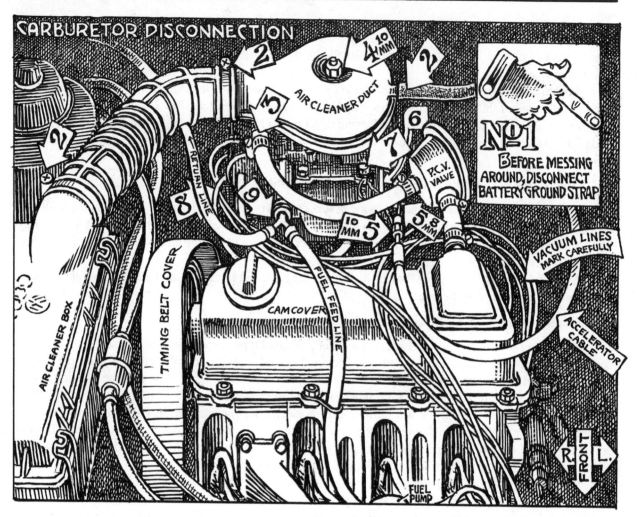

Remember **FRONT** is front of the car, and **LEFT** is the driver's side, in America.

Step 1. Disconnect Battery Ground Strap (10mm Wrench)

Tuck the strap out of the way so it doesn't accidentally touch the positive battery post. A stray spark may more than light up your life.

Step 2. Free Hoses

Remove the braided hose which goes from the metal air intake elbow on the top of the carb to the activated charcoal filter, a black container behind the firewall. Next use your phillips screwdriver to loosen the clamps on both ends of the large hose going from that air intake elbow to the air filter by the right fender. With the clamps loosened, pull off the hose and put it somewhere safe.

Step 3. Free Positive Crankcase Ventilation (PCV) Valve Hose

Use either a phillips or regular screwdriver to free the 25mm (1 in) hose running from the air intake elbow to the camshaft cover, at the cam cover end.

Step 4. Remove Air Intake Elbow

Remove the 10mm nut holding the metal elbow to the top of the carb. Then pull the elbow off and remove the rubber ring which goes between the elbow and the carburetor. Make a note to buy a new ring if it's broken or soaked with oil. Stash the ring and elbow.

Step 5. Disconnect Accelerator Cable (Standard Transmission)

Loosen the 8mm nut holding the end of the accelerator cable to the throttle linkage on the carburetor. Pull

Step 5. (Cont'd.)

the accelerator cable all the way out from the small barrel into which that 8mm nut screws. Stash the nut and barrel in a marked Baggie.

Automatic Transmission: See how the accelerator cable passes through the throttle linkage on the carb? On the end of the cable is a longish spring held by a small clip and washer. Use needle nosed pliers to remove the pin—be careful the washer and spring don't fly off into the blue yonder. Place the washer, spring and clip in a marked Baggie. If you weakened or destroyed the clip as you wrestled it off, make a note to buy a new one.

Step 6. Remove Cable Bracket and Dashpot Assembly

Keep the accelerator cable attached to the bracket so it won't need adjustment when you reinstall your newly rebuilt carburetor. Simply remove the three screws holding the cable bracket on the carburetor body. This bracket also holds a metal canister with two arms coming out of it—the dashpot. Unscrew the dashpot from the bracket. Some 1975 versions don't have a dashpot.

When the bracket is free from the car, tuck it and the cable out of the way and put the three screws back into the carb body for safekeeping.

Step 7. Disconnect Electrical Connections

Depending on whether your car has screw-on or push/pull type connections, either use a screwdriver to loosen and remove the nut holding the brown electrical ground wires to the carburetor body, or just pull the wires off. Mark the wires 'ground' with the indelible pen on masking tape. Now pull the plastic covered electrical connector from the electric idle cutoff valve and mark it ''idle cutoff valve.''

In addition, there may be a black plastic push-on electrical connector on the back of the vacuum unit bolted to a plate on the choke unloader mechanism. Look carefully and you'll see that the connector has two small ears, one on top and one below. Carefully pry them open with a small screwdriver and pull the connector off. No need to mark it as it can only fit in one place.

Now pull off the one or two wires going to the automatic choke. Mark them 'choke left' and 'choke right' (if there are two), or just 'choke' if there's only one.

Very early and California cars have a microswitch on the side of the carburetor with two electrical connections to it. The carburetor's jet system has been modified eliminating the microswitch, *except* in California where the switch still functions as part of the exhaust emission control system. If you are modifying your carburetor to present Environmental Protection Agency (EPA) emission standards, you can eliminate the microswitch—*except in California*. To do so, pull the two electrical connections off the switch and cut the metal connectors from the end of the wires. Use plastic electrical tape to individually insulate the ends of the wires, then bind them together with more tape. California people—pull the connections off the switch and mark them 'Microswitch Left' and 'Microswitch Right.'

Step 8. Remove Automatic Choke

The automatic choke is held to the right side of the carburetor body by three small screws. These screws go through a brass colored retaining ring which holds the choke body to the choke unloader mechanism which is bolted to the carburetor body. When you remove these three little screws, remember they are easy to drop and difficult to find. Hold your small magnet (if you've got one) right next to the screw as you unscrew it. Thus, if your reactions aren't up to par or the screwdriver slips, the magnet will save you from scratching in the dirt like a hungry hen. So remove the three screws, mark and Baggie them.

Now hold the choke body and **gently** pull it about 25mm (1 in) away from the side of the carburetor. There's a spring inside the choke which may still be connected to a delicate linkage arm inside the choke unloader mechanism. These two should be separated with care. Don't remove the two coolant hoses connected to the bottom of the choke body.

Notice two lines or punch marks on the top of the choke and unloader mechanism. They're there to help you line up the automatic choke when you stick it back in place.

Step 8. (Cont'd.)

While we're talking about chokes, if your vehicle is pre-1976, you may want to install the new style automatic choke which has a temperature switch in it. There's a kit for this and it's VW Part #055 198 580. You can, however, buy a whole new choke mechanism with the automatic choke temperature switch already installed.

In 1976, the carburetor was modified slightly to improve the emission control system. The catalytic converter was removed and some jets were changed inside the carburetor. This modification was not done in California. If you have less than 50,000 miles on your car, VW will do this modification under warranty. Beyond that mileage you're on your own unless you can talk sweetly to your service manager. Complain about a severe rattle from the catalytic converter and experiencing surging and hesitation while driving. Be insistent! No go? Chapter 13 tells how to remove the catalytic converter and this Chapter explains the jet changes. You *must* have VW check the carbon monoxide (CO) content of the exhaust gas after you do the modification. The law, my friends.

Also included in the warranty program was a change to strengthen the secondary throttle valve vacuum unit. The linkage on the unit was weak and broke easily; not an ideal situation. So while you're fiddling with your carb you might want to replace the linkage. Check that out with VW, too.

Step 9. Disconnect Fuel Line

The braided fuel line comes up from the fuel pump bolted to the bottom left side of the crankcase and forms a Y just in front of the carburetor. There, one arm of the Y goes to the carburetor fuel intake while the other is the return line to the tank. Remove the line at the carburetor by loosening the clamp and pulling the fuel line off. Plug the end of the fuel line with a pencil or punch and mark the hose with a piece of tape reading ''to carburetor.''

Step 10. Remove Carburetor

Loosen the four 10mm brass colored bolts inside the top of the carburetor. The two bolts closest to the firewall won't come all the way out with the carb on the manifold. Just loosen them for now and remove them after you've pulled the carburetor from the intake manifold.

When you've got the carb out, set it down in a safe spot. Put some clean rags into the now exposed hole in the intake manifold. Check the condition of the rubber plate on which the carburetor sits. It's held in place by four 10mm nuts and remains on the intake manifold. If it's worn, nicked, or scratched, make a note on your parts list to buy a replacement. Clean all four brass bolts and washers and stash them in a marked Baggie. With the carb off, take a break and read through the rest of the chapter before deciding whether to rebuild the carb yourself or have it done. If you decide to tackle the job yourself, here's how:

PROCEDURE 2: REBUILT AND/OR MODIFY ZENITH 32/2B2 CARBURETOR. Phase 2.

Condition: The carburetor needs to be rebuilt or modified to 1976 specifications,

Tools and materials: Phase 2 tool kit, can of carburetor spray cleaner, carburetor cleaner in a container big enough to immerse carburetor, rebuild kit, good quality pipe cleaners, lint-free rags, paper and pencil.

Now if your carburetor rebuild includes the update or modification, you will have to change two or three existing jets for different sizes. Volkswagen will sell you the whole 'update package,' including a new accelerator pump discharge nozzle, accelerator pump spring, EGR caps, jets and the gasket which goes between the throttle plate and carburetor body. Check your rebuild kit to see what comes with it.

Borrow a kid's bike pump with a needle attachment used to inflate footballs, or find a way to get to the local garage and use their air lines.

Remarks: Someone may have already replaced your carb's primary and secondary needles with a special kit. This kit (Part #055 129 201 REP) was supplied as a replacement for needles which had the bad habit of sticking. The replacement needles have three ridges equally spaced down the sides and fit into special housings pushed into the carburetor. If you discover that your needles are the ridged type, check that the ends

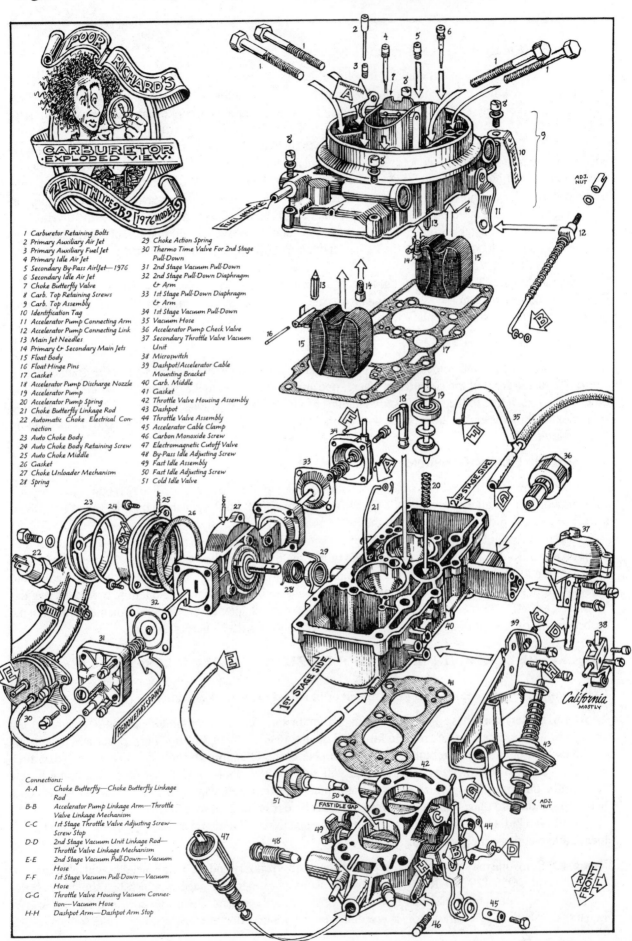

POOR RICHARD'S
CARBURETOR · EXPLODED · VIEW
ZENITH TYPE 2B2 1976 MODEL

1 Carburetor Retaining Bolts
2 Primary Auxiliary Air Jet
3 Primary Auxiliary Fuel Jet
4 Primary Idle Air Jet
5 Secondary By-Pass Air Jet—1976
6 Secondary Idle Air Jet
7 Choke Butterfly Valve
8 Carb. Top Retaining Screws
9 Carb. Top Assembly
10 Identification Tag
11 Accelerator Pump Connecting Arm
12 Accelerator Pump Connecting Link
13 Main Jet Needles
14 Primary & Secondary Main Jets
15 Float Body
16 Float Hinge Pins
17 Gasket
18 Accelerator Pump Discharge Nozzle
19 Accelerator Pump
20 Accelerator Pump Spring
21 Choke Butterfly Linkage Rod
22 Automatic Choke Electrical Connection
23 Auto Choke Body
24 Auto Choke Body Retaining Screw
25 Auto Choke Middle
26 Gasket
27 Choke Unloader Mechanism
28 Spring

29 Choke Action Spring
30 Thermo Time Valve For 2nd Stage Pull-Down
31 2nd Stage Vacuum Pull-Down
32 2nd Stage Pull-Down Diaphragm & Arm
33 1st Stage Pull-Down Diaphragm & Arm
34 1st Stage Vacuum Pull-Down
35 Vacuum Hose
36 Accelerator Pump Check Valve
37 Secondary Throttle Valve Vacuum Unit
38 Microswitch
39 Dashpot/Accelerator Cable Mounting Bracket
40 Carb. Middle
41 Gasket
42 Throttle Valve Housing Assembly
43 Dashpot
44 Throttle Valve Assembly
45 Accelerator Cable Clamp
46 Carbon Monoxide Screw
47 Electromagnetic Cutoff Valve
48 By-Pass Idle Adjusting Screw
49 Fast Idle Assembly
50 Fast Idle Adjusting Screw
51 Cold Idle Valve

Connections:
A-A   Choke Butterfly—Choke Butterfly Linkage Rod
B-B   Accelerator Pump Linkage Arm—Throttle Valve Linkage Mechanism
C-C   1st Stage Throttle Valve Adjusting Screw—Screw Stop
D-D   2nd Stage Vacuum Unit Linkage Rod—Throttle Valve Linkage Mechanism
E-E   2nd Stage Vacuum Pull-Down—Vacuum Hose
F-F   1st Stage Vacuum Pull-Down—Vacuum Hose
G-G   Throttle Valve Housing Vacuum Connection—Vacuum Hose
H-H   Dashpot Arm—Dashpot Arm Stop

are still sharp in Step 8. If you find them to be blunt, buy the above mentioned kit from VW because any other needle won't fit your carburetor.

When you're down at VW buy two replacement steel needle valves (Part #055 129 201 B) and a new type accelerator pump connecting rod spring (Part #055 129 143). You'll also need a new type accelerator pump discharge nozzle with two holes *unless* you're going to eliminate the catalytic converter. The parts person will know what you need.

If you don't live in California, buy a restricted orifice gasket to go between the EGR valve and the intake manifold. If you live in California, your orifice is already restricted.

More than anything else, you must have a clean work place. Clean your hands often and use only lint-free rags or good quality paper towels. As far as the Zenith carburetor is concerned, cleanliness is about equal to godliness.

Step 1. Inspection

Examine the carburetor in good light for cracks in the aluminum body. Check for cracks in the vacuum lines (see exploded diagram) and wear at the linkages. Take your time! If you discover that the first stage bowl is cracked after having sweated over it for an hour, you'll just have to throw the whole carb away and buy another. That's a drag.

Step 2. Remove Plate—1975 Only

Remove the two screws and a flattened triangular plate from the top right of the carburetor if it's present. Clean, mark and Baggie.

Step 3.   Mark First and Second Stage Carburetor Sides—All Models

Scratch on the *outside* of the carburetor with a sharpened knitting needle or similar tool to identify the first stage and second stage sides (also known as primary and secondary). It's important to know which is which because I refer to the first and second stage parts of the carburetor throughout this Procedure. It's the only way to differentiate between them.

Hold the carburetor in your hand; the *second* stage is the side to which the accelerator pump check valve is attached (see diagram). Scratch a '2' on the outside of the float bowl above the check valve. On the opposite side, scratch a '1.' Mark the top of your work bench 'first stage side' and 'second stage side' and keep all the pertinent parts in their respective places.

Look again at Peter's exploded view to familiarize yourself with the parts and their names.

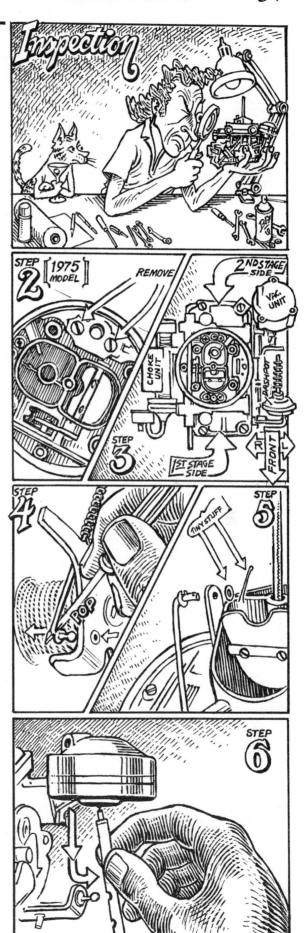

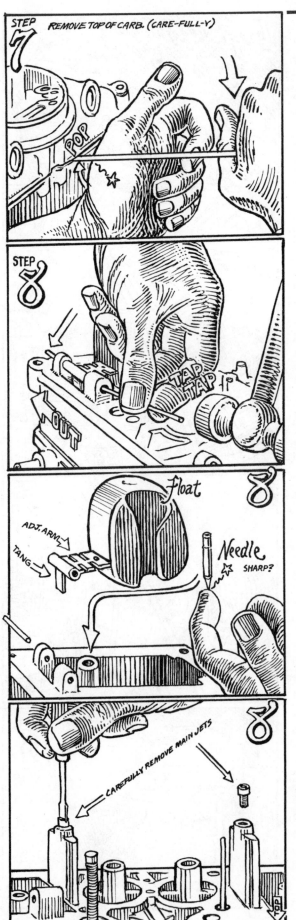

Step 4. Remove Accelerator Pump Linkage

On the left side of the carburetor (not the choke side) notice a metal rod attached to a lever. This rod has a spring around it and the end of the rod turns 90° (¼ turn) and goes into a part of the throttle linkage. Use a screwdriver to pry the bent end of this rod out of the little rubber bushing in the linkage. Leave the rubber bushing in place.

Step 5. Remove Choke Linkage

Look at the top of the carburetor; sticking up on the right side is a small rod linked to a butterfly valve at the top front of the carburetor. If you look very carefully, you'll see a small cotter pin or tiny circlip at the connection between the rod and the butterfly valve. Hold your magnet next to the cotter pin or clip and with tiny needle nose pliers or a small screwdriver, remove the clip or pin. Then remove the washer. Now pull the rod sideways to free it from the choke linkage. Inside the linkage is a tiny plastic bushing. Remove the bushing and place all these parts in a Baggie marked "choke linkage."

Step 6. Remove Rod from Secondary Throttle Valve Vacuum Unit

The rod is attached to the throttle linkage by a ball socket spring mechanism. Pull the brass rod down and away from the top of the vacuum unit and then to the right. It will pop off, leaving a ball attached to the linkage.

While you're here, check the ball for flat spots or hairline cracks. Also check that the spring inside the rod is not broken. Check the hole on the rod where the ball fits and make sure it's not elongated. If it is, make a note to buy a new rod. On early models, both the rod and ball on the linkage are often worn or broken. If so, replace them both.

Step 7. Remove Carburetor Top

The top of the carburetor is secured to the middle part by four slot-headed bolts. One bolt has one or more metal tags attached to it. Another may have an electrical ground connection. Remove the four bolts, mark and Baggie. Do not lose any of the tags. The numbers on the tag are necessary for ordering parts.

With the bolts off, pop off the carburetor top. If it doesn't come easily, use the heel of one hand as a fulcrum and a screwdriver in the other hand to lever the top off. Do not use the vacuum unit or choke housing as a leverage point. If the top still doesn't budge, tap it gently with a screwdriver handle or small rubber mallet.

This carburetor is aluminum and fairly delicate so resist the urge to pound.

When the top starts to loosen, the gasket between the top and the middle parts may stick. Don't worry, you're going to replace this gasket. Make sure the gasket doesn't hang on and bend the metal tongues on those two black plastic floats suspended under the top of the carburetor. If necessary, break the gasket with your fingers and gently remove the top of the carburetor. Remove and discard the gasket and lay the top of the carb on your bench. Look at the middle part of the carburetor. How much crud and water has collected in the bottom of the float bowls? If it looks murkier than Lake Erie, check the inside of the gas tank when you've finished this chapter. Chapter 12, Procedure 2, Step 3.

Step 8. Remove Floats, Needles and First and Second Stage Main Jets

Turn the top of the carburetor upside down on your sanitary work area. The hinged black plastic floats maintain the correct level of gasoline in the float bowls in the middle of the carb. Their adjustment is extremely critical, so use the utmost care when removing them. It's also vital not to mix up the first stage float with the second stage float. If you do, you'll spend hours trying to adjust your carburetor. My friend Ron, the Carburetor King, says mixing them up is a very common error, even with experienced carburetor rebuilders.

Do not scratch on the floats! They are attached by small pins through the ends of the hinges. Tap the pins from the inside with a thin nail, darning needle or something of that ilk to remove them. When the pins are halfway out, remove them with your fingers, or needle nosed pliers. Gently take off the floats and place them on their respective sides of your work area.

With the floats removed, you'll see the ends of two small cylinders sticking out of the carb body. These are the float needles. Their up and down action is regulated by the metal tongues on the plastic floats. The needles will slide out as you turn the top of the carb right side up. You will be replacing these needles with new steel ones bought in addition to the rebuild kit.

Turn the top of the carburetor upside down again. You'll see two brass colored slotted screws in the center of the two pillars, one on the first stage side and the other on the second. These screws are the primary main jet and the secondary main jet. Carefully remove them with a screwdriver. If, while removing any of the jets your screwdriver slips and messes up the slot in the top of the jet, make a note of which jet it is and a reminder to buy a new one.

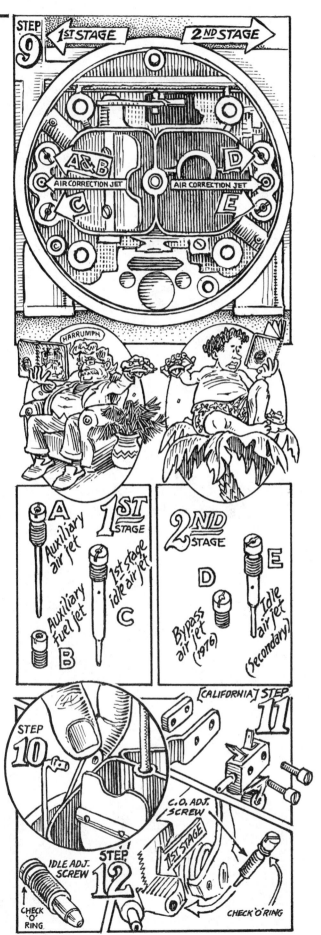

Step 9. Remove Fuel and Air Jets from Top of Carburetor

Hold the carburetor right side up and look into the mouth. You'll see six jets bunched in two groups of three. A 1975 carb has a hole on the second stage side toward the left where you'd expect to find a jet. There's nothing there. Don't worry, that's as it should be. Remember this when you put it back together. The '76 version has a jet in that spot.

Use your screwdriver to carefully remove the fuel and air jets. Place the jets on a sheet of paper divided into first and second stage sides and write underneath them what they are and where they came from. If you have a disaster like the cat chasing Erica's hamster across the table, don't panic; refer to the exploded diagram. When you've got the top three or four jets out, stick your thin screwdriver down the left side of the first stage where you removed the long auxiliary air jet (See diagram). Locate a slot in the top of yet another jet lurking in the hole. It's the primary auxiliary fuel jet. Loosen it completely, turn the carburetor top upside down, and let it fall into your palm. Place it on the first stage side of your paper.

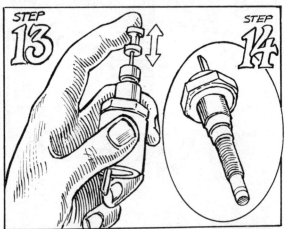

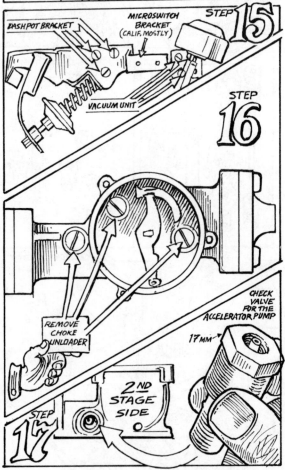

Step 10. Check Choke Butterfly

Look at the top of the carburetor and carefully check the pivot point of the butterfly on the first stage side. Use your fingers to move the arm connected to the hinge on the butterfly. Make sure it opens and closes smoothly. Check for metal burrs, loose pieces of metal, twigs, etc., stuck to the underside of the choke butterfly. If all's in order, place the top part of the carb in the large container, filled with about 15cm (6 in) of carb cleaner and let it relax and soak. Need to relax too? Do so.

Step 11. Remove Microswitch—California Cars and some '75 Models

The microswitch is just in front of the vacuum unit second stage on the right side of the carburetor. It's attached to the throttle linkage by two slot-headed screws. Remove the screws, pull off the microswitch, mark and Baggie it.

Step 12. Remove CO Screw and Air Mixture Screws

The CO adjustment screw goes into the base of the carb (the throttle plate) on the left toward the first stage side. You need a thin screwdriver to remove it and it's easiest to reach if you pivot the throttle linkage toward the rear of the carburetor. Unscrew the CO screw all the way and put it on your work area. On the right side of the carburetor directly opposite the CO screw is the idle adjustment screw. Use a larger screwdriver to remove it. Check the condition of the rubber O rings on the CO and idle adjustment screws. If they're nicked or worn, make a note to replace them. Your kit should include new rings. Mark and stash the two screws in separate Baggies.

Step 13. Remove Electric Idle Cut-off Valve

This valve is located in the base of the carburetor (the throttle plate) on the first stage side. Put your 17mm/wrench on the machined 'nut' that's an integral part of the valve just in front of the cylindrical part. Carefully loosen and screw out the valve.

Check the operation of the valve by holding the protruding shaft and pushing it in and out to see that it moves about 6mm (¼ in) without undue resistance. It's best checked by returning to the car, reconnecting the battery ground strap, then reconnecting the marked plastic covered electrical connector to the electric idle cut-off valve. The shaft should move in and out as Friend turns the ignition to ON and then off. There should be an audible click when this operation takes place. If it doesn't move and click, you need a new valve. Don't touch the valve against anything metal or you will blow a fuse. If you do, check to see which fuse is gone and replace it immediately. Disconnect the battery ground strap. Mark the electric cutoff valve and Baggie it.

Step 14. Remove Cold Idle Valve

The cold idle valve is located on the throttle plate on the right side of the second stage of the carburetor. You'll need your crescent wrench to remove it. Clean, mark and Baggie.

Step 15. Remove Secondary Throttle Valve Vacuum Unit

Remove the three screws holding the secondary throttle valve vacuum unit on the left side of the second stage of the carburetor. When you've got the vacuum unit off, inspect the rubber seal on its underside for cracks and wear. Also again check the condition of the shaft and internal spring for breaks. Clean the lot with a rag dipped in solvent (don't completely immerse it; you'll destroy the rubber), mark and Baggie.

Step 16. Remove Choke Unloader Mechanism

The choke unloader mechanism is attached to the right side of the carburetor. You'll recall having removed the automatic choke housing from this mechanism when you removed the carburetor from the intake manifold. Looking at the choke unloader mechanism, you'll see three screws, two inside the choke housing and one slightly to the rear. Loosen and remove the three screws, being careful not to damage the automatic choke linkage inside. Before pulling off the choke unloader, look inside the carburetor body and find the shaft coming from the unloader mechanism. This shaft connects to a brass internal linkage on which is attached that small bent rod going upward to the butterfly valve in the top part of the carburetor.

First remove the screw holding the internal linkage to the unloader mechanism. When the screw is out (don't lose it; it's impossible to get a replacement), remove the rubber hose running from the second stage vacuum pull down to the carburetor body. Refer to the diagram once again. Pull off the unloader mechanism, including the first stage vacuum unit pull down on the rear of the choke unloader mechanism and the second stage vacuum unit pull down on the front. Pull out the brass linkage from inside the carburetor and place it and the unloader mechanism in a marked safe place.

Step 17. Remove Accelerator Pump Check Valve

The check valve is screwed into the rear of the carburetor on the second stage side. Remove, clean, mark and Baggie.

Step 18. Remove Accelerator Pump Discharge Nozzle

This is the post sticking out of the top of the carburetor's middle section. It has a small arm sticking out to one side and looks like a miniature version of the olde worlde water pump in the middle of the village green. Its job is to discharge gasoline into the first stage side of the carburetor. It's just pressed into place between those two cylindrical barrels. Use your fingers to lift it out. Examine it carefully. The old type nozzle has one tiny hole drilled into the underside of the arm. The new type has two holes; one in the underside of the arm, the other at the end (see diagram). Keep the old type if you're eliminating the catalytic converter.

Check that the O ring at the bottom of the nozzle is free from cracks and nicks.

Remarks: If for some reason you don't have the new type discharge nozzle in your kit and have to get your carburetor back together pronto, don't panic. Use a fine embroidery needle to make a hole in the end of your

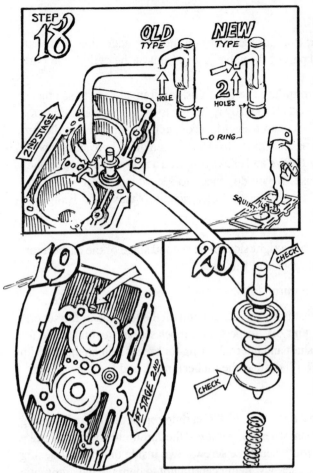

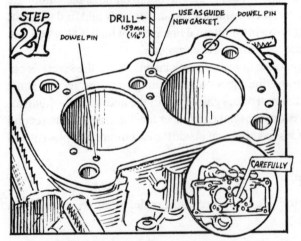

old type nozzle. It's best to get to VW and buy the correct part but . . .

Step 19. Remove Second Stage Bypass Fuel Jet (1976 only)

If you look at the second stage side of the carburetor from the top, you'll notice a small slot-headed jet in the bottom of the second stage float bowl. Remove this jet and add it to your jet stash with the appropriate marking.

Step 20. Remove Accelerator Pump Piston and Spring

The accelerator pump piston is a white plastic gizmo located next to the accelerator pump discharge nozzle. It must be removed with your fingers. After removing it, pull out the delicate spring directly beneath that piston. Clean the piston and carefully inspect the seal around the pump for abrasions and check the metal piston tip. You will replace the felt washer around the pump at reinstallation time. You may have a new pump piston in your rebuild kit. If so, throw the old one away.

Phew! This is a spot tricky, but you're doing great. Keep going...

Step 21.   Separate Carburetor Body from Throttle Plate

Turn the carb upside down and remove the one screw holding the throttle plate to the body. Pop the throttle plate off the body and remove the thick gasket sandwiched between the two. The gasket is held in position by guide pins. These guide pins remain in the body. The gasket should be discarded and replaced with the new one from your kit.

Temporarily put your new gasket in place. Notice the hole with a tiny brass bushing inserted. Does this hole line up with a hole in the bottom of the carburetor? If not, you must drill a new one in the carb. Find a 1.59mm (1/16th in) drill bit and drill completely through the carburetor base. Check the diagram to see if you're doing it correctly.

The newly drilled hole will come into the space where the bottom part of the choke linkage is, just to the right of the float chamber. Be sure not to drill into the float chamber itself. Nice 'n easy.

Step 22. Locate Accelerator Pump Check Ball (Early 1975 Models only)

Return the carburetor body to an upright position and find a thin plastic retaining ring holding the accelerator pump check ball. Don't be distressed if you can't find one. If you do find one, be sure the ball moves freely and has no dirt clogging it up. Clean it with carburetor cleaner and an old toothbrush.

Step 23. Clean It

Place the carburetor body in the container of carburetor cleaner.

Step 24.   Check Throttle Plate

Visually inspect the throttle plate and be sure all the linkages are operating smoothly, especially the linkage which was attached to the secondary throttle valve vacuum unit. Check the operation of the roller on the cam attached to the linkage, and make sure all the springs are in good condition and working.

Also be sure the butterfly valves on the inside of the throttle plate aren't rubbing the sides of the plate. Remove any crud trapped by the valves and tighten the screws holding them onto their shaft. When you're satisfied about its smooth operation, place the throttle plate in the carburetor cleaner. Don't leave your delicate carburetor immersed in the cleaner for more than an hour (or follow the cleaner manufacturer's instructions). If you leave it in too long, the special finish on the inside of the float bowls may be removed. Once it's gone, the finish cannot be restored—bad news. If there is stubborn dirt on the outside of the carb, help the cleaning process along by scrubbing with a used toothbrush. I say *used* toothbrush, don't make the mistake I did when I used a friend's Emu hair all natural soybean-handled brush to clean things. The repercussions lasted ages.

Step 25.   Retrieve Carburetor from Cleaner

Pull the lot out. If you have access to compressed air to blow the thing dry, wonderful. If not, let it air dry, then clean it with a lint-free cloth. Clean all the orifices with quality pipe cleaners. **DO NOT POKE A WIRE OR ANYTHING HARD AND SCRATCHY THROUGH THESE ORIFICES—USE A PIPE CLEANER.** Refrain from using your lungs to blow through the jet holes, gas intake lines, etc., because the moisture in your breath will condense on the inside and later cause rust problems if not removed. If you want to take the body parts to the local garage to blow them out, do it after the next step.

Step 26.   Clean and Identify Jets

Now's the time to be certain you have the correct parts for your carburetor before you begin the rebuild. If you're updating, you must eliminate the microswitch and catalytic converter (*not* California), because you will be changing the sizes of the jets. Jet sizes are stamped on the top of the jet.

Here's the jet sizes for the update: **1975** carburetors require changing both the primary (first stage) and secondary main jets. The new primary main jet is 112.5. The new secondary main jet is 120.

The **1976** version requires the 112.5 primary main jet only. Hopefully, the 120 secondary main jet already was installed. Check it. If it's the old 115, change it to the 120. You also have to change the primary air correction jet from a 130 or 135 (whichever is installed) to a 140.

People who live in Canada and California should check with VW to ask if VW has come out with any new jet sizes since this book was written. VW engineers have been playing around with jet sizes both to meet EPA egulations and maintain reasonable fuel economy. When inquiring, also specify whether you have an automatic or stick shift.

To ensure smooth reassembly, clean each jet individually (including the new ones) in *clean* carburetor cleaner by swishing them around and letting them air dry. Do NOT blow or poke anything through 'em except compressed air.

Break time . . . I'd like to resort to something totally hedonistic. Two weeks in the Bahamas, perhaps. Right . . . break over, time to get it all back together.

PROCEDURE 3: REASSEMBLY

Condition: Carburetor rebuild.

Tools and materials: Same as for Procedure 2

Remarks: Once again, make doubly and triply sure your hands are TV commercial clean and your work area is even cleaner. Those living in tents in the middle of the Mojave Desert had better be more careful than most,

especially if it's windy. Any dirt in the inside of the carburetor will severely impede its function. We should take note from Einstein's equation that $C+D \neq R+M$ (Carburetor plus Dirt is not equal to Rabbit plus Motion).

With your shiny carburetor pieces out of the cleaner, check for accumulated crud in any of the angled parts and passageways of the carb body. Especially check the mating surfaces (this is not a biological term) between the top and middle sections where the thin gasket is placed. If there's still evidence of the original gasket, spray it with gasket remover or carefully remove it with a sharp razor blade. Do not damage the ridge running along the top surface because it helps seal the two halves together. When everything's clean, use your lungs to blow out the carburetor bowl to make sure there's no gasket material left inside. If you have a Sherlock Holmes type magnifying glass, inspect the tiny orifices inside the carburetor for blockages and dirt.

Step 1. Install New Gasket

Make sure you have the new type thick gasket with the additional hole. With the middle of the carburetor body turned upside down, place the gasket on the guide pins. When you're sure it's mated correctly, (and you've drilled the new water drain hole for the choke into the base of the carburetor middle), replace the throttle plate on top of the gasket. No trapped dirt or lint should be between these two parts. When everything is aligned properly, replace the holding screw which goes through the bottom of the throttle plate into the carburetor body. Tighten it. Great.

Step 2. Install CO Screw and Idle Adjustment Screw

Spray some silicone lubricant on the replacement O rings (in your kit) for the idle adjustment screw and

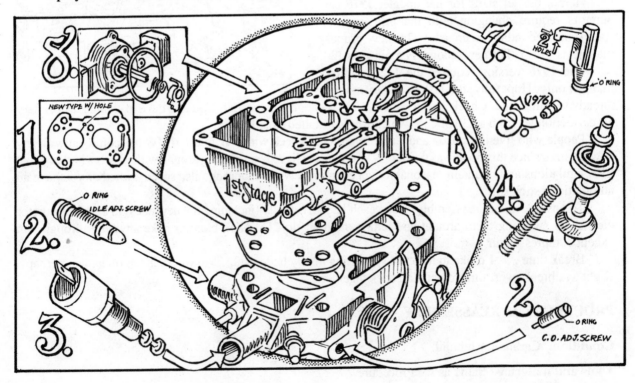

the CO adjustment screw and push the O rings into place on the screws. Turn the two screws into the throttle plate until they hit bottom, then back off four turns on each. This is a temporary adjustment which allows the car to start when the carburetor is reinstalled on the intake manifold.

Step 3. Install Electric Idle Cutoff Valve and Cold Idle Valve

Use your 17mm wrench to install these two items, noting that the idle cutoff valve goes into the throttle plate on the first stage side. Do not overtighten; remember you're putting hard steel into soft aluminum!

Step 4. Install Accelerator Pump Piston and Spring

First install the spring into the hole which accepts the accelerator pump piston. The piston is the white plastic thing with the metal cap and felt washer around it. Use the new one from the rebuild kit if it's included. Replace the felt washer with the new one from the kit. The wider part of the spring goes into the carburetor body first. When you're pushing in the pump piston, make sure the spring is centered around the plastic and is not pushed or trapped to one side. When the piston is centered, push it all the way home with your fingers. A 12 lb hammer is *not* needed.

Find clean machine oil—3-in-1 is fine—and add two or three drops to the felt ring on the shaft of the plastic piston. Be sure you've got the top of the plastic piston flush with the top of the carburetor body. If it's depressed below the surface of the body, it'll stick and fail to give the correct amount of gasoline required for efficient operation.

Step 5. Install Bypass Fuel Jet—'76 only

This is the small jet which fits into the second stage side of the carburetor float bowl. As you install this jet, or any other jet for that matter, be sure you don't get the threads crossed. You must be sure the threads seat properly or you'll have to buy yourself a new carburetor. It would be a pity to waste all your new-found expertise at this stage. When the jet is lined up, screw it in until it's tight. Again, remember that if your screwdriver slips and ruins the slot in the top of the jet, you must replace the jet or the carburetor won't work properly.

Step 6. Inspect Accelerator Pump Check Ball and Plastic Retainer—'75 Models

While the carburetor body was in the bath, the plastic retainer holding the check ball may have dissolved into oblivion. If so, just remove the remnants of the plastic and throw away the ball. It didn't work when they designed it anyway. Clean it if it remained intact.

Step 7. Install Accelerator Pump Discharge Nozzle

Make sure you have the correct type accelerator nozzle for your carb. Replace the O ring around the bottom of the nozzle with a new one from the kit. Then fit the nozzle into the top of the middle carb body. The nozzle arm points into the first stage bowl toward the left corner. Press the discharge nozzle in with your fingers only. Again, refrain from using the 12 lb hammer. Save it for later. The nozzle can only go in one way so make sure it seats correctly.

Step 8. Install Choke Unloader Mechanism

Find that unloader mechanism and make sure it's clean and shiny. Before you install it on the right side of the carburetor, find the choke butterfly valve connecting rod in your parts pile. If you disassembled the small lever which holds the rod, reassemble it with the straightest part of the rod going down into the carburetor middle. The lever arm points *toward* the first stage float bowl. Be sure the circlip is tight around the bottom of the lever, and the bent arms of the lever face the right side of the carburetor body. Look at the exploded diagram and see how it all fits. Check that the fast idle cam on the throttle plate is in the closed position as you slip on the unloader mechanism.

Lower the lever into position on the left side of the carburetor with the choke butterfly connecting rod in place. Now find the two springs which fit between the choke unloader mechanism and the carb body. Again, look at the exploded diagram. The spring with the long arm and the stepped backing plate on it fits against the side of the carburetor body with the arm pointing left. The small spring has a smaller arm on it which should

Step 8. (Cont'd.)

point toward the right. Loosely position these springs over the shaft sticking out of the choke unloader mechanism body. Then push the shaft through the left side of the carburetor body and mate it with the linkage inside. The adjusting screw on the fast idle cam should touch, or be aligned with, the stepped backing plate on the base of the big spring.

When you've got the mechanism in position, install and tighten the screw which goes through the linkage arm into the choke unloader mechanism shaft. The screw is quite long so it's easy to get in. Then install the three screws which go through the choke unloader mechanism into the side of the carburetor.

It's important at this stage to get the spring mechanism working properly. If you look inside the unloader mechanism and gently turn the lever which sticks out toward you, you'll see how it operates the linkage on the inside of the carburetor. When you let go, the lever should spring back into its original position by the action of those two springs behind the unloader mechanism. Check that the spring arms meet at the top, one facing right, one facing left. If it's not right, loosen the screw holding the linkage, withdraw the unloader mechanism, and correctly position the springs. Gently put the partially assembled carburetor body to one side.

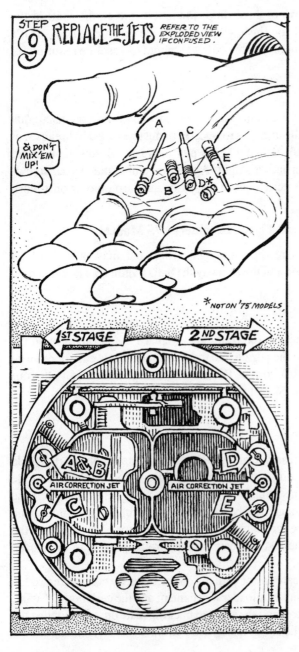

Step 9. Install Jets

Turn the top of the carburetor body upside down. Put the new primary and secondary main jets into the pillars. With the jets in place, tighten them up. Flip the top of the carburetor over and replace the four or five air and idle jets.

Don't forget to install the primary auxiliary fuel jet beneath the primary auxiliary air jet. The auxiliary fuel jet should be positioned first and screwed up tight with your screwdriver. Replace the auxiliary air jet with the new size (127.5) if you're doing the carburetor update.

Step 10. Replace and Adjust Floats

Before you begin this step, make yourself a float height template to the exact, and I mean *exact*, dimensions shown in the diagram. The diagram should

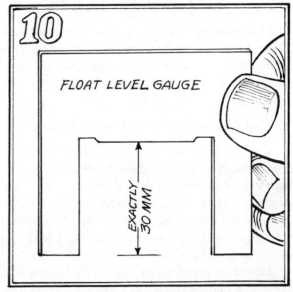

be transferred onto a thin piece of cardboard or aluminum. It's important to get the template height

Step 10. (Cont'd.)

correct and the edges square. Turn the carburetor top upside down and get the first and second stage ends clear in your mind. Find the new steel needles from your kit or parts pile. Do you have the needles with 3 ridges running along them? You bought special kit 055 129 201 REP and 2 needle housings were included in the kit. Use pliers to remove the old housings from the carburetor and install the new ones with the rubber 'O' ring end going in first. Give the O ring a shot of silicone spray before installing the housing. Tap them in with a light hammer.

Squirt a couple of drops of SAE30 oil into the holes which accept the needles. Install the needles with the pointed side *down*, i.e., the point goes into the carburetor top first. They'll thus be beneath the float arms when the floats are reinstalled.

Pick up the floats from the pile. Check them carefully and clean them thoroughly. Reposition one float into its hinge on the carburetor and then slide one metal pin through the hinged part of the float into the other half of the hinge on the carburetor. Make sure the metal pin is flush at each end. Now do the other one.

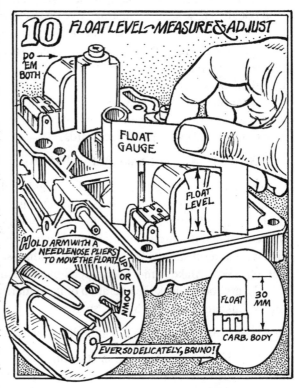

Now find the thin gasket which goes between the carburetor top and middle. Position it on top of the carburetor *middle*, not on the top of the carb. Gently lay the carb top down on the bench with the floats uppermost.

You are now going to check float height. Place your float height template diagonally across the *first stage* float with the two template arms touching the underside of the carb top. The first stage measurement from the bottom of the float to the underside of the carburetor top is 30mm. VW advises a 28mm gap but I think 30mm works much better. If you need to adjust the float height, take a pair of needle-nosed pliers and bend the metal ear on the float arm as close to the hinged part as you can. Make sure you don't twist the ear while you bend it. See diagram. If there's too little clearance, bend the ear *downward*. If there's too much, bend it *upward*. Do *not* adjust the clearance by manipulating the float body. You'll ruin the way the needles seat and the way the float aligns. When the first stage float height is correct, let's do the second stage exactly the same way.

Step 11. Install Accelerator Cable Bracket with Dashpot, Microswitch and Vacuum Unit Second Stage.

Find the three screws which hold the accelerator cable bracket mechanism, including the dashpot, on the side of the carb. Position the bracket, replace the screws and tighten 'em. Then (California cars only) install the microswitch with the two screws on the side of the bracket.

If you have an early '75 vehicle and live outside of California, you can disconnect the microswitch by taping up the ends of the two wires which were connected to the microswitch, then taping them together.

Use the screws to hold the secondary throttle valve vacuum unit on the left side of the carburetor body. When the screws are tight, connect the rod on the secondary throttle valve vacuum unit by pushing up the spring inside the rod with a thin screwdriver. Now pop the rod onto the ball on the throttle linkage, then pull the screwdriver out, allowing the spring to snap down. Be sure that the linkage operates properly—move the throttle linkage and see if everything's smooth. In fact, spray some silicone lubricant on the roller wheel on that throttle plate linkage.

Step 12. Install Carburetor Top

With the thin gasket on the top face of the carburetor middle, replace the top of the carb onto the carb middle. Take care that the upright rod which fastens to the choke butterfly is threaded through the hole in the

Step 12. (Cont'd.)

carburetor top. Also, make sure the accelerator pump connecting rod doesn't hang up on the side of the carburetor middle. Check that the choke butterfly connecting rod is firmly attached by the circlip on the choke unloader diaphragm arm. In other words, be sure you've got everything right before you install the top.

Temporarily install the four long bolts through the carb top to help locate the thin gasket correctly. When all lines up properly, gently position the top on and install and tighten the four outside screws, remembering to put the metal numbered tag and the electrical connector on the screws. The connector goes on the second stage right side and the tags go on the first stage left side. On '75 models, install the flattened triangular plate with its two screws into the right top part of the carb.

Step 13. Attach Accelerator Pump Linkage Rod

This linkage, you'll recall, is the shaft bent at 90° on one end, with a spring attached to its main body. You bought a new style spring from VW—remember? It differs from the old spring by having more windings.

To attach the spring, first remove the brass screw from the threaded end of the rod, and pull the screw through the bushing in the metal arm attached to the carburetor. Now pull off the old spring and replace it with the new. The narrow end of the spring goes on the rod first. Push the arm back through the bushings and install the brass screw.

The rod attaches to a lever on the top right part of the carburetor and snaps into the rubber bushing on the accelerator linkage. The bent arm of that linkage points *away* from the side of the carb, then goes through that rubber bushing. Don't get it backwards.

Step 14. Attach Choke Butterfly Valve

Find the tiny plastic bushing, washer and circlip or cotter pin. There are new ones in the kit. Attach the vertical rod from the choke unloader mechanism to the choke butterfly valve. First place the tiny plastic bushing in the lever on the side of the butterfly valve, push the vertical rod through the bushing, then replace the washer and the circlip or cotter pin. Emergency only: if you lose or break the cotter pin, you can use very fine wire as a substitute. Twist the ends together, secure the rod in the butterfly valve and snip off the ends to get 'em even. Make sure those snipped pieces don't disappear into the carburetor body.

Everybody: check the operation of the butterfly valve to be sure it works. Spray some silicone lubricant on the linkage assembly. So far, so good.

Step 15. Check Choke Unloader Mechanism and Install New Second Stage Diaphragm

VW has determined that a small spring they placed in the choke unloader mechanism should no longer be there. Some carburetors have it, some don't. Check to see if yours does.

Start by holding the carburetor with the first stage side toward you. Remove the four screws holding the plate on the face of the second stage vacuum unit pull down on the choke unloader mechanism. There is also a thermo time valve for second stage pull down attached to this vacuum unit. It's attached by the left two screws holding the vacuum unit to the choke unloader mechanism. With the screws removed, gently pry the unit apart and see if there is a spring between the vacuum unit and the body of the pull down mechanism. If there's no spring, fine; if there is one, remove it.

Look in your kit for a new second stage diaphragm with the hooked rod attached to it. Install it in place of the one already attached on your carburetor. No new diaphragm? Leave the old one in place.

Now put it all back together and install the four screws, remembering to install the thermo time valve as you do.

Step 16. Reinstall Vacuum Lines

Replace the vacuum lines onto the carburetor. One goes from the thermo time valve to a small pipe on the first stage side of the carburetor. Another goes from the thermo time valve to the second stage vacuum unit pull down. A third goes from the first stage vacuum unit pull down to the connection on the second stage side of the throttle plate.

Ole, the carb is back together. Take a few minutes to recover, then check that it's properly back together.

PROCEDURE 4: CHECK AND ADJUST OPERATION OF CARBURETOR. Phase 2.

Condition: Carburetor rebuild completed.

Tools and materials: Same as for Procedure 3. Include a 20cc calibrated glass vial (borrow one from your doctor/pharmacist), a 0.45mm (.018 in) drill bit, a 4.0mm (5/32 in) drill bit, millimeter ruler and a small plastic/glass funnel.

Step 1. Adjust First Stage Throttle Valve

Open the choke (get the choke butterfly vertical) and close the first stage throttle. The butterflies in the throttle plate will be closed, so turn the carb upside down to check that they are. You are going to adjust the

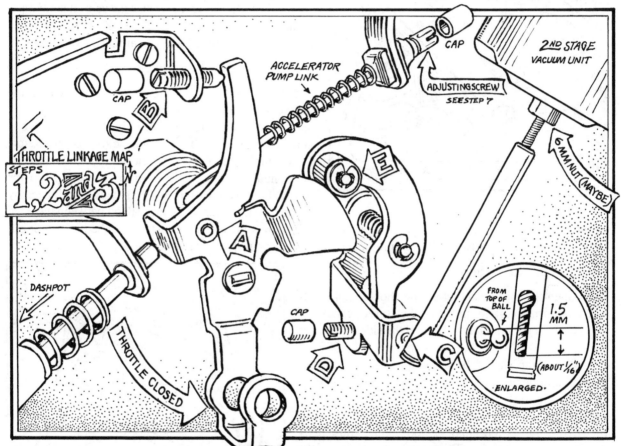

linkage into which the accelerator pump connecting rod is hooked through that little rubber bushing. (A) Just above the rubber bushing is an arm whose position is adjusted by a screw (B) going through the accelerator linkage. Pull off the plastic cap from this adjustment screw, and turn the screw *in* until there's a small gap between the throttle lever and the screw end. Now screw the screw in until it just touches the throttle lever. When it touches the lever, turn the screw in another ¼ turn toward the linkage. Stick the plastic cap back on the end of the screw.

Step 2. Check Secondary Throttle Valve Vacuum Unit Operation; Adjust if Required

Detach the ball on the throttle linkage from the spring inside the arm coming out of the vacuum unit base. Rest the arm next to the linkage and check that the distance between the top of the ball and the bottom of the socket in the linkage arm is 1 to 2mm. Look at the diagram. (C) I would shoot for 1.5mm. Use your millimeter ruler to measure the gap. This is a fairly critical adjustment. If yours measures under 1mm or over 2mm, correct it by loosening the 6mm lock nut at the top of the rod, then screwing the rod up into the unit or down from the unit as many turns as are required to correct this clearance. When it's right, screw the nut tight against the base of the vacuum unit to lock it into position. Finally, snap the linkage rod back onto the ball on the throttle linkage.

Step 3. Check and Adjust Second Stage Linkage

Open the choke by pulling forward the fast idle cam on the right side of the carb. You'll know the choke is open when the butterfly valve is vertical. When it's open, close the first stage throttle. With the butterfly valve vertical and the first stage throttle closed, you can adjust the movement of the wheel on the second stage linkage as it rolls across the cam on the throttle linkage. The linkage on the secondary throttle valve vacuum unit should be in place. See Step 2.

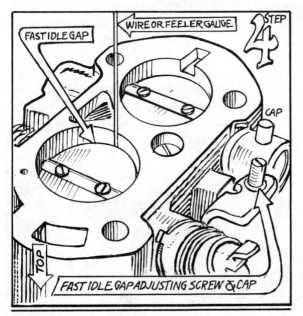

To adjust the second stage linkage clearance, screw in the adjusting screw, (D) on the diagram, until the small wheel (E) is pressed against the cam. It should just firmly touch; not forced, not loose. When the two meet, unscrew the adjustment screw ¼ turn. You've adjusted it.

Step 4. Adjust Fast Idle Gap

Use your 0.45mm (.018 in) drill bit to measure the gap between the carb and the butterfly valve in the first stage side of the throttle plate. This butterfly valve is connected to a lever on the outside of the carburetor. Make sure the choke is fully closed (butterfly valve is horizontal), then carefully turn the carburetor upside down. The position of the butterfly valve is adjusted by a screw on the lever. Push the drill bit between the edge of the butterfly valve and the carbueretor (see diagram). Screw the adjustment screw on the lever in or out until drill bit just fits between the carburetor and butterfly. The fast idle gap is now adjusted.

Step 5. Check Choke Gap

Open the throttle and close the choke (choke butterfly is horizontal). With the choke closed, check the gap between the butterfly valve and the side of the carb (see diagram). If your chassis number is 1753405708 or below, the gap should be 4.20mm (5/32 in). If your chassis number is higher than that, the gap should be 4.50mm. In fact, the gap isn't that critical, but you should do it anyway. Check the gap with the 5/32 in drill bit. If the gap is too small or too great, adjust it by turning a screw in or out. This screw is in the end of the protrusion (possibly sealed by yellow paint) on the end plate of the second stage vacuum unit pull down attached to the choke unloader mechanism. When the gap is correct, seal that screw with a drop of paint.

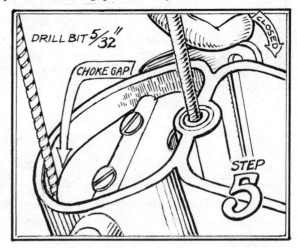

Step 6. Check Dashpot Adjustment (if you have one)

Open the choke and close the throttle. Push the rod sticking out the top of the dashpot all the way in. Remove any twigs or seeds. Loosen the locknut holding the dashpot to the accelerator cable bracket. Turn the dashpot in or out to adjust the gap between the dashpot rod and the carb bracket to 3mm (⅛ in) like in the

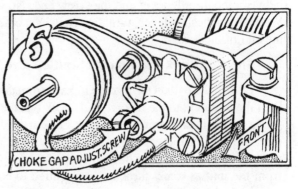

Step 6. (Cont'd.)

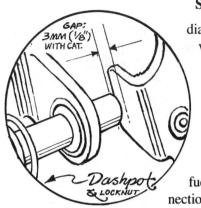

diagram. Make the gap 1mm (3/64 in) if you are eliminating the catalytic converter. To get this adjustment right, hold the dashpot rod in with your finger as you do the adjustment.

Step 7. Check Accelerator Pump Discharge Quantity

Do you have a small funnel which will fit beneath the carburetor and go into your glass vial? If not, find a small clean container, such as the plastic top of a spray can, etc.

Take the carburetor over to the car, remove the pencil plugging the fuel line and reconnect the line to the carburetor. Be sure all electrical connections around the carb aren't grounded and that they don't touch one another to cause a spark. It's a good safety idea to wrap a rag over the top of these electrical connections when you've got them tucked safely away.

Reattach the battery ground strap and ask Friend to crank over the engine about 15 or 20 times with the key to fill the float chambers of the carburetor with gasoline. Disconnect the battery ground strap and the fuel line and plug the line again.

Take the carb back to your workbench and find your calibrated glass vial. Hold the small container under the first stage side of the carb throttle plate. Open the choke and manually operate the throttle once. Now wait five seconds and operate the throttle again. Do it eight more times—a total of 10 strokes. Pour the gasoline into the calibrated vial to measure the quantity of fuel pumped out. You should have between 6.0cc and 9.0cc's. That's 0.6 to 0.9cc per stroke. 1975 Canadian models should pump 0.90 to 1.20cc per stroke.

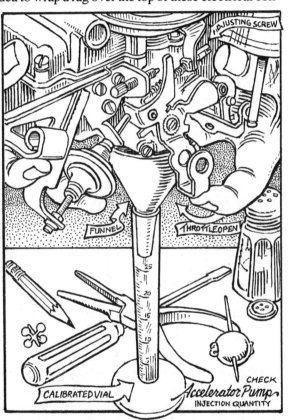

Look at the point where the rod goes through the linkage at the top right of the carburetor. You'll see a small brass slotted cylinder screwed onto the end of the rod. To adjust fuel quantity, turn the cylinder in for more discharge and out for less. It seems easier to turn it with a pair of needle nosed pliers, putting each of the needles in the slots on the end of the cylinder. Aim for the lower gasoline quantity; this will help decrease fuel consumption. Each time you adjust the pump quantity, fill the float bowls in the carburetor by attaching the fuel line, the battery ground strap, and asking Friend to turn the engine over a number of times.

Step 8. Check EGR Valve

This valve is held by two 10mm bolts to the rear of the intake manifold. All vehicles except California and automatic 1976's should have a special restricted orifice type gasket installed between the EGR valve and the manifold. Remove the thin plastic vacuum hose from the valve and take out the two 10mm bolts holding the valve. Clean the valve orifice with a Q-Tip soaked in solvent, gasoline or alcohol. Install the new gasket onto the end of the valve. If you push the 10mm bolts through the valve, the gasket won't slip off.

Hold the valve against the intake manifold and tighten the two bolts. Replace the vacuum hose(s)

1975 Models: Pull off the thin plastic vacuum hose from the top EGR valve connection. Trace the hose to a connection just behind the coil. Pull it off there and discard the hose. Prick a hole with a sewing needle through one of the plastic caps and put it on the EGR valve connection. No cap? Use a piece of plastic electrical tape.

Step 8. (Cont'd.)

1976 Models: Remove the vacuum hose as per 1975 (it probably isn't even there), then pull the other hose from the EGR valve connection. Plug the EGR with one of those pricked caps or a piece of tape. Follow the hose to a temperature control valve and pull it out here, too. Discard it. At the carburetor pull the vacuum hose at the angled connector to the right side of the electric idle cut-off valve. Follow the hose to a temperature control valve and pull it off there too and discard it. Plug the carburetor connection with a plastic cap or tape and all is done.

California cars: Leave things the way they are.

Step 9. Reinstall Carburetor

Remove the rags from the intake manifold. Check that the four 10mm bolts holding the rubber pad on top of the manifold are tight. Insert the four long brass bolts with their washers into the top of the carb, then gently lower the carb into position on top of the intake manifold. The first stage side points toward the front of the car. Tighten the four bolts finger tight, then diagonally torque them to 1 mkg (7 ft lbs).

Step 10. Install Automatic Choke

Reposition the automatic choke housing onto the linkage inside the choke unloader mechanism. Loosely replace the three screws into the retaining ring around the choke cover. Line up the two dots, one on top of the choke and one on the unloader mechanism. Then tighten the screws with your screwdriver.

Step 11. Install Vacuum and Electrical Connections

Do this by referring to the marked ends of your hoses and wires and the hose diagram at the beginning of this chapter.

Also, if you're eliminating the microswitch (not California) remove the electrical connections to it and tape them if you haven't yet done so. Remove the microswitch by taking out the two retaining screws and throw the lot away.

Step 12. Replace Fuel Line

Remove the pencil or whatever from the end of the fuel line and push the line onto its connection on the carb. Tighten the clamp.

Step 13. Install Accelerator Cable Bracket

Position the bracket on the side of the carburetor and secure it with the three screws from your Baggie. Find the small barrel (stickshift) and the 8mm nut which goes into it to secure the cable. Push the barrel into the hole on the throttle linkage and slip in the accelerator cable. Tighten the 8mm nut onto the end of the cable. Be sure not to have any strain on the cable because that will slightly open the accelerator linkage and cause problems when you're trying to get your final carburetor adjustments correct.

Automatics: pull the cable through the throttle linkage and replace the long spring, washer and tiny clip in the end of the cable. Be sure the clip is on tightly; if it comes off, your accelerator will not work at all. Use pliers to cinch the clip tight if it's loose.

Step 14. Catalytic Converter

Non-California residents won't be able to get the car to run well, idle smoothly and get decent gas mileage if the catalytic converter is in place after completing the carburetor modification procedure. So remove it (Chapter 13, Procedure 6). California folks, there's a $15,000 fine for removing the catalytic converter so don't do it.

Step 15. Start Car

Hook up the battery ground strap (10mm). You'll have to let the engine turn over seven or eight times before the fuel pump pumps sufficient gas from the tank to the carburetor float bowl. The car will probably idle very poorly, backfire and do all sorts of numbers. But you are ready to correct this weirdness.

PROCEDURE 5: ADJUST CARBURETOR. Phase 1.

Condition: Carburetor has been rebuilt, replaced or updated and needs adjustment.

Tools and materials: Phase 1 tool kit, VOM, Tach-Dwell meter.

Remarks: Make sure there's clean gas in the tank. If you've been following proper Maintenance schedules, you'll have installed a new air cleaner filter into the air cleaner at the right front fender. If you have not checked the condition of the filter lately, do so now. Pop the four clips holding the top half of the air cleaner box in position and see what your paper element looks like. If it's dirty and full of dust, replace it (Chapter 10, Procedure 10).

For now leave off the metal elbow that goes on top of the carb.

It's important to determine the CO level coming from the exhaust pipe, but you won't be able to do so without an accurate CO meter, an expensive item not normally owned by the backyard mechanic. Do this Procedure, then after your test drive, take the car to your local garage or VW dealer to have the exhaust gas CO content determined. It's not expensive and besides, it's illegal to drive a car which emits excessive CO exhaust levels.

While driving to the east coast one day, I was stopped on a freeway by the EPA people to have my exhaust gasses analyzed with their portable machine. They were courteous and friendly, but were looking for people who had tinkered with their exhaust and carburetor setups, thus not 'complying with the law.' Fortunately, I was clean. EPA has the power to prosecute and heavily fine an individual whose automobile pollution control system isn't functioning as it should!

Don't do the following carburetor adjustments in an enclosed, unventilated garage because carbon monoxide is deadly.

Step 1. Start Car

If you can't start the car, you may have forgotten to back off the idle screw. Use a short stubby screwdriver to turn the idle screw open four turns from the closed position.

Still won't start? Use a thin screwdriver to back off the CO adjustment screw on the side opposite the idle screw four turns from the closed position.

If the car still refuses to start, then, with the ignition off, look into the throat of the carburetor and open the choke butterfly and pump the throttle linkage with your hand a few times. Do you see atomized fuel vapor in the throat of the carburetor? If not, it's possible the fuel lines are blocked or the fuel pump has quit working. To remedy this problem, check Procedure 7 in Chapter 7. If you see gasoline being squirted in the carb throat in unvaporized form, you may have forgotten to install the main jets. It's unlikely, but I've seen this happen, and only you will know.

Fuel OK? Are all the spark plug and coil wires in place? Get Friend to turn the engine over with the key while you put the palm of your hand on top of the carb. When the engine's turned about four times, remove your hand. Do this two or three times and the car should start.

Step 2. Check Choke Action

The choke butterfly valve which you can see in the top of the carb should remain closed or partially closed for the first few minutes of operation. After about two to four minutes, the choke butterfly should open and the engine idle should drop. If this doesn't happen, check that the electrical choke is connected and that the dot on the choke housing lines up with the dot on the choke unloader mechanism. If everything is connected and lined up properly and the automatic choke still doesn't disengage, you must adjust it.

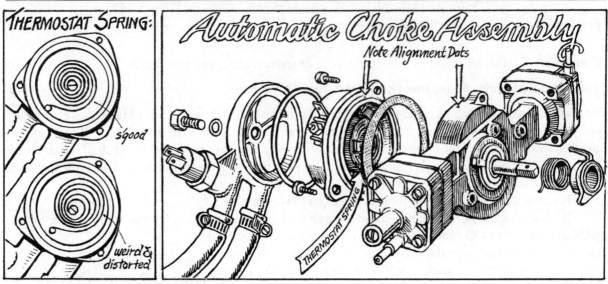

Step 3. Adjust Choke

To adjust the automatic choke, stop the engine and loosen the three screws on the retaining ring holding the choke cover on the unloader mechanism. Twist the choke mechanism about 6mm (¼ in) toward the *rear* of the car. The little dot on the top of the choke mechanism will move backward, right? Tighten the three screws.

Start the car again and the choke should open automaticaly after a few minutes. Conversely, if the choke opens too quickly, not allowing the car enough time to warm up, loosen the three screws and move the dot on the housing forward 6mm (¼ in). Retighten the screws and check again.

If you've had to move the dot, you must recenter the choke mechanism spring. To do so, loosen the 13mm nut in the choke mechanism (engine off) about one turn, then retighten it. See choke discussion at the end of this Chapter.

If you can't get the car to idle properly, check that all four leads to the spark plugs are still in position, that the distributor cap is held down tightly and that the wire from the distributor cap to the coil is firmly in place. These are things you could have disturbed when removing the carb. Did you install a new fuel filter between the gas tank and the fuel pump? Be sure you have the arrow on the side of the filter pointing forward toward the fuel pump. If it's backward, it will impede the flow of gas into the pump and the pump will not be able to properly supply the carb. When the choke butterfly is vertical (choke open), increase or decrease the idle so the engine doesn't race or stall.

Step 4. Test Drive

Remarks: Be aware that a leaky exhaust system will contribute to the rough running of your vehicle. So check the muffler and exhaust pipes.

Before embarking on your test drive, reinstall the metal air cleaner elbow on top of the carburetor and tighten the 10mm bolt holding it in place. Reconnect the large hose from the air cleaner box to the air cleaner elbow and tighten the hose clamps. Install the small hose running from the air cleaner elbow to the activated charcoal filter and tighten that hose clamp. Finally, hook up the PCV hose from the air cleaner elbow to the camshaft cover.

Now that it's all together, take the car for a drive. Warm up the engine and take it up into fairly high revs in all four gears. If you have an automatic, hold it in First, then Second and then Drive, to check that the engine doesn't miss and has good power all the way to maximum revs. All Models: As you fully depress the accelerator, the second stage vacuum unit should start working to give you extra gasoline to maintain the power you need.

Does the car seem sluggish? If so, pull over to the side of the road and turn off the engine. Lift and prop the hood and check that the secondary throttle valve vacuum unit linkage is squarely lined up with the throttle linkage. Check that the roller is riding smoothly on the throttle linkage cam. You might also check that the secondary throttle valve vacuum unit is correctly attached to its linkage via the ball and the spring inside the

Step 4. (Cont'd.)

rod. Keep the engine turned off and work the throttle by hand to see that the linkage is operating smoothly. It's possible that the nut holding the second stage linkage to the side of the carb has come loose. If so, tighten it with your 13mm wrench and again check the alignment of the two linkages. Take another drive. Better?

Swing by a gas station or VW dealer to get the exhaust CO content analyzed. Before you have the test done, have the test machine operator disconnect the air injection hose on the check valve and plug the opening in that valve. The check valve is the small cylindrical cannister which has a 13mm (½ in) pipe on its rear which attaches to a 13mm pipe attached by four bolts to the left side of the cylinder head just below the spark plugs. A large rubber hose runs from the check valve to the air injection pump (smog pump) below the alternator. Remove the hose clamp at the front of the check valve and pull off the hose. Plug the check valve orifice with electrical or duct tape. The test can now be done properly.

If your car still won't run right after the CO adjustment, go home and we'll check some more.

If the idle was properly adjusted while the car was stationary but the engine speed rises when you're waiting at traffic signs, etc., check the condition of the automatic choke temperature switch by disconnecting and removing the electrical leads that plug into the connectors on the outside of the switch. With your engine warm but off, put the probes of your VOM (set at RX1K) on the switch *connections* (not on the wires). The needle should remain at infinity (∞ ohms). If it doesn't, warm up the engine and test again. Still 0 reading? You need a new switch. Needle stays at infinity? Remove the switch with a 17mm wrench, cool the switch in the ice box for 10 minutes and test again. With a **cold** switch the results should be the reverse, that is, the switch needs replacing if the needle swings to infinity and is OK at 0 ohms. Replace it or read the choke rap.

That's about all the test we home mechanics can do. It's hard to imagine your carb is still messing up. But if so, other tests require a vacuum gauge. If you have one, follow the instructions in the *VW Service Manual*, 2nd Edition. If you can't get the engine to run right, turn to Chapter 13 and run through the tests for carbureted engines. If that doesn't help, take it to VW and let one of their carburetor specialists run checks with the vacuum gauge and CO meter.

THE CHOKE

Your Rabbit or Scirocco comes equipped with an automatic choke. John Muir didn't think much of automatic chokes; in fact, he claimed that manufacturers installed them so engines would wear out sooner. "Built-in obsolescence" he called them. It may be that the automatic choke is an unnecessary and harmful piece of equipment *most* of the time.

Now is the time to be honest! Can you truthfully say you'll warm up your engine every morning for about four minutes? Yes? Then read on. No? Quit right here.

If you disconnect the automatic choke it's really hard on your car to zoom off every morning without giving the engine time to wake up. Even in summer, the car needs a few minutes to regain internal warmth and stability. How would you like to be dragged to work with no time to thaw out in front of the stove? Not me.

The problem with these little items is that they automatically give you a richer mixture; that is, less air, more gas. Thirty percent of this gas isn't ignited, finds its way into the cylinders and washes off the life-saving oil. You thus wear out the cylinders or the piston rings quicker than you want.

If you disarm the choke, starting the car in the morning will require a couple of pumps on the gas pedal to let the fuel into the intake manifold and a few minutes to let the engine warm up. Earlier, you learned how to adjust it, now here's how to dismantle it.

AUTOMATIC CHOKE DISARMAMENT

All you need for this job is a small rubber band and a screwdriver. Remove the electrical connections going to the automatic choke body which is on the side of the carb facing the right fender. Tape the ends of the one or two wires with electrical tape and fasten them to the vacuum line coming out of the front of the choke to keep them from grounding against the engine.

Next remove the three screws going into the retaining ring holding the choke housing to the side of the choke unloader mechanism. Pull off the choke housing and carefully disengage the internal spring from the arm inside the loader mechanism. Hook the rubber band around the arm inside the unloader mechanism and over the top of the choke unloader mechanism. Pull off the metal air intake elbow from the top of the carb (10mm wrench) and see if the choke butterfly is in the vertical or open position. It should be. Reinstall the three screws through the retaining ring and put on the choke housing. The choke is now disarmed. From time to time remove the choke housing to check that the rubber band is still in position holding the butterfly valve open.

Should you move to either the North or South Pole or a severe winter sets in, you can re-arm the choke mechanism. Just remove the three screws from the choke retaining ring, taking out the rubber band and re-engaging the choke unloader mechanism arm with the spring on the inside of the choke body. Then reconnect the electrical connections or your choke will never turn off. Line up the dots on the top of the choke unloader mechanism with the dot on the choke body. If your choke is not turning off after three or four minutes, adjust the choke body—Procedure 5, Step 2, this Chapter.

CHAPTER 12

FUEL AND AIR DO MIX—PART 2

✒ Fuel Injection ✒

At the very mention of the words 'fuel injection,' some people, especially mechanical novices, think of future shock and space voyages, but consider this bit of early Anglo-Saxon history.

In ancient Britain there lived a lazy languid lad, a trainee insurgent under the ferocious leader King Bosch. His name was Ian Ject. Young Ian was so lazy and uninspired that he was unable to stand upright on the parade bog; much, I might add, to the annoyance of his leader.

King Bosch was always shouting at him ''Fool, stand up! Fool, Atten . . . Shun! Fool, Ian Ject . . . Shun!'' The name stuck.

One day during an encounter with another hostile band of Britains, the Strolling Rones I think they were called, young Fool decided to hot rod his steed by forcing food

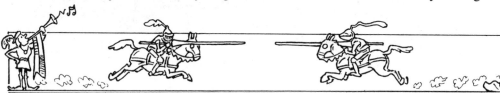

down its throat. He became the hero of the battle of the bands. Soon there was a whole platoon of food injected horses.

Of course, history credits King Bosch for the Bosch Fuel Injection System but now you know the real story.

Okay, already…all right! The inventors of the fuel injection system wanted an accurate, simple and efficient method to deliver a mixture of air and fuel into the cylinders. They got it. Not only that but a faulty part can be isolated and replaced easily. Carburetors, by comparison, are infinitely more complicated in operation and much more difficult to trouble shoot.

Imagine yourself in school with a test tomorrow and take this Chapter to bed. Look at the diagrams and become familiar with all the component names. There really aren't that many and once you know names you won't have to continually refer to the pictures to find out what's what and where it goes.

While trouble shooting you may have to run quite a few Procedures before locating the problem and its solution, but as they said in ancient Britain, ''Your Fuel Injection should not cause dejection.'' YOU can outsmart IT. The system works very logically and follows along from point A to point B (like bog drill) so it's easy to get on its wavelength and communicate. Here, I'll introduce you.

It's proper name is the Bosch Continuous Injection System (CIS) and it's hydraulic rather than electronic injection. Its heart and brains is a meter for fuel and air called the **mixture control unit.** Lift the hood and find it just to the rear of the battery. It has braided metal fuel lines bolted to its top. Found it? It consists of the **air flow sensor** and the **fuel distributor**, which together maintain the fuel-to-air ratio at 1 to 14 at all engine speeds. This ratio keeps toxic compounds in the exhaust gas at a minimum. The 1:14 ratio is a fair compromise between maximum power and optimum fuel efficiency.

As in the carbureted engine, we need a mixture of gasoline and air to produce the energy needed to run the engine. The amount of air entering the engine through **throttle valves** in the **intake manifold** is first measured by the **air flow sensor** as it flows over the **air flow sensor plate** in the mixture control unit. (Keep referring to the CIS system diagram). The *volume* of air and quantity of fuel available at the cylinders changes as you press down or release the gas pedal which affects the position of both the sensor plate and the throttle valves.

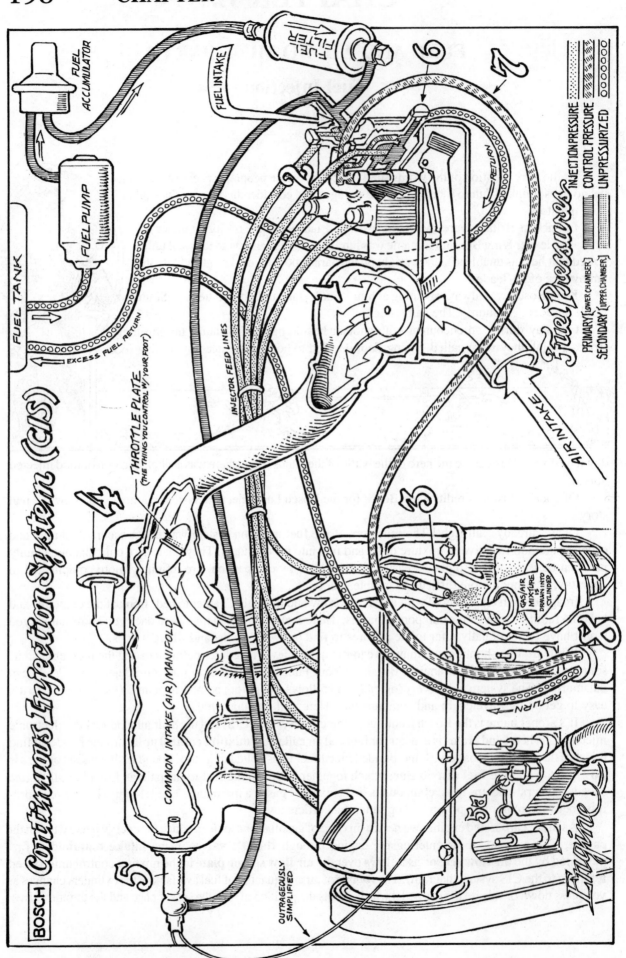

BOSCH Continuous Injection System (CIS)

FUEL ACCUMULATOR

FUEL PUMP

FUEL TANK

FUEL FILTER

FUEL INTAKE

EXCESS FUEL RETURN

INJECTOR FEED LINES

THROTTLE PLATE
(THE THING YOU CONTROL W/ YOUR FOOT)

COMMON INTAKE (AIR) MANIFOLD

OUTRAGEOUSLY SIMPLIFIED

RETURN

AIR INTAKE

GAS/AIR MIXTURE IS DRAWN INTO CYLINDER

RETURN

Engine

Fuel Pressures

	INJECTION PRESSURE
	CONTROL PRESSURE
	UNPRESSURIZED

PRIMARY (LOWER CHAMBER)
SECONDARY (UPPER CHAMBER)

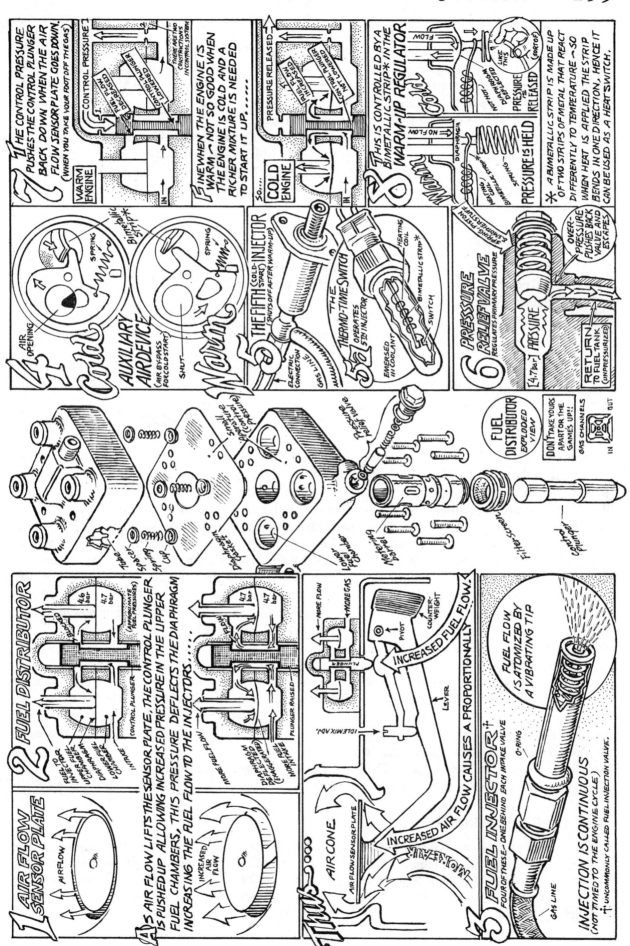

Once air is drawn into the engine's cylinders, an equal quantity of fuel is metered for each cylinder by the fuel distributor, and sent through **fuel lines** to four **fuel injectors** pushed into the cylinder head. Each injector pushes into a **manifold tube** in the intake air distributor on the right side of the cylinder head. Rubber O rings make an air tight seal between the injectors and the manifold tubes. When an intake valve opens, the air/fuel mixture is drawn into the cylinder to be compressed and ignited.

There are two pressurized fuel circuits in this CIS system: a **primary** fuel circuit and a **control** circuit. The primary fuel circuit operates under **system pressure**, which is between 4.5-5.2 bar (65-75 psi). The control circuit has a pressure varying between 1.3-3.8 bar (19-55 psi) depending on engine temperature. By the way, the word 'bar' refers to the international unit of pressure: 1 bar = 1 kg/cm^2 or 14 psi. Let's start with the primary circuit first.

PRIMARY FUEL CIRCUIT

The fuel is sent to the engine by an electrically powered **fuel pump** located just to the right rear of the fuel tank. The fuel pump is actually cooled and lubricated by the gasoline that flows through it. Never let your gas tank go completely empty. A dry, unlubricated pump burns up rather rapidly.

Once it leaves the pump, gas goes into a **fuel accumulator** just behind the right side of the rear axle beam. Its functions are to help the car start when the engine is hot and to prevent the fuel from surging and thereby varying fuel pressure.

From the accumulator, gas goes up the fuel line to the **fuel filter**. This paper and nylon cartridge strains any junk from the gas that could ruin the fuel distributor or clog the injectors. It *must* be changed every fifteen thousand miles.

Filtered gasoline now enters the **fuel distributor.** One end of the **control plunger** that's fitted into a barrel inside this distributor touches the arm of the **air flow sensor lever.** On the other side of the lever is the **air flow sensor plate.** The flow of air through the mixture control unit moves the plate, and the the lever, up and down. As the lever moves up it pushes the plunger up, exposing more area of the four gas **metering slits** around the middle of the barrel, thereby allowing more fuel to flow to the injectors.

Four **pressure regulating valves** ensure a constant and regular fuel flow. Each valve has a central thin steel diaphragm which effectively divides the pressure regulating valve into two **chambers**, each contaning fuel. The bottom **intake** chamber is constantly at system pressure. The top chamber (injector side) is constantly 0.1 bar lower than system pressure. This small difference deflects the steel diaphragm, opens the spring loaded **disc valve** in the top chamber, and allows fuel to flow through the metering slits and up to the injector. The volume of fuel is determined by the up and down movement of the control plunger inside the barrel and isn't affected by any pressure changes in the system. Refer to the diagram now and again.

The fuel pump actually supplies more fuel to the fuel distributor than it needs. The lower half of the pressure regulating valve has a **relief piston** on its side which opens and allows excess fuel to flow without pressure back to the tank. The circle is unbroken.

The injectors begin to spray fuel in an atomized conical pattern at 2.6-3.5 bar. A vibrating pin held inside a spring at the injector tip does the atomizing. Each injector has its own filter to catch tiny bits of crud that escaped the main fuel filter. The injectors operate continually above a certain pressure. The amount of fuel discharged from the injector changes only as your foot moves the gas pedal, which increases or decreases the air flow over the air sensor plate, raising or lowering the control plunger in the fuel distributor and covering/uncovering the metering slits. The injectors maintain 3 bars of pressure in the lines between the fuel distributor and the injector, so fuel is available immediately when you want to go on your merry way.

FUEL CONTROL CIRCUIT

The **control pressure regulator (CPR)** helps your engine start on cold December mornings. The CPR (also called the warm-up regulator) is connected by a fuel line to the top of the fuel plunger inside the fuel distributor. Another fuel line from the CPR joins the return line to the fuel tank. Let's dissect doctor.

Inside the guts of the CPR, there's a **heating coil** which receives juice from the battery when the engine is started. The heating coil is connected to a **bi-metalic strip** that moves as it heats up. On the end of the strip is a valve. When the strip is cold the valve is open, and fuel flows through the line to the CPR from the fuel distributor.

If we have a cold engine, we need a *low* control pressure so fuel flows to the CPR. Thus, the air flow sensor plate rises without any increase in air flow and in turn, raises the control plunger. Hooray! More gas flows through the metering slit for the same amount of available air without increasing the pressure at which the fuel is expelled from the injector. The fuel-to-air ratio is made richer in gasoline. As the engine gets warmer, the bi-metalic strip slowly straightens out, closes the valve and blocks the fuel flow. Control pressure returns to about 3.6 bar and the control plunger inside is pushed back down. Less fuel passes through the metering slits for the same amount of air—a leaner mixture.

Along with extra fuel, extra air is needed to prevent a cold engine from stalling. When the engine is cold and idling, the throttle valve (controlled by your foot on the gas pedal) is closed. The **auxiliary air regulator** allows air to bypass this valve by using another bi-metalic strip and heating coil arrangement inside the regulator. When the engine has that cold icy feeling, the bi-metallic strip inside the regulator holds open a rotary valve in the mouth of the regulator allowing more air to pass to the mixture control unit. As the engine warms up, the bi-metallic strip closes the gate valve and cuts the air flow to zilch.

WHAT ELSE?

We have two other items in the cold starting package: the **cold start valve** and the **thermo-time switch.** For just a few moments the cold start valve injects *extra* fuel into the intake manifold to be mixed with air, compressed and then burned. Its operation is controlled by the thermo-time switch (another bi-metallic strip and heating coil) which sits in the main coolant artery between the cylinder head and the radiator. Thus the temperature of the engine coolant controls the open/close mechanism inside the switch.

The same heating coil is also part of the starter circuit. Juice to the strip flows only when the starter is working. Clever, what?

For those who live above 5,000 feet, as part of the high altitude kit there's probably a barometric cell bolted onto the top of the radiator with a couple of red plastic hoses attached to it. We will locate and identify these parts as we get to them.

For those who want more details about their system, I recommend the Bosch Technical Instruction Manual for the Continuous Injection System. A translation from the German is available at your VW dealer. Another good VW publication is the CIS Fuel Injection Trouble-Shooting Guide (Part #W42-00-6957-1).

Here are a few words of advice before you start working on your fuel injection system. **FOLLOW THE INSTRUCTIONS TO THE LETTER.** Don't do anything unless I tell you to. Poor engine performance is due usually to infrequent and improper routine maintenance, not a screwed-up fuel injection system. Before laying a finger on your fuel injection system, examine the fuel lines for leaks, breakages, etc. None? Run through the Tune-Up Procedures in Chapter 10. This is important!! If the car still won't start or run right, come back here. Carefully read the Procedures all the way through before starting; then relax and enjoy the work.

At the end of this Chapter is a list of fuel injection problems and their cures. If you are stuck by the side of the road, run through as many of the Procedures as possible since I doubt if you've got your fuel pressure gauge along with you.

The remainder of the Chapter is laid out with the most common problems/repairs in logical order. Without question, the most frequent hassle with fuel injection is that the fuel pump relay goes bad, or a fuel injector decides on an early retirement. Funnily enough, one bad fuel injector can cause an engine to have terrible hot or cold starting problems.

Before beginning work on any fuel injector component, look at all the fuel line fittings for leaks. Tighten anything that's loose. Check that all four injectors are pushed fully into the cylinder head. Is the big rubber boot over the sensor plate properly secured by the hose clamp? How about the connection from the boot to the intake manifold? These should all be on tight. If anything splits when you're out in the boonies, tape the split with electrical tape. When you get home, change the oil and spark plugs (Chapter 10, Procedure 9 and Procedure 14, Step 12) as you'll have been running on a very rich mixture. Some of the excess gas will have found its way into the oil, so don't delay the change. Buy a new rubber boot and install it P.D.Q.

PROCEDURES FOR CHECKING OUT FUEL INJECTION SYSTEM. Phases 1 and 2.

Condition: You have been referred here from Chapter 7 because your engine won't start or run well, or you just love to read about fuel injection. Pervert!

Tools and materials: Phase 2 tool kit, including Tach Dwell meter and VOM, 1.5mm^2 (14 gauge) 8 amp

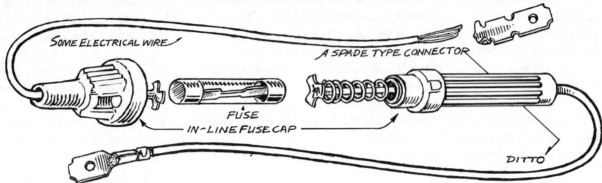

jumper wire, various electrical eyelet and in-line connectors, electrical tape and a fuel pressure gauge which reads from 0 to 6 bar (0 to 90 lbs psi) with a stop valve (gate valve) in the line. You can make one, rent or perhaps borrow this fuel pressure gauge. They'll let you have a look at the one at VW if you ask 'em nice.

Remarks: If you've never used a Volt Ohm Meter (VOM), read Chapter 20, Procedure 10. You can also use a test light for these Procedures.

Besides having the engine in good tune, you must have a good grade of gas in the tank. I have worked on an unusually high number of Rabbits whose fuel systems were clogged and partially ruined by dirty gas. See Chapter 20, Procedure 12 for a simple gasoline test if you think that your local gas contains weird contaminants.

PROCEDURE 1: CHECK FUEL PUMP. Phase 1 and 2.

Condition: Car won't start or run properly.

Tools and materials: Phase 1 tool kit, fused jumper wire, Friend.

Step 1.   Check Fuel Pump Relay and Fuse

Let's see if gas is being pumped from the tank up to the fuel distributor. The fuel pump is bolted to the car's underbody just in front of the right rear wheel. The most common cause for a fuel pump refusing to work is a blown fuse on the pump relay. It's in the relay plate just above the bank of fuses over the driver's legs. From now on I'll call the whole fuse box configuration by its proper name—the relay plate.

Remove the clip (if you've got one) from the center of the protective carpet and pull the carpet down. The fuel pump relay is one of those black boxes sticking up just above the line of fuses. It has a fuse under a plastic cover on the end facing you.

Examine the fuse and be sure the thin metal strip isn't broken. If it's blown, replace it. The fuel pump should now work and the car will start.

No luck or the fuse is OK? Let's check the relay itself. We have to bypass the relay with the fused jumper

Step 1. (Cont'd.)

wire to see if the relay is faulty. With the ignition turned off, pull the fuel pump relay out from the relay plate. Look carefully at the numbered slots on the relay plate from where you removed the pump relay. We are interested in the top and bottom slots #L13 and L14. Put one end of your fused jumper wire into slot L13 and the other end into slot L14. Get Friend to turn the ignition to ON while you hop back to the rear of the car and listen for a faint mechanical whirring at the fuel pump. Put your hand on the pump and feel the vibrations say 'Swami Balderdash.' No vibes—no working fuel pump. Either the fuse in the jumper wire has broken or the wiring to the pump is kaput so check the fuse first! Good vibes—a running fuel pump. In that case, your fuel pump relay is bad. Buy a replacement, put in the fuse and push the new relay into position. There you go.

If not, well weird things happen—even to Rabbits. Do you hear a soft whirring noise from the fuel pump even when you turn the ignition off? Lift the hood and make sure it's not the cooling fan. Keep listening. If the whirrs are still there, your fuel pump relay has stuck on so pull the thing out from the relay plate. The noise has stopped, I take it. Buy a new relay and install it as soon as possible. You will burn up your relay plate and drain the battery if you leave the relay in place. Just install it to drive down to VW to buy a new one.

Step 2. Check Fuel Pump

The fuel pump still doesn't work? Time to check the fuel pump itself. Keep the jumper wire in the relay plate and the ignition turned to ON. Tap the pump gently with a small hammer (It's in tiny pieces on the ground? I said gently.) Most of the time this will make the little bugger run. Fuel pumps are fairly expensive but if you're contemplating a long trip, consider replacing the fuel pump now. If you drive only in town, the occasional tap of the hammer will do the trick until you get money for a new pump or it gives up completely. I've known fuel pumps that required a tap every three months or so, but otherwise continued to work like Old Faithful. If tapping doesn't do it, let's check the fuel pump more closely.

Step 3. Check for Voltage at Fuel Pump

Remarks: Models up to mid-1977 have an electrical plug on the left side of the pump. Remove it to insert your VOM probes into the front of the plug when testing for juice. Later models have two wires secured to separate pump terminals by 8mm and 9mm nuts.

Chock, jack up the right rear of the car and block it safely.

Don't get confused between the fuel pump and the fuel accumulator. The accumulator is to the *rear* of the rear axle beam.

If you can't maneuver yourself into a position where you can reach the pump wires, do this. Remove the 10mm nut holding the front part of the fuel pump to its mount on the floor pan. Remove the 13mm nut from the right side bracket toward the rear of the fuel pump. Pull the pump from the bracket and loosely replace the pump nuts on the studs for safekeeping. Pull the fuel pump down toward you. Can you reach the wires now?

Find the two wires running to the pump. Either slide back the two rubber boots which protect the electrical connections on the front of the pump or pull the electrical plug.

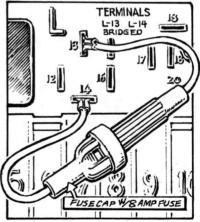

Step 3. (Cont'd.)

Find the two wires running to the pump. Either slide back the two rubber boots which protect the electrical connections on the front of the pump or pull the electrical plug.

Get out from under the car and remove the fuel pump relay and bridge #L13 and L14 slots in the relay plate with your short fused jumper wire if you haven't already done so. Turn the key to ON. Set the VOM to 15 VDC. Back under the car: either touch the positive VOM probe to the pump connection where the green wire with the black stripe goes (it might be solid green), or push it into the positive socket in the connector. Touch the other probe to the axle beam. Scratch through the protective underbody coating on the beam to make a good ground. If your VOM doesn't read at least 11.5 volts, switch the positive probe onto the other pump connection. No reading? There's no juice to the pump. Go to Step 4.

If you get a voltage reading, touch one VOM probe to the other wire on the pump, and ground the other probe on the axle beam. If your pump has plug type connections, stick the plug back onto the pump and push one of the VOM probes through the rear of the plug into the negative wire. Right. If this ploy suddenly starts the pump (the relay plate is still jumped), you have a bad ground connection between the fuel pump and the body of the car.

For those who managed to get a voltage reading at their fuel pump, but it still refuses to work after checking the ground wire, turn to Procedure 16 in this Chapter. If, however, your fuel pump checks out OK but the car still won't start, go to Procedure 2.

Come out from under the car, turn the ignition off, and pull the jumper wire from the relay plate.

You'll need 30cm (12 in) of 1.5mm^2 (14 gauge) wire with the insulation stripped from both ends to rig up a good permanent ground. If your pump is still bolted in position, remove the 13mm nut from the right side bracket and the 10mm nut holding the front part of the pump. Pull the pump downward and attach one end of your new wire to the stud which holds the right hand fuel pump support. If you have a biggish electrical eyelet connector with about a 9mm (⅜ in) hoe, crimp it to the wire first (Chapter 20, Procedure 14). If there's a rubber bushing over the stud, pull if off. After fastening the wire to the stud, slip a washer over it and replace the rubber bushing, the pump bracket and the 13mm nut. Thread the wire carefully over the top of the fuel pump.

1976 to mid-'77: Cut the old *ground* wire about 50mm (2 in) from the back of the electrical plug and strip a little insulation from the end of the wire still attached to the plug. Attach an in-line connector (splice) to the end of the wire and stick the other end of the connector to the stripped end of your new wire and crimp the two together. Push the plug back onto the pump. See Chapter 20, Procedure 14, if you've never spliced before.

Late '77 and on: Crimp a smaller eyelet connector to the end of the new ground wire and bolt it to the fuel pump ground stud. Roll back the rubber boots to keep the water out.

To check your work, either plug back the fuel pump relay jumper wire or put the pump relay back into the relay plate and start the car. In either case—the pump will work! Yes? Install the pump relay and stick the protective carpet back into position. Finished.

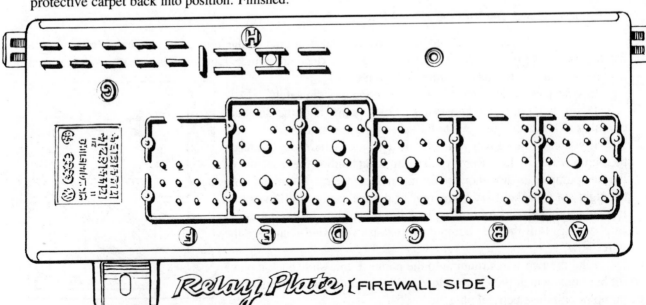

Relay Plate [FIREWALL SIDE]

Step 4. Liberate Relay Plate

Those poor souls who didn't manage to get a reading of 11.5 volts at the pump (or their test light didn't come on or was very weak), have to check the connections at the relay plate. Disconnect the battery ground strap (10mm wrench). Remove the single phillips screw holding the relay plate in position above the driver's knees. Lift the plate up slightly to clear the two metal retaining ears and pull it toward you. When it's free, carefully turn it around so all the plugs and wires in the back of the plate are facing you.

Step 5. Check Fuel Pump Power Source

At the bottom of the relay plate are lots of single wires fastened to the plate on two rows of brass-colored spade connectors. These connectors are on terminals G and H. Find the large square *white* plug with lots of wires in its back pushed into Terminal A. The terminal letters are stamped into the back of the relay plate.

Sort through the mass of wires running around the relay plate (gently now) and find a clear plastic 'Y' or 'T' connector. This has three or four separate wires running into it with brass spade connectors on their ends. The wire coming from the stem part of the 'Y' is red with a white stripe. The other two are green with a black stripe.

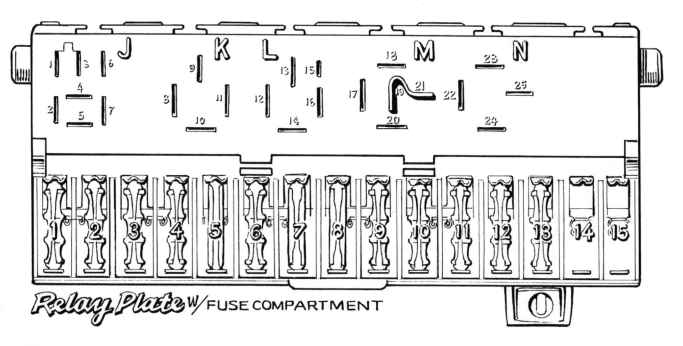

Relay Plate w/FUSE COMPARTMENT

(If yours doesn't have a stripe, don't despair, they ran out and switched to solid green.) One green/black wire goes to the *white* (not the clear) plug in Terminal A of the relay plate while the other runs to the fuel pump.

Make sure that the relay plate terminals don't touch against anything metal and reconnect the battery ground strap and turn the key to ON. Switch the VOM to 15 volts DC. Touch one probe to the connection in the clear plastic 'Y' containing the wire which goes to the white plug in the relay plate. Touch the other probe to the second brass spade connector prong from *your* right in terminal G at the bottom of the relay plate. (There may be a spade connector on that terminal with two black wires going into it.) You should get a reading of 12 volts. If you don't, move the probe one prong to your left. You will now get a reading. Turn off the ignition. The meter will return to zero. If it didn't, try the test again but use a different terminal G prong. Turn the key back to ON and the meter will read 12 volts. Off with the ignition, meter reading is zero. You are trying to find a connection that has power only when the ignition is turned to ON or the engine is running. Some have power all the time. When you've found one, keep both probes in position and ask Friend to check the fuel pump. If it's running, you have a problem with the wiring to the relay plate or the relay plate itself. Let's make a short-cut repair (see Step 6). If the pump still doesn't go, there's a break in the wire between the 'Y' and the fuel pump. We'll fix that one in Step 7.

Step 6. Relay Plate Short-Cut Repair

Additional materials: 8 amp in-line fuse, about 20cm (8 in) of 1.5mm^2 (14 gauge) wire, female spade connectors and an in-line connector, electrical insulating tape. See Chapter 20, Procedure 14, if you've never used electrical connectors before.

Pull the green/black wire running from the *white* plastic plug to the Y, out at the Y end. Cut the wire 50mm (2 in) from the plug and tape the end attached to the white plug with plastic electrical tape. Find a female spade connector from your stash that will attach to the male end in the clear plastic 'Y'. Attach the female spade connector to one end of the in-line fuse. Hook up the 20cm piece of wire with an in-line connector (splice) to the other end of the in-line fuse wire. If you don't have any in-line connectors, strip and twist the ends of the fused wire and new wire together and tape them with electrical insulating tape. Finally, attach another female spade connector which will fit on a terminal G prong to the other end of the 20cm piece of wire. All connected?

Push one end of your new wire into the clear plastic 'Y' and the other onto your pre-selected relay plate prong. Jump the relay plate with your jumper wire, reconnect the battery ground strap and listen to the fuel pump jump to life. Pull the jumper wire from the relay plate and remove the battery ground strap. Carefully replace the relay plate, watching that you fit it properly onto the metal ears. Replace the phillips screw, the fuel pump relay and the battery ground strap. Check that the fuel pump is secure to the car's underbody and you're on your way.

Step 7. Replace Hot Wire to Fuel Pump

Remarks: If you've never used electrical connectors before, read Procedure 14 in Chapter 20.

Additional materials: About 3 meters (10 feet) of 1.5mm^2 (14 gauge) wire and a few female spade connectors, one of which fits into the clear plastic 'Y'. A small eyelet type is needed for cars made after mid-1977, and an in-line connector (splice) for cars made before mid-1977.

Remove the battery ground strap (10mm wrench). Chock the car and then jack up the right rear and block it well. The fuel pump may still be unbolted from Step 1. If it isn't, loosen it unless you can easily get at the pump terminals. The older type fuel pump has its power plug connection in the left side (1976-mid-1977) so the pump doesn't have to be unbolted.

1976 to mid-'77: Cut the hot wire (see Step 3 if you don't remember which it is) about 50mm (2 in) away from the plug. Strip 13mm (½ in) of insulation from the end of the cut wire and attach it to one end of the in-line connector. Now attach the other end of the in-line connector to the stripped end of your new piece of wire.

Mid-1977 and on: Cinch the small eyelet electrical connector onto your new wire and connect it to the positive side of the fuel pump after removing the 8mm nut and washer holding the green and black hot wire to the pump. Slip the new and old wires on the stud and replace the washer and nut and tighten it up.

All Models: Thread the new wire carefully along the bottom of the car, following the plastic covered wiring harness across to the left side and up to the relay plate. Securely attach the new wire to the harness with pieces of plastic electrical insulating tape. When you reach the relay plate, pull up enough wire to give about 20cm (8 in) of slack at the plate. Find the clear plastic 'Y' again and pull out the green/black wire to the *fuel pump*. It's *not* the wire going to the big white plug. Attach a female spade connector to your new wire, and push it into the vacant slot in the clear plastic 'Y'. Tape the end of the old wire. The pump will work when you connect the battery ground strap and start the car. If it didn't, check the in-line fuse! Pull off the battery ground strap again, secure the relay plate with the phillips screw. Put back the battery ground strap again. If your fuel pump is hanging down, bolt it in and lower the car. Reinstall the fuel pump relay (check that the fuse is still OK).

PROCEDURE 2: FUEL SYSTEM, Phase 2.

Condition: Car won't start, quits while running, won't idle properly, or has no power.

Tools and materials: Phase 2 tool kit, a graduated 1000cc (one quart) container to catch the fuel, Friend, a fire extinguisher and a healthy regard for gasoline's explosive potential.

Remarks: **DO NOT SMOKE, LIGHT MATCHES, RUB TWO STICKS TOGETHER** or ignite anything during this test.

Step 1. Check Fuel Flow

The pump should deliver more fuel than the engine can use. Let's measure it. The fuel return line is the large braided metal hose (rubber hose in U.S. made Rabbits) that begins at the base of the fuel distributor. It is connected by two captive nuts to a thin metal line running back to the gas tank. Loosen and pull apart the return line connection (two 17mm wrenches). Stick the end of the hose into your graduated container. Pull the big central wire from the coil to prevent the car from suddenly starting, and have Friend turn the starter over for 30 seconds. No more, no less. You should get at least 758cc (¾ qt) of gas. Much less than this (500cc—½ qt—or so) with at least 11.5 volts to the pump (Procedure 1, Step 3) means that the pump is shot or the fuel filter or fuel lines are clogged. If you didn't get any gas, do Procedure 1 to check that the pump is working! I suspect the filter, so let's check it in Step 2. Lotsa gas? Reconnect the gas line to the fuel distributor and empty the gas into your fuel tank. Jump to Procedure 5.

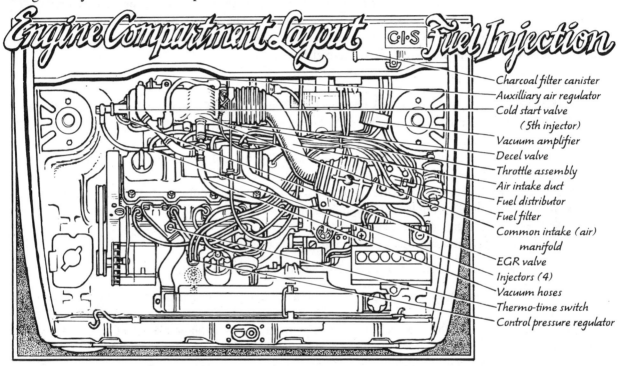

Engine Compartment Layout C·I·S *Fuel Injection*

- Charcoal filter canister
- Auxilliary air regulator
- Cold start valve
  (5th injector)
- Vacuum amplifier
- Decel valve
- Throttle assembly
- Air intake duct
- Fuel distributor
- Fuel filter
- Common intake (air)
  manifold
- EGR valve
- Injectors (4)
- Vacuum hoses
- Thermo-time switch
- Control pressure regulator

Step 2. Check Fuel Filter

If the filter hasn't been changed for a while, there's a good possibility it's full of junk or the internal cartridge is warped. There are a number of filter styles (I hear Christian Dior is doing one for next season) but they mount in the same position and do the same thing.

The filter is connected to the fuel lines with either 15, 17 or 19mm captive nuts. Loosen the line going from the filter to the fuel distributor at the filter end, then loosen the return line on the other end. Now loosen the 10mm nut holding the filter in its clamp, bend the front half of the clamp down and pull the filter free. Keep the filter level. Pour the gas from the filter into a glass jar. It should be clean and flow easily. A few specks of dirt are to be expected but if you have a poor flow along with vast amounts of dirt, the filter is more than a Golden Oldie and must be replaced. Take your old filter to the VW agency and swap it for an identical new one. Copious quantities of dirt mean that the fuel tank, lines and possible the injectors and fuel distributor are dirty. They must be cleaned. Go to Step 3.

Install the filter (new or OK old) with the arrow stamped on the body facing forward toward the headlights. Reconnect the fuel lines to the filter (15, 17 or 19mm wrench) and tighten the 10mm nut holding the filter into its clamp. Now try starting the car. No luck? Continue with Procedure 3.

Step 3. Check Fuel Tank and Lines—Side Mounted Sending Units

Remarks: Diesel and carbureted engine owners have been referred here also from different Procedures.

Before you can inspect the tank, you must remove the fuel tank sending unit. Early models and diesels have the fuel tank sending unit mounted on the right side of the fuel tank. Later models have the sending unit centrally mounted in the top of the tank. Disconnect the battery ground strap (10mm wrench). Side mounted sending units: check your gas gauge. You'll have to drain out everything over a quarter of a tank. Put your fire extinguisher someplace handy and find a large clean receptacle like a plastic dish pan to catch the gasoline. At the right rear of the gas tank is a hose connection from the fuel pump. Put the receptacle under the pump, loosen the clamp and pull off the hose. Gas will quickly drain into the bowl. When the tank is less than ¼ full, replace the hose. Again, **WARNING! DO NOT MAKE SPARKS.** Gasoline is explosive! If the tank was full, plug the end of the hose with a pencil and pour the gas already drained into a legal container or your neighbor's car. Repeat until the tank is less than ¼ full.

OK, go to the left side again. Pull off the electrical connection on the top of the fuel tank sending unit. Put a screwdriver blade into one of the slots on the outside circumference of the fuel tank sending unit and tap gently with a hammer in a counterclockwise ↺ direction. It will have to move about a tenth of a turn before you can pull the unit and rubber O ring free. Work it out carefully. There's a wire with a float on the end. Do not bend this wire! Put the unit down somewhere clean.

Step 4. Inspect Tank

Shine a bright *flashlight* into the tank and check the bottom for junk. Do not use a candle or a droplight; you might drop it, shatter the bulb and...bang! If the gas is a milky off-white color, you've got water in the tank. Among other things, this causes starting problems. Very carefully check the bottom of the tank for rust scales. They probably dropped off the rustfish. If you have any, the tank has to be replaced or very efficiently steam cleaned (Procedure 17).

If you can't see crud or water and the inside of the tank is a uniform color, it's OK. Carefully replace the sending unit and O ring. Tap it tight with a light hammer and screwdriver. Replace the electrical connection and battery ground strap and go to Procedure 3.

If you spotted crud or water, read the last paragraph of Step 5.

Step 5. Check Fuel Tank and Lines—Top Mounted Sending Units

Disconnect the battery ground strap (10mm wrench). To get at the fuel tank sending unit you must remove the rear seat.

Rabbits: First remove the seat back supports. These are hinged metal brackets, one on each side of the back of the rear seat. The brackets fit into metal ears on the floor of the car. Use a screwdriver to remove the clip holding the pin that goes through the hinged arm into the ear. Be careful. These clips often fly off and disappear into the wilderness. Now push the hinged arms toward the middle of the car to clear the ears. Do both sides.

Remove the seat from the car. The protective floor mat is held by two stiff plastic bands screwed into the floor. Don't remove the screws, just pull up on the rear of the band and free it from the slot in the carpet or rubber mat. Do both sides and roll back the carpet.

Put the fire extinguisher close to the car where you can reach it.

Sciroccos: Just pull the bottom of the rear seat upward. Simple.

All Models: The fuel tank sending unit is under the circular protective metal cap. Remove the three phillips screws, pull off the cap and there's the unit. Remove the electrical connector. With your screwdriver and hammer, tap the notched outer ring of the unit one tenth of a turn counterclockwise ↺ and pull the sending unit and gasket free. Don't bend the wire arm. Go back to Step 4 and inspect the tank, then return here. If your gas tank is OK, replace the sender unit, the gasket, the electrical connection and the protective cover. Replace the floor mat and back seat. Hook up the battery ground strap. If you determined earlier that you have a good fuel pump and an adequate supply of gas to the fuel distributor, but your car still won't start, more investigation is needed.

All Models: If you've got crud in the tank and fuel filter, you must remove and clean the tank (Procedure

Step 5. (Cont'd.)

18), clean the fuel distributor control plunger (Procedure 4), the control pressure regulator (Procedure 3, Step 3), do the injector test (Procedure 5) and replace the fuel filter, (Procedure 2, Step 2).

If the tank checked out OK, we'd better break out the gauge and get serious.

PROCEDURE 3: CHECK FUEL INJECTION SYSTEM AND CONTROL PRESSURE. Phase 2.

Condition: Engine won't or difficult to start (hot or cold).

Tools and materials: Phase 2 tool kit including the fuel pressure gauge described at the beginning of this Chapter.

Remarks: The following procedure is a basic test for any fuel injection problem, providing you're sure the fuel pump works and delivers sufficient fuel.

It's impossible to do the Procedure without a pressure gauge. It'd be like taking your temperature with your finger.

Clean off the top of the fuel distributor and make sure all the fuel line connections are sparkling clean. If there's no dirt in the fuel system, don't add any. These tests will be most accurate if the engine is cold. Cold means the engine hasn't been run for at least four hours. It's preferable to leave the car unused overnight. Before beginning work, find out the air (ambient) temperature. Use a thermometer or call a local radio station.

Step 1. Hook Up Fuel Pressure Gauge

Fuel line connections all clean? Good. At the Fuel distributor, remove the connection (14mm) on the fuel line running from the *top* of the distributor to the control pressure regulator. Connect the disconnected end of the fuel line into the output line on the pressure gauge. Now connect the intake line on the gauge to the fuel distributor. Use 14mm wrenches to tighten the line connections. Hang the guage with a chain, wire or string from the hood's underside. The gauge is now part of the fuel line from the fuel distributor to the CPR. Open the valve in the gauge.

Step 2. De-electrify CPR

Pull the elctrical plug from the face of the CPR and tuck it out of the way.

Step 3. Pressurize!

Remove the fuel pump relay from the relay plate and jump terminals L13 and L14 (Procedure 1, Step 1).

Go to the front of the car and make sure the gauge valve is *open*. What's the pressure reading on the gauge? Check the graph on the next page and compare your reading to the outside temperature. Let's say the outside temperature is 20°C (68°F). Your gauge should read between 1.35 and 1.75 bar (19-24 psi). You have just measured **cold control pressure.**

Now *close* the gauge valve and watch the dial. Keep the jumper wire in the relay plate. The pressure should rise to be between 4.5 and 5.2 bar (65-75 psi). You have just measured **system pressure.**

Open the gauge valve again. Take off the jumper wire from the relay plate and reinstall the fuel pump relay. Reconnect the CPR electrical plug. Ask Friend to turn the key so the engine turns over about eight times; or, if the car will start, keep the engine speed as close to idle as possible. Watch the pressure gauge. This time the needle should creep up the dial and then read between 3.4 and 3.8 bar (49-55 psi). You have just measured **warm control pressure.**

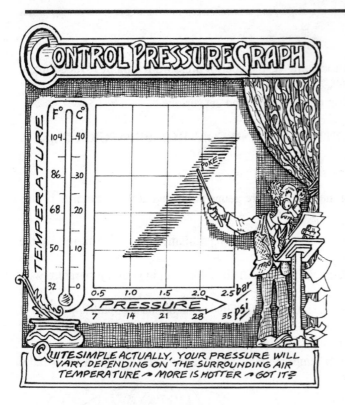

CONTROL PRESSURE GRAPH

QUITE SIMPLE ACTUALLY, YOUR PRESSURE WILL
VARY DEPENDING ON THE SURROUNDING AIR
TEMPERATURE ⌁ MORE IS HOTTER ⌁ GOT IT?

Step 3. (Cont'd.)

Keep the gauge valve open, operate the starter eight times to keep the engine running. Turn the engine off and watch the gauge. Does the needle slowly slip down the scale? It should stay above 1.6 bar (23 psi). Take a ten minute walk around the block and come back to check the gauge. Still above 1.6 bar? It should be. If it's just on the mark, wait another ten minutes and check again. Low? Let's isolate the problem.

Close the valve on the gauge, get Friend to operate the starter eight times or idle the engine if you can. Wait that endless ten minutes and have another look. 1.6 bar? If it's below the mark, then there's a leak somewhere. We can find it.

Pressure figures above 1.6 bar show that there are no leaks in either the primary or control systems. That's good. You people go to Procedure 5. The rest of you stay here.

Evaluation: Low Cold Control Pressure: The control pressure regulator is damaged and must be replaced. See Procedure 21.

Low Warm Control Pressure: Either the control pressure regulator is shot, or the juice to the CPR never made it. Check out Procedure 4.

Low System Pressure: Lots to do to find the cause of low system pressure.

Whatever your problems, continue.

Carefully check the tightness of all connections in the fuel system. This includes fuel pump connections, the hose between the fuel pump and fuel accumulator, all braided hoses from the fuel distributor to the injectors, the fuel pressure regulator, the cold start valve, etc. One of these is probably loose. If you find a loose connection, tighten it and do the pressure test again. Everything tight? Carry on.

Step 4. Try Again

If your gauge reads below 1.6 bar and all the connections are tight, close the valve on the pressure gauge line and run the engine for a few seconds. Off with the engine and another 20 minute run around the block. If the gauge reads 1.6 bar or above when the valve is closed, but was 1.6 bar or below when open, the control pressure regulator has an internal leak. It has to be replaced; Procedure 21.

If the gauge reads 1.6 bar with the valve open or closed, the regulator is OK but the fuel pump check valve is worn out or the fuel distributor rubber O ring has broken. Remove the three screws holding the fuel distributor to the mixture control unit and see what the O ring looks like. If it's broken or nicked, replace it. Give the new one a shot of silicone spray before putting it back on the base of the fuel distributor. Re-install and tighten the screws.

That wasn't your trouble? Try this.

Step 5. Fuel Pump Check Valve

Chock and then jack up the right rear of the car and block it well. In earlier model pumps the check valve is in the left side inside the pipe connecting the fuel line to the fuel accumulator. On later models this pipe begins at the rear of the pump. Remove the battery ground strap (10mm wrench). Remove the gas cap to relieve pressure in the system. Now, with a piece of rag moistened in kerosene, carefully clean the fuel pump check valve connection. Remove all traces of undercoating, mud, buffalo chips, etc.

To remove the check valve, remove the 17mm brass nut. Pull off the gasket, the brass line connection and the other gasket. Tuck the line where it won't touch dirt. Now screw out the fuel pump check valve and its

Step 5. (Cont'd.)

big gasket (15mm wrench). Watch for loose gas in the eyes! There's another gasket behind the check valve; remove it as you get the valve out. Jog down to your VW dealer and buy a new valve. Get new gaskets, too.

Install the new fuel pump check valve along with the gasket. Tighten it one turn past finger tight. Important! **DO NOT OVERTIGHTEN!** With the valve in, replace one gasket, put back the fuel line, then the other gasket and the 15mm nut. Tighten it. Check once more that all connections are good and tight.

Remove the blocks, lower the car and replace the battery ground strap. Do the pressure test again. If the readings are not within acceptable limits and all line connections are good, replace the control pressure regulator with a new one (Procedure 21). Still not right? Then:

Step 6. Check System Pressure Again

Keep your fuel pressure gauge between the control pressure regulator and the fuel distributor. Switch the valve to closed. Run the engine at idle and get the pressure up to 4.5 to 5.2 bar (65-75 psi). If the pressure is too high or too low, the fuel distributor or fuel distributor pressure relief valve is bad.

Step 7. Check Pressure Relief Valve

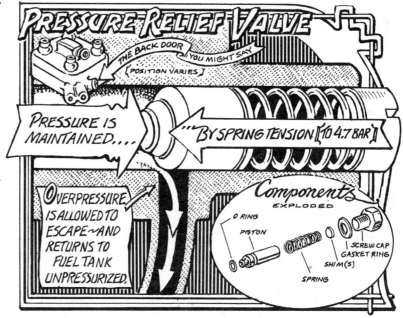

Remarks: The acceptable limits in system pressure is plus or minus 0.3 bar (8 to 10 lbs psi). Unless your system pressure is way beyond these limits, don't touch the relief valve, but the shims are the same.

If your pressure is way off, first call your VW dealer to see if they have a new valve or pressure relief valve shims. Without the shims you cannot do a repair! There are two sizes available, a 0.10mm shim (a 0.06 bar change, Part #063133489) and a 0.50mm shim (a 0.30 bar change, Part #062133489A).

The pressure relief valve is just to the left of the large braided or plastic return hose on the base of the fuel distributor. Remove the end plug (6mm allen or 13mm wrench). Don't lose the copper ring, the shims or the spring between the end plug and the piston inside the fuel distributor body.

Be very careful of this relief piston. If you drop it, kiss it goodbye. Pull it out with a thin wooden stick and not needle nose pliers! On the top of the piston is a rubber O ring so make sure it came out with the piston. Check for dirt or crud inside the piston's housing. Carefully flush the hole with gas.

If the relief piston did not move easily in its housing, carefully clean it and the rubber O ring with gasoline. Make sure that the small O ring on the tip of the piston is in good shape. Buy a new one if it's at all damaged. Install the piston, spring, and original shim, and tighten a new copper ring over the end plug. Do the fuel system pressure check again (Step 1) because you may have adjusted the pressure without changing shims if you found dirt.

If the pressure is still too high or low, change the shims. To increase pressure, use the larger shim. To decrease it, use the smaller shim. If this doesn't fix the pressure, buy your car a new fuel distributor and install it (Procedure 25).

Pressure OK, but the engine still won't run properly? Press on.

PROCEDURE 4: CHECK CONTROL PRESSURE REGULATOR. Phase 2.

Condition: Low *warm* control pressure

Tools and materials: Phase 2 tool kit, VOM

Step 1. Check Control Pressure Regulator (CPR) Electrical Supply

With the battery ground strap reconnected (10mm wrench), remove the plug from the rear of the alternator (8mm) and switch your VOM to 15 volts DC. Let's see if there's any juice to the CPR. Pull the plug from the front of the CPR and turn the ignition to ON. Insert the red (positive) VOM probe into one terminal in the plug on the end of the wire. Ground the negative VOM probe. If you get a reading of 11.5 volts (the minimum), go to Step 3. If there's no voltage, switch the positive probe into the other plug wire terminal. Nothing? Check the fuel pump relay and fuse (Procedure 1) and the electrical wire to the CPR for shorts and breaks. Still not running properly? Continue and...

Step 2. Check CPR Heater Coil Resistance

Disconnect the battery ground strap again (10mm wrench). Turn the VOM to the RX1K (ohm scale) and touch the VOM probes, one on each terminal in the connector on the face of the control pressure regulator. You should get a reading of around 20 ohms; if you do, move on. If not, replace the control pressure regulator with a new one (Procedure 21). Don't forget to put back the alternator plug in the rear of the alternator.

Pressure regulator OK but the car still won't start? Stay cool; there's another possible cause for the problem: dirt, filth or scum.

Step 3. Dirty Bertie?

Keep the battery ground strap disconnected and then clean and disconnect the two small braided fuel lines to the control pressure regulator (13 and 14mm wrenches). Be careful; a little gas will drain out from the lines. Shine a flashlight inside the regulator from where you removed the hoses. If the screen inside those holes is dirty or clogged, it must be cleaned. No dirt—go on to Procedure 5.

Remove the two 5mm allen head bolts holding the pressure regulator to the side of the crankcase. Pull the regulator off and clean the screens. If there are lots of particles in the screens, take the regulator to a gas station and blow it out with compressed air. Now check the condition of the gas tank if you haven't already done so (Procedure 2, Step 5).

Once you've done that, soak the regulator in clean gasoline without immersing the electrical connection. Find the line from the control pressure regulator to the fuel distributor. Remove the 13mm captive nut at the fuel distributor and blow through the line to blast out any dirt. Next pour a little gasoline down it to remove your breath moisture. Reconnect the line at the distributor and reinstall the regulator. Put back the two braided hoses and the battery ground strap and go to Procedure 6. Engine still doesn't work? Continue with Procedure 5.

PROCEDURE 5: CHECK AIR SENSOR PLATE POSITION AND CONTROL PLUNGER RESIST-ANCE. Phase 2.

Condition: Car won't start or run/idle.

Tools and materials: Phase 1 tool kit and a strong-ish magnet.

Remarks: Keep the gauge in position with the valve open.

Step 1. Sensor Plate Centered?

If the engine won't start, turn the engine over with the key for about 5 seconds to pressurize the fuel system. Turn the key off. With a screwdriver loosen the hose clamp around the big rubber elbow over the top of the air sensor plate. Next remove the hose clamp on the other end of the boot where it is fastened to the duct running to the throttle valve housing on the intake manifold. Pull the rubber boot completely free. Examine

Step 1. (Cont'd.)

the boot for cracks, etc., and make a note to buy a new one if it's at all damaged. Check carefully to see if the sensor plate is in the center of its conical housing. I will call this housing the air cone. You know, a being from Remulac in the South of France. Run a 0.10mm (0.004 in) feeler gauge blade around the gap between the perimeter of the plate and the air cone. If the feeler gauge binds at one or more positions, the plate is not centered. Use your 10mm socket to loosen the bolt holding the plate in position on the arm. Run the feeler gauge around the perimeter once more. When the plate is centered, retighten the bolt. Check with the feeler gauge to make sure the plate is *really* centered.

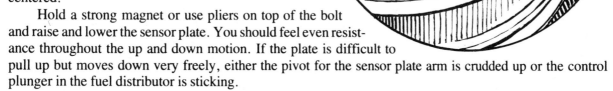

Hold a strong magnet or use pliers on top of the bolt and raise and lower the sensor plate. You should feel even resistance throughout the up and down motion. If the plate is difficult to pull up but moves down very freely, either the pivot for the sensor plate arm is crudded up or the control plunger in the fuel distributor is sticking.

Step 2. Check and Lubricate Sensor Plate Arm Pivot

Let's examine the pivot first. Remove the six 10mm bolts and the two 8mm nuts from the top of the mixture control unit and lift the top free. Clean any crud away from the pivot with a Q-Tip moistened in gasoline or solvent. Lubricate the pivot with a hit of WD-40 or even better, some Berryman Chem Tool B-12. That should make the arm move much more freely. Keep at it if there's a lot of junk around the pivot because erratic action of the arm will cause all kinds of starting problems and weird running conditions.

Carefully put everything back together and have Friend start the engine while you hold the sensor plate with your magnet. When the engine sputters, lift the plate and the engine should start. Lower the plate and the engine should idle. If not, go to Procedure 6 and free the binding control plunger.

PROCEDURE 6: CHECK FUEL DISTRIBUTOR CONTROL PLUNGER. Phase 2.

Condition: Car won't start, dirt in fuel system, runs poorly, low power output.

Tools and materials: Phase 1 tool kit, rubber O ring, maybe a new fuel filter, Berryman Chem Tool B-12 spray.

Step 1. Disconnect the battery ground strap (10mm wrench). Remove the three screws holding the fuel distributor on top of the mixture control unit and carefully pull it off. You may have to loosen one or more of the fuel lines to get at the screws. Hold your hand under the fuel distributor so the control plunger doesn't fall out. Turn it upside down and look at what you've got. If there's dirt or crud around that central shiny steel plunger, that's your problem. Gently pull the plunger out of the fuel metering barrel in which it sits. See if it's operating room clean. If so, install the fuel plunger by pushing it all the way in with your thumb, *small* shoulder first. Then turn the distributor over and be sure the plunger slides slowly but smoothly downward. If it sticks, clean the plunger very carefully with gasoline and reinstall it. Test the sliding action about 20 times. If it sticks even once, read on. If it's OK, skip the next paragraph.

Remove the lines from the top of the fuel distributor: first replace the three screws into the fuel distributor and screw it back onto the air flow sensor housing. Now loosen the five bolts holding the fuel lines to the fuel injectors and cold start valve on top of the fuel distributor (13mm wrench) after identifying and marking their positions with masking tape. Remove the fuel input line from the left side of the fuel distributor (17mm wrench) and the two small lines from the rear (13mm wrench). Remove the 17mm bolt holding the fuel return

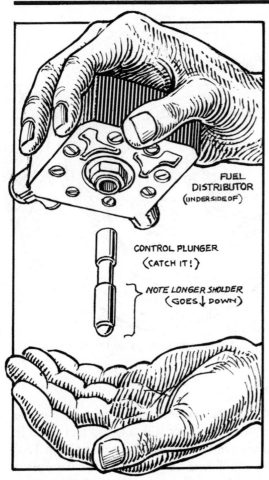

FUEL DISTRIBUTOR
(UNDERSIDE OF)

CONTROL PLUNGER
(CATCH IT!)

NOTE LONGER SHOLDER
(GOES ↓ DOWN)

Step 1. (Cont'd.)

line. When all is free, remove the three screws on top of the fuel distributor and lift the whole thing out, making sure you don't drop the control plunger. If you drop and damage the plunger, you'll have to buy a new fuel distributor! Lastly, remove the rubber O ring from the base of the distributor or the top of the air flow sensor housing.

Spray the plunger and the fuel metering barrel with Berryman Chem Tool B-12. Give everything a good soaking, then clean the plunger with a lint-free rag. Check inside the fuel distributor for minute particles of dirt. When you're sure everything is clean, flush it with gasoline. Again, don't build any fires close by.

Moisten the control plunger with gasoline and put it into the fuel distributor with the *small* shoulder going in first. The plunger should now move up and down freely. If it does, you've solved the problem. No? If the control plunger is binding and can't be freed, it must be replaced. Go to Procedure 26.

Put a new rubber O ring around the base of the fuel distributor before reattaching it to the mixture control unit. Tighten the three screws and all the fuel lines. Hook up the battery ground strap and if you found crud around the plunger, buy and install a new fuel and air filter! Starts and runs OK? Great.

If the car won't start now, you probably installed the control plunger upside down. The *small* shoulder goes in first. Do it again, Sam. Still won't start or runs terrible? OK, let's check the fuel quantity at the injectors.

PROCEDURE 7: CHECK INJECTION VALVES (FUEL INJECTORS). Phase 2.

Condition: Car won't start or run right, hesitation at all speeds.

Tools and materials: Phase 1 tool kit, four glass receptacles (numbered 1, 2, 3 and 4)—it's nice to have laboratory-type graduated flasks for this test but something like cigar tubes will do in a pinch (if you can't get four, one will suffice), an 8 amp fused jumper wire, Friend, maybe a new injector or two with new O rings.

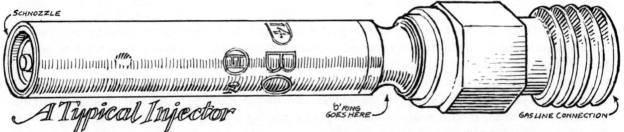

SCHNOZZLE

A Typical Injector

'O' RING GOES HERE

GAS LINE CONNECTION

Remarks: Remember gasoline is flammable so be careful and keep your fire extinguisher handy. If you found crud from Procedures 5 and 6, do Step 3 of this Procedure, then come back to Step 1.

Step 1. Test Injectors

Loosen the hose clamps on each end of the rubber boots above the air sensor plate housing. Pull the boot off to expose the air sensor plate (if you haven't done this step already).

Pull #1 injector out from the right side of the cylinder head. Just give it a firm tug to get it out; it doesn't screw in. Keep the fuel line attached to the injector and stick it into your receptacle. If you've managed to

Step 1. (Cont'd.)

obtain four receptacles, then pull the other three injectors and stick them into the containers. OK?

Remove the fused fuel pump relay from the relay plate (Procedure 1, Step 1) and bridge terminals L13 and L14 with your fused jumper wire. The fuel pump will spring into life pumping gasoline up to the fuel distributor.

Lift the air sensor plate all the way up with a magnet or needle nose pliers. Hold the center bolt, not the edge of the plate. Keep the plate up for 10 seconds. As the plate is lifted gas will flow out the end of the injector(s). The gas should spray out in an even cone shape. When you let go of the sensor plate, the gas flow should stop immediately. No drops or dribbles should form on the injector tip. Note the quantity of gasoline pumped out by the injector. Put a strip of masking tape to indicate the level in your receptacle. Great.

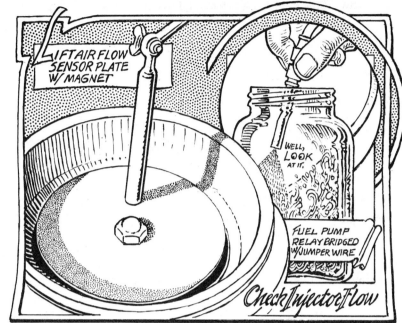

If you are testing one injector at a time, then install the injector you just tested back into the cylinder head, and test the other three using the above method. Remember to lift the sensor plate all the way up and hold it there for ten seconds. Also note the amount of gas the injector squirts.

Now what? Well, any injector which dribbles when the sensor plate is released or shoots anything other than a cone shaped spray is faulty and must be replaced. If one injector passes considerably more or less gas than the other three, either the injector is bad or the fuel line is blocked somewhat.

Step 2. Find the Problem

Swap the high or low injector with a brand new one from your parts pile (or buy one). Do the test again. If the injector installed on what is the high or low line gives the same quantity as the other three, then the old injector was faulty and you have solved the problem.

If the quantity is the same as it was *before* you installed the new injector, then the fuel line is blocked, or the fuel distributor is bad.

Put the new injector onto each of the other three fuel lines in turn if you suspect crud in the fuel lines. A new injector is the only sure test to determine if any of your old injectors are faulty.

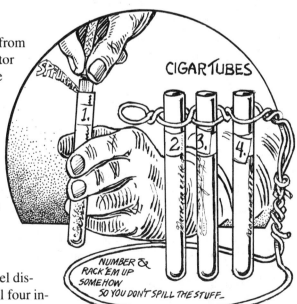

Step 3. Clean Lines

If you suspect junk in the line (or lines) from the fuel distributor to the injectors, let's clean them out. Remove all four injectors from their feed lines (11 and 14mm wrenches), keeping them in the 1, 2, 3, 4 order. Also remove the line from the cold start valve on the end of the intake manifold (13mm wrench). Place the fuel lines in the receptacles (or in one big one), bridge the fuel pump relay (L13 and L14) and lift the air flow sensor plate for 30 seconds to pump gas through the lines to clear them. Remove the relay

Step 3. (Cont'd.)

jumper wire, install the injectors and the cold start valve fuel line and do Step 1 again. If the flow hasn't equalized, the fuel distributor is shot and has to be replaced. See Procedure 26. Injectors OK—install the fuel pump relay back in the relay plate.

Now, if the engine starts but still has cold starting problems, let's find out why.

PROCEDURE 8: CHECK/REPLACE THERMO TIME SWITCH, ENGINE COLD. Phase 2.

Condition: Car difficult to start when cold.

Tools and materials: Phase 1 tool kit including test light or VOM, friend, maybe new thermo time switch.

Remarks: This switch controls the operation of the cold start valve which gets fuel only when the switch is cold. The workings of the switch are actuated by engine heat or the length of time the starter is operated. Before doing this test, check that the fuel lines to the fuel distributor are tight and that the rubber boot over the air sensor plate isn't cracked or loose. And check that the hose clamps are tight. See Procedure 14 for a hot engine test for the switch.

Step 1. Cool Thermo Time Switch

Skip this step if the engine hasn't been run for four hours. The thermo time switch is screwed into the top of the aluminum manifold on the left side of the cylinder head between the first and second spark plugs. A hose connects the manifold to the top rear of the radiator. Remove the electrical connection from the switch and unscrew it (22mm wrench or crescent wrench). You'll lose a little coolant, but don't fret. Put the end of the thermo switch in cold water with ice cubes if you have them. Don't immerse the entire switch, just the end that screws into the manifold. When it's cold, stick the electrical plug back onto the switch and lay the switch on top of the manifold so that the switch is grounded.

Step 2. Juice to Cold Start Valve?

Pull the big center wire from the coil to prevent the engine from starting and remove the electrical plug from the cold start valve. The valve is on the end of the intake manifold close to the right fender. Insert the probes of your VOM (switched to 15 volts DC) into the plug terminals on the end of the wire which was connected to the cold start valve. Have Friend operate the starter for 15 seconds without a pause. The VOM should zoom up to 12 volts DC, then ease down to zero volts. Did the VOM needle move backwards? Switch the probes in the plug and try again. If the needle stays at 12 volts, the thermo time switch is shot. If so, go to Step 4.

If you have juice and a good switch, go to Procedure 9. Nothing happened—did you have the switch grounded against the manifold. Yes? Continue.

Step 3. Try Again

Set VOM to 15 volts DC and put the negative probe onto a clean unpainted metal ground and push the other positive probe into one of the plug terminals on the cold start valve wire. Friend: turn the key and operate the starter. The needle should read 12 volts DC. No? Check the ground again. Still no? Put the positive VOM probe into the other plug terminal. Ask Friend to try the key again.

Step 3. (Cont'd.)

If the VOM needle reads 12 volts DC, there's juice to the switch but the thermo time switch itself is kaput and needs to be replaced. No electricity to the switch indicates a break in the wire which supplies power to the switch or that the wiring to the starter solenoid is faulty. See if you can find the break and splice in a new wire. See Chapter 20, Procedure 14, on how to splice.

Finally, if the VOM needle registered current *before* Friend operated the starter, the small wires to the solenoid on the starter are reversed. Terminal 30 wire has been switched with terminal 50 wire on the starter solenoid. Have you been messing with the starter lately? Check the wires.

Step 4. Replace Thermo Time Switch

If it's in place, remove the electrical plug from the top of the switch and use a crescent wrench to unscrew the switch from the coolant manifold. Screw in the new switch by hand until you're sure the threads aren't crossed, then tighten it with your crescent wrench. Replace the electrical plug and add a little antifreeze/water mix to the radiator to bring the coolant level up to the mark. Don't forget to re-install the big central coil wire. You're done.

PROCEDURE 9: CHECK COLD START VALVE. Phase 2.

Condition: Car difficult or impossible to start when cold, idles erratically, fuel consumption too high.

Tools and materials: Phase 2 tool kit, Friend, small glass receptacle to catch gas, maybe a new cold start valve. Keep your fire extinguisher handy. Engine cold?

Step 1. Isolate Valve From Thermo Time Switch

Since you just tested the thermo switch in the previous Procedure and found it to be OK (or replaced it), you must test the cold start valve to see if it's injecting gas into the intake manifold when it's supposed to.

Pull the electrical plug from the end of the cold start valve and put a piece of electrical tape over the electrical plug to prevent sparks flying about. Disconnect the plug from the rear of the alternator and pull the center wire from the coil.

Step 2. Remove Valve and Test It

Keep the fuel line attached to the valve but remove the two 6mm allen bolts holding the valve onto the intake manifold. Wipe the end of the valve clean. Jump the fuel pump relay as per Procedure 1, Step 1. Watch the nozzle on the valve for one minute. If gas squirts out the end or drops from the nozzle tip, the valve is defunct. Change it as per Procedure 23. No drips—remove the relay plate jumper wire and continue.

Step 3. Test Again

Reconnect the electrical plug onto the cold start valve (after removing the tape) and disconnect the electrical plug from the thermo time switch. Check to be sure the center coil wire is disconnected. Now you need a jumper wire to bridge the two terminals in the plug from the disconnected thermo time switch. Use a short piece of 15mm^2 (14 gauge) wire with the insulation stripped from both ends as a jumper wire. Put the cold start valve in the gas-catching receptacle, install the fuel pump relay and ask Friend to operate the starter for ten seconds. Watch the end of the valve. Gasoline should come out in an even cone-shaped spray and stop when Friend does. We don't want to see any drops form on the end of that valve when the engine stops turning.

Crud in the valve will give an erratic spray pattern. If yours sprays erratically or if drops form on the end of the valve, see Procedure 23 to change it. No gas sprayed at all? See Step 4.

If the valve tests OK, stick it back on the intake manifold and replace the electrical plug to it and the thermo time switch. Reconnect the coil wire and the alternator plug. If the engine still won't run right, go to Procedure 10.

Step 4. Why No Gas?

Keep the fuel pump relay in the relay plate and again disconnect the electrical plug from the cold start valve and examine the plug. It has a positive and a negative connection. Stick the positive probe of your VOM (set on 15 volts DC) into the positive terminal of the cold start valve plug and ground the other probe. Ask Friend to turn the engine over using the key for a second or two. The needle should read 12 volts DC. No? Try the probe in the other plug terminal and have Friend twiddle the starter again. Still nicht? Pull the fuel pump relay from the relay plate and bridge terminals L13 and L14 with your jumper wire (Procedure 1). Now try the above test again. 12 volts DC? The fuel pump relay is bad. Replace it. Whew. Replace the coil wire, the alternator plug and the thermo time switch plug or the thing will never start.

No voltage to the plug? There's a break in the wiring to solenoid terminal 50. Find the break and replace the wire—or have an auto electric shop do it for you.

PROCEDURE 10: CHECK AUXILIARY AIR REGULATOR. Phase 2.

Condition: Car impossible or difficult to start when cold, engine stalls just after starting on cold mornings, referral from other Procedures.

Tools and materials: Phase 1 tool kit, small piece of mirror, maybe a new auxiliary air regulator.

Remarks: The engine must be cold for this test, unless you've been referred here from Procedure 13. The regulator is located on the right side of the intake manifold with an air hose connected to the front and another to the rear.

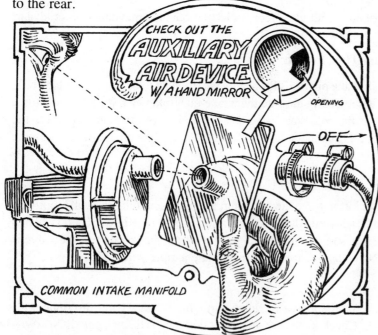

Step 1. Remove and Plug Hose

Loosen the hose clamps and pull both the hoses from the front and rear of the regulator. Put pencil stubs into the hoses to keep crud out.

Step 2. Pull Alternator Plug

Remove the big plug from the rear of the alternator after loosening the 8mm nut holding the metal clip securing the plug.

Step 3. Test

Turn the key to ON and watch the mirror to see if the rotary valve in the regulator is open. Keep looking and in about five minutes the rotary valve should begin to close. If you are freezing half to death on a Vermont January day, the valve will take a lot longer than five minutes to close. Perhaps you should pitch a tent. If the rotary valve closes, replace the air hoses, alternator plug and go to Procedure 11.

If the valve didn't close, you'll have to test for juice at the regulator. Proceed.

Step 4. Measure Resistance

Pull off the electrical plug from the rear of the regulator, disconnect the battery ground strap (10mm wrench) and insert the probes of your VOM (switched to RX1K) into the two terminals on the auxiliary air regulator. You should get a reading of 30 ohms. If the VOM reads infinity ∞, or much less than 30 ohms, replace the regulator with a new one. See Procedure 23. Correct resistance reading? Onward thru the fog.

Step 5. Check Power

Hook up the battery ground strap (10mm wrench), put the plug back into the alternator rear and switch the VOM to 15 volts DC. Put both probes of the VOM into the plug on the end of the wire running to the regulator and ask Friend to crank the starter. The car may start! The VOM should register 12 volts DC. If it doesn't, check for a break in the wires to the plug or check the fuel pump relay in the relay plate, see Procedure 1. If the regulator checks out OK but the engine still won't run as it should, try the next Procedure.

PROCEDURE 11: CHECK SENSOR PLATE HORIZONTAL POSITION. Phase 2.

Condition: Engine won't idle properly, stops when you lift your foot off the gas, runs erratically.

Tools and materials: Phase 1 tool kit, fuel pressure gauge.

Step 1. Hook Up Fuel Pressure Gauge (If It's Not Hooked Up Already)

Clean, then remove the fuel line running from the top of the fuel distributor to the control pressure regulator at the distributor end (14mm). Thoroughly clean the connections on the pressure gauge lines and hook it to the end of the CPR line and the vacant connection on the fuel distributor. Tighten the connections with the appropriate wrench and open the gauge valve. Hang the gauge from the hood with a piece of chain or string. Now remove the rubber boot from the top of the sensor plate. Check it for cracks, etc. while it's off.

Step 2. Pressurize!

Remove the fuel pump relay from the relay plate and jump terminals L13 and L14 with your fused wire (Procedure 1). Watch the pressure gauge; it should read 3.4 to 3.8 bar (49 to 55 psi). You may have to wait a minute or two for the pressure to get up there. Now pull the jumper wire from the relay plate and watch the pressure dial. It should fall no farther than 1.6 bar.

Let's take a look at the sensor plate position. The upper edge of the plate should be even with the bottom of the air cone taper. See the diagram. You have 0.5mm leeway. That means the plate can be 0.5mm below the bottom of the taper. If it's not level or is more than 0.5mm, adjust it.

To do so, put a magnet or pliers on the center bolt of the plate and lift the plate to its highest position. Under the plate there's a spring attached to a clip. This clip touches a small pin under the air sensor plate and determines the height of the plate when it's at rest. To raise or lower the rest position of the air sensor plate, raise or lower the height of the clip. Lift the sensor plate and use your fingers to pull off the spring and open or close the clip some. Reinstall the spring. If you drop the spring into the innards, unsnap the four clips holding the bottom part of the sensor housing and retrieve the spring from the top of the air filter.

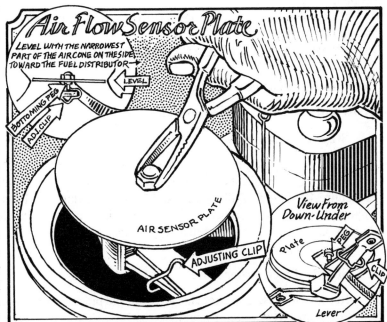

Step 2. (Cont'd.)

When you've got it right, start the engine, go through the pressure gauge test again as outlined in Procedure 3, Step 3. When that's done and checks out OK, remove the pressure gauge and reconnect the fuel lines. Install the fuel pump relay and the rubber elbow. The car will now start so turn to Chapter 10, adjust the idle speed (Procedure 18, Step 5) and then have the exhaust gas CO content adjusted.

 PROCEDURES FOR HOT STARTING PROBLEMS

You've got no gas in the tank if one of these procedures doesn't fix an engine that won't start, idle or stalls.

PROCEDURE 12: CHECK FUEL ACCUMULATOR. Phase 2.

Condition: Car won't start when weather is hot (above $32^{\circ}C$—$90^{\circ}F$).

Tools and materials: Phase 1 tool kit, maybe a new fuel accumulator.

Step 1. Chock, Jack and Block

Jack up the right rear side. Find the fuel accumulator nestled between the right rear wheel and the rear bumper about 8cm (3 in) inside the body overhang.

Step 2. Large or Small?

The fuel accumulator stores gasoline under pressure to help start your car when the engine is very hot. There are two types, a 20cc and a 40cc. The larger (40cc) version has a one inch long projection from the rear of the accumulator. Most hot-starting problems in early C.I.S. cars can be traced to small accumulators. If you have the small type, replace it with a large one from VW. (Procedure 24)

If you've already got the larger accumulator, have VW check the CO content of your car's exhaust gasses. Too high or low will make a hot fuel injected engine difficult to start. If this doesn't solve the problem…more checks.

Check Fuel Injectors once again (Procedure 7). If the injectors pass the test, keep reading.

PROCEDURE 13: CHECK AUXILIARY AIR REGULATOR (ENGINE HOT). Phase 1

Condition: Hot engine won't start.

Tools and materials: Phase 1 tool kit.

Step 1. Rotary Valve Closed?

Use vise grips to pinch closed the air hose on the left side of the auxiliary air regulator facing the left fender. The engine idle should remain the same or drop *very* slightly. If it changes more than 100 rpm, do Procedure 10, Step 5. Still won't start? Go to Procedure 14. If your car has a high altitude kit, check the vacuum hoses to the barometric cell on the radiator before following Procedure 14. Are the hoses secure? Pull off one of the hoses at the cell and blow, then suck on the connection. Reinstall the vacuum hoses and try the engine again. Nothing? Continue.

Step 2. Pinch Other Hose

Remove the vise grips from the left hose and pinch the right one. Any change? If so, you didn't pinch the left hose properly. Do Step 1 again.

OK . . .if your rpm's change only slightly when you pinch the hose, see Chapter 13, Procedure 5, Step 4, and check the deceleration valve. If that's not your problem, come back here.

PROCEDURE 14: CHECK THERMO TIME SWITCH (ENGINE HOT). Phase 2.

Condition: Hot engine won't start/idle.

Tools and materials: Phase 2 tool kit.

This test *must* be done when the engine is hot. Pull the electrical plug off the cold start valve on the end of the intake manifold and connect the test light to the terminals in the plug—not to the plug on the valve itself! Ask Friend to operate the starter. The test light should *not* light up. If it does, the thermo time switch is bad. Replace it (Procedure 8, Step 4).

If your test light doesn't light, the switch is probably OK but only a cold engine test (Procedure 8) will tell for sure. So check the position of the sensor plate (Procedure 11). If you still can't get your hot engine to start, run all the Procedures in the cold starting section (Procedures 1 to 11). Look for a leak around the fuel pump and all its line connections. Leaks not only cause problems when hot starting, but are **extremely** dangerous. A stray spark may barbecue the whole car. Be sure the injectors are pressed fully home in the cylinder head.

Check the O rings around the injectors and if they're funky, cracked or just plain missing, you'll have terrific starting problems, hot or cold. Soak the new rings in gasoline for five minutes before installing on the injectors.

PROCEDURE 15: CHECKLIST FOR SITUATIONS WHERE ENGINE STARTS BUT WON'T KEEP RUNNING. Phase 2.

Condition: You know all too well.

Tools and materials: Phase 1 and 2 tool kits.

Remarks: The ignition components have been checked (Chapter 10) and the rubber boot over the air sensor plate is intact and installed properly.

Step 1. Check Idle

Chapter 10, Procedure 18, Step 5.

Step 2. Check Injectors

Procedure 7. Also recheck the condition of the rubber O rings around the fuel injectors. Remember, those injectors have to be tight or you'll have air leaks that result in your engine constantly stalling out.

Step 3. Check Exhaust

If everything is OK so far, start the car and pass your hand along the length of the exhaust system (**don't** touch it). Feel for spurts of hot exhaust gasses from breaks and cracks in the pipe. Fuel injected engines run poorly when the exhaust system isn't in good shape. If you find any leaks, turn to Chapter 13, Procedure 3.

Step 4. Everything Tight?

If we still haven't cured your stalling problem, check the tightness of the cylinder head (Chapter 18, Procedure 11) and the intake manifold bolted to the cylinder head (Chapter 18, Procedure 10). Check that all the vacuum hoses are in their correct positions, that the line from the brake booster to the intake manifold is in good condition and that the boot over the mixture control unit is tight and has no cracks or breaks in it.

PROCEDURE 16: CHECK HIGH IDLE. Phase 2.

Condition: Engine idles too fast.

Tools and materials: Phase 1 tool kit.

Step 1. Adjust Idle Screw

Chapter 10, Procedure 18, Step 5.

Step 2. Check Throttle Valve

If adjusting the idle screw didn't set the idle right, do this. On top of the intake manifold, just to the left of where the accelerator cable attaches to the throttle valve linkage, is an 8mm nut with a screw inside it. This is the throttle valve adjusting screw. Loosen the 8mm nut slightly. Turn the screw clockwise ↻ until it just touches the cam of the throttle linkage, then another one half turn. Tighten the 8mm bolt, holding a screwdriver in the screw so it won't turn. Now try adjusting the idle again.

Step 3. No Go?

If you still can't get the idle down, the most likely suspect is the control pressure regulator (CPR). Do the test at Procedure 4. If the CPR checks out OK, take the car to VW and have them check the exhaust gas CO content. That'll fix it.

Step 4. Check Ignition Vacuum Advance/Retard Unit

Start the engine and pull the hose closest to the left fender from the vacuum unit on the side of the distributor. Seal the hose with a piece of tape. The engine revs should change; if they don't, check all vacuum line connections. Take a look at the hose diagram in Chapter 13 or the sticker on the underside of your hood for the hose layout. If your hoses are all OK, your distributor vacuum retard is bad. Replacing it is simple (Chapter 10, Procedure 26).

Did the idle drop? Reconnect the vacuum hose to the distributor. If your rpm's increase again, the auxiliary air regulator is open whereas it should be closed because the engine is warm.

Step 5. Check Auxiliary Air Regulator

See Procedure 13.

Step 6. Continue Dr. Watson

Check the position of the air flow sensor plate if you still have difficulty getting your idle correct (Procedure 11).

If the vacuum lines are where they should be and there's a good spray pattern at the injectors, something is wrong with the fuel distributor. Do the Berryman Chem Tool B-12 cleaning operation (Procedure 6). If that doesn't fix it, replace the fuel distributor which isn't a cheap item. Before you hit the bricks, take the car to VW and get the exhaust gas CO content analyzed and adjusted to finally verify that the fuel distributor is bad.

CIS COMPONENT REPLACEMENT PROCEDURES

The following procedures show how to change components in your fuel injection system. You have been referred here from other Procedures or Chapters while troubleshooting or adjusting your CIS system.

PROCEDURE 17: REPLACING FUEL PUMP. Phase 2.

Condition: Fuel pump tests show it's time to be retired.

Tools and materials: Phase 1 tool kit, container to catch gasoline, a plastic bowl, replacement fuel pump, two new copper fuel line gaskets.

Remarks: If it's July 4th, keep the fireworks away from your work area—every day, have the fire extinguisher handy.

Step 1. Remove Old Fuel Pump

First remove the gas cap to relieve pressure in the fuel system and then disconnect the battery ground strap (10mm wrench). Jack and block the right rear of the car and chock the front wheels to stop them from rolling and with your screwdriver in hand, twist yourself under the car into a position where gas won't drip into your eye. Place your container under the fuel pump and remove the hose clamp on the hose running from the gas tank to the pump. Plug the end of the hose with a pencil.

Remove the 10mm nut holding the front of the pump to the bracket on the floor pan. Next remove the 13mm nut holding the pump to the right side of the car body. Free the pump from the brackets and pull it down toward you.

Step 2. Remove Juice Supply

All Models: To remove the fuel line running from the fuel accumulator to the pump, take off the 15mm nut holding the fuel line in place; then remove the copper gasket, the metal line connector and another gasket. Don't get the end of the fuel line dirty! Now pull the fuel pump free.

Models from mid-1977 on: Push back the rubber boots on the ends of the two wires at the front of the pump. Remove the 8mm and 9mm nuts and pull off the wires and washers. Screw the nuts and washers onto the pump studs for safekeeping.

Early Models: Your pump has a simple, push-on/pull-off connection, so pull it.

Step 3. Connect New Fuel Pump

If your new fuel pump doesn't come with the 8 and 9mm nuts to connect the electrical wires, use the nuts from your old pump (if yours is so equipped).

OK, back under the car with your wrenches spread neatly within reach. Slip the new pump into the plastic mount and reconnect the electrical plug or the two wires. The hot wire goes to the positive pump terminal. On a screw type terminal don't forget to put on the brass washers before the nuts. Tighten the nuts and replace the line to the fuel accumulator. Peel the rubber boots back over the terminals. Install the new copper gaskets on each side of the fuel line. Tighten the 15mm fuel line nut and position the fuel pump on its mounting bracket. Tighten the 10 and 13mm nuts. Push the hose from the fuel tank onto the pump and tighten the hose clamp.

Reconnect the battery ground strap and start the car. Now go to the right rear of the car. Can you hear the fuel pump merrily whirring away? Hallelujah! Clean up. Gasoline will remove that nasty, sticky, underbody coating from your fingers.

PROCEDURE 18: REMOVE FUEL TANK. Phase 2.

Condition: Fuel tank requires steam cleaning/replacing.

Tools and materials: Phase 1 tool kit, large container to catch fuel, assortment of small hose clamps, new fuel tank if required, safety glasses.

Remarks: This Procedure works for carbureted and diesel engined cars. You may have less hoses than noted in the text but if you mark 'em, you're OK. Keep gas off exposed flesh—it burns. Likewise refrain from visiting "Marlboro Country" as you do this Procedure. Your fire extinguisher should be within a frenzied grasp. Disconnect the battery ground strap (10mm wrench) before you begin work.

Step 1. Remove Tank Sending Unit

Late models do it now; early models do it later. See Procedure 2, Step 3.

Step 2. Drain Fuel Tank

Place a container under the fuel pump. Loosen the clamp and pull off the hose which runs to the fuel

Step 2. (Cont'd.)

pump from the fuel tank. Drain the tank. If your container won't hold all the gas, drain it in two stages, putting a pencil in the line temporarily to stop the fuel. Pour the fuel into a gas can and stash it somewhere safe. When the tank is drained, go on.

Step 3. Chock, Jack and Block

Jack up the back of the car at least 64cm (24 in). Support and block it well, but don't support the rear axle beam which has to come off to get at the fuel tank. If you can get the use of a garage type lift, you've got it made.

Step 4. Disconnect Brake Lines

Before doing this on the right hand side, drop the fuel pump (not diesel or carbureted cars). See Procedure 17, Step 1. Then use two wrenches to separate the 11mm and 14mm captive nuts where the metal brake lines go through a bracket welded to the floor pan. Disconnect the right side, then do the left.

Step 5. Remove Fuel Filler Hose

This is the big hose connected to the back of the fuel tank. Loosen the hose clamp, then the clamp on the other end of the short pipe and pull the hose free.

Step 6. Lower Axle Beam

Remove the two nuts and washers from the right side of the axle beam (17mm socket). Now move over to the left side and do the same. When removing the last nut, be very careful the axle beam doesn't swing down and smack you in the teeth. The axle beam may be held up by a spring connected to the brake pressure regulator. If so, push up the axle beam and release the spring at the end of the axle beam. Leave the spring hanging on the brake pressure regulator.

Step 7. Disconnect Sending Unit (Early Models to mid-1977)

At the right side of the tank feel up and pull off the electrical connection to the fuel tank sending unit.

Step 8. Pull Return Hose—All Models

Feel further along the right front side of the tank for a small hose connected with a VW type clamp. Pull it off and remind yourself to replace the clamp with a new standard hose clamp.

Step 9. Remove Rubber Exhaust Hangers—All Models

Use a screwdriver to lever off the two rubber hangers holding the muffler to the floor pan and let the exhaust pipe hang loose, as surfers say.

Step 10. Remove Tank Retaining Straps—All Models

Remove the two 15mm nuts and washers holding the tank retaining straps to the floor pan. Now unhook the straps at the rear and remove them. Put your gas catcher under the rear of the fuel tank where you removed the fuel filler hose. Push your fingers into the tank where that hose was connected and move a small flap (if your model has one). This drains the last of the gas and saves you from getting drenched when you maneuver the tank out.

Step 11. Remove Vent and Return Lines—All Models

Turn the tank slightly to the left and pull it down toward you. As it starts to move, you'll see five (or less) colored vent lines on the right side of the tank. Diesels may only have one vent. Starting from the *front* of the car they are aquamarine, yellow, clear, green and pink. If there's also a bigger black return line, loosen the clamp and pull it off. The colored lines are held by VW clamps and are hell to get off. I use a pair of pliers around the clamp and pull gently but firmly. Don't bend or break the metal pipes on the tank where the vent lines connect or you'll need a brazing job, too. When the lines are disconnected, the tank is free.

Step 11. (Cont'd.)

Later Models: The Sending unit electrical connection is still connected to the top of the tank. Pull it off.

All Models: Carefully lower the tank to the ground. Remove two rubber protective pieces on the front seam of the tank. Stash 'em. Also remove the thin metal heat shield from the bottom of the tank—it just pries off.

By now your hands, arms, face and other parts are covered with a nasty combination of fuel and underbody coating. Use a gasoline moistened rag to get it off and finish off with soap or hand cleaner.

If your tank looks salvageable, take it to the steam cleaner. Stick around and when they've got the inside thoroughly clean, check it yourself. If there's still any rust or gunk inside, have them do it again. When it's done to your satisfaction, let it dry completely (for an hour or so). Now check it very carefully once more. Use your flashlight to poke into nooks and crannies. I had a tank that rattled after it was cleaned and close inspection revealed large chunks of loose solder. I got them out with a sharpened knitting needle, and was able to use the tank.

If you need to replace your tank with a new one, take the old one to the VW dealer and compare it with the new tank making sure it has the correct number of fuel and vent lines.

PROCEDURE 19: CLEANING FUEL LINES. Phase 1.

Condition: Dirt in fuel tank and therefore the fuel lines.

Tools and materials: Phase 1 tool kit, compressed air or good lungs, tea, juice or something to rinse away that awful taste after you blow out the fuel lines. New restrictor valve installed in fuel line for carbureted engines.

Step 1. Prepare to Blow

Carbureted engines: Remove the fuel return line from the Y connection between the carburetor, fuel pump and the tank return line. Cut off about 23cm (9 in) from the return line which will include the restrictor valve at the carburetor. Remove the fuel line from the fuel pump and blow down it from the carb end to eliminate any junk. Insert a plastic in-line hose connector (from VW) on the remaining return line and push on a new piece of hose with a restrictor valve installed in it. Use tiny hose clamps or VW type clamps to make an air and gas tight connection. Clean the fuel pump diaphragm screen with gasoline (See Chapter 7, Procedure 7, Step 7) and blow out any junk from inside the fuel pump.

Diesel: Remove the 15 and 17mm bolts holding the two lines in the fuel filter and remove the lines.

All Models: If you're lucky enough to have compressed air, insert the tip of the blowing tool into the end of the fuel line and give a few blasts. Remember, you're blowing from the engine compartment toward the rear. Those using lung power should give hard puffs. Pretend you're Louis Armstrong playing "The Saints". Blow three or four times, rinsing out your mouth between takes. Don't suck by mistake.

Ask Friend to crawl under the rear of the car and hold a hand against the end of the fuel line. If your breath doesn't reach the other end of the line, you'll have to resort to something a little more drastic.

Take a long piece of baling wire or something similar and wrap one end with electrical tape. This protects the fuel line from being gouged. Clean the end of the wire before taping it or the tape will come off and clog up the line. Poke the wire through the fuel line until it pops out the other end. Pull the wire all the way through and blow again. It's clear! Moby Dick would be proud of you.

Step 2. Check Fuel Lines

Look over the fuel lines in the engine compartment for cracks and breaks. Use a flashlight to check the metal fuel lines under the right side of the car, just inside the body overhang. These lines often have tiny holes from being battered by rocks and road junk. Leaks are easy to spot—a dark-colored stain around the hole where dirt has stuck to it. I've also seen fuel lines broken or badly damaged because someone tried to raise the car with the jack resting on the lines.

Step 3. Replace Damaged Fuel Lines

Damaged fuel lines should be replaced right away…a simple job. The lines are held in place to the underbody by metal clips. Bend down the clips holding the old lines, pull them out and install shiny new lines from VW. Push the clips back up to hold the lines and you're done.

PROCEDURE 20: REINSTALL FUEL TANK. Phase 2.

Condition: Fuel tank is out.

Tools and materials: Phase 1 tool kit, can of approved brake fluid and Friend.

Remarks: Install the heat shield, if you have one, onto the bottom of the tank.

Step 1. Install All Vent Lines and Hoses

Get under the car with the fuel tank and push on the return line closest to the right front of the tank and secure it with a hose clamp. If you have five colored vent lines, put them back in place. The order from the front is: aquamarine, yellow, clear, green and pink. Carbureted and diesel engines have one, two or three vent lines. When you put vent lines back, don't push too hard on the pipes where they connect. If you break a pipe, you'll have to have it brazed back on, so be careful. Fasten the lines with VW type clamps (they should still be on their hoses). For some reason I've had a lot of trouble with the clear one. The easiest way I've found is to hold the clamp with a pair of pliers and just push the line on.

Step 2. Install Sending Unit Wire

Very carefully thread the fuel tank sending unit electrical connection up through the hole in the floor if your sending unit is on the top. Get Friend to pull it into the car. If your tank's sending unit is on the side, just keep the wire tucked out of the way for now.

Step 3. Position Rubber Protective Pieces

Slip the two rubber parts on the front seam of the fuel tank. I didn't ask you to install these earlier because when you struggle to replace the tank, they normally get knocked off. Get them on securely because if one drops off, the tank will squeak like Mickey Mouse meeting Godzilla.

THIS IS HORRIBLE.

FORTUNATELY, MOUSE POSSESSES SUPERIOR INGENUITY & CUNNING.

CLIK

Step 4. Secure Fuel Tank

Slot the two tank retaining straps into position toward the rear and push the tank into place. With a nut and washer in one hand, push up one of the retaining straps so it fits into the stud sticking out of the floor pan. Put the nut and washer on the stud and tighten finger tight. Now do the same with the other side. If you can't get the nut started onto the stud, the tank is not correctly positioned. Wiggle it around. You'll feel when you've got it right. Tighten those two nuts (15mm socket).

Step 5. Install Filler Neck Hose

Slip the short thick hose which connects the gas tank filler with the tank onto the fuel tank. Now connect the other end to the filler neck and securely tighten the clamps.

Step 6. Reconnect Brake Lines

Screw the two disconnected parts of the brake line together (11 and 14mm). Be sure the 14mm nut first goes through the ear welded to the floor. These nuts are very tricky to get started. Do not crossthread them! Use your fingers until you're sure the threads are not crossthreaded, then tighten them with 11 and 14mm wrenches. After taking a break, do the other side.

Step 7. Install Axle Beam

Hook up the axle beam on the spring (if you have one) that's dangling from the brake pressure regulator. When it's hooked up, push the axle beam up and tighten a 17mm nut and washer with your 17mm socket. Replace the other three washers and nuts and torque them all to 4.5 mkg (32 ft lbs).

Step 8. Install Fuel Pump Connections

Install the electrical connections if you removed them. Push on the hose from the fuel tank to the pump and secure it with a clamp. If the pump is out, stick it back onto the two studs from the floor pan, and screw on and tighten the 10 and 13mm nuts.

Step 9. Check Your Work

Check the right side of the tank to make sure you replaced and tightened all the vent lines and hoses. This is important.

Step 10. Attach Exhaust Hangers

Use a screwdriver to lever the rubber exhaust hangers into position on the exhaust pipe and muffler ears. Replace any broken ones.

Step 11. Install Sending Unit

If your fuel tank has a side mounted sending unit, install it and the rubber ring by hand and then tap it slightly clockwise ⟳ with a screwdriver and hammer. Connect the electrical connection. If yours is top mounted, replace the unit and rubber O ring. Tighten the unit by tapping it just about a tenth of a turn with a screwdriver and hammer. That's all. Hook up the electrical connection and screw back the plate in the floor. Secure the plate with three phillips screws. Pull back the rubber mat and secure it with its two straps. Position the seat and make sure it's secure.

Step 12. Hook Up Battery Ground Strap (10mm Wrench)

Step 13. Fill 'er Up

If your engine uses unleaded gas, you'll need a funnel. The tank has a flap in the neck to accept only the thin gas pump nozzle for unleaded gas. Remember that crummy fuel caused all this trouble in the first place, so use clean gas. Same goes for diesel people.

Step 14. Bleed Rear Brakes

Chapter 14, Procedure 1.

Step 15. Lower Car and Clean Up

PROCEDURE 21: REPLACE CONTROL PRESSURE REGULATOR (CPR). Phase 1.

Condition: Your CPR is kaput.

Tools and materials: Phase 1 tool kit, new control pressure regulator

Step 1. Disconnect Battery Ground Strap (10mm Wrench)

Step 2. Remove Electrical Connection

Pull the electrical connection from the front of the control pressure regulator.

Step 3. Remove Fuel Lines

Remove the two fuel lines from the front of the CPR (13mm and 14mm wrenches).

Step 4. Pull Off Regulator

A 6mm allen bolt on each side of the CPR holds it to the engine. One bolt is slightly hidden by the face of the regulator. If the regulator is dirty, clean it and you'll see the bolts. Remove the bolts and pull off the regulator.

Step 5. Install New CPR

Clean the allen bolts and the crankcase where the CPR attaches. Push the CPR in place and finger tighten the two allen bolts. Now torque them to 2.0 mkg (14 ft lbs).

Step 6. Install Fuel Lines

You can't mix up the two fuel lines as the nuts will screw only on the right size thread. Don't try to prove me wrong! Pull the plastic protective caps from your new CPR. Screw on and tighten the fuel lines (13 and 14mm wrenches).

Step 7. Plug In Electrical Connector

It just pushes on.

Step 8. Hook Up Battery Ground Strap (10mm Wrench)

PROCEDURE 22: REPLACE AUXILIARY AIR REGULATOR. Phase 1.

Condition: Auxiliary air regulator died.

Tools and materials: Phase 1 tool kit, including 5mm allen wrench, new auxiliary air regulator.

Step 1. Remove Juice

Pull the electrical plug off the end of the auxiliary regulator.

Step 2. Remove Hoses

Loosen the hose clamps and pull the two hoses off the regulator.

Step 3. Remove Regulator

Remove the two 5mm allen head bolts securing the auxiliary air regulator and pull it off.

Step 4. Install New Regulator

Position your new regulator with the two allen bolts in the holes and start the bolts with your fingers. When you're sure the threads aren't crossthreaded, finish tightening with the 6mm allen wrench.

Step 5. Install Hoses

Check the length of the hoses for splits and if they're OK, slip them onto the regulator and tighten up the hose clamps. Replace any bad hoses.

Step 6. Reattach Electrical Plug

Make sure it's in the right place.

PROCEDURE 23: REPLACE COLD START VALVE

Condition: Faulty cold start valve.

Tools and materials: Phase 1 tool kit, including 6mm allen wrench. New cold start valve and gasket.

Step 1. Remove Battery Ground Strap (10mm Wrench)

Step 2. Remove Electrical Plug from Cold Start Valve

Just pull it.

Step 3. Remove Fuel Line

Remove the 13mm bolt holding the fuel line to the end of the cold start valve.

Step 4. Remove Cold Start Valve

Remove the two 6mm allen head bolts holding the cold start valve to the end of the intake manifold. Pull off the valve, then the gasket lying beneath it.

Step 5. Install New Cold Start Valve

Position the new cold start valve onto the end of the intake manifold after installing the new gasket. Then replace the two 6mm allen head bolts finger tight until you're sure they're not crossthreaded. Finish them off with your allen wrench.

Step 6. Reattach Fuel Line (13mm Wrench)

Again be careful not to get the threads crossed.

Step 7. Reattach Electrical Plug

Make sure it's properly inserted into the cold start valve—don't get it backwards.

Step 8. Reconnect Battery Ground Strap (10mm Wrench)

PROCEDURE 24: REPLACE FUEL ACCUMULATOR

Condition: Fuel accumulator bad or you want to replace an old 20cc with a new 40cc.

Tools and materials: Phase 1 tool kit, new fuel accumulator (40cc type only), safety glasses.

Remarks: A little gas will be spilled so be careful and keep the fire extinguisher handy.

Step 1. Disconnect Battery Ground Strap (10mm Wrench)

Step 2. Chock, Jack and Block

Jack up right rear of car and block it safely.

Step 3. Remove Accumulator Fuel Lines

Get under the car and remove the two fuel lines at the front part of the fuel accumulator (17 and 19mm wrenches). Careful of gas in your eyes.

Step 4. Remove Accumulator

Remove the two 10mm nuts holding the fuel accumulator in position in its housing and pull the accumulator out. *(Cont'd. on p. 192)*

TROUBLESHOOTING GUIDE

Here's a quick checklist of common fuel injection system problems and their cures. Turn back to the Procedure you need and do it.

PROBLEMS	SOLUTIONS
The engine won't start	1. Fuel pump working? Procedure 1. 2. Fuel flow blocked? Procedure 2. 3. Control and system pressure OK? Procedure 3. 4. Control Pressure Regulator OK? Procedure 4. 5. Fuel injectors plugged or leaking, lines plugged? Procedure 7. 6. Dirt in system? Procedures 2 and 7. 7. Control plunger sticking? Procedure 6.
Engine won't start when cold.	1. Thermo Time Switch bad? Procedure 8. 2. Cold start valve not working? Procedure 9. 3. Fuel filter plugged? Procedure 2, Step 2. 4. Auxiliary air regulator valve not closing? Procedure 10. 5. Air sensor plate out of position? Procedures 5 and 11. 6. Control pressure regulator doesn't have proper voltage? Procedure 4, Steps 1 and 2. 7. Fuel system doesn't have proper pressure? Procedure 3.
Trouble starting when engine is hot.	1. Fuel accumulator too small? Procedure 12. 2. Exhaust CO content too high? 3. Fuel injectors or lines plugged? Procedure 7. 4. Thermo time switch bad? Procedures 8 and 14. 5. Cold start valve stuck open? Procedure 9.
Engine starts, then stops.	1. No gas in tank? 2. Auxiliary air regulator doesn't close properly? Procedure 10. 3. Cold start valve doesn't close properly? Procedures 8 and 9. 4. Deceleration valve doesn't suck right? Chapter 13, Procedure 5, Step 4. 5. EGR valve plugged? Chapter 13, Procedure 5, Step 1.
Car runs, but idle is too high.	1. Idle screw out of adjustment? Chapter 10, Procedure 4, Steps 5 and 6. 2. Ignition vacuum unit not working? Chapter 10, Procedure 26. 3. Auxiliary air regulator not closing properly? Procedure 10. 4. Control pressure regulator bad? Procedure 4. 5. Idle Check. Procedure 16.
Idle stays high after engine is warm.	1. Idle incorrectly adjusted? Chapter 10, Procedure 18, Steps 2 and 6. 2. CO correctly adjusted? 3. Rubber boot over air sensor plate incorrectly positioned or split? 4. Idle check, Procedure 16.

TROUBLE SHOOTING GUIDE
(Continued)

PROBLEMS	SOLUTIONS
Engine hesitates when gas pedal is floored.	1. Control pressure regulator defective or has no voltage? Procedure 4, Step 2. 2. Incorrect position of air flow sensor plate in conical housing? Procedure 8. 3. Fuel control plunger sticking or binding? Procedure 6. 4. Cold start valve leaking? Procedures 8 and 9. 5. Injectors leaking? Procedure 7. 6. Idle or CO incorrectly adjusted? 7. Rubber boot over air sensor plate split or incorrectly positioned?
Engine hesitates around 45 mph.	1. Injectors defective? Procedure 7. 2. Rubber boot over sensor plate split or incorrectly positioned? 3. CO incorrectly adjusted? 4. Break in exhaust pipe? 5. Control pressure regulator has no voltage or kaput? Procedure 4, Step 2. 6. Accelerator cable kinked or incorrectly assembled? 7. Incorrect fuel pressure in control and main fuel systems? Procedure 3. 8. Fuel pump delivery rate too low? Procedure 1. 9. Driver too timid to go over 45 mph?
Fuel consumption much too high.	1. Control pressure regulator defective or has no voltage? Procedure 4, Steps 1 and 2. 2. Pressure in control system or main system too low? Procedure 3. 3. Fuel pump delivery too great? Procedure 1. 4. Cold start valve leaking? Procedures 8 and 9. 5. Air sensor plate incorrectly adjusted? Procedures 5 and 11. 6. Control plunger in fuel distributor binding or hanging up? Procedure 6. 7. Idle mixture too rich or CO content incorrect? 8. Potato or other object blocking exhaust system? 9. Boot over air sensor plate incorrectly installed or split? 10. Leaking or broken fuel injectors? Procedure 7. 11. Intake manifold loose on cylinder head? 12. Speedometer not giving an accurate reading?

Step 5. Install Accumulator

Install the new accumulator in its protective housing and attach it to the floor pan with two 10mm nuts. Tighten the nuts.

Step 6. Install Fuel Lines

Replace and tighten the two fuel lines at the front of the accumulator (17 and 19mm wrenches). It's impossible to get the two mixed up because their fittings are different sizes. Important: check that the connections are tight and won't leak.

Step 7. Reconnect Battery Ground Strap (10mm Wrench)

PROCEDURE 25: REPLACE FUEL DISTRIBUTOR

Condition: Fuel distributor shot.

Tools and materials: Screwdriver, new fuel distributor and O ring.

Step 1. Remove Old Distributor

Loosen all the fuel lines on the distributor (14mm) and then remove the three screws holding it to the air flow sensor housing. Lift the distributor off and don't drop the control plunger. Remove the gasket from the housing.

Step 2. Install New Distributor

Put the new gasket on top of the air flow sensor housing. Remove the plastic caps from the new fuel distributor, moisten the control plunger in gasoline and install the distributor onto the sensor housing. Stick the screws back and tighten them.

Step 3. Install Fuel Lines

Take one fuel line off the old distributor and install it onto the new in the *same position* as it was on the old. Now install the other fuel lines in the same way and tighten all the bolts. That's it.

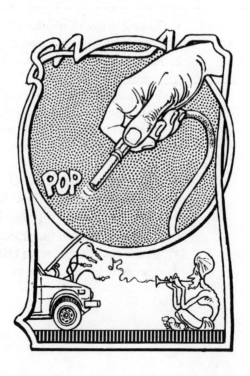

CHAPTER 13

∼❧ EXHAUST SYSTEM AND EMISSION CONTROL ❧∼

Exhaust gasses containing pernicious pollutants formed during combustion exit from the engine and enter the atmosphere by means of the exhaust system.

Car exhaust is one of the active ingredients in 'smog'—a product of hydrocarbons and oxides of nitrogen reacting chemically in sunlight. These two chemical pollutants are formed inside the cylinder head when gasoline is imperfectly burned, then spewed from the exhaust pipe ready to be turned into smog. So, VW has utilized a few techniques to significantly reduce pollution.

Pollution control devices must be in good condition so they can keep pollution to a minimum. If the smog control components are not properly maintained, not only don't they do their clean-up job, but they adversely affect the way your car runs.

The way you drive affects exhaust gas composition. If you floor the gas pedal at every green light, excess carbon monoxide and hydrocarbons are formed. Pollution! Gasp! Choke! By following the Maintenance Procedures (Chapter 10) on time, you'll help reduce pollution. A well-tuned engine is thus the first line of defense against SMOG.

A number of different emission control systems are used by VW. They range from the most complex used in California to hardly any on other parts of the globe. There's not a vast amount we can do to adjust the system but we can maintain it so it works as it was designed to.

Look at Peter's drawing of a typical carbureted emissions control system on the next page. When the engine starts, nitrogen oxides are formed in the cylinders. The amount of oxides sent out the tail pipe is reduced by rerouting the exhaust gas back into the intake manifold to be mixed with fresh air and gasoline and burned. What does that do?, you might ask. It reduces the peak flame temperatures as they're known in the trade inside the combustion chambers, resulting in lower amounts of oxides of nitrogen. You see, higher temperatures inside the cylinder head make for a higher pollution level.

Here's the first problem. Introducing exhaust gas into the combustion chambers only works well when the engine is turning over at highway speeds. At idle and low temperatures, the car engine would run like a dog with two legs. The 1975 solution was to put an exhaust gas recirculating (EGR) filter into the system to absorb the excess pollutants formed at low engine speeds. In 1976 VW abandoned the EGR filter as they'd devised a more efficient EGR system to take care of the low temperature hassle.

Diesel engine exhaust gasses cause similar pollution problems. Because diesel fuel is burned in the presence of large quantities of air, there are only a few percent of unburned hydrocarbons formed. However, the large amount of air in the combustion chambers helps form oxides of nitrogen. Here we go again— pollution.

Common complaints levied at diesel engines are that they stink and smoke a lot. The smoking problem is usually caused by a mechanical defect; probably one or more of the fuel injectors is faulty. The stinking problem is proving more difficult to solve. Presently a number of independent laboratories are trying to identify the odors and find a way to eliminate the unpleasant ones.

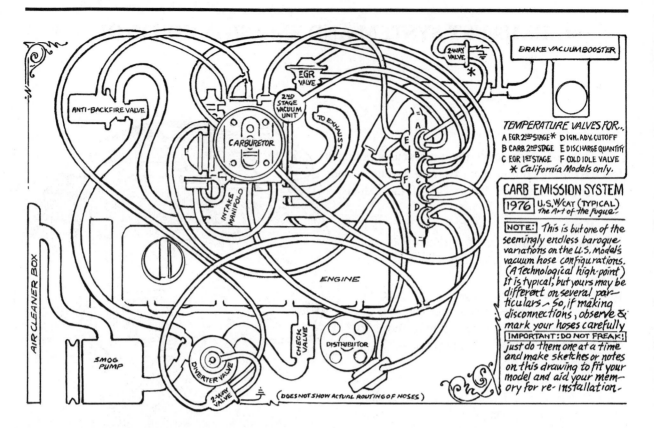

So the diesel engine isn't the pollution-free power plant thought by some people as one answer to our transportation-caused pollution problems. Far from it. Unless diesel engine pollutant control is improved, the diesel will not meet proposed Environmental Protection Agency (EPA) emission limits. Turbocharging and 'afterburners' are two ideas currently being investigated as solutions.

OK, let's take a closer look at the exhaust and emission control systems.

THE EXHAUST SYSTEM

Exhaust gasses coming from the cylinders rush by the exhaust valves into the **exhaust manifold.** This manifold is bolted to the right side of the cylinder head. Gaskets are fitted between the exhaust manifold and the cylinder head which allow for the different rates of expansion of the aluminum cylinder head and cast iron exhaust manifold. A **down pipe** bolts to the flange on the bottom of the exhaust manifold. The exhaust gas passes through this pipe into the **intermediate pipe**, through the **muffler** (which reduces engine noise), out the **tail pipe** and into our lungs. Metal and asbestos gaskets fit between the exhaust pipe sections filling any irregularities in the section joint flanges. A tight fit is what's needed to stop exhaust leaks.

California cars have an extra component: a **catalytic converter** is fitted between the intermediate pipe and the muffler. In 1980 all U.S. VW's will have a catalytic converter to comply with EPA emission limits. The catalytic converter is a metal canister with a specially treated ceramic insert to convert most of the **carbon monoxide** in the exhaust gas into harmless **carbon dioxide** and **water.**

All cars imported into the U.S. were originally fitted with catalytic converters. But in 1976 a recall program eliminated the converter and changed carburetor jet sizes for all cars except those in California. This change miraculously kept exhaust pollutants within EPA limits.

If you have updated the carburetor you should remove the catalytic converter.

If you have a cat, there is a box arrangement which is part of the exhaust down pipe. A small tube runs from the box into the base of the down pipe. At the top or back of the box another small pipe capped by a 19mm domed nut goes upward. This capped nut is removed when the carbon monoxide content of the exhaust gas is measured. Vehicles without catalytic converters have their CO content measured at the tail pipe.

OK. The exhaust system is held to the underside of the car by thick black rubber ovals called **exhaust**

hangers. Are all yours in one piece? A broken hanger puts strain on the exhaust system which eventually means a new pipe or two.

A leak in the exhaust system is usually accompanied by lots of noise and fierce stares from fellow motorists. Exhaust fumes escaping from the leak bypass the tail pipe and may find their way into the passenger compartment. If so, you could be in dead trouble. Literally.

Carbon monoxide is an odorless gas. First it makes you sleepy, then as you doze off, it kills you. It pays to keep the exhaust system in good condition, no? Check Procedure 6 if any of your pipes leak. An exhaust system check is part of the monthly routine in Chapter 10.

EMISSION CONTROL SYSTEM

Any emission control system is part of an on-going experiment by all car manufacturers to do the impossible—eliminate automobile-caused air pollution. The government has set certain standards as to what is 'acceptable pollution.' California has a fairly strict code and it seems more states will follow their example in the future.

Carbureted Engines

These engines use a combination of an **air injection** and an **exhaust gas recirculation (EGR)** system. Let's see, open the hood and prop it. A diagram is stuck to the underside of the car's hood showing the routing of the vacuum hoses and the components used in your system. The emission system relies on vacuum and temperature. When the engine's running, a partial vacuum is formed in the intake manifold. This vacuum is used to advance the ignition spark at the distributor and operate the emission control system.

The amount of vacuum needed is controlled by **temperature valves** screwed into a manifold to the rear of the cylinder head. The temperature of the coolant passing through the manifold determines when the valves open to allow vacuum to 'flow' and gradually bring into operation all the EGR components.

The **air injection system** is designed to reduce pollutants by oxidizing hydrocarbons (or most of them) as they come squirting out past the exhaust valves. The **air injection pump (smog pump)**, is a V-belt driven, silver coffee can sized cylinder, suspended under the alternator. It forces air into the exhaust port of each cylinder. A small copper colored cylinder (**check valve**) is attached to the pipe running across the left side of the cylinder head just below the plugs. This valve prevents exhaust gasses from reentering the pump and damaging it.

The exhaust gas, now mixed with air, is shot down the exhaust pipe, then through the red hot **catalytic converter** to emerge somewhat purged from hydrocarbons and carbon monoxide. Then the cleaned gas is converted to carbon dioxide and water vapor. If you don't have a catalytic converter as part of your exhaust system, the carbon monoxide/hydrocarbon content of your exhaust gas is higher than if you did.

Find the **diverter valve** bolted to the top right of the radiator. It senses changes in vacuum in the intake manifold when you take your foot off the gas pedal. Then a control valve opens letting more fresh air into the intake manifold and the fuel/air mixture inside the manifold is made leaner in gasoline to help prevent the engine from backfiring. To enable the system to work properly, there's an **anti-backfire valve** fastened close to the rear of the right fender and the firewall. Follow the hoses from the valve to see how it is also connected to the intake manifold. This anti-backfire valve comes into play only when you take your foot off the gas pedal. At that time, there's vacuum at the diverter valve and, for reasons you don't want to know, the valve prevents the engine from backfiring.

Attached next to the diverter valve there may be a small metal box or canister. This is the **second stage diverter valve.** It's also known as the two-way valve.

Feel around the rear of the intake manifold on the right side of the cylinder head and find a squashed metal cylinder. It's held to the manifold by two bolts. This is the **EGR valve.** Two small pipe connections on the cylinder part of the EGR have thin plastic vacuum hoses attached. Follow them to the carburetor and the temperature valves. No hoses? Then the connection(s) should have a yellow plastic cap to seal it. Someone has done the VW carburetor update.

On top of the carb is the black metal **air intake elbow.** A hose runs from the elbow through the firewall into the **activated charcoal filter** (a big black canister). Another hose coming from the air intake elbow ends at the rear part of the camshaft cover. There may or may not be a round plastic **positive crankcase ventilation (PCV) valve** halfway along this hose.

There's a CAT and an EGR light on the dash. The CAT light is there to remind California drivers to change the catalytic converter every 30,000 miles. If the CAT light flickers and the 30,000 maintenance period hasn't yet been reached, turn to Chapter 10, Procedure 14. A blazing EGR light is the EGR system's version of crying out for love and affection. Procedure 1 tells how to give it.

A few years ago a party of British rock 'n roll fans chartered an airplane to get to a distant concert. The leader of the group was a rather pushy, somewhat hysterical post-teen, who had recently acquired a lovely set of false teeth.

During the Atlantic crossing, the leader decided to see the cockpit. He burst into the hallowed area and began asking innumerable questions. The pilot became anxious and asked him to leave. He refused and the flight engineer decided to forcefully eject the unwanted guest. During the struggle, the group leader lost his bogus choppers at the very moment the pilot was yawning. Would you believe the teeth popped out of the prying fan into the flier!

Fuel Injected Engines

The emission control system on these engines is somewhat similar to the one on carbureted engines. At least, the idea is still to reduce exhaust air pollution. These engines have a simpler system so here I'll identify the parts and tell you what symptoms they demonstrate when they go wrong.

Take a look at the diagrams on this and the following pages to find your particular system. There's a sticker on the underside of your hood which shows the position of the vacuum hoses and shows what equipment is used.

Lift and prop the hood and find the intake manifold on the right side of the cylinder head. There's a hose running from it to the brake booster (if you've got one) just behind the brake master cylinder. Vacuum is

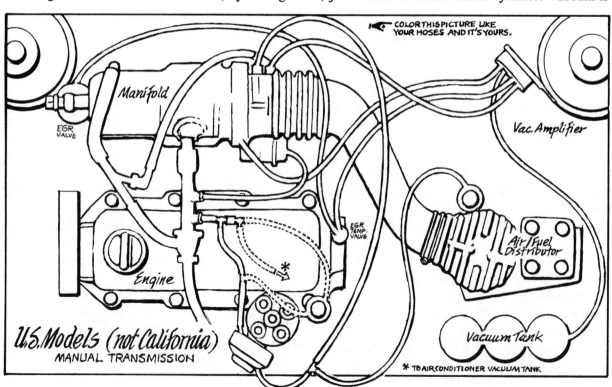

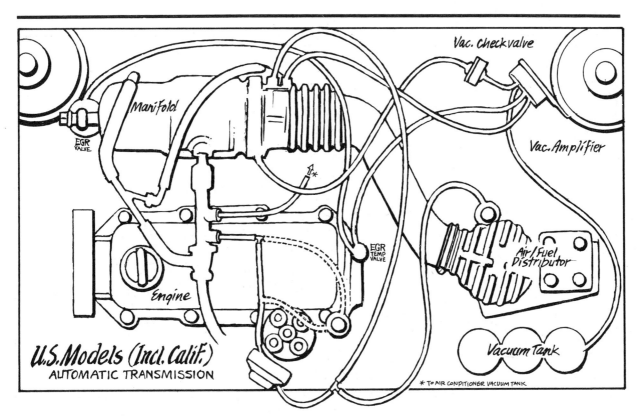

formed in the intake manifold to 'power' the emission control components as well as the ignition distributor vacuum advance/retard mechanism.

Another hose connected to the big intake manifold vacuum hose goes to the deceleration (decel) valve just below the intake manifold. This valve comes into operation when you take your foot off the gas pedal to limit vacuum in the intake manifold and thus lower the amount of exhaust emissions.

Yet another branch hose from that main vacuum hose runs to the vacuum unit on the distributor. A branch from that line goes to a two-way valve if you have an air conditioner. A hose from the distributor ends up at the charcoal filter canister check valve.

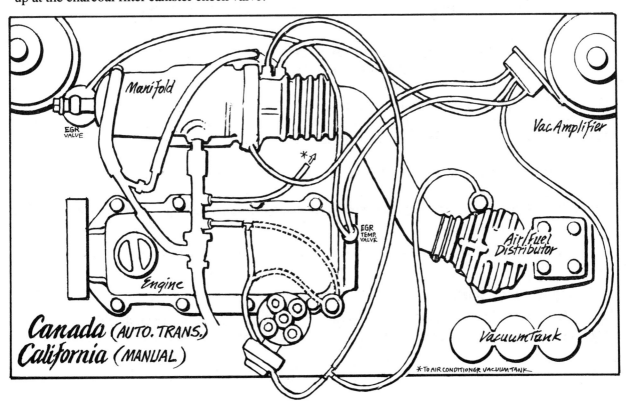

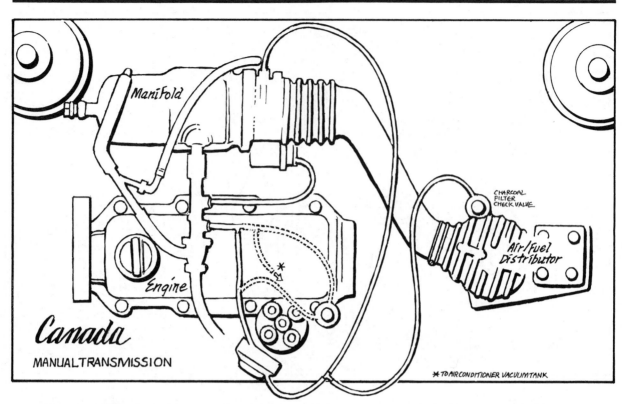

Find the EGR valve on the rear of the intake manifold close to the right fender. A vacuum hose connects it to the EGR temperature valve. Follow another vacuum hose to a flat cylinder bolted to the left front MacPherson strut (shock absorber) mounting on the left fender. This is the EGR vacuum amplifier. Another hose from that fixture ends up at the plastic vacuum tank someplace beneath the radiator.

You may have another of these funny looking vacuum tanks on the underside of the hood, especially if you have an air conditioner. The tank looks like three tennis balls glued together, but it doesn't bounce; it just 'stores' vacuum.

PROCEDURES FOR TROUBLESHOOTING EMISSION CONTROL SYSTEM (CARBURETED ENGINES) Phase 1

Before working on the emission control stuff, turn to Chapter 10 and do the tune-up Procedure.

The emission system differs from year to year and Canadian cars have less of it than U.S. cars. Differences in the systems will be noted as we go along.

PROCEDURE 1: CHECK EGR SYSTEM—CANADA 1975 and 1976 ONLY. Phase 1.

Condition: Engine won't start easily, idles poorly, hesitates when cold, stalls, poor power output, EGR dash light on. Engine in *good* tune.

Tools and materials: Phase 1 tool kit, Q-Tips and alcohol or solvent, thermometer, maybe a new EGR valve and gasket.

Step 1. Check Single Stage System

Find the EGR valve on the rear of the exhaust manifold facing the firewall. There should be a thin plastic vacuum hose running from it to a temperature valve screwed into the coolant manifold at the rear of the cylinder head. Another vacuum hose should run to the carburetor. Check the hoses for breaks and loose connections. Fix if you find any.

Step 2. Test

Start the engine and let it idle as best it can. Pull off the vacuum hose from the EGR valve, then pull the vacuum hose from the anti-backfire valve at the junction of the right fender and the firewall.

Slip the anti-backfire valve vacuum hose onto the vacant EGR valve connection. Does the engine idle speed fall? It should. If it does, go to Step 5 after reconnecting the vacuum hoses as they were. Idle remains the same? Continue.

Step 3. Check EGR Filter, 1975 only

The filter is housed in a tuna fish can sized container on the left side of the engine. Unscrew the wing nut holding the filter in place and check it by holding it up to the light. If it's dirty or torn, buy a new one and install it. No difference in the way the engine runs? Try this.

Step 4. Check EGR Valve

The valve is held onto the rear of the exhaust manifold by two 10mm bolts. A metal tube is screwed into the back of the valve. Remove the two 10mm bolts, then unscrew the valve from the metal line. Use Q-Tips soaked in solvent or alcohol to clean out all the crud and gum. When it's clean, hold one finger over one of the connections on the valve (if there are two) and suck on the other connection. The little plunger inside the valve should move. If it doesn't, try blowing, then sucking. Perhaps another cleaning will get the plunger to move. No? Then buy a new valve and gasket and install them on the exhaust manifold.

After hooking up the vacuum lines, try starting the engine again. That fixed it, yes? No? Go to Procedure 3.

Step 5. Test Temperature Valve

If your idle speed dropped during the test in Step 2, but the bloody car still runs like a jackalope with hiccups, there's a chance the temperature valve isn't opening. Let's test.

Remove the vacuum lines from the temperature valve, then use a crescent wrench to unscrew the valve from the manifold. Place the threaded end into a container of cold water with an ice cube or two to make things tinkle. Add a dash of bitters and a twist of lemon to bring out the true flavor of the valve. OK, remove the valve from the water and try to blow down the *angled* connection. You should get red in the face and no air should escape from the other vertical connection.

Now pour some warm water into a saucepan and balance the switch on the bottom of the pan; just enough water to cover the threads. Don't immerse the whole thing. If you have a thermometer handy, take the water's temperature. Heat the water until the temperature is above 50°C (122°F). That's hot, but not hot enough to burn your fingers. Take the valve out of the pan and try blowing down the angled connection again. Don't burn your lips. Air should be forced out the other connection. If so, the switch is OK. No air means the switch isn't opening at the correct temperature so it must be replaced. Buy a new one from VW and install it.

Screw the new or old switch back into the manifold and install the vacuum lines. Try the engine again. Better? If the engine still won't run like a kitten's purr, continue with Procedure 3.

Press the reset button on the EGR indicator box. It's a black box behind the left side of the firewall. A speedometer cable sprouts from its front and goes to the transmission. Found it? There's an illustration of the EGR box on the next page.

PROCEDURE 2: TEST EGR SYSTEM, U.S. 1975 AND 1976. Phase 1.

Condition: Engine won't start easily, idles poorly, hesitates when cold, stalls, poor power output, EGR dash light on. Engine in *good* tune.

Tools and materials: Phase 1 tool kit, Q-Tips and alcohol or solvent, thermometer, maybe a new EGR valve and gasket.

Remarks: The second stage connection on the EGR valve may be capped in *non*-California cars, that's OK.

Step 1.　Vacuum Hoses Correct

Compare your car's system with the diagram. Are the hoses correctly installed? Change them if they're not. When they are on the right places, start the engine and get it to idle as best it can. (There's another diagram on the next page.)

Step 2.　Check EGR First Stage

Find the EGR valve on the rear of the intake manifold and pull off the vacuum line from the connection on the end of the valve closest to the left fender. Now pull the vacuum line from the anti-backfire valve at the junction of the right fender and firewall.

Attach the anti-backfire valve vacuum line onto the vacant EGR valve connection. Does the engine idle speed fall? It should. If it does, reconnect the vacuum lines to their proper positions and go to Step 3. If the idle speed remained the same, go back to Procedure 1 and do Steps 3 and 4.

Step 3.　Test Temperature Valve

Go to Procedure 1 and Step 5. Valve OK, carry on with this Procedure (California) or go to Procedure 3 after reading the last paragraph of Step 5, Procedure 1.

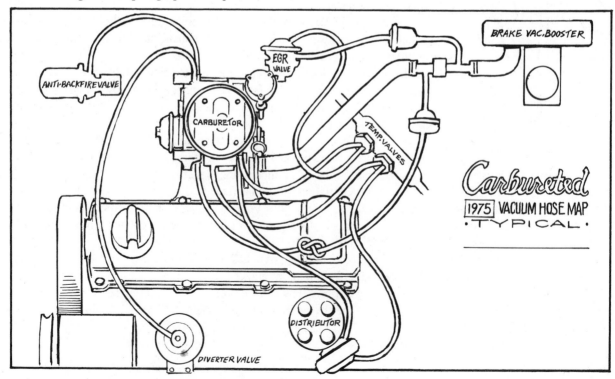

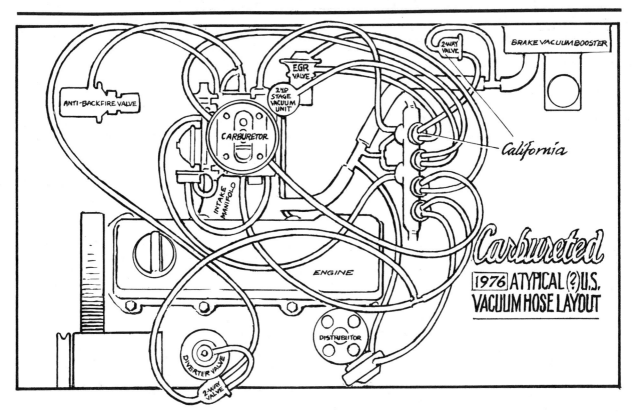

Step 4. Test EGR Second Stage (California Only)

You California people should have a microswitch fastened to the side of the carburetor. It's a small black rectangular box with two electrical connections on top of it and a little roller wheel underneath. This switch controls the operation of the two-way valve. Start the car and let it warm up. Move the roller on the base of the microswitch up; that is, 'switch' the microswitch on. The engine idle should drop or the engine should quit running. Let go of the roller and carefully listen to the two-way valve. Move the roller again (engine running) and listen. Does the two-way valve click when you push up the microswitch roller? Yes? All is well with the EGR system, so extinguish the EGR dash light by reading the last paragraph of Step 5, Procedure 1. No? Try this.

Step 5. Current to Switch and Two-Way Valve?

Crack out the VOM and set it at 15 volts DC. Pull off the microswitch electrical connection and test it for juice. If you don't know how, turn to Chapter 20, Procedure 10. Test the two-way valve for juice too; same way.

If you have a faulty microswitch buy a new one from VW and have them adjust its action because the operation requires a protractor and various other tools and experience. If you need to install a new two-way valve, do so.

Extinguish the EGR dash light by following the instructions in the last paragraph of Step 5, Procedure 1.

PROCEDURE 3: TEST AIR INJECTION SYSTEM—CARBURETED ENGINES. ALL MODELS. Phase 1.

Condition: Engine won't start easily, idles poorly, hesitates, stalls, has low power output and backfires when you ease off the gas pedal. Engine in good tune.

Tools and materials: Phase 1 tool kit.

Step 1. Check V-Belt

Find the air injection pump (smog pump) under the alternator and check that the V-belt which drives it is tight. Belt deflection should be 10mm-15mm (3/8-9/16 in). Sometimes the V-belt pulley breaks on the front of the air injection pump, so inspect it carefully.

Step 2. Check Check Valve

Find the 19mm (¾ in) pipe-like copper colored manifold which runs along the left side of the cylinder head just below the spark plugs. Attached mid-way along the pipe is a small round check valve. Loosen the hose clamp on the face of the valve and pull off the big rubber hose. Stick a rag into the check valve and start the engine. Air should pump out from the big hose. Feel it with your hand. If there's no air, the V belt on the air injection pump must be loose or broken (Step 1). I've never seen or heard of a bad pump, so continue…

Step 3. Clean Check Valve

Take the rag out of the check valve and examine the valve for dirt and grime. Filthy? If so, unscrew all the 17mm bolts holding the copper colored pipe to the cylinder head. Pull the pipe away from the cylinder head and remove the bolts and the two washers. Clean the pipe with solvent, then take it and the valve to the local gas station and use their free air to blow all the crud out. Blow *into* the check valve from the side to which the big pipe was connected. When it's all clean, reinstall it onto the cylinder head with one washer between the pipe manifold and the head and the other just below the bolt head. Tighten all four bolts and install the hose from the air pump on the check valve.

Start the car again. How is it? Still UGH? Continue…

Step 4. Check Anti-Backfire Valve

Loosen the hose clamp on the bottom hose on the anti-backfire valve located at the junction of the right fender and the firewall, and pull off the hose. Start the engine and run it for two minutes. Put your finger on the recently vacated hose connection on the bottom of the valve and pull on the accelerator cable to get the engine rpm's up high. Release the cable and feel a slight suck on the end of your finger. If so, the valve and vacuum hoses are OK. Go to Procedure 4.

No suck—no vacuum. Check that the vacuum hoses to and from the valve are in good condition and not kinky. Replace any faulty hoses. If all the hoses are OK, the valve is shot and needs to be replaced. Remove the old one and install the new. Switch the hoses from the old valve onto the new and listen to the sweet song of an engine that doesn't backfire.

PROCEDURE 4: TEST DIVERTER VALVE, CARBURETED ENGINES—U.S. AND CANADA. Phase 1.

Condition: Engine won't start easily, idles poorly, low power output, hesitates.

Tools and materials: Phase 1 tool kit, Friend, maybe new diverter valve, 63cm (24 in) of 15mm^2 (14 gauge) electrical wire.

Step 1. Check Valve (1975 U.S. and 1976 Canada)

If you have a 1975 U.S. car *without* the second stage diverter valve installed on top of the diverter valve on the top left of the radiator, you're at the right place.

Remove the vacuum hose from the single connection on top of the valve, then pull off the vacuum hose from the anti-backfire valve. Connect the anti-backfire valve vacuum hose to the diverter valve and start the engine. Let the engine idle while you hold your hand close to the slot in the gizmo on the side of the diverter valve. It's actually called the valve muffler. You should feel air pumped onto your hand. No air means the valve is bad because you've already checked the air injection pump. Buy a new valve and install it onto the radiator. Then, don't forget to put the vacuum hose back onto the anti-backfire valve.

Step 2. Check Diverter Valve, 1976 U.S.

This step is for people *with* the second stage diverter valve. First, disconnect hose A from the left side of the second stage valve, then hose B from the right side of the valve. Now connect hose B to the valve where A used to fit.

Start the engine. There should be air blown out from the slot in the gizmo (the valve muffler) on the side of the diverter valve. No air? Pull hose C from the second stage valve and put your finger close to the end.

Step 2. (Cont'd.)

When the engine is running there should be *no* vacuum sucking on your finger. If there's vacuum, the diverter valve is shot and must be replaced. Do it.

No vacuum, follow the vacuum hose and check the hose and its connections. Stick the vacuum hoses back onto the original connections and continue.

Step 3. Check Second Stage Diverter Valve

With the vacuum hoses back on the correct second stage diverter valve connections, pull the electrical plug from the valve. Strip 13mm (½ in) of insulation from each end of your piece of wire. Start the engine and hold one end of the wire on the *positive* battery post and the other end in the electrical connection on the second stage valve.

Ask Friend to step on the gas pedal or pull on the accelerator cable to increase the rpm's and feel for air blowing out of the muffler on the side of the diverter valve. None? Replace the second stage valve with a new one. It's an easy job.

PROCEDURE 5: TEST EGR SYSTEM (FUEL INJECTED ENGINES). Phase 1.

Condition: Fuel injected engine doesn't start easily and/or idle well, stalls, hesitates, low power output, EGR dash light on.

Tools and materials: Phase 1 tool kit, 40cm (18 in) of vacuum hose (buy the hose from VW), Friend.

Remarks: Run through the tune-up Procedure in Chapter 10 before you work on the emission control system.

Step 1. Check EGR Valve

Start the engine and let it idle as best it can. While it's warming up, check all the vacuum hoses for breaks and cracks. Tape up any broken hose as a temporary measure as we test the valve.

When the engine is warm, pull off the vacuum hose from the EGR valve that's located on the end of the intake manifold close to the right fender. Put the new piece of hose into the vacated vacuum connection on the EGR valve and, with the engine at idle, suck on the hose. The engine idle speed should drop or the engine should stall. If it does, not only do I want to meet you but the valve is OK. Reconnect the vacuum hoses to their original positions, then go to Step 2.

If your idle stays the same during the suck test, turn to Procedure 1 and clean or replace the EGR valve as per Step 4.

Step 2. Test Temperature Valve

Back to Procedure 1 and do Step 5 to see if the temperature valve still functions as it should. Install a new one if it's faulty. Return here if the valve checks out OK.

Step 3. Check Vacuum Amplifier

You should really use a vacuum gauge for testing this amplifier but we can give it the once over without it. Check the hoses to and from the amplifier for cracks. Replace any bad hose. Pull the hoses, one at a time, from the amplifier to see if there's crud inside. If it's cruddy, drive over to VW and have a mechanic test the valve with a vacuum gauge. The test takes about 30 seconds, but it's the only sure way to check if it's faulty. Replace it if it is.

Step 4. Check Deceleration (Decel) Valve (Manual Transmissions Only)

This is a weird one. A malfunctioning decel valve can cause diverse, but very strange engine problems. The most common are stalling at low engine speeds, hesitation, high fuel consumption and high idle.

Find the decel valve to the right of the cylinder head just below the throttle valve housing end of the intake manifold. If you can't get your hand in there, find someone with smaller mitts than yours. Ask Friend to start the engine and keep it at idle. Loosen the hose clamp on the small hose coming from the *right* side of the decel valve (the connection faces the firewall) and pull the hose off.

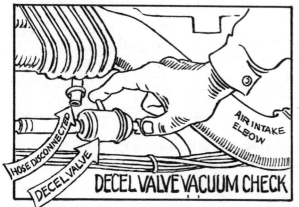

DECEL VALVE VACUUM CHECK

Keep the engine at idle. Put your finger on the end of the decel valve connection and have Friend floor the gas pedal for one second. No Friend, just pull on the accelerator cable to get the revs up to about 3000 rpm. If the engine died as soon as you took the hose off the decel valve, reconnect it and ask Friend to push on the gas pedal to keep the engine running, or you can pull on the accelerator cable.

When you have your finger on the decel valve you should feel suction from the connection as the engine speed is raised, then lowered (as you pull on the cable or Friend pushes on the gas pedal). If there's no suction, or the engine idle doesn't change when you pull off the hose, the decel valve is faulty. Let's make sure. Got suction—go to Step 6.

Step 5. Test Valve Again

Slip the hose back onto the decel valve and ask Friend to start the engine. Now pull the vacuum hose from the rear of the decel valve—the valve rear faces the left fender. Get the engine revs fairly high, about 3000 rpm's, pull off the hose from the right side of the valve again and do the suction test again. If you *have* suction, the valve is faulty. so install a new one. No suction, the valve is OK. So reconnect everything. Most times if you didn't get suction on the first test, you get it this time. This valve seems to fail quite often, especially at higher altitudes.

Step 6. Final Check For Those With Suction

Pull the vacuum hose from the rear of the decel valve (keep the engine running) and hold your finger over the end of the vacuum line or the end of the valve. Run the engine up to about 3000 rpm and put another finger on the hose connection on the right side of the valve. Suction? If so, the valve is faulty. Replace it. No suction? Valve is OK.

If none of the above tests find your problem, check the tightness of the intake and exhaust manifolds on the right side of the cylinder head, do a compression test (Chapter 10, Procedure 20) to see if your cylinder head gasket is blown, and check that the fuel injectors are tightly pushed home. If that doesn't do it, go back to Chapter 12 and track down the problem there.

PROCEDURE 6: GUT OR REPLACE CATALYTIC CONVERTER. Phase 2.

Condition: 30,000 mile maintenance (CAT light on), carburetor update, referral from other Chapters.

Tools and materials: Phase 1 tool kit, new cat converter and two new gaskets to fit between the cat and the exhaust pipe sections (California), old clothes, gloves, safety glasses, cap, painter's protective mask, Liquid Wrench, 2½ gallon bucket of water, heavy plastic trash bags, long screwdriver or metal rod.

Remarks: Ignore any snide comments and nasty remarks from onlookers when you don this gear for this Procedure. Just don't offer candy to children in that get-up.

Removal of the catalytic converter outside of California was the subject of a VW recall program quite some time ago. Maybe your dealer will do it for you?

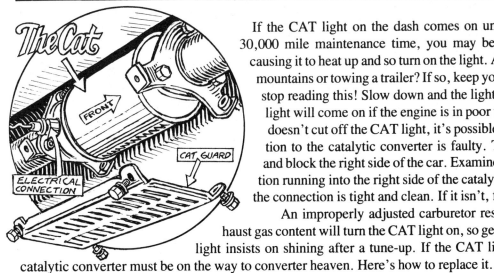

If the CAT light on the dash comes on unexpectedly before the 30,000 mile maintenance time, you may be straining the engine, causing it to heat up and so turn on the light. Are you speeding in the mountains or towing a trailer? If so, keep your eyes on the road and stop reading this! Slow down and the light will go out. The CAT light will come on if the engine is in poor tune. If a good tune-up doesn't cut off the CAT light, it's possible the electrical connection to the catalytic converter is faulty. To check, chock, jack and block the right side of the car. Examine the electrical connection running into the right side of the catalytic converter and see if the connection is tight and clean. If it isn't, fix it.

An improperly adjusted carburetor resulting in high CO exhaust gas content will turn the CAT light on, so get the CO adjusted if the light insists on shining after a tune-up. If the CAT light still flickers, your catalytic converter must be on the way to converter heaven. Here's how to replace it.

Step 1. Where's the Cat?

The catalytic converter is a round canister about the size of two 1-pound coffee cans held end to end. It's fastened to the exhaust system about halfway along the underside of the car. A metal heat shield held by four bolts is directly under the converter. On the right side of the converter a 17mm captive nut secures an electrical connection which ends up at the CAT light on the dash.

Step 2. Chock, Jack and Block

Jack up the right side of the car and block it carefully.

Step 3. Remove Heat Shield

Take out the four 10mm bolts holding the metal heat shield under the catalytic converter. Hand out the bolts and plate to Friend or place them where they won't get ground into the dirt.

Step 4. Take the Cat Out

Put on your protective clothes and unscrew the captive nut holding the electrical connection on the side of the cat (17mm wrench). Anoint the three 13mm nuts and bolts at each end of the cat with Liquid Wrench. Remove the two bottom bolts at each end, then adjust your mask and goggles.

Now remove the remaining bolt at each end of the cat and lower it gently to the ground. Treat the catalytic converter like a time bomb. If you inhale any of the inner contents, it's just as devastating.

Slide out from under the car, leaving the cat under there, and gather the bucket of water and trash bags around you. Reach under the car, pull out the cat and immerse it in the water. Make sure the inside of the cat gets well soaked. If you are eliminating the converter, do the next step. Replacing it with a new one? Go to Step 6.

Step 5. Gutting the Cat

Keep your protective gear on, pick up the long screwdriver or bar, and hold the cat over a plastic bag. You are going to knock the cat's guts into the bag. Push the screwdriver blade into the rear of the cat and poke. It'll love it. Immerse the cat in the water from time to time and keep poking until all of the ceramic insert inside the cat is in the trash bag. Tie closed the top of the trash bag and hide it until trash day.

Rinse out the inside of the cat with clean water, then pour all the nasty water down the drain.

Step 6. Install New Converter or Old Converter Case

Keep the weird clothes on.

The converter's electrical connection faces down and right. Install the cat with a new gasket between the cat and the two exhaust pipe sections. Install the top 13mm bolt on each end first, then screw on the nuts. Reinstall the two brackets which held the metal heat shield even if you've gutted the cat. The brackets are needed to take up the non-threaded portion on the bottom bolts. Stick the remaining two bolts through the exhaust pipe/cat flanges on each end, then tighten all six nuts to 2 mkg (14 ft lbs).

If you eliminated the cat's guts, cut off the electrical connection from the end of the wire which used to screw onto the cat. Tape up the ends of the wire with plastic electrical insulating tape.

If you've installed a replacement cat, screw the electrical connector onto the cat (17mm wrench). Tighten it.

Install the heat shield if you installed a new converter. Leave it off if you've gutted it.

Make sure the handbrake's on, gear shift lever in neutral (N) and the blocks and chocks are in place. Start the engine. Pass your hand around the cat to feel for leaks from either end. Check the tightness of the 13mm bolts if you feel a leak. While you're under there, check the entire exhaust system for leaks. Small holes can be welded closed by a local welding shop or muffler place. Big leaks are dangerous. Install a new exhaust pipe section if yours is holey. Procedure 7 tells how.

Step 7. Tidy Up

Remove the chocks and blocks, lower the car and put away the jack. Throw the old cat or bagged ceramic insert into the trash. If you got any of that insert on your clothes, throw them away too.

Step 8. Extinguish CAT Light

If you followed this Procedure to turn off the CAT light, you'd better do it. Lift the hood and find the black EGR box behind the left side of the firewall. There's an electrical plug and a speedometer cable coming out the front running to the transmission. Turn on the engine and press the CAT button on the box and check the dash to see if the light's out. Turn the engine off. Take a shower and call it a day.

PROCEDURE 7: REPLACE EXHAUST SYSTEM COMPONENTS. Phase 2.

Condition: The exhaust system has leaks.

Tools and materials: Phase 2 tool kit, new exhaust pipe sections, gaskets and rubber hangers.

Remarks: A sensible person takes the Rabbit to Midas and gets them to bust knuckles under the car sweating with the exhaust system. It'll probably be cheaper than buying the correct VW part. However, sometimes foreign parts places have good, relatively inexpensive exhaust parts that you'll have to install yourself. Same goes for 'free flow' systems.

The two exhaust sections which run under the car are called the intermediate pipe (the front pipe) and the muffler (the rear pipe). U.S. Rabbits with chassis numbers up to 175 3255 399 and Sciroccos up to 525 2032 546 use what's known as the 'old type' system. You can install a 'new type' muffler for an 'old type' intermediate pipe, but slight modifications are required.

Canadian Rabbits with chassis numbers up to 175 3255 399 and Canadian Sciroccos up to chassis number 535 2032 546 have the old type system also. Cars with chassis numbers in the U.S. and Canada higher than the ones listed are fitted with the new type system.

Canadian and U.S. systems are different, so if you're on holiday in Canada in a U.S. Rabbit and the muffler falls off…show this to the Royal Canadian Mounted Police. You can always trust a Mountie.

Step 1. Check What You've Got

OK, let's say that your intermediate pipe is shot and you want to replace it. You can only buy the new type. That means that the muffler presently fitted on your car won't fit the new type intermediate pipe. You will have to buy a new muffler, too. However, if your intermediate pipe is shot, it won't be long before the muffler wears away as well. Save yourself a grand hassle and change both of them right now. Steps 2 and 3 show how.

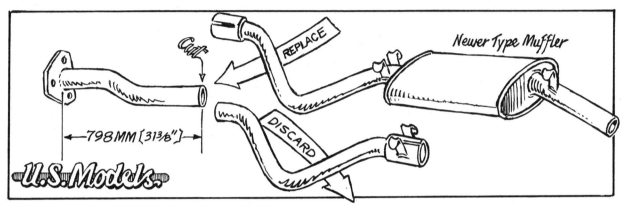

If you are here to change the muffler, and have bought a new type which will be fitted onto an old type intermediate pipe, then go to Step 4. If you have the new type intermediate pipe and are fitting a new type muffler to it, then go to Step 5. Compare what you've bought to what's fitted on your car.

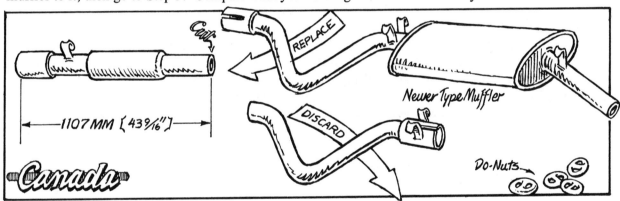

Step 2. Remove Intermediate Pipe

Liquid Wrench the three 13mm bolts holding the front part of the intermediate pipe to the down pipe. If you have a catalytic converter, anoint the three 13mm bolts holding the cat to the intermediate pipe. Remove the bolts. If they are badly rusted, use a hacksaw to get 'em off and make a note to buy new ones.

Unhook the rubber hangers holding the exhaust system to the underside of the car, and remove both exhaust sections.

Step 3. Install Intermediate Pipe

Install the new intermediate pipe onto the down pipe with a new gasket between the two. Install the three 13mm bolts and tighten them. Install the cat and its little pipe (if it's got one) and put a gasket between the cat and the intermediate pipe before you stick the three 13mm bolts back. All nice and tight?

Step 4. Adjust New Intermediate Pipe Length

Do this step only if you're installing a new type muffler onto an old type intermediate pipe.

First you people have to get the old muffler off. Since the intermediate pipe has to be cut, there's no need

Step 4. (Cont'd.)

to go through the trouble of loosening the clamp holding the muffler in place.

If you've got a catalytic converter, hold the new muffler against the one fitted to your car to see if you have any cuts to make. **U.S. cars:** Cut the intermediate pipe to 79.8cm (31⅜ in). **Canadian cars:** Cut the intermediate pipe to 110.7cm (43-9/16 in).

Don't cut the front part off the new muffler! Use a hacksaw to cut through the old intermediate pipe, then unhook the rubber exhaust system hangers and thread the system out from under the car. Go to Step 6.

Step 5. Remove New Type Muffler

Do this step if you have a new type intermediate pipe and a new type muffler.

Loosen the clamp holding the muffler onto the intermediate pipe (or the cat pipe). Spray copious amounts of Liquid Wrench around the clamp, let it soak in a little, then use a rubber hammer to beat on the front part of the muffler to get it off the intermediate pipe. If beating doesn't work, try levering the clamp open with a screwdriver. Get out your fire extinguisher and propane torch. *Carefully* heat the joint between the intermediate pipe and the muffler. That will help matters. You may end up chiseling the old muffler off the intermediate pipe. Don't damage the intermediate pipe!

Step 6. Install Muffler

All Models: Thread the new muffler over the rear axle beam and line it up so it fits onto the end of the intermediate pipe. Get the muffler the right way up so that the muffler is horizontal. Don't secure the muffler clamp just yet.

Hook the new rubber hangers onto the intermediate pipe or onto the muffler before things get bolted together. Are the hooks on the pipe lined up with the hooks on the underside of the car? Adjust the position of the muffler until they are.

Now hook one half of the rubber hanger onto the hook under the car and use your screwdriver as a lever to force the other half of the hanger onto the hooks on the intermediate pipe and muffler. Line up the muffler so it's not hitting the axle beam or the rear of the car and tighten the 13mm bolt holding the clamp in position.

Start the car. If the muffler rattles against the bottom of the car, you have not inserted the muffler far enough into the intermediate pipe. Loosen the clamp, push the muffler in further, retighten the clamp and test it once more. Start the car again and run your hand over the joints between the exhaust manifold, intermediate pipe, catalytic converter, and muffler section. If there are leaks, tighten the bolts in that connection to stop them.

Step 7. Tidy Up

Remove the blocks and lower the car to the ground. Throw away the old muffler parts and drive on.

CHAPTER 14

❧ BRAKES ❧

"The ability to stop is often more important than any other capability—humans, cars, whathaveyous. Do a good slow solid job on your brakes."

John Muir

THE WORKINGS

Pressing down your foot on the brake pedal initiates the chain of events which results in your car slowing down and eventually stopping.

The pedal is fastened to a rod which in turn presses against two **pistons** inside the **master cylinder** bolted to the firewall. Rubber caps on the pistons form a fluid-tight seal between the pistons and the smooth master cylinder wall. A **brake fluid reservoir** on top of the master cylinder ensures that the brake system is constantly full of brake fluid, which prevents air bubbles from entering the system.

The master cylinder works much like a hypodermic syringe to force brake fluid down **brake lines**. These thin metal lines carry fluid to the **wheel cylinders**. At the rear wheels the lines screw directly into the cylinders while up front, a flexible hose allows the front wheels to turn and move up and down.

On drum brakes, the wheel cylinder is bolted to the inside of the brake **backing plate** behind the wheels. When the pistons inside the master cylinder attempt to force brake fluid down the lines, the pressure pushes two pistons in the wheel cylinders outward against the top of the **brake shoes.** The shoes are hinged at the bottom and secured to the backing plate by a pin. The wheels are bolted to the heavy metal **brake drum** which has a smooth inside surface. The wheel cylinder pistons force the brake shoe linings against the drum as they move outward. Friction slows and stops the car.

On **disc brakes**, the wheel cylinder in the caliper has two pistons which move brake pads up against a two-surfaced **brake disc** (or **rotor**) bolted to the front driveshafts. The caliper, with its brake pads, surrounds the disc much like the way your fingers and thumb hold a frisbee. When the pads move, they grip the disc and stop the car.

Some cars have a **brake booster** (or **servo**) bolted to the firewall between the master cylinder and the brake pedal. This device, which uses vacuum formed in the engine's intake manifold, reduces the amount of 'push' needed at the brake pedal to stop the car. Diesels sometimes have a vacuum amplifier as well. The amplifier is fastened on the left side of the crankcase (where the ignition distributor fits on gas engines) and increases the amount of vacuum available for the booster.

This four-wheel braking system has a built-in safety mechanism. The master cylinder has a dual internal hydraulic circuit. One rear brake and one front brake are part of one circuit; the other rear and front brakes are part of the other. The dual-chamber master cylinder has two internal pistons, each working a separate circuit. Thus, if one of the piston seals inside the master cylinder circuits breaks, one circuit alone will do your stopping job for you.

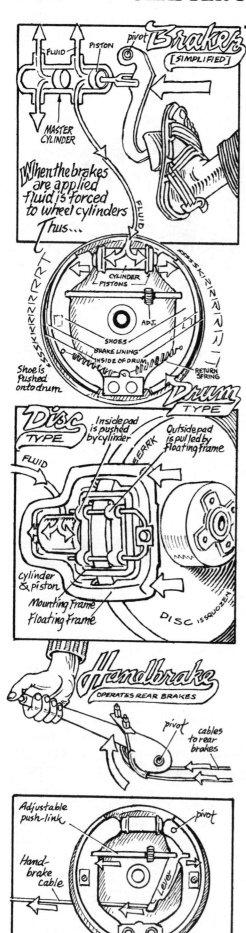

There's a brake light switch screwed into each brake circuit on the master cylinder. Fluid pressure inside the master cylinder works the switches to complete an electrical circuit that turns on the brake lights. A red brake warning light on the dash will come on if either brake circuits fail. This is the same light which reminds you that your handbrake is on.

When there's friction, there's also wear and tear. Naturally, it's best to have one surface (the cheaper one) wear out before the other. That's why replaceable brake pads and brake shoes are softer than the metal brake discs and brake drums they rub against. They're made of asbestos and other man-made fibers bonded together to form a surface that wears evenly and resists brake fade.

Fading is caused by the build-up of heat, a by-product of friction. Heat is retained by the friction surfaces, preventing them from grabbing the disc or drum with any degree of efficiency. Excessive heat build-up will put a glaze on the friction surfaces and boil the brake fluid; then you don't have any brakes at all. Nasty.

To get maximum stopping power the brake shoes should be as close to the drum as possible. Cars built before 1979 require the rear shoes to be adjusted manually while the front disc brakes are self-adjusting. 1979 and later cars were fitted with self-adjusting rear drum brakes so that no manual brake adjustment is required on these later models.

The handbrake or emergency brake is a mechanical brake that, despite its name, should be used only for parking. The handbrake lever between the front seats is connected to the rear brake shoes by two steel cables. If you are in the habit of driving with the handbrake on, you'll soon wear out the rear shoes.

Check your brakes every 10,000 miles or immediately if you've just bought a used Rabbit. Read on.

BRAKE PROBLEMS

The brake fluid level in the reservoir should be checked frequently. If it's low, don't add fluid until you've checked the brake adjustment. Adjusting the brakes may bring the fluid back to the correct level.

The most common brake problems are caused by improper adjustment and unavoidable wear. If the brake pedal goes halfway to the floor before you feel any resistance, it means the brake pads or shoes aren't making contact against the discs or drums as quickly as they should (see Procedure 1).

Sponginess is another problem. When you press down on the brake pedal, does it feel like you're stepping into a marshmallow pie? If so, you've got air in the hydraulic system, either from a leak or because you or someone else opened part of the system for inspection or repair. The system must be bled to remove the air. (Procedure 1)

Leaks work both ways; air can leak in or hydraulic fluid can leak out. Wheel cylinders may drool hydraulic fluid down the

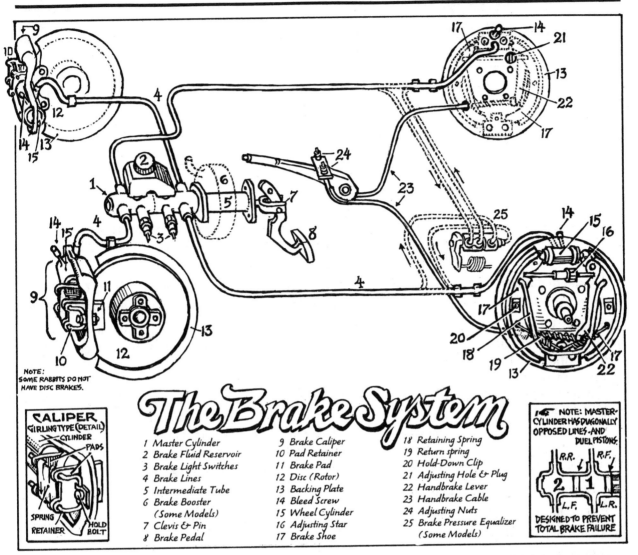

The Brake System

1 Master Cylinder
2 Brake Fluid Reservoir
3 Brake Light Switches
4 Brake Lines
5 Intermediate Tube
6 Brake Booster
  (Some Models)
7 Clevis & Pin
8 Brake Pedal

9 Brake Caliper
10 Pad Retainer
11 Brake Pad
12 Disc (Rotor)
13 Backing Plate
14 Bleed Screw
15 Wheel Cylinder
16 Adjusting Star
17 Brake Shoe

18 Retaining Spring
19 Return spring
20 Hold-Down Clip
21 Adjusting Hole & Plug
22 Handbrake Lever
23 Handbrake Cable
24 Adjusting Nuts
25 Brake Pressure Equalizer
  (Some Models)

NOTE: SOME RABBITS DO NOT HAVE DISC BRAKES.

CALIPER GIRLING TYPE (DETAIL)
CYLINDER
PADS
SPRING RETAINER
HOLD BOLT

NOTE: MASTER-CYLINDER HAS DIAGONALLY OPPOSED LINES AND DUEL PISTONS.
R.R. R.F.
2. 1
L.F. L.R.
DESIGNED TO PREVENT TOTAL BRAKE FAILURE

inside of the brake backing plate onto the inner side of the tire. Wet spots on the tire or the ground should be traced to their source. The rubber parts of the wheel cylinder could have deteriorated and caused a leak or, if you're lucky, it was just the neighbor's dog lifting a leg. Give the wet spot a delicate sniff, then compare the odor to the smell of brake fluid from the can you should have stashed in the trunk or garage. Is it the same? If it is, you'll have to replace or rebuild the wheel cylinder. (Procedure 6).

When you rebuild one wheel cylinder it's best to rebuild the one on the opposite wheel too. At the least, give it a very close inspection.

A leaky master cylinder is easy to spot because it's sticking out of the firewall or the brake booster in the engine compartment. Carefully check all the brake line connections at the master cylinder for leaks. The white plastic brake fluid reservoir is on top of the master cylinder. Make sure it's pushed firmly onto the master cylinder and doesn't have any cracks in it.

If the master cylinder is leaking, don't try to rebuild it yourself. Take it to an expert! It is **vital** that the job be done perfectly. (Procedure 10)

Disc brakes: Always adjust the rear brakes before you bleed. (Procedure 1)

Drum brakes: Adjust the shoes (Procedure 1) before you bleed.

All Models: Always adjust/bleed front and rear. Believe me, it's worth the time and effort. Before you bleed, pump the brake pedal about 20 times to work the air out of nooks and crannies in the system.

Check the brake fluid level in the reservoir during the pump/bleed procedures. Don't let it get more than 25mm (1 in) below the full line.

Early '75 Rabbits have drum brakes on all four wheels so the adjustment and bleeding procedures apply to all four wheels. Late '75 and on cars have self-adjusting disc brakes on the front. When the front disc brake pads reach their wear limit, change them. Then check and maybe work on the rear brakes. '79 and on cars have self adjusting rear drum brakes, too.

All Sciroccos and Rabbits with automatic transmissions have wear indicators embedded in the front disc brake pads. When the pads wear below the safety limit, the indicators cause the brake pedal to pulsate, reminding you that the pads must be changed. Do your periodic maintenance rather than wait until the pads are shot—it's a lot safer.

PROCEDURE 1: ADJUST AND BLEED BRAKES. Phase 1.

Condition: Your car doesn't stop as well as it used to (or at all); the brake pedal goes halfway to the floor before the brakes take hold; you've installed new pads/shoes; or the pedal feels as though the master cylinder has been replaced by a can of mush. Adjust and bleed the system whenever you have it apart—whatever the reason.

Tools and materials: Phase 1 tool kit, fresh can of heavy duty brake fluid (SAE J1703, 116 DOT 3), a small glass jar, a 45cm (18 in) piece of 4mm (5/32 in) internal diameter plastic hose, flashlight and safety glasses.

Remarks: Wear those safety glasses and some kind of filtering mask to avoid inhaling brake dust. It's really nasty stuff. Brake fluid is *extremely poisonous*. Use the glass jar to catch excess fluid, then properly dispose of both. Brake fluid also ruins paint; if any gets on the car, wipe it off immediately and wash the spot with warm soapy water.

Adjust and/or bleed the brakes in this order. Begin at the right rear, then do the left rear, the right front and finally the left front. This bleeding pattern helps to properly eliminate all the air from the lines.

Don't reuse fluid pumped out during the bleeding process. It's become aerated and thus useless.

If you're stuck on the road, you can bleed the brakes without the glass jar or plastic hose. Hold a rag over the end of the bleeding nipple to keep the fluid off the tires and out of your eyes.

Step 1. Check Brake Fluid Level

If the level is less than 13mm (½ in) low, leave it alone. During the adjusting and/or bleeding procedure, keep checking it. If more than one half inch low, fill to the half inch level.

Step 2. Chock, Jack and Block

Release the handbrake. Put the car in first gear or Park with chocks in front of and behind the front wheels. Place the jack under the triangular jacking mark just in front of the right rear wheel and raise the car until the wheel is off the ground. Block it up in case the jack fails (Chapter 1).

Step 3. Release Brake Pressure Regulator (if you have one)

Cars not equipped with a brake booster (the big black flattened cylinder behind the master cylinder on the firewall) have a brake pressure regulator to prevent one rear wheel from locking up when the brakes are out of adjustment. This regulator is just above and behind the rear axle beam on the left side of the car. A lever on the back of the regulator is held to the axle beam by a large spring. Press the lever toward the body of the regulator to release pressure in the right rear brake line, allowing the wheel to turn easily.

NOT ON ALL MODELS

PRESSURE RELEASE

TO R. REAR TRAILING ARM

BRAKE PRESSURE EQUALIZER

FRONT

Step 4. Check and Adjust Brakes

Remarks: Adjust and bleed the brakes at the same time to save time and energy. Begin with the right rear wheel. If you have a 1979 and on car, the rear brakes are self adjusting—go to Step 5.

Read this Step all the way through before you start work.

Look behind the wheel at the backing plate attached to the rear axle. This plate is the base for the brake components and prevents dust and moisture from entering the mechanisms. Looking at the plate from the rear, notice a

Step 4. (Cont'd.)

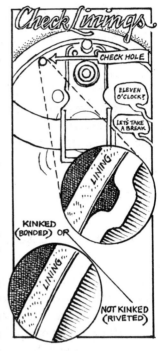

small plastic plug fitted into the plate at the 11 o'clock position. Pull it out.

When the plug is out, shine your flashlight through the hole and look at the amount of friction lining remaining on the shoe. If the lining material looks almost worn down to the metal part of the shoe, both shoes need to be replaced.

Look carefully at the metal shoes. A 'kink' in the shoe indicates the friction linings are bonded to the shoe. A regular, non-kinked metal shoe has the linings riveted on.

Replace bonded linings when they get to be 1.5mm (0.06 in) or less, and riveted linings when they are 2.50mm (0.100 in) or less. Don't include the metal shoe in your measurement. Procedures 4 (front drums) and 5 (rear drums) explain how to change brake shoes, so do it now before you adjust and bleed.

Inside the hole in the backing plate is an adjusting star connected to a threaded bar. Turning the star moves the threaded bar in and out. When it moves out, the bar pushes both brake shoes out toward the brake drum.

Stick a medium-sized regular screwdriver into the hole and fit the blade into the space between points of the star. Now push the handle of the screwdriver upward to move the star clockwise $\bigcirc$, thus moving the brake shoes closer to the brake drum. Pushing down on the screwdriver moves the shoes away from the drum. Turn the star until the shoes tighten against the drum. You'll know they're

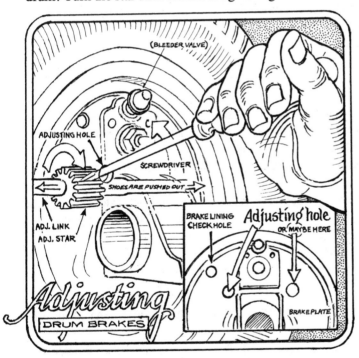

tight when the wheel is difficult to spin.

When you've adjusted the brake shoes until the wheel barely turns, back off the star a couple of notches by pushing down on your screwdriver. The wheel should turn easily with a minimum of scraping. Don't worry if you hear an occasional scratch; you don't want the wheel to bind up. When it turns easily, reinstall the rubber plug in the backing plate, check the brake fluid level in the master cylinder reservoir and add fluid if necessary. Now bleed that right rear brake (read the next three Steps). When that's done, lower the car and repeat the adjust/bleed Procedure on the left rear wheel. You won't need to push the lever on the brake pressure regulator when you work on the left wheel.

Step 5. Brake Bleeding People Get Ready

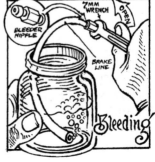

Read through the next three steps before you actually do them. They go too fast to thumb through while you're under the car. Remember: adjust the drum brakes before you bleed them (1978 and earlier).

Remarks: Air in the brake system will be compressed more readily than hydraulic fluid. If there's air in there you'll experience that spongy feeling when you push down the brake pedal. You need to pump pressure into the hydraulic brake lines to bleed off unwanted air through a nipple (basically a bolt with a hole drilled into it) screwed into the back of each wheel cylinder.

Step 6. Pump Pressure into Brake Lines

Put on safety goggles and lay a rag over the inside of the tire to protect it from any brake fluid you may spill.

Position yourself with a 7mm box end wrench, the hose and glass jar where you can easily reach the bleeding nipple but won't get brake fluid in your eyes if the hose slips off when the nipple is open. Pour 13mm (½ in) of brake fluid into your jar.

Remove the rubber nipple cap. If it doesn't have one, thoroughly clean the nipple with a rag and slip the 7mm box end wrench onto the nipple. Now push one end of the hose onto the nipple and put the other end into the glass jar. Set the jar on a block or something else solid. You don't want the end of the hose to flap about wildly. If you're stuck on the road, hold a rag over the nipple end to keep fluid off the tires and out of your eyes.

Have Friend pressurize the system by pumping the brake pedal 20 times, then hold it down hard to keep the pressure in there.

Step 7. Bleed Air Out

Check the hose end is in the fluid at the bottom of the jar. Now pull on the 7mm wrench on the nipple and open it a quarter of a turn. Fluid and/or air will shoot out and bubble into your jar. Friend's foot will sink with the pedal to the floor. Close the nipple quickly; it should be open for only one second. Keep the end of the hose in the fluid at the bottom of the jar.

Have Friend pump seven more times and hold. Meanwhile you should open the nipple for one second again, then close it. If you goof and open the nipple while Friend is pumping, brake fluid will spew out into the jar. Don't worry. Close the nipple and have Friend check the fluid level in the master cylinder reservoir. If it's more than 13mm below the full mark, add some.

Continue pumping and bleeding until you're satisfied there's no more air in the line. When just fluid is pumped down the plastic hose, all the air is out of that line. If your brakes are very spongy, but no air came out in the first try, do it three or four times to be sure. Replace the rubber nipple cap and wipe any spilled fluid off your tire. Brake fluid eats rubber.

Now go back with your screwdriver and adjust, then bleed the left rear brakes. When that's done, adjust and bleed the right front drums, then the left front. If you've disc brakes on the front, just bleed them—they don't have to be adjusted first, disc brakes are self-adjusting you know.

When all four are bled, check the master cylinder reservoir level and add fluid to bring it up to the full mark.

If the pedal still feels mushy after doing this Procedure, your wheel cylinders and/or master cylinder are suspect. However, if you've cured the mushiness, but still have more than 4mm (5/32 in) of free play in the brake pedal, you must adjust the push rod between the brake pedal and the master cylinder. (Procedure 2).

To check free play, push the pedal down with your fingers. That easy distance (shouldn't be more than 4mm (5/32 in) is the free play before you come up against resistance in the master cylinder.

PROCEDURE 2: ADJUST MASTER CYLINDER PUSH ROD AND/OR BRAKE PEDAL. Phase 1.

Condition: More than 4mm (5/32 in) of free play in the brake pedal after installing new brake shoes/pads, adjusting and bleeding the brakes or replacing the master cylinder.

Tools and materials: Phase 1 tool kit.

Open the driver's door and get down on your knees. If you have a fancy Rabbit or Scirocco, remove the protective carpeting from the space between the pedals and the bottom of the dash. It's held in the middle by a plastic clip. Now thread your way between the bottom of the steering wheel and the brake pedal. A push rod with a threaded end comes from the master cylinder through the firewall and is attached to the top of the brake pedal by a U-shaped linkage called a clevis. A 15mm nut screwed hard against the clevis linkage prevents the push rod from turning.

Manual Transmissions: Before adjusting the master cylinder push rod, check that the brake pedal is the same height from the floor as the clutch pedal.

Remove the protective carpet above the pedal cluster and notice how the top of the brake pedal rests against a threaded bolt. That bolt determines how far up the pedal travels. Loosen the 10mm nut holding the bolt against the bracket and screw the bolt in or out until the pedal height is correct. Tighten the 10mm nut and try the free play again. Still too much? Read on.

Automatic Transmission: If you have more than 6mm of free play, adjust the pedal position to take up 2mm of the play (as described above), then have at the push rod adjustment.

All Models: To adjust the master cylinder push rod, loosen the 15mm nut on the rod behind the clevis. Turn the push rod in or out until you get 4mm (5/32 in) of free play. Some free play is important; otherwise, you could have the push rod working the brakes without help from your right foot. A situation to avoid.

Remember to retighten the 15mm locknut on the push rod.

PROCEDURE 3: CHANGE HYDRAULIC BRAKE FLUID. Phase 2.

Condition: After you have owned the car for two years or 30,000 miles have gone by, the brake fluid must be changed. Brake fluid absorbs water and will speed corrosion in the mechanical and hydraulic parts of your brake system. Please don't neglect to change the fluid. It may save a life. Yours, perhaps.

Read Procedure 1 in this Chapter before doing this Procedure.

Tools and materials: 7mm combination wrench, two small clear jars, two 45cm (18 in) pieces of 4mm (5/32 in) internal diameter plastic hose, can of brake fluid meeting SAE recommendation J1703 and Motor Vehicle Safety Standard 116 DOT 3, Friend.

Remarks: This procedure is usually performed with a machine called a pressure bleeder, but we can do it without one.

Step 1. Position Hoses

Take the rubber protective caps from all four bleeding nipples and slip the plastic hoses on the end of the right front and left rear nipples. Put the ends of the hoses into the small jars.

Step 2. Pump Fluid Out

Lift and prop the hood. Remove the cap from the brake fluid reservoir on top of the master cylinder, fill it to the top with brake fluid and have Friend pump the pedal five times and take his/her foot off the pedal. Open the right front and left rear bleeding nipples with the 7mm wrench.

Ask Friend to pump the brake pedal twenty times and keep foot on the brake while you close the two open nipples. Friend: pump pedal five more times and take your foot off the pedal.

Step 3. Do the Other Two

Fill the brake fluid reservoir to the brim with new fluid, switch the hoses and jars, then open the left front and right rear bleeding nipples. Set the hoses into the jars and ask Friend to pump the brake pedal another twenty times. Check the fluid reservoir and fill it again. Have Friend pump another five times.

Close the two open nipples and check the tightness of all four.

Step 4. Replace Fluid

Slowly fill the reservoir with new fluid as Friend slowly pumps the brake pedal seven times. Now go to Procedure 1, adjust the brakes and very thoroughly bleed all the air from the system.

PROCEDURE 4: INSPECT AND/OR REPLACE FRONT DRUM BRAKE SHOES (EARLY '75 RABBITS ONLY). Phase 2.

Condition: The car has been pulling to one side when the brakes are applied, indicating grease or fluid on the front brake pads or brake shoes or the shoes have worn out.

Tools and materials: Phase 2 tool kit, new brake shoes, Locktite, Liquid Wrench, safety goggles, painter's protective mask, fine emery cloth, clean rags, rubber band, pipe cleaner or soft wire, solvent and stiff brush.

Remarks: Take your time on this Procedure—brakes are important! (Rear brakes see Procedure 5, Disc Brakes see Procedure 7.)

Step 1. Chock, Jack and Block

While the car is on the ground, put it into first gear or Park (P) and remove the hubcap or plastic covers on the lug nuts. Now loosen the lug nuts one turn, then chock the rear wheels front and back so the car can't roll. Jack up the front wheel and put a block under the car in case the jack fails.

Step 2. Remove Front Drums

Go to Procedure 1, Step 5, and move the adjusting stars until the brake shoes are as far away from the drums as possible, then remove the lug nuts and pull off the wheel.

Sprinkle Liquid Wrench on the phillips screw holding the drum to the front wheel hub. Let it soak in awhile and then remove the screw. If it's stuck, put the car in gear to prevent the drum from turning. If the screw won't turn, grip the blade of the screwdriver with vice grips (or a wrench) for added leverage (buy a new screw if the head gets mangled). Pull the brake drum off and don't drop it. Now go inside the car and press the brake pedal down gently about 50mm (2 in) and release.

Step 3. Identify Front Brake Components

The top part of the brake shoes fits snugly against the wheel cylinder piston. The bottom part touches and pivots on a bar attached to the backing plate by two rivets. Two springs, called the lower return springs, on the bottom of each brake shoe keep the shoes under tension when they move outward. A pin sticks through the backing plate and the center of the shoes, and is held in place by a retaining clip. At the top, just below the wheel cylinder, is the adjusting bar and star. Below the bar are the upper return springs.

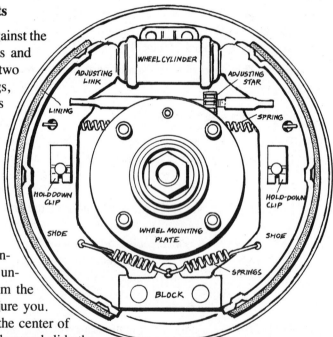

Step 4. Remove Front Brake Shoes

Safety glasses on? Use a pair of pliers to unhook both lower return springs. It seems easier to unhook them from the brake shoe rather than from the other end. Make sure they don't fly out and injure you.

Now let's remove the clip from the pin in the center of each shoe. Push the face of the clip toward the shoe and slide the clip up from the little pin. Pull the pin out from the back of the backing plate. Grab the bottom of the brake shoes and pull them apart away from the bottom bar. Lift 'em over the wheel hub and unhook the two upper return springs. Be careful. The adjusting bar is held to the backing plate by a weird little spring called the brake adjuster locating spring. Unhook that spring and remove the two shoes and adjusting bar.

Watch the wheel cylinder carefully. If either piston starts to move the rubber seals on the end of the wheel cylinder outward, hold the pistons inside the cylinder with your thumb and forefinger. Hook a rubber band or pipe cleaner or soft wire around the wheel cylinder to hold the pistons together. This is why I asked

Step 4. (Cont'd.)

you to tap on the brake pedal in Step 2. Doing so prevents the pistons from moving outward.

If the wheel cylinders are leaking inside the brake mechanism or the rubber boots are split or cracked, do Procedure 6 before reinstalling your brake shoes. Whatever the problem, wear your protective mask and clean the backing plate until it shines with the stiff brush and solvent.

Step 5. Examine Front Brake Shoes and Brake Drums

If the lining on the brake shoes is worn down or soaked with oil and grease, don't try to recondition them. Trade them in for new ones.

Brake drums must be inspected carefully. If you are here from the rear brake Procedure, the rear drums are still attached to the wheel. Run a fingernail across the inside friction surface of the drums. If there are very deep grooves, scores or ridges, you can get things back in order by having a certain amount of metal taken off the drum on a lathe (called 'turning the drums'). Auto parts stores or VW will do this job. Remove the lug nuts if the drums need to be turned.

However, very deep grooves cannot be eliminated entirely so you may have to buy new or used brake drums. Tell the person doing the turning that the minimum drum diameter is 180.5mm (7.105 in) *after* turning. The wear limit on your brake drum is 181mm (7.125 in). If they are past that, get replacements. Check junk yards for good used ones, although good ones are hard to find.

Measure the thickness of the front brake *linings* with a rule. Don't include the metal shoes in your measurement. Linings that are bonded to the brake shoes (no rivets) should be 1mm (0.039 in) thick at the very minimum. If your front brake linings are rivetted to the shoes with eight rivets, the lining thickness should measure at least 1.5mm (0.059 in).

Compare the surface of rivetted linings with the rivet heads. If the rivets are close to being worn down, trade your brake shoes in for new ones. Don't throw them away. Trade them in. $$

Step 6. Clean All Parts

Use your stiff cleaning brush and solvent to clean the brake backing plate and all the other parts you removed if you haven't done so already. Don't use solvent on brake linings which are going to be reinstalled. You'll make them unuseable. OK...your hands are clean too and there isn't a five gallon can of paint to knock over and step in.

Step 7. Install Front Brake Shoes

Wash your hands completely free of grease and tidy up the work area if it's a disaster. Hook the upper return springs into the two holes on the tab on the backing plate just below the wheel cylinder. Let one spring dangle to the left, the other to the right. Use your fingers to screw the brake adjusting bar all the way into the star. Fit the bar into that weird little brake adjuster locating spring. Fit that spring into the holes in the tab. Now put one return spring into the *rear* of one brake shoe. Insert the other spring while getting the brake adjusting bar into the two nose-shaped cutouts in the top of the brake shoes. Then remove the rubber band or wire from the wheel cylinder.

Be sure the two top edges of the brake shoes are properly in position on the ends of the wheel cylinder pistons. They should touch the pistons, not the rubber boots. Hold the bottoms of the brake shoes, spread them apart and push them over the wheel hub. Position them beneath the short bar rivetted to the bottom of the backing plate.

Now push one of the retaining pins through the rear of the backing plate and through the hole in one of the brake shoes. To secure the retaining pin, hold the retaining clip just above the pin and push the surface of the clip toward the shoe as you slide it downward. The head of the pin will fit into the small recess in the clip. Now do the other side. Finally, install the bottom two retaining springs from the front. Check your work.

Step 8. Install Brake Drums

All that remains is to install your beautifully clean and shiny brake drum. If you didn't have any solvent handy to clean the drum, use the liquid soap/detergent you use for washing dishes. Use fine emery cloth to

Step 8. (Cont'd.)

lightly scratch the shiny friction part of the drum. Use a side-to-side motion, not round and round.

Push the brake drum over the brake shoes and line up the hole in the wheel hub with the hole in the brake drum. These holes accept the phillips screw. Put a dab of Locktite on the screw, then screw it through the brake drum into the axle hub. Make sure the brake drum is fully home. Push it on hard with both hands or both feet if necessary, but don't push the car off the blocks! Get the screw as tight as you can. Install the wheel and the four lug nuts. Now do the other side of the car.

PROCEDURE 5: INSPECT/REPLACE REAR BRAKE SHOES AND DRUMS. Phase 2.

Condition: Brake linings worn beyond safe limit.

Tools and materials: Phase 2 tool kit, new brake shoes, safety goggles, painter's protective mask, clean rags, fine emery cloth, rubber bands, pipe cleaner or soft wire, stiff brush and solvent.

Remarks: Before you start work, push the brake pedal down gently about 5mm (2 in) and release. This helps prevent the pistons in the wheel cylinders from popping out when you remove the brake shoes.

Step 1. Adjust Brake Shoes Away From Drums (Pre-1979 cars only)

Depress the lever on the brake pressure regulator (Procedure 1, Step 4) if you have one. Move the adjusting stars until the brake shoes are as far away from the drums as possible. Procedure 1, Step 5.

Step 2. Chock, Jack and Block

Chock both front wheels in front and back. Release the handbrake. Jack up a rear wheel and block the car safely in case the jack fails.

Step 3. Put on Safety Goggles

Pre-1979 models have the rear brakes held in position by a very strong spring. If you're not careful, this spring could fly out and slap you in the face so keep your eyes protected whatever car you work on.

Step 4. Remove Wheel

There's no need to remove the wheel from the drum unless the drum has to be 'turned.' Remove the hubcap or the four plastic lug nut covers and pull the plastic dust cover from the center of the wheel. Use two screwdrivers or a pair of water pump pliers (big pliers) to lever the metal grease cap from the center of the brake drum. Do it slowly; it will eventually work its way off. Using a hammer will dent it.

On the stub axle behind the grease cap is a funny looking serrated metal washer held in place by a cotter pin. Squeeze the two arms of the cotter pin together and pull it out. Pull off that serrated washer. It's covering a nut and prevents it from coming unscrewed. The nut can be removed easily with a crescent wrench, vice grips or a 24mm (15/16 in) socket. It shouldn't be too tight. If it's very tight, your rear wheel bearings may be shot. We'll check in a minute.

Put everything somewhere safe and clean. Put a clean cloth or strip of paper towel on the ground under the place where the stub axle sticks through the wheel. Now hold the tire at the 9:00 and 3:00 o'clock positions and pull it toward you about 20mm (¾ in). Then push it back on the axle again. You will have brought to light a washer and wheel bearing. Pull them off and put them into a clean marked Baggie. If the bearing gets dirty or falls in the mud, put it into a can of clean solvent and swish it around from time to time. You're going to repack the bearing with grease later.

REAR WHEEL BEARING ASSEMBLY
EXPLODED

Now grab the tire again and pull the whole thing free from the axle. If it won't come off, you turned the

Step 4. (Cont'd.)

adjusting star the wrong way and have the brake shoes hard against the drum, or (right wheel) you forgot to release pressure in the brake pressure regulator.

With the wheel off, you'll see the brake backing plate holding the brake shoes, various springs, levers, etc. No bearing should be attached to the stub axle. If there is one, the rear hub bearing has been left on the axle instead of being in the rear of the brake drum. Lever it off by using the same two-screwdriver method you used to remove the metal grease cap in Step 4. Keep rags on the floor beneath the axle in case you overdo it and the bearing comes shooting off the axle straight into the dirt. It did? Put it in another can of solvent. Behind the wheel bearing is a plastic dust cap. Put the rear bearing and cap into a marked Baggie. Don't mix up the two bearings!

Step 5. Remove Rear Brakes Shoe Retaining Springs (Pre-1979 Cars)

Remarks: 1979 and on, see Mini-Procedure coming up.

The rear drum brakes are similar to the front ones with addition of the handbrake cable opeating lever and a large U-shaped spring. (European cars also have two upper return springs.) Look carefully at the way everything is installed.

Be very, very careful! This large U-shaped spring is under a lot of tension and can fly off and severly injure you or a bystander. Put a glove or rag on one hand and hold the spring against the backing plate with your palm. With the other hand use a pair of pliers or a screwdriver to lever one arm of the spring out of the brake shoe. When the spring is removed from one shoe your hand is preventing it from flying off. Now that the tension is off, unhook the other arm of the U-spring from the other brake shoe and lay the spring down somewhere safe.

Next, remove the ends of the bottom two retaining springs from the open chain link with a pair of pliers. Again, pay attention to what you're doing because these springs are also under tension.

Step 6. Free Handbrake Cable

The cable fits into a lever and is secured to the bottom of the brake backing plate by the open chain link which held the ends of the two bottom retaining springs. Twist this link out of the hole in the backing plate. With pliers hold the long spring which is around the handbrake cable and slide it forward and away from the lever on the shoe. When the spring has come forward about an inch, you can twist the cable out from the arm. It might take two tries. Won't come? Try this.

Get in the car and remove the plastic cover from the bottom of the handbrake lever between the seats. The two handbrake cables are attached to this lever. Use two 10mm wrenches to loosen the nuts on both cables. Remove the top one and continue to loosen the bottom one until it's at the top of the cable. Don't remove that lower nut. Do both cables.

Now when you're down at the rear brakes trying to pull the spring up the cable, life will be a lot easier.

Step 7. Remove Brake Shoes

Remove the spring clip from the center of each brake shoe by pushing the face of the clip in toward the axle and then sliding it up from its retaining pin. Slide the pin out from the rear of the backing plate. Do the pin on the other brake shoe and put them both in a marked Baggie along with the clips.

Step 7. (Cont'd.)

Now take off the brake shoes and secure the pistons in the wheel cylinder with a rubber band or soft wire. Take a good look at the wheel cylinder. If it's leaking or deteriorated, it needs to be rebuilt. Procedure 6. Now do the other side of the car and examine the components. If you broke any springs, buy new ones before replacing shoes.

Step 8. Examine Brake Shoes and Drums (Procedure 4, Step 5)

Examine the shoes and trade 'em in on new ones if needed. Bonded rear brake linings should be at least 1.5mm (0.059 in) thick, rivetted linings at least 2.5mm (0.097 in) thick. Don't include the metal brake shoes in your measurements.

Carefully check the new ones you buy against the old. They should be the same.

Step 9 follows the Mini-Procedure for 1979 and on cars.

MINI-PROCEDURE: REMOVE REAR BRAKE SHOES (1979 AND ON MODELS)

These later cars have self-adjusting rear brakes. A nice touch, I suppose. The self adjustment mechanism uses a triangular spacer between the wheel cylinder and the leading brake shoe (the one toward the front of the car). When the linings wear a little, the triangular piece is pulled down by a spring to take up the space vacated by the worn linings. The system is designed so that it's difficult to reach the absolute wear limit and thus destroy your brake drums. If you insist on never checking your brakes, however, the linings will eventually wear out and deface the drum. Try to avoid that.

Put on your safety glasses before beginning work.

Step 1. Remove Top Spring

That's the one which fastens into the trailing shoe (the one toward the car's rear) and hooks over the end of the horizontal metal bar. Use a small screwdriver to lever it out. Be careful, the spring can fly out easily.

Step 2. Remove Shoe Retaining Clamps

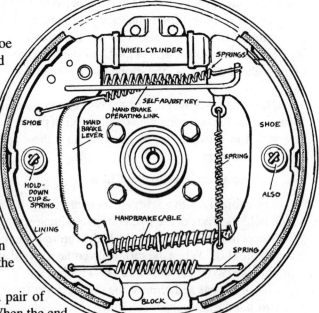

These clamps are comprised of a shaft, spring and cup. The shaft, shaped like a nail with a flattened point, fits through the rear of the backing plate and sticks through a hole in the middle of the brake shoe. Next comes the spring and finally the cup. The cup has a slot and a small depression in its center. The nail tip fits nicely into the depression and prevents the shoe from moving away from the backing plate.

To remove the clamp, hold the cup with a a pair of pliers and push the cup toward the backing plate. When the end of the nail is out of the depression, turn the cup 90° (¼ turn) so the nail can slide out through the slot in the cup. Remove the spring and pull the nail out from the back of the backing plate. Now do the other one and Baggie the lot.

Step 3. Secure Pistons

Wrap some soft wire or a stong rubber band around the wheel cylinder to prevent the pistons from falling out and sucking air into the hydraulic system.

Step 4. Free Brake Shoes

Hold the shoes at the top and pull them sideways away from the wheel cylinder. Next pull them toward you a little and then upward away from the bottom rivetted plate. The bottom spring should now be loose and can be removed from the two shoes. Flip the trailing shoe over and unhook the handbrake cable. Use needle nose pliers to pull the spring down the cable, then twist the shoe so the cable can be pulled out of the lever rivetted to the shoe. Now remove the springs and horizontal bar from the other shoe. Lay down all the springs, bar, spacer and shoes and clean the backing plate with your stiff brush and solvent.

Examine the wheel cylinder and check the rubber boots for splits. If any fluid is leaking or if the thing looks rusty, rebuild or replace it (Procedure 6). If required, do the wheel cylinder Procedure now, then install the brake shoes before you go to work on the other rear wheel. You may need to see what a properly put together rear self-adjusting brake assembly looks like before you reinstall yours.

If the shoes on one side are worn, you can bet that both rear brake assemblies will need new shoes. Hotfoot it to the parts store and get shoes for both sides. You can take the old shoes back to the store later to get your trade in $—don't lose your receipt.

End of Mini-Procedure.

Step 9. Install Rear Brake Shoes—Pre-1979 Cars

Gather your new rear brake shoes and all the parts you took off when you removed your old shoes. First install the leading shoe. That's the one closest to the front of the car. Hold it on the backing plate by installing the pin through the rear of the plate and into the shoe. Hook the spring clip over the top of that pin. Next, install the bottom retaining spring on that shoe. Make sure the top of the shoe is in contact with the wheel cylinder. The pistons on the rear wheel cylinders have a step cut out of them, which should face *toward* the backing plate. Thus the brake shoe can't slip sideways off the piston. Now insert the cylinder on the end of the handbrake cable into the lever on the trailing shoe. Turn the shoe over and slide the cylinder on the end of the cable into the arm. You may have to pull back the spring on the cable before you can get it into the arm properly. In? Great.

Find the adjusting bar and screw the star in as far as it will go. Position one end of the adjusting bar into the nose-shaped cutout on the leading shoe. Get the other end of the bar into the similar cutout on the trailing shoe. Push the trailing shoe against the backing plate. Make sure the end of the handbrake cable is in the lever and the cutout on the wheel cyclinder piston faces the backing plate. Put both shoes under the rivetted bottom bar on the backing plate and hold the trailing shoe with the pin and spring clip. Replace the bottom retaining spring.

Right…here comes the hard part. Safety glasses properly on? Find the large U-shaped spring. Push one side of the spring into the trailing brake shoe, then lever the other arm of the spring into the leading shoe. If you hold the spring flat against the shoes with the palm of your hand (wear a glove or wrap a cloth around your hand), you can use a screwdriver to lever the right arm into the shoe. Now if the screwdriver slips, the spring won't fly away and decapitate the poodle. When the spring is in, check everything very carefully. Slide the handbrake cable into the open chain link. European cars: Replace the top two retaining springs. Now move over to the other side and, using the above Procedure, remove/install the other rear brake shoes.

Step 10. Install Rear Brake Shoes—1979 and On

First check that your new shoes have the handbrake cable lever attached to the trailing shoe. If not, remove the lever from the old shoes (it's held by a pin and a clip) and transfer the levers to the new.

Put on your safety glasses and lay out all the clean brake parts. Put the end of the metal bar without the little turn-up into the top of the leading shoe. It fits into the top slot. Slip the little triangular metal self-adjuster between the shoe and the bar. The little nipple on the rear of the adjuster *faces* the backing plate. Slip the top spring in through the *rear* of the shoe and hook the other end over the turn-up on the end of the metal bar. Use needle nose pliers to get the spring on. It will probably take a couple of attempts but Percy Veer. Next hook one end of the weak spring into the bottom of the self-adjuster and the other into the hole in the bottom of the shoe. Look at Peter's diagram on the next page or take the partly assembled shoe to the other side of the car (if the

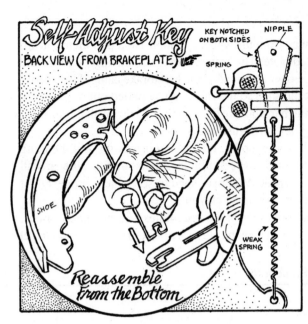

Self-Adjust Key

BACK VIEW (FROM BRAKEPLATE)

KEY NOTCHED ON BOTH SIDES

NIPPLE

SPRING

SHOE

WEAK SPRING

Reassemble from the Bottom

Step 10. (Cont'd.)

wheel and drum are off) and check it against what you see.

Everything fine so far? Primo. Pick up the trailing shoe and move the handbrake lever away from the shoe. Hold the cylinder on the end of the handbrake cable with a pair of pliers and use needle nose pliers to pull the spring up the cable about 10mm. Be sure the little washer is up the cable too. Hold the spring away from the cylinder and fasten the cable end into the rear of the handbrake lever. Another pair of hands is most welcome. If you simply can't hold that cable spring away from the end, here's another way:

Get in the car and remove the plastic cover from the bottom of the handbrake lever between the seats. The two handbrake cables are attached to this lever. Use two 10mm wrenches to loosen the nuts on both cables. Remove the top one and continue to loosen the bottom one until it's at the top of the cable. Don't remove that lower nut. Do both cables.

Now when you're down at the rear brakes trying to pull the spring up the cable, life will be a lot easier.

Back to the shoes. Take the leading shoe assembly and slide the end of the metal bar attached to the shoe up the handbrake cable lever on the trailing shoe. Pull the lever away from the shoe a little. When the bar is at the top, pull the lever back toward the shoe and fit the end of the bar into the slot at the top of the trailing shoe. Got it? Now replace the bottom spring into both shoes.

Position the shoes over the small bar at the bottom of the backing plate and engage the top of the shoes onto the wheel cylinder. Check that the shoes fit properly on the pistons in the wheel cylinder. You will see that the pistons have a step cut out of them. This step *faces* the backing plate so the shoes won't slip away from the wheel cylinders with alarming results.

Install the thin top spring. The short end hooks onto the horizontal bar. Pull the other end through the slot in that bar and hook it to the hole closest to the lining on the brake shoe. Check it against the still intact side to see if it's right.

Find the nails, springs and cups and push one nail through the rear of the backing plate and through the hole in one brake shoe. Hold the cup with a pair of pliers, replace the spring over the nail and replace the cup. Hold the nail in place by keeping your finger on the head in back of the bacing plate. Be sure the nail sits properly in the cup's depression. Remove the rubber band or whatever from the wheel cylinder and give your work a final check. Now do the other side.

Step 11. Check and Install Rear Wheel Bearings

Additional tools and materials: Copper or brass drift, wheel bearing grease, new inner wheel bearing seals, maybe new bearings and races.

The wheel bearings revolve in what's known as a wheel bearing race. The outer race is pressed into the front of the brake drum and the inner race into the rear of the drum. Check the surface of the outer race for grooves, scratches, even nicks. If there is *any* damage, the race must be removed and a new one pressed in. To do this, take off the lug nuts and remove the wheel from the drum. Now find a copper or brass drift. Don't use a steel punch; it can destroy the inside surface of the brake drum where the race presses in and you'll have to buy a new drum. I would examine the inner bearing and race if you find the outer one is at all damaged. To get at the inner bearing and race use a screwdriver to lever the inner seal out from the brake drum. Remove the bearing and check it and the race for damage.

To remove the race: tap gently from *inside* the brake drum all the way around the inside circumference of the race until it begins to move out through the front of the brake drum. Keep tapping until the race falls out. Have a look at the illustration on the next page.

Step 11. (Cont'd.)

It's best to take the brake drum to VW and have new wheel bearing outer races pressed in with a hydraulic press, but you can do it by laying the race on the face of the drum and tapping it gently with a hammer. Move the hammer around the circumference and get the race down. Don't get the race sideways or it won't seat properly. Remove it if it gets awry and start again. Use the drift to seat it down in there.

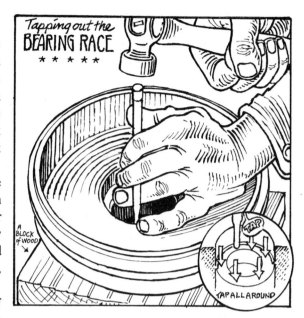

If you dropped your bearings in the dirt, retrieve them now from the can of solvent, swish them around in new, clean solvent and examine them very carefully for scratches and dirt. Use a small toothbrush to totally eliminate all traces of dirt. Now let's replace the cleaned or new wheel bearings with wheel bearing grease only, not Vaseline or Brylcream.

Let's do the inner bearing first. Plop a blob of grease about the size of an egg yolk in the palm of one hand. Push the grease thoroughly into the roller bearing assembly with your fingers. The wheel bearing must be completely full of grease. This job takes five minutes to do properly. Wipe off any excess grease and slip the inner wheel bearing into the clean race in the rear of the brake drum. The narrower side of the bearing goes in first.

Tap on the rubber seal that prevents dirt, dust and moisture from entering the bearing. If the seal is cracked or goes in too easily, get a new one. Tap alternate sides of the seal until it's fully seated.

Next pack the outer wheel bearing with grease (as above) and put it into a clean sealed Baggie where it won't get damp or dirty.

Step 12. Install Rear Brake Drum

Turn the adjusting star inside the brake backing plate until the brake shoes are as close together as possible. Now push the brake drum over the stub axle and when it's home, slip in the outer wheel bearing. Narrow part goes in first, remember. Push on the clean washer and screw on the nut. Tighten the nut with whatever you've got and then back it off until it's loose again. Tighten the nut once more until the washer is just touching the nut.

Insert a screwdriver between the washer and the brake drum and using finger pressure on top of the

screwdriver, try to push the washer downward. If it moves easily, the nut is too loose. On the other hand, if it won't move at all, it's too tight. Adjust the nut pressure until that thrust washer, as it's called, can be moved slightly with finger pressure on your screwdriver as a lever to move the thrust washer.

Here's another trick if you happen to have a 24mm socket: use a torque wrench to tighten the nut to 3.5 mkg (25 ft lbs), then back off the nut and retorque it to 1 mkg (7 ft lbs). That does the same thing as the screwdriver method.

Replace the serrated metal washer and slip a new cotter pin through the hole in the stub axle. Use needle nose pliers to spread the arms of the cotter pin around the stub axle. Hold the wheel at the 9 and 3 o'clock positions and rock the wheel side to side. There should be no play. There is? Remove the

Step 12. (Cont'd.)

cotter pin and serrated metal piece and tighten the nut ½ turn. Install the lot and test again. OK? Install the grease cap after sticking a fingerful of grease into it. Tap the cap on with a rubber hammer or put a piece of wood over it and tap on the wood with a regular hammer. Make sure it seats properly.

Step 13. Adjust and Bleed Brakes (Procedure 1)

Do the same Procedures on the other wheel.

PROCEDURE 6: OVERHAUL WHEEL CYLINDERS (SLAVE CYLINDERS). Phase 2.

Condition: Your wheel cylinders (front or rear) are leaking or rusty.

Tools and materials: Phase 2 tool kit, 5mm allen wrench, wheel cylinder rebuild kit or new wheel cylinders, safety glasses, fine steel wool and alcohol, VW brake paste, recommended brake fluid.

Remarks: The wheel cylinders bring the brake shoes into contact with the brake drum. If they're leaking fluid or admitting air, they won't do their job properly, and therefore you risk a dent in your fender at the very least. There are two ways to go. You can buy new wheel cylinders from VW or a foreign car parts store, or you can rebuild the existing cylinder for about one third the cost.

However, when you get the thing apart and find that the inside of the wheel cylinder is badly rusted, scored or nicked at all, don't try to save money by installing a rebuild kit. The cylinder won't work properly and may contribute to your demise. Buy a new cylinder. If you can't decide whether to replace or repair, take the cylinder to someone who knows.

If you're reconditioning the old wheel cylinder you can buy a wheel cylinder hone from an auto parts store which fits into an electric drill. This hone will polish and remove any residual junk from inside the wheel cylinder. Hones are fairly expensive, however, and steel wool works just as well, though it takes longer. If you buy a hone, make sure it's the right size for those tiny VW wheel cylinders. Hones made for U.S. sized cylinders won't do.

Step 1. Remove Wheel and Brake Drums and Shoes

Procedures 4 (front drum brakes) and 5 (rear drum brakes).

Step 2. Remove Wheel Cylinder Components

Remove the dust cap and loosen the bleeding nipple on the rear of the wheel cylinder one turn (7mm wrench). Pull the rubber boots from the ends of each side of the wheel cylinder. As you remove the boot, out will come the piston. Beneath the piston is a rubber cup and a long spring. An identical setup of cup, piston and boot is installed on the other side of the wheel cylinder. Note how the cup is positioned behind the piston. The large flange on the cup faces toward the *center* of the wheel cylinder. If the whole thing messily disintegrates as you're pulling it out, look at   the diagram.

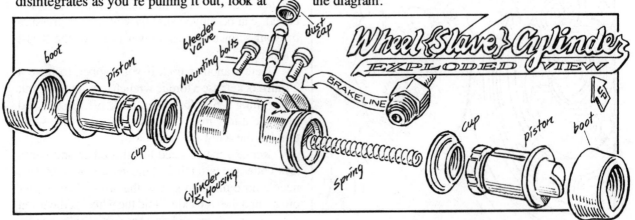

Step 2. (Cont'd.)

Use your fingernail to check inside the wheel cylinder for grooves, scoring and dirty deposits. If it's scored and groovy, remove the cylinder and either take it to VW or the parts store and ask if it should be replaced or cleaned, or make up your own mind. If it's not too bad, you can clean it out as per Step 3. To get the rear wheel cylinder off the backing plate, first remove the brake line that runs into the back of the wheel cylinder. Loosen the 12mm captive nut completely and gently pull the brake line away from the cylinder. You don't want to kink the line. Now remove the two 5mm allen bolts holding the wheel cylinder to the backing plate and take the wheel cylinder off. Put the allen bolts into a marked Baggie.

Before removing the front cylinders, you must separate the brake hose from the metal line (12mm and 14mm wrenches). Then unscrew the hose (14mm) from the wheel cylinder. Put a Baggie over the open end of the metal brake line.

Before you go to VW or the parts store, clean the parts you're having checked and put them in a cardboard box.

Step 3. Rebuild Wheel Cylinders

If the power that be advised that one or more of your wheel cylinders was beyond hope and you bought new ones, go to Step 4. If you're going to clean and rebuild them, here's how:

Dip a piece of steel wool in alcohol and push it into the wheel cylinder. Stick a screwdriver into the center of the steel wool and twist it around and around so the steel wool tangles with the blade but the blade doesn't touch the side of the cylinder. Put a good shine on the inside of the cylinder. Don't push the steel wool backward and forward—only 'round and 'round until it looks like a new mirror. You can stick another screwdriver into the steel wool via the other end of the cylinder for better action. When it's clean, break out your can of brake fluid and pour some into a clean container.

Wash your hands thoroughly to remove any traces of grease. Dip a corner of a clean rag or your forefinger into the brake fluid and thoroughly swab the inside of the wheel cylinder. Remove the bleeding nipple (7mm wrench) and clean it too.

Take the wheel cylinder rebuild kit out of the box and get your VW brake paste. Smear a little paste onto the pistons and the two internal cups. Dip the spring into your cup of brake fluid. Do not soak the large rubber boots . Take one of the pistons and one of the rubber cups and slip the cup into the groove on the rear of the piston. The large shoulder faces the rear of the piston. The cups in rebuild kits from anywhere but VW may not have one shoulder larger than the other. With these it doesn't matter which way 'round you put them Thought I'd tell you this to prevent your getting paranoid if your components aren't exactly as described. However, the rebuild stuff should be the same size as the originals.

Next, slide the front part of the piston into one of the rubber boots and push the piston into one end of the wheel cylinder. Snap the end of the boot over the groove on the end of the wheel cylinder so the piston won't fall out. Put the other cup onto the other piston and put the piston into its boot. Don't install this piston into the cylinder yet

Slip the spring into the wheel cylinder making sure it fits into the hole in back of the piston that's already been inserted into the cylinder. Now, hold that piston in place with your forefinger, and push the piston you're installing into the cylinder making sure the spring fits into the hole in the back. Hold the pistons in with your thumb and forefinger and fasten the rubber boot around the groove on the end of the wheel cylinder. Turn the step cut out of the pistons (if present) toward the backing plate. Hold the pistons in with a rubber band or soft wire. Replace the bleeder nipple and the new dust cap.

Step 4. Install Rebuilt or New Wheel Cylinder

Keep the rubber band around the wheel cylinder to prevent the pistons from popping out and fit the cylinder into position on the backing plate. Rear brakes—make sure the brake line is clean, then put the line into the rear of the cylinder and screw up the captive nut with your fingers. Take care not to cross the threads. Front brakes—screw the flexible hose into the cylinder and tighten it (14mm). Front and rear—Push the wheel cylinder onto the backing plate, reinstall the two 5mm allen-headed bolts and tighten the 12mm captive nut on the brake line (or 14mm brake hose). Front brake people screw the metal brake onto the hose and

Step 4. (Cont'd.)

tighten it (12 and 14mm wrenches).

Looks OK? Check your work, then turn to Procedure 4 or 5 and install the brake shoes and drums.

DISC BRAKES

All Rabbits manufactured after the end of 1975 have disc brakes on the front wheels. There are three brands, Teves, Girling and Kelsey Hayes. The name is stamped on the caliper. The three are very similar but parts are not interchangeable.

Disc brakes derive their name from the strong metal **disc** (or **rotor**) bolted onto the front drive shaft which rotates along with the wheel. A 'floating caliper' surrounds this disc. Pressed into the caliper is the **brake cylinder** housing the **brake pistons.** Brake pads with a friction surface on one side press up against the pistons. When you press the brake pedal with your foot these pistons move outward and push the brake pads against each side of the smooth disc to stop the wheel. Imagine your thumb and forefinger (the pads) pinching against a dinner plate (the disc). Disc brakes are very efficient and are used on most high performance and racing cars, usually on all four wheels. The pads wear out faster than the linings on drum brakes, so inspect them regularly.

How To Check For Wear (See 1980 changes, p. 235)

Check the pads for wear every 6,000 to 10,000 miles, Some cars have pads with a built-in wear indicator. There is a lug on the disc which touches part of the pad when the pad is worn and when you press the

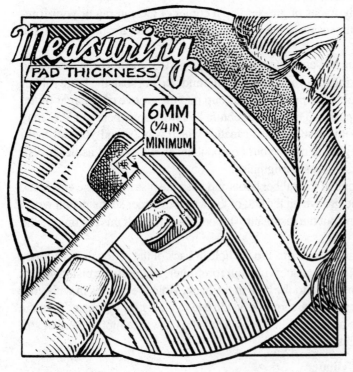

Measuring
PAD THICKNESS

6MM
(¼ IN)
MINIMUM

brake pedal you can feel it pulsate. Time to change pads! Since not all cars have the wear indicators, it's wise to measure the thickness of the pads to be sure there's a safe amount of friction material remaining on them. Use a small rule to check pad thickness without removing the wheels. Stick the rule through one of the slots in the wheel and measure the thickness of the pad. *Include* the metal backing part of the pad in your measurement but not the thin metal spacer behind the pad. The spacers are just under 1mm thick. The brake pad should measure at least 6mm (¼ in). Replace *both* pads in one caliper even if only one is worn to the limit. Always replace the pads on both wheels even if one side measures OK. They usually wear about the same amount, but for safety's sake replace all four.

If the pads have worn down to the metal, then I bet that the disc has some nasty looking scars. Let's do the pad change and see…

PROCEDURE 7: CHANGE FRONT DISC BRAKE PADS. Phase 2.

Condition: Brake pads are worn (see 1980 changes, p. 235).

Tools and materials: Phase 2 tool kit, small punch (for Teves calipers), four new pads, recommended brake fluid, chalk, safety glasses (put 'em on right now), two new retaining springs (Teves).

Step 1. Chock, Jack, Block and Remove Front Wheel

Loosen the lug nuts first, then jack the car up. Rock the car to be sure it's safety blocked.

Step 2. Remove Old Pads

Girling Calipers: Turn the ignition key to ON and move the steering wheel until the front of the caliper faces you. Ignition off. Pry off the thin metal spreader spring from the front of the caliper. Use a screwdriver blade between the spreader spring and one of the retainer arms for best leverage.

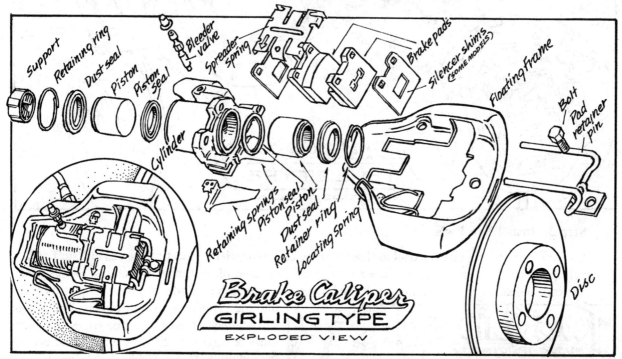

Now remove the 13mm bolt holding the retainer onto the caliper frame. When the bolt's out use a pair of pliers to remove the retainer from the two brake pads. Mark the inner pad 'I' and the outer one 'O' with chalk, then simply pull them out by the ears. There may be a thin metal spacer behind each pad, pull them out also. They are supposed to cut down brake squeal. If you're going to reuse the old pads, it's important to put them back where they came from. If you don't, the braking action is somewhat uneven.

Teves (ATE) Calipers: The pads are held in place by two pins and the pins are secured by a retaining spring. Lever the spring out of the pins, then use your small punch to remove those pins. Put the punch on the end of the pin where the retaining spring fits and drive it out. Don't get the punch stuck in the caliper! Next take out the spreader spring and use the chalk to mark the edge of each pad with an 'I' (inner) or 'O' (outer). If you decide to reuse the old pads they must go back from whence they came or uneven braking is the order of the day. Pull the inner pad out by the ears. Ouch.

When that pad is out, push the floating frame and its brake cylinder inward to free the outer pad from a notch. Now pull the pad out.

(Illustration of Teves caliper is on next page.)

Both types: Inspect the spreader spring, pins and clips and make a note to replace any damaged ones. Examine both pads for scoring or uneven wear. If the pads are very worn or down to the metal backing, inspect the disc for scoring. In fact, inspect it whatever your pads look like. Run your fingernail across the disc. Does your nail hang up on ridges and scoring? If so, the disc will have to be removed and turned on a lathe. See Procedure 8.

Is there any brake fluid on or around the pads or any part of the brake mechanisms? Yes? Then the brake cylinder will have to be rebuilt. Check the brake mechanism on the other side to see if there's leakage there. If just one side has a leak, rebuild *both cylinders!* (Procedure 8). All looks well…? Proceed.

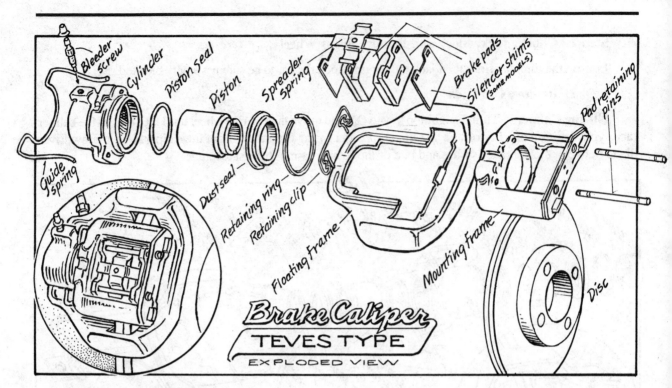

Brake Caliper TEVES TYPE EXPLODED VIEW

Step 3. Install New Pads

Use a clean cloth dipped in alcohol to clean the crevice into which the pads fit. You can buy stuff called brake cleaner which just sprays on any brake component. It flushes off dirt, then evaporates. Works well.

Teves: Loosen the 7mm bleeding nipple slightly on the front of the cylinder and push the pistons back

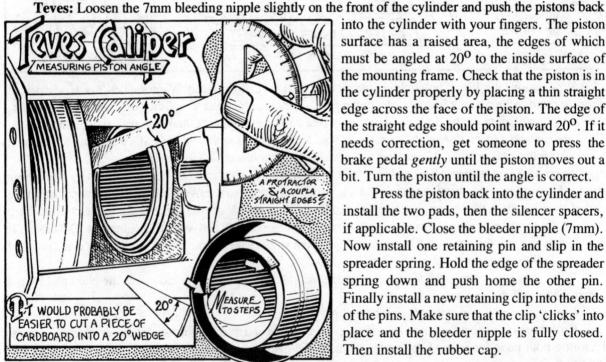

into the cylinder with your fingers. The piston surface has a raised area, the edges of which must be angled at 20° to the inside surface of the mounting frame. Check that the piston is in the cylinder properly by placing a thin straight edge across the face of the piston. The edge of the straight edge should point inward 20°. If it needs correction, get someone to press the brake pedal *gently* until the piston moves out a bit. Turn the piston until the angle is correct.

Press the piston back into the cylinder and install the two pads, then the silencer spacers, if applicable. Close the bleeder nipple (7mm). Now install one retaining pin and slip in the spreader spring. Hold the edge of the spreader spring down and push home the other pin. Finally install a new retaining clip into the ends of the pins. Make sure that the clip 'clicks' into place and the bleeder nipple is fully closed. Then install the rubber cap.

Girling: Loosen the 7mm bleeding nipple back into the cylinder. Install the two pads and silencer spacers (if present) and close the bleeder nipple. Put the pad retainer back through the ears on both pads and replace the 13mm bolt through the retainer and into the caliper. Tighten the bolt. Put the spreader spring back over the two arms on the retainer (the little cutout arrow faces down).

All Models: Put the wheel back on, lower the car, tighten the lug nuts and check the brake fluid level in the reservoir. Now do the other side. As I said before, you should replace all four pads at the same time. It's cheaper and quicker than a stay in the infirmary. Now turn to Procedure 1 and bleed the front brakes.

PROCEDURE 8: REMOVE AND INSTALL FRONT DISC AND CALIPERS. Phase 2.

Condition: You found a fluid leak in one or both of the brake cylinders. Remove them and take them away for overhaul. The pads had worn to the metal and gouged the discs so they need to be removed and turned or replaced.

Tools and materials: Phase 2 tool kit, two new phillips screws to hold brake disc on.

Remarks: Please don't try to remove the calipers if they are hot, Also, *always* remove the caliper before removing the disc. You will bust the caliper frame if you force matters.

Step 1. Chock, Jack and Block

Loosen the lug nuts first, jack the car up, make it safe, then remove the wheel.

Step 2. Remove Brake Pads

Procedure 7, Step 2.

Step 3. Remove Calipers

If you're here to just remove the disc, the caliper can remain attached to the brake hose. If the brake cylinder is to be rebuilt, the cylinder has to be released from the hose. Don't try to unscrew it yet.

The brake caliper is held onto the wheel bearing housing by two 15mm bolts. Put a short extension onto your socket and remove the bolts. They are tight so use Liquid Wrench and watch your knuckles. Mark and Baggie the bolts.

If you are just going to remove the brake disc, pull the caliper off and hang it onto the steering tie rod with a strong wire hook. Do *not* let the caliper hang just by the hose. You'll weaken it and you may do the same to your head if the hoses fail.

To remove the caliper, pull it off the wheel bearing housing (steering knuckle) and unscrew the hose from the caliper (14mm). Girling calipers have a *left hand thread,* so remove the hose by turning it clockwise ↻ .

Put a plastic bag over the exposed end of the hose and tie it up out of the way. Keep the end of the hose pointing up; that way you won't lose all the brake fluid. Now do the same thing to the other side and take the calipers to the rebuild shop.

Step 4. Remove Brake Disc (if it's worn)

The disc is held onto the wheel hub by a phillips screw. Soak the screw with Liquid Wrench and let it stew. Use vise grips, your screwdriver, a sharp punch or a diamond tip chisel to get the screw out if the screwdriver won't budge it. Remember to buy two new screws.

The brake disc pulls off the hub when the screw is out. Take it to VW and get it turned (resurfaced) if it needs it.

Step 5. Install Disc

Line up the hole in the disc with the hole in the hub and push the disc into position. Secure it with a *new* phillips screw. Get the screw tight.

Step 6. Install Calipers

Before you leave the brake shop check that the cylinders are complete with rubber dust boots and the piston rotated into the correct position (Teves). See Procedure 7, Step 3. Also check that the cylinder is properly fitted into the floating caliper with the spring attached. See drawing on next page. Inspect the brake hose and replace it if it's in poor condition. See Procedure 9. Girling calipers have a left hand thread; turn the hose clockwise ↻ to remove and counterclockwise ↺ to install.

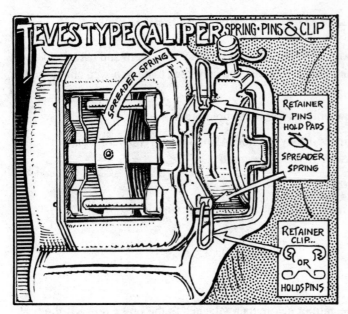

Step 6. (Cont'd.)

Unhook your caliper from the tie rod where you hung it for safety. Position the caliper onto the wheel bearing housing and install the two 15mm bolts. *Leave off* the spring washers if your car originally had them. Torque to 6.0 mkg (43 ft lbs). Go back to Procedure 7, Step 3, and install new pads. Finally, bleed the system (Procedure 1) and put the wheels back on. Don't forget to tighten the wheel lug nuts when the car's on the ground.

PROCEDURE 9: REPLACE FRONT BRAKE HOSES. Phase 1.

Condition: The hoses are worn, split or bulging in places.

Tools and materials: Phase 1 tool kit, new hoses, can of recommended brake fluid.

Remarks: Girling hoses are shorter than Teves' and have a left hand thread where they screw into the calipers. The Girling hose also has a groove around the connection which threads into the caliper. Don't mix the two up. When you buy a new hose, compare the length of the new against the old.

Step 1. Remove Worn Hose

It's possible to do this Procedure with the car on the ground and the wheels on, but it's less hassle if it's up and off as it were. Besides, it keeps the brake fluid from dripping into your mouth. Chock and block the car if you jack it up.

Use 11mm and 14mm wrenches to separate the brake hose from the metal brake line. They meet at a tab welded onto the inner fender well. There's a spring clip on the metal pipe which presses against the tab; don't lose it when the pipes are divorced, I mean separated. Put a plastic bag over the thin pipe end.

Now remove the hose from the caliper with a 14mm wrench. Teves hoses unscrew counterclockwise ⟲ and Girling uses a left hand thread, so screw clockwise ⟳ to get that hose off.

Step 2. Install New Hose

Having checked the length of your new hose against the old, install it into the caliper. Girling owners screw counterclockwise ⟲ to install. Remove the plastic bag from the metal line. Slip the rubber grommet off your old line and put it onto the new to protect the hose from chafing against the support tab. Screw the metal line into your new hose (11mm and 14mm), then push the rubber grommet into the support tab.

Do the other side and then bleed the front brakes (Procedure 1). When the brakes have been bled, get someone to press the brake pedal a few times as you watch the hose connections for leaks. Don't forget to replace the dust caps on the bleeding nipples. That's it.

PROCEDURE 10: REMOVE BRAKE MASTER CYLINDER FOR OVERHAUL. Phase 2.

Condition: Master cylinder leaking.

Tools and materials: Phase 1 tool kit, large syringe.

Step 1. Remove Master Cylinder

The master cylinder sticks out from the left side of the firewall and has a semi-opaque white plastic hydraulic fluid reservoir on top. If your car has a black cylindrical brake booster, the master cylinder sticks out from the front of it. Removing the master cylinder is the same for both versions.

Step 1. (Cont'd.)

Pull off the two electrical brake light connections from the sides of the master cylinder. You'll see them—they're in different positions for different years. Let the connections dangle down. Now place a thick rag under the master cylinder to catch stray drops of brake fluid. Brake fluid is harmful to eyes and paint, so be careful.

Find some kind of syringe like a meat baster to empty the brake fluid reservoir. Don't suck the stuff out—**POISON!** Remove the four brake lines to the master cylinder (11mm wrench) and pull them just slightly clear; don't kink the lines. Put a Baggie onto the end of each line to keep them clean. Remove the two 13mm nuts holding the master cylinder to the brake booster or the firewall and carefully pull the master cylinder free. Tip the remaining brake fluid into a container, then pull off the plastic reservoir.

Stuff a clean Baggie or piece of rag into the hole left by the departed master cylinder. Clean the master cylinder before you take it to a brake specialist for rebuilding.

Step 2. Install Master Cylinder

Reinstall your clean master cylinder fluid reservoir on the top of the master cylinder by pushing it down firmly. Make sure it's seated properly. Remove the Baggie or rag from the hole and loosely install the master cylinder on the firewall or the brake booster with the two 13mm nuts.

Remove the protective Baggies and put the four brake lines onto their respective holes in the master cylinder. Get the threads started on all four lines *by hand*. Please make sure they're not cross threaded; then tighten the two 13mm nuts holding the master cylinder in position. Next tighten the four 11mm captive bolts on the brake lines.

Reconnect the electrical connections on the two brake light switches. Fill the master cylinder reservoir with fresh clean brake fluid to just above the line. Have Friend pump the brake pedal about 20 times while you check the level of the fluid and add some if necessary. Replace the cap on the fluid reservoir.

Now bleed the brakes at all four wheels. Procedure 1. Don't neglect this step.

PROCEDURE 11: BRAKE PRESSURE REGULATOR. Phase 1.

Condition: Right rear wheel won't turn, uneven braking.

The brake pressure regulator cannot be serviced or repaired by you. Fortunately, it very rarely goes bad, so if your right wheel won't turn, try pressing the lever on the rear of the regulator to equalize the pressure. Has the spring broken? If so, buy a new one and replace it. Adjust the rear brakes (Pre-1979) to equalize rear braking action, then bleed the brakes (all models).

If that doesn't work, you'll have to take the car to VW for testing on their pressure regulator machine.

PROCEDURE 12: FIX BRAKE LIGHT SWITCH. Phase 1.

Condition: Rear brake lights don't come on.

Tools and materials: New bulbs, new switch?

The two switches on the master cylinder work only when your foot presses the brake pedal. This closes a contact inside the switches to make the rear stoplights shine. If one or both brake lights refuse to work, first check the fuses in the relay plate and the bulbs (Chapter 19); then check the switch.

Step 1. Check Switch

Pull one of the electrical connectors from one of the switches on the master cylinder and see that the wires in the back of the connectors are in place. Find a short piece of electrical wire and strip 6mm (¼ in) of insulation from each end of the wire. Now stick the ends of the wire into the opposite slots in the connector which plugs onto the switch. Have Friend check the rear brake lights. If your brake lights go on, the switch on the master cylinder is bad. Check both switches.

Step 2. Remove Bad Switch

Unscrew it with a crescent wrench.

Step 3. Install New Switch

Buy a new switch and screw it into the master cylinder with your fingers, then tighten it with a crescent wrench. Don't overdo it. The switch has pipe threads that tighten themselves as you screw in the switch. Plug in the electrical connections and admire your brake lights.

THE HANDBRAKE

The handbrake (emergency or parking brake) is operated by a black lever between the two front seats. Two steel cables run from the lever to the brake shoes at the rear wheels. When the handbrake lever is pulled up, the cables tighten and push the rear brake shoes against the brake drum. The lever is held up by a notched locking arrangement—pawl teeth fall into ratchet teeth. To release the brake, just press the button at the end of the handbrake lever. This knocks the pawl away from the ratchet teeth and lets you push the handle down.

PROCEDURE 13: ADJUST HANDBRAKE. Phase 1.

Condition: There is too much play (goes up more than three notches) in the handbrake, and the rear brakes are adjusted properly (Procedure 1).

Step 1. Chock, Jack and Block

Get both rear wheels off the ground.

Step 2. Adjust Cable Nuts

Release the handbrake lever. Remove the plastic shield from the handbrake lever by putting your fingers at the bottom of each side of the cover and pulling them sideways to clear the lever. Pull the cover upward toward the top of the windshield. It might be stuck so give it a good pull to bring the two cables to light.

Loosen the top nut on each cable (two 10mm wrenches). Tighten the bottom nuts on each cable into the bar until you are unable to spin the rear wheels by hand. Now loosen these bottom nuts a couple of turns. Pull the handbrake lever up and down to make sure the cables are moving properly. Turn the cable nuts until the wheels are able to roll without binding up.

Have Friend give the wheels a spin and pull the handbrake lever up two notches. The wheels should slow down or stop. Now pull the lever up to the third notch. You shouldn't be able to turn the wheels at all by hand. Release the brake lever and the wheels should turn easily.

Get the same amount of stopping power on each wheel—adjust the nut on the right cable for the right wheel and left nut for the left wheel. When your brakes are tight at three notches and completely free when the lever is released, it's right. (If you can't get it right at three notches, go to four.)

Step 3. Tighten Cable Nuts

Hold the bottom cable nut still while you tighten the top one onto it (two 10mm wrenches). Do both cables. Put the plastic protective cap back on the lever, remove the blocks and lower the car. The handbrake is adjusted and you're on your way.

PROCEDURE 14: FIX HANDBRAKE LEVER. Phase 2.

Condition: The handbrake won't stay in the UP position; probably the pawl tooth has fallen down. The long wire with the spring on it (attached to the bottom at the end of the handbrake) can't engage with the pawl and force it into contact with the ratchet teeth.

If you keep the rear brake shoes adjusted close against the drum, the only maintenance at the handbrake lever will be to adjust the tension in the handbrake cables. If you become lax on either of these two Procedures, the pawl tooth is going to slip out.

Tools and materials: Phase 1 tool kit.

Step 1. Take Handbrake Lever Apart

Take the plastic cover off (Procedure 13, Step 2). Remove the four 10mm nuts holding the brake cables in position. To free the handbrake lever, remove the snap ring (thin screwdriver) from the end of the pivot at the base of the handbrake and pull out the pin holding the handbrake lever in its mount. Remove handbrake lever.

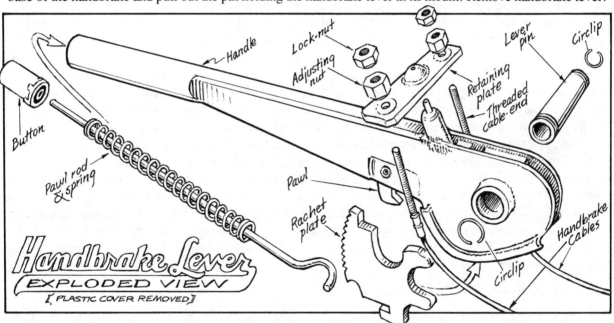

If the whole thing falls apart in your hands, you'll have to put it back together. Insert the ratchet bar (the piece of metal with the U-shaped scoop cut out of it and the teeth on one edge) into the center part of the handbrake lever with the U-shaped scoop around the hole into which the pins fit. Fit the end of the pawl that's shaped a bit like a crooked finger into the ratchet gizmo.

The opposite end of the pawl has a round shape that goes into the long metal shaft with the spring around it. This spring attaches to the button in the end of the handbrake. When you have the pawl engaged in the ratchet, fit that long metal shaft over the top of the pawl lever. Once it's together, it'll stay together unless you drop it.

Step 2. Put Handbrake Lever Back Into Car

Thread the two handbrake cables coming up through the car floor through either side of the ratchet plate. Slip the metal bar over the cables and screw one of the domed bottom 10mm nuts onto each cable. The domed side fits into the small depression in the bar.

Smear a little grease on the handbrake pin and fit the handbrake lever into its mount. Slip the pin through the mount and through the lever, then replace the snap ring. Be sure the clip is in the groove on the outside of the pin. Screw on the two cable nuts and adjust the handbrake action, Procedure 13.

PROCEDURE 15: REPAIR HANDBRAKE CABLE. Phase 2.

Condition: One or both handbrake cables have broken.

Tools and materials: Phase 1 tool kit, new handbrake cables.

Step 1. Find Broken Cable

Remove the plastic molding from the bottom half of the handbrake lever (Procedure 13, Step 2).

The threaded ends of the handbrake cables poke through holes in a small metal bar and are held in position by 10mm nuts on each cable. Grab either one of the cable nuts with a pair of pliers and pull it upward. A broken cable will come out in your hands. Let's assume the left cable is broken; the Procedure for replacing the right cable is identical.

Step 2. Replace Left Cable

Loosen (but do not remove) the two 10mm nuts from the *right* cable. Unscrew the nuts all the way to the top of the cable. Pull out the broken piece of the left cable and remove the two nuts from it.

Now go back to the left rear wheel. If you're doing a brake job, the brake shoes are already exposed. If not, go to Procedure 5 and expose; there's no need to take the shoes off the backing plate.

The handbrake cable is held to a lever attached to the back of the trailing brake shoe. The cable has a long spring around it and may be held in place on the backing plate by an open chain link. Twist that chain link around with a pair of pliers so the cable with the long spring is more easily maneuvered. Pull the spring away from the lever on the rearmost brake shoe to which it is attached, i.e., pull it toward the front of the car. You can now unhook the rear part of the cable from the lever. On the end of the cable is a kind of squared-off cylinder. Free it from the arm, then pull the cable completely out of the backing plate. Thread the rest of the broken cable from its attachments and discard it. Keep the two 10mm nuts, though.

Slight Problem: On 1975 cars, the handbrake cable is held under the car on the rear axle beam by a welded metal bracket. From '75 on, a wire clip was attached to the rear axle beam instead of the bracket. Some early models have problems with squeaking and grinding noises caused by the old type mounting system. If you have those noises, stick a strip of weather-stripping foam onto the axle beam to keep the handbrake cable away from the axle beam. This will stop the squeaking noises. The proper modification includes cutting and grinding away part of the rear axle beam to remove that bracket. See your VW service manager and s/he will tell you what to do and how to do it if you want to replace the bracket with the clip. The foam method is easier, cheaper and faster.

Step 3. Install New Handbrake Cable

Remove the two 10mm nuts if they came with the new cable. Grease the first 30cm (12 in) of the cable. Push this greased portion through the floor from under the car to between the seats and up to the handbrake lever (in the off or down position). Push it through the handbrake lever, then through the bar that fits into the top of the lever. Screw on the two 10mm nuts. One of the nuts has a domed bottom (don't we all) that fits into the recess in the bar. Just run the nuts onto the end of the cable; but not all the way down. Now thread the other end of the cable through the support brackets or clip under the car. Thread the end of the cable into the rear of the backing plate. Pull the spring on the cable forward and fit the flattened cylinder into the lever on the trailing brake shoe. This secures the cable to the backing plate. Let the spring snap back into position. Make sure it fits correctly. Install the split link if you've got one. The cable is installed.

You cannot adjust the action of the handbrake until the brake drum is installed and the rear brakes are properly adjusted (Procedure 5). You also want to check the rear wheel bearings before adjusting the handbrake (Procedure 5, Step 11).

When everything is back together, adjust the handbrake action (Procedure 13) before you drive the car. When you've done the handbrake Procedure, change your clothes, wash up and take a test drive.

1980 Changes

P. 226 Disc Brakes How to Check for Wear, 1980 Changes To inspect the pads on the new ATE or Kelsey-Hayes brakes, you must first remove the wheel. With the car chocked, jacked and blocked, measure the thickness of the brake pad from the backing plate to the brake disc (rotor). Do not include the pad backing plate in your measurement. If either pad is less than 2mm (.080 in) thick, it's time to replace *all four* front pads.

P. 226 PROCEDURE 7 Change Front Disc Brake Pads, 1980 Rabbit. The new style ATE and the Kelsey-Hayes brakes are a snap to work on.

Step 1. Remove Springs First chock, jack and block the car. Then use a screwdriver to pry off the top and bottom thin wire anti-rattle springs. Note that the loops on the end of the springs face inward.

Step 2. Free Bolts Use a 7mm allen wrench to remove the inner top and bottom retaining bolts which are hidden inside the black rubber bushings. They may be covered with mud. When the bolts are out, note that the top bolt is longer than the bottom one.

Step 3. Remove Cylinder Assembly Pull the bottom part of the assembly toward the front of the car so that it comes off the caliper frame. Now hang the cylinder assembly from the car body with a piece of wire.

Step 4. Remove Pads Simply slide 'em off. Mark which is inner or outer in case you decide to reinstall them.

Step 5. Check Bushings Are the bushings which hold the cylinder assembly onto the caliper frame bolts in good condition? Replace them if either the rubber outer or inner plastic sleeve is cracked or worn. Also check the anti-rattle springs and allen bolts. All OK?

Step 6. Clean Caliper and Cylinder Assembly Remove all dirt and debris with a stiff paint or toothbrush. Wear a mask to protect your lungs.

Step 7. Check Brake Disc (Rotor) Run your fingernail across the disc to check for scoring. If it's rough, it needs to be removed and turned on a lathe. A VW agency or other machine shop will do it for you.

Step 8. Install New Pads Check your new pads against the old. The same? First install the inner pad (this has a chamfer on the edge of the lining), then the outer. Check that they fit snugly up against the disc.

Step 9. Install Cylinder Assembly Use something like a basting syringe to remove a little brake fluid from the master cylinder. Push the piston into the cylinder assembly as far as it will go. Now install the assembly onto the caliper frame. It's a tight fit but don't use a hammer. If it won't go, the piston isn't pressed in far enough. Push a little harder and get it in.

Step 10. Tighten Up Give the allen bolts a shot of silicone spray, put a few drops of Loktite on the threads and screw them into place. Torque 'em to 4 mkg (30 ft lbs). Hook the anti-rattle springs into position (loops inward).

Step 11. Check Up Check your work carefully. Press the brake pedal a few times to seat the pads. Put the wheel back on and do the other side. When both the wheels are on, check the fluid level in the master cylinder reservoir and add some fresh fluid if needed. Finished.

CHAPTER 15

SUSPENSION AND STEERING

Instead of a white water kayak trip, you're embarking on a tour of the dark underside of your Rabbit in this Chapter. You can run the river some other time. As we proceed, refer to Peter's diagram to see what the different components look like and what they're called. I'll use the proper names used by parts people and put the common name, if different, in parentheses.

Sticking out of the dash in front of the driver is the **steering wheel** which is attached to an energy absorbing **steering column**. Two **universal joints** at the bottom of the column route it through the firewall onto the **pinion shaft** of the **rack and pinion steering** gear. This **steering rack** (steering box), bolted to a bracket welded to the bottom of the firewall, has a steering **tie rod** attached to each end. The tie rod on the right can be adjusted to alter the direction the wheels point (toe-in). A **ball joint** on the end of each tie rod sticks through the **steering arm** on the **wheel bearing housing** (steering knuckle). The bottom of the wheel bearing housing clamps to another ball joint on the end of the **control arm** (wishbone). (The other ends of the control arm are attached to the car's underbody via rubber bushings.) The top part of the wheel bearing housing attaches to a long vertical tube surrounded by a **coil spring** and is called the **MacPherson Strut**. The top part of the strut is bolted to a flexible mount inside the fender well which is accessible from the engine compartment. These struts move up and down independent of one another.

The MacPherson strut is not, as some people believe, a new disco step, although it does demonstrate what's known in the trade as 'negative roll radius.' That mouthful means that the car will continue to move straight ahead even if you were to have a tire blow out.

Wheel camber (vertical wheel position) is adjusted by turning the top bolt attaching the MacPherson strut onto the wheel bearing housing. The **driveshaft** (front axle) passes through the middle of the wheel bearing housing and is held onto the wheel hub by a big nut. Each of the two driveshafts have two **constant velocity (CV) joints** which allow the wheel to turn and move up and down as they transfer energy to the wheels. The brake calipers are bolted to the wheel bearing housing and the brake disc is screwed onto the hub. Four lug nuts hold the wheel tightly to the hub.

The rear wheels are bolted to a brake drum which is attached to a stub axle. This short axle in turn is bolted to a **trailing arm** which is part of the rear torsion **axle beam** (rear axle). The axle is securely bolted to the car underbody via hinged plates. The bottom of the rear MacPherson strut is attached to the trailing arm and the top to the fender well.

Checking the Front End

If you're having front end troubles like clunking, steering wheel vibration or knocking when you hit a bump, be sure the tires are all inflated to $1.90Kg/cm^2$ (27 psi), then drive the car onto hard level ground. Get the wheels pointing straight ahead and bounce the front of the car up and down a few times by pushing on the front fender. With healthy struts, you'll feel a lively resistance from the MacPherson strut and when you stop

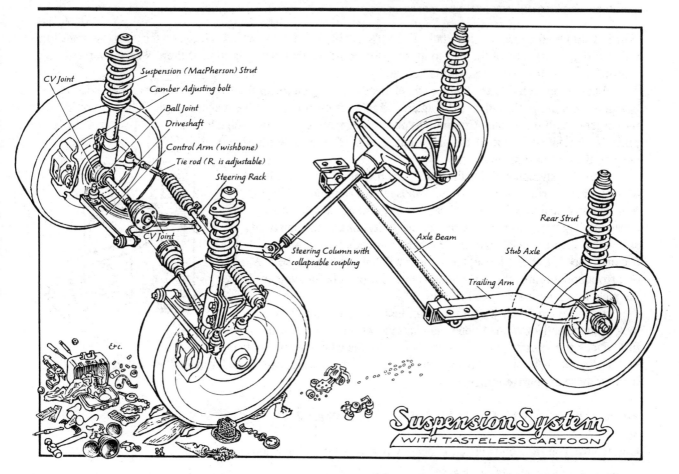

CV Joint
Suspension (MacPherson) Strut
Camber Adjusting bolt
Ball Joint
Driveshaft
Control Arm (wishbone)
Tie rod (R. is adjustable)
Steering Rack
CV Joint
Steering Column with collapsable coupling
&c.
Rear Strut
Axle Beam
Stub Axle
Trailing Arm

Suspension System WITH TASTELESS CARTOON

your pushing, the car should not wallow up and down like an aging porpoise. If the fender droops when the cat sits on it, the shocks are worn out, probably the coil spring, too. Sometimes worn shocks make a loud knock when you push down on the car and let it spring back up. Also do the bounce test on the rear (push on the bumper). Sagging? (Procedure 6 or 7 in this Chapter). If the front end acts weird and the steering wheel wobbles when you drive, check the wheel rims for missing balance weights. A clean spot at the wheel rim indicates you've lost a weight. Take the car to a tire store and have the wheels balanced. A dynamic balance is more accurate. For that process the wheel is spun very rapidly on a machine which automatically determines how much weight the wheel needs for balance. It's a fairly expensive process ($2.50-5.00 per wheel) as compared to static balancing which uses a pivot with a bubble (like a builder's level) to determine what weights are needed. Check tire condition before having the wheels balanced because one or more may need replacing. Buy good quality radial tires from a tire store, not a service station, because they're cheaper.

Open the driver's window and turn the steering wheel as you watch the left front wheel (the key has to be turned to ON to release the lock). How much does the steering wheel move before the front tire does? This difference in movement is termed steering play and should be no more than 13mm (½ in). A number of components contribute to excessive steering play so let's find out the cause.

Lift and prop the hood and find the steering rack. It's bolted to the firewall directly behind the transmission. An accordian type rubber boot protects the steering column universal joint where it is fastened to the pilot shaft sticking out the top of the rack. Similar boots protect the tie rods where they attach to the ends of the rack.

Follow one of the tie rods out through the fender well and see how it's attached via a ball joint to the steering arm of the wheel bearing housing. Ask Friend to hang onto the steering wheel while you try to move the tie rod by hand. Watch the ball joint as you grunt; it should have no play at all. Now do the same test to the other tie rod on the other side of the car. No play? Let's be more thorough.

Chock, jack up the front of the car and block it safely. Get both front wheels off the ground.

Here's how to test the ball joint on the wheel bearing housing for play. Hold the tire at the 12 o'clock position with both hands and push/pull. If there's any movement, the wheel is loose on the hub (check the lug nuts for tightness), one of the ball joints is worn or the wheel bearing is shot. If there's no movement, the steering rack is probably loose or maladjusted.

Ask Friend to hold the steering wheel steady while you grasp the front wheel at the 9 and 3 o'clock positions. Do the push/pull cha-cha again and feel for movement. If the wheel bearing is loose, you'll feel movement in all directions. Continue to push hard, feeling for more unhealthy play. If you detect it, one of the ball joints is loose or the rubber bushings holding the control arm are worn.

There's a slight possibility the MacPherson strut isn't securely bolted to the wheel bearing housing, so check those two 17mm bolts. The top bolt is eccentric and adjusts wheel camber so don't use a cheater bar to tighten it. Tighten the nut on the rear of that bolt, holding the bolt head still with a 17mm wrench. Check the other 17mm bolt below the eccentric one, too. If either is loose, the camber will have to be reset by VW or a front end alignment shop. Tighten any loose bolts before you go! If the wheel bearing is shot, see Procedure 9.

If a loose strut wasn't your problem, lie under the front of the car and look at all the ball joints. As Friend cha-cha's the wheel again at 9 and 3, carefully check the joint which fits into the bottom of the wheel bearing housing.

Let's check ball joint play. VW measures it with a vernier caliper and a special lever, but we can do it without these expensive things.

PROCEDURE 1: CHECK BALL JOINT PLAY. Phase 2.

Condition: The front end clunks, knocks, vibrates—something is loose.

Tools and materials: A jack, Friend, pencil and rule.

Remarks: The car must be on solid, level ground and the tires properly inflated to 1.90 Kg/cm^2 (27 psi).

Step 1. Eliminate Ball Joint Play

Place the jack under the control arm directly beneath or as close as possible to the ball joint. Pump the jack until the ball joint is fully compressed; that is, all the slack is removed from the joint. Nothing except the control arm should move as you take up the slack. If the chassis moves at all, the results will be incorrect.

Measuring the Ball Joint Play

CHASSIS SHOULD NOT MOVE! — NEITHER SHOULD THIS STUFF

CONTROL ARM (WISHBONE)

MEASURE AS CLOSE AS POSSIBLE TO TIRE

MUTTER, MUTTER

PUT JACK AS CLOSE AS POSSIBLE TO THE TIRE

THE BALL JOINT

A FLAT SURFACE

JOINT ARM PLAY

YOU CAN DO IT WITH A VW JACK, BUT YOU WILL HAVE TO MONKEY WITH THE HANDLE A BIT, SO DO IT A COUPLE TIMES TO MAKE SURE.

Step 2. Measure

Put the end of the rule firmly on the ground next to the control arm as close to the ball joint as possible. Have Friend mark the rule where the top of the control arm touches it.

Step 3. Measure Ball Joint Play

Keep the rule in place, slowly release the jack and pull down on the tire. Mark the low position of the control arm on the rule. Now do the process again. When you get two identical sets of figures, subtract the low number

Step 3. (Cont'd.)

from the high. The difference between the two measurements shouldn't exceed 2.50mm (just over 3/32 in). If the difference is greater, the ball joint must be replaced. It's a job you can do—Procedure 5. Measure the ball joint play on the control arm at the other side of the car and replace it if necessary.

If the ball joint play is OK, check the rubber bushings at the ends of the control arms where they bolt to the car underbody. If the rubber is hard and crumbly or the control arm is loose in the rubber, that's your trouble. See Procedure 5.

After examining all the components of the front suspension and finding them to be fit and well, you may still have sloppy steering. The steering rack is probably loose. Let's adjust it.

PROCEDURE 2: ADJUST/LUBRICATE STEERING RACK. Phase 2.

Condition: There's play in the steering wheel, or rattles and groaning from the rack. The ball joints, rubber control arm bushings and tie rods are OK.

Tools and materials: Phase 1 tool kit, Friend.

Remarks: Check that the rack is securely bolted to the firewall before you begin.

Step 1. Chock, Jack and Block

Chock the rear wheels, get both front wheels off the ground and block the car safely.

Step 2. Find Adjusting Screw

This screw is behind and below the rubber accordian boot protecting the pilot shaft fastened to the bottom of the steering column. It's a tricky little bugger to get at, so watch your knuckles. If you have a 17mm box end wrench you can bear to mutilate, as in the diagram, you'll have a much easier time getting at the locknut which secures the adjuster. Loosen the locknut about two turns.

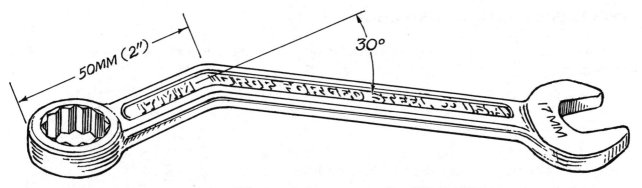

17MM BENT WRENCH FOR STEERING RACK LOCK·NUT

Step 3. Adjust

Screw the adjuster in (7mm) until the screw just touches bottom. Then tighten the locknut while holding the adjuster with your wrench. Try the steering wheel for play. If it feels stiff, the adjuster is too tight. Try again. If it feels OK and the play is correct (13mm or ½ in), lower the car to the ground and check the play again. A test drive will tell for sure.

If steering play is fine but turning the wheel produces a groan, the rack is in dire need of lubrication.

PROCEDURE 3: HOW TO CURE STEERING GROAN. Phase 2.

Condition: The rack has a hard time and makes noise during movements. I mean the steering rack, not the one used to extract information.

Tools and materials: Spray can of Dow Corning Molycote_R #321 lubricant, screwdriver.

Remarks: If you can't find the right spray at your local auto parts store, call VW and ask the service manager what they use and where they get it. Do not use oil, WD-40, or anything else for that matter.

Step 1. Uncover Cause

Turn the steering wheel all the way to the left (first turn the key to ON to disengage the column lock). Right hand drive owners turn to the right. Loosen the clamp holding the rubber boot around the right (right hand drive—left) side of the rack and pull the boot down the tie rod.

Step 2. Clean Rack

Wipe off any grease or crud on the geared end of the rack with a clean rag.

Step 3. Lubricate

Point the spray at the rack and apply a thin coat of lubricant. Let it dry for at least ten minutes, then pull the rubber boot back onto the rack. Install the clamp and tighten it. Move the steering wheel around and experience the sweet sound of silence. You may now need to adjust the steering play so see Procedure 2.

You may find that your rack is worn beyond adjustment and replacing it is the only way to cure sloppy steering. As yet I haven't seen a worn out rack. VW says the rack will outlast the useful life of the car and I believe 'em. The only time you will probably have to replace the rack is if your car's involved in an accident. I hope the insurance company pays for the work. I have the replacement Procedure in my files and if you ever need a copy, please write.

PROCEDURE 4: REPLACE TIE RODS. Phase 2.

Condition: The left or right tie rods are bent or the ball joints on the ends of the rods are worn and need replacement.

Tools and materials: Phase 1 tool kit (you'll need two medium sized hammers or a ball joint puller), paper and pencil, new tie rod, metal mm scale (rule), two medium cotter pins, tape measure.

Remarks: The original factory-installed left tie rod isn't adjustable; the right one is. All replacement tie rods from VW are adjustable.

TieRodEnd
BALLJOINT

Step 1. Remove Wheel

Point the wheels dead ahead and remove the plastic lug nut covers or the hub cap and loosen the four wheel lug nuts. Chock, jack up the front of the car and block it well. Remove the appropriate wheel.

Step 2. Remove Bent/Worn Tie Rod

The tie rod is attached to the steering rack by an inner ball joint protected by an accordian type rubber boot. There's a lock nut on the rack which prevents the ball joint from turning and before the tie rod can be removed, you have to loosen the ball joint from the steering arm on the wheel bearing housing. So first remove the cotter pin from the bottom of the ball joint where it sticks through the steering arm. Then use a 19mm wrench to loosen the castellated nut   from the ball joint and run the nut down the thread (but don't remove it yet).

Step 2. (Cont'd.)

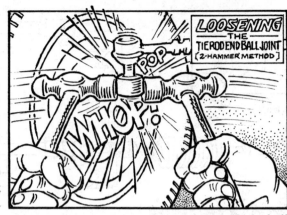

If you have a wheel puller handy, use it to break loose the tie rod ball joint from the wheel bearing housing arm (Chapter 20, Procedure 9). If not, you can use two hammers to break the ball joint free. Put on your safety glasses, then sprinkle some Liquid Wrench around the tie rod ball joint where it goes through the wheel bearing housing and wait a few minutes for it to seep in. Use both hammers to simultaneously smack the *arm* through which the ball joint fits. **On no account** hit on the ball joint itself or hit the castellated nut upwards in hopes of popping the ball joint out of the arm. The two hammer method on the arm will make the ball joint jump out. When it's loose, remove the nut, pull the ball joint out of the arm and screw the nut onto the ball joint for safekeeping.

Step 3. Remove Tie Rod from Steering Rack

Remove the clamp from around the accordian rubber boot protecting the tie rod ball joint where it screws onto the steering rack. Turn the rubber boot inside out to expose the ball joint and lock nut. Use a pair of vise grips and a crescent wrench to remove the ball joint from the steering arm. Loosen the lock nut ¼ turn, then simply screw off the tie rod counterclockwise.

Step 4. Adjust New Tie Rod

If you're replacing the old solid left tie rod with a new one, adjust the length of your new tie rod to dimension Z in the chart on the next page. It should be exactly equal to the old tie rod length. To adjust length simply screw it in or out.

On the road or stuck in some impossible situation? Here's a quick method that'll get you home. Screw the new tie rod onto the steering rack until it just touches the lock nut. Use a crescent wrench and vise grips to tighten the locknut. Pull the rubber boot over the ball joint and secure it with the hose clamp. Go to Step 7 but remember to do Step 5 and the rest of this Procedure when you're home.

If you've a decent place to work, continue…

Step 5. Measure Steering Rack Dimensions

Now we have a few awkward measurements to take. On top of the steering rack is a pinion shaft attached to a pinion gear inside the steering box. That's where the term rack and pinion comes from. The rack must be correctly centered inside the housing so the tie rods move both front wheels an equal distance.

Inside the car, center the steering wheel spokes (the remaining front wheel will be pointing straight ahead), then screw the new tie rod onto the steering rack. If you're replacing a right hand tie rod, measure the distance between the end of the rack and the inner flange on the right tie rod. This is dimension "X." Check the table for the proper "X" dimension for your car's chassis number stamped in the engine compartment on top of the right suspension strut mounting. If the dimension is right, go directly to Step 7.

If not, remove the rubber boot from the other end of the rack and measure the distance from the flange *inside* the rack to the inner flange on the left tie rod. The two measurements should be equal and should correspond to "X" figures in the chart. If not, you'll have to remove the tie rods and centralize the rack.

Step 6. Centralize Steering Rack

Remove both tie rods (Step 2) and adjust them so they're equal to dimension "Z" in the chart. Measure dimension "Y" on the steering rack and get Friend to turn the steering wheel until dimension "Y" is equal at both ends. Adjusting the rack may make the steering wheel spokes slightly off center. You can fix that later when you're finished with this Procedure.

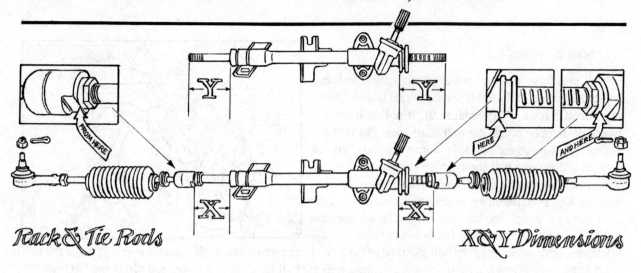

Rack & Tie Rods   *X & Y Dimensions*

STEERING RACK DIMENSION

Scirocco through Chassis # 535 2500 000

Rabbit through Chassis # 176 3002 647

$X = 67mm$ (1.638 in)

Scirocco (manual transmission) from
Chassis # 536 3000 001

Rabbit (manual transmission) from
Chassis # 176 3002 648

$X = 69mm$ (2.716 in)

Sciroco (automatic transmission) from
Chassis # 536 3000 001

Rabbit (automatic transmission) from
Chassis # 176 3002 648

Left tie rod
$X = 69mm$ (2.716 in)

Right tie rod
$X = 67mm$ (2.638 in)

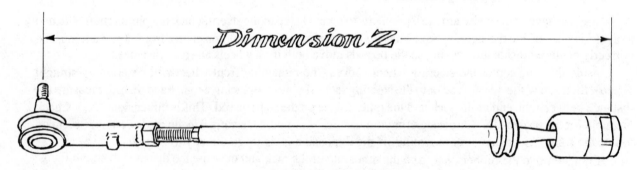

Dimension Z

TIE ROD DIMENSION

Scirocco through Chassis # 535 2500 000

Rabbit through Chassis # 176 3002 647

$Z = 38.1cm$ (15 in)

Scirocco from Chassis # 536 3000 001

Rabbit from Chassis # 176 3002 648

$Z = 37.9cm$ (14-59/64 in)
(38.1cm (15 in) for right tie rod on cars with
automatic transmissions)

Step 6. (Cont'd.)

Install the left tie rod onto the rack and screw it in until you reach dimension "X." Put the ball joint on the other end of the tie rod into the arm on the wheel bearing housing and replace the castellated nut. Don't disturb the position of the rack or you'll have to centralize it again.

Now install the other tie rod and get dimension "X" correct by screwing the tie rod in or out. Pull the ball joint into the steering arm and replace the castellated nut. Tighten the lock nuts on the tie rods where they fit into the steering rack, pull the rubber boots back into place and tighten the clamps. The hard part's over, go to Step 8.

Step 7. Secure Tie Rods

If you didn't have to centralize the steering rack or you're out on the road, put the ball joint on the end of the tie rod into the steering arm on the wheel bearing housing, then replace the castellated nut. Tighten the locknut on the tie rod where it fits onto the steering rack, pull the rubber boot over the tie rod and install the clamp.

Step 8. Torque Castellated Nuts

Torque the castellated nuts to 3.0 mkg (22 ft lbs) or tight if you don't have a torque wrench. Install a new cotter pin into the hole through the ball joint. If the pin won't go all the way through, advance the nut a little until the pin slips into place. Bend the arms of the pin around the nut, then do the other side. Install the wheel, then get VW or an alignment shop to adjust the wheel toe-in.

Turn to Procedure 8 if the steering wheel spokes aren't centered.

PROCEDURE 5: FIX CONTROL ARMS. Phase 2.

Condition: The control arm ball joint is worn, the rubber bushings are shot or the control arm is bent.

Tools and materials: Phase 1 (or 2) tool kit, a steel straight edge, Loctite, a torque wrench, and new ball joints.

Remarks: Removing the left control arm on an automatic car is a bit of a swine. You have to loosen some of the engine/transmission mounts to get the thing off. Not overly hard, but you'll need an hour or so to do it.

Cars built before October 1974 have the ball joint attached to the control arm by two 8mm bolts. You have to enlarge the holes in the replacement ball joint to 8.3mm and install the joint onto the arm with two 8mm bolts, spring washers and nuts. Later models have the joint attached by three rivets. Installing a replacement ball joint onto an old control arm requires enlargement of the two outer holes a mite, use 8mm (the size of the bolt—not the head) nuts, bolts and spring washers to hold the replacement ball joint in place.

New style rivetted ball joints are removed from the control arm by chiseling or drilling the rivets out (6mm drill) and installing the new ball joint with three 7mm bolts (the size of the bolt, not the head), nuts and spring washers.

You'll have to take the control arm to VW or a machine shop to have the ball joint or rubber bushings replaced unless you have a drill press at your disposal and know how to use it.

Check
FRONT EDGE
OF
CONTROL ARM
W/
STRAIGHT EDGE

Step 1. Chock, Jack and Block

Chock the rear wheels, loosen the lug nuts and jack up the car. Block it well and remove the wheel. Put a jack under the wheel bearing housing and give it a couple of pumps upward.

Step 2. Check Control Arm

Put your steel straight edge along the front of the control arm and check that it's true (square, straight). Now put the straight edge along the top and bottom lips to see if they're true. Sounds like a sweet-

Step 2. (Cont'd.)

heart's prayer. If the arm is bent at all, the wheel camber angle is wrong. That's why your tires are wearing out so fast. You have to replace the control arm. Look for a *good* used one in your local junkyard or buy a new one from VW.

Step 3. Free Ball Joint

Remove the 13mm nut, bolt and washer which hold the ball joint into the wheel bearing housing. A sprinkling of Liquid Wrench may help matters. The arm holding the joint is split, so insert a screwdriver blade to widen the split and lever out the ball joint.

Step 4. Remove Control Arm, Standard Transmission

Take out the two 15mm bolts which hold the rear U-clip pivot, that's around the control arm, to the car underbody. Finally unscrew the 19mm bolt which secures the control arm front hinge. The arm's free.

Step 5. Remove Control Arm, Automatic Transmission

Place a jack under the transmission and pump it up until it's snug. Crawl under and remove the two 13mm nuts from the right engine/transmission mount just next to the exhaust pipe. Those two nuts hold the mount onto the transmission. Don't remove the two 17mm nuts from the middle of the mount.

Come out from under the car and remove the 17mm bolt from the rear transmission mount where it bolts inside the left fender. You may have to raise the jack a bit to get the bolt out. Now remove the two 17mm bolts holding the transmission to the left front engine/transmission mount which is bolted to the front crossmember below the radiator. Jack up the engine/transmission until you can unscrew the front 19mm bolt holding the control arm in place.

Step 6. Install New Joint

Take the control arm to VW or a machine shop and have them replace the ball joint and rubber bushings. It is very important to use the correct size drill bit to enlarge the ball joint mounting holes and that the holes are square to the control arm. A dull drill bit and a shaky arm won't do, so spend a few dollars to get it done properly in a drill press (see this Procedure's 'Remarks.'). Buy a new 19mm bolt and lockwasher to secure the control arm's front pivot to the car. Take the old bolts to VW to compare and make sure the new bolt is **exactly** the same size as the old.

Step 7. Install Control Arm

Remove any trace of oil or grease from your new 19mm bolt and put the lockwasher onto the bolt with the convex surface of the washer facing the head of the bolt. The concave (dished) surface will be facing the threaded part of the bolt. Push the bolt through the front pivot and screw it into the captive nut. Be careful not to cross-thread it. Wiggle the control arm around until the bolt correctly lines up with the nut. Screw it in a few turns, then tighten the U-clip bolts until they're just snug. Remove the 19mm bolt and apply a film of Locktite to the threads. Install the bolt and tighten it a little.

The control arm should move up and down easily. If it won't, loosen the U-clip bolts and play with the position of the clip until the arms moves freely. Tighten the bolts and try again. All moves sweetly?

Torque the 19mm bolt to 6 mkg (43 ft lbs) and the U-clip bolts to 3 mkg (22 ft lbs).

Step 8. Secure Ball Joint

Push up the control arm until the ball joint fits into the wheel bearing housing. Install the 13mm bolt. If it won't go in, you haven't pushed the ball joint up far enough into the wheel bearing housing. When the bolt's in, install the washer and nut and torque them to 3 mkg (22 ft lbs).

Step 9. Automatics Only

Get under the car with your 13mm wrench and torque wrench and the two 13mm nuts. Lower the jack until you are able to install the two 13mm bolts into the engine/transmission mount next to the exhaust pipe. Torque 'em to 2.5 mkg (18 ft lbs).

Step 9. (Cont'd.)

Reinstall the 17mm bolt into the rear transmission mount and the two 17mm bolts into the left front engine/transmission mount attached below the radiator. Remove the jack, center the rubber part of that mount, then torque the bolts to 4 mkg (29 ft lbs).

Step 10. Finish Up

Check each bolt carefully to see that they're all tight. Then remove the jack from under the control arm and install the wheel. Lower the car to the ground and tighten the wheel lug nuts, replace the hub cap or plastic nut covers and go for a test drive. Isn't it amazing how well it rides now?

PROCEDURE 6: REPLACE SHOCK ABSORBERS IN FRONT MAC PHERSON STRUT. Phase 2.

Condition: The front shocks are worn and maybe the front coil springs are worn or broken as well.

Tools and materials: Phase 1 tool kit, torque wrench, Friend.

Remarks: The shock absorber sits inside the MacPherson strut and it's dangerous for you to replace without proper tools. It's like this—the coil spring surrounding the strut is under extreme tension and will fly off and seriously hurt you if an attempt is made to remove it without the right tools. Remove the entire strut from the car and take it to VW for a shock change.

Step 1. Chock, Jack and Block

Loosen the wheel lug nuts before you get it up.

Step 2. Free Bottom Part of Front Strut

Look at the way the bottom of the strut is held to the wheel bearing housing. The top bolt is specially shaped (eccentric) and is used to adjust wheel camber. To maintain the proper camber when you put things back together, bang a punch mark on the face of the top bolt and another on the strut next to it. Check the diagram.

Put another jack or block under the control arm to prevent the control arm from dropping and stretching the brake hose when the strut is removed. No other jack or blocks? Tie the control arm up with a length of wire.

Now remove both 17mm bolts, washers and nuts holding the strut to the control arm and stick one bolt back through either hole. This will prevent the control arm from falling when you remove the top of the strut from the car body.

Pull the flexible brake hose out from the ear on the side of the strut.

Step 3. Free Top of Strut

Lift and prop the hood. Remove the plastic cap from the top of the strut where it pokes through the fender inside the engine compartment. Next remove the two 13mm bolts holding the top of the strut (the cap assembly) onto the fender. Mark the pieces 'Top' and Baggie them.

Step 4. Remove Strut

Pull out that lone bolt holding the strut to the wheel bearing housing and thread the strut out from the car. Put the bottom bolts, etc., into a marked Baggie.

If necessary, remove the other strut in the same manner (don't forget the punch mark routine) and take them both to VW for a shock and/or coil spring change. If your rear shocks are bad too, do Procedure 7 and take the lot to VW at the same time.

Step 5. Install Strut

When you get your suspension goodies back from VW, lay out the Baggies with the nuts, bolts, etc., where you can reach them. Lift and prop the hood. Ask Friend to position the strut through the fender well so the studs on the top stick through the holes in the fender. Install the two 13mm nuts and washers and torque them to 2 mkg (14 ft lbs). Snap the plastic cover back on the cap assembly. Do the other side the same way.

Twist the bottom of the strut until it lines up with the arm on the wheel bearing housing. Install the regular 17mm bolt, washer and nut in the *bottom* hole and tighten it a little. Push in the top eccentric bolt and line up the punch mark on the face of the bolt with the one on the strut. Slip on the eccentric washer, regular washer and nut and get it all tight. Torque both upper and lower bolts to 8 mkg (58 ft lbs). That's tight, so give your socket an extra ¼ turn tug if you don't have a torque wrench. Be sure the punch marks still line up, then push the brake hose into the little ear on the side of the strut and stick the wheel back on. Do the other side, lower the car and tighten the lug nuts. Finito.

Make an appointment with VW or a front end shop to align the front end if your tires are worn unevenly.

PROCEDURE 7: REPLACE SHOCK ABSORBERS IN REAR MAC PHERSON STRUTS. Phase 2.

Condition: The rear shocks are worn and/or the coil spring may be worn or broken.

Tools and Materials: Phase 1 tool kit, Friend.

Remarks: The shock absorber sits hidden inside the MacPherson strut making it difficult and dangerous to replace. Like the front ones, the coil spring surrounding the strut is under extreme tension and will fly off and seriously injure you if you attempt to remove it without the correct tools. Remove the entire strut from the car and take it to VW for a shock change.

Step 1. Expose Top Bolts

Lift the trunk and move the parcel shelf out of the way. On top of both rear fender wells at the left and right side of the trunk is a rubber cap which covers the top of the strut. Peel off the caps and lay them on the floor of the trunk.

Keep the car on the ground and loosen the wheel lug nuts.

Step 2. Chock, Jack and Block

Chock both front wheels, put the handbrake on, jack up the rear of the car and support it well on both sides. Now pull the rear wheels off. Make sure the car is very well supported because you've got some levering to do that may shift the car a bit.

Step 3. Free Bottom Strut Mount

Remove the 17mm bolt which holds the bottom of the MacPherson strut to the rear axle beam trailing arm. You may need a thin punch to get the bolt out once you've removed the nut. Use a big screwdriver or wrecking bar to lever out the bottom part of the strut from the hole in the trailing arm. You need quite a lot of leverage to free that strut, so keep your fingers clear of the base of the strut. Once the bolt's out, put it into a marked Baggie.

Step 4. Free Top Mount

Get Friend to hold the strut as you remove the 17mm nut from the top of the strut where it mounts to the fender well inside the trunk. Once the nut's free, take off the metal plate and rubber bushing. Put them into your Step 3 Baggie and have Friend slide the strut out from under the car.

Now remove the strut on the other side of the car in the same manner, if necessary, mark and Baggie the pieces and take both MacPherson struts to VW for a shock and/or coil spring change.

Step 5. Install Strut

Ask Friend to sit by the side of the car and thread the strut over the rear axle trailing arm until the top of the strut protrudes through the hole in the wheel well inside the trunk. Meanwhile, have your head in the trunk helping Friend line things up. When the top of the strut pokes through the wheel well, put back the rubber bushing, plate and 17mm nut. Torque the nut to 3.5 mkg (25 ft lbs) and put the rubber cap back on (it's lying on the trunk floor or in a Baggie).

Come out from the trunk and twist the strut until the bottom fits through the hole in the trailing arm. Line it up with the hole which accepts the 17mm bolt, push the bolt through the arm and strut and replace the 17mm nut. Torque it to 4.4 mkg (38 ft lbs). Install the other strut the same way, stick the rear wheels back on and lower the car to the ground. Tighten the wheel lug nuts, check your work and you're finished.

PROCEDURE 8: CENTRALIZE STEERING WHEEL. Phase 1.

Condition: You have centralized the steering rack or the steering wheel is off center and driving you crazy.

Tools and materials: Phase 1 tool kit and a 24mm socket (15/16 in).

Remarks: This Procedure will take only 15 minutes and it's well worth the time to get the spokes on the steering wheel centered. If you are going to sell or trade the car, fix this because a misaligned steering wheel puts off prospective purchasers.

Step 1. Turn to Chapter 19, Procedure 9 and do Steps 1 through 5 inclusive.

Step 2. Remove Steering Wheel

Hold it! Before you pull off the steering wheel decide which direction and how much the wheel needs to be turned to get the spokes centered. If the front wheels are pointing dead ahead you can see how far the steering wheel needs to be moved. The difficult part is getting the wheels to point straight ahead. Anyway, when they are, pull the steering wheel off the column and replace it with the spokes centered.

Step 3. Install Steering Wheel Nut

Slip the washer onto the steering column and replace the nut. Tighten the nut with your socket and go for a test drive.

Steering wheel centered? Good. No? Then remove the nut again and check the punch marks. You will know how much to move the wheel to get the spokes centered so use the punch marks as a reference point. When you think it's properly aligned, install the washer and nut and take another test drive. Right this time?

Step 4. Tidy Up

Torque the center steering wheel nut to 5.0 mkg (54 ft lbs) and replace the horn ground wire to the horn bar.

Rabbits: Push the horn bar back onto the steering wheel after repairing any breaks in the plastic horn bar with plastic cement if need be.

Sciroccos: Install the rubber steering wheel center. First get it started on the top part of the rim. Make sure the thing is fully over the little lip, then work it all on. Just use your fingers; a screwdriver will poke holes through the rubber and make it look terrible.

PROCEDURE 9:   REMOVE/INSTALL FRONT WHEEL BEARING HOUSING (STEERING KNUCKLE) TO REPLACE WHEEL BEARINGS. Phase 2.

Condition: The front wheel bearings are worn.

Tools and materials: Phase 2 tool kit, 30mm socket to remove the front driveshaft nut, wire clothes hanger, new wheel bearing.

Remarks: After removing the wheel bearing housing, take it to VW or a machine shop to get the new bearing pressed in with their heavy duty press.
Work on one side of the car at a time.

Step 1. Loosen Driveshaft Nut

Remove the hubcap (or plastic lug nut covers and center cap). Use the 30mm socket on your breaker bar to loosen the driveshaft nut. Don't remove it yet. Loosen the wheel lug nuts.

Step 2. Chock, Jack and Block

Chock the rear wheels and jack up the front side of the car. Support things with a sturdy block. Remove the driveshaft nut, washer and lug nuts. Pull off the wheel.

Step 3. Remove Front Brake Drum (Drum Brakes only)

Chapter 14, Procedure 4, Step 1. Then remove the brake shoes, Chapter 14, Procedure 4. Unscrew the brake hose from the metal brake line (12mm and 14mm wrench). Cover the end of the brake line with a clean rag or Baggie. Now unscrew the brake hose from the wheel cylinder (14mm wrench). Baggie the hose.

Step 4. Remove Brake Caliper (Disc Brakes only)

Chapter 14, Procedure 8. With a piece of string or wire, hang the removed caliper out of the way on the coil spring.

Step 5. Remove Brake Disc (Disc Brakes only)

Back to Chapter 14, Procedure 8, Step 4.

Step 6. Remove Tie Rod End

See Procedure 4, Step 2, in this Chapter.

Step 7. Free Control Arm Ball Joint

See Procedure 5, Step 3, in this Chapter.

Step 8. Free and Support Driveshaft

Put a shot of Liquid Wrench or WD-40 on the splined part of the driveshaft sticking out through the center of the wheel bearing housing. While the oil is penetrating, make a medium-sized hook out of a wire clothes hanger.
Crouch by the side of the wheel bearing housing, grasp it with both hands and pull it away from the driveshaft. If Friend is around, get a helping hand to support the driveshaft as you grunt and groan. You only want to get the splined part of the driveshaft free from the wheel hub, not all the way out from the wheel bearing housing. If you can't get the driveshaft to move, flood the splines with more Liquid Wrench. Find a wooden block, hold it against the end of the driveshaft and strike it smartly with a big hammer. Don't beat directly on the driveshaft. You'll mess up the threads and that's a drag. Life is difficult enough right now.

Step 9. Free MacPherson Strut (this is not a political statement)

Turn back to Procedure 6, Step 2. When that's done come back here and get Friend to again support the driveshaft and wheel bearing housing as you remove the second of the two strut bolts.

Step 10. Remove Wheel Bearing Housing

Pull the wheel bearing housing free from the driveshaft and hang the driveshaft from the coil spring with your wire hook. Put the washer and nut back onto the end of the driveshaft for safekeeping.

If required, take out the other wheel bearing housing the same way.

Step 11. Off to VW or Machine Shop

Call them before you hotfoot over to see if they can deal with you now.

When you get home with the rebuilt wheel bearing housing, gather all your tools and materials around your work area.

Step 12. Install Wheel Bearing Housing

Remove the nut and washer from the end of the driveshaft. Line up the wheel bearing housing on the end of the driveshaft splines so that the MacPherson strut will fit onto the arm on the housing. Now push the housing onto the driveshaft and loosely screw on the driveshaft washer and nut.

Step 13. Secure MacPherson Strut

Reinstall the two bolts into the strut and the housing. Turn to Procedure 6, Step 5, in this Chapter.

Step 14. Secure Control Arm Ball Joint

This Chapter, Procedure 5, Step 8.

Step 15. Secure Tie Rod End

This Chapter, Procedure 4, Step 7.

Step 16. Install Brake Disc (Disc Brakes only)

Chapter 14, Procedure 8, Step 5.

Step 17. Install Brake Caliper (Disc Brakes only)

Chapter 14, Procedure 8, Step 6.

Step 18. Install Brake Shoes (Drum Brakes only)

Chapter 14, Procedure 4. Then screw the brake hose into the rear of the wheel cylinder (14mm wrench) and then into the metal brake line (12mm or 14mm wrenches). Next install the brake drum, Procedure 4 in Chapter 14.

Step 19. Put Wheel Back On

Install but don't tighten the lug nuts yet.

Step 20. Do Other Side

Install the other wheel bearing housing if it's been removed.

Step 21. Bleed Brakes

Chapter 14, Procedure 1, and bleed the front brakes.

Step 22. Tighten

Lower the car to the ground and tighten the wheel lug nuts. Torque the driveshaft nuts to 24 mkg (173 ft lbs) Chapter 20, Procedure 8.

It's worth the time and effort to get the front wheel camber and toe-in checked and adjusted, if necessary, at VW or a good front end alignment shop. Although you've got the punch marks lined up on the MacPherson strut's eccentric bolt, it may have been out of line to begin with.

CHAPTER 16

⚞ CLUTCH, TRANSMISSION AND DRIVE SHAFTS ⚟

All cars with standard transmission (also called manual or stick shift) have a clutch mechanism to link the engine with the transmission. Without it the engine would be directly connected to the front wheels, constantly trying to pull the car along. Stopping and starting would be like riding a bucking bronco.

When you push down the **clutch pedal** inside the car, the **clutch cable** pulls the **release lever** on the side of the transmission which moves a **pushrod** inside the transmission to force the **clutch release plate** hard against powerful spring fingers on the **clutch pressure plate.** Thus pressure is taken off the two-surfaced **clutch disc.** The clutch is now **disengaged,** allowing the engine to turn free.

The metal clutch disc has a hard wearing asbestos compound bonded to each face which requires periodic replacement as it wears. How often depends on how well you shift gears and the amount of city driving you're forced to endure. Driving with your left foot resting on the clutch pedal (riding the clutch) will hasten clutch disc replacement time.

When your foot comes off the clutch pedal, the springs in the pressure plate trap the clutch disc between the flywheel and the pressure plate. The clutch is **engaged,** allowing power produced by the engine to be transferred via the transmission and drive shafts (axles) to the front wheels.

In place of a clutch mechanism an automatic transmission uses a fluid filled **torque converter** to transfer power from the engine to the transmission. It's the transmission's job to get power through the driveshafts (axles) and finally to the front wheels.

While you're driving, road conditions change. It takes a lot of power to move a heavy car full of passengers from a dead stop or up a steep grade. Less power but more speed is needed when you're just cruisin'.

When the clutch is engaged, the gears inside the transmission mechanically link the engine to the drive shafts and the front wheels. First gear allows the engine to produce and transfer lots of power, but the car won't achieve much in the way of speed.

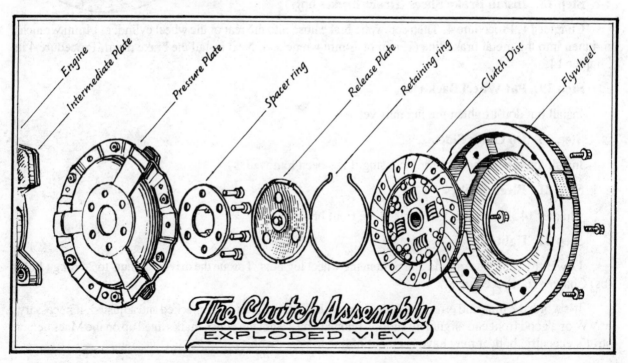

The Clutch Assembly
EXPLODED VIEW

Engine — Intermediate Plate — Pressure Plate — Spacer ring — Release Plate — Retaining ring — Clutch Disc — Flywheel

Second gear takes over where first gear leaves off (the engine speed is approaching its maximum rpm's), and the car picks up speed. The cycle continues until fourth or fifth gear is engaged. In the higher gears the car rolls merrily along at a fair lick, but the engine power output is fairly low, which conserves gasoline and keeps drive train wear to a minimum.

An automatic transmission does the same thing as the standard type, but the gear selection is determined automatically. It's possible to keep the automatic transmission in one gear for prolonged periods by moving the gear select lever in the car. That's great for climbing hills when extra power is required, but normally the select lever should be in 'drive' (D) allowing the transmission to work most efficiently.

CLUTCH MALADY TROUBLESHOOTING GUIDE

1. Clutch slips on hills or during acceleration (engine speed increases but the car slows down), smell like 6-month-old gym socks wafts into the car when accelerating.

   Clutch disc is worn; oil on the disc, flywheel or pressure plate. Procedures 4 and 5.

2. Car jerks forward after gear is engaged and clutch pedal is released; clutch 'grabs.'

   Clutch disc, pressure plate or flywheel worn; bad bearings in transmission. Procedures 4 and 5.

3. Squealing from transmission when the car's in gear.

   Clutch disc, pressure plate or flywheel worn; bad bearings in transmission. Procedures 4 and 5.

4. Loud knocking when starter is engaged.

   Faulty starter, teeth missing from starter drive gear or edge of flywheel. Procedures 4 and 5.

5. Clutch pedal pulsates when depressed.

   Very worn clutch disc, broken pressure plate, loose bolts. Procedures 4 and 5.

6. Difficulty engaging gears.

   Worn clutch disc (Procedures 4 and 5), clutch cable out of adjustment (Procedure 7), gear relay levers out of adjustment (Procedure 7). Transmission innards worn. Remove the transmission and get it rebuilt. Procedure 4.

7. No resistance at clutch pedal or pedal is flat on the floor.

   Clutch cable broken. Procedure 2.

8. Oil dripping from bottom of transmission.

   Rear crankshaft seal blown. Procedures 4 and 5.

9. Noise and slight jerk from front end when pulling away.

   CV Joints worn/loose. Procedure 8.

All these problems except clutch cable adjustment/replacement, and gear relay lever adjustment mean pulling the transmission from the car (Procedure 4). You won't have to pull both the engine and the transmission unless the engine also needs work. Separating the transmission from the engine while they're in the car is easy.

Hotshot VW mechanics can take the transmission out, replace the clutch, stick it all back together and road test it in less than two hours. It will take us about a day, including coffee and smoke breaks. Just make sure you can get to VW for parts when you need them.

PROCEDURE 1: ADJUST CLUTCH CABLE (STANDARD TRANSMISSION). Phase 1.

Condition: The clutch pedal has more than 15mm (5/8 in) of free play.

Tools and materials: Phase 1 tool kit.

Remarks: Free play is the distance the clutch pedal moves before the release lever on the side of the transmission disengages the clutch mechanism. The clutch cable stretches with use, increasing the free play at the pedal and making it difficult to release the clutch and change gears. During normal use the lining on the clutch disc wears away reducing clearance between the clutch release lever and the pushrod inside the transmission. Unless the cable tension is periodically adjusted, the clutch disc will burn to ashes. Too little free play keeps the clutch partially disengaged all the time. Check the diagram and measure your free play.

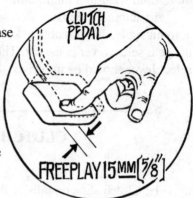

Step 1. Take A Look

Lift the hood and prop it. The clutch cable runs through an ear on the left side of the transmission. See the white plastic cylinder attached to a threaded rod on the end of the clutch cable? The inner part of the cable sticks through the ear and is secured by a square metal clip underneath the release lever on the side of the transmission, just below the ear. The lever actuates the clutch release mechanism when it's pulled up by the cable.

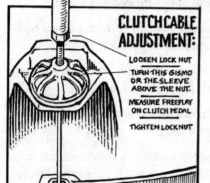

Step 2. Adjust Free Play

Slightly loosen the nut just below the white plastic cylinder (17mm wrench). To increase pedal free play, screw the flat-bottom disc counterclockwise ↺. Watch the release lever move down as cable tension is released. To take up excessive free play, screw that 17mm nut down the threaded shaft. Then screw the plastic disc down a bit by hand. When the free play at the pedal is 15mm, hold the plastic cylinder with a 14mm wrench to keep it from moving and then tighten the 17mm nut snug against the cylinder. Measure the free play again to check that it's right.

PROCEDURE 2: REPLACE CLUTCH CABLE (STANDARD TRANSMISSION). Phase 1.

Condition: Broken clutch cable.

Tools and materials: Phase 1 tool kit, new clutch cable.

Step 1. Get the Car Home (if you're already home, go to Step 2)

When the clutch cable breaks in the middle of town, don't despair. You can still drive on. Race car drivers often shift gear without using the clutch pedal, and so can you. Here's how:

If you're in rush hour traffic, push the car to the side of the road, turn off the engine and wait for things to slow down a bit. Ready? Don't turn the engine on yet and shift into first gear. Check that the road is clear and start the engine. Since you have no clutch, the starter motor will pull the car along with a jerk. When the engine starts, the starter motor disengages and you are away. Accelerate to about 15 miles per hour, then take your foot off the gas pedal and pull the gear shift lever into second. Accelerate to 25 mph, release the gas pedal and shift into third. Easy. On the freeway you can get up to 40 mph in third and use the same technique to get into fourth. In town stay in third! Try to anticipate the traffic light change sequence so that you don't have to stop. This may be some kind of traffic violation in your state. If you must stop, shift into neutral and coast to a stop. Turn off the engine. Do the start procedure in first gear again and get on home or to VW.

Practice this technique on an empty parking lot some Sunday afternoon and you'll be ready for anything.

Step 2. Remove Broken Cable

If you've got a protective carpet above the driver's legs, remove the plastic clip from the center and take the carpet out. Now unhook the plastic gizmo on the end of the clutch cable from the clutch pedal.

Lift the hood and prop it. Remove the metal clip and a strangely shaped metal spacer from under the clutch release lever on the left side of the transmission. Pull the cable through the lever. If the cable broke while on the road you probably lost the metal clip and spacer. Buy new ones from VW or a junk yard.

Pull the plastic adjustment cylinder out from the ear on the transmission and pull the other end of the cable through the firewall.

Step 3. Install New Cable

Push the slotted plastic gizmo end of the new cable through the hole in the firewall. Hook the plastic piece over the clutch pedal.

Find the metal clip and spacer that hold the cable to the transmission lever. If the 17mm nut on the threaded rod below the plastic cylinder is tight against the cylinder, loosen it. Turn the bottom plastic disc all the way up into the cylinder. Push the cable through the rubber in the ear on the transmission until the white plastic disc fits snugly against the ear. Now pull the end of the metal inner cable through the slot in the clutch release lever. Take a look at the clutch pedal to see if the cable is still attached at that end.

Put the dished metal piece over the cable with dished part facing down. Now slip the metal clip (with its depression also facing down) over the cable end. The little ball will fit into the clip and be secure. You may find it easier to put the clips on from under the car. Measure the clutch pedal free play and adjust it if need be (Procedure 1). Check that the cable isn't snagged on anything. Clean your tools and hands, brush off your clothes and you're done.

Write yourself a note to recheck the free play after 300 miles.

PROCEDURE 3: REMOVE/INSTALL/ADJUST AUTOMATIC TRANSMISSION GEAR SELECTOR CABLE. Phase 2.

Condition: The gear selector cable has broken or needs adjusting.

Tools and materials: Phase 1 tool kit, Friend, new cable. Give the parts person at VW your chassis number when buying a new cable, as there are a few different types.

Remarks: Before you rip the cable out of the car check that the end of the cable is attached to the selector lever on the side of the transmission. Cable clamp loose or missing? Step 8 tells how to adjust it.

If you can't get the transmission to kick down into a lower gear when you stomp on the gas pedal, turn to Chapter 7, Procedure 1, Step 3.

As you do this Procedure be aware of the difference between the **gear shift lever** inside the car and the **transmission select lever** on the transmission.

Step 1. Disconnect Battery Ground Strap

Remove the strap (10mm wrench) and tuck the cable out of the way.

Step 2. Free Cable From Transmission Select Lever

Put the gear shift lever inside the car into Park (P) and pull the handbrake on. Now loosen the 13mm nut on the cable clamp on the end of the transmission lever. It's easiest to get at by lying by the left front wheel. When the nut's off, pull the cable out of the clamp, remove the rubber accordian and put the clamp, washer, nut and accordian into a marked Baggie.

Stay on the ground and feel up the cable. Removing the rubber accordian will have brought to light a 12mm nut holding the cable sheath against the transmission bracket. If you're having difficulty getting your hands/tools up in there, let's remove the transmission guard from under the transmission. It's bolted to each end of the transmission by two 13mm bolts. Remove all four bolts, pull the guard off, and lay the guard and bolts in the trunk. Better?

Step 2. (Cont'd.)

Ask Friend to hold another 12mm wrench (or crescent wrench) on the cable at the other side of the transmission bracket. Friend: lean over into the engine compartment for easy access to the cable nut.

You, meanwhile, should loosen the 12mm nut, then pull the cable out from the transmission bracket.

Step 3. Remove Gear Shift Lever Knob and Console

Turn to Chapter 7, Procedure 11, and do Steps 1 through 3, and then return here.

Step 4. Free Cable From Gear Shift Lever

See how the cable fits over a pin on the left bottom side of the shift lever? Well, remove the little circlip securing it and put the clip in a marked Baggie.

Now loosen the 12mm nut holding the cable sheath to the front part of the gear shift lever mount. You'll need to put another wrench on the forward part of the cable to get sufficient leverage on the rear nut. Turn the rear nut all the way off the cable sheath and push the sheath forward so you can free the cable from the shift lever mount. OK?

Step 5. Remove Cable

Go to the front of the car and follow the cable across the engine compartment to the firewall. The cable goes through the firewall and is protected by a rubber grommet. Hold the cable just in front of the grommet and pull the cable out. Friend can guide the cable out from inside the car.

Pull the cable out from the engine compartment like a champion fisherman.

Step 6. Install New Cable

Roll the firewall grommet off the old cable unless your new one came equipped with one. Install Friend in the car as you carefully thread the shift lever cable end through the firewall. Push it until Friend can grab it from the inside.

Friend: Pull the cable until there's enough of it to get the cable sheath into the front of the shift lever mount. Unscrew the rear nut a few turns if need be, then position the cable in the mount. Tighten the nut using two wrenches. Now slip the end of the cable onto the shift lever pin and secure it with the circlip. Cinch the ends of the clip together with needle nose pliers if the clip's loose.

Now position the grommet in the firewall; use a thin screwdriver if you're having difficulty getting it in.

It's time to turn your attention to the transmission end of the cable. The two rubber washers fit one at each side of the transmission bracket. Run the end nut down the threads a little. Guide the cable down toward the transmission levers and be sure it follows a nice gentle curve and isn't hung up on anything. Lie down again by the left front wheel and position one rubber washer on each side of the bracket; show 'em Pierre. (See illustration on next page.) Have Friend help you position the cable from above if your fingers are getting cramped. Slide the rubber accordian onto the cable and maneuver the cable clamp (get it out of the Baggie) onto the cable end.

Push the threaded end of the cable clamp through the hole in the end of the transmission lever and install the washer and nut. Don't move the transmission lever or you'll spend more time on this Procedure than needed.

Pull the end of the inner cable with pliers and tighten the 13mm nut on the cable clamp in the transmission lever. Get it tight.

Now go inside the car again, start the engine and shift gears. Does the lever engage all gears including Park (P) and Reverse (R)?

Step 7. Test For Sure

Take your tools and drive the car down the road apiece and check that you can smoothly change gears using the shift lever. Stop and then try backing up. Everything OK? Drive home and go to Step 9. If the gears aren't shifting properly, find Friend and continue with the next step.

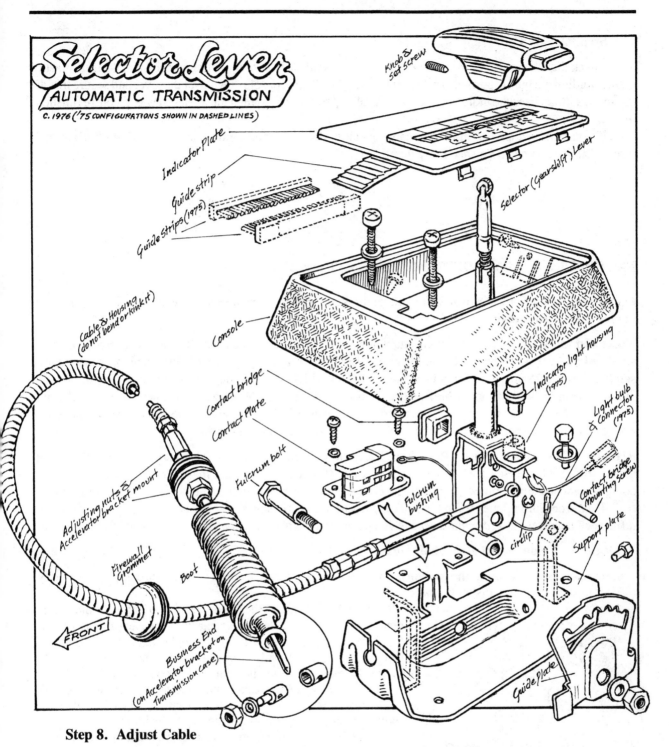

Selector Lever
AUTOMATIC TRANSMISSION
C. 1976 ('75 CONFIGURATIONS SHOWN IN DASHED LINES)

Knob & set screw

Indicator Plate

Guide strip

Guide Strips (1975)

Selector (Gearshift) Lever

Cable & Housing (do not bend or kink it)

Console

Contact bridge

Contact Plate

Fulcrum bolt

Indicator light housing (1975)

Light bulb & connector (1975)

Adjusting nuts & Accelerator bracket mount

Fulcrum bushing

Contact bridge mounting screw

Firewall Grommet

Boot

circlip

Support plate

FRONT

Business End (on Accelerator bracket on Transmission case)

Guide Plate

Step 8. Adjust Cable

Put the shift lever in P and loosen the 13mm cable clamp nut on the transmission lever. If your cable clamp is missing, buy a replacement from the dealer. Ask Friend to push the transmission lever all the way to the left while you pull on the end of the cable with pliers and tighten the cable clamp nut. Try to engage all the gears or take another test drive. No go? Move the gear shift lever to P, loosen the clamp nut and pull the transmission lever to the right, but don't pull too far or you'll engage another gear. Give Friend the pliers and 13mm wrench to get the clamp nut tight.

Still no go? Put the shift lever in P once more and loosen the 13mm nut holding the cable sheath onto the bracket. Make sure the cable sheath is pushed fully into the bracket, then tighten the nut again. That often fixes a stubborn cable. Try engaging gears again. Got it finally?

Step 9. Tidy Up

Check that all the electrical wires are connected around the base of the shift lever and that the little plastic gizmo holding the bulb is pushed in place. Now slide the plastic console down over the lever and secure it with the screws. Snap back the indicator plate and install the shift knob; tighten the allen screw and you're finished inside.

If you removed the transmission guard, install it using the four 13mm bolts. Can't find it? It's in the trunk. That's it—you're finished lying in the dirt.

PROCEDURE 4: REMOVE TRANSMISSION. Phase 2.

Condition: Clutch mechanism worn out or broken, transmission needs to be overhauled, rear main crankshaft oil seal blown.

Tools and materials: Phase 2 tool kit, including the CV joint tool (See Chapter 4, Phase 2 tools), piece of stout 4x4 timber (or nail two 2x4's together) 132.13cm (50½ in) long, a 91cm (36 in) length of strong chain, safety glasses, a 75mm (3 in) bolt with a washer and nut which will fit through the chain links, Friend. Rent a 30mm socket (1-3/16 in) and a breaker bar to fit it, find a 61cm (24 in) piece of pipe to use as a cheater handle. Make sure the pipe fits over the end of the breaker bar. 1978 on standard transmissions need the polygon socket tool to remove the starter. See Phase 2 tool list in Chapter 4.

Remarks: This is not a difficult Procedure, but try to rent garage space with a hydraulic jack for a day. It makes lifting much easier and the job much quicker. If that's not possible, make sure your jack is in good condition and use strong blocks to support the car's weight and chocks to prevent the rear wheels from rolling.

This Procedure applies to both standard and automatic transmissions. On automatics be aware of the difference between the *gear shift lever* inside the car and the *transmission select lever* on the transmission.

Step 1. Remove Left Driveshaft Nut

The driveshafts go from the transmission to the centers of the two front wheels. Two constant velocity (CV) joints are integral parts of the shaft.

Chock the rear wheels, pull up the handbrake and put the car into gear. Don't attempt to remove the driveshaft nut with the car supported by a jack. It's dangerous! Pry the hubcap or the plastic lug nut covers and center plastic cap off the left front wheel. Slide your cheater handle over the breaker bar. With the 30mm socket on the breaker bar, put the socket on the left driveshaft nut. Get the cheater pointing forward and horizontal, then stand on it. Bounce gently up and down until the nut begins to loosen. Don't use a hammer.

Put the driveshaft nut and washer into a marked Baggie, then loosen the wheel lug nuts.

Step 2. Disconnect Battery

Remove both battery connections (10mm wrench) and tuck the cables out of the way.

Step 3. Disconnect Clutch Cable (Standard; automatics go to Step 4)

Completely loosen the white plastic disc (Procedure 1, Step 1) on the clutch cable to increase free play, then lift the clutch release lever on the side of the transmission and remove the metal clip from the bottom of the cable. Remove the metal spacer at the same time. Baggie the pair. Pull the clutch cable through the rubber bushing in the ear on the transmission. Now tuck the cable up behind the firewall out of the way.

Step 4. Disconnect Cables (Automatics)

Three cables attach to a bracket on the left side of the transmission case. Ask Friend to move the gear shift lever back and forth a few times and depress the gas pedal so you can watch the levers move on the bracket. Have Friend put the gear lever in Park. The automatic gear selector cable is the one with the little plastic slotted gizmo on the end hooked over one of the transmission levers. (The other end is attached to the gas pedal.) Use your hand to lift the transmission lever high enough to unhook the end of the cable.

Next loosen the 13mm clamp nut holding the gear shift cable onto the smallest lever. Pull the cable out of the clamp.

Finally, pop the cable off the lever which points straight up. That cable runs from the throttle mechanism on the carburetor or fuel injection assembly. Don't mess with any of the nuts holding the cables to the bracket, instead remove the two 13mm or 15mm bolts holding the bracket to the transmission. Push it aside and put the bolts back on the transmission for safekeeping.

Step 5. Detach Speedometer Cable (Everybody)

The speedometer cable runs from the black EGR box on the left side of the firewall into the top of the transmission. Remove the phillips screw or 13mm bolt from the cable; hold down the clip at the transmission and pull the cable out. Reinstall the screw or bolt through the clip back into the transmission for safekeeping. Stick the end of the cable in a Baggie to keep the cable gear clean.

Step 6. Remove TDC Sensor and Inspection Plug (Standard; Automatics go to Step 9.)

Early Rabbits have an electrical plug attached to the top dead center inspection hole plug in the top of the transmission. It's part of the computerized diagnostic system. Pull it and mark it 'TDC' plug.

On later models a plastic 'pop' cover fits in the TDC plug. Unpop it.

All models: Unscrew the TDC plug by hand or with a pair of needle-nosed pliers or vice grips. There's a special VW tool US 4463, if you like special tools, but you don't need it. The spark plug wrench VW used to give with the Bug just fits that plug. Mark and Baggie the plug.

Step 7. Line Up the Flywheel (Standard)

Turn the ignition key to ON and turn the steering wheel all the way to the right. Friend: Put a 19mm socket with a short extension on the crankshaft sprocket bolt. It's most easily accessible through the right wheel well. Meanwhile you will be watching the inspection hole on the transmission. Use a flashlight if necessary.

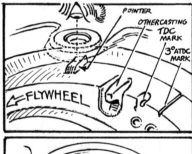

Have Friend turn the socket clockwise $\circlearrowright$ while you watch through the TDC hole for a 6mm (¼ in) square lug on the upper flange of the flywheel. It's important to get the correct lug lined up with the triangular pointer in the TDC hole. If things are incorrectly lined up, it will be impossible to separate the transmission from the engine. Look at the diagram.

Remarks: Don't get the square lug mixed up with the TDC mark or that raised line just to the left of the TDC mark. The lug is actually 330° before top dead center.

Engine Transmission WILL SEPARATE ONLY WITH THE POINTER IN POSITION IN THE TIMING HOLE →

Step 8. Unhook Shift Linkages

Ask Friend to shift gears as you watch the rods and levers move on the right side of the transmission close to the firewall.

The short vertical rod (the relay lever) has an arm on top that points forward. A shaft runs from the relay

Step 8. (Cont'd.)

lever towards the left fender and connects to an arm on the transmission (see diagram). Use needle nose pliers to pull the pin out of the shaft where it connects to the vertical relay lever and reinstall the pin into the shaft for safekeeping.

Behind the shaft you just liberated is another smaller shaft. It is secured to the transmission lever by a white or black plastic cap. Clean the cap if it's dirty. Use a small screwdriver to pry the clip on the cap end open. Peter shows you how on the diagram below. Pop the shaft off the transmission lever. Leave the disconnected shafts lying loose.

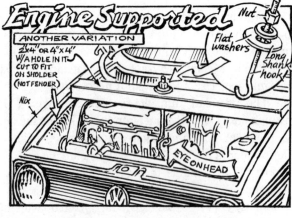

Step 9. Disconnect Backup Light Switch

The switch is screwed into the transmission or attached to the right side near the relay levers. Pull the two wires at the switch and mark them 'backup right and left.'

Step 10. Support Engine

Lay your piece of 4x4 across the inside of the fenders, not on top of them or you'll have two lovely dents. Wrap the piece of chain around the 4x4, above the hole in the end of the cylinder head. Slip a washer onto the 75mm (3 in) bolt and push it through one end of the chain, then through the cylinder head hole and into the other end of the chain. Get a bit of tension on the chain so things don't sag too much when the transmission is free. If the engine drops too far, you'll break the exhaust pipe or the rubber exhaust system hangers. Put the nut and washer on the bolt.

Step 11. Remove Top Two Engine/Transmission Mounting Bolts

Remove the two 19mm bolts and washers from the top of the transmission where it bolts to the engine. Mark and Baggie.

Step 12. Support Transmission

Place your jack under the transmission and pump it up until it's a snug fit between the transmission and the ground. This helps when it's time to remove the transmission mount bolts. Don't move the transmission up at all.

Step 13. Free Rear Transmission Mount (Standard; Automatics go on to Step 14.)

Remove the four 13mm bolts holding the rear of the transmission to its mount at the left fender. Mark and Baggie the bolts and go to Step 16.

Step 14. Free Rear Transmission Mount (Automatics)

Remove the 17mm bolt from the rear mount where it attaches to the left fender just below the battery. Mark and Baggie it.

Step 15. Remove Skid Plate (Automatics)

The protective plate underneath the transmission is held by four 8mm, 10mm or 13mm bolts. Put on your safety glasses, crawl under the car, remove the bolts and mark and Baggie. Clean and stash the plate.

Step 16. Chock, Jack and Block (All Models)

Remove the jack from under the transmission and place it beneath the stamped triangular mark behind left front wheel. Chock the rear wheels, then jack up the car and support it with a strong block or a jackstand. Lower and remove the jack and get the right front side up in the air. Block that side well also. You are going to work under the car so *block it safely*. Standard transmission go to Step 19.

Step 17. Remove Torque Converter Cover Plate (Automatics)

Slide under the car with a 10mm and 13mm socket in hand, with your head facing the left side of the car so you can see the transmission. Remove the three 13mm bolts holding a plate to the bottom of the transmission. Pull the plate off and pass it and the three bolts to Friend. Ask Friend to clean, mark and Baggie them. Don't move, there's more to do under there.

Step 18. Free Torque Converter from Drive Plate (Automatics)

Swap your 13mm socket for a 10mm one. Ask Friend to put the shift lever in Neutral (N); then have Friend turn the crankshaft via the right front fender well with a 19mm socket. Below the spot where the cover plate was attached you'll see the drive plate turn before your very eyes. Yell 'halt' when a 10mm bolt appears. Remove the bolt, then ask Friend to turn the crankshaft again until another 10mm bolt appears. Remove that one, then go through the same routine until another 10mm bolt rears its head. Remove it; then stash all three in a marked Baggie.

Step 19. Free Driveshafts

Stay under the car, ask Friend to pass you your safety glasses, and clean the dirt from the six socket head bolts (allen bolts) in the CV joint closest to the transmission on the left driveshaft. A small electrician's screwdriver is best for the job. Don't use a 6mm or 7mm regular allen wrench to remove the CV joint bolts. The tool will round off the points inside the bolts and you'll have to use a vise grip or other drastic measures to remove them.

Put the splined CV joint tool onto your ratchet handle and push the tool firmly into the bolt at the top of the joint. Put your back against the wheel (or ask Friend to hold it for you) and loosen the CV joint bolt. Stuck? Leave that bolt for a minute and try the opposite one. Turn the front wheel until that bolt is up in the 12 o'clock position. That way you don't have to fight the rubber boot. While you're at it, check the condition of the boots. If any are split, replace them when the transmission is out.

If any of the CV joint bolts are really difficult to remove, slip an 8mm box end wrench over the splined socket for added leverage. Should you strip the internal splines in any of the bolts, you'll need to use a pair of vise grips to remove the bolt.

Remove all the bolts and curved spacers beneath them. Mark and Baggie. Now remove the bolts from the inner CV joint on the other drive shaft. Make a note to buy replacements for any mangled bolts.

Step 20. Remove Left Driveshaft

Automatics: It may be necessary to jack the transmission up slightly to get the driveshaft away from the transmission. Read through the step before you jack, however.

All Models: Squirt some Liquid Wrench onto the driveshaft splines which stick through the outside of the left wheel. Now get back under the car and use a big screwdriver or breaker bar to lever the driveshaft away from the side of the transmission. Don't split the rubber boot over the CV joint. When it's free, pull the driveshaft out from the center of the wheel.

Driveshaft stuck? Ask Friend to find a block of wood and hold it over the threaded end of the driveshaft sticking through the wheel. Have Friend hit the block smartly with a big hammer while you pull on the driveshaft from under the car. Friend: Don't beat directly on the threaded end of the driveshaft or you'll never get the nut back on. It's free? Remove the driveshaft and protect the exposed CV joint with a plastic bag. Dirt in the CV's is a disaster. Put the shaft in a safe place. Now remove the left front wheel.

Time for a story break, I reckon.

Many years ago a certain well known dairy company started a nationwide competition to find a catchy jingle to promote their canned milk. A cowboy from the midwest sent in the following prizewinning entry:

> No tits to pull,
>   no hay to pitch,
> Just punch a hole
>   in the son of a bitch!

(Un)fortunately this jingle was never used.

OK, back to work.

Hang the right driveshaft up out of the way with a length of strong wire and put the CV joint in a plastic bag. Put plastic bags over the CV joint drive flanges on the side of the transmission. Automatics go to Step 23.

Step 21. Remove Starter and Left Engine/Transmission Mount (Standard)

Jack up the transmission just enough to take a little weight off; don't try to lift the car any higher than it already is.

Late model vehicles require the special polygon allen socket to remove the starter bolts.

The starter is a large black cylinder with a smaller one (the solenoid) on its top. It's bolted on the left side of the engine/transmission. Remove the 13mm nut holding the big wire coming from the battery to the solenoid. Pull off the wire and the spring washer, then put the washer and nut back on the solenoid for safekeeping. Now remove the two small connections to the right and left of the 13mm nut on the solenoid. Mark them right and left.

There are two methods of attaching the starter to the transmission. One uses two long 15mm bolts (or the polygon socket head bolts) which go through the starter, the transmission and into captive nuts welded onto the engine/transmission mount. With this type, get under the car and use a 15mm wrench to remove the lower bolt first. Now get up out of the dirt and remove the top bolt. Pull the starter free by twisting it slightly and easing it out. Lay the starter in the trunk. Thread the mount out from the car and Baggie it along with the two bolts.

If you have the other type starter, slide under the car with a 13mm socket. Remove the one or two 13mm bolts that hold the support bracket (on the rear of the starter) onto the transmission. Now remove the three 13mm nuts holding the front part of the starter in place. Again, these are easier to get at from underneath. Pull the starter out of the car.

There are two 17mm bolts holding the left engine/transmission mount in position. Remove the bolts (one has a nut) and pull off the mount. Mark and Baggie the mount and bolts.

Step 22. Free Intermediate Plate and Cover Plate (Standard)

The intermediate plate is a thin metal plate trapped between the engine and the transmission. Remove the three bolts holding the plate onto the bottom edge of the transmission (11mm socket). Pass the plate and bolts to Friend for marking.

The cover plate is in the two o'clock position next to the *right* drive shaft. It may be obscured by grime so rub around a bit if you can't find it easily. It's half moon shaped, about 75mm (3 in) long. Remove the two 11mm bolts holding the plate, then remove the 19mm bolt securing the transmission to the engine. The 19mm bolt was partially hidden by the cover plate. Mark and Baggie (sounds like a firm of private investigators). Go to Step 24.

Step 23. Remove Starter and Left Engine/Transmission Mount (Automatics).

This is one of those times you might wish you had a standard transmission. Please turn to Chapter 7, Procedure 9 and do Steps 1, 2 and 4. You'll need the tools listed at the beginning of that Procedure.

When the starter is out, remove the two bolts from the left engine/transmission mount. Remove the mount and Baggie it all.

Step 24. Remove Exhaust Pipe Support

Back under the car. Find the exhaust pipe and notice how it's supported by a bracket where it begins to sweep up toward the exhaust manifold on the cylinder head. The exhaust pipe is held by two 13mm bolts that go through a flange on the pipe and bolt to two support brackets. The right side support is usually a piece of pipe with a metal flange at each end. Remove the two 13mm bolts from one end and the two 17mm bolts at the other where the pipe bolts to the engine. Pass the unbolted treasures to Friend for cleaning and Baggie-ing.

Step 25. Remove Bottom Transmission Mount

The mount which bolts to the bottom of the car supports the right side of the transmission. Stay under the car and remove the two 17mm nuts holding the mount to the underbody. Then remove the two 10mm or 13mm nuts from the ears at the front of the mount. Be sure the mount doesn't fall and ruin your smile. Crawl out to inspect the rubber part of the mount for cracks and wear. Make a note to replace if necessary. Clean and stash the mount and nuts. Standard transmission go to Step 27.

Step 26. Remove Rear Mount (Automatic)

It makes life much easier if you first remove the three 15mm bolts from the rear transmission mount close to the left fender. One of the bolts secures the battery ground strap. Slide the mount out from the car and Baggie it with the bolts.

Step 27. Separate Engine from Transmission (All Models)

Check that all nuts and bolts holding the engine and transmission together have been removed. Is the chain that's supporting the engine safe and tight? Check the blocks supporting the car. Be sure the square lug on the flywheel is lined up with the pointer in the TDC hole (Step 7).

Lower the jack under the transmission a little and get help to pull the transmission toward the left fender. When the transmission starts to move, raise the jack a little to support the weight. Wiggle the transmission if it sticks. If it won't move, check again for any overlooked securing bolts. Automatic people check that you did Step 17.

When the transmission is almost free from the engine, prepare to take the weight. Let the jack take the strain and gently lower the transmission to the ground.

Automatics, when the transmission is free from the engine, don't let that big round thing (the torque converter) hang up on the engine. Push it back into the transmission. When you get the transmission on the ground, hold the converter in place with a few lengths of wire.

All Models: If your transmission is kaput, take it to a specialist. They have the correct tools and know-how to repair it. Have a look at it before you go.

Time for a refreshing drink methinks. Automatics, go to Step 29.

Step 28. Inspect Transmission (Standard)

Gently pull on the rod sticking out from the center of the transmission bellhousing. Move it in and out to see if its action is smooth. That rod (part of the clutch release mechanism) slides in a bronze bushing. Check the bushing for cracks and wear. Below the bushing is a rubber seal, check it carefully. If there's any oil or black sticky gunge around the seal or on the inside of the transmission, have the bushing and seal replaced by the transmission specialist. Take the transmission to VW and ask for advice if you feel lost.

Step 29. Inspect Transmission (Automatic)

Spin the torque converter. It should turn very easily, unaccompanied by any scraping sounds. Pull the converter out of the transmission. Any leakages from the seal? Get VW to install a new seal and check the transmission and torque converter bushing. Tell them that the wear limit diameter is 34.25mm and the out-of-round maximum is 0.003mm. Put the converter back into the transmission and secure it with wire before you go.

Step 30. Check Transmission Case (All Models)

Check that the transmission case is free from cracks and holes. Try to buy a used, but guaranteed, transmission from a junkyard if your case is shot.

If you are here to replace the rear main crankshaft seal, the next Procedure's for you. To install the transmission see Procedure 6.

PROCEDURE 5: REPLACE CLUTCH COMPONENTS AND/OR REAR MAIN CRANKSHAFT SEAL. Phase 2.

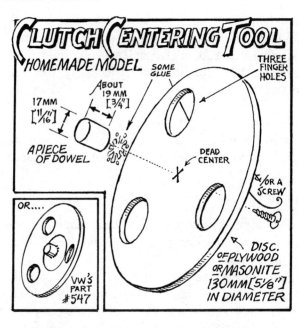

Condition: Clutch mechanism is worn or there's oil on the clutch components indicating a blown rear main crankshaft seal.

Tools and materials: Phase 2 tool kit, clutch centralizing tool (make one like the sketch or buy VW Part #VW 547), a tube of Loctite, fine emery cloth, non-petroleum base cleaner/solvent, new clutch disc, maybe a new pressure plate and flywheel (I hope not $$), a rear crankshaft seal, SAE 80W-90 transmission oil, Friend, rags and solvent, spray can of silicone lubricant, steel straight edge, torque wrench, baling wire.

Remarks: Give the parts person your engine and chassis number when you buy parts. It's especially important to get the correct size seal.

Automatics start at Step 1, then to Step 5 if your rear main seal is leaking. Standards begin at Step 2.

Before you begin work on the rear of the engine to mess with the clutch mechanism or drive plate, check the blocks supporting the car. You have some fairly heavy duty pulling to do, so everything had better be safe.

If you've rented a garage and a lift, raise the car until you can stand underneath and work.

Automatics start at Step 1, then go to Step 5 if your rear main seal is leaking. Standard begin at Step 2.

Step 1. Remove Drive Plate from Engine (Automatics)

This Step applies to rear crankshaft seal replacers only.

To prevent the drive plate from turning, lie under the car and thread some wire through any hole on the outer edge of the drive plate into a hole on the edge of the crankcase. Diagonally loosen, then remove the six bolts (17mm socket with a short extension). Baggie the bolts along with the big metal spacer washer fitted under them. Remove the wire and pull the drive plate off the crankshaft. Don't drop it.

Remove any thin metal spacers between the drive plate and the crankshaft. Then clean, mark and Baggie them. Go to Step 5.

Step 2. Remove Flywheel and Clutch Disc from Crankshaft (Standard)

Remarks: Check the support blocks beneath the car; you're going to do a lot of pulling with your precious head under all that Volkswagen.

Step 2. (Cont'd.)

The flywheel is the large round piece of metal with all the teeth around the outside edge. Scratch a line across the outside edge of the flywheel onto the pressure plate. That will help you get it back together properly. Get Friend to hold the 19mm socket on the front of the crankshaft to prevent it from turning. Loosen the six 11mm bolts on the flywheel in diagonal sequence and take them out. Pull the flywheel and clutch disc away from the engine. The clutch disc is directly under the flywheel and will fall onto your face if you're not careful. Come out from under and lay the flywheel and disc carefully on your work table.

Step 3. Examine Clutch Assembly and Remove Release Plate

Start with the flywheel. If any outside teeth are missing you'll have to get a new flywheel. A junkyard is the first place to look. Inspect the inside machined surface which mates with the clutch disc. Any deep scoring? If so, it will have to be resurfaced by VW or a machine shop. Resurfacing is a lot cheaper than buying a new one.

Check the two small metal dowels (pegs) on the inside of the flywheel. If they're loose or missing, get replacements from VW. When you have 'em, tap them into position with a light hammer.

Next look at the clutch disc: there should be at least 2mm (1/16 in) of friction material remaining above the top of the rivets in the disc. The disc should be evenly worn; if one side is substantially thinner than the other, the pressure plate is suspect or the flywheel bolts were loose. We'll check in a moment.

Time to remove the clutch release plate. Get back under and look how the release plate is held onto the pressure plate by a spring wire retaining ring. The upturned ends of the wire ring fit between two slots on the retaining plate. Insert a screwdriver blade under one of the ends of the wire ring and carefully lever it out. When it's free, pull off the retaining plate. Clean and Baggie.

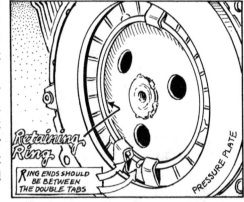

Retaining Ring

RING ENDS SHOULD BE BETWEEN THE DOUBLE TABS

PRESSURE PLATE

How does the pressure plate look? Is there any deep scoring on the friction surface? If there is, you need a new one. Hold the plate firmly and try to pull it off the crankshaft. It should be firm and not rattle. The metal fingers around the inner circumference of the plate shouldn't be broken or worn. Replace the plate if anything is broken. Oil on the plate indicates a blown rear main crankshaft seal, but the oil can be cleaned off and the plate can continue in faithful service.

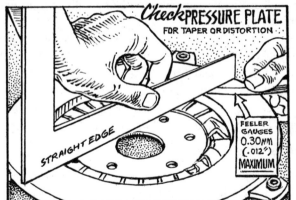

Check PRESSURE PLATE FOR TAPER OR DISTORTION

STRAIGHT EDGE

FEELER GAUGES 0.30MM (.012") MAXIMUM

Lay your steel straight edge across the friction surface of the pressure plate. Try to push a 0.30mm (.012 in) feeler gauge blade beneath the straight edge. If it *just* fits with no room to spare, the plate's OK. If a thicker blade will fit below the straight edge, the plate is worn beyond tolerance and must be replaced.

If you're here to check/replace the rear crankshaft seal, go to Step 4. Component replacers check the six 17mm bolts holding the pressure plate to the crankshaft. If any are loose, take them all out in diagonal order, and put a few drops of Loctite onto the threads. Ask Friend to hold the front crankshaft nut still (19mm) while you torque the bolts to 7.5mkg (54 ft lbs). If everything is OK so far and you're here to replace your clutch components, go to Step 7. If you're plate isn't quite kosher or you're replacing the crankshaft seal, continue.

Step 4. Remove Pressure Plate (Standard)

Screw one of the bolts into the plate that held the flywheel to the pressure plate. They're in a marked Baggie, I hope. Now wrap some thick wire around the bolt and through one of the holes in the crankcase to

Step 4. (Cont'd.)

stop the pressure plate from moving. A 19mm socket on the front crankshaft bolt won't do; it will only loosen the bolt.

Diagonally loosen the six bolts holding the pressure plate (17mm socket and a short extension). Remove them and the thin metal spacer. Note that the spacer has a lip which faces you. Remove the wire you used to retain the plate, then pull the pressure plate off the crankshaft. Use two screwdrivers as levers if it's stuck and ask Friend to hold on tight. Careful, if it suddenly comes off the crankshaft, you don't want to drop it.

Now you can see the rear main seal held by the seal plate. There should be no oil on or around the seal. If there is, you now know the source of the oil that was dripping onto the garage floor.

Step 5. Remove Rear Main Seal

Use a large screwdriver blade to pry out the old seal. Don't scratch the inner edge of the seal retaining plate. Work on the inside of the seal. Carefully clean away any pieces of the broken plastic seal and wipe around the crankshaft with a clean rag.

Step 6. Replace Rear Main Seal

Compare your new seal to the old one. Same size I hope. Spray the seal with a little silicone lubricant if you have any. If not, do not fret. Start the seal into the retaining plate (with the big groove facing in towards the crankcase). Tap around the outer edge of the seal with a small hammer. Make sure the seal is going in straight. Keep tapping the outer edge until the seal is flush with the plate. Now find a wooden dowel and continue tapping around the edge until the seal is about 8mm (5/16 in) below the lip of the plate.

Step 7. Install Pressure Plate (Standard) or Drive Plate (Automatics)

Standard: This step applies to people installing a new or reinstalling the old pressure plate. Clean the friction surface of the pressure plate with a non-petroleum based cleaner. Spot remover or a spray can of brake lining cleaner is best, organic cleaning solution is OK. (Dry things off after rinsing with water if you go the organic route.) Next, lightly rub emery cloth horizontally *across* the pressure plate. Then rub again but at an angle, so the pressure plate ends up with a crosshatch pattern of tiny scratches.

Automatics: Just clean the drive plate.

All Models: Find the Baggie with the 17mm bolts and the metal spacer washer, along with any spacers that were between the crankshaft and the drive plate or pressure plate.

Position the pressure plate or drive plate onto the end of the crankshaft, remembering to install the spacers if you had any. The plate only fits one way, so make sure all the holes line up. Put a few drops of Loctite on two bolts. Push one through the spacer (the lip faces you) and through the pressure or drive plate into the crankshaft. Now screw in the other bolt. Loctite all the remaining bolts and screw them in.

Ask Friend to hold the crankshaft tight with a 19mm socket on the other end as you diagonally tighten the bolts to 7.5 mkg (54 ft lbs). Automatics can now jump to Procedure 6 to install the transmission.

Step 8. Install Clutch Release Plate and Retaining Ring (Standard)

Find and clean the release plate and retaining ring. The release plate fits into the center of the pressure plate. It only fits one way so move it around until the slots on the release plate line up with the fingers on the pressure plate. When it's in position, pop in the retaining ring. Be sure the upturned ends of the retaining ring fit between the two upturned bits on the clutch pressure plate. Go back to Step 3 and see how it all looks when assembled. Put a drop of lithium or multi-purpose grease into the hole in the center of the retaining ring. Don't overdo it; wipe off any excess.

Step 9. Install Clutch Disc and Flywheel (Standard)

If you're replacing your flywheel with another, you must file a new timing notch. Do it just as in the diagram on the next page. Now clean the flywheel and rough it with emery cloth as you did the pressure plate in Step 7. Don't use emery paper on the clutch disc or clean it with anything but spray or brake cleaner or a clean rag if it's dirty but reuseable.

Step 9. (Cont'd.)

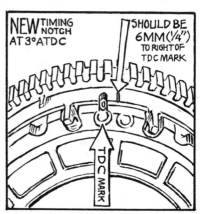

Place the clutch disc on the inside of the flywheel. On one side of the disc you'll notice that the metal center part sticks up in the middle while on the other side it's flat. The flat side goes *against* the pressure plate. The other side pokes out of the flywheel when it's installed.

Position the flywheel over the pressure plate and turn it until it mates with the locating dowels. Push it home. The line you scratched on the flywheel and pressure plate at the beginning of the Procedure will help you get things right. Screw two of the Baggied 11mm bolts through the flywheel into the pressure plate.

Slip the middle dowel of the clutch disc centering tool into the hole in the center of the clutch disc. Move things around until the tool fits snugly into the center of the flywheel. Install all four remaining 11mm bolts and gently tighten them with a socket. If you can remove the centering tool and put it back in easily, the disc is centered properly—OK?

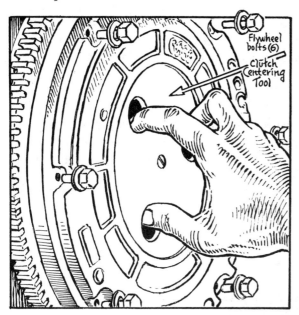

Ask Friend to hold the crankshaft still (19mm) and diagonally torque the 11m bolts to 2 mkg (14 ft lbs). No more, no less. Remove the centering tool.

Step 10. Align Flywheel (Standard)

Get under the car and position Friend at the front of the engine with the 19mm socket. The flywheel has a scoop cut out of the outside edge. If necessary, turn the engine over until that scoop aligns with the scoop cut out of the intermediate plate on the right side of the engine. That puts the lug at the 2 minutes before 12 o'clock position.

PROCEDURE 6: INSTALL TRANSMISSION—ENGINE IN CAR. Phase 2.

Condition: The transmission is out.

Tools and materials: Phase 2 tool kit, Friend, lithium-based CV joint grease.

Step 1. Get It In

Automatics: Remove the wire holding the torque converter in place. Make sure the torque converter stays fully inside the transmission during installation.

Standard: Spray a little WD-40 onto the splined shaft sticking out of the transmission.

All Models: Slide the transmission under the car. Make sure the driveshafts are still held up with wire. Lift the transmission onto the jack or connect it to your hoist and gently lift it.

Pump the jack to get the transmission up until it lines up with the engine. Get the splined shaft into the center of the clutch and then push the transmission into place. You may have to rock the transmission a bit to get it home. Keep the transmission as horizontal as possible, lift it at the rear and push it on.

Standard: If the transmission won't slide home, get Friend to move the 19mm front crankshaft bolt back and forth slightly to allow the splined shaft to line up with the splines inside the clutch disc.

All Models: When the transmission is on, install one bottom 19mm bolt through the transmission into the engine to hold the two together. Keep the jack under the transmission to support it until the mounts are installed.

Step 2. Install Engine/Transmission Securing Bolts (All Models)

Install the top two 19mm bolts through the top of the transmission into the engine and tighten them enough to pull the engine and transmission together. Now install the remaining bottom bolt.

Step 3. Install Rear Transmission Mount (Automatic)

Reinstall the mount onto the rear of the transmission with the three 15mm bolts, making sure you rehook the battery ground strap onto one of the bolts. The ATF filler tube also has a tab secured by one of the bolts. When the bolts are tight, install and tighten the 17mm bolt through the ears inside the left fender into the rubber bushing in the top part of the mount. You may need to jack the transmission up and down a bit to get the bolt in. Remove the jack.

Step 4. Install Rear Transmission Mount (Standard)

Reinstall the four long 13mm bolts through the rear transmission mount into the transmission. One of the bolts holds the battery ground strap. Use the jack to lift the rear of the transmission if the bolts won't start by hand. Don't crossthread them. When they're in, tighten them with your wrench. Remove the jack.

Step 5. Install Bottom Mount

Get under the car with the mount, its Baggied bolts, and a 10mm or 13mm socket and a 17mm socket. Position the mount over the two studs sticking out from the floor and put the two ears at the front of the mount onto the transmission. Loosely install the nuts. Tighten the two 10mm or 13mm nuts to 2 mkg (14 ft lbs). If the mount is under sideways strain, just tighten the 17mm nuts enough to support the transmission. If it lines up OK, torque the 17mm nuts to 4 mkg (29 ft lbs). Stay under, there's more to come.

Step 6. Install Exhaust Pipe Support

Remove the jack from under the transmission if it's still there. Ask Friend to pass you the support and a 13mm wrench. Position the support between the exhaust pipe and the engine. It fits in there very neatly, so turn it end-over-end if at first you don't succeed. Put the two 13mm nuts and bolts through the exhaust pipe flange and into the support. Install the two 17mm bolts through the other end of the support and into the engine. Tighten the 17mm bolts but leave the others loose. Automatics go to Step 8.

Step 7. Secure Intermediate Plate and Cover Plate (Standard)

Install the three 11mm bolts that hold the intermediate plate to the bottom edge of the transmission. While you're down there, check that the 19mm bolt holding the engine to the transmission is tight. Position the small cover plate onto the transmission next to the right drive shaft. Secure it with the two 11mm bolts. Come out from under and remove the 4x4 support from the engine and then go to Step 10.

Step 8. Secure Drive Plate and Replace Converter Cover Plate (Automatics)

Ask Friend to turn the crankshaft with the 19mm socket until a hole in the drive plate appears. Line up the drive plate hole with a threaded hole in the torque converter and install a bolt. Do the other two and torque them all 3 mkg (21 ft lbs).

Now install the thin metal cover plate and secure it with the three 13mm bolts. Come out from under and remove the 4x4 support from the engine.

Step 9. Install Starter (Automatics)

Turn back to Chapter 7, Procedure 9, Step 12, and do it, but don't hook up the battery ground strap yet. Come back to Step 11 when you've done the starter installation.

Step 10. Install Starter and Left Engine/Transmission Mount (Standard)

If your starter was secured by the engine/transmission mount bolts, first loosely position the rubber part of the engine/transmission mount into the other half of the mount still bolted to the front crossmember. Then push the starter into place with the solenoid facing up and slip in one of the 15mm allen or polygon socket

Step 10. (Cont'd.)

bolts. The top bolt screws into a captive nut welded onto that small black metal pipe. If the bolt won't start in the thread, bend the tab which holds the captive nut with a pair of vise grips until it's square with the bolt. Now put the other bolt in and tighten them both to 3 mkg (22 ft lbs). Install the electrical connections and go to Step 11.

If your starter was held by three 13mm nuts, position the starter into the transmission and loosely install the nuts. Push the starter fully into place and install the one or two 13mm bolts holding the rear support bracket onto the transmission. All this is best done from underneath. Tighten all the nuts to 3 mkg (22 ft lbs). Install the electrical connections.

Next position the engine/transmission mount into the other part of the mount still bolted to the front crossmember. Replace the top 17mm bolt that secures the mount to the engine/transmission. Now put the other bolt in and tighten them both. Now, put back the wheel and screw on the lug nuts.

Step 11. Install Left Driveshaft

Remove the plastic bags from the CV joint and the left CV joint drive plate on the side of the transmission. Check the CV joint for dirt. If it's OK shoot a dollop of special VW CV joint grease into it. Don't use anything else. A cruddy CV joint must be cleaned and repacked with grease. Procedure 8 tells how.

Slide the splines on the end of the left driveshaft through the center of the left wheel bearing housing and out through the wheel. Loosely install the 30mm nut and washer. Line up the inner CV joint with the drive plate on the transmission. Use a big screwdriver to lever it if need be. Put one CV joint socket head bolt through a curved spacer (they're in a Baggie) and screw it into the drive flange with your fingers. Install all six bolts and three spacers. Tighten them to 4.5 mkg (33 ft lbs). Hold your back firmly up against the left wheel as you apply torque or ask Friend to hold the wheel or step on the brake pedal.

Step 12. Secure Right Driveshaft

Same as Step 11.

Step 13. Install Skid Plate (Automatics)

Clean the plate and bolt it to the transmission. Go to Step 15.

Step 14. Install Shift Linkage Rods (Standard)

Remove the pin from the horizontal shaft (you put it there for safekeeping) and push the shaft through the vertical relay lever. Pop the other loose shaft onto the small ball on the transmission lever. Close the clip with a screwdriver and go to Step 16.

Step 15. Install Bracket and Cables (Automatics)

Attach the cable bracket to the transmission with the two 13mm or 15mm bolts. Hook the automatic gear selector cable (the one with the slotted plastic gizmo on the end) over the lower transmission lever. Next pop the throttle cable onto the tallest vertical lever. Check that the shift lever inside the car is in Park (P) and loosen the 13mm nut on the clamp in the third lever. There will be a slight dent in the cable where it was originally held by the clamp. Try to tighten the clamp on the cable at that same spot.

Step 16. Install Backup Light Connections

You marked the end of the electrical connections earlier. Plug them into the switch.

Step 17. Install Speedometer Cable

Remove the phillips screw or 13mm bolt from the clip attached to the top of the transmission where the speedometer cable fits. Remove the Baggie from the end of the speedometer cable and push the cable into the transmission. You may have to turn the end of the cable around a bit before it clicks home. Secure it with the clip and tighten the bolt or screw. Automatics, go to Step 19.

Step 18. Install Clutch Cable

Turn to Procedure 2, Step 3, and do it. Then adjust the free play as described in Procedure 1, Step 2.

Step 19. Install Battery Cables

Clean the battery posts and cable terminals if required, tighten the cable clamps onto the posts (10mm wrench) and coat each post with Vaseline or the like.

Screw in the TDC hole plug, pop on the cap or reconnect the TDC electrical sensor if you've got one.

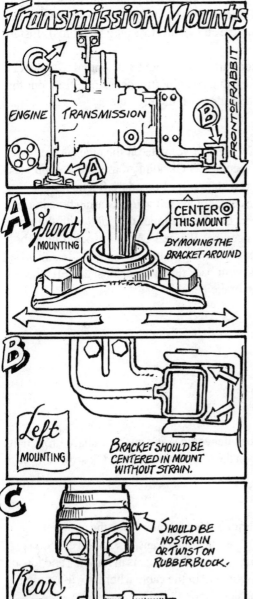

Step 20. Line Everything UP

Refer to the drawings as you do this Step. Loosen the 17mm bolt in the rear transmission mount and the two 15mm bolts holding the left engine/transmission mount to the front crossmember.

Get under the car and check that the rubber part of the bottom transmission mount isn't being strained. Loosen the 17mm nuts if the mount is twisted and ask Friend to move the engine/transmission assembly from side to side. Use a big screwdriver or crowbar to line things up.

Torque the nuts in the bottom transmission mount to 4 mkg (29 ft lbs).

Check that the rear transmission mount is centered like in the drawing. Lever the transmission from front to rear to get the thing centered. Torque the bolt to 4 mkg (29 ft lbs).

Finally, get the round rubber part of the left engine/transmission mount centered in the other half of the mount bolted to the front crossmember. Lift the engine with a crowbar to center it if need be. Tighten the two 15mm bolts.

Now inspect the transmission to see that all the bolts are tight. Only empty Baggies left? Good. Lower the car off the support blocks, then tighten the left driveshaft nut to 24 mkg (173 ft lbs). Chapter 20, Procedure 8, tells how to tighten that nut.

Check the engine and transmission oil levels, Chapter 10, Procedures 1 and 25 tell how. Try shifting gears (did you install the linkage rods?), then start the car. If the exhaust pipe bangs against the underbody, one or more of the rubber hangers broke and must be replaced. Did you tighten the two 13mm bolts that hold the exhaust pipe to the support bracket?

Take the car out for a drive and feel what an amazing difference a new clutch or rebuilt transmission makes. It's worth all the work.

If you can't shift easily into all gears, turn to Procedure 7 in this Chapter and adjust the shift linkage.

I did a clutch job one bright afternoon, in record time to boot. I waved my goodbyes to all and started the engine. There was the most most horrific noise coming from the transmission. It sounded like a twelve-ton rattlesnake with palsy. I initially thought I had installed a faulty part. I turned off the engine.

Later that night, contemplating the penguin on the overstuffed chair, I listed the changes made to the car during the course of the overhaul. One of the bolts securing the tiny cover plate near the driveshaft had been missing, so I replaced it with a new bolt. Perhaps the new bolt was too long? I rushed into the cold night, loosened the new bolt a couple of turns and started the engine. No more noise! I removed the bolt, replaced it with a shorter one and paid homage to Sherlock Holmes.

PROCEDURE 7: CHECK/ADJUST SHIFT LINKAGE—STANDARD TRANSMISSION. Phase 2.

Condition: Difficulty engaging gears, you've had the engine/transmission out of the car and now it's hard to get the shifter into the gears. The clutch cable free play is OK.

Tools and materials: Phase 1 tool kit, Friend, molybdenum grease, maybe new shift rod bearing.

Remarks: If you haven't had the engine/transmission out of the car, first do the 'pop' test described in Chapter 3, Procedure 1, Step 4.

Step 1. What's Wrong

Lift and prop the hood. Peer over the transmission and check the relay levers and rods on the transmission's right side. Are all the rod end connections popped into place on the selector levers? Also check that the long rods which just push through metal levers are secured by   clips. If any of the clips fall out, the rods move in their mounts and make it diffucult to change gears.

Wipe a little molybdenum grease on everything that moves. Take your hands off that turtle! Install Friend in the car and ask him/her to move the gearshift lever to engage all gears. Lubricate! No better? Press on.

Step 2. Check Shift Lever

Put the gearshift lever in Neutral and wiggle it from side to side. It should move easily and not bind up at all. Go to Step 3 if it sticks. **Pre-1975 cars:** When the shifter's in Neutral, check that the bottom part of the shift lever (pull the rubber boot down to reveal it) is vertical. No? Go to Step 3. Yes? Go to Step 4.

1976 and on cars have a differently shaped shifter which wasn't designed to be vertical. Let's see if it sits in its bearing plate correctly.

Step 3. Check Lever Plate

Unscrew the gear shift knob counterclockwise ↻. Now peel the rubber boot from around the base of the shift lever and slide it off. Before your very eyes is the oval lever bearing plate with a white plastic bearing in the middle that's about the size of a half smooth golf ball. Is the golf ball cracked? If so, don't do anything yet.

The plate is held in position by two 10mm bolts. If your 1975 car's shifter isn't vertical, loosen the two bolts and move the plate until it is. Tighten the bolts. Now try shifting gears. Better? That's often the trouble.

1976 and on cars have two small round holes in the lever plate. These holes must line up with two similar holes in the housing below the plate. Look carefully. Loosen the two 10mm bolts and move the lever plate until all the holes line up. Install the rubber boot and shift knob if it does. Does that fix your shifting problem? If not, try this.

Step 4. Check Clevis Bolt

Chock, jack and block the left front of the car; make sure those blocks are safe. Loosen the two 10mm bolts in the lever plate around the base of the gearshift lever, then get under the car. Peel off the weatherseal boot from the bottom of the shift lever (you're under the car, remember). If it's stuck, come out from under and loosen the two lever plate bolts a tad more. Now dive under again and pull off the boot.

The vertical shaft lever is attached by a clevis bolt to the horizontal shift rod which runs forward to the relay levers on the side of the transmission. Is the bolt tight? I've seen those bolts with nuts missing, so replace any missing nuts and try the shift action again. **1975 cars** go to Step 6.

Step 5. Check Stop Finger Position (1976 and On)

Ask Friend to put the shift lever in Neutral (N), then center the lever. It's most accurate if Friend moves the lever all the way left then all the way right, then stops the lever in the center.

Measure the gap as shown in the diagram. It should be *exactly* 19mm (¾ in). To adjust it, loosen the 13mm bolt holding the front part of the shift rod in its clamp and move the shift rod until you get the 19mm gap. Friend: make sure the shift lever stays centered. When the gap's correct, tighten the 13mm bolt, center the shift lever again and remeasure the gap. Keep at it until the gap is exactly 19mm. Now try the shift action. If it's fixed, install the rubber boot, lower the car and tighten the two 10mm bolts at the lever plate. Slip the rubber boot back on and screw on the shift knob. Non-fixers continue.

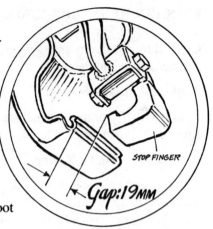

STOP FINGER

Gap:19MM

Step 6. Check Shift Rod Bearing Assembly

Find the bearing plate bolted to the underside of the car. The shift rod passes through the center of it, and the bearing in the center of the plate is protected by two rubber boots. Peel back the boots and slide them down the shift rod. You can use a small screwdriver to free the boots from the bearing plate if needed.

You will have brought to light two 10mm nuts and bolts which secure two thin triangular shaped thin metal plates to the bearing plate. Remove the 10mm nuts and pull back the metal plate on the *shift lever* side of the bearing plate. Now you should see a white plastic somewhat oval bearing. Pull it away from the bearing plate.

Now push the other half of the white bearing out from the bearing plate and let it hang on the shift rod. Looking carefully at the shift rod you should see a black plastic semicircle about 15mm (9/16 in) wide pushed onto the shift rod. Missing? That's your trouble.

Even if the semicircle bearing is present, carefully examine all the plastic bearing parts for signs of wear; like nicks and scratches. If the rubber boots were torn, dirt could have gotten into the bearings and rendered them useless.

Step 7. Replace Bearing Assembly

Buy a whole new gear shift bearing assembly from VW including the semicircle bearing, the setscrew (1975) and rubber boots if they're worn.

Loosen the 13mm nut (1975 models, remove the 10mm setscrew) at the front end of the shift rod, then remove the two 13mm nuts holding the bearing plate to the car's underbody. Pull the shift rod out from the front clamp and pull off the rubber boot, the metal plate and the white plastic bearing. Take off the bearing plate, the other metal plate and the rubber boot if you're replacing that boot. Pop off the semicircle bearing and clean the shift rod until it shines. Slide on the new boot, plate and bearing plate.

Clip on the new semicircle bearing and put the new white oval bearing onto the rod with the half shoulder

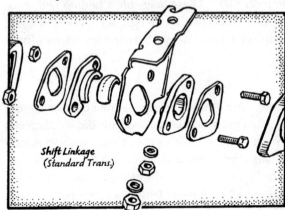

Shift Linkage
(Standard Trans)

going on first. Now slide the metal plate back on and lastly the rubber boot with the wide end going on first. Place the front end of the shift rod into the clamp and loosely install the bearing plate back onto the car's underbody with the two 13mm nuts.

Wipe a smear of molybdenum grease onto the inside of the bearings and then position the semicircle bearing until it sits in the center of the bearing plate. Slide the front half of the white bearing over the semicircle. Pull the other white bearing half back so the two halves fit together snugly. Now position one metal plate on each side of the bearing and install the two

Step 7. (Cont'd.)

10mm nuts and bolts. They go through the bearing plate as well as the metal plates. Tighten the 10mm bolts and then the 13mm bolts. Fit the rubber boots over each side of the bearing plate and (1976 and on) go back to Step 5 and adjust the stop finger position. 1975 models should center the shift lever in the Neutral position (Step 5), then install a new set screw into the front clamp.

All Models: Check your work, then lower the car to the ground.

PROCEDURE 8:   REMOVE FRONT DRIVESHAFTS, Phase 1. REBUILD CONSTANT VELOCITY (CV) JOINTS. Phase 3.

Condition: Worn CV joints, referral from Chapter 10, bent or broken driveshaft.

Tools and materials: Phase 2 tool kit including 30mm (1-3/16 in) socket and breaker bar (rent it if necessary), cheater, molybdenum CV joint grease (available from VW), maybe new rubber boots for protecting joints, large and small hose clamps to fit rubber boots, CV joint tool (Phase 2 tool list in Chapter 4), Liquid Wrench, circlip pliers, maybe a new driveshaft, new CV joint circlips, waterproof marker.

Remarks: The two front driveshafts are of different lengths. The right one is solid and is 658.0mm (25-29/32 in) long and the left one, which is tubular, is 445.5mm (17-17/32 in) long. Also note that there are two types of CV joints, inner and outer. The driveshaft removal Procedure is the same for automatic and standard transmission cars and applies to left and right drive shafts. This is a difficult Procedure but attempt it anyhow. If you get stuck, a VW mechanic can easily remedy your mistake.

Read Procedure 15, Chapter 20, before you begin work.

Step 1. Check CV Joints

Lay something down under the transmission so you won't get dirty. Grasp one of the driveshafts (close to the inner CV joint) and try to move it forward and backward (front to rear). There should be no play. If there is, the driveshaft will have to come out and the CV joint repacked with grease or replaced. Do the push/pull motion again on the driveshaft close to the other (outer) CV joint. Now, grasp the same driveshaft again and move it toward and away from the transmission. There should be some play but no nasty noises. If you hear noises, the lot has to come out and be repaired. Do the same tests on the other driveshaft.

Step 2. Remove Driveshaft Securing Nut

Pry off the hubcap or the blackplastic center cover. Slip your socket and breaker bar onto the large nut. Ask Friend to depress the brake pedal and pull on the handbrake while you put chocks in front of and behind the two rear wheels. Stick the cheater over the breaker bar and remove the driveshaft nut. Do *not* attempt to remove the driveshaft nut when the car is supported by a jack or hoist. The force required to remove it could bring the car down on top of you. Put the driveshaft nut in a marked Baggie.

Step 3. Remove Driveshaft

Chock, jack up the vehicle and block it well. Put the gearshift in Neutral and don your safety glasses. Take a small electrical type screwdriver and remove all the crud from inside the socket headed bolts holding the CV joint to the transmission. Spin the wheel to bring the CV joint bolts into view. When they're clean, take your 12 point CV joint tool and put it on a short extension and snap on your ratchet handle. Insert the tool into the CV joint bolt at about the 11 o'clock position and put your back hard against the tire or ask Friend to hold the wheel for you. Remove the bolt. Now spin the wheel about 20° and remove the next CV joint bolt.

If you can't get enough leverage to remove the bolts, slip an 8mm box end wrench around your allen socket and use that as extra leverage. If the insides of the CV joint bolts are stripped, you will have to resort to more drastic measures. Remove as many of the bolts and half moon shaped spacers below the bolts as possible and put them in a marked Baggie. You will have to remove the stripped bolts with a pair of vise grips. Pull the CV joint tool off the ratchet and push it into the stripped bolt. Now tap it with a small hammer. The socket

Step 3. (Cont'd.)

inside the bolt prevents the bolt from being squashed, making it difficult to grip. Get your vise grips and grip tight the stripped bolt head. Unscrew the bolt. You will be able to remove any stubborn bolt in this manner. Buy new bolts to replace the stripped ones.

Don't beat on the CV joint with a hammer and chisel or any other tool for that matter. It's expensive to replace. When all the bolts and spacers are removed, put a large plastic bag around the CV joint and tape it to keep the dirt out. Turn the steering wheel as far to the left as possible (ignition key to the first 'on' position) and withdraw the splined part of the driveshaft from the center of the wheel. You might have to jiggle things around, especially if you have an automatic transmission, but it will come. If the driveshaft splines are stuck in the center of the wheel, squirt some Liquid Wrench around the splines and wait a few minutes. If you still can't pull it out, find a big hammer and block of wood. Put the wood on the end of the driveshaft where it sticks through the wheel and give it a few sharp whacks with the hammer. That will free it. Don't beat on the driveshaft without the piece of wood in between. That's a dangerous and costly procedure.

Step 4. Stop, Look and Listen

It's rather nice to have a vise; or at least a Friend to help with this Procedure. It's a greasy little job, so work somewhere where a bully isn't going to kick sand in your face. Look at Peter's exploded view of the driveshaft and CV joints. You will see that the outboard CV joint (the one closest to the wheel) has a little

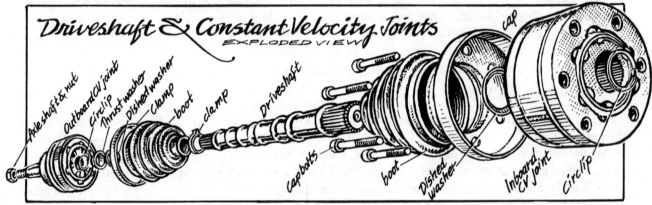

splined shaft which protrudes through the wheel. Between that outboard constant velocity joint and the inboard CV joint is the forged metal driveshaft. Even if your outboard CV joint is more worn than the inboard one, repack them both. It makes sense since you've got the whole thing half apart anyway. So, let's deal now in detail with that outboard joint.

Step 5. Liberate Outboard CV Joint

First pry off the large clamp holding the rubber boot around the CV joint. Leave the small clamp in place. Turn the rubber boot inside out as you peel it away from the outboard CV joint. If the rubber boot is split or worn, remove both clamps and pull the boot off. Secure the driveshaft in a vice. Examine the outboard

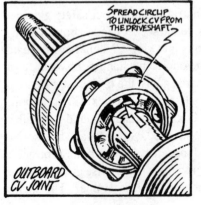

constant velocity joint from the driveshaft side and you'll see there's an opening in the innards. Twist the opening around until you see the ends of a circlip. Break out your circlip pliers and use it to expand the circlip. Now grab hold of the small splined axle onto which the large driveshaft nut fits and give it a strong tug. Use a rubber hammer to drive the CV joint off from the driveshaft if you can't pull it off by hand.

Put that outboard CV joint on a clean surface and remove the circlip, thrust washer and dished washer from the driveshaft. Note that the thrust and dished washer fit with the *convex* side of the dished washer up against the shoulder on the driveshaft. If either of the washers are distorted, buy replacements.

Step 6. Disassemble Outboard CV Joint

If you have decided to examine/repack both inner and outer CV joints, please *do one at a time*. If you mix up any of the ball bearings or CV joint components, you will have made a frustrating and expensive mistake.

VW does not sell CV joint parts. If any component is broken or worn, the whole joint has to be replaced. It's not possible to use the balls from one joint in another as they wear at different rates. The components of each CV joint are carefully selected at the factory and cannot be interchanged.

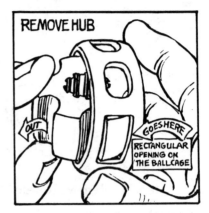

Wrap the splined shaft of the outboard CV joint with masking tape and put it between the jaws of your vise so the balls and cage are facing you. Clean off any dirt or grease and make a mark with a waterproof felt-tip pen across the outer ring, the ball hub and the ball cage of the CV joint. Do not put a saw or scratch mark onto these components. Next tilt the ball cage upwards to remove the balls. Now turn the ball cage and ball hub until you see two large rectangular openings. The ball cage is in a vertical position with the rectangular opening facing you so you can withdraw the cage and the hub from the outer ring. To remove the ball hub from inside the cage, turn the hub so that one ridge in the hub is in line with one of the large rectangular openings in the cage. Now pull the hub out of the ball cage.

Step 7. Examine CV Joint Components

First examine the balls for scoring, flat spots or flaking. If any of the balls is in any way defective, you have to replace the joint. Are the balls OK? Examine the ball hub and cage. There will be a bright ring where the cage containing the balls runs around the inside of the hub. That's OK. If you don't feel you can make a satisfactory diagnosis of the CV joint's condition, take the components to a service person at VW and ask for advice. If everything seems OK, let's reassemble the works.

Step 8. Reassemble Outboard CV Joint

Make sure your felt tip pen marks are still visible. Thoroughly clean the ball hub until it shines and reapply the felt tip pen mark. Next clean the ball cage, making sure the felt tip mark is still visible. Dip all the balls in solvent and clean them. Then clean the ball hub. Coat all parts of the joint with that special molybdenum CV joint grease. Install the ball hub in the ball cage. It goes in the same way it came out. Next thoroughly coat each ball with grease before you slip it into the ball cage and hub. Add an extra dab of grease to hold the ball in position as you rotate the cage and hub to get the balls in one by one.

Now you have to get the balls, hub and cage into the outer ring. Remember all the marks must line up. You have to tip the cage upward to get the whole works into the outer ring. Be sure you haven't installed the cage upside down in which case your felt tip pen marks wouldn't show. It's very important to have it the right way up. When everything is properly together, pack the joint with molybdenum grease. Use your forefinger to make sure the grease penetrates the ball cage. Wipe a thick smear of grease over the inner and outer faces of the joint.

Step 9. Install Outboard CV Joint Onto Driveshaft

If the old rubber boot is in good condition, you can install the CV joint straight away. If you are replacing the rubber boot, first tape the ends of the driveshaft with masking tape to protect the new rubber boots as you slide it onto the shaft (if you neglected to do so earlier). Fit the end of the boot between the cast ridges on the

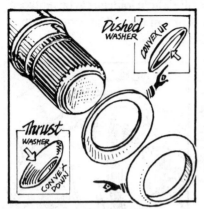

driveshaft and install the clamp. Turn the boot inside out and remove the tape from the driveshaft splines. Next, install the dished washer with the dished convex part *against* the shoulder on the driveshaft. Now slip on the thrust washer; the convex side *toward* the CV joint. Install a new circlip in the groove inside the CV joint ball hub so the ends of the circlip are visible through the opening. Lightly grease the end of the driveshaft, fully expand the circlip with your circlip pliers and push the CV joint onto the driveshaft splines. If you're lucky, the driveshaft will snap in place. If not, use a rubber hammer to drive down the end of the axle shaft until the CV joint pops onto the driveshaft and the circlip snaps into the groove. You'll hear it when the circlip snaps into position. Be sure the joint is packed full of grease, pull the rubber boot over the CV joint and secure it with the large clamp.

Step 10. Remove Inboard CV Joint

Remarks: You will have to take the driveshaft to VW or a machine shop to get the driveshaft pressed out of the inboard CV joint. *Do not* attempt to drive the driveshaft out of the joint with a hammer or chisel. You will deteriorate the end of the driveshaft, making it impossible to reinstall it into the inboard CV joint. You

will also have to take the driveshaft and CV joint back to VW or the machine shop to have the rebuilt joint pressed back onto the driveshaft. Let's do it.

Place the driveshaft in a vise and examine the inner part of the inboard CV joint. Use your circlip pliers to remove the circlip around the part of the driveshaft which sticks through the CV joint. Buy a replacement circlip. Remove the clamp which holds the boot around the CV joint and use a hammer and drift to drive the metal cap off the outer part of the CV joint. The cap is the metal part that fits over the CV joint just adjacent to the boot. Turn the boot inside out over the driveshaft.

Once you've got the cap and boot off, don't tilt the CV joint. If the ball hub inside the joint tilts more than 20°, the balls will fall out. OK,

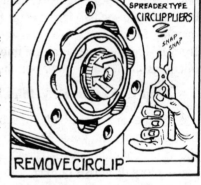

truck on down to VW or the machine shop and have them press the driveshaft out from the CV joint. While you're there, buy yourself a new circlip and a new rubber boot and clamps if your boot is damaged at all. Once the CV joint is off, remove the dished washer from the driveshaft.

Step 11. Disassemble Inboard CV Joint

Clean the CV joint and mark the top part of the ball cage, ball hub and outer ring with a waterproof felt tip pen. Now turn the ball hub and cage 90° from the outer ring. Line up the ball cage and hub so the two opposite balls line up with the grooves of the outer ring. You can now push the ball cage and hub out of the outer ring. Take care not to drop the six balls. Carefully take those balls out of the ball cage and put them in a Baggie.

Now turn the ball hub so the groove in the ball hub lines up with the outer edge of the ball cage. Gently twist the hub out of the cage. Clean everything, but don't rub the mark off the top of all three components.

Step 11. (Cont'd.)

Examine the balls, cage, hub and outer ring for damage. The outer ring will have a bright line on the inside where the balls have been running. That's OK, but if there are any marks, deep scorings or pitting on the balls or outer cage, the CV joint is useless. If you are unsure of the condition of the joint, take it to VW and get their expert opinion.

Step 12. Assemble Inboard CV Joint

When all the components are clean and shiny, coat them with molybdenum grease. Install the ball hub in the ball cage. It goes in the

REMOVE THE HUB

same way it came out. Now coat each ball with a good smear of grease and install the six balls back into the cage and hub. Put an extra dab of grease on the balls to hold them in place. You now have to get the ball hub and ball cage containing the balls into the outer ring. This is the tricky part. Be sure your felt tip pen marks are still visible. The ball and hub assembly should be positioned at a 90° angle to the outer ring. If you rotate the

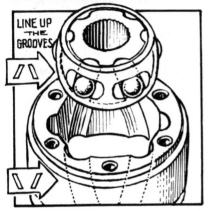

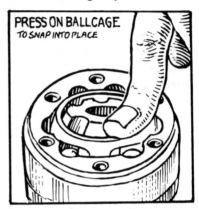

larger diameter portion of the outer ring you will see that the grooves of the outer ring which accept the balls are of unequal spacing. As you begin to slide the ball and hub assembly into the outer ring, line up the balls with the grooves in the ring so when you tip the ball hub 90°, the balls will easily slide into the grooves. The important thing is to have the correct side of the ball hub assembly and outer ring facing you. That's the side with your felt tip pen mark on it. Should the marks rub off, align things so the chamfer (bevel) on the splines of the ball hub are on the *same* side as the larger diameter side of the outer ring. Do not beat on the inner hub cage with a hammer or anything else to get things in position. Pressure with your thumbs is sufficient. If you just can't do it, try again. No? Take the whole thing to VW and they'll do it for you. You'll be amazed at how simple it really is.

When the assembly is together, be sure everything revolves smoothly , then fully pack the joint with molybdenum grease, turning the ball cage and hub around as you work in the grease with your forefinger. Smear both sides of the joint with a layer of grease.

Step 13. Reinstall Inboard CV Joint Onto Driveshaft

Have VW or a machine shop press your CV joint onto the driveshaft. Also get them to install the circlip for you. Buy a new rubber boot and clamps (if necessary) before installing the CV joint. To protect the boot from damage put masking tape onto the splined end of the driveshaft before pushing on a new boot. Push on the boot until the end of it is between the two cast ridges on the driveshaft, then secure it with a clamp. Put the dished washer on the end of the driveshaft, the *convex* side goes against the shoulder on the driveshaft.

Dished Washer

When the joint is properly installed, reposition the cap and boot on the outer surface of the CV joint. Tap the metal cap over the end of the CV joint until it's secure. Tighten the clamp around the rubber boot.

Step 13. (Cont'd.)

Make sure the head of the clamp isn't going to foul the socket head CV joint securing bolts when the driveshaft is reinstalled.

If you decide to take a break before reinstalling the driveshaft into the car, slip a Baggie over each CV joint and tape it securely to keep things clean.

Step 14. Install Driveshaft

Remove the Baggies from the CV joints and gather your socket head bolts and half moon-shaped spacers. If you destroyed any of the bolts getting them out, use replacements. Put a couple of drops of oil on the splined part of the shaft which fits through the wheel.

Slide under the car and push the splined shaft through the wheel. Find one socket head CV joint bolt and one spacer, slide the spacer onto the bolt and push the bolt through the inboard CV joint. Line up a hole in the CV joint drive flange in the transmission so the bolt can screw straight into it. Install the bolt fingertight. Slip another bolt through the same spacer, CV joint and into the flange. Install all the bolts. When they're all in, use your CV joint tool to gently tighten the bolts in diagonal sequence. When the socket head bolts are fairly tight, torque them to 4.5 mkg (32 ft lbs). Hold your back against the wheel to stop things from turning as you apply the torque. Remove the blocks and lower the car to the ground. Install the driveshaft nut. Torque it to 24 mkg (173 ft lbs). See Chapter 20, Procedure 8, for the method. Push on the plastic dust cover or hub cap and you're finished.

TALLYHO

CHAPTER 17

~ COOLING IT ~

THE COOLING SYSTEM

As soon as your engine starts, heat is produced. Rabbits like a little heat, but too much will send them scurrying for their burrows. Excess heat can build up and totally destroy an engine in no time, so there are two cooling systems in water-cooled VW's to carry heat away. One system uses oil which lubricates as well as cools. The other, the subject of this chapter, uses water, actually a mixture of water and antifreeze, called the **coolant**.

The 40% water and 60% *phosphorous free* ethylene glycol antifreeze mix is circulated around holes inside the crankcase called the **water jacket**. The coolant is pumped throughout the engine and cylinder head by the V-belt driven **water pump** hung on the left side of the engine. A **thermostat** in the base of the water pump acts as a faucet to control the amount of coolant flowing into the **radiator**. When the coolant is cold (engine just started) the thermostat stays closed and the water pump circulates the coolant only around the engine and cylinder head, not into the radiator. As the engine warms up as a result of internal friction and heat produced by the burning of fuel, the temperature of the coolant increases. When it gets up to 80°C (176°F) the thermostat slowly opens, allowing the coolant to flow into the hallowed area of the radiator.

The radiator is the big flat box filled with lots of thin tubes. Metal fins surround the tubes to increase the cooling surface area. Some models have a plastic **expansion bottle** connected to the top of the radiator by a thin hose. Others have a **header tank** inside the top of the radiator. The tank or expansion bottle allows the coolant to expand as it heats and is sealed by a pressure sensitive cap.

Because the radiator is right at the front of the car it constantly receives hits of onrushing air. The hot coolant coming into the top of the radiator is cooled by air flowing over the tubes and fins. By the time the coolant flows out from the radiator's base, it's cool enough to be pumped back into the water jacket to begin its cooling journey again.

If there isn't enough cooling air flowing through the radiator (like when fuming in traffic jams), an electric **cooling fan** automatically switches on when the coolant reaches 90°C (194°F). A **thermoswitch** on the left side of the radiator switches the cooling fan on and off. The engine doesn't have to be running for the fan to switch on. In fact, the key can be in your pocket and the fan can turn on. The fan stops running when the coolant temperature gets down to around 85°C (184°F).

Inspect the front of the radiator every week or so for dead penguins, toffee wrappers, Zig Zag papers and other debris that can block the air flow and prevent the radiator from adequately cooling the coolant.

When winter looms (a weaving term), especially check the pressure cap, all the joints, hose clamps and the cooling fan electrical connections. Most cooling system problems are caused by neglect. Radiator hoses very rarely just burst; it takes a while for a weak spot to develop. If you examine the hoses regularly you'll avoid getting stuck after gathering mushrooms on top of Mt. Washington. Keep the coolant level up to the top mark and resist cooling system additive advertisements.

TROUBLESHOOTING GUIDE

Here are some basic cooling system problems, symptoms and where to find help:

ALRIGHT, WHO'S HAVING THE
Broiled Rabbit?

Problem	Solution
Pump squeaks. This often happens first thing in the morning and goes away after a few moments. As time goes by, the squeak gets worse.	Procedure 1.
Engine overheats.	Procedures 2, 3 & 4.
Poor passenger heater output but water temperature gauge (or the thermometer symbol) stays at normal.	Procedure 5.
Engine takes a long time to warm up on cold days and heater output to heat the inside of the car is poor.	Procedure 2, Step 7; Procedures 5 & 6.
Engine temperature is normal and heater output is good, but water temperature gauge or symbol stays low.	Procedure 6.

PROCEDURE 1: FIX SQUEAKY PUMP. Phase 2.

Tools and materials: Phase 1 tool kit, perhaps a new pump, receptacle for drained coolant, maybe new container of phosphorous-free antifreeze, Permatex. Buy the rubber O ring that fits between the water pump and the crankcase and the paper gasket that fits between the two halves of the pump. If you can't find them, speak to the person at VW who rebuilds engines. There's always a huge box of gaskets somewhere around the rebuild room. Be nice but firm. They sell VW's and you need to be able to fix 'em.

Remarks: Some mechanics add oil to the coolant to lubricate and quiet a squeaky pump. Don't do it; oil will quickly rot the rubber hoses and clog the tiny tubes inside the radiator. Don't even add water soluble mineral oil. Put nothing in your cooling system except water and phosphorous-free antifreeze.

Step 1. Check the V-Belt

Did you work on the alternator or change the V-belt recently? If so, the water pump may have developed a squeak a week or so after a belt change or adjustment. This means the belt tension is too tight. Even if you didn't change belts, the tension could be wrong. The belt should deflect about 10mm to 15mm (3/8 to 9/16 in). Press on the belt with your thumb half way between the water pump pulley and the alternator. If the deflection's less or more than 10-15mm, turn to Chapter 8, Procedure 2, Step 3, and adjust it. If the belt tension is OK, please continue.

Step 2. Examine Pump

Loosen the alternator and remove the V-belt (Chapter 8, Procedure 2, Step 3). Spin the water pump V-belt pulley with your hand. Is it difficult to turn or does it make nasty noises?

The pulley should turn easily, but not spin freely like a bicycle wheel. If it groans, wheezes or squeaks, at all, the pump must be replaced. Call VW or a foreign car parts store to check if they have a pump in stock. You replace only the front half of the pump, because it has all the guts. It's a much easier task to unbolt the engine pump from the crankcase than to mess with the pump while still attached to the engine. You'll save time, believe me.

Step 3. Drain Coolant

If you've recently been driving the car, wait 15 minutes or so until the engine cools down. Get inside the car and slide the heater temperature control to the right—all the way on. Next place your clean catch pan under the water pump. If you keep it clean you'll be able to reuse the drained coolant. Unscrew the radiator pressure cap or the cap from the top of the expansion bottle.

Lie under the car but keep your face away from the water pump. Remove the two 10mm bolts from the metal pump base on the bottom of the pump. The large hose running from the radiator attaches to this base. When the two bolts are out, pull the base down and move fast to avoid gallons of coolant running down your arm. Feel up inside the pump for the thermostat. All you can see of it is a brass colored metal disc. Use your fingers to pull it all the way out of the pump. Screw the 10mm bolts back into the pump for safekeeping and let the pump base (still attached to the big hose) hang down loosely.

Loosen the clamps securing the two hoses to the back of the water pump, then pull the hoses free. Don't use anything like a screwdriver to lever them off unless they're damaged already. As you pull on the hoses be careful not to slip and skin your knuckles.

If the drained coolant in the catch pan is a clear green, pour it from the catch pan into a screw top container and stash it. If it's milky, discolored with rust or generally cruddy, go to Procedure 2, Step 8, and flush the cooling system with water. Then come back here.

Step 4. Clear the Decks

Begin by removing the V-belt pulley from the front of the water pump. The pulley is usually held by three 13mm bolts and washers. Mark and Baggie. If your model has an air injection pump, loosen the 13mm nuts holding it to the bracket and swing it toward the engine, then remove the V-belt. Next remove the alternator, the how-to is in Chapter 8, Procedure 1, Step 3.

Now you must remove the T-head bolt which holds the drive belt guard to the water pump. Remove the 10mm nut and pull it and the washer off the bolt. Next pull the bolt out from the rear of the pump and Baggie the lot. Leave the two metal washers and the rubber grommet through which the bolt goes in the drive belt guard.

Step 5. Remove Water Pump

If you have an air injection (smog) pump and air conditioning, the injection pump may be held to a bracket bolted onto the water pump. It's also possible that part of the air conditioner mount is secured by the bolts holding the water pump onto the crankcase. There are lots of combinations so figure out which is yours and deal with it. Remove and Baggie the three or four 13mm bolts holding the water pump to the crankcase.

Hold the pump firmly with both hands and pull it away from the engine. You might have to wiggle and hassle with it a bit but don't use anything to lever it off. It'll come. Thread the pump out of the engine compartment and drain out any coolant left inside.

Step 6. Disassemble Water Pump

Remove the seven 10mm bolts that hold the two pump halves together and pry the pump apart. Don't worry about breaking the paper gasket, you have to replace it anyway. Scrub the rear part of the pump clean and remove *all* traces of rust and gasket material from the machined face that mates with the front half. You might have to use a razor blade or spray it with gasket remover. Whatever you do, get it shiny bright.

Step 7. Assemble New Water Pump

Take your new pump out of its box and examine it very carefully for cracks or unwanted pieces of metal stuck to the rear machined face. Hold it against the old other pump half. It fits? Wunderbar! as they say in Germany. Apply a thin line of Permatex to both mating surfaces and stick the gasket onto the rear half of the pump. It fits only one way. Match the two halves and install all seven bolts. Torque them diagonally (Chapter 20, Procedure 7) to 1 mkg (7 ft lbs). That's not very tight, so those of you who don't have a torque wrench use a gentle arm. Now install the V-belt pulley and torque the 13mm bolts to 2 mkg (14 ft lbs).

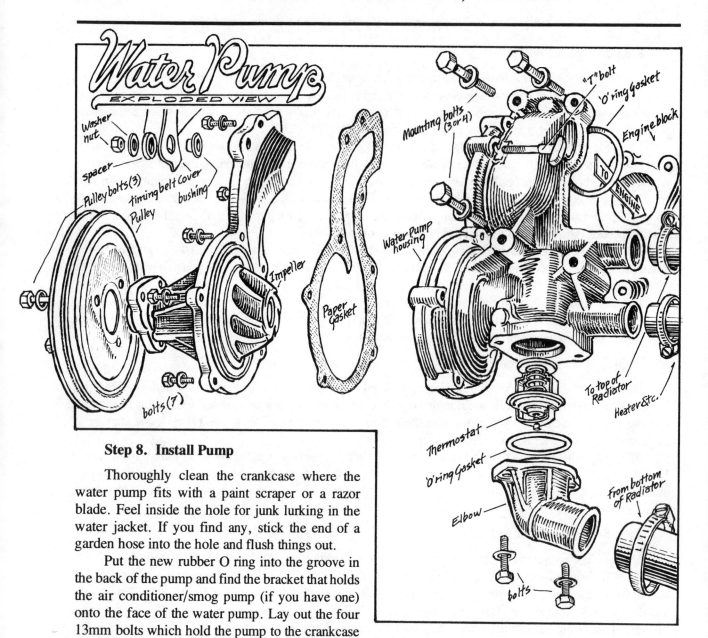

Step 8. Install Pump

Thoroughly clean the crankcase where the water pump fits with a paint scraper or a razor blade. Feel inside the hole for junk lurking in the water jacket. If you find any, stick the end of a garden hose into the hole and flush things out.

Put the new rubber O ring into the groove in the back of the pump and find the bracket that holds the air conditioner/smog pump (if you have one) onto the face of the water pump. Lay out the four 13mm bolts which hold the pump to the crankcase (the two short ones go at the top). Stick one of the four bolts through the bracket, into the water pump and screw it into the side of the crankcase—fingertight. Install the other three bolts and torque them all to 2 mkg (14 ft lbs).

Step 9. Install This and That

Put the T-head bolt through the back of the water pump and push it into the drive belt guard. Don't knock the washers or the spacer out of the guard. Install and tighten the nut.

Install the smog pump, then the alternator (Chapter 8, Procedure 2, Step 3). Install the V-belt on the water pump pulley, alternator pulley and crankshaft pulley after checking the belt for tears and cracks. Replace it if it's worn. Make sure you've got the correct belt; it's the longer of the two you removed. Adjust the V-belt to 10mm to 15mm (3/8 in to 9/16 in) deflection. Replace the V belt on the smog pump if you have one and get 10-15mm (3/8-9/16 in) deflection here also. The belt deflection Procedure is the same as described in Chapter 8, Procedure 2, Step 3.

Step 10. Install Hoses and Thermostat

Use a cloth to wipe the insides of the two hoses that attach to the rear of the water pump. Now push the hoses back onto the pump and tighten the hose clamps. If the clamps aren't in good condition, replace them

Step 10. (Cont'd.)

with new ones. Push the thermostat back into the water pump, narrow disc goes in first. Position the rubber O ring on the pump base (still held onto the large radiator hose) and bolt the base back onto the pump using the two 10mm bolts.

Step 11. Fill With Coolant

If your old coolant is clean (a clear green) pour it into the radiator or expansion bottle. Keep the heater control lever on the dash fully on so the coolant can entirely fill the system. The coolant should be up to the top line in the radiator or expansion bottle.

If your old coolant was foul and dungy, refill the system with a fresh 60% phospherous-free antifreeze, 40% water mix. Use 2.6 liters (2.76 U.S. quarts) of water to 3.9 liters (4.14 U.S. quarts) of antifreeze. Coolant in? Check all the hoses and clamps and then start the engine and run it for a minute. Turn if off and check the coolant level. If it's low add enough so it's up to the top mark but don't overfill it. Start the engine and run it for five minutes, then turn it off and remove the radiator expansion bottle cap and check the coolant level again. OK? Pour leftover coolant mix into a screw top container to use for future "topping ups." Dispose of old cruddy antifreeze by bottling it and giving it to the trash collector. Please don't pour old coolant down the drain; you might end up drinking it someday.

PROCEDURE 2: CHECK CAUSE OF ENGINE OVERHEATING. Phase 2.

Condition: Red light (thermometer symbol) comes on and/or the engine overheats.

Tools and materials: Phase 2 tool kit, safety glasses, maybe more coolant, new hoses and clamps, rule or tape measure.

Remarks: If the car overheated but the red thermometer symbol warning light didn't go on, go to Chapter 8, Procedure 1, Steps 3, 4 and 5 and check the bulb (the Procedure's the same as for alternator bulb). If the bulb checked out OK but there's something else wrong, go to Procedure 5 in this Chapter to get the warning system working. Then come back here to fix the overheating problem.

Do not remove the radiator or expansion bottle cap if the engine is very hot. Wait fifteen minutes or so for things to cool down.

The electric cooling fan should be spinning its blades off. No? Do this Procedure before turning to the fan Procedure 3 in this Chapter. Check that the ignition timing is correct before you begin (Chapter 10, Procedure 16).

Step 1. Check Brakes

Put the car in Neutral, handbrake off, and push. The car should move. If it doesn't, the brakes are stuck so go to Chapter 14 and read it.

Step 2. Check Coolant Level

If the engine is very hot, lift and prop the hood, then relax a while until the electric fan turns off. People with plastic expansion bottles: see if the coolant is below the bottom line or is missing altogether. Radiator cap models: you're risking bad hand and face burns if you try to remove the cap when the coolant is boiling hot. When things are cool, remove the cap, keeping your face and body away from the car. With the cap off, see if the coolant is up to scratch. If it's on the mark, go to Step 3.

Step 2. (Cont'd.)

If it's low, ideally you should add an antifreeze/water mixture but if you're out on the road find some clean water.

Don't use dirty bile from the roadside ditch; it'll clog the cooling system. Start the engine and pour coolant (or the water) into the radiator or expansion bottle until it's up to the bottom mark. Screw the cap back on and leave the engine running. After a minute or two turn the engine off and check the level again. OK? On your way. If you used water only, remember to add antifreeze when you get home and the engine is cold. If the coolant level is low again, continue...

Step 3. Check Hoses

Check inside the engine compartment for broken hoses. Put your safety glasses on. Squeeze the hoses with your hands and look for cracks, especially around the hose clamps. Watch and be wary of coolant escaping from cuts, cracks or pinholes. Don't forget the small hose at the rear of the cylinder head while checking.

Examine the metal pipe running from the small hose to the water pump. If your car is carbureted, check the two small hoses running to the automatic choke. If your hoses are OK, go to Step 4.

Broken hoses are a cinch to replace. If any of the lower hoses have bust or split, first drain the coolant into a clean catch pan (Procedure 1, Step 3) before installing a new hose. Replacing the top hose will cause a little coolant to be lost, but not enough to warrant the hassle of draining the coolant into the catch pan. Anyway, if anything is broken you've probably lost the coolant already! If any of the clamps on any hoses are rusty or deformed, buy new ones.

Buy new hoses from VW if possible. They usually have the correct hose in stock and they fit better than copies.

To remove an old hose, first completely loosen the hose clamps at each end and slide them up the hose away from the ends. Hold the hose tightly just behind the hose clamp and pull. If it won't come off easily, cut the hose off with a sharp knife. Don't use a screwdriver to lever a hose off, especially if it's stuck hard onto the radiator. You may ruin the brazed connection and that's an expense and a time waster.

When the old hose is off, clean the connections with a rag until they shine. Slip the hose clamps onto the center of the new hose. Moisten the inside of the hose with water and slide the hose onto its connections. Push the clamps into place about 10mm - 15mm (3/8 in - 9/16 in) from the end of the hose and tighten them with your screwdriver.

Replace any lost coolant.

Step 4. Check Water Pump V-Belt

Examine the V-belt at the front of the engine to see if it's broken. If it is, go to Chapter 8, Procedure 2, Step 3. If not, check that it has the 10mm - 15mm (3/8 - 9/16 in) deflection (Chapter 8, Procedure 2, Step 3). It's OK? Continue.

Step 5. Does Electric Fan Work?

If your engine is very hot, the electric fan should be whirring away like a hungry banshee. Fan works? Go to Step 6. Silence? The fan or the thermoswitch is broken. I hope it's the switch. Check it by reading through Procedure 3 in this Chapter.

Step 6. Does Water Pump Work?

Drain the coolant through the pump base: remove the two 10mm bolts, then remove the thermostat from inside the pump body (Procedure 1, Step 3). Install the pump base (Procedure 1, Step 10) and fill the system with clean water.

Loosen the hose clamp around the end of the large hose on the top of the radiator, pull the hose away and start the engine. A steady stream of water should be pumped out of the disconnected hose. A *steady* stream, not a trickle. If you don't get a good flow, first check all the hoses for obstructions by taking them off and looking through them. If you don't see daylight, flush them out with the garden hose. Replace any cracked,

Step 6. (Cont'd.)

worn or crudded up hoses. If the hoses are OK, the water pump is broken (Procedure 1).

If water flowed freely through, let's make sure there's no junk clogging the system anywhere. Do the next Step even if you've installed new hoses.

Step 7. Flush Cooling System

If you've been pouring a leak sealer or flushing agent into the radiator, there's a good chance the stuff has dislodged rust and junk from inside the water jacket and the stuff has collected in the water pump or one of the hoses.

The coolant is already drained from Step 6. Take a look at it. If it's brown and dirty, with plastic ducks floating on top, get rid of it and buy a new bottle of phosphorous-free antifreeze. Reconnect all the radiator hoses (except the top radiator hose) and secure them with hose clamps. Put the garden hose back into the top of the radiator or plastic expansion bottle and flush the system once again. Flush 'til the water runs clear or for a couple of minutes and then start the engine, run it for five minutes, turn it off and pull the base of the water pump off (two 10mm bolts). If the water draining out still isn't clear, reinstall the pump base and go through the routine until it is clear. When you get a clear rush, leave the pump base off, but reconnect the hose to the top of the radiator.

If you've been referred here from elsewhere, remove the thermostat, Procedure 1, Step 3, then come back here.

Time to make a refreshing drink—a thermostat glace. Put the thermostat in a bowl of cold water and toss in a few ice cubes. Soak it for ten minutes. Get your rule or tape measure and measure the thermostat and check it against the 'cold' dimension in Peter's drawings.

Boil a pan of water, let it cool for five minutes, then drop the cold thermostat into the hot water. Ouch. Let it stew for three minutes. Take it out of the pan with a fork, lay it on the table and measure it. Compare your dimension to the 'hot' dimension in the drawing. If either the cold or hot dimensions aren't as in the diagram, buy a new thermostat. Test your new thermostat in the same manner. One hellish day my brother ran through five before he finally got one that worked.

If the thermostat tested OK, put it back into the pump and pour in the coolant (Procedure 1, Steps 10 and 11). Start the engine. Does it run cool? If not, continue.

Step 8. Check Valve Timing

Turn to Chapter 10, Procedure 23. If that doesn't help, the radiator cap or expansion bottle cap is possibly faulty, or the radiator is clogged or damaged. If you've been using antifreeze containing phosphorous, the radiator could be clogged. Only steam cleaning can cure it.

Step 9. Check Pressure Cap

Testing the pressure cap has to be done by a garage with a special tool. It's easier to buy a new cap. Gas engines use Part #171 121 321 and diesels use #171 121 321B.

Step 10. Here's a Weird One

It seems that the radiator can corrode internally if the electric cooling fan motor is faulty. Pull off the two wires from the thermoswitch on the left side of the radiator. Find your VOM and switch it to 15 volts DC. Put the negative VOM probe on the negative battery post and touch the positive probe to the fan motor housing. If there's a positive reading (if the needle moves up the scale at all) the fan motor is faulty. Change it (Procedure 4). You'll also have to remove the radiator and get it steam cleaned (Step 12).

A slight negative voltage reading is fine, so reattach the thermoswitch wires.

Step 11. Remove Radiator

Loosen the hose clamps on the three hoses attached to the radiator and pull the hoses off. Unplug the cooling fan and thermoswitch wires. Remove the 10mm nuts which hold each side of the radiator to the bottom front crossmember. Disconnect the diverter valve or barometric cell from the top right of the radiator. Lift the radiator clear of the studs, and free the U- or Z-shaped wire holding it to the top crossmember. Turn to Procedure 4 in this chapter and do Steps 1 and 2 to remove the electric fan and its shroud. Take the radiator to the shop and ask their advice on the radiator's condition.

If the radiator shop people tell you your radiator is done for, ask them if they've got a decent one lying around. If not, look in a junkyard for a used one. Check used radiators very carefully before you buy and insist on a written guarantee. Screw your thermoswitch out of the old radiator to put into the new.

Step 12. Install Radiator

First install the cooling fan (Procedure 4) and screw in the thermoswitch on the side of the radiator if you haven't done so yet. Push the U- or Z-shaped clip into the top of the radiator and hook it into its slot on the top front crossmember. When the clip's in, lower the radiator onto the bottom crossmember studs and screw on the two 10mm nuts. Push the coolant hoses into position and secure them with hose clamps. Connect the thermoswitch electrical wires, snap in the cooling fan plug, install the diverter valve or barometric cell and you're done.

PROCEDURE 3: CHECK COOLING FAN OPERATION. Phase 2.

Condition: Cooling fan doesn't come on when engine is hot.

Tools and materials: Phase 2 tool kit, fuses, test light or Volt-Ohmmeter (VOM).

Remarks: Check all the fuses in the relay plate above the driver's legs before you begin work. Flip open the hinged plastic cover to replace any blown fuses (the thin metal strip down the face of the fuse is broken) with one of the same color.

Step 1. Check Electrical Connections

Open the hood and prop it. Feel down the left side of the radiator for the thermoswitch. Keep your fingers away from the fan blades in case the fan suddenly decides to switch itself on. The thermoswitch has two electrical connections. Pull them off. Check that the two connectors are clean and in good condition. If not, clean them with a small wire brush. Examine the ground connection at the end of the brown wire which starts at the switch and ends up grounding on the body just below and in front of the battery. Now look at the two connecting terminals on the thermoswitch itself. Clean them if they don't shine. Plug the wires back in, start the engine and run it until it's hot. Still no fan motions? Shut off the engine and read on.

The fan motor has either a rubber plug or a wire in the back. If yours has a wire, follow it for about 15cm (6 in) until your fingers trip over a two-piece plastic electrical connector. Check it for dirt, grime and loose wires. Clean it if need be and make sure the two halves of the connector are firmly pushed together. If there's a plug in the back of your motor, check it for inner cleanliness and tight fit.

Start the car again and get the engine hot. If the fan still doesn't work and you have an air conditioner, check the relay which partially controls its operation. No air conditioner—go to Step 3.

Step 2. Check Fan Relay—Air-Conditioned Cars Only

The function of the relay is to turn on the radiator cooling fan as soon as the air conditioner is used. This prevents the engine from overheating and cools the freon in the condenser fitted just in front of the radiator. Factory installed air conditioners have the relay installed inside the engine compartment on the left front part

Step 2. (Cont'd.)

of the fender just in front of the battery. The relay could be anywhere in the engine compartment if the air conditioner was installed by a non-VW agency or private party.

To check the relay, lift and prop the hood and ask Friend to push the air conditioner temperature control lever to the coldest setting. Then turn the key to ON and push on the air conditioner fan lever. The radiator cooling fan should burst into life. No? Switch your VOM to 15 volts DC and pull off the top right wire (probably brown) from the relay. Put one VOM probe on the vacant relay connection and the other into the connector on the wire you pulled off the relay. You should get a 12 volt reading with the ignition switch ON and both air conditioner controls on. No? Bad relay. Buy a new one from VW and install it.

Step 3. Check the Thermoswitch

Keep the key turned to ON. If you don't have a VOM or test light handy, find a short piece of electrical wire about 15cm (6 in) long, and strip 25mm (1 in) of insulation from each end. This will be your jumper wire. Find the electrical connector on the wire which runs to the fan motor connection from the thermoswitch on the side of the radiator. This is the hot wire; pull it at the thermoswitch end. Leave the ground wire connected to the thermoswitch. Push one end of your jumper wire or positive VOM probe (switched to 15 volts DC) into the end of the connector you just pulled and touch the other end (or other probe) to the metal electrical connection on the thermoswitch which still has the wire attached to it—the ground. Make sure there are no loose fingers, noses or elbows in the fan blades. If the fan starts to turn (VOM reads 12 volts DC), the thermoswitch is bad and must be replaced (go to Step 4). If the above test didn't get your fan working, we must suspect that the wiring or the fan motor is bad. In that case, go to Step 5.

Step 4. Replace Thermoswitch

Buy a new one as soon as possible. It's important not to run the engine without the fan being 'fully operational' as they say in the armed forces. Stick the electrical connection back onto the switch. When you've got a new thermoswitch, pull off the two electrical wires and use a crescent wrench to unscrew the faulty thermoswitch from your radiator. Screw in the new thermoswitch and tighten it up. Don't overdo it. Install the electrical connectors, and you're finished.

Step 5. Check Power Supply To Cooling Fan

Find your VOM (or test light) and switch it to 15 volts DC. No VOM? Check your test light by touching the probes to the battery posts. It should light.

Leave both electrical wires connected to the rear of the thermoswitch. Turn the key to ON and push the positive probe of the VOM or test light into the rear of one of the hot connections on the thermoswitch. (There are two wires running to this single connector.) Put the negative probe onto the ground connection on the switch. The needle on the meter should read 12 volts DC or your test light should shine. Put the red probe onto the other wire on the hot side of the switch and touch ground again with the other probe. A reading of 12 volts DC or the shine of the test light indicates power to the switch. No power, check the wires to the switch for breaks, etc., and check for shorts (Chapter 20, Procedure 10).

If you have power to the switch, the fan motor is burnt out or there's a break in one of the wires running to and from the motor.

Let's check the wires to the fan motor for cracked insulation. It's possible that the wire is grounding against something. Out with the VOM again and check continuity in the wires.

Remove the battery ground strap (10mm wrench) and tuck it out of the way. Switch your meter to RX1K and test the wires running to the fan. Chapter 20, Procedure 10, tells how to do this test.

If the wires are OK, the fan motor is shot and you will have to replace it! Comparison shop by telephoning a few electric motor shops to ask how much they charge to rebuild a motor like yours. Compare this price with a guaranteed motor from a junkyard. Then call VW to ask the price of a new one.

PROCEDURE 4: REPLACE COOLING FAN. Phase 1.

Condition: The fan motor is shot.

Tools and materials: Phase 1 tool kit, new or rebuilt cooling fan motor.

Step 1. Pull Electrical Connection from Back of Fan Motor

You've begun.

Step 2. Remove Motor and Shroud

If yours is a carbureted model and you don't live in Europe, there's a diverter valve bolted to the top right of the radiator. If yours is fuel injected and you live at a high altitude, there's a barometric cell bolted to the top right of the radiator. Remove the bolts (10mm or 13mm wrench) holding your particular piece of equipment to the radiator. Push the valve or cell to one side and screw back the bolts into the radiator for safekeeping.

Two bolts on each side of the rear face of the radiator hold the fan shroud to the body of the radiator. Remove all four bolts (10mm wrench). Next remove the U- or Z-shaped piece of wire from the top of the radiator. Use a pair of pliers or a screwdriver to wiggle it free. Now lift out the shroud containing the fan motor and the rubber flaps. Loosely install the four 10mm bolts into the holes in the rear of the radiator for safe-keeping.

Step 3. Free Motor From Shroud

Lay the shroud face down on your work table and remove the three 10mm nuts and bolts holding the fan motor to the shroud.

Use a screwdriver to lever open the metal clip holding the electrical cable (if you have one) on the shroud. Pull the fan motor clear.

Step 4. Install New Motor

Take the fan blade off your old motor and install it onto the new motor if it doesn't have one. Place the new motor onto the shroud, install the three 10mm nuts and bolts and tighten them. Fit the electric cable (if any) under the metal clip and close the clip with a screwdriver (without cutting the cable insulation).

Step 5. Install Fan and Shroud

Remove the four 10mm bolts from the rear of the radiator and position the shroud so the holes in it match up with the holes in the radiator. Screw in all four bolts with your fingers and when they're in place, tighten them. Use a pair of pliers to put the U- or Z-shaped piece of wire between the top of the radiator and the top front crossmember.

Step 6. Install Diverter Valve or Barometric Cell (if present)

Position the valve or cell on the top right of the radiator and secure it with the 10mm or 13mm bolts. Tighten the bolts.

Now all that remains is to plug in the wire to the back of the fan motor and hook up the battery ground strap (10mm wrench). Check all electrical connections, including the thermoswitch on the side of the radiator. Start the engine and when it's hot, the cooling fan will whirr into action.

PROCEDURE 5: CHECK INTERIOR HEATING SYSTEM. Phase 2.

Condition: Interior heater output poor but the engine temperature is normal, heater motor doesn't work.

Tools and materials: Phase 1 tool kit, flashlight, maybe a new thermostat or radiator thermoswitch.

Step 1. Check Heater Cables

Pull the handles off the heater control levers sticking out from the dashboard. Give them a firm tug to get them off. Now pull off the heater fan motor knob if you have one. Use your fingernails to carefully lever the

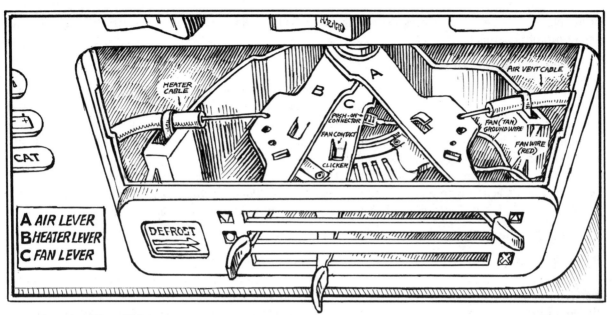

Step 1. (Cont'd.)

plastic panel around the heater levers out from the dash.

Each heater control lever is fastened to a wire secured to the end of the lever by a metal clip. Check the clips carefully—you may need a flashlight to see in there. If a wire has slipped off the lever, the clip is probably missing. You wondered from whence cometh that little metal thing that the baby was sucking on.

Buy a new clip from VW and reattach the wire to the lever. Look at the way the clip holds the wire on the other levers. The clip must go on and secure the plastic wire sheath. All on? Reinstall the panel, the heater fan knob and the lever handles.

To replace a broken heater control wire, leave the old broken wire in there and run the new wire alongside it. Follow the old wire from the lever to the heater box fitted under the dash and unhook the old wire and put on the new. I'm sorry I can't be more helpful, but it would take 50 pages to describe exactly how to do it and really, it's an easy job. Reinstall the lever, knob and panel when you're finished. If the cables were OK and the motor works but puts out cold air, go to Step 5.

Step 2. Check Electrical Components (1975 and 1976 Models)

These cars have an electrical contact on the right hand heater lever switches to turn the heater motor on. Pull off all the lever handles and pop out the plastic panel from the dash. Clean the electrical contacts with a fine emery board. Turn the key to ON and push the heater fan motor lever all the way right to ON. If the heater motor still won't go on, check the electrical wire and the spade connection on the end. It fastens to the connection on the right side of the bottom heater control lever. If that won't fix it, test the continuity of the wire (Chapter 20, Procedure 10). Replace a bad wire. A good wire means that the heater motor is burnt out. Go to Step 4.

Step 3. Check Switch Components (1977 and on models)

These cars have a separate rotary 'click' switch to the left of the heater control levers to turn on the heater fan motor. The switch sometimes gives out or will work only in one position. If the heater motor refuses to work at all, reach up behind the dash and check that the electrical plug to the back of the switch is pushed fully home.

If the plug is on, the switch is probably defunct. Pull off the plastic heater control levers and the heater fan motor knob, and gently pry the plastic panel out from the dash. The switch is held to the dash by two spring metal ears. Squeeze the ears between your thumb and forefinger and pull the switch forward out of the dash.

Buy a new switch, push the plug onto its back and install the switch into the dash. Do this in the dealer's parking lot so if a new switch doesn't change things, you can return it. If a new switch doesn't fix it, the wiring or the electric motor is bad. Check the wiring with a VOM (Chapter 20, Procedure 10). Wiring OK? The heater motor is defunct.

Step 4. Liberate Heater Fan Motor

If the heater fan motor should go to motor heaven, you'll have to pry open the heater housing at the base of the dash to get at the motor. It's the big black thing that fits in that space between the driver's and passenger's legs. The two halves of the housing are held together by metal clips and the motor is held inside the housing by two screws or clips. I don't mess with this stuff often, it's a pain in the butt. I've never actually seen a bad motor, the switch is usually faulty.

However, when you get to the motor, test it with your VOM (Chapter 20, Procedure 10) and replace it if need be. Test its action before you install the housing. OK? Put everything back together, push the heater panel into the dash, put the levers and heater fan motor control knob back on and you're done.

Step 5. Check Electric Radiator Cooling Fan

Remarks: Air-conditioned cars turn your air conditioner control levers off.

Lift and prop the hood and ask Friend to start the engine. Does the electric radiator fan switch on immediately after starting the car? If so, the thermoswitch on the side of the radiator has decided to stick in the closed position. Buy a new one from VW, pull off the two electrical wires and unscrew the old one (crescent wrench). Carefully screw in the new one with your fingers and tighten it with the crescent wrench. Not too tight, please. Reinstall the electrical wires and start the engine. The fan won't switch on until the coolant gets hot. You'll now get a good blast of heat from the heater.

Was your cooling fan working OK? If the engine stays cool, then the thermostat in the water pump is warped and must be replaced (Procedure 2, Step 9).

PROCEDURE 6: CHECK COOLANT TEMPERATURE SENDING UNIT. Phase 1.

Condition: Water temperature gauge reads low or high but the engine stays cool, the radiator cooling fan works, and the heater works OK.

Tools and materials: Phase 1 tool kit, new sending unit.

Step 1. Check That Idiot Light is Working

The bulb behind the thermometer symbol on the dash can be checked using the same method to check the alternator bulb in Chapter 8, Procedure 1, Steps 3, 4 and 5. Bulb OK? Continue.

Step 2. Test Sending Unit

The sending unit is the metal cylinder screwed into the small aluminum manifold on the rear of the cylinder head. A heater hose also attached to the flange goes through the firewall.

Does the idiot light go on or the needle on the gauge swing up to red every time the ignition is switched to ON? If so, leave the ignition switched to ON. Pull the wire off the sending unit and clean the wire with a cloth. Touch the end of the wire to a clean unpainted metal ground (like the cylinder head). If the gauge moves upward or the idiot light comes on, the sending unit is bad. Go to Step 3 and replace it. If the needle stays put or the light stays off, either the wiring is bad (check it with the VOM meter, Chapter 20, Procedure 10) or the gauge has retired from active service. You must pull off the dash panel to replace it. Ask VW to do it for you.

Step 3. Replace Sending Unit

Pull the wire off the sending unit and unscrew the unit with a crescent wrench. You'll lose a little coolant but don't worry. Screw a new sending unit into position, hook up the electrical connection and top up the radiator or expansion bottle with your stash of water/antifreeze mixture.

CHAPTER 18

➤ ENGINE REBUILD ➤

This Chapter is about how to rebuild your Rabbit or Scirocco gasoline engine. In this edition I don't get into rebuilding the diesel engine, although it's very similar to the gasoline version.

The in-line water cooled engine is a high revving little rabette, and was built with all its internal parts carefully fitted and balanced. It likes to remain that way. However, if you're on your way to Alamogordo and your engine destroys a rod bearing, you are, as the matador might comment, on the horns of a dilemma. If you're short of time and cash, you can pull off the oil pan and if the crankshaft's undamaged you can slip in a new rod bearing, change the oil, and limp the rest of the way home. But you *must* overhaul the engine properly at your first available opportunity. If you don't have the money to do it right now, park the car and hide the key under the bed so you're not tempted to keep using it.

A friend of mine replaced a rod bearing on the road, then flew to Spain for a deserved holiday. While he was away, his cousin borrowed the car for a quick run to Los Angeles. A hundred miles east of L.A. the car melted part of its crankshaft. The reason? After my friend had installed the new rod bearing, he unfortunately neglected to torque the rod bolts correctly and one of the nuts came off. It jammed between the side of the crankshaft and the crankcase and whupped the crankshaft beyond recognition. The chap had a very expensive trip to L.A. and back. Let this be a warning. Make sure a temporary repair becomes a permanent one very shortly afterwards.

Notes on the cylinder head: The overhead camshaft engine must have its valves correctly adjusted. If you've driven the last 10,000 miles with the valves too tight, the lobes of the camshaft are going to complain. Read Chapter 10, Procedure 22, and avoid a valve job. Valve jobs I don't do. I have neither the tools nor the inclination because the people at Elmer's machine shop are a thousand times better and quicker than I.

If you destroy a valve or two somewhere on the road, pull the cylinder head off and take it to the closest machine shop or VW dealer to get a valve job. If you want to really keep your engine alive, this is not a vehicle in which you can pull the head, slip in a used valve and make it. No cash? Take the head to a machine shop, and either wire Mum for $$ or work in a local store for a day or two until you have enough money to get the head out of the shop and back into your car.

I usually replace all the bearings when I overhaul an engine. Since I've gone to all the trouble to get the engine out of the car, disassembled and cleaned, it's worth replacing all those bearings, especially if the engine's innards were sprinkled with thousands of broken up bearing remnants. Please resist the temptation to

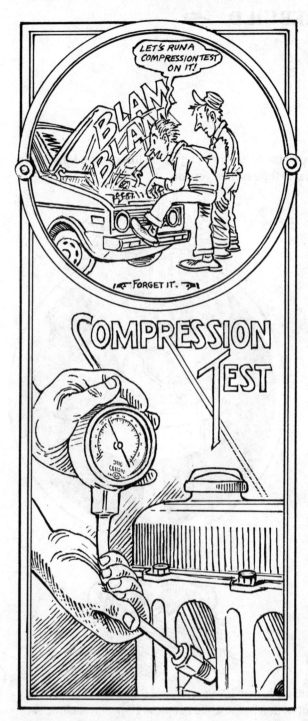

think that if a part looks alright, it *is* alright. Only Superperson has the ability to see through steel with X-ray vision. You and I mortals must first visually inspect the bearing surfaces for nicks, dents, scratches, etc., then measure them.

Why does a perfectly healthy sounding engine with 50,000 miles on it suddenly start sounding like a steam locomotive with square wheels? Well, it's usually due to simple neglect. I just rebuilt a Rabbit with only 28,000 miles on it. It had surprisingly (for the owner) developed an incredible knock. When I lifted the hood and inspected the dipstick, I could not find the slightest evidence of that vital ingredient—oil. When I drained the 'oil' from the engine, I managed to get enough to lubricate my daughter's tricycle. No wonder the engine was knocking. It's amazing it was still in one piece, and not a molten blob.

Periodic maintenance saves time, trouble, paranoia and expense. When engines begin to approach 100,000 miles, things will have worn a little but I see no reason why a well-maintained Rabbit shouldn't hop along for 150,000 trouble-free miles.

Your car, however, might need an engine overhaul at 40,000 miles if the person who previously owned it didn't maintain it properly, constantly loaded it to the gills and drove stop-start in downtown Suburboville. So…what *you* have to rely on is regular maintenance, a compression check every six months and interpretation and correction of any strange noises the engine makes. Chapter 10, Procedure 20, tells how to do a compression check and interpret your findings.

The Diagnosis, Please, Doctor!

The compression check is not all, by any means. The number of miles on your odometer gives an indication of wear, as does the scum and grime collected on and around the engine. A recent noticeable lack of power, even after a Chapter 10 Tune-up, indicates overhaul time is imminent. A cross country trip in a car with low compression, loaded with four persons and towing an Air Stream trailer will do your engine no good at all. This is a sure way to hasten overhaul time. High mileage, low compression, big appetite for oil and smoky exhaust add up to the inescapable fact that it's time to get your hands really greasy.

There are more considerations: noises. My companion has threatened to kick me out of the car when she's driving and I suddenly awaken from a deep sleep shouting, ''Pull over, pull over!'' The startled look on her face is matched by mine—due to the pain in my shoulder from the blows that I receive. The ear, however, has often saved us from the greasy nose.

Any slight change in the noises coming from the engine compartment should immediately make you perk up and listen more attentively to what's going on. If you hear new noises and dismiss them with, ''Ah blast it, it'll be OK in a while,'' you'll become accustomed to the noise even if it gets louder. First look around for little things like a frayed timing belt or a twig caught in the drive belt guard. Perhaps some junk is caught in one of the V-belt pulleys, which'll make a ticking noise as the V-belt passes over the offending garbage. Found nothing? A noise can sometimes be traced to improperly adjusted valves. Read Procedure 22 in Chapter 10.

Noise Checks

If after adjusting the valves, you still have unusual engine noises, further investigation is needed. A loud knocking from the engine means that something's amiss so you may as well get ready to rebuild. In which case, *don't* start the engine, you may do more damage.

Do the following checks (unless your engine noise is very loud). Start the engine and let it warm up. Get out of the car, lift and prop the hood and rev the engine by pulling on the accelerator cable. Hold it there for a few seconds, then let go of the cable and listen for a tick-tick-tick at the moment you release the cable. Repeat this six or seven times. If you hear the tick you have a rod knocking. This is neither an infectious nor pernicious disease. It can be cured by an immediate engine overhaul. You could drive the car very carefully for 2 or 3 more weeks but beyond that, you're well into the badlands. If you're on the road and hear the tick-tick-tick, do this 'hill test.'

Drive it up a hill in third gear with the gas pedal to the floor for a few seconds, then release it. Listen for the tick. If you hear it, baby the car for the rest of your journey. If it's really loud, pull over and save the crankshaft! Ask Friend to tow you home (Chapter 6).

A knocking sound from the engine may be indicating worn main bearings. As with a bad rod, this noise too, will be louder when the engine is suddenly relaxed after having been under load (the hill test). In this case, the knocking sound is deeper. The nasty noises may be symptoms of a broken piston ring, cracked or broken cam follower in the head, sticking valves, loose rod bearing caps, or your grandma's false teeth chattering in the trunk.

If you hear any strange noises as you're driving, pull over to the side of the road and remove the cam cover and carefully check the cam follower adjusting discs under the camshaft lobes. If one is cracked, replace it and check all your valve clearances (Chapter 10, Procedure 22). Finally, if you hear a noise like it's raining cannon balls, remove the cam cover and tighten the cylinder head bolts in diagonal sequence as per Procedure 9 in this chapter.

When you've come to the inescapable conclusion that the engine needs overhauling, what are you going to do next? You have three choices: buy a new engine, overhaul it yourself or have it done by a VW dealer, an independent mechanic or the local butcher who repairs engines on weekends. Take your choice. The first two will do a good job and guarantee their work. The third person will *probably* do a good job, but then again . . . You might be able to connect with a Volkswagen mechanic who does outside work in the evening and on weekends.

If you're not into doing the overhaul yourself, there are still ways to save $$. You can remove the engine and the transmission, separate them, remove the hardware, then take the engine to the rebuild person or shop to let them have at it. Try to talk the owner of the machine shop into charging you wholesale prices for the new parts required. Maybe you could sweep out the shop a few times to return the favor. When the engine is overhauled, drag it home and reinstall it yourself.

Before you take your engine to a machine shop, however, call the local hotrod places and car dealers and ask the service managers who has the best machine shop in town. Everybody usually comes up with the same name. That's the person for you. Now check the cost of an overhaul at the VW dealer against one at this primo machine shop.

If you have to replace the pistons, connecting rods and crankshaft, you're going to spend a lot of money. If the crankshaft is regrindable and the pistons and rods are OK, you'll save! If you do all the work yourself, you'll eliminate labor costs and profits.

An overhaul takes about a week: one day to get the engine/transmission out and to split the transmission from the engine, at least three days in the machine shop and then another day to put it all back together.

Another consideration: How about installing a used engine? It may be possible to come across a Rabbit that has just been wrecked and towed into a junkyard. Check out the number of miles on the odometer and if the engine still runs, do a compression check. If you decide to go this route, you can have your old engine out and the new used one installed in two days. Plus, you can trade in your old engine to the junkyard—every dollar helps. I've successfully been this route a number of times.

Before you plunk down the cash, however, check the engine out as carefully as possible. Read the tests in Chapter 3. You will find that most junkyard dealers will give a guarantee with their engines.

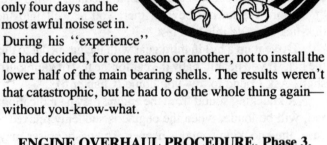

As you begin your overhaul, think about the cast of thousands who are probably doing the same thing at the same time. Draw strength in numbers and in the fact that you know that you can do it. Follow the Procedures carefully and mark and Baggie every nut, bolt, washer, etc. You will come to the conclusion that rebuilding an engine is FUN.

A guy I know decided to make his engine rebuild even more fun and enlightening with the help of a well-known hallucinogen. He did wonderfully. The engine was back in the car after only four days and he managed a journey of almost 600 yards before the most awful noise set in. During his ''experience'' he had decided, for one reason or another, not to install the lower half of the main bearing shells. The results weren't that catastrophic, but he had to do the whole thing again—without you-know-what.

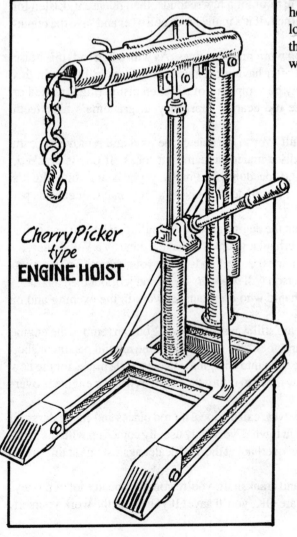

Cherry Picker type
ENGINE HOIST

ENGINE OVERHAUL PROCEDURE. Phase 3.

Remove and Strip Engine
Separate Transmission from Engine
Take off Engine Hardware
Tear the Engine Apart
Put Engine Back Together
Bolt Engine and Transmission Together
Install Engine Hardware
Put it all back into the car
Celebrate

Condition: The engine needs an overhaul.

Tools and materials:

Phase II tool kit	3M weatherstrip adhesive
12 point CV joint tool	tube of Permatex
10mm allen wrench or	piles of rags
polygon cylinder head	Liquid Wrench
bolt wrench	gallon of solvent
two jacks	parts cleaning pan and
strong blocks	stiff brush
plastic garbage bags	small roll of soft wire
paper & pencils	rubber hammer
assorted paper bags	inspection magnet
Baggies	roll of emery cloth
masking tape	electric drill and bits

small propane torch	assembly lubricant	oil filter	oil
coolant drain pan	air filter	fuel filter	EGR filter (1975 cars)
clean work space	clean work bench	strong hoist	Friend
indelible pen	*hone and honing bits	oil drain pan	*cylinder bore dial tester

Try to rent an engine stand which will hold the Rabbit engine. It's easier to work on the engine bolted to a stand than wrestle with it on a bench. Those little tags ⌐⌐⌐stores use to show prices are great to use as markers. A spray can of gasket remover and a gasket scraper is nice but not essential.

*The machine shop has these tools, so don't buy them.

Remarks: Rebuilding an engine is a big job but you can do it. Where most people run into trouble isn't in the overhaul itself but in getting the wires back onto their proper terminals. Pull off a vacuum hose one Friday evening, forget to mark it carefully, and a week later you can't remember where it came from. Mark everything and take it off and put it back on two or three times to help keep it in your memory.

If you get confused or bogged down halfway through a Procedure, don't lose heart; you can do it! Put your tools away, have a cup of something nice, take a walk…relax. When you can face it again, everything will go much easier.

Find a clean, well-lighted place to do your rebuild. If you plan to do it on the kitchen table check with friends or family before you plop a greasy engine down in front of them. The same goes for the living room floor, especially if there are curious kids around who might decide to help before you crawl out of bed some morning.

So you need a good work area and a tight system of bagging and marking parts. If you lose or misplace something, write it down immediately on two sheets of paper and replace the part. Draw diagrams of anything you find difficult to assemble. Do whatever makes life easier!

When the time comes to pull the engine from the car, invite a few friends over for a snack. They'll come in handy. The same goes for when you're ready to drop it back in or carry it up from the basement. My friend Eddie The Huge can just about lift an engine out with one hand, tuck it under his arm and carry it to the shop. You and I lesser mortals have to rely on friendship and a strong hoist.

Read each procedure thoroughly before you reach for your tools, and do everything *by the book*. Find a loyal Friend to read the instructions aloud as you work; it'll be a great help.

While you're doing the overhaul you might also want to replace the clutch and perhaps the engine/transmission mounts. We'll look into those when we come to them.

Take engine and chassis numbers along with the old parts when you go parts shopping.

Get Ready: Drive or tow the car to a car wash and thoroughly clean the engine and engine compartment. You'll be glad you did when it comes time to put tools in your hands.

If you're going to pull the engine on the street or in the front yard, clean your chosen area well, then park the car over it. Make sure you can rent a hoist when you need one and that all your friends haven't left town.

Before starting work, read Chapter 1, 4, 7, 20, and Chapter 12 if you've got fuel injection.

Where Am I? When I say the FRONT of the car I mean the front, the end that goes down the road first. The LEFT side is the driver's side, except in England and other weird places.

The *front* of the *engine* is where the timing belt and alternator V-belt are located. This means that the left side of the engine is where you'll find the spark plugs and the right side is where you'll find the intake and exhaust manifolds.

When you are facing a nut, bolt or screw and want to loosen it or take it out entirely, turn it COUNTERCLOCKWISE ↺ . This is to the left, the direction opposite to the movement of the hands of a clock. Those with digital watches will have to learn this now. Clockwise ↻ screws it back on.

PROCEDURE 1: STRIP AND REMOVE ENGINE/TRANSMISSION. Phase 2.

Put the car in Neutral, pull on the handbrake and chock the wheels. You don't want it moving around when you lift the engine out. Arrange all of your tools neatly around you. A table (got a fold-up picnic table?) is nice to have for laying out nuts, bolts and parts in a logical order before cleaning and labelling them. Here we go.

Step 1. Remove Hood

Although you can remove and install the engine with the hood in place it does tend to get in the way, especially if you're using a cherry picker type hoist. The hood is easy to remove and I suggest you do so to keep head bruises to a minimum.

Remove the two bolts from the hood hinge by the rear of the left or right fender (10mm socket). Drop the hinge and put the bolts back into the hood, fingertight. Have Friend hold the unsupported side as you go around and remove the other two 10mm bolts. Lift the hood clear and put it where it won't blow over and get banged up. Don't forget to screw in and fingertighten the other two bolts in the hood for safekeeping.

Step 2. Remove Battery

Remove both battery cables from the battery posts (10mm wrench) and the bolt on the clip that holds the bottom of the battery (13mm socket and extension).

Slide out the battery and store it somewhere safe. Remember it's full of acid so be careful. If you set it on a cement floor put a piece of wood or three or four newspapers down first. The New York Times Sunday edition works well. This prevents the battery from draining its current to ground. Cover it with a cardboard box to prevent children/pets from licking or sitting on it.

Step 3. Drain Oil and Remove Filter

Place an oil catch pan under the engine and remove the oil pan drain plug. Remove the filter from the left side of the engine with a filter wrench. Never done an oil change? Go to Chapter 10, Procedure 9, Steps 2 and 3. Put the filter into the oil drain pan. While the oil drains go to…

Step 4. Drain Coolant and Remove Thermostat

Move the heater temperature control all the way on. This drains any coolant from the heater. Put a clean catch pan under the car; a plastic dishpan works well. If you keep the coolant mixture clean, you can reuse it. Go back to Chapter 17 and do Procedure 1, Step 3; then come back.

Leave the catch pan under the car; you'll need it again in a minute.

Step 5. Remove Radiator and Cooling Fan

If you're here to pull the cylinder head, skip this Step.

Head back to Chapter 17, Procedure 2, Step 12. Mark the electrical connections 'fan' and 'thermo-switch' with tape and an indelible pen.

Store the radiator in a safe place. It's an expensive item and you don't want the kids to knock it over. Store the coolant in a closed container.

Step 6. Remove Air Conditioner and Condenser (not for Cylinder Head Removers). If you don't have air conditioning, go to Step 7.

WARNING! Do not loosen any air conditioner or compressor hoses! Just remove what I tell you; nothing more or you'll get a face full of freezing freon.

Snap open the connection in the wire going to the air conditioner compressor (a large silver gadget driven by a belt on the front left of the engine) and mark the ends. If there's a brown ground wire from the unit, remove it and mark it.

So many types of compressor mountings are used that you'll have to figure this one out for yourself. Check the bolts carefully and remove what you must—but don't remove the mounting bracket from the engine. Leave it in place for now.

When the compressor is loose, put it on the protected right fender. A hose runs from the compressor to the condenser (an additional radiator at the front of the car). Cover the condenser's inside face with a thick piece of cardboard and tape it in place to protect it while the engine is being lifted out.

Step 7. Electrical Disconnections

Take a close look at Peter's drawings on the following pages and compare them to your own car. By studying the diagrams you'll see what goes where and why. Follow the ABC order and nothing will go wrong. If you have any extra wires, just mark the wire and to what it fits. OK?

Arm yourself with your price tags, masking tape and an indelible pen. Clean the wires as you remove them so the tape or tags will stay put. Mark them clearly.

If you just want to remove the cylinder head for a valve job, remove only the electrical connections around the carburetor (fuel injection, around the intake manifold) and at the rear of the head.

You may have to cut some of the little plastic straps around the wiring harness in order to make the disconnections. Don't worry about it; you can replace them with electrical or telephone cable clips later (buy them at an electrical supply store) or just use good old fashioned black electrical insulating tape. Tuck loose wires away after labelling them.

People just removing the cylinder head to A, B, C and D only.

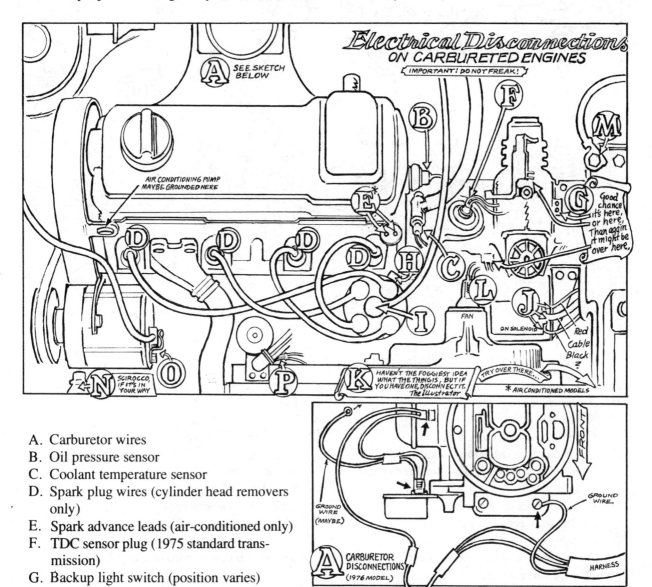

A. Carburetor wires
B. Oil pressure sensor
C. Coolant temperature sensor
D. Spark plug wires (cylinder head removers only)
E. Spark advance leads (air-conditioned only)
F. TDC sensor plug (1975 standard transmission)
G. Backup light switch (position varies)

Step 7. (Cont'd.)

H. Thin wire from coil

I. Thick wire from coil

J. Starter leads (one 13mm, two push-on wires; Automatics, see Chapter 7, Procedure 9, Steps 3 and 6)

K. Radiator thermoswitch (2 wires)

L. Radiator cooling fan

M. Ground strap on rear transmission mount

N. Bulb cap, Scirocco only

O. Alternator plug (8mm)

P. Diverter valve (was bolted to radiator)

Now check all your wires to see if everything's disconnected. Air-conditioned cars may have an extra ground wire somewhere.

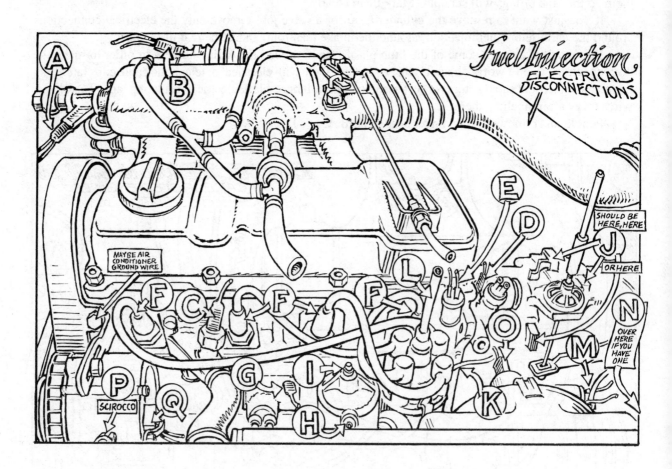

People just removing the cylinder head do A, B, C, D, E and F. OK?

A. Cold start valve

B. Auxiliary air regulator

C. Thermoswitch

D. Coolant temperature sensor

E. Spark advance leads (air-conditioned only)

F. Spark plug wires (cylinder head removers only

G. Control pressure regulator

H. Oil pressure sensor

I. Oil temperature sensor (Scirocco only)

J. Backup light switch

K. Thin wire from coil

L. Thick wire from coil

M. Starter leads (one 13mm, two push-on wires)

N. Radiator thermoswitch

O. Radiator cooling fan

P. Bulb cap (Scirocco only)

Q. Alternator plug (8mm)

Now check all your wires to see if everything's disconnected. Air-conditioned cars may have an extra ground wire somewhere.

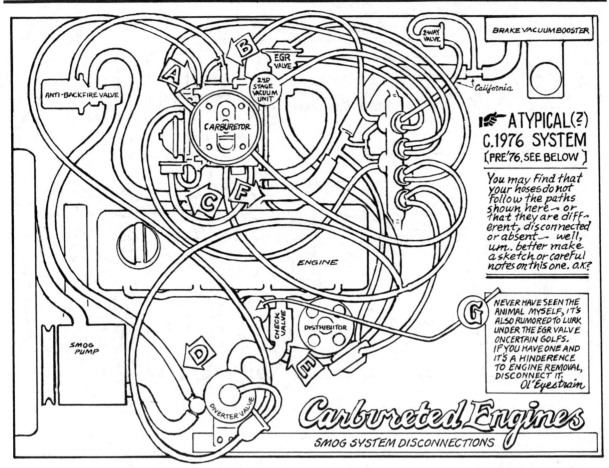

ATYPICAL(?) C.1976 SYSTEM [PRE'76, SEE BELOW]

You may find that your hoses do not follow the paths shown here — or that they are different, disconnected or absent — well, um.. better make a sketch or careful notes on this one. o.k?

NEVER HAVE SEEN THE ANIMAL MYSELF, IT'S ALSO RUMORED TO LURK UNDER THE EGR VALVE ON CERTAIN GOLFS. IF YOU HAVE ONE AND IT'S A HINDERENCE TO ENGINE REMOVAL, DISCONNECT IT.
Ol'Eyestrain

Carbureted Engines
SMOG SYSTEM DISCONNECTIONS

Step 8. Vacuum and Smog System Hose Disconnections

A. Hose from diverter valve (rear of carburetor)
B. Anti-backfire valve (rear of carb)
C. Anti-backfire valve (at intake manifold)
D. Anti-backfire valve (from air injection (smog) pump)

E. Check valve
F. Brake booster to intake manifold (if present)
G. EGR filter (two 10mm nuts on top of oil filter)
Cylinder head removers can skip G.

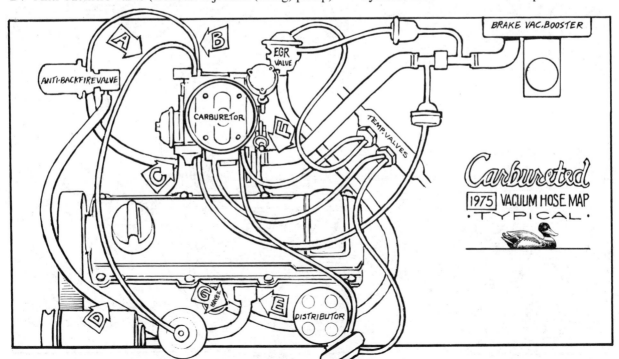

Carbureted 1975 VACUUM HOSE MAP ·TYPICAL·

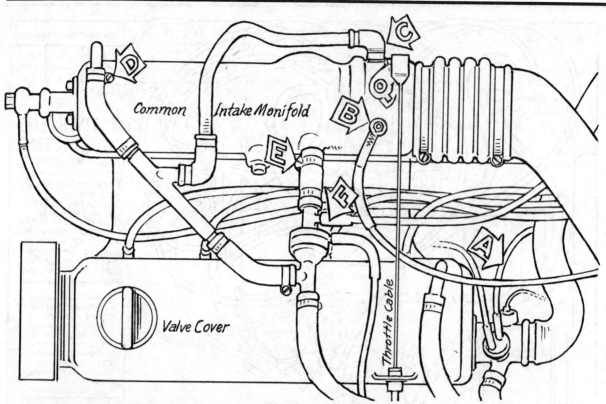

Fuel Injected Engines Vacuum Hose and Smog Control Disconnections

A. Thermoswitch vacuum hose (from vacuum amplifier)

B. Throttle valve housing left vacuum hose
    (from vacuum amplifier)

C. Throttle valve housing rear vacuum hose (from distributor)

D. Intake manifold front vacuum hose

E. Intake manifold left vacuum hose

F. Vacuum hose from deceleration valve

Step 9. Carbureted Engines Coolant Hose Disconnections

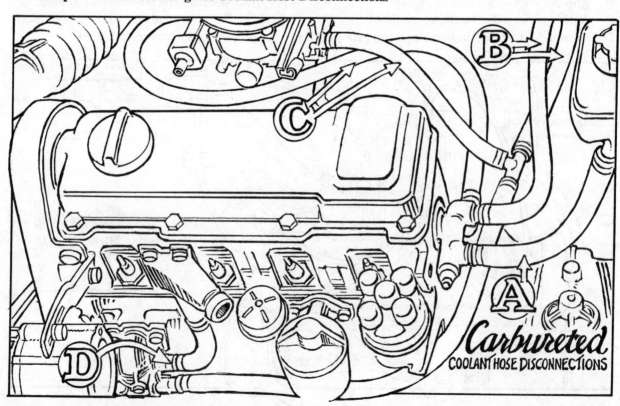

Carbureted
COOLANT HOSE DISCONNECTIONS

Step 9. (Cont'd.)

A. Hose to expansion bottle (1975 and mid-76)   B. Two heater hoses
C. Two hoses (may go to intake manifold)   D. From water pump

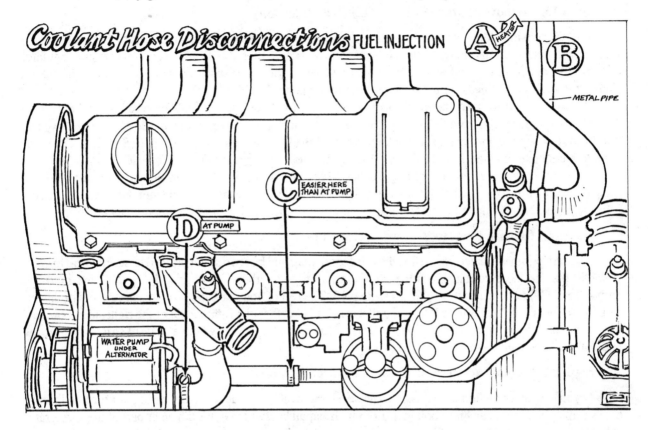

Coolant Hose Disconnections FUEL INJECTION

A. From heater   C. End of metal pipe
B. From thin metal pipe D. From water pump

Step 10. Line Up Flywheel, Standard Transmission (not Cylinder Head Removers)

Turn to Chapter 16, Procedure 4, Steps 6 and 7, then return here.

Step 11. Remove Air Cleaner and Ducts, Carbureted Engines

Remove the 10mm nut holding the black metal air intake elbow on the top of the carb. Then loosen the hose clamp holding the hose running from the air intake elbow to the plastic PCV valve on top of the cam cover. Pull the hose free from the air intake elbow. Now pull the hose on the left of the elbow. It goes to the charcoal filter.

Next use a phillips screwdriver to loosen the clamp on the large corrugated hose running from the air cleaner (the large plastic box fastened inside the right fender) to the exhaust manifold baffle connection. Pull the hose free from the exhaust manifold baffle. Cylinder head people go on to Step 12. Pull off the small hose that runs to the air injection pump from the front of the air cleaner housing. Mark these hoses "To Air Cleaner."

The air cleaner is held to the body by one wire snap clamp similar to one that used to hold the cap on old-fashioned lemonade bottles. Snap open the wire clamp from the left side of the bottom of the cleaner and pull the cleaner box slightly to the left to free it from the rubber mounts. Now that the whole air cleaner assembly is free, lift it out of the engine compartment. Screw back the 13mm nut on the rod sticking up from the center of the carburetor for safekeeping. Stuff a piece of clean rag into the carburetor mouth.

Step 12. Remove Intake Manifold (Fuel Injection, Cylinder Head Removers Only)

Loosen the hose clamp holding the flat rubber hose onto the intake manifold. It's the one which starts at the mixture control unit. Free the hose from the manifold.

Step 13. Remove Mixture Control Unit (Fuel Injection)

Pull the fuel injectors out from the manifold tubes on the right side of the cylinder head. Then remove the fuel line from the cold start valve (13mm). Next remove the two fuel lines from the control pressure regulator (13 and 14mm). Remove the fuel line from the fuel filter to the fuel distributor at the filter end (17mm) and finally the fuel return line from the back of the mixture control unit (17mm).

Remove the hose from the cam cover which runs from the base of the mixture control unit. Two accordian-type hoses run from the base of the mixture control unit. One goes to a baffle plate on the exhaust manifold. Loosen the hose clamp and pull the hose off the baffle (head off people go to Step 15). The other goes to a connection at the front of the car; loosen that hose clamp and pull off the hose.

Now loosen the hose clamp holding the flat rubber hose to the intake manifold and pull that hose off. Snap open the clip on the back of the unit (facing the firewall) and take the complete unit out of the car and lay it in the trunk. Now remove the battery ground strap from the rear transmission mount (13mm).

Step 14. Remove Fuel Hoses (Carbureted Cars)

The fuel pump is located just below the third spark plug and has two small braided hoses running from it. Remove the fuel hose coming from the fuel pump up to the carburetor. Plug with a pencil and mark 'to carburetor.' Cylinder head off people, go to Step 15. The rest of you mark the hose which runs out of the left side of the fuel pump 'fuel pump left' and pull it off. Pull the other one running out of the right side of the fuel pump and mark it 'fuel pump right.' Tie the two fuel lines up out of the way with a piece of string and plug the ends of the lines with a pencil.

Step 15. Unhook Accelerator Cable (Carbureted Cars)

If you've got a standard transmission, the accelerator cable is attached to the carburetor throttle linkage by a small cylinder with an 8mm bolt in it. Loosen the small bolt which holds the inner part of the accelerator cable to the carburetor linkage. Draw the cable free of the linkage. Now use two 10 or 13mm wrenches to loosen the two nuts holding the outer sheath of the cable onto the bracket on the side of the carburetor. The nut closest to the carburetor must be removed so the cable can be pulled out from the bracket. Screw the nut on the threads on the outer cable for safekeeping.

Automatic transmission owners have their accelerator cable held to the carburetor throttle linkage by a bracket. The cable goes through the linkage, then passes through a spring. At the end of the spring is a small circlip. With your fingers, pull the spring back slightly from the clip, then remove the circlip with needle nosed pliers. Pull out the accelerator cable. Put the clip in a Baggie marked "accelerator cable linkage." With your screwdriver, remove the two or three screws which hold the accelerator cable bracket to the side of the carburetor. On top of the accelerator cable bracket is another bracket which holds the dashpot to the carburetor. When you've removed the cable attached to the bracket, remove the small barrel remaining on the carburetor throttle linkage through which the accelerator cable passed. Baggie it marked "accel. cable linkage." Remove the brackets and put back the two or three screws into the side of the carburetor.

Step 16. Unhook Accelerator Cable (Fuel Injection)

Your accelerator cable is held onto a ball located on top of the throttle linkage on the intake manifold. To remove the cable from this ball, just grasp the cable and pull it up to free it from the throttle plate assembly. Now find two 10mm wrenches and loosen one of the two nuts on the cable sheath. The cable will now slide free from the bracket on the cam cover. Tuck the cable out of the way somewhere.

Step 17. Detach Speedometer Cable

Turn to Chapter 16, Procedure 4, Step 5. Then return.

Step 18. Free Exhaust Down Pipe—All Models

Find your can of Liquid Wrench and find the exhaust manifold bolted to the right side of the cylinder head below the intake manifold. Feel down the exhaust manifold about 10cm (4 in) and you'll find a flange with two rows of three 13mm nuts underneath. These nuts hold the exhaust down pipe to the exhaust manifold. Liberally douse each of those 13mm nuts with Liquid Wrench. While you're waiting for the stuff to soak in, find a 13mm socket and a 13mm open end wrench. You'll need the socket for the four end nuts and the wrench for the two central ones. Remove the six nuts. If any of the nuts are stuck and you can't remove them, or if you've been tugging so hard on your wrench that you've rounded the head off the nuts, quit right now. You people can disconnect the bottom section of the down pipe from the intermediate pipe running under the car. I'll show you how to do this in a few minutes.

People who have managed to loosen and remove the six 13mm nuts from the exhaust manifold should now notice a metal tube running from the EGR valve just to the right of the exhaust manifold. This pipe attaches to two of the studs between the exhaust pipe and the exhaust manifold. Push down on the pipe slightly so that the ears welded onto the pipe will clear the two studs and prevent things from hanging up when you remove the cylinder head or engine.

Step 19. Free EGR Valve (Carbureted Engines)

Feel around the back of the intake manifold until you find the small pie dish shaped EGR valve. It's attached to the rear of the intake manifold by two 10mm bolts. Remove 'em. There's a gasket between the EGR valve and the intake manifold. Remove the gasket and put it in a Baggie along with the bolts. There's a pipe which runs from the EGR valve down to the exhaust down pipe. There's no need to try to remove the valve or the pipe from the car. It stays in the engine compartment as you lift the engine out. *If you're taking the engine out, go on to Step 29. Head off people, please continue.*

Step 20. Remove Exhaust Baffle Plate (Carbureted Engines)

Remove the three 13mm nuts holding this baffle plate to the right side of the exhaust manifold. You earlier disconnected a large hose which went from the base of the air cleaner to this baffle plate. Sprinkle some Liquid Wrench on the three nuts holding the plate in position, wait a few moments, then remove the nuts and the plate. When it's off, screw the three nuts fingertight back on the studs.

Step 21. Loosen and Remove Alternator V-Belt

First, loosen the 13mm nut and bolt which goes through the curved support bracket on the right side of the engine (FRONT is front of engine, remember), then goes through an ear on the alternator. When the nut and bolt are loose, you can push on the alternator and slip off the belt. Check where the alternator ground strap bolts to the crankcase. If it's fastened to the cylinder head or the timing belt cover, remove it from the alternator by unscrewing the 8mm nut holding the strap to a stud on the back of the alternator. When the nut's off, remove the strap and screw the nut fingertight on the alternator's stud so's you don't lose it.

Step 22. Remove Camshaft Drive Belt Cover and Maybe Alternator

Unhook the fuel line from the clip on the camshaft cover.

Four 10mm nuts and bolts hold the camshaft drive belt cover in position. The bolts go through metal washers and rubber vibration spacers set in the cover. Feel around the outside perimeter of the cover for the four bolts. The bottom one is tricky, it may be easier to get at it from underneath. Remove 'em all, then thread the cover out of the engine compartment. Place the bolts, spacers and washers into a marked Baggie; put it with the belt cover.

If you can't maneuver the cam belt cover free with the alternator in place, remove the alternator (Chapter 8, Procedure 2, Step 3, tells how). With the alternator removed the drive belt cover will come away more easily. Air-conditioned cars have the alternator located below the air conditioner compressor, but mounted the same as above.

Step 23. Remove Drive Belt

Tension on the toothed camshaft drive belt is maintained by a wheel bolted to the front of the cylinder head, and held by a 15mm nut. Loosen the nut, then slide the belt off the drive belt sprocket with your fingers. When it's off, inspect it for cuts and nicks. Buy a new one if it's oily or damaged.

Step 24. Remove Camshaft Cover

Remove the eight 10mm bolts or nuts which hold the camshaft cover on the cylinder head. One of the left side bolts/nuts holds a spring clip holding the carburetor fuel line. Some fuel injected engines have a hose held by the left rear bolt. Remove the long metal spacers from each side of the cover and pull the camshaft cover off the head. Don't worry if the cork gasket below the cover sticks and breaks, you're eventually going to replace it. Remove and discard the half moon plug from the back of the head and the thin rubber strip from the bearing cap at the front of the head. Clean the cam cover, bolts/nuts and spacers and stash them.

Step 25. Remove Camshaft Drive Belt Sprocket

Slip a piece of wood or the handle of a plastic screwdriver through one of the right holes in the sprocket. The handle will act as a stop when you apply force to the 19mm bolt holding the sprocket on to the camshaft. Unscrew the bolt, then pull the sprocket off. Stuck? Screw the 19mm bolt back fingertight, then give the head of the bolt a whack with a hammer. If that doesn't shift the sprocket, try levering it off with a couple of screwdrivers. Don't lever on the outside sprocket edge; you may bust a tooth, the screwdriver or your knuckles.

When the sprocket's off, find the half moon shaped Woodruff key either in the slot in the center sprocket hole or stuck to the camshaft. Carefully remove it (small screwdriver) and stash it along with the sprocket in a marked Baggie.

Step 26. Free Coolant Pipe

A small coolant pipe runs from the water pump to the intake manifold. It's held onto the rear of the cylinder head by the lower of two 10mm bolts. Loosen the bottom bolt and free the tab holding the pipe. Put the bolt back into the cylinder head for safekeeping.

You may have a 19mm (¾ in) hose attached to the top of the intake manifold. Loosen the hose clamp and pull the hose free from the manifold. Mark it. If you couldn't loosen the six 13mm nuts from Step 18, go to Step 31, then return here.

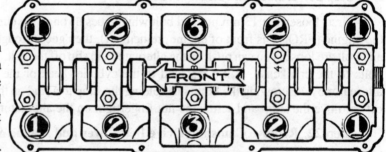

Step 27. Free Cylinder Head

Vehicles up to 1978 use a 10mm allen wrench while later models use a special polygon wrench to unscrew the cylinder head bolts. There are ten and they must be loosened in order. First loosen the four corner bolts ½ turn. Then loosen the bolts closest to the four outside ones ½ turn. Finally, ½ turn on the two center ones. Continue loosening in increments of ½ turns until they're free.

Step 28. Remove Cylinder Head

Grasp the head at the front and rear and pull it upward. If you can't get it to budge, find your rubber hammer and tap the head lightly at each end to loosen it. When it's loose, lift it carefully. The cylinder head gasket may be stuck either to the underside of the head or to the surface of the engine block. Don't worry about bending or breaking it. It has to be replaced. Lay the head down on a clear surface and stuff clean rags into each of the four cylinder bores in the crankcase.

Cylinder head people go to Procedure 2.

Step 29. Remove Driveshafts from Transmission—All Models

Turn to Chapter 16, Procedure 4 and do Step 19. Hang the disconnected driveshafts up out of the way with wire hooks. Make them out of wire clothes hangers. Don't wire them to any part of the engine!

Step 30. Remove Exhaust Pipe Support

See Chapter 16, Procedure 4, Step 24.

Step 31. Free Exhaust Down Pipe

People unable to remove any of the six 13mm nuts (from Step 18) holding the exhaust pipe to the exhaust manifold should now remove the three 15mm nuts and bolts from where the horizontal intermediate pipe mates to the vertical down pipe. The three bolts go through a flange welded onto the ends of each pipe. These flanges are just before the pipe begins its upward sweep to the exhaust manifold. A more than liberal dose of Liquid Wrench is usually needed as a prelude to removing the bolts. Wire brush off all the crud that has accumulated on these bolts.

If you can't get the bolts loose, try a little heat from your propane torch on the nuts. **Be Careful!** Make sure the gas or fuel injection return lines are safely tucked away and the fire extinguisher's handy. If heat won't budge them, saw 'em off. Put the hacksaw blade *between* the nut and the flange and saw away. Watch your knuckles. I hope you don't have to remove all three bolts using this method! Whatever you saw off has to be replaced, so note that on your parts shopping list.

Step 32. Remove Bottom Transmission Mount

Turn to Chapter 16, Procedure 4, and do Step 25, then...

Step 33. Remove Starter and Left Engine/Transmission Mount (Standard Transmission)

Turn again to Chapter 16, Procedure 4, and do Step 21.

Step 34. Remove Left Engine/Transmission Mount (Automatic Transmission)

It's held by two long bolts (15mm or polygon head).

Step 35. Disconnect Cables (Automatic Transmission)

It's in Chapter 16, Procedure 4, Step 4.

Step 36. Remove Shift Linkages (Standard Transmission)

Chapter 16, Procedure 4, Step 8.

Step 37. Support Engine

Attach the hoist lifting chain to the two ears on the left side of the cylinder head. Then attach the chain to the hook on your hoist. Raise the hoist slightly so there's just a slight amount of tension in the chain. When you remove the engine and transmission mount bolts, you'll want the engine/transmission unit to be fairly well balanced.

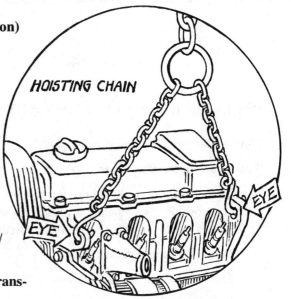

HOISTING CHAIN

EYE

EYE

Step 38. Remove Front Engine Mount and Rear Transmission Mount

A 17mm socket will remove the bolts from both mounts. First remove the bolt from the mount at the front of the engine. This mount bolts the engine to the inside of the right fender. If, when you get the bolt loosened, you are unable to remove it, lift the hoist slightly so you can pull the bolt free. Put the bolt in a Baggie marked 'front engine mount.'

Standard transmission: The rear transmission mount is held to the transmission by four 13mm bolts but keep those bolts in place! Remove the 17mm bolt which goes through the rubber and metal part of the mount

Step 38. (Cont'd.)

just to the rear of the battery. Take the bolt out and slip it into the marked Baggie. If you can't easily get the bolt free, raise or lower your hoist a bit.

Automatics: Remove the 17mm bolt from the rear transmission mount. Now remove the mount. It's secured to the transmission by three 15mm bolts. One of the bolts also secures the battery ground strap. Slide the mount out from the car and Baggie it along with the bolts.

The engine and transmission are now free from all restraint and can be lifted out. However, check that everything is disconnected and out of the way. Be sure that fuel lines, driveshafts, etc., are free from the engine and transmission.

Step 39. Remove Carburetor (Automatics Only)

The automatic transmission is bigger than the standard and you need more room to maneuver.

Remove the four 10mm nuts which hold the carburetor to the intake manifold. Put them in a marked Baggie.

Finally, unhook the two small water hoses from the base of the automatic choke on the side of the carburetor facing the right fender. Pull off the carburetor, put it in a big plastic bag, seal and stash it in the trunk.

Step 40. Remove Engine and Transmission

When you're sure that everything is clear and out of the way, begin pumping the hoist. The engine and transmission will clear the front and rear mounts and begin to move upward. Be very careful that the engine and transmission unit doesn't swing backward and smack the carburetor if it's still attached. It's very handy to have a couple of friends to help guide the engine out. When you're clear of the mounts, pump the hoist higher until the engine is completely out of the car. Guide the engine/transmission unit very carefully to avoid damaging the paintwork. Now wheel the hoist backward until the engine is away from the car. Don't leave it dangling in the air, as the hoist may tip over. Lower the engine/transmission unit until it's resting on the ground—Safety! Clear the space where you are going to do the engine work and ask Friends to help carry it to that place (or use a wheelbarrow).

The next Procedure deals with the stripping and preparation of the cylinder head for people having a valve job done at the machine shop. Call and make an appointment at the machine shop so they'll be ready for you.

PROCEDURE 2: STRIP CYLINDER HEAD. Phase 1.

Condition: Engine rebuild, valve job.

Tools and materials: Phase 1 tool kit

Remarks: This Procedure's for people who've removed the cylinder head and intend to take it to the machine shop for work. Engine rebuild people skip this Procedure for now and go to Procedure 3. You'll be referred back to this Procedure when you're ready to disassemble your engine.

Step 1. Remove Spark Plugs

Just screw them out and discard.

Step 2. Remove Head Bolts and Washers

Turn the cylinder head upside down and slide out the ten bolts and washers. Count the bolts and washers; you must have ten of each.

There is a small plastic half-moon shaped end plug at the rear of the cylinder head. It's just pushed into place. Remove and discard it if you haven't done so already.

Step 3. Free Exhaust Manifold

Use a 12mm socket on a medium extension to remove the eight nuts holding the exhaust manifold on the cylinder head. Apply some Liquid Wrench to the nuts before attempting to remove them. When you have them free, place them in a marked Baggie.

Step 4. Free Intake Manifold

Remove the six 6mm allen bolts which hold the intake manifold to the side of the cylinder head. Pull out the bolts and place them in a marked Baggie. The air heater hose manifold may prevent you from putting the 6mm allen wrench on the two left bolts if it's still in place. In this case, remove the manifold by taking off the 12mm nuts and washers holding the intake manifold to the exhaust manifold. Remove the two 6mm allen bolts from the intake manifold, then reinstall the heater hose gizmo back onto the exhaust manifold with the 12mm washers and nuts fingertight.

Step 5. Remove Intake and Exhaust Manifolds

Pull firmly on both the intake and exhaust manifolds and they'll come free from the side of the cylinder head. The gaskets beneath both manifolds should be removed and discarded.

Step 6. Remove Tensioner Pulley

Remove the 15mm bolt holding the pulley onto the front of the cylinder head. Put the nut and pulley into a Baggie marked 'tensioner pulley.'

Step 7. Remove Oil Pressure Sensor (if present)

Use a crescent wrench to unscrew the sensor from the rear of the head. Mark and Baggie.

Step 8. Remove Coolant Manifold

This small manifold is held onto the rear of the head by two 10mm bolts. The bottom bolt is loose already so remove it and the top one and stash the manifold and bolts in a marked Baggie.

Step 9. Remove Left Coolant Manifold

Take out the three 10mm bolts and washers holding the coolant manifold to the left side of the cylinder head. Clean, mark and Baggie.

Step 10. Remove Check Valve Manifold (Carbureted Only)

It's held to the left side of the cylinder head by four 15mm bolts. Remove them and the washers; Baggie the lot.

Step 11. Clean Cylinder Head

Use a stiff brush and solvent to clean off the worst of the dirt.

Step 12. Inspect Cylinder Head

Look it over very carefully for cracks on the underside.

Step 13. A Machine Shop Interlude

Take the cylinder head to the machine shop with the camshaft still bolted in place. Ask to speak to the person who will be working on your cylinder head and give 'em the following tolerances if they need them. The maximum cylinder head distortion is 0.1mm (0.004 in) and the maximum runout on the camshaft is 0.01mm (0.0004 in). Those figures indicate how much bend there is in the camshaft before it's considered unuseable. Also ask the people there to inspect the camshaft bearing caps. If they're worn, you'll need a new head. Bearing caps are not replaceable. If you want to do your own cylinder head work, look at Section 15 in the *Volkswagen Repair Manual, Second Edition, for the Type 17 Rabbit and Type 53 Scirocco*. It's all laid out there. However, please do *not* attempt it unless you have access to the correct tools and know-how to use them.

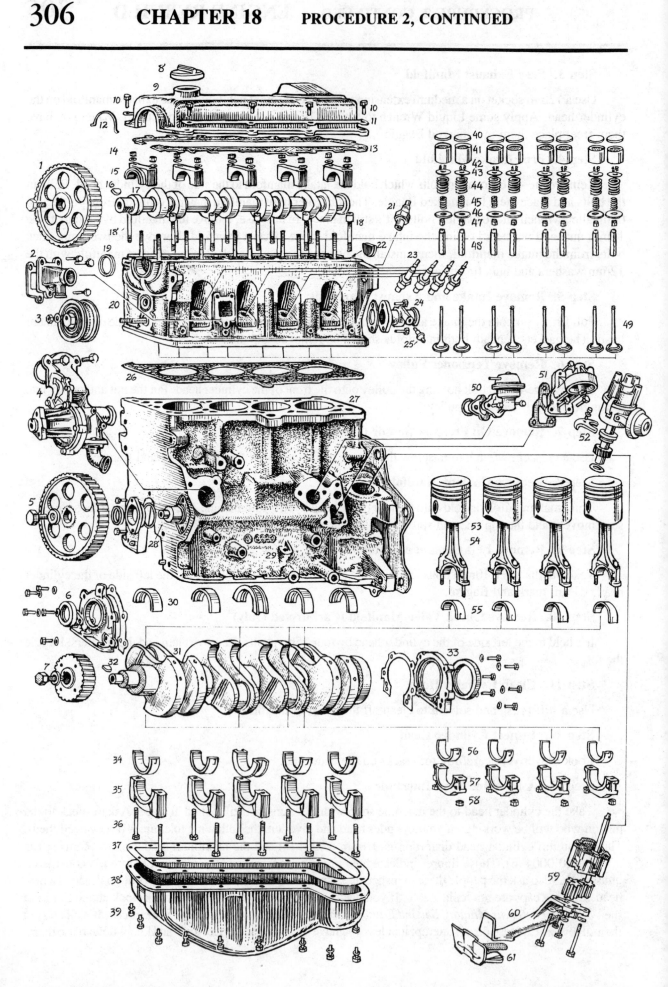

Step 13. (Cont'd.)

Before the people at the machine shop actually start work on your cylinder head, get an estimate of their costs. Call VW and ask them how much an exchange cylinder head would cost. Some of the early models had inferior cylinder heads and were covered under some kind of warranty exchange program which went up, I think, to 30,000 miles. Whatever it is, it's worth investigating to see if you could get a new head for a price close to the cost the machine shop is going to charge. If you decide to buy a new head, you'll have to strip all the pieces from your old head, including the camshaft, and reinstall them on your new head, then get the valve clearances adjusted. See Procedure 8 in this Chapter.

If the machine shop people find the camshaft bearings are worn beyond the wear limit, the cylinder head will have to be replaced. The wear limit is checked by measuring the axial play on the camshaft. This means how much end to end movement the camshaft has while being retained by the bearings. Ask the machinist to check this play for you. Maximum play should be 0.15mm (.06 in).

PROCEDURE 3: DISMANTLE ENGINE—ALL MODELS

Condition: Your engine is out of the car waiting to be rebuilt.

Tools and materials: Phase 2 tool kit, Liquid Wrench, cleaning equipment and clean rags, clean place to work, Baggies, masking tape, indelible marker, notepaper and pencils, Friend.

Step 1. Clean Engine and Transmission

Now that the unit is out of the car, you can load it into the back of your pickup and take it to a steam cleaning place to get the engine and transmission shiny. This is a big psychological boost as well as making things easier to identify and remove.

Step 2. Separate Engine from Transmission (Standard)

First, free the intermediate plate (the thin metal plate which fits between the engine and transmission). There are three 11mm bolts going through the intermediate plate into the transmission. Remove the bolts, then mark and Baggie 'em. The intermediate plate remains on the engine when the transmission is removed.

Next, remove the inspection cover (another small pressed piece of metal the same thickness as the intermediate plate). It's next to and just above the right driveshaft and is held into the transmission by two 11mm or 12mm bolts. Remove the two bolts and the inspection cover. Clean the cover thoroughly, then stash it in a marked Baggie along with the two bolts.

Check that the TDC lug is still lined up with the TDC hole pointer in the transmission. No? Line it up using the 19mm socket on the crankshaft. Get it right!

Remove the 19mm bolts holding the transmission to the engine. One is just below the right driveshaft and the others are on the top of the engine/transmission. Put them in a marked Baggie. Now you and Friend position yourselves on each side of the transmission. Grasp the transmis-

Step 2. (Cont'd.)

sion firmly and pull it backward. If it won't move, make sure the lug on the flywheel is still correctly lined up and that you removed all the bolts from the intermediate plate and small inspection plate and the 19mm bolts holding the transmission to the engine. If you can get it so far but no further, wrap some cloth around the end of a large screwdriver or bar and insert it between the transmission and engine. Levering gently on that bar will pop the transmission loose from the engine block.

With the transmission free, check around the spline shaft. Is there a thick oily mess adhering inside? If so, the transmission oil seal has failed and needs to be replaced. Take the transmission to a transmission shop or VW and have the seal replaced along with the bronze bushing. If everything looks OK, wipe it out with a rag and put it safely out of the way. Now it's the hour to turn your attention to the engine.

Step 3. Separate Engine from Transmission (Automatic)

Since the engine and transmission are in the breeze, as it were, let's remove the starter. Sometimes the teeth on the starter mechanism hang up on the flywheel and make it difficult to remove the transmission from the engine. You will have already removed the two 10mm nuts which hold the rear of the starter in position on the rear support bracket when you removed the tin cover, so now remove the three 13mm nuts holding the starter to the transmission. Mark and Baggie them and loose the 13mm bolt holding the rear starter mount on the crankcase. Pull the starter free. Tighten the 13mm bolt holding the starter mount on the crankcase for safekeeping. Turn back to Chapter 16, Procedure 4 and do Step 18.

Now remove the three 19mm bolts holding the engine and transmission together. Put them in a marked Baggie. Separate the engine from the transmission: find Friend and, standing one at each side of the transmission, firmly, pull it away from the engine block. If it won't come easily, check to see that all the retaining nuts and bolts have been removed. Especially check that all three 10mm bolts are removed from the drive plate. If you're unable to split the two apart, insert a large screwdriver or bar with some cloth wrapped around the blade between the engine block and transmission, and lever the transmission slightly rearward until there's a slight crack. Now the transmission will pull away freely. Be careful of the torque converter, that squashed round thing with the serrations on the face inside the transmission which floats on a long shaft and bearing inside the automatic transmission. When you have the transmission and engine separated, be very careful that the torque converter doesn't fall to the floor. You can remove the converter by gently pulling it out of the transmission case, then set it down somewhere level. Leave the shaft the converter turns on inside the case.

Check the condition of the oil seal inside the automatic transmission (it was hidden by the torque converter). It should be intact. Also check the condition of the splined shaft sticking out through the oil seal. If the oil seal is cracked, have it replaced by VW or a transmission specialist. It's important that it's put in properly because, if not, automatic transmission fluid will leak out and render your transmission inoperative. Don't squirt gasoline or petroleum-based cleaning solutions on or around the transmission oil seal. This silicone seal is very easily damaged by petroleum products. Use rags to clean the inside of the transmission.

If your car is getting on in years, take the torque converter to VW and have them check the inside of the converter bushing for scoring. That's the bushing on the inside of the torque converter which slips over the shaft protruding through the oil seal in the automatic transmission. Ask the folks at VW to measure the converter bushing for you. You may need a new converter bushing installed onto your torque converter and VW have the special tool to press the bushing into place.

Step 4. Support Engine

You'll need the help of at least one friend to lift the engine onto your clean work surface or engine stand. If you have an engine stand, remove the arm from the stand, then bolt the engine onto the arm and lift it onto the stand. Now that the engine's firmly on the bench or stand, it's time to collect your thoughts and begin dismantling.

You can leave some stuff attached to the crankcase, such as the fuel pump, distributor, oil filter manifold, etc. However, it makes those pieces very difficult to clean and they sometimes get in the way. So I suggest removing them.

Step 5. Remove Water Pump

The water pump is held to the side of the crankcase by three 13mm bolts. If your car is air conditioned and carbureted, a long 13mm bolt goes through the bottom part of the air conditioner compressor bracket, the water pump and into the crankcase. Remove all three 13mm bolts and washer. Mark and Baggie them. Pull the water pump away from the block, clean and stash.

Step 6. Remove Alternator (if you haven't already done so)

First remove the alternator ground strap from the rear of the alternator by removing the 8mm nut holding it in position. Pull off the ground strap and replace the 8mm nut fingertight for safekeeping. You may need two 13mm wrenches to remove the nut and bolt holding the top of the alternator onto its curved adjusting bar. The bar is also attached to the smog pump (if you have one) or the air conditioner support bracket (if you have one). Remove the nut and bolt and put them aside for a moment. Stick your 6mm allen wrench into the socket head bolt on the bottom of the alternator and remove the 13mm nut from the other end of that bolt. Remove the socket head bolt and the alternator. Reinstall the nut and bolt through the alternator and tighten them fingertight. There's a spacer on the 13mm nut and bolt which goes through the adjusting arm on '75 and '76 models. Put it on the 13mm bolt and loosely install the nut and bolt back onto the adjusting bar.
Air-Conditioned Models: To pull the alternator free from the a/c mounting bracket, you will have to pull back the long socket head bolt and twist it toward the firewall to clear the rear ear on the support bracket. Slide the alternator off the bolt and lift it off. Push the bolt back into its ears and put the nut back onto the bolt for safekeeping.

Step 7. Remove Smog Pump ('75 and '76) and Air Conditioner Bracket (if you have one)

The smog pump is held onto that curved adjusting bracket by a 13mm bolt. Loosen and remove the bolt. The other side of the pump is held by a longer 13mm bolt and nut. Remove the nut from the bolt, pull the bolt out and the smog pump is free.

On '75 models with air conditioning, the smog pump is attached to part of the air conditioner support bracket. The pump is held onto that bracket by a long 13mm bolt through two ears on the bottom of the a/c bracket. Remove both the 13mm nut from the end of the bolt and the other 13mm bolt holding a bracket on the front of the crankcase on the other side of the smog pump. With the bolts removed, pull off the smog pump. Reinstall all the nuts and bolts through the pump; do them up fingertight for safekeeping. Remove the bolts holding the air conditioner bracket.

Step 8. Remove Oil Dipstick

Put it where you won't lose it.

Step 9. Remove Distributor

Mark the wires running to the spark plugs 1, 2, 3 and 4 from the front (if your cylinder head is still in place). Then pull the wires off the top of the spark plugs. Remove the distributor by taking out the 13mm bolt which holds the U-clamp around its base. This U-clamp holds the distributor to the crankcase. Remove the U-clamp and pull out the distributor and stash it somewhere safe. Put the bolt and U-clamp in a Baggie marked ''distributor.''

Step 10. Remove Oil Filter Manifold

It's held to the crankcase by three 6mm allen bolts. Remove the bolts and stash them along with the manifold.

Step 11. Remove Fuel Pump

The pump is held onto the left side of the crankcase by two 6mm allen bolts. Remove the bolts and pull off the fuel pump. Beneath the fuel pump is a thick plastic block with a small nipple on the top facing outward. Pull the block off; use a screwdriver if necessary. Mark and Baggie the pump, block and bolts.

Step 12. Remove Control Pressure Regulator (Fuel Injection)

Remove the two 6mm socket head bolts holding the CPR to the left of the crankcase. Pull it off and stash in a marked Baggie.

Step 13. Free Intake and Exhaust Manifolds

At the rear of the cylinder head a small manifold houses the water temperature sensor.

If it's still in place, loosen the hose clamp from the pipe on the right side of the small manifold and pull off the coolant hose. Held onto that small manifold is a metal pipe that ran from the water pump, along the left side of the engine, to a rubber pipe which fits onto the intake manifold. Loosen the bottom 10mm bolt and pull the pipe free, then loosen the hose clamp to remove the rubber pipe where it meets the metal pipe.

Step 14. Remove Exhaust Air Heater Baffle Plate—Carbureted Models Only

If you haven't already removed this, you'll need a 13mm socket to remove the three nuts holding this baffle plate to the right side of the exhaust manifold. Sprinkle some Liquid Wrench on the three nuts holding the plate. Remove the nuts and plate, stash the plate somewhere safe and replace the three nuts fingertight on the studs for safekeeping.

Step 15. Remove Drive Belt Cover—All Models

Four 10mm bolts hold the camshaft drive belt cover in position. The bolts go through a metal washer, a rubber vibration spacer and another metal washer before they screw into the crankcase. Remove all four 10mm bolts, then slip off the cover. Put the bolts, spacers and washers into a marked Baggie. Clean the drive belt cover and stash it with the Baggie.

Step 16. Remove Camshaft Drive Belt

The toothed camshaft drive belt (timing belt) has its tension maintained by a pulley bolted to the cylinder head, secured by a 15 or 17mm nut. Loosen the nut and remove the belt.

Step 17. Remove Camshaft Cover

Models up to '78 have the cylinder head camshaft cover held on by eight 10mm nuts. Later models have bolts in place of nuts. Remove the nuts or bolts and the long metal spacer from each side of the camshaft cover. Pull off the camshaft cover along with the cork gasket. There is a thin rubber strip which fits over #1 bearing cap on the end of the camshaft. Remove and discard the strip. Remove the half-moon end plug from the other end of the head. Clean your camshaft cover and put it and the nuts and metal spacers in a safe place.

Step 18. Remove Cylinder Head

Turn back to Procedure 1 and do Steps 26, 27 and 28.

Step 19. Remove Oil Pan (Sump)

If your engine is on a stand, tip the engine over so the oil pan is facing up. If you're working on a bench, lay the engine carefully on its side. The oil pan on early models is held by twenty 5mm allen bolts while later models are held by twenty regular 10mm bolts. Use the appropriate tool to remove all the bolts and washers; put them in a Baggie marked 'oil pan.' Pull off the oil pan and its gasket. A little oil may drain out at this stage. Clean the oil pan with solvent and put it in your parts pile.

Step 20. Remove Oil Pump and Check Backlash

Now that the oil pan has been removed, you can see the metal crankshaft with connecting rods that fasten to the pistons. The oil pump is that silver thing with the protruding arm. On the bottom of the arm is a deflector plate and inside the plate is a strainer. The deflector plate helps combat oil surge occurring when you drive around corners too fast. Anyway, the pump is held inside the crankcase by two 13mm bolts. Remove the two 13mm bolts and attendant washers, withdraw the oil pump and clean it.

Lever off the deflector plate so you can get at the strainer, then clean out any foreign particles which may have accumulated. Squirt some solvent up inside that arm to get into the body of the pump.

Disassemble the pump to clean it more thoroughly by removing the two 10mm bolts and washers holding the arm to the body. Pull off the arm and you'll see two pump gears. Carefully clean any junk out from inside the pump body and arm.

You now have to check the operation of the pump by measuring the backlash. Turn to Chapter 9, Procedure 5 and do Step 8. Then return here.

If your pump measurements are borderline, you can reinstall it when the engine's rebuilt but make a mental note to replace it within five thousand miles or so.

If your pump tested OK, lubricate the gears with engine oil. Install the strainer and oil deflector plate. Use vice grips to pinch the ears on the deflector plate to hold it firmly onto the arm. Turn the vertical main shaft sticking out from the top of the pump to check that the gears turn smoothly. Put the pump into a big plastic bag, seal it and store it somewhere. Discard the oil pan gasket.

Step 21. Remove Drive Plate (Automatics)

The drive plate is held to the rear of the crankshaft by six 17mm bolts.

Find a 15cm (6 in) piece of 50mm x 100mm (2 in x 4 in) wood and put it between one of the crankshaft counterweights and the *right* side of the crankcase. This enables you to apply enough force to undo, without damaging anything, the 17mm bolts holding the torque converter drive plate to the crankshaft.

Loosen the six bolts in a diagonal order, then remove them and the metal disc held by the bolts. Stash the bolts and disc in a Baggie. Note that the drive plate has three ears on its circumference which face the transmission. Now pull off the plate by holding it at its extreme edge and gently pulling it free from the crankshaft. If it's stuck, squirt some Liquid Wrench around the joint between the crankshaft and the inside of the plate and wait a few moments. On no account, beat on the drive plate with anything. A little wiggling will free it.

Step 22. Remove Flywheel (Standard Transmission)

The flywheel is held to a part of the clutch mechanism called the pressure plate by six 11mm bolts and washers. Put a piece of 50mm x 100mm (2 in x 4 in) wood between one of the crankshaft counterweights and the right side of the crankcase. Remove the six 11mm bolts in diagonal order from the flywheel, loosening each a ½ turn at a time until loose, and gently remove the flywheel. Directly beneath the flywheel is a clutch disc which will drop onto your big toe as you pull the flywheel off. Try to avoid that mishap. Put the flywheel and clutch disc into your parts pile. Keep the wooden block inside the crankcase.

Step 23. Remove Release Plate and Clutch Pressure Plate (Standard Transmission)

The large piece of machined metal now facing you is the clutch pressure plate. Its machined face rides on one side of the clutch disc. The just-removed flywheel has an inner machined face which rides on the other side of the clutch disc. To remove the clutch pressure plate you first have to remove the release plate. The release plate is held on the pressure plate by a retaining spring (a circular piece of spring wire) with its two ends slightly upturned. Remove the retaining ring by inserting a screwdriver between the rim of the release plate and the retaining ring itself. Once it's sprung free, remove the wire and the release plate; clean, mark and Baggie. You are now faced with six 17mm bolts holding the clutch pressure plate to the rear of the crankshaft. Remove the six 17mm bolts in diagonal fashion, then pull out the metal disc through which the bolts passed before bolting into the rear of the crankshaft. You'll note that the disc has a little lip on its circumference which 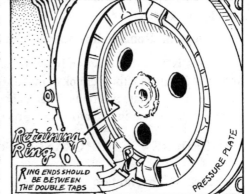 curves up toward you. With the bolts removed, pull off the clutch pressure plate by holding it at the 9 and 3 o'clock positions and working it gently toward you. Don't drop the pressure plate on the floor. When it's free, gently lay it down in your parts pile.

Step 24. Remove Rear Crankshaft Oil Seal Plate

The seal plate is a cast piece of aluminum with a brown or black plastic seal pressed into the middle. It allows the crankshaft to turn while preventing the escape of any oil onto the flywheel. There's a similar seal at the front of the crankshaft; one, too, for the intermediate shaft. This seal plate is held on the engine block by 10mm bolts and nuts. Loosen and remove the 10mm bolts, then pull off the rear crankshaft seal plate. If it won't come off easily, insert a screwdriver between the rear of the plate and the crankcase and carefully lever it free.

The oil seal has to be replaced so you may as well remove the seal from the plate right now. Lay the seal plate down on its face and using a hammer and short wooden dowel, tap the brown or black plastic seal from the rear, pushing it in in increments out toward the front. Tap gently around the circumference of the seal. When you've got it almost out, turn the plate over and lever the seal the rest of the way out with a small hammer or screwdriver handle. Don't use a screwdriver blade between the seal and the seal plate; you'll mess up the plate. When the seal is out, discard it, then clean the seal plate and place it along with the six bolts and washers in a Baggie marked 'rear seal plate.'

Step 25. Remove Crankshaft Drive Belt Sprocket

This drive belt sprocket is bolted to the front of the crankshaft by a 19mm bolt and washer. Four 6mm allen bolts (or 13mm bolts) hold the V-belt pulley to the front of the drive belt sprocket. Put the piece of 2x4 between the crankshaft and crankcase as per Step 21 or 22. Remove the 19mm bolt and washer and pull off the drive belt sprocket. Examine the small end of the crankshaft that's protruding through its oil seal and you'll see a half-moon shaped Woodruff key. If for some reason it's not on the crankshaft, it will be inside the drive belt sprocket. Wherever it is, find it and put it in a marked Baggie along with the sprocket, bolt and washer.

Step 26. Remove Intermediate Shaft Drive Belt Sprocket

The last sprocket is fastened to the intermediate shaft. Stick a screwdriver through one of the holes in the sprocket and use it as a lever to counteract the force needed to remove the 19mm bolt securing the sprocket. Don't let anything slip! Remove the Woodruff key from the end of the intermediate shaft. Place the sprocket, bolt, washer and Woodruff key into a Baggie marked 'intermediate shaft.'

Step 27. Remove Front Crankshaft Oil Seal Retaining Plate

Retaining plates come in two different styles. One version is attached to the crankcase by three 10mm bolts and one 13mm bolt; the other by four 10mm bolts.

Remove the bolts, pull off the seal retaining plate, clean it, and remove the seal using the same method used in Step 24. Put the retaining plate and bolts into a Baggie marked 'front oil seal.' If your front seal retaining plate has another extra little gizmo known as the drive belt guide, you'll have to get it off from the oil seal retaining plate by removing two 5mm socket head bolts. Put the guide along with the seal retaining plate into the Baggie.

Step 28. Remove Intermediate Shaft Oil Seal Retaining Plate

This is held into position by two 13mm bolts. Loosen and remove the bolts and pull off the oil seal retainer. It's quite a thick chunk of metal. Beneath the seal plate is a thin rubber O ring. Discard it. Mark and Baggie the seal plate and bolts. That's about all the stuff you need to remove from the crankcase. Now, I'll treat the crankcase innards to a new Procedure because these steps are getting a little too high. Are you?

PROCEDURE 4: STRIP CRANKCASE INNARDS

Step 1. Orientation

If your crankcase is on an engine stand, flip the engine over so the crankshaft is facing up. If you're working on a bench, make sure the top of the bench is clear, lay some thick paper towels or rags on the bench and lay the crankcase on its side so the crankshaft faces you. The crankshaft is immediately visible as you look into the interior gloom. Notice the eight large flattened counterweights (part of the crankshaft). Some have

Step 1. (Cont'd.)

partially drilled holes in them. These were drilled by the factory to make sure that the crankshaft is perfectly balanced. Opposite those counterweights you'll see the four connecting rod bearing caps held onto the connecting rods by two nuts. If you peer deeper inside you'll see that the connecting rods are fastened to the pistons. At this stage you can only see the scooped out underside of the piston.

Running parallel to the crankshaft is the intermediate shaft with a gear on the end. A little further forward from the geared end is a lobe that actuates the fuel pump on carbureted models. The oil pump has a shaft fitted into the bottom part of the distributor shaft. When the geared end of the intermediate shaft turns the distributor shaft, it also works the oil pump. Very clever. Pull the intermediate shaft out from the front of the crankcase and wrap it with rags.

Have a look at the main bearing caps which hold the crankshaft in position. Main bearing Cap #1 is on the sprocket end of the crankcase (the *FRONT*). Main bearing cap #5 is on the flywheel side (the *REAR*) of the crankcase. These main bearing caps have numbers stamped into them; they should be in sequence, 1, 2, 3, 4, 5. There's a possibility that any of the numbers other than 3 could be out of sequence, i.e., #2 could be in the #5 position. If so, make a note because it's **very** important that when the main bearing caps are reinstalled, they go back in the position they came off. It's also important that they aren't turned 180°. They're made so it's difficult but not impossible to turn them around when reinstalling them. #3 main bearing cap is slightly wider than the other four.

Bearing shells are thin metal pieces which fit between the bearing caps, the crankcase saddles and the crankshaft. The bearing shells are designed to wear and be replaced. There's a half shell (called the upper and lower shells) on each side of the crankshaft. #3 bearing shell is different than the other four. There are also bearing shells between the connecting rods and connecting rod caps. These shells are also in two halves, one half pressed onto the connecting rod and the other into the connecting rod bearing cap. Before you remove the crankshaft, you need to identify which piston fits in which bore. So...if you've got an engine stand, turn the crankcase over again so the machined upper surface is facing you.

Step 2. Identify Pistons

The top of the pistons will probably be coated with a thick layer of carbon. Stamped into the top of each

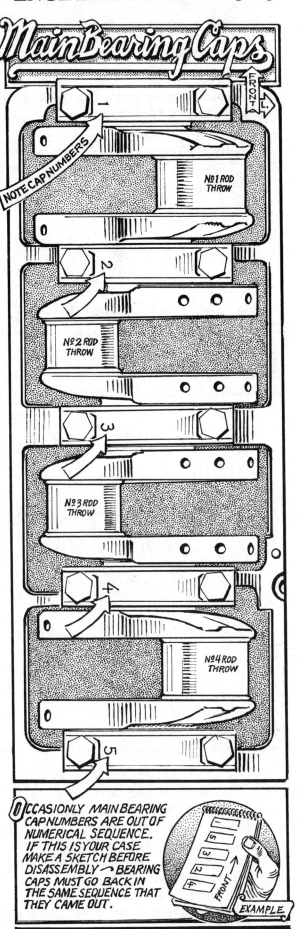

Step 2. (Cont'd.)

piston is a number and an arrow which you won't be able to see because of the carbon. Use a sharp center-punch to punch a dot at the *front* (the sprocket end) of #1 piston. Then put two punch marks on the front of piston #2, three on #3 and four on #4. Make sure the punch mark on the piston penetrates the carbon coating

into the piston head itself. Don't do it with a 10 lb hammer and all your might; you'll drive the punch straight through the piston. A medium tap will suffice. Now that the pistons are identified, turn the crankcase so the crankshaft is facing you once again.

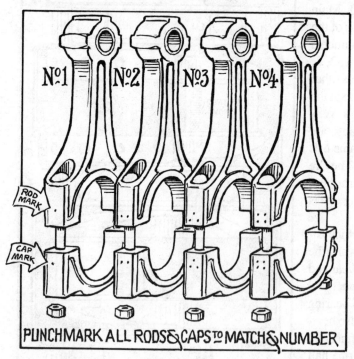

Step 3. Remove Rod Bearing Caps

Rotate the crankshaft by either levering it around with a wooden hammer handle or by reinserting the 19mm bolt into the end of the crankshaft and turning it with your socket. You want to move the crankshaft until you can work on the connecting rod bearing caps. Move the crankshaft until #1 cap is closest to you. That'll bring #4 close also, while #2 and 3 will remain down in the bores. First let's mark each connecting rod bearing cap and connecting rod, so arm yourself with your sharp punch and hammer and put one punch mark on the *side* of #1 bearing cap and on the same side of the connecting rod. Then put *four* punch marks on the #4 cap and four punch marks on #4 connecting rod. Turn the crankshaft up so #2 and #3 are up high and put two marks on #2 cap and rod and three dots on #3 cap and rod. Now you can't mix up the rods and caps when it's time to reassemble.

Loosen the two 14mm nuts half a turn at a time on each side of #2 and #3 connecting rod bearing caps. Remove the nuts and washers and pull the bearing caps off. If the caps stick, use a brass or rubber hammer or a small piece of wood and a ballpeen hammer to lightly, and I mean lightly, tap the threads sticking through the bearing caps to loosen the connecting rod from around the crankshaft. Put the wood between the threads and the hammer! When you've moved the rod a little, remove the bearing cap. Do the same for #1 and #4 rods. When the caps are off, inspect the surface of the bearing shells inside for wear. There's a possibility the bearing shells won't come off with the caps, but will remain stuck to the crankshaft. If so, remove the shell with your fingers. Put the bearing caps and shells on your bench in 1, 2, 3, 4 order. All these orders make it sound a bit like you're in the Army, but it's important. The next time you overhaul an engine, you won't even need to read this book.

Step 4. Remove Main Bearing Caps

Remember the rap about the numbers on the main bearing caps and my request to make a note of the order? Remove the two bolts securing main bearing cap #3 around the crankshaft and then put them back into

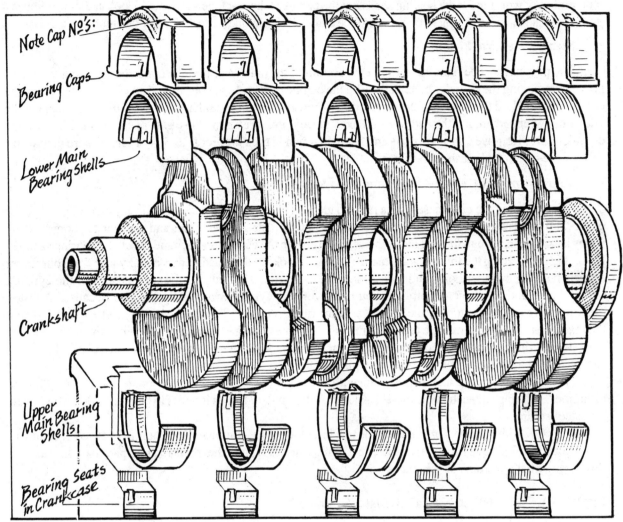

Note Cap Nº's:

Bearing Caps

Lower Main Bearing Shells

Crankshaft

Upper Main Bearing Shells

Bearing Seats in Crankcase

the rod cap, but don't screw them up. Now remove the other four bearing cap bolts and let them rest in the caps too. Use the two bolts resting in main bearing cap #3 as levers to wiggle the main bearing cap free from the crankshaft. *DO NOT USE A SCREWDRIVER OR ANYTHING ELSE AS A LEVER TO GET THAT BEARING CAP OFF*. It's tight but will come with lots of wiggling. When you have #3 off, remove the main bearing shell too. It may have stayed in the cap or remained around the crankshaft. Remove the other four main bearing caps along with the bolts and bearing shells and put them in the 1, 2, 3, 4, 5 order. **Remember**—if your main bearing caps are not in 1, 2, 3, 4, 5, order, put them on the bench in the order *they were installed in your engine*. Very important.

Step 5. Remove Crankshaft

Grasp the crankshaft at the front and rear and just lift it away from the crankcase. Be careful because it's heavy. Put it somewhere safe below your bench where it won't roll away.

Step 6. Remove Bearing Shells from Bearing Saddles

The five bottom halves of the crankcase bearing shells are probably still in the crankcase bearing saddles. Leave the bearing shells in position and examine 'em carefully for scratches after wiping off the oil from their surfaces. If, for example, #2 looks badly scratched, examine the machined surface of the crankshaft (the throw) which revolved in that bearing shell. Check the crankshaft for scratches, nicks, etc. After inspecting

Step 6. (Cont'd.)

the bearing shells, remove them from the saddles by pushing them out with your thumbs. Do not lever them out with a screwdriver or anything of that ilk. Put them in 1, 2, 3, 4, 5 order along with the main bearing caps. You probably won't reuse the bearing shells but the people at the machine shop should look at them. If you *are* going to reuse them, stick a piece of masking tape onto their backs and write their position numbers on the tape.

Step 7. Remove Pistons

The pistons must be removed through the bottom of the crankcase past the crankshaft bearing saddles to prevent damaging the cylinder bore walls. Flip the engine over and use your fingers to push a piston down the cylinder bore. Hold the bottom of the connecting rod away from the cylinder walls. Now use a hammer handle with a rag wrapped around the end of it and exert steady pressure on the top of the piston to slide it down the cylinder bore. Remove all four pistons and lie them down in their correct 1, 2, 3, 4 order. Be sure they won't roll off the bench and crash to the floor.

Step 8. Inspect Cylinder Bores and Crankcase

After cleaning the crankcase with a rag and clean solvent, check the crankcase very carefully. Look for cracks and deep scores in the bores. Look for cracks between the cylinder bores and between the bores and the water jacket holes around the outside of the crankcase. Flip the crankcase over and check the bearing saddles. If you see any cracks, the thing is shot (the first place to look for a replacement is a junkyard). Put your finger into each of the cylinder bores and feel for a ridge at the top. This ridge is the original size of the cylinder before the up and down motion of the piston rings wore the cylinder walls away slightly. Because the piston rings don't reach to the top of the bores, a slight ridge remains. The wear should not be excessive, but the machinist can determine the exact amount of wear by measuring it with a micrometer. If the bores are only very slightly ridged, and have no deep scratches or score marks in them, they can be honed and the old pistons can be reused after refitting them with new piston rings.

Tie the crankshaft to a nail in the ceiling with a strong piece of string. Tap one of the *counterweights* with a hammer. If it rings like a bell the metal is sound. A dull thud indicates it needs to be melted down and made into steel soldiers.

If it's OK with no scores or marks on the machined surfaces, continue. Bad crank? Go on to Procedure 6.

Procedure 7 gives a rundown on the crankshaft, crankcase and other parts in anticipation of the machine shop visit; what questions to ask, etc.

PROCEDURE 5: CHECK CLEARANCES. Phase 2.

Condition: Your engine is torn down and you wish to determine the condition of the crankshaft bearing shells.

Remarks: To measure the clearance you need a substance called Plastigage. Buy the green Plastigage; it's available at your machine shop or any parts house.

If your engine has many thousands of miles on it, you'll need to buy a packet of red Plastigage. The red stuff measures greater clearances (more wear). Plastigage is a thin strip of plastic which, after being compressed, is compared against the scale on the packet the stuff comes in. This reading will give you the clearances between the surface of the crankshaft journal (or throw) and the bearing shell. It's a highly accurate and very simple operation to perform. If *any* of your old bearings have the slightest scratch in them (or you've decided to replace them anyway), throw the lot away, buy new ones and forget this test. People with bad crankshafts should also skip this test and go to Procedure 6.

Step 1. Check Crankshaft Bearing Clearances

Clean the crankshaft until it's completely free of oil, grease, gunk, etc. Do the same thing with the bearing saddles in the crankcase. There mustn't be *any* grease or oil on either the saddles or the bearing shells. Reinstall the five bearing shells into the bearing saddles *in the same order* they came out. If any of the bearing caps or shells get mixed up, throw the shells away. If you reinstall the wrong bearing shell into a cap, you will have wasted all your efforts to make your engine like new. Stop here and buy new bearing shells. Continue with Procedure 6!! All in order? Continue.

Notice the little notch in the saddle which corresponds to a notch in the bearing shell. Line up the notches and press in the bearings with your thumbs. Don't use any oil or grease on the bearings.

When all five bearings are in position, lower the crankshaft into the crankcase. The sprocket end of the crankshaft goes toward the front of the crankcase. When the crank is seated on the bearings, find the cleaned main bearing caps and corresponding bearings. Press the bearing shells into the caps, making sure the notches on the shells line up with the notches on the caps. The *upper* halves of the main bearing shells that fit into the saddles have a lubrication groove in them. Be especially sure that main bearing cap #3 has its bearing shell correctly aligned; it has two outside lips which fit over the bearing cap.

Step 2. Measure Clearance

Lay a short piece of Plastigage across all five main crankshaft throws (see the diagram). Now reinstall the main bearing caps with the bearing shells in place onto their correct positions. Install the bolts in each bearing cap. Start with #3, go to #1, then #5, #2 and #4 and torque the bolts to 6.5 mkg (47 ft lbs). *Do not* turn the crankshaft for any reason or you will ruin the Plastigage strips. When you reach correct torque, *carefully* remove all five bearing caps and shells starting with main bearing #3.

Step 3. Measure Plastigage Strip

As you remove the main bearing caps, you'll find the flattened Plastigage strip stuck to the surface of the crankshaft. Using the scale on the side of the Plastigage packet as a guide, match the width of the Plastigage to the markings on the side of the package. The package marks

are in thousandths of an inch or in millimeters. The less wear in the bearing shells, the wider the strip of Plastigage will be. Conversely, if the bearing shells are worn, the Plastigage strip will not have compressed as much so it will not be as wide. Measure *both* ends of the strip. If there is a difference between ends, the crankshaft is unevenly worn. Make a note to have it checked by the machine shop.

If the bearing shells are in good condition, they will measure between 0.03 and 0.08mm (0.001 to 0.003 in). The wear limit for these main bearing shells is 0.17mm (0.007 in). So, if you have a measurement which is approaching 0.17mm (0.007 in), your bearing shells are worn out. Remove the Plastigage strip from the crankshaft journals with solvent, not a metal tool.

Step 4. Check Connecting Rod Bearing Clearances

If your main crankshaft bearings are worn out, you can bet your bottom dollar, yen, pound, peso, that the connecting rod bearings are also worn. I wouldn't even bother to measure them, just buy new ones. However, if you are in or around the grey zone of wear, it's worth measuring the connecting rod bearing clearances. You only need measure one of the bearings. I'd do #3. Find #3 piston and the connecting rod bearing cap and clean the bearing areas and bearing shells very carefully free from oil and grease. Place the clean crankshaft onto your clean work bench and put the #3 upper bearing shell into the connecting rod. Now fit the connecting rod around the #3 crankshaft journal (throw) with the arrow on top of the piston (and the dots you have made with your punch) facing forward. Lay a strip of Plastigage across the crankshaft journal, then install the connecting rod bearing cap with the bearing shell in the cap. Remember to line up your punch marks. Screw back the two nuts onto the connecting rod threads and tighten them to 4.5 mkg (33 ft lbs).

Step 5. Measure Plastigage Strip

Remove the two nuts from the connecting rod and pull off the cap. The flattened piece of Plastigage can now be compared to the scale on the packet. The clearance should be 0.028 to 0.088mm (0.0011 to 0.0034 in). The wear limit is 0.12mm (0.0047 in). Check both ends of the Plastigage strip. If the wear limit is approaching 0.12mm, your bearing shells are worn out and must be replaced. Remove the compressed Plastigage strip from the crank with solvent, not a metal tool. Remove all the bearing shells. If you're going to re-use them, stick a piece of masking tape onto their backs and write their number position on the tape.

Put a film of oil on all crankshaft bearing surfaces to prevent rust. In humid climates, it's surprising how fast rust can act. Wrap the crankshaft in a clean rag and stash it.

PROCEDURE 6: CHECK PISTONS AND CONNECTING RODS. Phase 2.

Condition: Engine overhaul.

Tools and materials: Phase 2 tool kit.

Step 1. Look

Problem pistons are easily detected. The top surface of the pistons will be very much blackened with carbon and other flaky deposits. See how the three piston rings are spread slightly away from the pistons. Be sure all three of the rings are intact (not broken) and that the bottom oil scraper ring has its thin inner spring in position. The sides of the pistons will have a bloom (or lightly colored wear patch) on them. This is normal. Check that the sides of the pistons are free from scratches and cracks.

The connecting rod is fastened to the piston by a piston pin held in position by two circlips. Hold the connecting rod tightly in one hand and try to rock the piston from end to end with the other hand as shown above. Don't slide it, just rock it. If it rocks, the piston pin or bushing on the rod have worn out. The machine shop can press a new bushing into the connecting rod and you can buy new piston rings if needed.

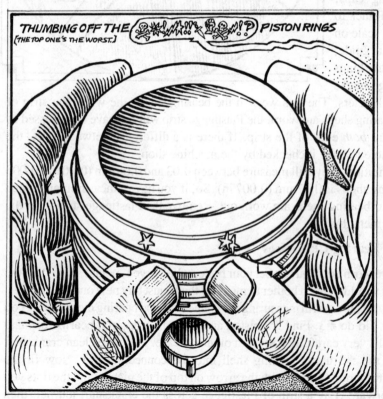

THUMBING OFF THE @*!!!¿@*&!? PISTON RINGS
(THE TOP ONE'S THE WORST.)

Step 2. Remove Piston Rings

Hold the connecting rod in a vise with layers of cloth around the rod for protection. Don't tighten the vise too much, you're just trying to stop the rod from moving. Put your two thumbs on the ends of the top ring and your two forefingers toward the center of the ring. Stretch the ring slightly with your thumbs and slide it upward over the top of the piston. Don't bend the ring—bent rings are useless. Place the ring on your bench with its top facing up; the same way it was installed on the piston. Now, remove the second ring using the same method and lie it down next to the first ring. Remove the third (the oil scraper ring) and bench that. Beneath the oil scraper ring is a thin, tightly coiled spring which may or may not come away with the ring. The spring is not one continuous piece like it looks,

Step 2. (Cont'd.)

but has a thin piece of wire crimped into one end into which the other end fits. Expand the spring slightly with your fingers and pull it away from the piston.

Look carefully at the piston rings and you'll see the top two rings (the compression rings) are slightly different. The second (middle) ring has a notch out of its lower outside surface. The top compression ring has a slight bevel on the top inside edge. Both rings have the word "top" engraved on one end. The oil scraper ring has two U scallops taken out of the inside and outside edge. This ring can be installed either way up.

Remove the rings from all four pistons and lay them down on a sheet of paper with the numbers 1, 2, 3 and 4 written on it. Pile up the rings in the order they came off. Again, if you're going to reuse these rings, the correct ring must go onto the correct piston. It's important.

Step 3. Separate Piston from Connecting Rod

First remove one piston pin circlip. To do this, use a thin drift or punch and insert it into the notch on one side of the piston. Carefully lever the circlip out holding your fingers just over the clip to prevent it from flying into orbit. When the clip's out, you can remove the piston pin by pushing it out through the side of the piston from which you have just removed the circlip. See the diagram. If you can't push the pin out using your fingers, find a piece of dowel that is bigger than the pin but will easily fit inside the hole and push the pin out. If you still can't get it out, put the whole lot into the oven and warm it to about 60°C (140°F). It will be a bit too warm to grasp tightly but won't sizzle your fingers. Don't get the works too hot. While it's hot, remove the pin with your fingers or a dowel.

Remove the pins from all four pistons and lay them down in 1, 2, 3, 4 order. When the pistons are cool, dip them into clean solvent and remove the carbon deposit from their tops. You can use a soft wire brush and a blunt knife or scraper. Don't touch the piston sides.

Clean the piston ring grooves with a toothbrush or a piece of broken piston ring. *Don't use* a wire brush on the sides of the pistons! Carefully examine the ring grooves for any nicks or trapped dirt. The top compression ring groove is more likely to wear than the other two, so pay close attention to it. Clean those pistons with a soft rag until they shine. Use the edge of the rag to eliminate any traces of dirt in the piston ring grooves. If you see burr damage in either of the top two ring grooves, clean the burr away with a tiny file. Do not file the outside edge of the piston.

Step 4. Check Connecting Rods

Find your four connecting rod bearing caps and install them onto their respective connecting rods. Be sure the forge marks and punch marks on the caps and rods line up. Screw the two nuts onto each rod. Clean the rods and caps with solvent and dry them off with a soft clean cloth. Check the bearing surfaces for nicks and scratches. Also check that the connecting rods are free from cracks, especially around the bearing surfaces.

Take a look at the top of the connecting rod through which the piston pin fits. There is a replaceable bronze bushing pressed into the connecting rod. Check the bushing for uneven wear, scratches and nicks. If there was rocking when you tested the connecting rod by trying to rock the piston, this connecting rod bushing is probably worn and will need to be replaced. The machine shop will check it for you. If you see any scratches or abrasions, you'll have to replace the piston pin and the connecting rod bushing.

Severe wearing of the upper part of the connecting rod is most unusual, unless the engine has received a violent shock such as seizing up. In this case, the piston pin could be bent and will need replacing. The possibility is discussed in Procedure 7. Don't despair! Maybe it can be saved.

PROCEDURE 7: ORGANIZE FOR MACHINE SHOP VISIT

Condition: The engine requires rebuilding and is in pieces.

Tools and materials: Notebook and pencil.

Remarks: Telephone the machine shop for an appointment.

Step 1. Evaluation

There are certain variables you now have to take into consideration. Let's say you stripped your engine because of excessive oil consumption and low compression. Measurement of the bores may show that the cylinders need boring out and this means you'll need oversized pistons and rings. If so, you *must* replace all the bearings in your crankcase. If the cylinder walls have worn so much that they need reboring, you can be sure every bearing needs replacing. Do not try to save money by reinstalling any of the old bearings.

Did you dismantle the engine because a valve dropped and broke one of the pistons? This can happen with few miles on the engine in which case the main rod bearings will be well within wear tolerance. You can save a little money by reusing your old bearings but putting in new ones gives your engine an extra lease on life, as it were. The rule of thumb seems to be that if there are 50,000 or more miles on your engine, replace *all* the bearing shells and also the piston rings. With anything below that mileage, you can possibly reuse the piston rings and the Plastigage test will have answered the bearing question.

The next variable is the crankshaft. Even if you find heavy damage to the crank, it's unlikely you'll have to replace it. Abrasions in the bearing surfaces of the crankshaft can be turned out on a lathe by the machinist.

Wrap the crankshaft with foam or clean rags to make sure it's not going to roll around and damage itself or anything else. Lay it in the trunk of the vehicle taking you to the machine shop.

Find the cylinder head with the camshaft and valves still installed, clean it as best you can and stick it in the trunk of the car.

Load up the crankcase and pistons and connecting rods (carefully wrapped in rags) and take along the bearing shells if the Plastigage test results were in the grey zone. Drive on down to the machine shop and enjoy the scenery on the way.

Step 2. Inspect Crankshaft

Unwrap the crankshaft and let the machinist inspect it. If it obviously needs machining, then oversize main and rod bearings will have to be installed.

Crankshaft Journal Sizes

| Sizes | Crankshaft main bearing journal | | | | Crankshaft connecting rod journal | | | |
| | Diameter | | Maximum out-of-round | | Diameter | | Maximum out-of-round | |
	mm	in	mm	in	mm	in	mm	in
Original								
grade 1	54.00–0.04	2.126–.0015	0.03	.0012	46.00–0.04	1.811–.0015	0.03	.0012
grade 2	54.00–0.06	2.126–.002	0.03	.0012	46.00–0.06	1.811–.002	0.03	.0012
Undersize 1								
grade 1	53.75–0.04	2.1161–.0015	0.03	.0012	45.75–0.04	1.8012–.0015	0.03	.0012
grade 2	53.75–0.06	2.1161–.002	0.03	.0012	45.75–0.06	1.8012–.002	0.03	.0012
Undersize 2								
grade 1	53.50–0.04	2.1063–.0015	0.03	.0012	45.50–0.04	1.7913–.0015	0.03	.0012
grade 2	53.50–0.06	2.1063–.002	0.03	.0012	45.50–0.06	1.7913–.002	0.03	.0012
Undersize 3								
grade 1	53.25–0.04	2.0965–.0015	0.03	.0012	45.25–0.04	1.7815–.0015	0.03	.0012
grade 2	53.25–0.06	2.0965–.002	0.03	.0012	45.25–0.06	1.7815–.002	0.03	.0012

If your engine seized up, there's the possibility the crankshaft is bent. Ask the machinist to test for crankshaft straightness. It's called checking 'crankshaft runout.' If the crankshaft passes that test, the machinist will measure the journals with a micrometer to finally determine if machine work is needed. On page 320 is a table of sizes to show the machinist if the crankshaft needs regrinding.

If the spirits weren't on your side and the crankshaft is not grindable, you'll have to buy a new one. They're not cheap, I'm sorry to say, but you do get some money back on your old one. When you buy a new crankshaft, also order new correct size main and connecting rod bearings (unless the machine shop is getting that all together).

If the journals on the crankshaft need grinding, the connecting rods will probably need reconditioning. Show the connecting rods and caps to the machinist, and s/he will decide what to do with them.

If one of your rods is badly damaged, ask if it can be remanufactured. If the bearing surface is damaged, they can bolt the cap and rod together and turn a new bearing surface on a lathe. The size of the new hole has to be matched with the bearing shells available and with the crankshaft journal sizes. If the rod was damaged, the crankshaft will definitely have to be reground.

Step 3. Inspect Crankcase

The crankcase bores will need to be measured by the machinist at three points. The first is taken 10mm (⅜ in) from the top of the bore; another at the same distance from the bottom of the bore and the third in the center of the bore. The same measurements are taken again with the micrometer twisted 90°. There are eight different sizes acceptable for these cylinder bores: a standard size for the 1.5 liter (89.7 cu in) engine and a standard size for the 1.6 liter (96.9 cu in) engine. The bores can be enlarged by drilling them out to accept larger pistons (reboring, it's called). Boring is done by the machine shop. The following table shows both piston diameter and the cylinder bore size required for the correct oversize piston.

Piston and Cylinder Diameters

Engine	Repair stage	Piston diameter		Cylinder bore	
		mm	in	mm	in
	Standard dimension	76.48	3.0110	76.51	3.0122
		76.49	3.0114	76.52	3.0126
		76.50	3.0118	76.53	3.0130
	First oversize	76.73	3.0209	76.76	3.0221
		76.74	3.0213	76.77	3.0224
		76.75	3.0217	76.78	3.0228
1471 cm³ (89.7 cu in)	Second oversize	76.98	3.0307	77.01	3.0319
		76.99	3.0311	77.02	3.0323
		77.00	3.0315	77.03	3.0327
	Third oversize	77.48	3.0504	77.51	3.0516
		77.49	3.0508	77.52	3.0520
		77.50	3.0512	77.53	3.0524
	Standard dimension	79.48	3.1291	79.51	3.1303
		79.49	3.1295	79.52	3.1307
		79.50	3.1299	79.53	3.1311
	First oversize	79.73	3.1390	79.76	3.1402
		79.74	3.1394	79.77	3.1406
1588 cm³ (96.9 cu in)		79.75	3.1398	79.78	3.1409
and					
1457 cm³ (88.9 cu in)	Second oversize	79.98	3.1488	80.01	3.1500
		79.99	3.1492	80.02	3.1504
		80.00	3.1496	80.03	3.1508
	Third oversize	80.48	3.1685	80.51	3.1697
		80.49	3.1689	80.52	3.1701
		80.50	3.1693	80.53	3.1705

The machinist will also inspect the bearing saddles and general condition of the crankcase.

Now, if the crankcase checks out OK and doesn't need boring, it still needs to be lightly honed. You can ask the machine shop to do it for you (cheap job) or you can rent or borrow a hone and do it yourself. The how-to is in Procedure 8.

Step 4. Inspect Pistons

If you think that you need any new pistons, get the machinist to look at the piston pin (wrist pin) bushings in the top of the connecting rods. S/he will also measure the pistons for wear and then finally check the piston-to-cylinder clearance in the crankcase.

Step 5. Buy Parts

With your machinist's recommendations and sizes, go to VW or a European parts shop. Find the list you made as you dismantled the engine and add to it the following list:

1. New connecting rods. Did the machinist recommend them? If so, make sure they'll fit the new or reground crankshaft.

2. Connecting rod bearings. Ask the machinist for the correct size to buy.

3. Main bearings. The machinist will have told you the correct size.

4. New piston or pistons? Again, the machinist will have told you the correct size to buy after consulting the sizes listed earlier in Step 2. A replacement piston must be the same weight class as the old ones.

5. New piston rings.

6. A complete engine rebuild gasket set. Buy this from VW. You can buy them from parts houses or from discount mail order places, but I don't recommend them. VW built the engines and the gaskets to fit them.

7. Nuts and bolts. Replace any rounded off nuts or bolts. Take the old nut/bolt with you for comparison. It's important to get the same thread size. Also buy a selection of spring or lock washers. Get eight new 14mm (head size) connecting rod cap nuts.

8. Loc-Tite. This thread cement is an extra insurance policy on those nuts and bolts that'll be torqued.

9. Miscellaneous—Points, condenser, distributor cap and spark plugs. Also check the materials listed at the beginning of the chapter.

Remarks: The gasket set you buy from VW includes new seals for each end of the crankshaft and a new one for the intermediate shaft. These seals can be easily installed using a block of wood and a hammer. It's not difficult but if you don't feel confident you can correctly install the seals into their seal plates, take the three seal plates and their new seals from the gasket set to the machine shop and ask them to press in the new seals for you.

PROCEDURE 8: PRE-ASSEMBLY

Condition: Engine requires rebuilding.

Tools and materials: A bucket of clean solvent and a stiff brush to clean parts, clean rags or a roll of lint-free paper towels, an old toothbrush, a ring groove cleaner or pieces of old piston rings, toothbrush, a small fine toothed file, access to a gram scale.

Remarks: Keep your hands, tools and work area spotlessly clean.

Step 1. Cleaning

You've been to the machine shop and have determined which old parts are going to be reinstalled into your engine. You will also have done your shopping and have those new parts at hand. Clean everything until it's shinier than my brother-in-law's scalpel. After all, a chance to clean is a chance to cure.

Step 2. Check and Balance Pistons

If you bought new pistons, check once again that the weight class number stamped on the top of your old piston(s) corresponds with the number on your new piston(s). The numbers and letters designate size as well

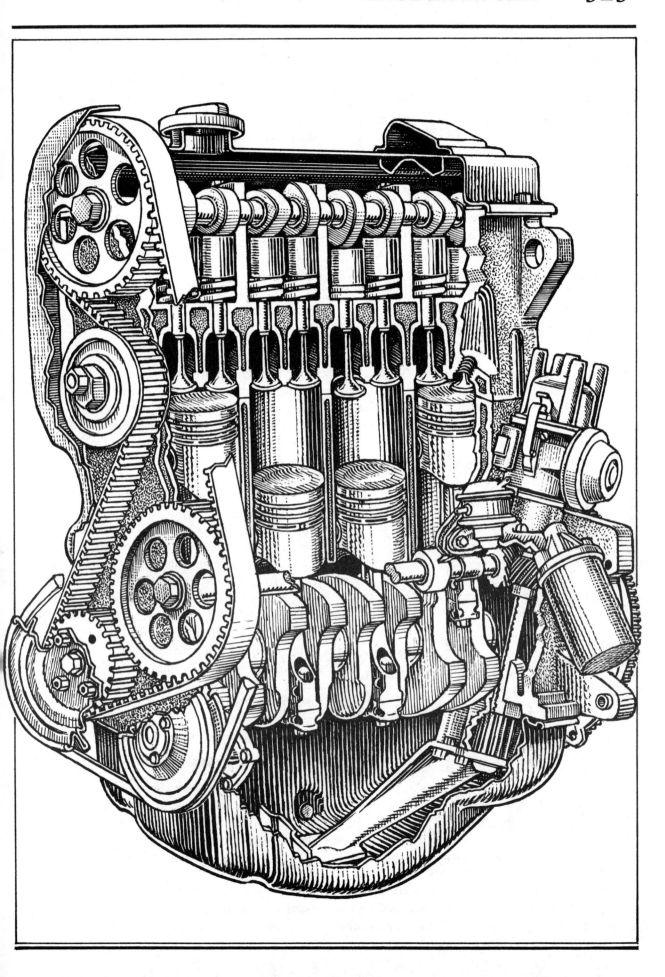

Step 2. (Cont'd.)

as weight class. If you had to buy four new pistons they should weigh the same. If you bought just one new piston, use a gram scale to check that your new one weighs the same as your other three. Weigh them all to find the lightest one. There shouldn't be more than 2.5 grams between the heaviest and lightest piston. That'll help maintain the internal stability we all crave. File metal from the heaviest until they all weigh the same. If you have to remove metal from the piston for balance, do so at the skirt (the bottom part of the piston). See the diagram. When filing any metal, hold the pistons in your hand—*do not put them in a vise!*

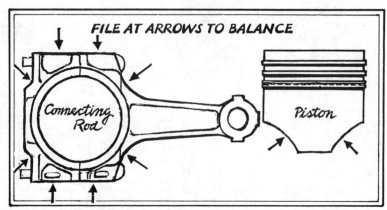

Step 3. Balance Connecting Rods

Balancing the connecting rods so's the difference between the heaviest and lightest is within 5 grams will help your engine stay alive for another 200,000 miles. If you have had one connecting rod remanufactured, or are only replacing one, you must balance the other three so that all four rods weigh the same. Use a gram scale. Find the connecting rods and their respective bearing caps and the new nuts. Push on the connecting rod

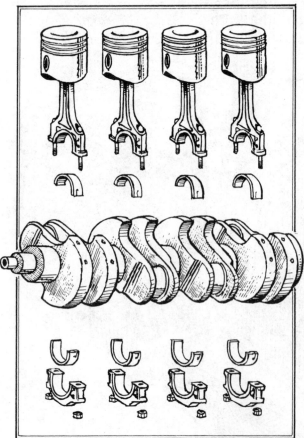

bearing caps without the bearing shells installed. Remember the punch and forge marks on the connecting rods? Well, match them up with the caps. Then screw on the two new nuts. With everything assembled, weigh each connecting rod on the gram scale and write down its weight.

There should be no more than 5 grams difference between the lightest and the heaviest connecting rods. If there is a greater difference than that, you must file away metal from the heavier rods. The diagram shows where. A medium file will remove about .2 gram per stroke. File slowly and gently and weigh the connecting rod after every few strokes. If you have, for example, five grams to remove from one connecting rod, remove 2½ grams from around the outside circumference of the connecting rod and 2½ grams from the outer circumference of the connecting rod bearing cap. Don't leave any jagged edges; keep it nice, neat and smooth. Keep the cap bolted onto the rod as you file.

Step 4. Assemble Pistons onto Connecting Rods

The pistons and rods are clean and balanced. If you're using one or more of your old pistons and had difficulty removing the piston pins, you'll probably have the same problem reinstalling them. Lay out the pistons in the 1, 2, 3, 4 order with their respective pins and circlips. Lay the connecting rods next to the pistons in the same order.

Before you install any of the rods onto the pistons, familiarize yourself with the position of the piston on the rod. The arrow on the top of the piston faces forward toward the *front* of the engine while the forge marks at the bottom of the rods face *left*. Thus, when the pistons are installed in the crankcase, the forge marks will point toward the intermediate shaft.

Wrap some cloth around the connecting rod and hold it firmly in the vise. Firm—not squashed! Remove the circlip from one side of any new pistons. Squirt oil into the piston hole and smear a drop of Lubriplate onto the piston pin. Push the piston pin into the piston from the side where you removed the circlip. Keep pushing until the pin sticks about 5mm (3/16 in) into the middle of the piston. Now make sure the forge mark on the connecting rod faces left in relation to the arrow on top of the piston and slip the rod onto the 5mm of piston pin. Push the pin until it slides through the rod and into the other side of the piston. When the pin is all the way in, install the circlip and check your work.

If you can't get the pin in, warm up the piston to no more than 60°C (140°F) in the oven and cool the pin in the freezer. When it's warm, use a rag to hold it so you won't be uncomfortable. Smear the piston pin with Lubriplate before you attempt to install it and use a rubber hammer or a piece of dowel and regular hammer to tap the piston pin into place.

When all the pistons and connecting rods are installed, hold each piston one at a time and let the connecting rod swing free. It should pivot very easily like the pendulum on Grandfather's clock. Test all four pistons. If any are tight, take the offending one(s) to the machine shop and ask for advice.

Now remove the rod cap nuts from the connecting rods and pull the caps off. Don't mix them up. Smear a film of oil onto the bearing surfaces of the rods and wrap some masking tape around the bottom of the rod threads onto which the caps fit. This will prevent the sharp threads from scratching the cylinder walls when the pistons are installed.

Step 5. Hone the Cylinder Bores

Remarks: Lightly hone the bores even if there's no ridge at the top of the cylinders unless the machine shop did it.

The ridge at the top of each cylinder bore is removed with the hone. Fit the hone into your electric drill and make sure the engine block is steady on your stand or bench. Push the hone into the cylinder and switch on the drill. Move the hone up and down the bore *twice*, then smartly withdraw it. Feel around the top of the cylinder. Has the ridge disappeared? If not, do the up-down motion twice again. That'll do it. Do all four bores, then wipe the bores with a clean oiled rag.

Step 6. Install Piston Rings

You're installing old pistons with new rings or installing new pistons and rings. Right? Right.

New pistons don't always come with new rings installed; the rings are usually in a separate little box and you have to install them yourself.

If you're using old pistons, you should have removed the rings already. Take #1 piston and a new set of rings. New rings are wrapped in oily plastic, so unwrap them and lay them on a clean paper towel. Before installing them onto the piston you must check the end gap of each ring. How? Find the oil ring, that's the one with the spring on the inside, and carefully remove the spring. Slide this ring about 15mm (5/8 in) into #1 cylinder bore and get it square with the top surface by *carefully* pushing it down with the top of the piston. Insert a 0.025mm feeler gauge blade between the two ends of the ring and try different blade sizes until you're able to accurately measure the tap. It should be between 0.25 and 0.40mm. Remove the ring and similarly put the middle compression ring into the #1 bore. That ring gap should be 0.3 to 0.45mm. Next the upper compression ring; the gap should also be 0.3 to

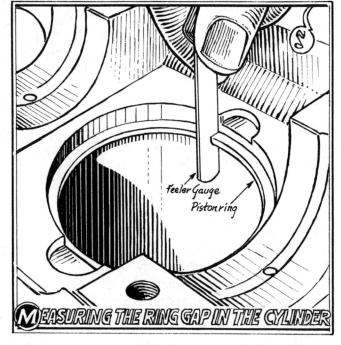

feeler Gauge
Piston ring

MEASURING THE RING GAP IN THE CYLINDER

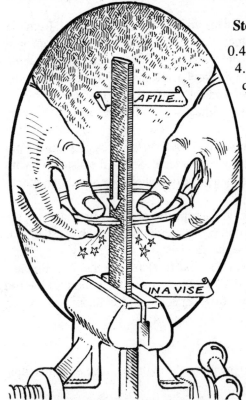

A FILE...

IN A VISE

WIDENING THE RING GAPS

Step 6. (Cont'd.)

0.45mm. Check the three piston rings which fit in bores #2, 3, and 4. If any ring gap you measured is smaller than the minimum required, there isn't enough clearance and you must increase it.

Put the tail of a small flat file in the vice, hold the ends of the piston ring in both hands and enlarge the gap by pressing down each end of the piston ring simultaneously on each side of the file. See the illustration.

Gaps correct? Now let's see if the piston rings bind up in their groove on the piston. Hold the ring and roll it around the groove. If it binds anywhere, check the inside of the piston ring groove for burrs, nicks or anything else. Clean any junk away with a tiny file or broken ring.

If you break or bend a ring, you have to buy a new set of three because they don't sell them individually. Also, if you bend one, please replace it; don't try to bend it back into shape. Once it's gone, it's gone.

Wrap a rag around the connecting rod and put it into the vice. We'll first install the third or bottom piston ring (the oil scraper ring). It's in two parts. The internal part is a spring which must be placed into the groove first. Expand the spring slightly by finding the ends and pull one end away from the other. One end has a piece of wire crimped into it as a guide for the other.

Slide the spring into the bottom ring groove and push it in place with your fingers. Now put your thumbs on the end of the oil scraper ring, cradle it between your thumbs and index fingers, stretch the ring slightly and slide it over the top of the piston into the bottom groove, over the spring. This ring doesn't snap into the groove flush with the sides of the piston; rather it sticks out a bit all the way around.

Look at the other two rings. They each have the word 'top' or a dot punched into their tops close to the ends. The middle ring has its bottom outside corner cut away in a step making the top of the ring slightly wider than the bottom. Maneuver this ring onto the piston using the same method used on the oil scraper ring.

The top ring has a bevel on its inside top edge that will face the inside of the piston groove. Install it. When all the piston rings are properly in

Replace the Rings

BOY, IF THIS KEEPS UP I'M GOING TO GET A RING EXPANDER.

place, stagger the gaps. Put the gap in the top ring at the 12 o'clock position facing forward, the gap in the middle ring at 12:20 and the gap in the bottom ring at 12:40. Now install the rings on the other three pistons and stagger the gaps the same way. This stagger prevents the compressed fuel/air mixture from escaping past the rings.

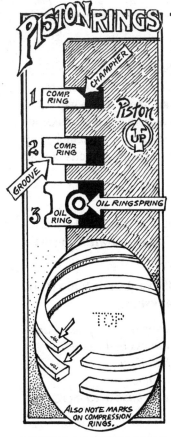

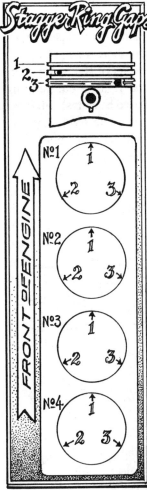

PROCEDURE 9: CRANKCASE (ENGINE BLOCK) ASSEMBLY

Condition: Your engine block is back from the machine shop having been bored, honed and cleaned and you have all the information the person at the machine shop has given you. Pistons and connecting rods have been balanced and piston rings installed. You have your new or reconditioned crankshaft and its size-matched bearings clean and at your disposal. The Baggies containing all the gubbins from the engine disassembly Procedures are laid out neatly in your work area.

Tools and materials: Phase 2 tool kit, torque wrench, Permatex, 3M weather-strip adhesive, Lubriplate, an oil can full of the same oil you're going to use in your engine, that piece of clean 2x4 wood, clean rags and paper towels, Friend, rebuild gasket kit from VW, all the parts you bought from your shopping list, crankshaft seal plates with the seals installed by the machine shop if you were too unsure to do them yourself.

Step 1. Pep Talk

Well team, you have done remarkably well so far. You've been learning where all the parts came from and how they fit together. It might look a little weird with hundreds of marked Baggies strewn asunder, but there's no mystery. The things are made of metal, they were designed by people to be put together by people. If you've followed the Steps so far, putting the thing together is a doddle (simplicity itself). Telephone the machine shop and ask for advice if you get stuck; they'll help.

Step 2. Dry Run

Look in your new parts pile and find the packet of new main bearing shells. (Using the old bearing shells? Do this too.) Four bearing shells are identical; the fifth has two ridges which fit over #3 bearing saddle in the crankcase. Five bearing shell halves have a lubricating groove running end to end. These *upper* bearing shells fit into the bearing saddles in the crankcase. All the bearings have a notch on one of their edges which line up with an indentation in the bearing saddle. There is a similar indentation in the main bearing caps in which fits the *lower* main bearing shells.

If you decided to reuse your old bearing shells, they have to be installed in the same position from where they were removed. Remember, if the crank has been reground, *USE NEW BEARINGS!*

Find and unwrap the crankshaft. Remember, the crankshaft sits on the upper main bearing shells fitted into the bearing saddles with the pointed end (which accepts the sprocket) facing *forward*. If you're using new bearings, wipe a smear of clean oil on the bearing shell face and then fit both halves around a crankshaft *main* journal. *Don't* put them around a connecting rod journal. You should be able to squeeze the two halves of the shells together so that the edges touch and easily turn both bearings around the crankshaft. Does it feel right? If you have doubts, you can do the more positive Plastigage test (next Step). If both ends of two halves of the main bearings won't touch when around the crankshaft journal, you have the wrong size bearing shells. Nip down to the machine shop with your crankshaft and bearing shells after doing the following connecting rod bearing test and ask their advice.

The connecting rod bearing shells are eight identical half shells without a lubricating groove in them. They are thinner than the main bearing shells.

Step 2. (Cont'd.)

However, they do have the little notch in them which corresponds to the notch in the connecting rod and connecting rod bearing cap. Wipe a smear of oil on the face of a pair of these bearing shells, and fit them around one of the crankshaft connecting rod journals and see if they fit. If they're too small, there'll be a gap when you put the two halves together. If they're too big, you will have too much clearance between the crankshaft and the bearing halves. Again, if you feel it's not correct, do the Plastigage test and return to the machine shop for help and advice. If anything's wrong, check to see if you fitted the connecting rod bearing shells around the *connecting rod journal* on the crankshaft, not on a main.

Step 3. Plastigage Test

Wipe all oil traces off the bearing shells and do Steps 2, 3 and 5 of Procedure 5. Don't do Step 4. Also do Step 5 of this Procedure if the Plastigage test shows that your old bearings are OK. Tighten down all the main bearing caps before you do the test.

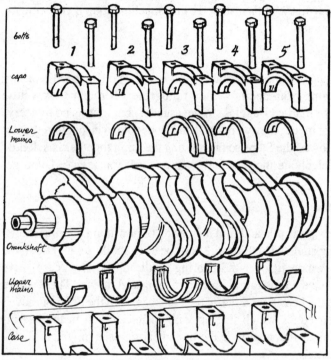

Step 4. Install Crankshaft Main Bearing Shells and Crankshaft

There was a young fellow named Hank
Who had a few bucks in the bank
He got dirt in his engine
From lack of attention
Now Hank and his bank need a crank.

Flip the crankcase so that the main bearing saddles are facing upward.

Wipe each of the bearing saddles with a piece of clean rag or lint-free paper towel, making absolutely sure there's no grit left on those saddles. Lay the set of five main bearing shells on the table (remove the masking tape from the rear of used bearings). Find #3 upper shell. It's the one with the flanges on the outside. Upper shells have the lubricating groove in them. Wipe #3 upper clean and place into #3 bearing saddle, matching the notch in the bearing with the notch on the saddle. Press it firmly in place with your fingers. Now, insert the other four upper bearing shells after cleaning them and press each one firmly into its saddle bearing. If you're using the old bearings, insert them onto the same bearing saddle from whence they originally came. Take a fingerful of Lubriplate and wipe the face of each bearing shell with a thin smear. Clean your fingers.

Take the spotlessly clean crankshaft and gently lower it into the new bearings. Retrieve the main bearing caps from the bench pile and clean them all with an ultra-clean rag. Fit #3 lower bearing shell into #3 cap. That's the shell with the flanges on the outside. Make sure the notch in the bearing shell lines up with the notch in the bearing cap. The numbers stamped into the base of the main bearing caps point *away* from where the intermediate shaft fits in the crankcase. These main bearing caps fit only one way so if you reverse one 180°, it won't fit properly around the crankshaft. The diagram shows an exaggerated view of how *not* to install your main bearing cap.

With #3 bearing shell firmly inserted into bearing cap #3, wipe a smear of Lubriplate over the shell and fit the cap around the crankshaft so

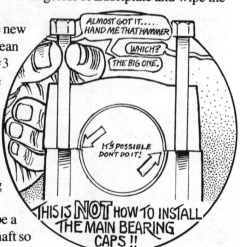

it lines up with #3 upper bearing saddle. Install the two 17mm bolts through the main bearing cap and into the saddle and screw the bolts up fingertight. Press down #3 bearing cap with your fingers so it fits snugly onto its saddle. If it won't fit properly, it's turned 180°. Check. OK? You can use a hammer handle to press the cap down onto the saddle if fingers won't do it. Remember that you wrote down the order in which the main bearing caps came off? Possibly the numbers stamped on the main bearing caps were not originally installed in numerical order. You could, for example, have 2, 1, 3, 5, 4 instead of 1, 2, 3, 4, 5. Press the cleaned main bearing shells into the remaining main bearing caps. Install used bearings into their original positions if you're using 'em. Now smear a thin film of Lubriplate onto the surface of those bearing shells.

Everything OK so far? Great—wipe your hands and position the bearing caps over the crankshaft and line them up with the bearing saddles. Get them in the correct original order and check that you've got the numbers all on the same side toward the intermediate shaft hole. Install the 17mm bolts and tighten 'em all up fingertight. Push down the bearing caps until they all seat correctly. Wonderful, it's going beautifully. Now take your 17mm socket, stick it on the torque wrench and, starting with #3, get a little tension on the bolts. After #3, tighten them a little in the following order: 1, 5, 2 and 4. When they are somewhat tight, torque them to 4.0 mkg (29 ft lbs). Torque all the main bearing cap bolts in the 3, 1, 5, 2, 4 order as above, starting with #3. When they're torqued to 4 mkg (29 ft lbs), torque all ten bolts to 6.5 mkg (57 ft lbs) using the same order. Go around the bolts once more—it's important that the torque is correct. Now check if the crankshaft turns easily. Yes? Marvelous.

Step 5. Measure Axial Clearance

Now that the crankshaft is in, you have to check the axial play (the gap between both edges of the #3 main bearing and the side of the crankshaft throw). Hit one end of the crankshaft smartly with a rubber hammer, or piece of wood and regular hammer to push it up the crankcase. Measure the gap between the side of bearing #3 and the crankshaft. The gap should be between 0.07 and 0.17mm (that's 0.003 to 0.007 in). The wear limit is 0.37mm

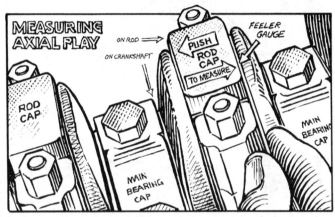

(0.015 in). Now hit the other end of the crankshaft to move it the other way and check the gap on the other side of #3 bearing. If you can't get a 0.07mm feeler gauge blade between #3 main bearing and the crankshaft, first make sure that the crankshaft is all the way forward (or backward). Hit it again with your hammer and remeasure the axial play. If the 0.07mm blade still won't fit, go to the machine shop and ask them to measure the axial play with a micrometer. A wider than specified gap can be corrected by installing new bearing shells if you're using your old ones. If, indeed, the play is too small then you will have to take the crankshaft out again and file a little off both sides of #3 main bearing. I've never had to file Rabbit bearings. In these days of computer quality control, main bearing sizes are usually extremely accurate. You should have no problem unless you're using inferior (cheap) parts. However, if necessary, file both bearing halves evenly using a very fine flat file. It's very tricky to file both halves of the bearing shells identically so you'll have to reinstall all the bearings and caps to accurately measure how much metal you've removed.

If nightfall is drawing nigh or friends have come for a binge and you decide to quit for the day, please cover your work with clean rags or paper towels and weight the covers down.

Step 6. Remove/Install Crankshaft Front and Rear Main Seals into Seal Plates

If the machine shop installed the seals into the retaining plates, go on to Step 7. If not, stay here.

Lay down the cleaned oil seal retaining plate on its face and, using a small wooden dowel and a hammer, tap the rear of the seal out of the plate. When the seal is flush with the face of the retaining plate, rest the edges of the plate on two small blocks of wood and continue tapping the rear of the seal until it's all the way out of the seal plate. Hang onto the seal. Clean the inside of the seal retaining plate thoroughly with solvent and dry it. Remove the seal from the other retaining plate in the same manner.

Find the large oil seal you removed from the rear oil seal retaining plate. The gasket set will include two different rear crankshaft seals (the flywheel side). There'll be a brown one and a black one. Check your old seal against the ones in the kit and make sure you install the correct one. The difference between the two is on the inner circumference in which the flange on the end of the crankshaft rides. Lay the rear of the oil seal retaining plate on a solid flat surface. Give the seal a shot of silicone spray if you've got some and place your new oil seal on top of the retaining plate. The rear of the seal has a big groove which must face down. Use a small ball peen hammer to gently tap all around the outer seal edge until it slides into the retaining plate. When it's in about 3mm (⅛ in), lay a flat piece of wood on top of the seal. Gently tap the center of the wood while moving the wood around the outside of the seal. Continue tapping until the seal begins to slip further into the plate. When the seal is flush with the face of the plate, find a wooden dowel and continue tapping around the edge of the seal until the rear of the seal is flush with the rear of the plate.

Now do exactly the same thing with the front oil seal.

Step 7. Install Seal Plates

Look at each end of the crankcase where the oil seal retaining plates fit. If there are any pieces of old gasket still sticking, apply gasket remover spray (if you've got any) and scrape it all off with a sharpened paint scraper or razor blade making positively certain that none of the pieces of gasket go inside the crankcase. Don't nick the metal. When all the old gasket is gone, dry the crankcase with a rag.

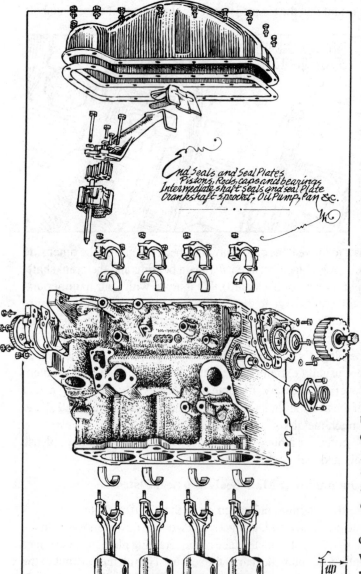

End Seals and Seal Plates. Pistons, Rods, caps and bearings. Intermediate shaft seals and seal Plate. Crankshaft sprocket, Oil Pump, Pan &c.

Look in your gasket set for the two oil seal retaining plate gaskets. They're the same shape as the plates, so match the gaskets with the retaining plates to make sure you have the right ones. The gaskets in some gasket sets have a silver side and a side with writing; others are silver on both sides. Both types are fine. Fit the front gasket onto two metal pins (dowels) on the front of the crankcase. Carefully slide the oil seal retaining plate over the crankshaft and push the plate onto the two pins sticking out of the engine. You'll have to turn the plate side to side a little to get the lip of the oil seal to ride over the front part of the crankshaft.

Find the 10mm bolts and washers from your marked Baggie. If your retaining plate has a 13mm bolt going through it or your model has a separate drive belt shield, install these on the face of the oil seal retaining plate. Now screw the bolts through the retaining plate into the crankcase. Tighten them fingertight. When you're certain the oil seal is properly located around the crankshaft and the plate is flat against the crankcase, torque the bolts in diagonal sequence to 2 mkg (14 ft lbs).

Now install the rear oil seal retaining plate onto the rear of the crankcase in exactly the same way. Remember to install a gasket between the rear retaining plate and the crankcase! Torque the plate bolts to 2.0 mkg (14 ft lbs).

Step 8. Install Pistons in Crankcase

The pistons (with rings) are already installed onto the connecting rods. Recheck that the gaps in the rings are staggered evenly around the circumference (see diagram in Procedure 8, Step 6).

Let's start with piston #1. Turn the crankshaft so #1 and #4 connecting rod throws are at the *lowest* position. Get a new bearing shell out of the box and clean it well with a cloth. Push the bearing shell into the connecting rod and be sure the little notch on the shell lines up with the notch in the connecting rod. Press the bearing fully home and smear a little Lubriplate onto the bearing shell. Turn your engine over if it's on a stand, or set it on two pieces of wood so there's no weight on the crankshaft. Squirt some oil on your fingers and smear the oil on the inside of #1 cylinder bore. Wipe it all the way around. Pour oil on the piston rings too.

Point the arrow stamped on top of the piston toward the front of the crankcase and check that the forge marks on the bottom of the connecting rod point toward the intermediate shaft hole. If the marks point away from the hole, you'll have to remove the piston pin circlip and piston pin and turn the piston around.

Gingerly lower the piston into the cylinder bore from the top. Take care the connecting rod does not bang against the cylinder walls. Place your ring compressor around the piston rings and tighten the compressor so the rings are completely in their grooves and flush with the side of the piston. No ring compressor? Read on. When the rings are compressed, check again that the arrow on the piston top is pointing directly toward the front of the engine. Push the top of the piston down with your hand or a hammer handle. When the oil scraper ring is down inside the bore, loosen the ring compressor and move it up to compress #2 and #1 rings. Continue pushing the piston down until all three rings have disappeared into the cylinder bore.

If you don't have a ring compressor but have strong fingers, use them to hold each ring against the piston side. It is also possible to use an 11cm (4 in) hose clamp to compress the piston rings but you'll have better luck with your fingers. Get Friend to help if necessary. Be especially careful not to bang the piston against the machined upper crankcase surface. Go slow 'n easy.

With #1 piston in place, repeat the process with #4 piston. Don't forget to insert the connecting rod bearing shell.

With two pistons in, carefully flip the crankcase so the crankshaft is facing you. #1 and #4 throws on the crankshaft will be pointing upward toward you. Feel past #1 throw, grasp the connecting rod and pull it up

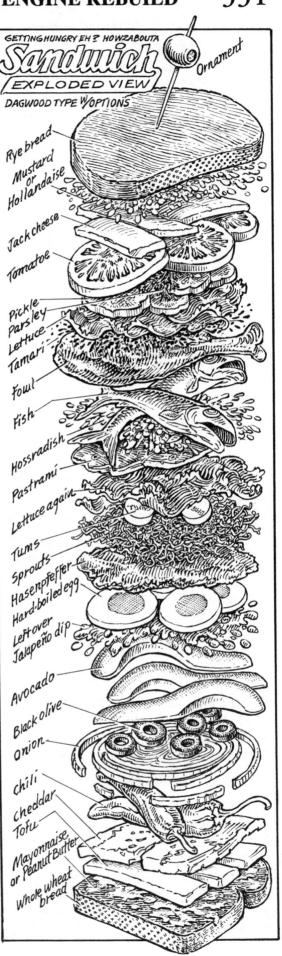

GETTING HUNGRY EH ? HOWZABOUTA

Sandwich

EXPLODED VIEW

DAGWOOD TYPE W/OPTIONS

Ornament
Rye bread
Mustard or Hollandaise
Jack cheese
Tomatoe
Pickle
Parsley
Lettuce
Tamari
Fowl
Fish
Hossradish
Pastrami
Lettuce again
Tums
Sprouts
Hasenpfeffer
Hard-boiled egg
Leftover Jalapeño dip
Avocado
Black olive
Onion
Chili
cheddar
Tofu
Mayonnaise or Peanut Butter
Whole wheat bread

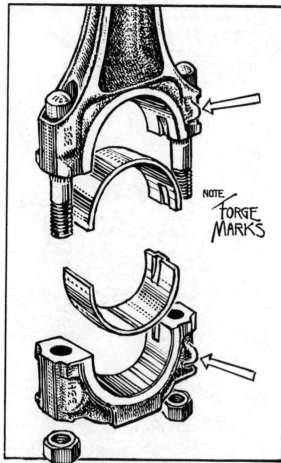

NOTE
FORGE
MARKS

Step 8. (Cont'd.)

until the connecting rod bearing insert mates with the crankshaft. Check that the bearing shell is still installed and hasn't fallen out somewhere as you were pushing on the piston. Remove the masking tape from the studs.

Find #1 connecting rod bearing cap and install the cleaned connecting rod bearing shell. Smear some Lubriplate on the face of the shell and install the connecting rod cap onto the studs of the connecting rod.

Be sure the forge and punch marks on the side of the connecting rod and the connecting rod bearing cap line up. Put on two new 14mm nuts fingertight. Now go through the same process with #4. Don't forget to install the bearing shell in the connecting rod cap.

Flip the crankcase again after turning the crankshaft so that #2 and #3 throws are in the lowest position. Install piston #2 and piston #3. *Don't forget to install the bearing shells into the bottom of the connecting rods.* Turn the crankcase over once more and install the connecting rod bearing caps (with bearing shells installed) and the new 14mm nuts. Now find your torque wrench and slip on a 14mm socket. Torque the #2 connecting rod bolt nuts in ½ turn stages until you reach 4.5 mkg (33 ft lbs). When #2 is done, then do #3.

Rotate the crankshaft so #1 and #3 connecting rod bearing caps are facing you. Torque the 14mm nuts to 4.5 mkg (33 ft lbs). Turn the crankshaft (it's hard to turn with all the pistons installed) and check your work. Stick a clean rag into the top of the cylinder bores to protect them and the pistons.

Step 9. Install Intermediate Shaft and Oil Seal

Remove the old intermediate shaft oil seal from the plate and install a new one. Use the same method described in Step 6 of this Procedure. Dig through your gasket set for a thin rubber O ring about 38mm (1½ in) in diameter. Stretch the O ring over the rear shoulder of the retaining plate. Smear Lubriplate on the toothed end of the intermediate shaft and the small cam lobe in the middle of the intermediate shaft (if present). A final smear on the front part of the intermediate shaft behind the oil seal and you can slip the intermediate shaft into position. Push it into the crankcase making sure the rear part of the shaft fits well in its little hole.

Look at the intermediate shaft oil seal plate. It may have a hole in the rear close to the seal. There is a similar hole in the bottom part of that depression in the crankcase where the intermediate shaft sticks out. The hole in the plate *MUST* line up with the hole in the crankcase. Turn the plate over until they do. Install the two 13mm bolts and washers and torque them to 2.5 mkg (18 ft lbs).

Step 10. Install Drive Belt Sprocket on Front of Crankshaft

First install the half moon key (Woodruff key). Lubricate the key slightly with oil and put the *round* side into the slot on the crankshaft. Tap it down snug with a small hammer. Find the correct drive belt sprocket. Clean it with solvent and dry it. Put your new (or old) drive belt (timing belt) on the drive belt sprocket if the V belt pulley is still bolted onto the sprocket. Slide the drive belt sprocket onto the crankshaft. Line up the slot on the inside of the sprocket with the Woodruff key. Get your 19mm bolt with its thick washer and put three drops of Locktite on the threads. Insert the bolt through the drive belt sprocket into the end of the crankshaft. Tighten the bolt. Find your faithful short piece of 2x4 wood and stick it between one of the crankshaft counterweights and the left side of the crankcase. Torque the 19mm crankshaft bolt to 8 mkg (58 ft lbs). I hope

Step 10. (Cont'd.)

you remembered to install the drive belt if your V-belt pulley is bolted to the sprocket. Forgot? Remove the 13mm bolts or 6mm socket head bolts which hold the V-belt pulley on the drive belt sprocket and pull off the pulley. Slip the drive belt on and reinstall the pulley and torque the bolts to 2 mkg (14 ft lbs). Keep the piece of 2x4 between the crank and the engine block.

Step 11. Install Intermediate Plate and Pressure Plate (Standard) or Torque Converter Drive Plate (Automatics)

You have checked your pressure plate for looseness and general good health (Chapter 16, Procedure 5, Steps 3 and 4). If your car is automatic, check the torque converter drive plate for missing teeth.

Standard transmission: Find your intermediate plate and clean it. Remove your crankcase from the engine stand. You'll need Friend to help. Put the crankcase on your bench and fit the intermediate plate on the crankcase rear, making sure the plate fits on the dowel pins sticking out. Put the crankcase back on to the stand.

Automatic transmission: Don't worry about the intermediate plate right now.

Standard or Automatic: Push the pressure plate or the torque converter drive plate on the rear of the crankshaft and line up the irregularly spaced holes in the plate with the holes in the crankshaft. Find the six 17mm bolts and metal spacer that goes between the bolts and the plate. Apply Locktite on the bottom part of the threads of those bolts and screw them into the crankshaft.

Automatic people: The ears on the outside circumference of the torque converter drive plate face *away* from the engine. Torque the 17mm bolts to 7.5 mkg (54 ft lbs) in a diagonal pattern.

All: Remove the piece of wood from between the crankshaft counterweights and the inside of the engine.

Step 12. Install Oil Pump

You have previously inspected the internal workings of your oil pump and found all specifications to be within tolerance or you have a new oil pump.

Find the Baggie with the two 13mm oil pump bolts and washers in it. Lubriplate the end of the oil pump drive shaft; a little dab'll do ya. Lower the oil pump into the crankcase with the scavenger pipe pointing forward diagonally across the crankcase underside, below the crankshaft. Refer to the full page exploded engine if you're lost. Torque the two 13mm bolts to 2 mkg (14 ft lbs).

Step 13. Install Oil Pan

Your oil pan is thoroughly clean inside and out. No? Clean it.

Squeeze a thin line of 3M weatherstrip adhesive around the lip of the oil pan and smear it all around. Wipe a cloth along the bottom of the crankcase to remove any oil. Find the oil pan gasket from your set and lay it on the bottom of your crankcase. When you've got the gasket to fit the shape of the engine, flip it over and stick it on the oil pan. Smear some weatherstrip adhesive on the bottom of the engine and install the oil pan, lining up the holes so the oil pan bolts can go in. The socket bolts have both a round and square washer; the hex bolts have just a regular washer. Install all twenty bolts and washers, then tighten them until the pan is fairly secure. First torque the four extreme corner bolts to the following values: the socket headed bolts are torqued to 1 mkg (7 ft lbs); the hex headed bolts to 2 mkg (14 ft lbs). Then tighten and torque the remaining oil pan bolts. Remove the oil pan drain bolt and slip on its new copper washer from the gasket set. Screw it into the oil pan and torque it to 3 mkg (22 ft lbs).

Step 14. Install Oil Filter Manifold

Check the crankcase for traces of the old gasket and remove them. Find the new manifold gasket and compare it to the manifold to see if it's the right one. The scrupulously clean manifold is attached by three 6mm socket headed (allen) bolts and washers. Position the gasket and manifold against the engine, screw in the bolts and torque them to 2 mkg (14 ft lbs). 1975 models may have an EGR filter which is part of that oil filter manifold.

Step 15. Install Fuel Pump (Carbureted Models)

Dip into you gasket set and find a black or brown plastic block about 8mm (5/16 in) thick. This block fits between the fuel pump and the crankcase. Also find another thin rubber O ring about 38mm (1½ in) in diameter. Press this O ring into the rear of the fuel pump in a plump Figure 8 shape. The plastic block has a small nipple at the top which fits into a small recess on the back of the fuel pump. Find the 6mm allen bolts and washers in the marked Baggie and fasten the fuel pump to the engine. Torque the two 6mm bolts to 2 mkg (14 ft lbs).

Step 16. Install Control Pressure Regulator (Fuel Injection)

Remove the clean CPR from the Baggie along with the two 6mm bolts and washers. Fit the CPR on the side of the crankcase, screw in the two 6mm bolts and torque them to 2.0 mkg (14 ft lbs).

Step 17. Install Water Pump

Pump clean? Check that it still works by turning the front pulley. It should turn fairly easily but not spin around like a bicycle wheel. If it either spins too freely or is difficult to turn, the pump is shot and you must replace it. See Chapter 17, Procedure 1.

OK. With a good pump in your frenzied grasp, rummage through your gasket set once more for a 50mm (2 in) rubber O ring and press it into the rear of the pump casting which fits on the engine. Install the upper two 13mm bolts and washers if your car is air conditioned or has a smog pump. If not, install the lower 13mm bolt (or bolts) through the pump into the crankcase. Torque the bolts to 2 mkg (14 ft lbs).

Don't put in that central bolt yet; it's the one that secures the air conditioner compressor bracket. Let's put the bracket on first.

Step 18. Replace Mounts (Air Conditioner and/or Smog Pump Models only)

You may have to use a little intuition when replacing your air conditioner support bracket since there are lots of styles.

The bottom part of the smog pump bracket is fastened across the face of the water pump. Install the one or two 13mm bolts and torque to 2 mkg (14 ft lbs). In early air conditioned carbureted cars, the smog pump attaches to the bottom part of the air conditioner bracket. The alternator goes between the smog pump and the upper part of the air conditioner bracket and is fitted in various ways. Tricky.

Clean the air conditioner bracket if you haven't done so already, and find all the rubber and metal inserts and spacers which fit into the air conditioner bracket. Line the bracket up with the two holes in the engine and the water pump. Fit all the rubber spacers and metal washers into the bracket before attempting to install it on your engine. Loosely install all the bolts with your fingers. When everything is installed, torque all the bolts to 2 mkg (14 ft lbs).

Step 19. Install Intermediate Shaft Drive Belt Sprocket (All Models)

Find your intermediate shaft drive belt sprocket in its handsome, tight fitting Baggie along with the 19mm bolt and thick washer which secures it to the intermediate shaft. Lurking in the bottom of your Baggie is the half moon shaped Woodruff key.

First, lightly oil the Woodruff key and then tap it into the slot on the intermediate shaft, then slide the drive belt sprocket onto the shaft. Check that it's on correctly by looking at the crankcase from the side to see if it lines up vertically with the drive belt sprocket on the crankshaft. There's a punch mark (a dot) on the *outside* face of the intermediate shaft. The dot is used to get the valve timing correct later. Put a few drops of Locktite on the bolt threads, then tighten the 19mm bolt. Stick a thick screwdriver through one of the holes in the drive belt sprocket and use it as a lever against the force which you exert as you torque the bolt to 8 mkg (58 ft lbs). Don't let the screwdriver slip.

Step 20. Install Distributor

Carefully check the distributor shaft gear for signs of wear and/or broken teeth. If any teeth are broken, you will have to replace the distributor. Try to buy a used one. It's important to get the same distributor as the

Step 20.   (Cont'd.)

one originally fitted to your car. They have advance/retard units on them.

Clean your distributor, especially the insides. Install new points (Chapter 10, Procedure 14, Steps 5-9). Leave the cap off for now. Find a new flat paper gasket which goes between the distributor and the crankcase from the gasket set. Peer into the gloom where the base of the distributor fits onto the crankcase. You will see a lip in the center of the oil pump drive shaft. A slot in the base of the distributor shaft fits into the lip. Get the lip running parallel to the crankshaft by using needle nose pliers. Find the 13mm bolt and washer along with the U-shaped clamp that holds the distributor on the crankcase. Install the paper gasket onto the distributor and lower it into the engine keeping the thin line in the top edge of the distributor at about a 30^0 angle to the crankcase. This means the vacuum advance/retard canister on the side of the distributor will be pointing diagonally away (toward the rear) from #3 cylinder bore.

Put on the new rotor and align the end of the rotor with the thin line on the top edge of the distributor. Point both marks (the one on the rotor and the one on the distributor) to about 50 mm (2 in) behind #4 spark plug hole. Don't worry about getting it perfect because you'll have to adjust things when the engine is fully assembled anyway. Secure the distributor with the 13mm bolt and use a wrench to tighten it ½ turn beyond fingertight. Pull off the rotor, put the dust shield on the distributor and reinstall the rotor.

Step 21. Install Clutch (Standard Transmission)

Please turn to Chapter 16, read through Procedure 5 and do Steps 8 and 9.

Well, that's just about all the junk that has to go on the crankcase; next comes the cylinder head. Even if you've been working continuously, do the next Procedure.

PROCEDURE 69: RESTORE SANITY

Condition: Engine overhauler approaching the abyss.

Tools and materials: Baggie/bottle of Mother's little helper.

Step 1. Get Ready

Gather your tools and materials around your favorite armchair and settle back.

Step 2. Unscrew Cap/Roll Numbers

Introduce bottle/number to lips. "Lips, this is bottle/number. Bottle/number, this is Lips."

Step 3. Chug-a-lug

You can do it.

Step 4. Howd'ya Feel?

Better, I hope.

PROCEDURE 10: READY CYLINDER HEAD. Phase 1.

Condition: Valve job, engine rebuild, head swap.

Tools and materials: Phase 2 tool kit.

Remarks: If you're swapping heads, then follow this Procedure to install the stuff from the old head onto the new. If you've had your old head worked on by the machine shop, do the assembly steps (begin at Step 6) in this Procedure to reinstall the goodies you removed in Procedure 2. The machine shop may or may not have installed a new oil seal in the front of the head. If not, then remove the camshaft sprocket as per Step 2 (get Friend to support the head) and install the seal (Step 4). Then continue with Step 6, OK?

Step 1. Remove Camshaft

First, check that the camshaft bearing caps are numbered 1 to 5 in sequence. #1 is at the front of the head (the drive belt end). If they are out of sequence and you are here to work on your old head for any reason, the camshaft bearing caps must be reinstalled in your head in the same order in which they came out. People changing the camshaft from the old cylinder head to a new one won't need the bearing caps from the old one anymore. Having made note of the order, remove bearing caps #1, 3 and 5 by using your 13mm socket to remove the nuts, then pulling off the caps with your fingers. Now loosen one turn the right nut on bearing cap #2, then the left nut on #4. Now loosen one turn the left nut on #2 and the right nut on #4. This loosening sequence is to prevent the camshaft from bending. If you decide to remove the camshaft bearing caps in a different order, you may bend the camshaft. Continue loosening the nuts from bearing caps #2 and #4 until there's no tension on the nuts. That tension is valve spring pressure. Remove bearing caps #2 and 4 and put them in order with the other three. Lift out the camshaft. Examine the camshaft carefully for scratches and chips out of the lobes, then clean and wrap it with a soft rag.

Step 2. Remove Drive Belt Sprocket from Camshaft

Note that the sprocket has a punch mark

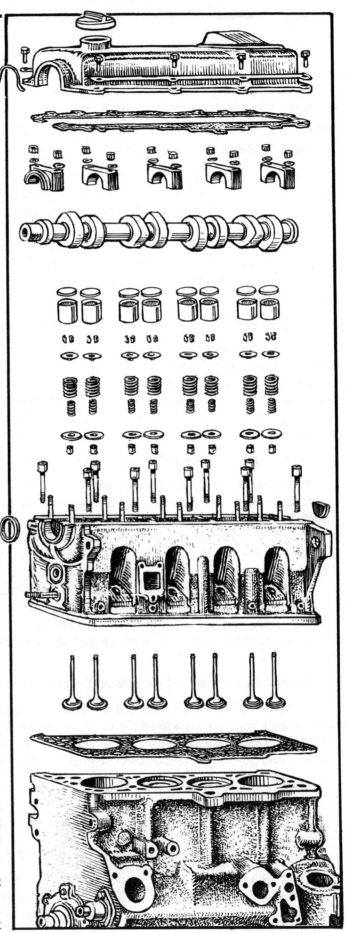

Step 2. (Cont'd.)

(dot) on its *rear* face. Put the drive belt sprocket with the camshaft bolted to it into your vise. Don't clamp the camshaft in the vise! Use your 19mm socket to remove the bolt and thick washer holding the sprocket onto the camshaft. When the bolt is loose, hold the camshaft with one hand and unscrew the bolt with the other hand. Keep the oil seal and put the 19mm bolt and washer and the drive belt sprocket into a marked Baggie.

Step 3. Remove Cam Followers

Lay your new cylinder head alongside the old one. Squirt some oil onto your forefinger and smear it inside the eight large holes in the top of your new cylinder head. You're going to remove the cam followers from the old head and immediately put them into the new. The cam followers are easily removed using your thumb and forefinger only; *don't* use pliers. If one is stuck, squirt it with a little oil or Liquid Wrench.

Start at #1. Pull out #1 cam follower (it has a valve adjusting disc in the top which stays put in the follower). Clean the cam follower with a lint-free rag and slide it into the new head. Do the same with all the remaining cam followers. Keep them in order. In other words, if you take out #8, put it into #8 hole in your new head.

Step 4. Install Oil Seal and Camshaft Drive Belt Sprocket

Root around in your gasket set to find a circular oil seal identical to the one originally fitted around the camshaft in your old cylinder head. Place the oil seal over the end of the camshaft. Install the Woodruff key into the slot in the end of the camshaft. Now slide the camshaft drive belt sprocket onto the camshaft (with the punch mark *facing* the camshaft). Put Locktite on the 19mm bolt and install it and the thick washer. Hold the drive belt sprocket in the vise and, holding the camshaft with one hand, torque the 19mm bolt to 8 mkg (58 ft lbs). Be careful not to trap the oil seal between the sprocket and the camshaft.

Step 5. Install Camshaft in New Cylinder Head

First remove the camshaft bearing caps from the new cylinder head. Look at the numbers stamped on the top of the bearing caps. Remove them and lay them on the bench in the same numerical order they were installed. Smear Lubriplate on the inside bearing surface of the bearing caps and bearing saddles in the cylinder head. Lower the camshaft into your new head, making sure the front oil seal is positioned in the groove. Now find bearing caps #2 and 4 and install them onto their correct positions around the cam. Install the two washers and 13mm nuts on each of the two bearing caps and begin to tighten them diagonally (right #2, left #4, etc.) with your socket. When valve spring pressure is felt, tighten the four nuts one turn at a time until the bearing caps come into contact with the bearing saddles.

Now install and secure the other three bearing caps making sure the front oil seal is correctly aligned in the groove under #1 bearing cap. Screw on the remaining nuts and washers and torque them all to 2 mkg (14 ft lbs).

Step 6. Install Timing Belt Tension Pulley Stud

Your new cylinder head probably doesn't have a threaded stud sticking out from its front face. This stud holds the pulley which adjusts timing belt tension. Place a vice grip on the *unthreaded* part of the stud in your old cylinder head. Turn the stud out ⟲ , clean the threads, apply Locktite on the threads and screw the stud into your new cylinder head. Use vise grips to tighten it.

Step 7. Install Oil Pressure Switch (if present)

Unscrew the oil pressure switch from the rear of your old head with a crescent wrench, clean it and screw it into the new.

Step 8. Remove/Reinstall Check Valve Manifold (Carbureted only)

This manifold is held by four 17mm bolts to the left side of the cylinder head. There's a washer on the front and rear of the bolt. Loosen all four bolts, remove them from the manifold and pull the manifold off. Clean it and the bolts and washers with a wire brush and cloth. Install the manifold on your new head. Put a

Step 8. (Cont'd.)

washer on the bolt before it's pushed through the manifold, then put another washer between the manifold and the cylinder head. Torque the 17mm bolts to 2 mkg (14 ft lbs).

Step 9. Remove/Reinstall Rear Coolant Manifold

This manifold is held to the head by two 10mm bolts. Remove the two bolts and pull off the manifold. Clean it thoroughly, scraping away any remnants of gasket.

Find a new gasket in the gasket set, apply a thin layer of Permatex both on the rear of the manifold and also on the new cylinder head. Place the gasket on the manifold after inserting the two bolts through the manifold so the gasket lines up properly. Install the manifold, resplendent with its gasket, on the head and torque the two nuts to 1 mkg (7 ft lbs).

Step 10. Install Left Coolant Manifold

Unscrew the three 10mm bolts and washers and remove the old manifold from the head. Scrape off any gasket still sticking to the rear of the manifold. Apply a thin layer of Permatex to the rear of the manifold and another thin smear on the new cylinder head. Position the new gasket and install the three 10mm bolts. Torque them to 2 mkg (14 ft lbs).

You can now reinstall the old camshaft bearing caps onto your old cylinder head and put the old head into a box to take to VW in exchange for $$. Your new cylinder head is now ready to bolt onto your crankcase.

PROCEDURE 11: INSTALL CYLINDER HEAD. Phase 1.

Condition: The old cylinder head has been overhauled by the machine shop or your new cylinder head is ready to go.

Tools and materials: Phase 2 tool kit, gasket set.

Remarks: If you're following this Procedure after having had a valve job (engine remained in car), you'll first have to reinstall the exhaust and intake manifolds on the cylinder head.

Step 1. Prepare Thyself

Carefully remove the four rags from the cylinder bores and clean any drops of oil or Lubriplate which may have found their way onto the machined upper surface of the crankcase. Now clean off any grease or whatever from the underside of the cylinder head. Find the new cylinder head gasket from your gasket kit and compare it to the old one. The same? Lay the new cylinder head gasket on top of the crankcase so the word ''Oben'' or ''Top'' faces up toward the cylinder head. You can thus read the 'Oben' when the gasket is installed on top of the crankcase.

Step 2. Install Cylinder Head

Find and clean in solvent the ten 10mm bolts and washers which hold the cylinder head to the crankcase. Make sure there are ten bolts and ten washers. If you've lost a washer, buy a new one—don't attempt to install the head without washers below the bolts.

Place bolts into the center holes on both sides of camshaft bearing cap #3. Lift the head and lower it onto the crankcase.

Note to people who are reinstalling the cylinder head onto the engine in the car: be sure to line up the six studs in the base of the exhaust manifold with the flange on the top of the exhaust down pipe. It's handy to have Friend hold the cylinder head as you line up the studs. When they're lined up and in position, lower the head down and continue.

Push two bolts through the holes in the cylinder head gasket, then thread them by hand into the crankcase. Now put in the four corner bolts making sure all the while that the cylinder head gasket stays in place. Now you can put in the other four bolts. When you're sure everything is correctly lined up, tighten the ten bolts until there's a small amount of tension on them. When there's tension, torque the head bolts in the order

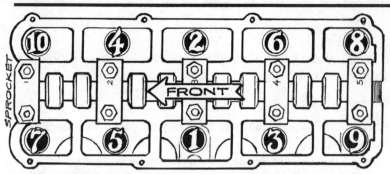

Step 2. (Cont'd.)

shown in the diagram to 7.5 mkg (54 ft lbs). If you've got polygon head bolts, after arriving at 7.5 mkg, tighten the bolts ¼ turn clockwise ⟳ more. These polygon socket head bolts will not need to be retorqued in 1,000 miles unlike the regular hexagon socket head bolts. I'll remind you about retorqueing those bolts at the end of the Chapter. If you lose a bolt, buy one of the same type you already have. Don't intermix the old socket head with the new polygon socket head type bolts.

Step 3. Install Camshaft Cover

Find the rubber plug from the gasket set which fits into the end of the cylinder head and the thin rubber strip which goes over camshaft bearing cap #1. Now get your beautifully clean cam cover with its long thin spacers. Fit the new cork gasket into the camshaft cover. Models up to 1978 have tongues (lick, lick) on the cork gasket which fit into slots in the base of the camshaft cover. Models made after 1978 do not have the slots in the camshaft cover nor tongues on the gasket. Make sure your camshaft cover is fitted with the correct gasket.

Position the camshaft cover on top of the cylinder head, put one of the long metal spacers on top of the camshaft cover and hold it with the four 10mm bolts or nuts. Now do the other side.

Very early '75 models don't have a long metal spacer between the bolt and the camshaft cover; they have individual metal washers.

Carbureted models have a wire fuel line holder which goes on bolt #2 on the left side. Air conditioned models have a spark advance valve which goes on bolt #4 on that same side, but it's not installed until you get the engine back into the car. Fuel injection has a hose securing gizmo on the last bolt on the left side.

All: Torque the 10mm bolts or nuts to 0.6 mkg (4.3 ft lbs).

Step 4. Install Intake and Exhaust Manifolds

Gravitate toward your gasket set and find the long paper gasket which goes between the intake manifold and cylinder head. Also dig out the four thick oval shaped gaskets which fit between the exhaust manifold and cylinder head. Place the four exhaust manifold gaskets into position on the cylinder head. Install them the right way up so that the insides of the holes on the gasket will line up perfectly with the holes in the cylinder head.

Your exhaust and intake manifolds are hopefully still attached to each other, so slide them onto the side of the cylinder head. Don't push them all the way home yet. Find the paper intake manifold gasket: push two of the socket head (allen) bolts through the intake manifold, then through the gasket into the cylinder head. Now install the other four bolts through the intake manifold.

Notice that two of the 6mm socket head bolts are longer than the others. As logic would have it, they fit in the thickest part of the manifold. With the gaskets correctly lined up, push the manifolds hard up against the cylinder head and install the eight 13mm nuts and washers on the studs which stick out through the exhaust manifold. Torque all the bolts and nuts to 2.5 mkg (18 ft lbs). Put a rag in the top of the intake manifold.

Step 5. Install Drive Belt Tension Pulley—All Models

Slip the pulley onto the stud sticking out from the front face of the cylinder head and put on the washer and 15mm or 17mm lock nut to hold the pulley in place. Just tighten the nut fingertight for now.

Step 6. Air-Conditioned Models Only

Look through your Baggies until you find one containing the nuts and bolts which hold the drive belt guard in position on the front of the engine. You will have one T-shaped bolt lurking in the bottom of the Baggie. Find the 10mm washer and nut which fits onto the end of that bolt and slip the bolt through the hole in the top part of the water pump. Put the washer and nut on the bolt and get it fingertight. This is just a little trick to enable you to put the drive belt guard on without spending 15 hours lining up the bolt. If you don't do it now, you'll see what I mean when you come to replace the drive belt shield.

Step 7. Install Camshaft Drive Belt—All Models

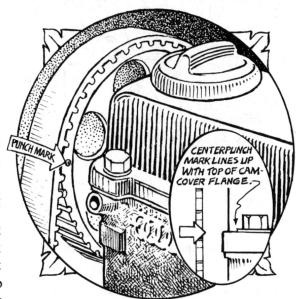

Put your 19mm socket on the bolt holding the camshaft drive belt sprocket to the camshaft and line up the punch mark on the rear of the sprocket with the left side of the camshaft cover. Check that #1 cylinder camshaft lobes are pointing up. If not, turn the camshaft until they do. Is the dot on the front of the sprocket? The sprocket is on backwards. Remove the bolt and turn it around.

Now put your 19mm socket on the *crankshaft* bolt and set the notch in the V-belt pulley at the 1 o'clock position. Turn the intermediate shaft drive belt sprocket so the punch mark on the face of the sprocket lines up exactly with the V-notch on the crankshaft pulley. Move either of those two sprockets around until those line up correctly.

Lift the rotor and pull off the dust cover from the distributor. The small line on the sparking end of the rotor should align with a line on the rim of the distributor. If it's not quite aligned, turn the distributor body (loosen the 13mm nut holding the U-clip if necessary) until the line of the rim is lined up with the mark on the rotor tip.

Find the drive belt from the parts pile (if it's not yet installed), and slide it over the sprockets and around the tensioner pulley. Turn to Chapter 10, Procedure 23 and do Step 11.

Step 8. Tidy Up

First gap (0.60 to 0.70mm, 0.024 to 0.028 in) and loosely install the new spark plugs. Chapter 10, Procedure 14, Step 12, tells how to gap the plugs. Then loosen the lower 10mm bolt holding the small coolant manifold on the rear of the cylinder head. Hook up the small ear on the metal pipe to the loosened bottom bolt. The pipe runs from the water pump to a rubber hose which attaches to the intake manifold. Make sure the pipe ear is on the bolt and then tighten the bolt. Push the end of the rubber hose onto the intake manifold. The hose slips onto the connection furthest away from the cylinder head. The other connection on the intake manifold is connected to the small coolant manifold on the rear of the cylinder head by a rubber pipe. Tighten the rubber pipe with its hose clamp. Fasten the big hose from the water pump to the underside of the left coolant manifold.

BEFORE INSTALLATION

FLYWHEEL

PLATE

LINE UP THE LARGE NOTCH ON THE FLYWHEEL WITH THE INDENT ON THE INTERMEDIATE PLATE.

PROCEDURE 12: MATE CRANKCASE TO TRANSMISSION. Phase 1.

Condition: Both your engine and transmission are out of the vehicle and require union.

Tools and materials: Phase 1 tool kit.

Step 1. Align Flywheel (Standard Transmission)

You will remember that before you could separate the transmission from the engine you had to line up a lug on the flywheel with the pointer inside the transmission top dead center (TDC) inspection hole. Get the lug pointing up again. Look at the flywheel and you'll see a scoop cut out of its outside circumference just behind the teeth. Face the flywheel and turn the 19mm bolt on the front of the crankshaft until the scoop lines up directly with the scoop in the intermediate plate. Go to Step 4.

Step 2. Install Torque Converter Into Transmission (Automatic Transmission)

Slide in the torque converter by inserting the long shaft through the bushing in the center of the transmission. Make sure it's fully home and spins freely.

Step 3. Install Intermediate Plate (Automatic Transmission)

If you're using an engine stand, get Friend to help you take the engine off it and lower it to the floor. Put the cleaned thin metal intermediate plate onto the engine. Note the plate has a hole cut out of it where the starter fits. Make sure the hole is on the right side of the engine.

Step 4. Push on Transmission—All Models

Support your engine on the hoist with the oil pan just touching the floor. Find your marked Baggies containing the nuts, bolts and washers to bolt the transmission to the engine. Lay the bolts out so you can reach them but won't kick them into the undergrowth. Find Friend, position yourselves at each side of the transmission and carefully slide the transmission onto the rear of the engine.

If you've got automatic transmission, don't let the weight of the transmission exert any stress on the torque converter. If this happens, you'll bend the shaft which the torque converter spins on and problems with your automatic transmission will start here. Check that the intermediate plate isn't fouling the studs preventing the transmission from sliding into place.

Standard transmission: if the transmission won't go on, check that the lug on the flywheel is going to line up with the mark in the TDC inspection hole in the transmission case.

Slide the transmission fully up against the engine. When everything is mated up beautifully, screw in the 17 and 19mm bolts which hold the two items together. Tighten them. Remember the mount which fits on the 17 and 19mm bolts on the left side of the engine/transmission? Well, torque all the engine/transmission bolts and nuts except the two which are going to hold that left engine/transmission mount to 5.5 mkg (40 ft lbs).

Standard transmission—go to the next Procedure.

Step 5. Install Starter (Automatics Only)

Clean the starter of all grease and slime and find the starter mounting bolts in your Baggie selection. Install the starter on the transmission and find the rear support bracket if it's not still bolted on the side of the engine. Position the rear bracket on the two studs sticking from the rear of the starter, then screw in the three 13mm bolts which hold the starter to the transmission. Screw one 10mm nut onto the stud sticking through the rear starter support bracket. When it's tight, torque the three 13mm bolts holding the starter to 2 mkg (14 ft lbs). Now begin to tighten the 13mm bolt holding the rear starter support bracket to the side of the engine.

Step 5. (Cont'd.)

Pull off the 20mm nut from the back of the starter and put it back into your marked Baggie. Please be sure the large hose clamp is still around the starter body. This clamp will secure the cover later.

Step 6. Link Torque Converter to Torque Converter Drive Plate (Automatics Only)

Find the appropriate Baggie and fish for the three 10mm bolts which hold the torque converter to the drive plate. There are three holes on the torque converter drive plate which are probably outlined in white. Turn the crankshaft with the 19mm socket until the drive plate hole lines up with a threaded hole in the torque converter and install a bolt. Do the other two and torque them all to 3 mkg (22 ft lbs). Now reinstall the thin metal cover plate and secure it with the three 13mm bolts.

PROCEDURE 13: REINSTALL ENGINE AND TRANSMISSION INTO CAR. Phase 2.

Condition: The engine and transmission have been out and apart: they're now back together.

Tools and materials: Phase 2 tool kit, a floor jack and plenty of time, a Friend or two.

Step 1. Get Ready

Brush all the leaves and cobwebs out of your engine compartment. If your car is an air-conditioned model, make sure the air conditioner compressor is safely tucked away and the condenser is still protected by a stout piece of cardboard. Please be sure the wheels are chocked to prevent the car from rolling.

Lift the engine and transmission unit up by your hoist and wheel the hoist to the car. Swing the engine and transmission around until the front of the engine is pointing toward the right fender. Lay out all your engine mounting bolts, brackets, etc., from your marked Baggie stash.

Step 2. Lower Away

Note for automatic owners: Your transmission is bigger than the standard type, so you'll have to thread it into the engine compartment, then support it on a jack while you lower the engine.

All models: Start lowering your engine/transmission. Arm yourself with the 17mm bolt which holds the front engine mount to the flanges on the inside right fender. Continue lowering the engine into the engine compartment being sure the right hand driveshaft is correctly aligned so that it'll mate with the drive plate on the side of the transmission. You may have to lift the engine slightly and thread the drivshaft over the exhaust pipe support so the shaft will line up. Check that the six studs on the bottom of the exhaust manifold are going into the exhaust down pipe correctly. With all the wires, etc., out of the way, lower the engine. Place a jack under the rear part of the transmission to use as a fulcrum. Continue lowering the engine until you're able to insert the 17mm bolt into the front engine mount and screw it into its captive nut. Use your socket to tighten the bolt. If the socket turns, turns, turns and isn't screwing the bolt into the nut, slide the nut back or forward until it does. Move it until the point on the end of the 17mm bolt engages the hole in the nut. When the bolt has protruded through the nut, stop screwing; that's far enough for now.

Step 3. Install Rear Transmission Mount (Standard Transmission)

Find the 17mm bolt which holds the rear transmission mount to the ears welded on the left fender. Pump up the hoist until the rear transmission mount lines up with those ears and slip the 17mm bolt through. If the engine is tipping too far back, move the jack a little to the rear and pump it up so the engine squares itself with the rear mount. Go to Step 6.

Step 4. Install Rear Transmission Mount (Automatic Transmission)

Keep the rear of the automatic transmission as low as you can and install the rear mount. There are a couple of things to get straight here. The automatic transmission filler tube has a support bracket which fits between the rear of the transmission and the mount. Look at it from the top and you'll see where it goes.

Step 4. (Cont'd.)

Position the mount on the rear of the transmission and find the battery ground strap which goes on the 17mm bolt before the bolt goes through the mount. Slip that bolt in first, do it up fingertight, then install the remaining two 17mm nuts and washers on the studs. When they're on, torque them to 4.0 mkg (29 ft lbs).

Now jack up the rear of the transmission until the upper part of the mount slides into the mounting ears on the fender. When it's in, slip in the 17mm bolt and get the threads sticking through the nut on the other side of the mount. Do not tighten it! Now remove the hoist and get it out of the way so you won't trip on it.

Step 5. Install Left Front Engine/Transmission Mount (Automatic Transmission)

Find your mount and remove the 17mm bolt and the 19mm bolt and nut (if they're installed) which hold the left side of the engine and transmission together. Once they're out, install the mount with the rubber part mating into the other half of the mount bolted to the car's front crossmember. The two ears on the mount have holes to accept the bolts. Slip the bottom 19mm bolt through first, screw the nut on and tighten it with your socket. Now push the mount toward the engine and put in the 17mm bolt. This bolt may screw into the captive nut welded to the metal pipe which is part of that plumbing mechanism running from the water pump to the intake manifold. The left ear of the mount goes between the captive nut and the engine. Push in the 17mm bolt and tighten it. Now torque both bolts to 5.5 mkg (40 ft lbs).

Step 6. Install Starter and Left Engine/Transmission Mount (Standard Transmission)

The bolts which hold your starter are also the ones which hold the left engine/transmission mount. Position the starter (with the solenoid facing up) into the transmission and slip through the polygon socket-headed bolts or the long 15mm bolts. When the starter's in its hole, ask Friend to pass you the mount. Put the rubber part of it into the other half of the mount which stayed bolted to the front of the car. When it's in right, push a bolt through the bottom hole in the starter, through the transmission case into the nut welded to the other side of the mount. Push the other bolt through the starter.

There's a nut welded onto a tab which is part of that metal pipe. If the tab is bent so the nut is not square with the bolt, bend the tab with vise grips enough so you can screw the bolt into the nut. When the nut's in right, tighten the bolts and torque them to 3.0 mkg (22 ft lbs).

If your vehicle doesn't have the type starter which bolts to the left engine transmission mount, just install the mount. Then install the starter with the three 13mm bolts and tighten the rear 13mm nuts, making sure there's no strain on the rear mount. If there is strain, please turn back to Chapter 7, Procedure 8 to install starter in car. When all's in order, torque the three 13mm bolts to 1.6 mkg (11 ft lbs).

Step 7. Install Bottom Mounts—All Models

Get the cleaned mount from your parts pile and the 13mm and 17mm nuts from your marked Baggie. Get under the car and slip the mount onto the transmission. Secure it with the nuts. Now push the mount onto the two threaded studs sticking out from the underbody. Put the jack under the rear part of the transmission and jack it up until the mount slides onto the studs. When you've got the two 17mm nuts started, tighten them just a little. You're leaving all the mounting bolts loose because you have to align the engine and transmission later.

Step 8. Secure Exhaust System to Engine

If you split your exhaust down pipe at the manifold, then install the six new 13mm nuts on the studs protruding through the flange on the top part of the exhaust pipe where it meets the exhaust manifold. Set the ear on the EGR manifold pipe on one of the studs, if you have an EGR pipe, that is. Torque those six 13mm nuts to 2.5 mkg (18 ft lbs).

If you split the exhaust pipe at the bottom, find the three 13mm nuts and bolts along with the gasket that goes between the two exhaust sections. Slip through one bolt (put in the gasket) and screw it into the nut. Now install the other two bolts and nuts. Put the socket on one end of the nut and the torque wrench on the other and torque the nut to 2.5 mkg (18 ft lbs).

Step 9. Install Left Drive Shaft, then Right Drive Shaft

See Chapter 16, Procedure 6, Steps 11 and 12.

Step 10. Install Carburetor (Carbureted Models)

Remove the rag from the mount of the intake manifold and place the carburetor on the manifold with the choke mechanism pointing toward the right fender. Seat the carburetor onto its rubber mount atop the intake manifold and secure it with the four 10mm nuts and washers. Just tighten the nuts until they're snug.

Step 11. Install Air Injection (Smog) Pump (Not Fuel Injection)

The pump is held by a long 13mm bolt and nut going through ears on the support bracket. It also has a curved adjustment bracket which, in some cases, is held to the alternator, and in other cases, is held to the front of the engine. Whichever you have, install the long 13mm bolt through the rear ear on the support bracket, then through the smog pump and out the front ear. Screw on the 13mm nut. Install the 13mm bolt onto the curved adjusting bracket or put the 13mm bolt through the bracket into the front of the engine if you have air conditioning. Torque the long 13mm bolt to 3.0 mkg (22 ft lbs). If your smog pump has the bracket which goes into the front of the engine, tighten that bolt to the same torque.

If you have an early '75 with an air conditioner, install the hose running from the smog pump to that air filter mechanism a little to the left of, or bolted to, the oil filter. Tighten the rubber hose with the hose clamp.

Step 12. Install Alternator—All Models

On non-air conditioned cars, the alternator is slipped into position very easily. Find the long 6mm socket head bolt (and the spacer if you have one), install the alternator in its mounting bracket and push the long bolt through. As soon as the bolt goes through the bracket, slip the spacer between the front of the alternator and the bracket. Continue pushing the bolt through the alternator mounting ears and out through the rear part of the support bracket. Put on the washer and 13mm nut. Hold the other side of the alternator onto the curved adjusting bar and push the 13mm bolt with its nut through the bar into the alternator. Tighten this nut with your fingers.

Air-conditioned model folks should take the nut off the end of the long allen bolt which holds the alternator in place, and withdraw the bolt from the front ear of the support bracket until there's enough room to slip the alternator between the two ears. Jockey the alternator down under the compressor and fit it into the mounting bracket. Push the bolt through and put the spacer between the front of the alternator and the frontmost supporting ear. Push the bolt all the way through and put on the 13mm nut. The bracket which is attached to the other side of the alternator can now be attached to the side of the air conditioner support bracket that's also held by a 13mm bolt. Tighten the 13mm nut on the end of the long socket head bolt. If you can get your torque wrench in, torque it to 3.0 mkg (22 ft lbs).

Step 13. Install Dipstick

Please make sure your dipstick is shiny clean.

Step 14. Install New Oil Filter and EGR Air Filter, if Applicable.

Smear a few drops of oil onto the rubber ring on the top of the new oil filter. Screw in the filter on the oil filter attaching point on the left side of the engine and when the rubber ring touches the face of that manifold, screw the filter in ¾ turn more. Early 1975's install a new EGR filter, and retain it in its housing with the plastic wing nut and washer.

Step 15. Install Air Conditioner Compressor

Carefully position your air conditioner compressor on its mounting plate. First attach the alternator ground strap to whichever bolt on the engine it was originally attached. Now install the bolts which hold the air conditioner to the plate through the plate into the air conditioner compressor. Leave the bolts loose because you have to install the belt before you can correctly position the compressor.

Step 16.   Install Cable Bracket (Automatics)

The bracket is held to the right side of the transmission by two 13mm bolts. On some vehicles the battery ground strap is attached to one of these 13mm bolts. If your car is like this, please install the ground strap. Tighten the bolts to 3.0 mkg (22 ft lbs).

Step 17.   Install EGR Valve (if your model has one).

Find the two 10mm bolts in the EGR Baggie and slip them through the EGR valve located behind the rear of the exhaust manifold. You may also have a gasket that goes between the exhaust manifold and the EGR valve. If you do, place it between the valve and the manifold. Put in the two 10mm bolts and tighten them.

Step 18.   Install Shift Linkage Arms (Standard)

Turn to Chapter 16, Procedure 6, Step 14.

Step 19.   Check Engine/Transmission Alignment

See Chapter 16, Procedure 6, Step 20.

Step 20.   Install Speedometer Cable

Back to Chapter 16, Procedure 6, Step 17.

Step 21.   Install Clutch Cable

See Chapter 16, Procedure 2, Step 3. Then adjust the free play as described in Procedure 1, Step 2 (Chapter 16).

Step 22.   Attach Accelerator Cable Bracket to Carburetor and Install Accelerator Cable (Carbureted Automatics)

The bracket is still attached to your accelerator cable and is probably tucked away somewhere over the firewall. Find your dashpot assembly if you removed it along with the accelerator cable bracket. Find the three slot head bolts which hold the bracket to the carburetor. Position the dashpot, then slip a bolt through the dashpot mount into the accelerator cable mount and into the body of the carburetor. Install all three bolts.

While you're here you may as well install the accelerator cable on the accelerator throttle mechanism. On the end of the cable there should be a spring and a little circlip. Remove them. Push the accelerator cable through the small barrel on the throttle linkage (prevent the linkage from moving with one hand), slip on the spring and put the clip on the back of the cable. Make sure the clip is firmly seated before you let go. Tighten the large nut on the accelerator cable sheath against the end of the bracket. Check that the bracket is lined up correctly with the throttle linkage mechanism. If you bashed it while working around the engine, it will have to be lined up correctly before the accelerator will work smoothly.

Step 23.   Attach Cables to Automatic Transmission Bracket (Automatic)

See Chapter 16, Procedure 6, Step 5.

Step 24.   Install Accelerator Cable (Standard)

Find the Baggie containing all the parts needed to reinstall this cable. Remove one of the 10mm or 13mm nuts screwed onto the outer sheath of the accelerator cable and slip the cable through the bracket on the camshaft cover (or a bracket on the side of the carburetor). Install the 10 or 13mm nut onto the cable which protrudes through the bracket. Don't tighten it yet. Now (carburetors) find the little barrel which holds the cable in the throttle linkage on the carburetor. Insert the barrel into the carburetor linkage arm, push the inner part of the cable through and screw in the 8mm bolt in that barrel, cylinder or whatever you want to call it. Nip into the driver's compartment and check that the accelerator cable is still attached to the gas pedal. If so, turn your attention to the carburetor linkage once more. Pull on the inner cable and tighten the 8mm nut into the small cylinder. Now tighten the two 13mm nuts on the outer sheath where they attach to the bracket.

Step 25. Install Accelerator Cable (Fuel Injection)

Your accelerator cable attaches to the ball on top of the throttle linkage on the intake manifold. First attach the outer sheath of the cable onto its support bracket on top of the cam cover. Then pop the plastic and brass attachment that's on the end of the cable onto the throttle linkage. Tighten the two 10mm nuts, then pop the accelerator cable onto the throttle plate.

Step 26. Install Injection Equipment (Fuel Injection only)

Take the injection equipment out from the trunk and clean up anything that's dirty. Gingerly position the mixture control unit onto its little shelf at the left fender and snap closed the clamps holding the base of the mixture control unit into place. Connect the flattened plastic tube running from the mixture control unit to the intake manifold and secure both ends with the large hose clamps. Hook up the fuel lines to the fuel filter. Remove your four Baggies or pieces of rag from the right of the cylinder head where the four fuel injectors fit. Check the valves for cleanliness and replace the rubber O rings around the base of the injectors. Spray the four O rings with a shot of silicone before you insert the four injectors into their holes and push them home hard. Remove the 13mm bolt from the end of the cold start valve and slip on the fuel line. Install the 13mm bolt and tighten it.

Now put back the two fuel lines which run to the control pressure regulator (CPR). They are held by a 13 and a 14mm bolt. Remove the two bolts from the CPR, slip on the fuel lines, screw in the bolts and tighten them. Finally, put back the two fuel lines running into the CPR. One from the fuel filter and the other is the fuel return. Replace the fuel filter unless the filter is fairly new. Some models have hoses running from a branch on the exhaust manifold to the bottom part of the mixture control unit. Install the hoses and tighten the hose clamps.

Step 27. Install Radiator

First remove the cardboard from the air conditioner condenser (if you have one), then slide in the U- or Z-shaped wire that holds the top part of the radiator onto the front crossmember. When it's in, lower your radiator into the engine compartment onto the two bottom studs. Screw on the two 10mm washers and nuts and tighten them. While you're here, if you have a thin hose running to a white plastic expansion bottle, attach one end of it to the left side of the radiator at the top and tighten the hose clamp.

Step 28. Reinstall Bottom of Water Pump

In your gasket kit find the remaining thin rubber O ring, look in your parts pile for the thermostat and find the two 10mm water pump bolts in the Baggie. Lie under the car with your 10mm socket and insert the thermostat into the water pump housing, put the O ring inside the housing, then mate the bottom part of the pump still attached to the radiator hose on the bottom of the radiator. Screw in the two 10mm bolts and tighten them to 1 mkg (7 ft lbs).

Step 29. Install Diverter Valve or Barometric Cell

The diverter valve (and the second stage diverter valve if you've got one) or barometric cell is somewhere stashed and marked, so please reattach it to the top right portion of the radiator. It takes two 10mm (or 13mm) bolts to hold the item in position.

Step 30. Install V-Belts

If you have an air-conditioned model, install the air conditioner compressor belt first. It goes on the crankshaft V-belt pulley position *closest* to the front of the engine, then slips over the pulley on the air conditioner compressor. The other belt fits around the middle V-belt pulley position on the crankshaft, onto the alternator and then around the water pump. The outside crankshaft V-belt pulley position accepts a belt from the smog pump. First adjust the belt tension on the air conditioner compressor by sticking a stout screwdriver or bar between the compressor and the support bracket. Pull up on the screwdriver or bar and tighten the bolts holding the compressor onto its bracket. You should aim for 10mm to 15mm (3/8 in to 9/16 in) of belt deflection. Be sure the compressor is square on its bracket and the pulley on the front of the compressor is square with the pulley on the end of the crankshaft.

Now tighten the belt on the alternator by levering it up with the same screwdriver and tighten the adjusting bracket which goes up to the air conditioner compressor mounting bracket. Aim for about 10 to 15mm (3/8 to 9/16 in) belt defection. When you have the correct belt tension, tighten the bolt running through the support bracket to 2 mkg (14 ft lbs).

If your car isn't fitted with an air conditioner, the V-belt tension is much more easily adjusted. See Chapter 8, Procedure 2, Step 3.

Step 31. Electrical Reconnections

Install the distributor cap with the four wires running to the correct spark plugs and attach the long wire running from the coil to the condenser. Don't forget the dust cover and rotor.

Standard transmission people should turn to the beginning of this chapter and use the diagram to reconnect all the electrical disconnections.

Automatic owners should first attach the long cable which runs to the starter/solenoid. The thin red wire which attaches to the solenoid goes on the connection closest to the engine. The other connection fits on the other side of the solenoid. When all three electrical connections on the solenoid are connected, slip the protective tin plate over the starter/solenoid, making sure the two holes in the back of the plate line up on the two studs protruding through the rear of the starter mount. Tighten the hose clamp around the starter protective plate and put the two 10mm nuts on the rear of the studs. Tighten them. Now reconnect everything electrical you disconnected. Refer to the diagram in Procedure 1, Step 7, at the beginning of this Chapter.

Step 32. Vacuum Reconnections

Reconnect all the vacuum disconnections by referring to the diagram in Procedure 1, Step 8.

Step 33. Coolant Hose Reconnections

Back once more to Procedure 1, Step 9.

Step 34. Oil It Up

Fill engine with engine oil and the automatic transmission with DEXRON (R) BASE A.T.F. Please read the beginning of Chapter 10 on oil and lubricants.

The engine holds 3.7 U.S. quarts (3.5 liters/3.1 Imperial quarts).

The automatic transmission holds 12.8 pints. If any leaked out, drain the remainder and replace it with fresh stuff. Chapter 10, Procedure 25, tells how.

Step 35. Pour in Coolant

If you managed to keep your old coolant clean, pour it back into the radiator or expansion bottle. If necessary, top off with a mixture of 40% water and 60% phosphorous free antifreeze. If you threw your old coolant away, mix an antifreeze/water coolant mixture and put it into your radiator.

Step 36. Hook Up Fuel Hoses

Carbureted cars need the fuel pump hoses restored to the carb. Fuel injection lines should be installed already.

Step 37. Install Battery

If this rebuild has taken six months, the battery is probably dead. Take it to the gas station for a trickle charge! Clean the battery terminals with a wire brush and bicarbonate of soda (Chapter 9, Procedure 1, Step 1). When the battery's recharged (or OK) install the two battery cables and tighten the terminal bolts with your

10mm wrench. Get the positive terminal onto the positive post and the negative (the ground strap) onto the negative (ground) battery post.

Step 38. Check...

Now...there are a few pieces left over. The drive belt guard is not yet installed, and carbureted model owners have not yet installed their air cleaner mechanism. That's fine, because at this stage before you finally bolt everything together, see if you've put on the drive belt properly. Ask Friend to put the key in the ignition (shift lever in Neutral or Park–P), the handbrake on and start the engine. It will take a while for the fuel to find its way into the carburetor or injection equipment before the engine will fire. Don't try to press the gas pedal through the floor. Continue turning the key for 5 second intervals until the car starts. Let it run just above idle. Don't be put off by the smell from the engine. That's just the Lubriplate heating up and giving off vapor. If it's the middle of winter and very cold, people with carburetors might like to close the butterfly valve in the top of the carburetor to richen the mixture. If the car just won't start, check that the rotor is inside the distributor cap, all the ignition wires are properly connected and the spark plug wires are in the correct order.

Short story break: The folks at my local VW dealership here in Santa Fe have provided the best help and encouragement anyone could possibly wish for. Just after installing one of the many engines I rebuilt in their workshop, a couple of mechanics gathered around to hear the initial start-up. I had been especially careful with this engine and had someone run through the Procedures with me to check that everything was right. I got into the driver's seat, turned the key, worked the starter a few seconds and it started. I climbed out of the car very pleased with myself—everything was running beautifully. I walked around to the front to admire my handiwork when I detected a slight knocking noise from the engine. My heart sank. I peered in, *knowing* nothing was wrong, yet fearing the worst. The knocking increased. I revved the accelerator a little, the knocking continued to get louder; it rose with the revs and died when the revs died. My face was long.

While pondering deeply, I happened to notice a smirk on Joe's face. ''Ah-hah!'' thought I. Up to dirty tricks and suddenly I realized the knocking was not quite in sync with the engine. Under the car was young Maggie tapping the body with his hammer handle. The rest is up to your imagination.

Now that your engine is running, turn to Chapter 10, Procedure 14, and do a complete tune-up. Check that the drive belt is properly installed and that all the punch marks, notches, etc., line up correctly. When you've done that, come back here to Procedure 14.

PROCEDURE 14: FINISH AND TIDY UP. Phase 1.

Condition: Your engine has been rebuilt and tuned up.

Step 1. Install Drive Belt Guard

Clean the drive belt guard, especially on the inside, and find the four 10mm bolts which held it to the engine. If you have an air-conditioned model, you'll have already installed one of the bolts which goes through the water pump to hold the left side of the drive belt cover in place. Be sure the rubber vibration spacers and metal washers are installed so the shoulder on the inner metal spacer goes into the rubber vibration spacer from the inside. Put the four 10mm bolts through the cover into the engine fingertight. Make sure the cover isn't fouling the drive belt, then tighten all four bolts.

Step 2. Install Exhaust Manifold Baffle Plate

This baffle plate is held by three 13mm nuts and washers to the side of the exhaust manifold. Install the plate and tighten the three nuts.

Step 3. Install Air Cleaner Stuff (Carbureted Engines)

Put the air filter housing into the two holes on the inside of the right fender. Now thread the hose with the metal air intake elbow into position on top of the carburetor and secure it with the 10mm nut on top. Connect the PCV valve to the top of the camshaft cover and secure it with a hose clamp. Install the short hose which runs from the base of the air cleaner housing to that exhaust baffle plate. Secure it with hose clamps.

Step 4. Fuel Injection

Did you install a new air filter in the base of the mixture control unit? If not, please do so. Connect all the hoses to and from the mixture control unit.

Step 5. Install Hood

You'll need Friend to help you or you'll scratch the paint beyond belief. Get the hood and hold it so you're able to screw the bolts through the hinges and into the hood. Reposition the braided ground strap if you've got one, onto one of the hood bolts. Tighten the four 10mm bolts and try the hood for snugness. You may have to monkey around with it to get it to fit properly.

Step 6. Install Windshield Washer Hose

The hose will probably be lying somewhere inside the firewall. Push it onto the base of the gizmo which jets the water onto the windshield.

Step 7. Final Check

Give everything a thorough final check. Take your time over this. All OK? Clean yourself and your tools.

Make a note of the mileage reading on the odometer. You will have to change the oil and filter in 300 miles. When 1,000 miles have elapsed, turn to Chapter 10 and run Procedure 2. 1,000 miles up means that you must retorque the cylinder head bolts (when the engine is cold unless your engine has the polygon type bolts). Just remove the camshaft cover, back off the head bolts ¼ turn, then torque them to full torque value once again. Procedure 11, Step 2 shows the way.

Drive the car as per Chapter 5, Step 4, and do your maintenance Procedures on time. 'Bye.

CHAPTER 19

◆ ODDS 'N ENDS ◆

This Chapter deals with repairs needed to keep your car safe and legal, such as broken or defunct windshield wipers and washers, lights, horn, etc. It also deals a bit with the adjustments of small things which haven't been covered elsewhere; a broken gas gauge, for example.

If your state or country has an inspection program, run through this Chapter to fix any minor problems which could fail your car.

When anything electrical goes bonkers, first *check the fuses* in the relay plate. Nine times out of ten, the problem can be traced to a blown fuse. The fuses all live in the relay plate above the driver's knees. Remove the clip from the center of the protective carpet (if you've got one) and pull the carpet down. There's the relay plate in all it's glory with the fuses under a hinged clear plastic cover. Now, there are fuses and there are relays. Fuses are the weak link in an electrical circuit. If the circuit is overloaded, the thin metal strip on the fuse face burns out and the circuit is no longer a circuit. Thus, the sensitive (and expensive) electrical components are protected from damage caused by a surge in electrical current.

Replace any burned out fuse with one of the same amperage. The white fuses are 8 amp, the pink 16 amp. Don't intermix the two. It's a bad idea to wrap aluminum foil around a fuse if one blows. Use a new fuse from your stash—keep some in the glove compartment.

OK, sitting above the fuses are a motley assortment of black and silver boxes; the relays. A relay is nothing more than a switch worked by electricity. There's nothing for you to flip or press. The current flowing through the relay does all the work.

If you have a problem with things electrical and all the fuses are intact, the next move is to check the electrical connections on the malfunctioning piece of equipment. Clean off any crud and corrosion. All electrical connections must be free from scuz to work properly. If any of the lighting circuits fail, check the bulb and its holder.

A hassle with the starter/solenoid and stuff like the dash lights dimming when you turn on the key is probably a result of corrosion on the battery terminals. Chapter 9, Procedure 2, Step 1, shows how to clean them.

For electrical things to work properly, the battery/alternator/voltage regulator system has to be in good shape. Check 'em in Chapter 8.

Let's begin with a simple and common problem.

PROCEDURE 1: FIX HEADLIGHTS. Phase 1.

Condition: Both (or all four) headlights don't come on or quit at the same time. If just one headlight doesn't light, go to Step 2. Fuses are OK.

Tools and materials: Phase 1 tool kit and any parts you find that are defective and need replacement.

Remarks: Scirocos have four headlights; two operate on low beam and all four operate on high. This Procedure applies to Sciroccos as well as Rabbits, except that you have to replace either the high or low beam light, depending on which is broken or burned out.

Step 1. Broken headlight or Dimmer Relay?

Lift and prop the hood and check the connections on the rear of the bulbs. Are they pushed on tightly? Free of crud?

Turn the key to ON. If none of the headlights work when you turn on the main headlight switch, pull on the headlight dimmer switch on the left of the steering column. Do the lights come on now? If both (or all four) headlights are still off and your car was built before 1977, immediately suspect a broken headlight relay. 1977 and on, diesels and U.S. Rabbits have no relay, so don't bother to look for it.

Step 2. Check Relay (1975 and 1976)

Lights still don't work? We'll check the dimmer switch relay. Keep the ignition and headlight switches on. Operating the headlight dimmer switch should produce an audible click from the relay. This relay is in the relay plate above the driver's left knee probably hidden by a protective carpet. If the relay's not clicking, it's definitely broken. If possible, drive to VW and ask to borrow a headlight dimmer relay for a few minutes so you can be sure it's the cause. Leave your watch or children with the parts person as security.

To examine the old dimmer relay, turn off the ignition and headlight switches. Examine the relay plate and pull out the relay from the socket marked "J." That's the one on *your* left as you look at it. Pull out the old relay and in with the new. Turn the ignition to ON, turn on the headlights and see if they're shining. If so, pay VW for the relay and you're off. If they don't, return the borrowed relay and continue...

Step 3. Replace Headlights

If your relay clicks, but one or more headlights doesn't work, you'll have to replace them. They are of the sealed beam type. That means you have to replace the whole unit, glass included. If both headlights burned out at once, maybe you have a faulty voltage regulator or alternator. Read Chapter 8.

If you need to replace a headlight, first buy a new unit (any auto store or VW). When you get home, lift and prop the hood and see how the grill at the front of the car is secured.

PLASTIC GRILL CLIP & PIN

PUSH 'EM THROUGH

Sciroccos have phillips screws holding the plastic grill. Early Rabbits have phillips screws but in mid '75 the top screws were abandoned in favor of plastic clips.

Remove the phillips screws and the broken headlight and, if applicable, remove the clip(s) from the top of the grill. Push the round center of the clip in toward the engine. Use a thin screwdriver or knitting needle. Feel over the front crossmember to behind the clip and pull the round bit out. Now you can pull the clip out from the grill. If you can't easily get to the headlight with the grill partially in place, remove all the clips and screws.

The headlight itself is held by two or three phillips screws going through a chrome rim around the outside of the headlight. Don't mess with the two phillips screws with a spring on them. To remove the blown headlight, unscrew the phillips screws from the chrome retaining ring and pull the ring off. Slide the light toward you about 15cm (6 in) or so and remove the electrical connector from the rear of the headlight. The light can now be pulled clear.

To install a new headlight, first be sure you have it the correct way up (look at the other one), then connect the electrical connector to the rear. Slip the chrome headlight retaining ring over the light and screw in the two or three phillips screws. You may have to turn the ring around a few times until you get the screw holes lined up.

Reinstall the front grill. Screw back the phillips screws first, then push in the plastic clips. Don't insert the round center part until the clip body is pushed home. Push the center bit in with a screwdriver handle if it's a tight fit.

Step 4. Align Headlights

Tools and materials: Builder's level, chalk, tape measure, Friend.

Remarks: Some states have laws requiring an 'official' state approved service station to adjust your headlights. This is how they'd do it if they didn't have a machine.

Check the pressure in all tires, fill the gas tank about halfway and find a level ground surface next to a vertical surface like a door or wall. A level driveway and garage door, for example. Roll the car up to the wall and make a chalk mark on the wall directly opposite the center of the hood. Using a level, extend the chalk mark to a long *vertical* line. This is the vehicle "center line." With Friend in the car to push on the brake and keep the front wheels pointing straight ahead, push the car backward until it's 3.5 meters (12 ft) from the wall.

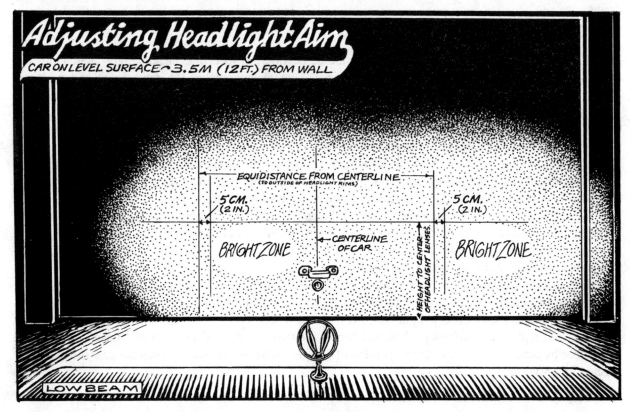

Friend still in car, measure the distance from the ground to the center of one of the headlights. Transfer this measurement to the wall and make a mark across the vehicle center line. At this mark make a horizontal line with the level extending past the two outermost headlights.

Measure the distance between the centers of the outermost headlights. Halve this distance and draw a vertical line on the wall this distance from the vehicle centerline. Draw another vertical line this distance on the other side of the vehicle centerline. OK so far?

Ask Friend to turn the ignition to ON and flip the headlights to low beam. Cover one of the headlights and see if the other one shines in the bright zone as in the sketch. Then cover the other light, uncover the covered one and see if that light is in the bright zone. No? Lift and prop the hood and adjust. German-made Rabbit headlights are adjusted by screwing the top phillips screw on the rear of the headlight in or out. If the bright zone is too high, turn the screw counterclockwise ↺. Too low, clockwise ↻. Sciroccos have a plastic knob on the inside of the headlight mounting bracket, so twiddle that. Another set of screws/knobs on the side of the light move the light either right or left to adjust the sideways aim of the bright zone. U.S. Rabbit rectangular headlights are adjusted from the *front* of the car. The up/down screw is just above the glass part of the headlight, and the side-to-side screw is to the left of the right headlight and to the right of the left headlight.

Erase the chalk marks from the wall when you've finished.

Remarks for Procedures 2 through 5: If you replaced what you thought were burned out bulbs and still didn't get illuminated, check that the spade connectors running to all lighting assemblies are OK. If they look dirty or corroded, clean them with emery paper and push them back into position.

PROCEDURE 2: REPLACE BACKUP LIGHT SWITCH AND ALL REAR LIGHT BULBS. Phase 1

Condition: One or more of these lights doesn't work. If the turn signal is blitzed, read Procedure 8.

Tools and materials: Phase 1 tool kit, new switch and gasket and/or bulbs.

Remarks: If none of these lights work, first check the fuses, then check the electrical connections and the bulbs.

Step 1. Backup Lights

If both backup lights refuse to work at the same time, suspect the backup light switch on the transmission. There are three possible switch locations. Two types screw into the transmission and the other fits on the right side of the transmission notched by the shift linkage. Lift and prop the hood and see what kind you have.

To test the backup light switch, ask Friend to stand at the rear of the car while you turn the ignition to ON. Pull off one of the two electrical connections to the backup light switch on the transmission and touch it to the metal part of the other connection on the other side of the switch. Both backup light bulbs in the tail light assembly should now light. If they don't your bulbs are blown or the wires are broken. It's probably the bulbs. See Step 2. A blazing swath of light at the rear means that the backup light switch is broken.

To replace the screw-in type switch, turn off the ignition, pull off the two electrical connections which go to the backup light switch and use your crescent wrench to screw out the switch. Buy a new one, slip on a new gasket and screw the switch in with your fingers, tighten it with your crescent wrench, torque to 2 mkg (14 ft lbs), and slip on the two electrical connections.

If your type switch attaches to a bracket and has an arm worked by the transmission shift levers, first remove the two electrical wires going to the switch, then use your 19mm socket to remove the large bolt holding the bracket and backup light assembly on the transmission. Position the new switch on the transmission, replace and tighten the bolt and slip on the two electrical wires. You may have to adjust the switch bar by bending it backward or forward until you get the lights to come on when the gear shift lever is pushed into reverse.

Step 2. Replace Bulbs

Assuming your switch is OK, one or more of the rear light bulbs may be burned out. Let's check. To get at the bulbs, lift the hatchback and unscrew the white plastic knob from the rear of the taillight assembly. Pull off the black plastic protective cover and you're faced with an aluminum plate with the rear of the bulbs and a few wires and connectors sticking through it. The plate is held into position by a plastic tab close to the fender. Slightly push back the plastic tab and pull out the plate containing the bulbs, etc.

Your car may have a Volkswagen type plastic clip around the main wiring harness running into the underside of the taillight assembly. If it prevents you from pulling out the plate, snip the clamp and you'll be able to get the plate out much easier.

A burned out bulb is removed by holding the glass part of the bulb between your thumb and forefinger, pushing it in slightly and turning it counterclockwise ⟳ . Look at the bulb filaments inside the glass. Tap the glass with your finger and see if the filament is broken. You can further check a bulb with your VOM switched to RX1K. See Chapter 20, Procedure 10.

Install a new bulb by firmly pushing it into the plate with the two little nipples (one on each side of the bulb) in line with the slots inside the bulb holder and turning slightly clockwise ⟳ . Reinstall the plate by placing it under the tiny plastic ear on the side of the light assembly closest to the fender, then clicking it home past the black plastic tab on the other side. Reinstall the black plastic protective cover by lining up the white plastic knob with its threaded insert in the hole in the taillight assembly. Screw it in fingertight. Don't go crazy, it'll crack if tightened too much.

Step 2. (Cont'd.)

If bad bulbs aren't your problem, use your VOM to check the wires and connections. Chapter 20, Procedure 10 tells how.

PROCEDURE 3: REPLACE TAILLIGHT LENS ASSEMBLY. Phase 1.

Condition: Broken lens.

Tools and materials: Phase 1 tool kit, new lens.

If you back into a wall, someone runs into you or your taillight lens gets broken mysteriously, replace it by first opening the rear hatch. Use an 8mm socket or wrench to remove the four 8mm nuts and washers holding the plastic taillight assembly in position on the rear body panel. With the nuts and washers removed, pull the taillight assembly off. Replace it with a new assembly, making sure you don't have it upside down, push it back through the body work and replace the washers and nuts. Don't screw them too tight. Those suckers are expensivo!

PROCEDURE 4: REPLACE SIDE MARKER LIGHT BULBS. Phase 1.

Condition: Burned out bulbs. Fuses and electrical connections are OK.

Tools and materials: Phase 1 tool kit, new bulbs.

The side marker lights are located on the side fenders; orange ones at the front, red ones at the back. To replace the bulb behind these markers, remove the two phillips screws holding on the lens protective cover, hold the bulb between your thumb and forefinger, push it in slightly, turn it counterclockwise ⟲ , then withdraw it. Push in the new bulb and turn it slightly clockwise ⟳ to locate it properly. Reinstall the side marker cover with the two phillips screws. Don't tighten the screws overzealously or you'll crack the lens.

PROCEDURE 5: REPLACE LICENSE PLATE LIGHT. Phase 1.

Condition: Burned out bulb. Fuse and electrical connections OK.

Tools and materials: Phase 1 tool kit, new bulbs.

You will have one or two separate light assemblies for your license plate lights. Each assembly is held by two phillips screws on the underside of the body just above the license plate. Remove the two phillips screws and pull off the license plate light lens. Remove the bulb as described in Procedure 4 and replace it with a new one. Then put on the license plate lens assembly and screw in the two phillips screws.

PROCEDURE 6: FIX INTERIOR LIGHT. Phase 1.

Condition: You grope in the dark for that elusive button. Fuses and connections are OK.

Tools and materials: Your fingers, new bulb.

The interior light is just pushed into place in the left side of the roof. Remove it by pushing in the little metal tab on the rear of the light with your thumb. Ease out the light assembly and you'll see a capsule type bulb held between two copper spring contacts. Pull out the bulb and replace it with a new one. Check that the spade connectors are clean and in position. Reinstall the interior light assembly by just pushing it back into the roof. Make sure the headliner is in position and not bunched up or loose.

PROCEDURE 7: REPLACE BULBS: FRONT PARKING AND TURN SIGNAL LIGHTS. Phase 1.

Condition: Burned out bulbs in front. If it's a turn signal on the blink, read Procedure 8. The fuses and electrical connections are OK.

Tools and materials: Phase 1 tool kit, new bulbs.

This lot is located in the front bumper. All you need do is remove the two phillips screws holding the lens cover in position in the bumper and remove the burned out bulb. Replace it with a new one and secure the lens cover with the two phillips screws.

PROCEDURE 8: FIX TURN SIGNALS (WINKERS, FLASHERS, SEMAPHORES). Phase 1.

Condition: It works, it doesn't; it works, it doesn't, it doesn't, it doesn't. Fuses and connections are OK.

Tools and materials: Phase 1 tool kit, maybe a new switch or relay.

If one of the four turn signal bulbs burns out it causes both the relay and the light on the dash to click much faster (or slower) than normal. For example, when a right rear bulb burns out, the right front turn signal light and the flasher relay on the relay plate will click on and off twice as fast (or slow) as usual. Here's a test: If none of the turn signals work, click on the "Hazard" flasher switch and look to see if any of the four turn signals work. If the relay clicks on, but some of the lights don't work, turn off the hazard flasher and check for a burned out bulb(s) or corrosion on the base of the bulb holder. To replace a bulb, use Procedure 2 or 7.

If nothing lights when you turn on the hazard switch, you probably have a kaput flasher relay. Go to VW and borrow a flasher relay. Pull out the broken relay from position N in the relay plate above the driver's knees. Position N is all the way to the right as you look at the plate. When the new relay's in place, turn the ignition to ON and try the switch again. If the signals all work, wonderful. They don't? Continue, we'll fix them.

If all the turn signals light when you turn on your hazard switch but none of them do when you work the turn signal lever (hazard switch off), you have a problem with the turn signal switch itself. Turn off the ignition and remove the two phillips screws holding the black plastic cover on the underside of the steering column. This will expose a maze of wires running up toward the steering wheel. If you get upside down and look up, you'll see three plastic multipoint connectors (MPC's). One goes into the rear of the ignition switch in which the key fits, and the other two sit under the steering column. We're interested in the one on the right under the steering column. Pull off that MPC by grasping the black plastic part of it and pulling it down toward the foot pedals. Check that all the wires in the back of the MPC are pushed fully home. You may have to use part of a matchstick or toothpick as a wedge to make sure the wires are in tight. Reinstall the MPC, turn the ignition to ON and try the turn signal lever again. Problem solved? Good. Reinstall the black plastic protective cover on the underside of the steering column with the two phillips screws.

Another problem can be worn contacts on the turn signal lever. This problem is indicated when you have to keep holding the turn signal lever in position to get the lights to flash. Replacing this mechanism is a bit of a trip so we'll do it as a full Procedure.

It's possible that a bad relay plate is causing your flasher problems. An electric shop (or VW) can fix it for you.

A harrassed New York office worker rushed out of his apartment house only to see his bus roar off. He decided to chase it and despite a few close calls ended up running all the way to the office.

Later, recounting the ordeal to his partner in papers, he resolved to run to work every day. "I'll save myself 50 cents."

"Big deal," his pal retorted, "You should run behind taxis and save $3.50!"

PROCEDURE 9: REPLACE TURN SIGNAL LEVER/WINDSHIELD WIPER SWITCH MECHANISM. Phase 2.

Condition: Turn signal lever malfunctions, bad windshield wiper motor switch.

Tools and materials: Phase 1 tool kit including a 24mm or 15/16 in socket, new turn signal lever/windshield wiper switch mechanism.

Remarks: This mechanism is an expensive item to replace because it's also the windshield wiper switch mechanism. You might want to live with the problem of having to hold the turn signal lever in position for a while.

Step 1. Align Front Wheels

Turn the steering wheel until the front wheels are facing straight ahead.

Step 2. Disconnect Battery Ground Strap (10mm wrench)

Step 3. Remove Horn Bar (Rabbits)

Pull off the central steering wheel cover (that's the horn bar) by grasping it with both hands, thumbs at the bottom, fingers at the top, and giving it a hard tug toward you. If it's difficult to pull off, insert a thin screwdriver under the plastic cover halfway between the center crest and the outside of the cover and locate one of the springs holding the cover in position. There's one on the right side, one in the middle and one on the left. With the screwdriver in the spring, gently pry the cover upward. If you hear a nasty cracking noise, you've broken the plastic plate beneath the cover. But don't worry; I do the same thing every time, and it's easily repaired with plastic cement. With the cover off, disconnect the small electrical wire running to the connection in the middle of the plastic cover. That's the horn ground wire. Go to Step 5.

Step 4. Remove Rubber Horn Cover (Sciroccos)

Peel the rubber center part of the steering wheel away from the center rim. Use your fingers. When it's free, take that rubber part out of the wheel.

Step 5. Scribe, Scribe

In order to reinstall the steering wheel in its original position, mark the plastic under the steering wheel with a pencil and inscribe a like mark on the steering column switch cover. Also put a punch mark on the face of the threaded steering wheel column which is surrounded by that big nut in the center of the steering wheel. Make another punch mark on the steering wheel recess opposite the one you just made as close to the first one as possible.

Step 6. Remove Steering Wheel

With your 24mm (15/16 in) socket, remove the center nut holding the steering wheel on the steering column. The nut's fairly tight so you'll have to grasp the wheel with one hand and turn your socket with the other. Don't slip or you'll require two new front teeth. Pull off the steering wheel; the nut and washer will remain inside the wheel recess.

Step 7. Remove Turn Signal Mechanism

Models up to 1978 have a separate turn signal and windshield wiper switch. '78 and on cars have the two switches combined in one unit. To take off the turn signal/windshield wiper switch unit, first remove the three or four long screws facing you which go through the switch mechanism. Mark and Baggie them. Then pull off the two multipoint connectors (MPC's) under the steering column which plug into the back of the wiper/turn signal switch mechanism. Hold the black plastic socket; do *not* tug on the wires. When the MPC's are removed, slide the windshield wiper/turn signal switch mechanism up the column toward you.

Step 8. Install New Switch

Slide the new switch mechanism down the steering column and line up the three or four screw holes. Take the screws from your Baggie and slip them into the new switch mechanism. Tighten them *gently*.

Slip the two MPC's onto the prongs on the rear of the switch mechanism. Make sure they're properly pushed home.

Step 9. Test Mechanism

Before you put back the steering wheel and cover, replace the battery ground strap and turn the ignition to ON and try the turn signals and windshield wipers. OK?

Step 10. Reinstall Steering Wheel and Cover

If all is well, line up the steering wheel with the marks you scribed and punched and reinstall the washer and nut lying in the recess of the steering wheel. Torque the bolt to 5.0 mkg (36 ft lbs).

Rabbits: Before you put back the steering wheel cover, first repair the plastic plate, if you broke it, with plastic cement. Then reconnect the spade connector on the end of the small electrical wire into the cover. Snap the cover back onto the steering wheel.

Sciroccos: Hook up the ground wire and peel the plastic cover back onto the steering wheel. Just use your fingers to get the rubber on. Avoid using a screwdriver or anything sharp; you'll rip the rubber. You know how disastrous that can be.

Step 11. Tidy Up

Reinstall the plastic steering column protector on underside of steering column with two phillips screws.

PROCEDURE 10: FIX HORN (HOOTER, BEEPER, BUZZER, BIP-BIP OR HONKER) Phase 2.

Condition: The horn won't work.

Tools and materials: Phase 2 tool kit, Volt Ohmmeter (VOM) or test light, Friend, electrical wire.

Remarks: Fuses are OK.

Step 1. Test Horn

The horn can be a tricky little doodad to mend as there are quite a few things to check when it's silenced. We'll start with the simplest, the electric part of the horn itself. Test the horn with the ignition turned to ON. Ask Friend to keep pushing on the horn bar on the steering wheel, then go to the front of the car with a small hammer. Locate the electric horn under the front of the car about 18 inches in from the left front wheel. (Sciroccos have two horns.) Check that the electrical connections are tight on the back of the horn and corrosion free. Have Friend continue pushing the horn bar down. If no sound is heard, tap the horn with your hammer. Sometimes the plate which vibrates inside the horn and makes the noise gets stuck, and the good old hammer trick can free it. Also check that the horn isn't hard up against the body. This happens if you've hit it with a stone or something like that. Bend it away from the body if it's touching.

Step 2. Is There Juice?

If the above methods don't get the horn to work, let's see if there's juice going to the horn. Find your VOM and turn it to 15 volts DC. With the ignition key still ON and Friend pushing the horn bar, insert one probe of the VOM (or test light) into the electrical connector on the end of the black/yellow (hot) wire which connects to the horn and ground the other probe on the chassis (ground). You should get a reading of 12 volts DC. If not, insert the probe into the other electrical connector and test again. Still no reading? Ask Friend to move the horn bar up and down and side to side to try to get electrical contact. If the needle on the VOM jumps around, the problem is probably with the horn bar, Step 5. If the needle stays at rest, let's check further.

Step 3. Hot Wire

Strip the insulation from both ends of two 1 meter (3 ft) lengths of electrical wire. Wrap one end around the battery positive post and hook the other to the hot horn terminal at the front of the car. Fasten one end of the other wire to the negative battery post and the other end to the ground terminal on the horn. If there's no sound, the horn is kaput. Unhook the wires, buy and install a new horn, and you've finished.

Horn works? There's a problem with the wires, the horn bar or the relay plate. Reconnect the two horn wires.

Step 4. Check Wiring

First look under the steering column and check the wires in the right multipoint connector (MPC), (not the one at the base of the ignition switch). Push on the brown/blue wire in that MPC; ignition ON, horn bar down. Any noise? Push a matchstick or toothpick into the connector to ensure a good connection if the horn now sounds. Nothing? Find a length of electrical wire, stripped at both ends (or your VOM set at 15 volts DC). Pull the MPC off the base of the steering column and stick the wire end (or VOM probe) into the MPC opposite the brown/blue wire. Ground the other end of the wire/probe onto a clean unpainted metal surface. The horn hoots? Go to the next Step. Nothing? The electric shop or VW beckons, since the problem's in the relay plate.

Step 5. Check Horn Bar

First, turn off the ignition.
Rabbits: See Procedure 9, Step 3, and remove the horn bar.
Sciroccos: See Procedure 9, Step 4.

Under the horn bar is a small brown wire with a female spade connector on its end coming up from the steering column. Has your connection fallen off? If so, push back the connection, push the horn bar back on and the horn will work when the ignition is turned to ON.

If your connection is good but the horn won't work, we'll have to check the horn bar. Remove the steering wheel as described in Procedure 9, Step 5, and clean the contact between the steering wheel and the steering column switch. The contact is a bronze piece of metal which is slightly springy and faces you as you pull off the steering wheel. Clean off any grease and rub it with a piece of emery paper 'til it shines.

While you're here, let's measure and possibly correct the distance between the steering wheel and the steering column spacer. With the steering wheel off, you can see a black plastic spacer sleeve pushed over the steering column. That spacer sleeve keeps the underside of the steering wheel the correct distance from the contact on the steering column switch. Get the dimensions correct.

If any of these distances are too great or too small, adjust the spacer sleeve by prying it up or knocking it down a bit. These measurements are fairly critical for correct horn operation. When you're sure they're correct, reinstall the steering wheel, put the horn bar back on with the brown wire connection on the underside in place. Don't forget to replace the MPC on the steering column switch if it's still off. Try the horn again. Yes?

If your horn still has a problem, there's trouble with the connection in the relay plate. Messing with the relay plate is not really in the realm of your capabilities. It's sensitive and messing with the wires can cause new problems greater than your horn problem. I would buy one of those marine type horns which work on compressed air and have it somewhere inside the car so you can pass inspection. If you want to pursue horn problems further, the whole thing is laid out in Section 90.7 of the VW Official *Repair Manual Type 17 Rabbit, Type 53 Scirocco*.

PROCEDURE 11: FIX SPEEDOMETER. Phase 2.

Condition: Your forward speed is a mystery.

Tools and materials: Phase 1 tool kit, new cable maybe.

Step 1. Check Transmission Cable

If your speedometer suddenly quits, hope it's only a broken cable. Actually, there are two cables in your Rabbit or Scirocco, one running from the transmission to the black EGR counter box on the firewall, and another from the rear of that box through the firewall into the rear of the speedometer on the dashboard. Let's check which cable is broken before buying a replacement. Start with the long one from the transmission to the EGR box. Find a large phillips screwdriver or 13mm wrench and remove the screw or bolt holding the speedometer cable in the right top part of the transmission. Pull the cable from the transmission and screw back the phillips screw or bolt into the transmission for safekeeping.

Scirocco speedometer cables may be held to parts of the body with plastic clips. If so, free them before attempting to remove the cable.

The cable has a white plastic gear arrangement on the end. Use your thumb and forefinger to unscrew the metal ring holding the other end of the speedometer cable in the black EGR counter box. Pull the cable free. Twist the gear end of the speedometer cable round and round and see if the other end of the cable turns. If it doesn't, the cable is broken. If it does, it's OK, but you should check it more thoroughly by pulling on the non-geared end of the cable to see if the inner cable is in one piece. Sometimes the cable can break, then remesh itself together, making you think the cable is intact. When you're sure the cable is OK, reinstall it and go to Step 3.

If that cable is broken, you must buy a new one. Take the old cable with you to VW to make sure you buy the correct one. The new cable won't have the white plastic speedometer drive gear installed. You have to take it off the old one and put it on the new one.

Step 2. Switch Gears

There are two types of speedometer drive gear ends. The older type has the plastic speedometer drive held in place by a small half moon shaped retaining clip just below the gear part. To pull that drive off, insert a thin screwdriver blade under the clip and pry it of. Be careful, that clip can fly half-way to Timbuktu. The plastic gear will now slide off.

The new type has a hole just below the geared part. Find a pointed object that will fit inside the hole. Before inserting your tool, look through the hole for a circlip on the inside of the speedometer drive. You may need to clear out oil from the hole before you can see the clip. Line up the hole with the clip and push your tool through the hole onto the clip while pulling the speedometer drive gear away from the cable. You have to pull quite hard to get it off.

To attach it to your new cable, push the new cable onto the geared speedometer drive without pushing anything through the hole. Push it on hard and make sure it's clicked home. When the speedometer drive gear end is attached to the new cable, put the cable back into the top of the transmission and secure it with the phillips screw or 13mm bolt. Now push the other end into the black EGR counter box. Do not kink the cable while doing these operations! If it becomes kinked, the cable will not work properly and the speedometer will not read correctly. Tighten the cable in the EGR counter box with your thumb and forefinger. *Don't* use pliers to tighten.

Step 3. Check Small Cable

If your old cable checked out OK and is reinstalled, we must check the other, smaller cable running from the back of the box to the rear of the speedometer. Get inside the car and feel up behind the speedometer for the place where the speedometer cable joins the speedometer. Unscrew the retaining ring with your thumb and forefinger and pull the cable out of the back of the speedometer. Next remove the retaining ring from the rear of the EGR box and pull the cable through the firewall toward the engine.

With the short speedometer cable removed, twist one end of the inner cable between your thumb and forefinger and see if the other end moves. If it's broken, the other end won't turn. A good final test is to grasp both ends of the inner cable and pull in opposite directions. Does it pull apart? If broken, get a new one and thread it through the firewall from the engine compartment end, push it into the rear of the speedometer and tighten the retaining ring. Now replace the other end in the back of the EGR counter box. Again, do not kink the cable.

If the cables are both OK, the speedometer head is broken. It's an unusual condition. You have to remove the dash insert, take off the printed circuit and unscrew the speedometer and install a new one. I've never had to do one.

I once replaced a speedometer cable only to have it break again. Another replacement broke 20 miles later. It turned out that the black EGR box was faulty causing the cables to break. A new one was installed and nary a cable has broken since.

PROCEDURE 12: FIX FUEL GAUGE. Phase 1.

Condition: Shows full when empty or empty when full or doesn't work at all.

Tools and materials: Phase 1 tool kit, Friend.

Remarks: If your gauge always registers full, do the Steps, too.

Step 1. Find Sending Unit Connections

The sending unit is in one of two different locations depending on your model and year. Models up to '76 and most diesels have the unit on the right side of the gas tank. You'll have to get on your knees to see the connection.

Later models have the sending unit on the top of the tank. To get at it: **Rabbit** people have to remove the rear seat. **Sciroccos**—just lift the rear seat bottom up and out. To remove the Rabbit seat, first remove the rear seat back supports. These are hinged metal brackets, one on each side of the seat. They fit into ears welded to each side of the car floor. You need a screwdriver to remove the clip holding the pin through the hinged bracket arm into the ear. Be careful; these clips often fly off and disappear into the wilderness. With the clips off, push the hinged arms toward the center of the car to clear the ears. Do both sides. Remove the seat assembly through a door. Now pull back the protective floor mat held by two stiff plastic bands. They are screwed into the car floor. Don't remove the screws; just pull the rear of the band upward and it will come free from the slot in the carpet. Do both sides and roll back the carpet or rubber mat.

The fuel tank sending unit is under the circular protective metal cap held by three phillips screws. Remove the screws and pull off the cap.

Step 2. Check Electrical Connections (Carbureted and Diesel)—Fuel Injection go to Step 3.

A brown ground wire should be connected to a terminal on the sending unit. Check the tightness and cleanliness of the connections. Turn the ignition ON and see if the gauge works. No? If your gauge always registers full, take the violet/black wire off the sending unit (ignition ON) and see if the gauge needle falls. If

Step 2. (Cont'd.)

so, you've got trouble with the sending unit. If not, the wire is grounded somewhere. Follow the wire and find the break. Chapter 20, Procedure 10 tells how to use a VOM in troubleshooting electrical problems.

If your gauge doesn't register, pull the violet/black wire off the sending unit connection and touch it to a clean unpainted metal surface. Ask Friend to turn the ignition to ON and watch the gas gauge. It moved up to full? You have a problem with the sending unit or the brown wire isn't grounded properly.

Use your VOM to check the wire resistance with the battery ground strap disconnected (Chapter 20, Procedure 10). If the wire's OK, the sending unit is bad. Go to Step 4 and change it.

Step 3. Check Electrical Connections (Fuel Injection)

The sending unit electrical connection has a plastic plug on its top. Pull the plug and check the tightness of the wires in the plug. If they're OK, use your VOM to check wire resistance (Chapter 20, Procedure 10).

Step 4. Check/Replace Sending Unit

If the electrical connections turned out to be OK in both cases but the fuel gauge still doesn't work, you must remove the fuel tank sending unit to check it more carefully. The tank should be below ¼ full if you have a side mounted unit. First, disconnect *both* terminals of the battery (10mm wrench). The method for removing the sending unit is identical whether you have a top or side mounted unit. Use a screwdriver and hammer to tap the unit's notched outer ring about one tenth of a turn counterclockwise ↻ . Now pull the unit free. Carefully thread it out of the fuel tank. Push the electrical connection back onto the top of the fuel tank sending unit and install the two battery connections. Ask Friend to turn the ignition to ON as you slowly move the arm sticking out of the sending unit base *slowly* through its arc of travel. The fuel gauge on the dashboard should move correspondingly. If there's still no reading on the dashboard gauge, reinstall the fuel tank sending unit and truck on down to VW, leave your car outside, explain your dilemma to the parts person and ask for the loan of a new sending unit. Plug the new unit into the electrical connection which was plugged into your old unit (no need to remove the old sending unit) and again go through the test of slowly pushing the float through its arc of travel. Remember, the ignition must be turned to ON. The fuel gauge will now work. You've hopefully found the source of your trouble. If you want to spring for it, buy the new unit and install it in your car.

No luck? The connection from the gauge to the relay plate is bad, or the relay plate itself is kaput. Go to VW or an auto electric shop.

Another Little Trick: If your sending unit seems to check out OK but your fuel gauge needle wanders a little, the voltage stabilizer is shot. This voltage stabilizer also has an effect upon the coolant temperature gauge (if you have one). The stabilizer is inserted into the printed circuit on the rear of the instrument cluster and held by a tiny screw going through the stabilizer into the printed circuit backing. To get at the tiny stabilizer, disconnect the battery ground strap (10mm) and lie inside the car with your back and posterior on the driver's seat and your head under the steering wheel. It's position 37A in the Kama Sutra. Remove the screw from the center of the stabilizer and, holding the stabilizer's body, gently push it upward to free it

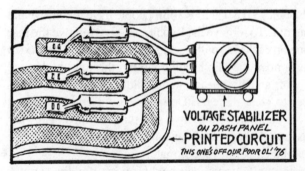

VOLTAGE STABILIZER
ON DASH PANEL
←PRINTED CURCUIT
THIS ONE'S OFF OUR POOR OL' '76

from its three connections in the printed circuit. When you've got the stabilizer out, go to VW and buy an identical one. With your new voltage stabilizer in hand, look at it carefully and you'll notice that on some stabilizers there's a metal plate on the back. When you install the stabilizer, be sure the plate is facing toward the metal speedometer housing. It's important! Get back into Position 37A and slip the three prongs of the voltage stabilizer into the prongs on the printed circuit board. A very painstaking, frustrating job, I may add. When you've got them in, replace the screw in the center of the stabilizer and tighten it into the printed circuit backing. Then feel below the connections on the printed circuit to the voltage stabilizer and smooth out any 'bump' which may have formed as you pressed in the new stabilizer. Reinstall the battery ground strap (10mm) and test the gauge.

If that doesn't fix it, the printed circuitry on the back of the instrument cluster is in question. You need to remove the dash insert, disconnect all the wires, etc., unbolt the printed circuit and install a new one. They rarely go wrong.

Now it's time to talk about certain biological aspects of your Rabbit or Scirocco. Rabbit has more of a biological ring to it. Scirocco is more meteorological. VW designers have seen fit to include two venomous, yet useful species of snake in their automobiles; the Vindscreen Viper and the Rear Vindow Viper.

On the Scirocco they mainly put on only von vindscreen viper; on the Rabbit, two. It is up to us to maintain the creatures which work for us in good health and spirit. Let's proceed to nurture our viper tenderly.

PROCEDURE 13: REPLACE WORN WIPER BLADES. Phase 1.

Condition: Worn or damaged wiper blades which streak or don't do the job adequately.

Tools and materials: Phase 1 tool kit, new blade(s) or arm(s).

Remarks: When buying new blades for your vehicle, you must specify whether it's the Scirocco with one viper or the Rabbit with two. The procedure for changing the rubber blade is the same for front and rear vipers.

In the olden days when windshield wiper rubber (or blades) wore out, parts stores sold a whole new blade assembly. In modern times all you can buy is the rubber blade which makes contact with the windshield. I can't say it's any cheaper! To replace the blade on the windshield wiper arm, first free the rubber portion from the two retaining arms. These arms have fingers on their ends which clip around the two metal spacers and into the rubber. If you carefully look at the arm, you'll see the rubber portion is open at one end and closed at the other. Grasp the rubber at the closed end and firmly pull it out of the retaining arms. Two metal pieces will slide out with the rubber.

Insert the two metal spacers in the new blade, one at each side and slide the new rubber with spacers in place into the finger parts of the wiper arm. Thread the rubber carefully through all fingers until it comes to the end where the fingers fit into two tiny slots in the closed end of the rubber piece.

Everything fits properly? The blades not going to slip out?

If for some reason the bracket is broken, you'll have to buy a new one from the dealer. To remove the bracket from the arm, pull the arm away from the windshield and point the blade upward. Then squeeze together the U end of the arm, slide the bracket down (towards windshield) and remove it as shown. To replace it just slip the slot on the bracket onto the arm. Line it up with the U and pull it up to snap it in place. Then give it a tug in the opposite direction to make sure it's properly located.

PROCEDURE 14: ADJUST WIPER ARMS. Phase 1.

Condition: The wiper blade(s) don't wipe enough of the windshield.

Tools and materials: Phase 1 tool kit.

When the windshield wipers are turned off (at rest, as it were), the distance from the bottom of the rubber blade to the top of the rubber part at the bottom of the windshield should be as follows: on the **Rabbit**, the left blade should be 35mm (1⅜ in), the right 65mm (or 2½ in). On a **Scirocco** with the two-armed wiper system, the left blade should be 25mm (1 in), the right 30mm (1-3/16 in). On a **one-armed Scirocco** the distance should be 55mm (2-3/16 in).

To see if the arm needs adjustment, run your wiper motor for a minute (be sure to throw some water onto the windshield before you do this to prevent scratching the glass). Turn off the wiper motor by using the lever on the steering column (not the ignition switch), then measure the distances. If they are more than 5mm off, adjust them.

The arms of your wiper or wipers are connected to a crank on the wiper shaft by a 10mm nut. To get at this nut, you have to remove the black plastic cap from the base of the wiper arms just below the windshield. Pop off these caps with a screwdriver and there's the nut. To adjust the arm(s), remove the 10mm nut and lift off the wiper arm from the shaft protruding through the body work. Both the inside of that wiper arm and the shaft have serrations. Press the wiper arm back onto the shaft after moving it slightly in the direction needed to correct the distance. Measure the distance from the blade to the windshield rubber. When it's right, tighten the nut and press the protective cap back on. The rear windshield wiper (if you have one) is adjusted similarly.

PROCEDURE 15: CHECK AND REPAIR NON-FUNCTIONING WINDSHIELD WIPERS. Phase 2

Condition: Windshield wipers do not work or work only intermittently (remember, Sciroccos and deluxe late model Rabbits have a position on the wiper column switch where it's *supposed* to work intermittently!).

Tools and materials: Phase 1 tool kit, VOM.

Remarks: To do the tests properly, the battery must be fully charged and the battery terminals on tight. The ignition should be turned to ON and the air conditioner, if you have one, should be running.

Step 1. Check Voltage to Motor

Your ignition is turned to ON, OK? Now move the wiper control lever on the right side of the steering column to the on position and break out your VOM. Lift and prop the hood. Locate the wiper motor slightly to the left and just behind the firewall below the windshield. Remove the plastic 'drip tray' above the motor. It may be held by clips. Be careful not to break it, especially on U.S. cars. Pull off the multipoint connector (MPC) on the motor by grasping the plastic connector part (not the wires). With the VOM turned to 15 volts DC, insert one probe of the meter into terminal 53 (that's a green wire with a black stripe or a black wire with a green stripe) and ground the other probe. If there's voltage present at this MPC, your VOM needle will swing over to 12 volts. If your VOM did not show a reading, there's a break in the wire from the switch on the steering column to the wiper motor (Step 3). If you get a 12 volt reading, the wiper motor is defective. Let's be sure.

Step 2. Check Wiper Motor

Find two longish pieces of electrical wire and strip the ends. Connect one end of the wire to the positive battery terminal and stick the other end into terminal 53 of the connection on the wiper motor. Now attach one end of the other wire to terminal 31 of the connection on the wiper motor and the other end to the negative battery terminal.

If the wiper motor runs, you have a faulty ground wire. If so, repair it by simply running a piece of wire from the rear of terminal 31 in the connector on the wiper motor to a good ground. If you can't think of another place, attach it to the negative battery post.

However, if your wiper motor didn't run, it's defective and has to be replaced. Turn to Procedure 16 in this Chapter.

Step 3. Check Wiper Switch

First reconnect the MPC on the wiper motor itself. Now go inside the car. Using your phillips screwdriver, remove the plastic protective piece from the underside of the steering column. The MPC's will now be exposed. The one we're interested in is the one furthest to the left (remember FRONT is FRONT). Don't pull the MPC off yet but keep the ignition turned to ON and the wiper lever in the full ON position. Look at all the wires running into the rear of the MPC and wiggle them around a bit, pushing them into the MPC more than pulling them. See if the wiper motor starts. Especially check the green and black wire. It is not unusual to have a loose connection inside the MPC. The easiest way to repair it is to find a wooden matchstick or toothpick, cut it in half and insert it into the rear of the MPC to press the end of the wire tightly against the metal connector for a good flow of current.

If that didn't make your wiper motor run, let's test some more.

Step 4. Test Continuity from Switch to Wiper Motor

Pull off the MPC from the wiper motor switch (the left one, remember) and find one of your electrical wires. Insert one end of the test wire into terminal 53A (the black and grey wire) and the other end into terminal 53 (the green/black wire). In effect you're jumping the switch. Be sure your ignition is turned to ON. If the wiper motor runs, your wiper motor switch is kaput. To replace it, see Procedure 9 in this chapter. If your wiper motor doesn't run, there's a break in wire 53A or 53 between the relay plate and the wiper motor switch. That means trouble. We can, however, check this malfunction.

Step 5. Check Continuity Between Relay Plate and Wiper Motor Switch

First disconnect the battery ground strap (10mm), then remove the phillips screw holding the relay plate in position above the driver's knees. Pull the relay plate slightly upward to clear the two ears which hold the plate in position. Turn the plate around and pull out the black plug from position E. Reconnect the battery ground strap. Get your test wire and look into the now vacated spot on the relay plate and find terminals E15 and E16. If you look very carefully into the relay plate you'll see the numbers above the pins sticking out from the plate. Stick one end of your wire into E15 and the other onto E16. Ask Friend to reconnect the MPC into the base of your windshield wiper switch. Make sure the ignition is turned to ON and watch your wiper motor run. If the wiper motor does run, you have to replace wire 53 or 53A running from the black connector pushed into the relay plate to the MPC pushed into the windshield wiper motor switch.

First remove the battery ground strap (10mm), ignition off, then remove wire #53 from the MPC at the windshield wiper motor switch and gently pull it through the wiring harness until it reaches the rear of connector E. Measure the length of the wire against a new piece of wire, cut the new wire the same, then thread the new wire through the wiring harness and insert it into the rear of the MPC at the steering column switch. Insert the other end into the back of connector E. Reconnect the battery ground strap, turn the key to ON and see if the motor runs. If it doesn't, replace wire 53A by the same method.

People who didn't get their wiper motor to run when E15 and E16 were bridged with the test wire have a break in the relay plate.

Step 6. Check Relay Plate

Disconnect the battery ground strap (10mm) and remove E and C connectors in the back of the relay plate. Turn your VOM to RX1K. Touch one probe to E16 and the other to C9. Your meter should read 0 ohms. Then check E15 to C13; your meter should still read 0. If you get a 0 reading in both cases, your relay plate is OK but the wiring harness from the relay plate to the wiper motor is broken somewhere.

If you get an infinity reading when you touch the probes to the above connections, the relay plate is shot and has to be replaced.

Replacing the wiring harness from the relay plate to the wiper motor is something you shouldn't attempt. Take the problem to VW or a qualified and reliable auto electrical shop. Talk to the person who is going to work on your car and explain the tests you've done so far.

Step 6. (Cont'd.)

If you have to replace your relay plate, get a new one from VW, quoting your chassis number. Just transfer every electrical connection from your old plate to your new one, one step at a time so they don't get mixed up. Reconnect your battery ground strap and test every electrical function of your car before calling it a day. I've heard of cases of faulty relay plates being obtained from VW and the headaches that ensue are worthy of 25 minutes of TV headache remedy advertisements. If a new relay plate is required, speak to your service manager about the possibility of a warranty repair.

PROCEDURE 16: REMOVE/REPLACE WINDSHIELD WIPER MOTOR. Phase 1.

Condition: Wiper motor shot.

Tools and materials: Phase 1 tool kit, new wiper motor.

Step 1. Disconnect Battery Ground Strap (10mm)

Step 2. Unhook Motor

First remove the flimsy plastic 'drip tray' from between the top of the firewall and the base of the windshield apron. The tray may be held by clips. The wiper motor is below this tray. Pull the electrical plug from the side of the motor and tuck the wire out of the way.

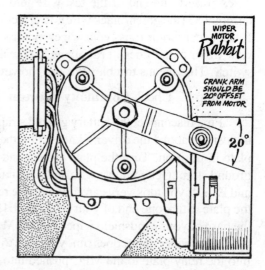

Use a screwdriver to pop off the connecting rod from the drive crank bolted to the top of the motor. The drive crank is the metal arm held to the motor by the 10mm nut. Leave the nut alone for the moment, just pry the crank off. When it's off, remove the 10mm nut which holds the crank and take it off. Remove the four nuts/bolts which hold the motor in position on its bracket, and thread it out of the car.

Step 3. Install New Motor (Rabbit and '75 Sciroccos)

Take the new motor and temporarily hook it up to its electrical plug. Reconnect the battery ground strap

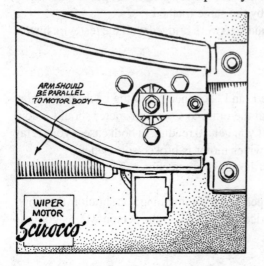

and run the motor for three minutes. Turn off the wiper switch on the steering column (don't pull the motor plug) and install the wiper motor crank as per diagram on previous page. Reinstall the motor, tighten the nuts/bolts and pop back the connecting rod after giving the crank pin a shot of grease. Push back the plug, reinstall the drip tray and you're done.

Step 4. Install New Motor ('76 and on Sciroccos)

Install the motor with the nuts/bolts *before* installing the drive crank. Hook up the electrical plug, put back the battery ground strap and run the new motor for three minutes. Turn the motor off using the steering column switch (don't pull the motor plug) and attach the drive crank as per the diagram. Pop back the connecting rod after giving the crank pin a shot of grease. That's it.

CHAPTER 20

MECHANICS' TIPS

AND GENERAL INFORMATION

This chapter contains information for proper identification of chassis, engines, transmissions, etc. There's also a few tips on how to correct seemingly impossible situations, such as stripped nuts and broken studs, as well as a few how-to's.

Let's start with **general information**.

The vehicles covered in this book are the Rabbit Type 17 (the Rabbit 2-door sedan is Model 171, and the Rabbit 4-door sedan is Model 173), and the Scirocco Type 53 (Sport Coupe Model 531).

Rabbits and Sciroccos were first sold in the U.S.A. in 1975, with 1.5 liter engines having the code letters FC or FG. The manual transmission code for that year is GC and the automatic transmission EQ. These designations apply to both the Rabbit and Scirocco transmissions. In 1976 the engines were available in 1.5 and 1.6 liter sizes. The 1.5 liter engine kept the same designation, and the 1.6 liter fuel-injected engine was given the FN code and the 1.6 liter fuel-injected engine was coded EE or EF. In 1977 the 1.5 liter diesel engine was introduced and its code is CK. 1978 brought us the EH engine code, and in 1979 Sciroccos were fitted with a 1.6 liter engine coded EJ. That engine is identical to the EE/EF types. The codes for the automatic and manual transmissions remained the same. European cars have engines with different codes.

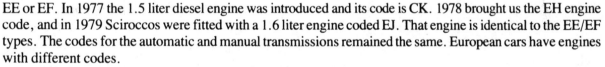

1975 Rabbits and Sciroccos have drum brakes on all four wheels, but in 1976 disc brakes became standard on front wheels of all models. Drum brakes remained on the rear. The picture is the same to date. Automatic transmission and air conditioning have been available as factory options on all models except the diesel. Air-conditioned diesel engines have been available since 1978 when they were installed by the dealer.

Engine and Chassis Numbers:

The Rabbit chassis number is on the top of the dashboard on the left side. Read it through the front of the windshield. The number is also in the engine compartment on top of the right suspension strut mounting. The Scirocco chassis number is on the driver's side of the windshield pillar (that's the left side) and also in the engine compartment on the right suspension strut mounting. In both models engine numbers are found on the crankcase just above the fuel pump (or, fuel injection, just above the control pressure regulator).

Manual transmission serial numbers are stamped below and to the left of where the inboard right hand constant velocity joint on the driveshaft bolts to the transmission. The transmission number gives you the day, month and year of its manufacture. The automatic transmission has its number stamped on the top of the transmission where it mates to the engine.

The transmission type number (010) is stamped on the top middle of the transmission between the driveshafts. Rabbits and Sciroccos also have an identification plate on the upper front cross member. That's the thing you put your elbows on when you lean to look into the engine compartment. The plate is a little to the right of the hood latch.

Volkswagen Part Numbers:

To obtain the correct part for your particular model, you have to give the parts person a nine digit chassis number. These numbers are computerized which helps the Volkswagen distribution network find any piece in the country. It's best if you can take your old used part into the dealer for comparison with the picture on their microfiche viewing screens. These visual display units show a picture of the part and its computerized number. Likewise, if you need a part for your engine, supply the parts person with your engine and chassis number.

     MECHANICS' TIPS

PROCEDURE 1: SOME TOOLS AND HOW TO USE THEM

By definition (mine) a mechanic's tool is an instrument used to improve the mechanical capability of any person attempting any Procedure. Most tools use either a twisting or linear action. In the twisting category we have wrenches, sockets and screwdrivers. The most basic linear tools are hammers, files and saws.

The hammer is probably the most commonly abused tool in auto mechanic-ing. Although it's usually not the right tool for the job, it certainly is an essential ingredient in any tool box. But use it with a great deal of prudence.

The socket on its ratchet handle, and the combination or open end wrench are the most useful tools in your tool box. Choose a wrench or socket that properly fits the nut or bolt you are trying to remove or install. Turn it clockwise ◯ to tighten and counterclockwise ◯ to remove. When removing a nut or bolt in easy view, use the box end wrench because it completely surrounds the nut and efficiently grips all of its faces. If the nut is difficult to get at, use the open end side of the combination wrench.

How to Use A Torque Wrench:

A torque wrench measures the force you are applying to a nut or bolt. Thus, the tighter you get a nut, the higher the torque value. Torque is measured in foot pounds, meter/kilograms, inch pounds or centimeters per kilogram. These words mean the number of pounds or kilograms being applied to a wrench one foot or one meter away from the center of the nut. Inch pounds means the number of pounds applied to the nut so many inches away.

Torque wrenches come in three styles. The simplest (and cheapest) is just a bar with a head on it to accept your socket on one end. It has a plate on the other end with the inch, foot or meter value stamped on it. Attached to the end which accepts the socket is a pointer which indicates the foot pound or meter kilograms you apply.

The second type has a dial on one end with a needle set inside. The needle turns when you pull on the wrench.

The third and most expensive torque wrench is the click set type. With this one, you screw the handle of the torque wrench in until the handle lines up with the torque number stamped into the tool. An audible click is heard when the desired torque is reached as you pull on the nut or bolt.

Whichever kind is yours, first be sure to have the correct torque for the particular nut or bolt you are tightening. If you apply too much torque, you'll strip the thread or worse, break the stud.

To torque a nut/bolt, rest one hand on the head of the wrench just above the socket and steadily pull on the handle of the torque wrench with the other hand until correct torque is reached.

If a number of nuts or bolts have to be torqued at once, first tighten all of them to ¾ of the required torque. There is a predetermined pattern on items such as the cylinder head which you should follow closely; otherwise distortion will occur. A good rule of thumb is to tighten in a diagonal sequence. See Procedure 7.

When you've obtained ¾ of desired torque, adjust your wrench to full torque value and proceed. When the nuts or bolts are fully tightened, go round once more reversing the sequence to make sure they are all correctly torqued.

If you've torqued something too tight, loosen the nuts or bolts in the diagonal sequence, reset your torque wrench to ¾ torque, tighten them to that partial value, then continue to full torque.

Sometimes you have to retorque cylinder head bolts after a certain mileage interval. Always loosen the bolts ¼ turn (in a diagonal pattern), then torque them back to full torque.

If you have to torque something and just cannot fit the torque wrench in position, use a regular socket or wrench and some arithmetic. Let's say a nut has to be torqued to 2 mkg (14 ft lbs). Hold your regular wrench or socket handle about 15 cm (6 in) from the center of the nut and give a steady hard pull. Don't jerk or pull too hard. You just want to get the thing tight, not welded into position.

Magnetic Magic; A Clumsy's Must:

When removing small screws, nuts or bolts, undo them with a wrench or socket in one hand and in the other hand hold your inspector's type magnet close to the item being unscrewed. This way, if your socket slips when the nut comes to the end of its thread, the nut will stick to the magnet instead of getting lost in the dirt below. If you do manage to drop something in the dirt, the magnet is great for finding it. It's wonderful for retrieving washers from the innards of the front crossmember.

Ivory Magic:

If you dig your fingernails into a bar of soap before beginning work, grease and grime will have a harder time penetrating as the space under the nails is already occupied by soap. You can wash it and the grime out from under when you're finished.

PROCEDURE 2: REMOVING FROZEN AND/OR ROUNDED OFF NUTS, SCREWS AND BOLTS

Liquid Wrench and patience are your two best friends. Heat is a big help but must be used with extreme caution, as an automoblile engine contains a very explosive mixture—gasoline and air. Careless waving of flames can cause more than a fright. Don't use vast quantities of heat on any of the nuts or bolts on the cylinder head. It's made of aluminum and distorts when heated to high temperatures. Anyway, there's nothing on the cylinder head that's going to get that stuck.

The biggest problem nuts are the six holding the exhaust down pipe to the exhaust manifold. They're made of soft steel and round off very easily. Apply lots of Liquid Wrench and give it time to penetrate before attempting to remove them.

If you round off the corners of a nut, try holding it with a pair of vise grips. Turn the handle of the vise grips just as you would a wrench and screw it off. If that doesn't work, try tapping the next size smaller socket over the head of the wasted nut, and turn it off with a ratchet handle. No luck? Try filing two new flat places on opposite sides of the nut and use your wrench or socket in a final attempt to get the thing off.

If I can't remove a nut or bolt within five minutes, I use more drastic ways, such as the chisel method. A diamond tip chisel is the best for this job. Don't use a chisel designed for woodworking. Put on your safety glasses and hold the sharp chisel blade on one of the flat sides of the nut or on top of the nut if the side is inaccessible. Hit the head of the chisel one good solid blow with your hammer to make an indentation in the nut. If you don't trust your aim, hold the chisel with a pair of vise grips. Continue beating the chisel firmly onto that nut. When the nut starts to turn, make another indentation on another flat side so that you can continue turning the nut off the stud. When the nut moves easily, use vise grips or a wrench to remove it. Copious amounts of Liquid Wrench and small amounts of heat can be used here to good advantage.

After the socket has loosened a nut down in the depths of the engine compartment, you may be unable to reach in there to screw it off by hand. Here is the ancient veritable newspaper trick. Place a folded piece of newspaper over the mouth of the socket, put the socket on an extension and push the socket over the nut. Put the ratchet handle onto the extension and loosen the nut. Thus, when the nut is undone, it will stay inside the socket and not fall into the great void. Likewise, when you need to screw on the nut, put another piece of newspaper over the mouth of the socket and push the nut into it. The newspaper (or two zig-zag papers) will prevent the nut from falling out of the socket. Remember to remove the paper from the socket when the exercise is finished.

Another method to use on a tough-to-remove nut is to split it. Here's how:

If there's enough space, saw through the side of the stubborn nut with a hacksaw, trying not to saw into the stud on which the nut is screwed. When you've sawed the nut, insert a chisel or screwdriver blade into the saw cut and twist. This will open the nut slightly and allow you to turn it off the stud with a chisel, wrench or or your fingers. If you can't turn it off, hit either side of the saw cut with a punch or chisel and knock the nut off. It will eventually break.

If there's not enough space to get at the nut with a hacksaw, use a sharp chisel to beat on the underside of the nut, staying well away from the threads of the stud. Beat in a counterclockwise ↺ direction so that if the nut loosens, it'll turn off the stud. Continue hitting the nut until it cracks, then insert your chisel or screwdriver blade and break the nut apart. It takes a lot of energy and concentration to hit something in a confined place so make sure that if your chisel slips, it doesn't damage something important close by.

When you get the offending nut off, check the threads of the stud and if necessary, replace the stud using Procedure 4.

PROCEDURE 3: STARTING NUTS, BOLTS AND SCREWS

Nuts usually won't start because the stud is dirty from accumulated engine crud and grease. So, clean the stud with a wire brush and solvent and get the threads inside the nut clean.

Turn the nut over if it won't start on one side and try again. If the thread inside the nut is stripped, buy a new nut. Alternatively, it may be that the end of the stud is slightly chewed up, preventing the nut from starting. Try this: hold the nut squarely on the stud with your fingers, then gently tap the nut with the hammer to get it over the first screwed up part of the thread. Now try turning the nut clockwise ↻ with your wrench. If you can't reach the stud with a hammer, use a piece of wood, hammer handle or an extension from the ratchet set to tap the nut onto the stud. That method doesn't work? Try screwing the nut on in a counterclockwise direction half a turn until it bites, then continue in the clockwise ↻ direction. Finally, should all else fail, either replace the stud (Procedure 4) or cut new threads with a thread chaser or die.

If the threads on the stud and nut are OK, it's sometimes impossible to get a nut started in a place where your fingers can't fit. In this case you need a screwdriver whose blade will just fit into the hole of the nut. Put the nut onto the end of the screwdriver blade and give the nut a slight tap to hold it there. Position the screwdriver with the nut on the end over the stud or whatever you're trying to turn it onto. Make sure the nut is square to the stud. When the nut is started, withdraw the screwdriver and continue with your socket and extension.

If the screwdriver won't fit but your forefinger will, put a dab of thick grease on the end of your finger and stick the nut to your forefinger. Press your forefinger and the nut hard up against the stud and try to turn it on with your other hand or a wrench. If you can't reach it with your other hand, use the greased forefinger as a wrench and turn it slightly backward and forward until the nut starts.

Maybe you can hold the nut on the end of the stud with your forefinger and start the nut by using the end of a thin screwdriver on the side of the nut to try to get it started. If this doesn't work, try stuffing some paper into the end of a socket, put a dab of grease onto that paper and put the nut inside the socket so that it's stuck onto the grease. Put an extension onto the socket and try turning the nut on. The paper prevents the nut from being pushed all the way inside the socket and makes it possible to see what you're doing.

If you're trying to start a tiny nut or bolt, put the nut on the end of your inspection magnet and try to start it with that.

Difficult-To-Get-At Screws:

If you can't get a direct grip on a screw with your screwdriver blade (the condenser, perhaps), slide the screwdriver blade sideways into the screw slot and use the screwdriver like a lever. When the screw is half out, finish it off with your fingers. Hold a magnet close to the screw. There is a tool called a right angle screwdriver to take care of such tricky jobs but the old side-of-the-blade trick works every time for me. **Tiny screws:** A dollop of Vaseline applied to the head of the screw will hold it on the screwdriver blade as you thread the blade toward home. Don't use Vaseline when replacing the points. You don't want it inside the distributor.

You can achieve the same holding power by *magnetizing* the end of a screwdriver. If one of the kids has a bar magnet, borrow it and stroke the screwdriver blade in one direction (away from you) across the length of the magnet. Continue the stroke about 30cm (12 in) past the magnet, then circle the blade back (toward you) over the magnet about 30cm from the other end of the magnet. Do this about 50 times and you'll have a magnetic screwdriver.

PROCEDURE 4: REMOVE OR INSTALL STUDS

Sometimes when you're trying to turn a nut off a stud, the stud comes out with the nut. Don't despair! Try this: some studs have a part in the center with no thread. Put this unthreaded part into a vice or clamp it into a pair of vise grips. Sprinkle Liquid Wrench over the nut still sticking onto the stud and turn it off with a box end wrench. If the stud has threads all the way, find two more nuts the same thread size as the stud. Twist the nuts onto the end of the stud opposite the stuck nut. Turn them down the stud about 7mm (¼ in). Get two wrenches the same size as the nuts and tighten those two nuts onto one another. When you've got them very tight, put the stuck nut into the vise grips or vise and sprinkle with Liquid Wrench. Put your box end wrench on the bottom nut of the two you just threaded onto the stud and turn in a clockwise ⟳ direction to remove the stud from the stuck nut.

If you have to remove a stud from the cylinder head or crankcase, put on two nuts as described above and remove the stud by turning the inside nut counterclockwise ⟲ .

When it's time to reinstall a stud, do so by turning the outside nut clockwise ⟳ .

Studs occasionally have a tendency to pull themselves out of the engine or wherever as you tighten the nut. In this case the stud thread or nut thread has stripped. If it's a stripped stud, you'll have to remove it and install the next larger stud size. If you're installing a larger stud into an aluminum head, use the two nut method and let the new stud make its own threads in the aluminum.

However, if the stud is going into iron or steel you'll have to buy a tap with the same thread size as your new stud and make a new thread.

Novice's Catastrophe:

Everything is going smoothly while you're replacing a nut on a stud, when suddenly the stud breaks. It usually breaks flush with the surface of the object you're working on. If there's even a small amount of stud sticking out, try sawing a slot into the top of the stud to accept a screwdriver blade. Sprinkle lots of Liquid Wrench around the stud and try to ease the broken stud out with your screwdriver. If the stud is in a place where you can apply heat, do so before trying to remove it. No luck? Go to the next Procedure.

PROCEDURE 5: HOW TO USE AN EASY-OUT. Phase 1.

Condition: Broken stud.

Tools and materials: Drill, bit, Easy-Out[tm], Phase 1 tools. The best Easy-Out's I've ever seen are made by Snap-On Tools. If you don't have a set or a drill bit, take the broken remainder of the stud to the parts store and ask for an Easy-Out and drill bit of the correct size.

When you have your tools at hand, put a punch mark smack in the center of the broken stud. Next drill down about 13mm (½ in) or half the stud length. Snap-On Easy-Outs require you to tap the Easy-Out into the new hole with a hammer, then turn the piece of old stud out with a wrench or Easy-Out handle. The more conventional type of Easy-Out has a wide left hand thread. Screw this type into the stud in a counterclockwise ⟲ direction and as the Easy-Out screws into the stud, it will turn the stud out. Use plenty of Liquid Wrench during this operation.

If the Easy-Out method doesn't work (sometimes the tip of the Easy-Out breaks), you'll have to drill the whole stud out using a drill bit the same size as the stud, then use a tap to make a new thread for the next larger stud size. Remember to buy nuts to fit the new larger stud.

PROCEDURE 6: HOW TO RECONDITION SPARK PLUG HOLES

Condition: Spark plug hole threads ruined.

Tools and materials: Thread chaser.

Perhaps in your haste to get to a concert, you crossthreaded a spark plug when installing it into the cylinder head. If you didn't tighten it down too hard and it came out easily, it's possible to clean the thread inside the head with a thread chaser which works well in the case of minimal thread damage. The Volkswagen dealer or your local machine shop will have one which they may lend you. Position the chaser in the spark plug hole, apply some thin oil around the chaser and screw it in. When it's fully in, remove it and clean out any debris from the new threads. You may as well clean out the other three spark plug holes while you're at it.

Install brand new spark plugs to start with a clean slate, as it were.

If you attempted to tighten a plug down hard, the threads in the cylinder head are ruined and you'll have to take the head to VW or a machine shop to have a helicoil inserted into the stripped hole. It's not something to do yourself. If the cylinder head is still on the engine, drive or tow the car to the machine shop because they can insert the helicoil with the engine still in the car.

The moral to this story is obvious—don't overtighten (or crossthread) spark plugs.

PROCEDURE 7: TIGHTEN/LOOSEN IN DIAGONAL SEQUENCE

Start with #1, then go through the sequence as in the diagram. This is how to loosen and tighten bolts on a circular plate:

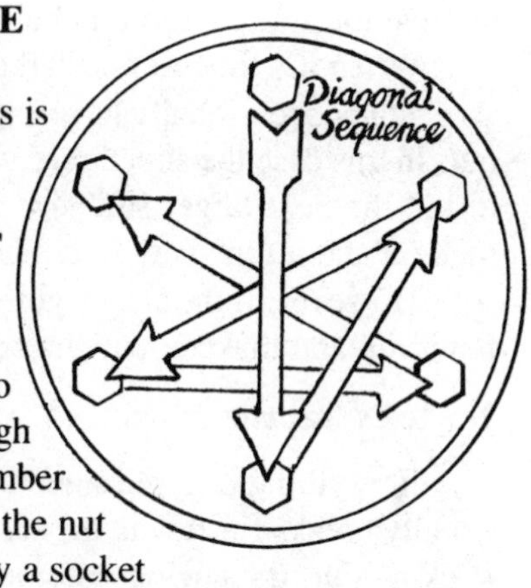

PROCEDURE 8: HOW TO REMOVE AND INSTALL FRONT DRIVESHAFT NUT

Use the correct size socket (30mm or 1-3/16 in). It's impossible to remove the driveshaft nut with a hammer and chisel. There's not enough room in the center of the wheel to fit a chisel onto the nut. I've tried it a number of times on screwed-up drive shafts and have never been able to remove the nut without destroying the driveshaft threads. Spend what's necessary to buy a socket from Sears.

The driveshaft nut is torqued to 24 mkg (173 ft lbs). That's a lot! Do not try to remove it when the car is jacked up; the force required will inch the car forward off the jack and onto your cranium. It's important—**remove front driveshaft nut only while all four wheels are on the ground!**

Removing:

Pull on the handbrake, put the car in gear and put chocks in front of the rear and front wheels. Slip the socket onto your breaker bar and find a piece of metal pipe (a cheater) to slip over the breaker bar to increase leverage. Have the breaker bar and cheater handle pointing forward horizontally and carefully stand on the end of the cheater to loosen the nut.

Installing:

When reinstalling the driveshaft nut, you must get it torqued to 24 mkg (173 ft lbs). Your torque wrench doesn't read that high? Here's a way to work it out.

First you must know your own weight. Measure from the center of the socket to the place on the cheater where you're applying force. Measure in centimeters or feet and multiply the distance in centimeters/feet by your weight. For example, if you weigh 54k (120 lbs) and are applying that huge bulk on the cheater 45 cm (18 in) from the center of the socket, you are applying 53 x 45.7 (120 x 1.5) which works out to 24 mkg or 180 foot pounds—about the perfect torque for the front driveshaft nut. When it no longer moves with your weight on it (don't bounce up and down), it's tight enough. If you're heavier or lighter than the example, adjust the distance between the nut and the place you're applying the force.

PROCEDURE 9: HOW TO USE A PULLER

A puller is a device that grabs onto something and pulls it off or out. Two items on your Rabbit might require a puller to remove them. The first is the ball joint on the tie rod end. A ball joint puller is merely two claws with a big bolt in the center. The claws hold the steering arm and when the center bolt on the puller is screwed in, the ball joint pops free of the arm. Simple and effective.

The other puller you may need is for a wheel drum, but only if the car's had no maintenance for 25 years or it's spent most of its life on a river bottom causing the brake drums to rust in place.

Before trying to remove the brake drums, first back off the brake shoe adjusting mechanism so the brake shoes are not in contact with the drums. Now if the drums won't come off, you need the puller. There's a plate on the wheel drum puller that uses the wheel lug nuts to attach the puller to the drum. In the center of the puller is a tower with a large bolt in its center. If the drum seems to be welded in position, use judicious amounts of heat on the drum and slowly turn the large center bolt on the puller and eventually the drum will pop off the axle. Resist the temptation to beat on the drum with a heavy hammer. You'll break it.

PROCEDURE 10: "HOW TO USE A VOLT OHMMETER (VOM)" by John Muir

First take a look at Peter's drawing on the next page.

The VOM you have may look different and use different names or symbols for the various scales but they all measure the same electrical phenomena: volts (both AC and DC), resistance (in Ohms) and amperes (Amps). Voltage is like water pressure (the force with which it comes through the hose), and resistance is like friction (rubbing against the sides of the hose). You have continuity when there's zero resistance. Amps are like measuring the amount of water. You have to relate amount to time and an ampere a second is called a coulomb. Batteries are rated by ampere hours. They will put out so many amps for so many hours. If the rating of a 12 volt battery is 70 amp-hours, it'll put out 7 amps for 10 hours at 12 volts. That's what they guarantee you. When you check resistance, you're making sure the path the electricity takes is clear. An electrical short is a little like the hose being cut and the water (electricity) running out.

Take a good look at your VOM. It has a needle which moves to tell you the answer you're seeking. You have to read the needle on some scale. Notice there are several, like OHMS (Ω), V-AC (AC volts), V-DC (DC volts), etc. Below the needle is a dial with a pointer. You set the pointer to what you are measuring, like Volts AC, OHMS (if you're going to measure resistance or check continuity), Volts-DC or DC ma-uA (AMPS)…this means milli or micro amps. Look at the two leads (wires). Notice that the connectors (probes) are shorter on one end than on the other. The shorter ends are plugged into the VOM. Plug one into the hole in the VOM that says Common (or 'COM' or 'COM−' or just '−'). This is the common lead for all VOM operations, also the negative terminal, which in Rabbit means 'ground.' The other connector goes into various places depending on what you are going to measure. For now, put it into the + hole. This hole might say '+ volts-ohms-mA,' 'V-ohm-ma,' '+ v Ω MA' or just '+' on yours. Now twist the dial with the pointer so the pointer points to Rx10K (or 10K) in the OHMS section. This means resistance times 10,000. Touch the probes together and watch the needle; it should swing to somewhere around zero. Now find the "adjust ohms" (Ω adj.) knob and turn it until the needle is exactly at 0 on the OHMS scale. This means no resistance; the other end of this scale means infinite resistance where no electricity could possibly pass through. Now what kind of resistance can you measure? How about yourself? Every patch of skin on your

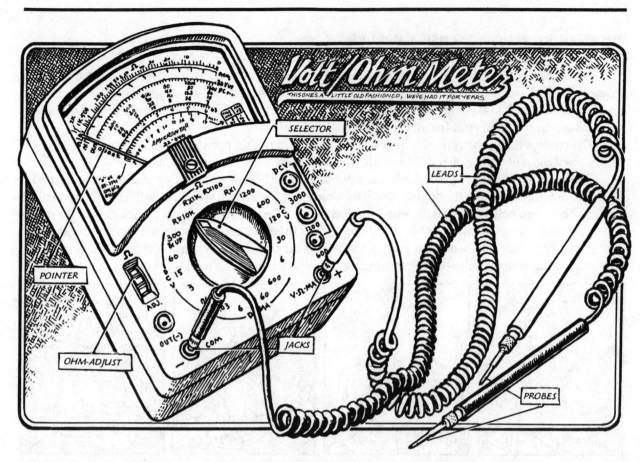

body has a slightly different resistance, so put the probes on the palm of your hand and watch the needle move. If the probes are about 13mm (½ in) apart on me, they make the needle swing to about 50 on the ohms scale, so multiply 50 times 10k which gives 500,000 ohms resistance for 13mm (½ in) of my palm skin. Put the two probes to your forehead, 13mm (½ in) apart. For a 13mm of forehead skin, I get 10 x 10,000 (10k) or 100,000 ohms, so there's more resistance in my palm skin than in my forehead skin…interesting. Move the pointer to Rx100 and my palm doesn't give a reading even when the probes are very close but when the probes are about ⅛ in apart, the needle reads 200 which times 100, gives 20,000 ohms resistance in damp forehead skin.

Find other things to test and practice reading the needle so you can read it accurately on any scale. Move the dial so the pointer points to 250 volts AC—make doubly sure you turned it to 250 V-AC—then carefully insert one probe into one hole in a wall plug and the other into the other hole in the same wall plug. Read the needle on the ACV scale; it will swing to 115 volts or thereabouts if you're in the U.S.

The VOM is a very sensitive instrument and you should just lightly touch the probes either together or to whatever you're testing, so you can quickly see if you have the dial set to the wrong scale—the needle will jump. Setting the VOM to the wrong scale can burn it out. *Never* test resistance on anything that's plugged in; use the ACV scale if you plug it into the wall socket or the DCV scale if it runs off a battery. If, with the dial set to DC volts, you touch your probe to a battery and the needle takes a dive to below zero, you have the wrong polarity so switch probes…put one where the other was.

To Check Continuity:

First, you *must* know that the item you're going to check is attached to no current so switch it to "OFF," disconnect it, unplug it, etc. Set the pointer on the dial to an OHMS scale (like Rx1, Rx10, Rx1K—some VOM's just say x1, x10 or x1K), with one probe in the + hole and the other in −, touch the probes together and adjust the needle to zero. Now you can put one probe on one end of what you're checking and the other at the other end. If the resistance is 0 ohms, you have continuity. If the needle doesn't go all the way to 0− try a smaller scale, like if the pointer is at Rx1K, try Rx10—you have resistance, probably caused by a bum connection so check any splices or connections until you do get continuity.

To Check Fuses (car, house, boat—any fuse):

Put the connectors in the + and − holes, set the pointer on the dial to the voltage you would expect, like 115 volts AC if you're testing something in the U.S. that plugs into house current (unless it's a 220 volt appliance, in which case set the pointer to 220 volts AC or over). The needle should swing to 115 volts on the AC scale. If you're checking auto fuses and it's a 12 volt system, set the pointer on the dial to 30 volts DC or 50 volts DC—whatever your VOM has that's over 12 volts DC. The needle should swing to 12 volts on the DC scale. You'll notice there are several DC scales you can read for the needle so read the scale that shows 12 volts DC most accurately.

The idea in checking a fuse is to find if there's voltage to both sides of the fuse, so put the probe plugged into − to any ground and the other first to one side of the fuse, then to the other. If the needle swings to the expected voltage on both sides, the fuse is OK. If the needle swings to the expected voltage on one side of the fuse but not on the other, the fuse is bad or has a bad connection.

To check continuity in a fuse, you must remove it from its receptacle. If the needle swings to zero, the fuse is OK, if it stays at infinity, the fuse is nowhere.

OK, to check *continuity*, use the *OHM* scale and the thing you're checking must *not* have electricity to it. To check a *hot* line, fuse, switch, you *must* use a *voltage* scale, either AC or DC.

To Check Amperes:

The VOM is not a very good ammeter. The amps produced by the Rabbit alternator are beyond the VOM's capacity to measure. Mostly, if you know the voltage and can measure the resistance, you can figure the amps using the formula below.

For those of you who would like a little theory about electricity, here's a short story: There are two basic kinds of current, alternating current (AC) and direct current (DC). When you rotate a wire in a magnetic field (between North Pole and South Pole), the wire cuts through the field and picks up electricity. Take a piece of paper and draw a horizontal line across the center. Put the point of a pencil on the left side of the line and imagine your body is a wire rotating through a magnetic field (force created between two magnets). The magnetic field is strongest when you are closest to a pole (magnet) and gets weaker as you rotate away from a pole. So now draw a line as you rotate. Start on the line you already drew; this is zero. As you rotate closer to a pole the line you draw will go up, then, as you leave the most concentrated field area, the current becomes less so make your line head down—you've made a hill. The other pole is minus (or below the line), so draw your line down toward the other pole and as you rotate away from it, your line will head back to zero—you've made a valley. If you've drawn rounded curves, you have a sine curve of alternating current electricity. All electricity made by rotating a wire (or bunches of wires) through a magnetic field is alternating current.

But our cars use direct current because AC cannot be stored in a battery. The generator uses a commutator (that round thing that brushes run on that has copper strips with insulation between them) to lop off all the electricity below the line so the curve you draw is nothing but hills with no below zero valleys. The alternator used in Rabbits makes AC, then uses diodes to separate out the hills and valleys so the valleys are reversed and become hills and thus acceptable to the battery. From the battery comes direct current which makes a straight line running parallel to the line you drew first—the zero line on your paper. In a 12 volt system, this line is 12 units up off zero (that is, the distance between the two straight lines is 12 units or volts).

The number of wires you rotate in the field and the strength of the field determine the voltage and the number of times you rotate the wires (speed) in the field determines the amperage. They are a little more mixed up than that, but this is just a short story. The usual automobile generator or alternator produces between 12 and 15 volts and between 30 and 50 amperes. The voltage regulator keeps the voltage down to what the battery can absorb and also decides how much amperage the battery can use. The voltage regulator controls the amount of magnetic field present in the generator and thus, the amount of amperage. When the headlights are on, the product of the generator is used directly by the headlights as long as the generator is turning.

So now you can see that in an automative system, the voltage is regulated to an almost constant value and the amperage is controlled by the needs. And so what are the needs called? The needs or demands put on the electrical system are the resistances. So it figures that the amperage required by any electrical device is the voltage divided by the resistance. E (voltage) = I (amperage) x R (resistance) $E = IR$, $I = E/R$, $R = E/I$. W (watts) = EI (volts × amps) and by messing around with algebra, $W = I^2R$ (heat loss). There, you have the basic formulae for direct current. The same formulae apply to alternating current except that R (resistance) gets complicated by the addition of Capacitance and Induction to Resistance, and the whole schmutz is called Impedance (the AC equivalent to resistance). OK, OK, you don't have to know any of this to run a VOM but it's nice to know what you're measuring.

PROCEDURE 11: HOW TO PUSH START A CAR (STANDARD TRANSMISSION)

If one bleak morning the car won't start with the key, all is not lost. At least it isn't if your transmission isn't automatic.

If you're fortunate to have had the foresight to park your car on a hill, this procedure is a cinch. If you're on the straight and level, you'll need help. (Isn't that the truth!) I take it there's some gasoline or diesel fuel in the tank. Diesel people should pull out their pre-glow knob all the way and wait a minute or two.

Get in the car and turn the ignition to ON. Put the car into second gear and roll down the window. Check that the coast is clear, release the handbrake and depress the clutch pedal. Get your friends to start pushing you forward. When your friends break into a run or fall to the ground clutching their chests, pop your foot off the clutch pedal and hit the gas. The car will buck a few times before the engine fires so make sure you're not pointing toward the prize rose bush. The engine will start so depress the clutch and keep revving the engine by using the gas pedal. Park the car and leave the engine running to give the battery a few minutes to begin to recharge itself. Thank your friends; you may need them again if you stall on the next corner.

PROCEDURE 12: HOW TO TEST GAS FOR WATER CONTENT

Adulterated gasoline is a big problem these days, so if you have doubts about the purity of gasoline from your local filling station, buy a gallon from them in a clean, legal container and take it home. Or…siphon a gallon from your tank.

Pour some of this gas into a clean glass jar, put the jar in a safe place and let it stand overnight. In the morning see if the gasoline has stratified (separated into layers). Water, having a greater specific gravity than gasoline, will sink to the bottom of the jar.

If your gasoline stratifies or has particles on the bottom, inform the gas station owner that there's water in the gas. What they'll do about this substandard gasoline, I don't know, but at least you've done them (and yourself) the favor of pointing out the problem.

It is very important to use clean, pure gasoline, especially if your car is fuel injected. Water in the lines will create havoc with the fuel distributor, control pressure regulator and the rest of the fuel injection system.

Once you have performed this test, put the gasoline back into the legal container and dispose of, or thoroughly clean, the glass bottle. Be very careful when doing this test; don't smoke or leave the bottle lying around, especially if it still has the apple juice label on it. Fatal accidents can occur very easily.

PROCEDURE 13: HOW TO CHECK BATTERY WITH A HYDROMETER

You can buy a cheap, battery test hydrometer from any auto parts store or large discount house. Put on your safety glasses and remove the top or tops from the battery. The electrolyte (water-acid) in each battery cell is of a certain specific gravity which we measure to find out a battery's condition. The hydrometer has an inner float with numbers on it (you'll check them all in time). Unscrew or pop off the battery caps, squeeze the ball on the end of the hydrometer, then put the tip into the first battery cell. Slowly release your grip and electrolyte will be sucked into the hydrometer. The float will sink or float inside the electrolyte and your job is to read the number on the float which corresponds with the top level of the electrolyte. If the syringe sucked up too much electrolyte so the float hits the top of the instrument, squeeze a little back into the cell. A fully charged cell will read 1.275 to 1.380 on the float scale. A cell in reasonable condition will read from 1.250 to 1.275. A poor cell reads from 1.225 to 1.250. Anything below that means the battery's deceased. The battery needs recharging if the reading in any cell is between 1.225 and 1.250.

Use a battery charger to 'trickle charge' the battery or take it to your local service station. It's important to get the thing trickle charged and not 'boosted;' otherwise you'll drastically shorten battery life. If you're charging the battery yourself, take hydrometer readings in all cells every half hour. Sometimes a battery will not hold its charge in which case you need a new one. A reading of 1.275 to 1.380 indicates a fully charged battery.

PROCEDURE 14: HOW TO SPLICE ELECTRICAL WIRE

When you need to add a length of electrical wire to a piece too short for the job, make sure your new wire is the same gauge or thicker than the wire you're adding to.

First I'll deal with a splice that doesn't use an insulated connector. Remove 10mm (⅜ in) of insulation from one end of the new and old wire. Use stripping pliers if you have any. If not, a penknife or, in an emergency, your teeth will suffice. Next, twist the bared end of the wire around between your thumb and forefinger until there are no loose wire hairs. Lay the two wire ends side by side and twist them together to make one long wire. Next pull the two wires gently away from one another to test the strength of the twist. Wrap insulating tape around the splice starting 13mm (½ in) in front of the splice and ending 13mm behind it.

A more professional looking but no more effective way of splicing is to use an in-line insulated connector. You can buy these in various gauges to match the wire you're using. Remove the insulation from one end of your wires, twist the ends and push one into the end of the connector. Use your crimping/stripping pliers to pinch the connector onto the wire. Insert the end of the other wire into the other end of the connector and crimp that tight. Give a gentle tug on both wires to be sure your splice is tight.

If you need to splice a male or female spade-type connector onto a wire, first check that your connector has an insulated cover on the part which receives the wire. Some connectors are sold with a separate short piece of insulation. If that's the case, cut the insulation to cover the end of the spade connector and your wire, slide it onto the wire, strip the insulation off the end of the wire and insert it into the spade connector. Crimp the ends of the connector firmly onto the wire, then slip the piece of insulation over the end of your freshly installed connector.

PROCEDURE 15: HOW TO REMOVE AND INSTALL VW TYPE HOSE CLAMPS

These things were designed by someone with a wry sense of humor. They are impossible to get off and even more difficult to get on. However, despair ye not! I have a solution.

A small electrician's screwdriver and a pair of pliers will do the trick. To get such clamps off, place the small screwdriver blade under the tail of the clamp and lever the tail upward. This will free the slots in one end of the clamp from the little ear on the other end. That's simple and it's off.

Getting it on is another matter. I reinstall hoses with regular hose clamps—saves time and effort—but if you insist... First flatten the little hump in the clamp a bit with your pliers. Next put the clamp where you want it to go. Put the blade of the small screwdriver through one of the slots in the clamp and use the little ear on the other end as a levering point. Lever the other end of the clamp until the slot is just past the ear. Now pull on the screwdriver until the clamp slides down the screwdriver blade and fits over the ear. If the clamp is too loose, release it and again put the screwdriver blade in the next furthest away slot. Still too loose? Again . . . and again.

PROCEDURE 16: HOW TO TURN THE ENGINE OVER WITHOUT FRIEND

This trick works only for vehicles with a standard transmission and is useful when setting the point gap. Make sure the handbrake is on and the stick shift is in Neutral (N). Remove the large wire from the center of the coil to prevent the engine from starting. Use a screwdriver with a wooden or plastic handle to short across the two big nuts on the starter and solenoid. A small spark will accompany the starter motor as it turns the engine over.

Keep any loose clothing, fingers, ears, jewelry, etc., out of the way of the alternator and air conditioner V-belts.

Another way to turn the starter motor over is to remove the coil wire, then attach one end of a jumper wire to the solenoid and touch the other end to the positive battery post. You can make yourself a jumper wire by attaching crimp or screw-type alligator clips to insulated electrical wire about 1 meter (36 inches) long.

PROCEDURE 17: JOE'S WAY TO ADJUST THE TIMING BELT

Condition: Referral from Chapter 10, Procedure 23.

Tools and materials: Phase 1 tool kit, strong fingers or two pairs of hands, crescent wrench.

Step 1. Loosen Belt Tensioner

HOLD IT. Read on before you do it. Put the 15mm or 17mm wrench on the tensioner locknut. Put the Crescent wrench on the tensioner and keep clockwise ↻ pressure on the Crescent wrench. Loosen the locknut and move the tensioner about 30 degrees. You'll still have some tension on the drive belt. It's important to have the tension. Tighten the tensioner locknut.

Step 2. Remove Belt

Here's where the strong fingers come in. Gradually work the belt off the camshaft sprocket. If you really can't get it off, loosen the tensioner a bit more. Just a bit.

Step 3. Try Again

When the belt's off, align the dots and notches. Put the belt back onto the crankshaft and intermediate shaft and pull it upward. Has the notch or dot moved? If so, release the belt and move the notch on the crankshaft pulley about five degrees in the opposite direction to the way it moved when you pulled up on the belt.

Step 4. And Again

Pull up on the belt again and see if the notch and dot line up. If so, install the belt onto the camshaft sprocket. Because the tensioner isn't totally loose, this is the hard part. Tip the back of the belt up toward the edge of the sprocket and work it slowly into place. Don't use anything to lever it on; you'll nick the belt and screw it up.

Or ask Friend to help you finger power it on. Keep all the marks lined up. As the belt starts to slide onto the camshaft sprocket, check that the marks stay aligned. If they move, turn the offending pulley a few degrees in the opposite direction to the way it moved when the belt tension increased. Keep trying. When the belt is finally on all the sprockets, adjust the belt tensioner until you can turn the belt 90°.

Then recheck the timing as per Chapter 10, Procedure 23.

PROCEDURE 18: MECHANICS' QUICK DWELL TEST

You need Friend for this one. Hook up the tach/dwell meter and install Friend in the car to turn the engine over five times using the key. Watch the dwell reading on the meter. Off a few degrees? Remove the distributor cap, rotor and dust shield. Loosen the point holding screw and insert your medium screwdriver blade between the nipples and the point slot. Ask Friend to turn the engine over again as you adjust the point gap by twisting the screwdriver blade. When the gap's correct (44° - 50° new points, 42° - 58° old points), tighten the holding screw. Install the distributor dust cover, rotor and cap and ask Friend to start the engine. How's the dwell?

PROCEDURE 19: MISCELLANEOUS TIPS

Need a Drop of Oil?

Should you be out in the proverbial boonies and stuck for a spot of oil, remove the dipstick and use the oil adhering to the tip. Clever, huh?

The world record for transferring a pint of oil from the engine to a container using the "1 drop at a time" method is 4 hours, 26 minutes, 12 seconds. I know because I hold it.

V-Belt Broken?

Sometimes one of the V-belts at the front of the engine breaks and you don't have a spare. You can substitute the leg of a nylon stocking or pair of tights for a belt. That is, if you're wearing nylon stockings or tights. Remove the tights and cut one of the legs off close to the crotch. Slip the liberated leg over the two V-belt pulleys and tie a square knot in the stocking leg as tight as possible. Cut off any excess nylon. Buy a new belt at the next store you pass.

If you don't have a nylon stocking, nylon string will sometimes work if you can tie it tight enough. This method won't work for your timing belt; a new belt and a reading of Chapter 10 is the only solution.

Using Jumper Cables:

Keep the Samaritan's engine running and use one jumper cable to connect the positive terminals on the two batteries. Now hook the other cable to both negative terminals. Check your work and start your car. As soon as your car's engine bursts into life, take off the jumper cables and thank your helper kindly.

Gas Tank Leak?

During one of my travels, I bounced off a sand dune into a pile of rocks, one of which put four tiny holes into the Rabbit's gas tank. Since welding equipment is hard to find in the middle of the Mojave, I whipped out a bar of Dial and had at the tank. If this disaster should happen to you, rub bar soap into the offending split or pin-hole. Of course, if you've trashed out your gas tank on a rock and there's a huge gash in it, this method won't work. However, it works beautifully for small holes. Continue rubbing the soap into the holes until the gas or diesel fuel no longer flows. Repair the gas tank as soon as you have access to tools. The temporary repair on my Rabbit has lasted three years. You might say it's part of a continuing experiment.

Shelter:

Let me dispel one myth. It isn't a good idea to keep a car in a heated garage. It's lovely to have heat when working on a car but storing a car in one is not so good. If the car underbody is coated with salt from winter roads, the warmth of the surrounding atmosphere will accelerate the rusting process. Rinse off salt and road dirt from beneath the car before putting it into any garage; warm or freezing.

That's all the tips I can come up with at the moment. If you come across a time-saving idea, please let me know.

CHAPTER 21

❧ DER DIESEL ❧

Rudolf Diesel

First, a little history. A 34 year old German named Rudolf Diesel (1858-1931) built a modified internal combustion engine in 1892 and tried to run it on a mixture of coal dust and compressed air. It blew up. Undaunted, he built another engine that managed to run on a mixture of crude oil and air. Clever Rudolf patented his compression ignition Diesel engine in 1895, and it enjoyed a varied and productive life in Europe.

In 1912, the engineers in the United States began research into diesel power, and various people came up with modifications so it could be used as a power plant for cars, trucks, boats and railway engines. Mercedes Benz was the second auto manufacturer to put a diesel engine into a car; Peugeot tried it first in 1922 and had moderate success. VW was the first company to build a lightweight, high speed diesel automobile engine in 1977. Good move, VW. They now put a turbo-charged diesel engine into a Rabbit which holds numerous world speed and endurance records. It's a lovely piece of engineering.

The VW diesel uses the same 1600cc crankcase (engine block) as the regular gas-powered engine. The crankcase is machined to accept larger pistons than gas-powered models. The cylinder head is very different from the gas engine. It has a specially designed swirl type combustion chamber which incorporates the piston. Also, the compression ratio is much higher than the gas engine.

The diesel engine has no spark plugs, distributor, coil, carburetor or emission control stuff to maintain. Read Chapter 2 to find out how the gas engine works, and fill in the diesel gaps here.

Intake Stroke:	As the piston moves down in the cylinder bore, the intake valve opens and fresh air is drawn in.
Compression Stroke:	The intake valve closes as the piston begins its upward stroke. Air inside the cylinder begins to heat up as it is compressed. As the piston nears the top of its compression stroke, diesel fuel is sprayed into the swirl chamber through the injector. The air is now compressed to almost 1/25th of its former volume, causing the temperature to rise to around 900°C (1650°F). When diesel fuel is injected into this hot air, it immediately ignites. The design of the swirl chamber ensures that the fuel is well mixed with hot air.
Combustion Stroke:	As the fuel burns, heat energy forces the piston down the cylinder bore and thus turns the crankshaft.
Exhaust Stroke:	Just before the piston reaches the bottom of its stroke, the exhaust valve opens. The piston again begins to move upward (as a piston in another cylinder is forced down on its ignition stroke) pushing the spent gasses out through the open valve, down the exhaust pipe into the outside air.

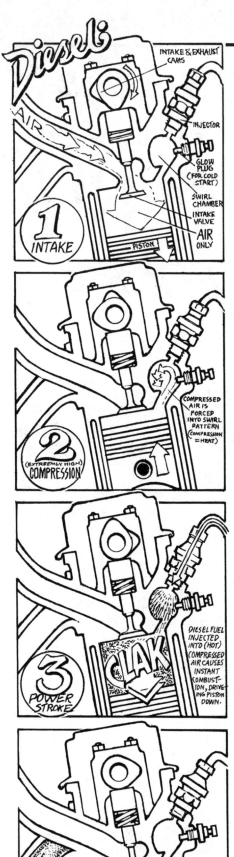

The diesel engine has only one way to regulate the amount of fuel available to the injectors. A lever on the fuel pump is connected to the accelerator pedal. The position of the lever is thus determined by the driver's foot on the pedal. Simple.

The passages from the air cleaner to the intake valves are large and unrestricted. When the diesel engine is idling or running slowly, lots of extra air is available to the cylinders. It is this extra air, plus very high compression in the cylinders that causes more thorough combustion and reduces exhaust gas emissions.

A traditional problem with diesel engines is difficult starting at low temperatures. To remedy this, an electric glow plug is screwed into each swirl chamber. The plug is connected to a relay inside the car. When the ignition key is turned to ON (pre-glow), current to the glow plugs heats up the air inside the swirl chamber. A red light on the dash indicates how long the plugs are on. On a '79 and on, the plugs stay on for 15-25 seconds after the light goes out. When you pull the knob just to the left of the steering wheel the timing of fuel sent from the pump to the injectors is altered. Use it only when the engine is cold. Once the engine has started, push the knob back in. There's no need to wait for the glow plugs to heat the chamber if you turn a running engine off for a minute and want to start it again. In warm weather there's no need to wait until the red light goes out.

Although the diesel engine has no ignition stuff, there's no excuse to neglect maintenance. Just the reverse. You should be able to get at least 200,000 miles from a well-kept diesel engine before rebuilding it. If you want yours to last long, do the following maintenance Procedures at the correct mileage intervals. They are specifically designed to keep your diesel engine alive. The rest of your maintenance stuff is in Chapter 10.

PROCEDURE 1: EVERY 3,000 MILES

Step 1. Change Oil and Filter

Chapter 10, Procedure 9.

Step 2. Clean and/or Replace Air Filter in Dusty Areas

Chapter 10, Procedure 10, Step 6.

Step 3. Check Vacuum Booster (if fitted)

The booster is the mechanism fitted on the left side of the crankcase below the rear spark plug. Check the coiled tube from the booster where it fits into the crankcase. The connections get loose sometimes.

PROCEDURE 2: 15,000 MILE MAINTENANCE

Step 1. Change Fuel Filter

See Procedure 3.

Step 2. Clean/Replace Air Filter

Chapter 10, Procedure 10, Step 6.

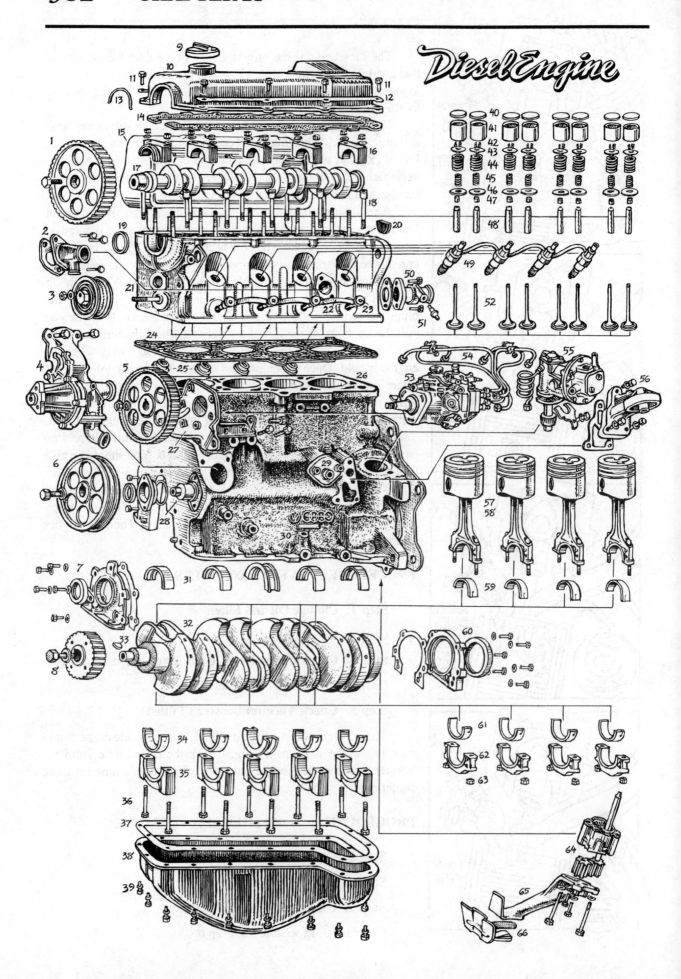

Diesel Engine

Step 3. Check/Adjust Valves

Chapter 10, Procedure 23.

Step 4. Check Idle and Maximum RPM

Procedure 16.

Step 5. Go to VW and have them check:

Compression and injector pump timing.

PROCEDURE 3: CHANGE FUEL FILTER. Phase 1.

Condition: 15,000 mile maintenance, you just bought a used diesel, fuel filter and lines clogged, referral from elsewhere.

Tools and materials: Phase 1 tool kit, new fuel filter, fire extinguisher, empty container.

Remarks: Warning! Diesel fuel will leak out as you do this Procedure. Don't smoke or light matches! If you have any cuts on your hands, cover them with a water proof adhesive bandage. Diesel fuel will also irritate the heck out of tender skin.

Step 1. Liberate Filter Assembly

Lift and prop the hood, then remove the two 13mm nuts holding the filter assembly to the bracket on the suspension strut mount on the inside of the right fender. Leave the fuel hoses alone.

Step 2. Remove Filter

All models have a bleed plug on the bottom of the filter assembly for draining out water and contaminated fuel. Later models don't have a big plastic priming pump knob on top of the filter housing as do the older versions.

All Models: Unscrew the filter housing by hand. If it's tight put a crescent wrench on the 22mm nut at the bottom of the housing. Beware of spilling fuel on the paint work; lay rags over the fender and work over a container. When the housing is fully unscrewed, pull it away from the top part of the assembly, pour the fuel out, remove the fuel filter and discard it.

Step 3. Install New Filter

Before installing the new filter into the housing, wet your fingers with a drop of fuel from your container and lubricate the top seal of the filter. Slide the filter into the housing and fill the filter housing almost to the top with clean diesel fuel. Screw the housing back onto the top of the assembly, fingertight only.

Step 4. Install Filter Assembly

Position the assembly onto the two studs, and screw back and tighten the two 13mm nuts.

Step 5. Bleed the Lines (Early Models)

You've got a primer knob? This Step is for you. Open the vent screw on top of the filter assembly and depress and release the primer knob until the fuel coming from the vent screw doesn't have any air bubbles. Some cars have a clear plastic fuel line running from the filter to the fuel pump and you can see when the

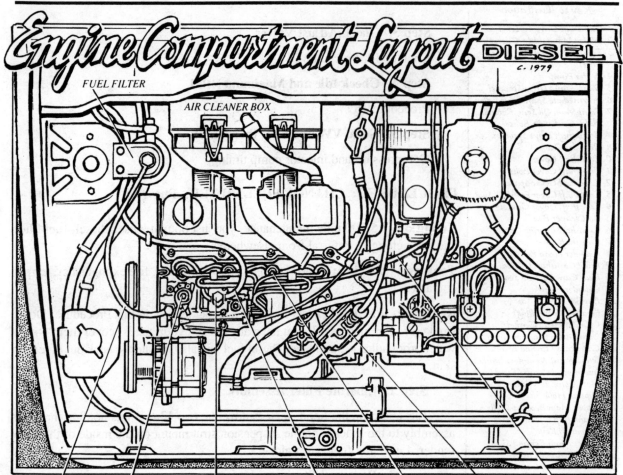

Engine Compartment Layout DIESEL
c. 1979

FUEL FILTER

AIR CLEANER BOX

FUEL LINE • THROTTLE LEVER • INJECTION PUMP • FUEL RETURN LINE • INJECTOR • VACUUM PUMP • COLD START CABLE

Step 5. (Cont'd.)

bubbles are no more. Close the screw and start the car. Check around the joint in the filter assembly for leaks. If fuel leaks out, stop the engine and tighten the filter housing by hand. If you aren't strong enough, find someone to help you tighten it. Don't use a wrench on the nut at the bottom of the filter, please. You may be tempted to overtighten.

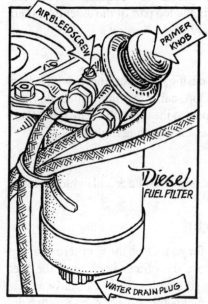

AIR BLEED SCREW

PRIMER KNOB

Diesel
FUEL FILTER

WATER DRAIN PLUG

Step 6.   Bleed the Lines (Late Models)

Open the vent screw (if you've got one) on top of the filter housing. Next loosen the fuel line connections (17mm) on #2 and #3 fuel injectors on the left side of the cylinder head.

Ask Friend to crank the starter (using the key) without pulling the cold start (glow plug) knob beside the steering column. Watch the loosened connections on the injectors and tell Friend to stop cranking when fuel is pumped out.

Tighten the 17mm fuel line connections and do up the vent screw on top of the fuel filter housing. Start the car (use the glow plug knob this time) and check around the filter housing and injectors for leaks. If you find any, stop the engine and tighten loose joints. Don't tighten the filter housing with anything other than human hands. Get another pair to help if needed.

Take a test drive. If the engine stalls out at all, go back home and bleed the system again. This time loosen all four fuel line connections at the injectors. OK?

DIESEL ENGINE TROUBLESHOOTING GUIDE

Engine Stalls	Procedure 1, 3, 6, 14
Car difficult to start	Procedure 1, 4, 10, 11, 12, 14, 15
Car won't start	Procedure 4, 10, 11, 12, 14, 15
Engine loses power	Procedure 5, 14
Engine idles too fast or too slow	Procedure 6
Glow plug indicator does not work	Procedure 13
Fuel consumption too high	Procedure 1, 7, 14
Excessive exhaust smoke	Procedure 9, 14
Loud knocking fan engine	Procedure 8

Use this guide to find and repair your problem. Do the Procedures in the above order.

PROCEDURE 4: DIESEL ENGINE DIFFICULT OR IMPOSSIBLE TO START

Condition: Fuel in tank, correct viscosity oil in crankcase.

Tools and materials: Listed in referred Procedures.

Step 1. Battery and Cables OK?

Turn to Chapter 7, Procedure 3, and check.

Step 2. Does the Starter Work?

Back to Chapter 7, Procedure 6.

Step 3. Check Stop Solenoid

See Procedure 11 in this Chapter.

Step 4. Check Cold Starting Cable

Procedure 10 tells how.

Step 5. Check Glow Plugs

Go on to Procedure 12.

Step 6. Check Fuel System

Procedure 14, begin with Step 2.

PROCEDURE 5: DIESEL LOSES POWER. Phase 2.

Condition: The engine can't reach top speed anymore, pick-up is poor, car is very sluggish.

Tools and materials: Phase 2 tool kit.

Step 1. Check Tires

Are they all properly inflated? A low tire will cause you to think that the engine's down on power. Inflate the front tires to 1.9 kg/cm^2 (27 psi) and the rear to 1.9 kg/cm^2 or 2.1 kg/cm^2 (27 or 31 psi) depending on your load.

Step 2. Check Brakes

If the front or rear brakes are sticking against the disc or drum, the engine will labor. Touch the center of each wheel after a drive. Hot? The brakes are indeed touching the drum or disc. Turn to Chapter 14 and read it.

Step 3. Clutch Slipping?

Turn to Chapter 16 and do the slip test at the beginning of the Chapter.

Step 4. Check Air Filter

It must be clean. Chapter 10, Procedure 10, Step 6, shows how to check/replace the filter element.

Step 5. Check High Idle

Procedure 6 in this Chapter explains how.

Step 6. Accelerator Cable Sticking?

Turn to Procedure 15 in this Chapter and check the cable.

Step 7. Check Fuel System

Procedure 14 gives the fuel system rundown.

Step 8. Check Valves

Turn back to Chapter 10, Procedure 22, and check the valve clearance. Go to VW and have them change the adjusting disc if necessary.

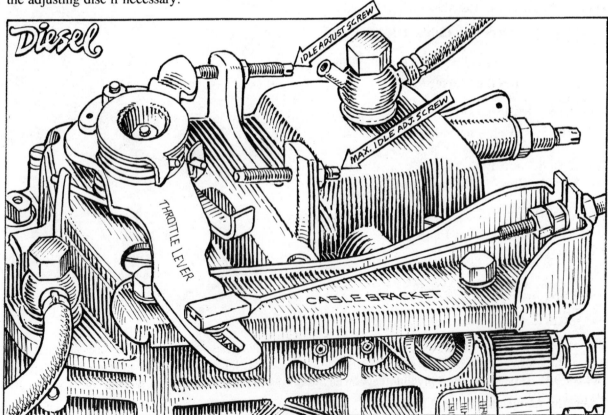

PROCEDURE 6: ADJUST IDLE OR MAXIMUM RPM SCREWS. Phase 1.

Condition: If your car is down on power, start with Step 1 to find the Maximum RPM Screw, then go to Step 3 and adjust it.

If the engine races at 'idle' or stalls at traffic lights, find the idle screw in Step 1 and adjust it in Step 2.

Tools and materials: Phase 1 tool kit.

Step 1. Find Idle Adjusting Screw and Maximum RPM Adjusting Screw

The injection pump is the silver thing with four silver fuel lines coming from its rear. On top of the pump there's a lever attached to a cable (the accelerator cable). When your foot is off the accelerator pedal, the lever touches the idle adjusting screw. Pull the pump lever all the way back and its movement is stopped by the Maximum RPM Screw.

Step 2. Adjust Idle Adjusting Screw

The warm engine should idle between 770 and 870 rpm. If it stalls while you're waiting for a light, the idle's too low. If the engine roars, the idle's too high. Because we don't have a special idle tool like they do at VW, we shall have to use our ears.

Loosen the locknut (which may be covered in yellow paint) on the idle screw (10mm open end wrench). Turn the screw about one turn clockwise . Put the car in neutral and be sure the cold start knob is pushed in fully. Ask Friend to start the engine and push the clutch pedal down. How does the engine idle? If it's too slow, screw in the idle screw a little clockwise . Too fast? Unscrew it a little counterclockwise . Tighten the locknut when it's correct.

Step 3. Adjust Maximum RPM Screw

On the back of the maximum RPM screw there's a 10mm locknut held in place by a dab of yellow paint. Has the nut come loose or disappeared? If so, the screw may have shifted forward, preventing the lever (and so the accelerator pedal) from opening all the way.

Maximum diesel engine revolutions are supposed to be 5400 to 5450 rpm. The VW dealer adjusts this limit with a special adapter attached to a regular Tach/Dwell meter. We can fake it, however. Measure the distance from the end of the screw to the fuel pump flange. This distance should be 9mm (23/64 in or a hair under ⅜ in). If it isn't, move the screw in or out with a screwdriver. You may have to loosen the locknut (10mm wrench) before the screw will turn. When the distance is correct, tighten the locknut while holding the screw in position with a screwdriver. Measure the distance again and take the car for a test drive. If it's a lot better, but still won't go as fast as before, turn the maximum RPM screw out one more turn. Tighten the locknut again.

Still no power? Go to Procedure 14.

PROCEDURE 7: FUEL CONSUMPTION TOO HIGH

Condition: Visits to the diesel pump are too frequent—you are getting below 40 miles per gallon overall. The engine should have more than 3,000 miles on it before you start worrying about fuel consumption.

Tools and materials: Phase 1 tool kit and materials as noted.

Step 1. Check For Leaks

Are there drops or puddles of fuel on the ground beneath the fuel tank? Climb into the back seat and sniff around for a strong smell of diesel fuel. If you discover leaks in the tank, it will have to be removed for repairs. (Chapter 12, Procedure 18). Tiny pinholes can be stopped by rubbing a bar of soap over the hole (Chapter 20, Procedure 19).

Step 2. Check Tire Pressure

This Chapter, Procedure 5.

Step 3. Check Fuel Filter

Turn to Procedure 3 in this Chapter and especially check the connections on the ends of the fuel line running from the fuel filter to the injection pump. How's the fuel line? Is the filter housing tightly screwed onto the filter assembly?

Step 4. Check Air Filter

Chapter 10, Procedure 10, Step 6 shows how.

Step 5. Check Idle

Procedure 6 tells how.

Step 6. Check Brakes

Are they binding? See Procedure 2.

Step 7. Check Clutch

Turn to Chapter 16 and do the slip test at the beginning of the Chapter.

Step 8. Check Injectors

The fuel lines on the injectors and on the back of the fuel pump should be tight. Are the little rubber plugs in place on #1 and #4 injectors? Buy new ones or plug the nipple with tape (in an emergency) and try a test drive. If all is OK, go on to Procedure 14 and start with Step 3 and go through all the steps. One of the injectors might be stuck open. If not, the pump is out of adjustment or faulty. You'll have to take the car to VW and get them to fix it.

Step 9. Check Sending Unit

There's a remote possibility the fuel gauge sending unit is loose and fuel is spilling out. The sending unit is on the side of the fuel tank (Chapter 19, Procedure 12).

PROCEDURE 8: LOUD KNOCKING NOISE FROM ENGINE. Phase 1.

Condition: When at idle, the engine 'knocks' louder than normal.

Tools and materials: Phase 1 tool kit, maybe a new injector.

Remarks: If this is your first day with a new diesel Rabbit, be aware that the engine makes a knocking noise all the time.

Step 1. Check Oil

Read Chapter 10.

Step 2. Check Injectors

Procedure 14, Step 4, in this Chapter.

Step 3. Check Compression

Take the car to VW. If your car fails this test, I hope it's still covered by warranty!

PROCEDURE 9: EXCESSIVE SMOKE FROM EXHAUST PIPE. Phase 1.

Condition: You have lots of black, blue or white smoke belching from the exhaust pipe, compression check indicates engine is OK.

Tools and materials: Phase 1 tool kit.

Step 1. Driving Correctly?

Starting out in second gear or lugging around town in fourth is murder on the engine and clutch. Read Chapter 5.

Step 2. Cooling Fan On All the Time?

Lift and prop the hood and start the engine. The radiator fan shouldn't come on for quite a time. If it switches on as soon as the engine is started, the engine won't be able to reach proper operating temperature and it'll belch out excess black smoke. Turn to Chapter 17, Procedure 3, and especially check the thermo switch. Fan OK? Continue…

Step 3. Check Injectors (Procedure 14, Step 4, in this Chapter)

If an injector drips fuel after the engine stops cranking, the injector is staying open too long and pumping excessive fuel into the cylinder. This fuel is mostly blown out the exhaust pipe.

If none of these three steps cure the smoking, the injection pump is mistimed or faulty. The VW service people will be happy to see you. Tell them what tests you've done and the results.

PROCEDURE 10: CHECK COLD START CABLE. Phase 1.

Tools and materials: Phase 2 tool kit, Volt Ohmmeter (VOM) or test lamp. If you're here from Chapter 7, welcome.

Step 1. Check Cold Start Cable

When you pull the cold start knob on the dash the injection pump timing is advanced 2.5°. This means a few cc's of vaporized fuel is injected into the combustion chamber to help start the engine. Sometimes the cable breaks or slips off the lever on the *right* side of the injection pump. A screw holds the cable into a pivot pin in the top of the cold start lever. Has the screw come out allowing the cable to hang free? If so, the screw and pin may have fallen onto the Interstate. Go to VW, get replacements and continue with Step 2. If you find the cable broken, buy a new one and go to Step 3 in this Procedure.

BACKSIDE OF DIESEL PUMP
COLD START CABLE & LEVER
Cable
Locking screw
Lever
Barrel Clamp

Step 2. Put Cable Back On

Push the cold start knob in. Slide the pivot pin into the hole at the top of the injection pump lever. Slip the end of the cable through the hole in the pin and replace the screw (not too tight). Push the cold start lever as far forward as it will go, toward the right fender. Pull the cable tight and tighten the locking screw. Get in the car and pull out the cold start knob. Smooth as satin sheets?

Step 3. Remove Broken Cable

If the cable is broken, we have a bigger job on our hands. Get inside the car and unscrew the cold start plastic knob from the old cable. Next remove the circlip holding the cable on the bracket just to the left of the steering wheel. Pull the old cable out of the bracket and through the firewall (leaving in place, I hope, the rubber grommet). If the cable is still attached to the injection pump lever, remove the locking screw and withdraw the cable end.

The cable is held by a bracket on the injection pump end. Remove the U-shaped clip (the locking washer) from the end of the cable sheath. The open part of the clip may be upside down (in which case you can't see it) so turn it with needle nose pliers and pull it off. Don't lose it.

Slide the assembly out of the bracket and remove the top washer.

Step 4. Install New Cable

Push the threaded end of the new cable through the firewall. The rubber grommet should still be in place. If not, slip it around the cable and work it into the firewall with a small screwdriver. Get in the car and push the end of the cable through the bracket next to the steering column. Install the circlip and screw on the plastic cold start knob. Push the knob fully in. Come on 'round to the front of the car again and find the two washers from the old cable. Slide the plain washer onto the cable until it touches the sheath. Push the cable through the rubber bushing and pull it tight. Replace the locking washer and wiggle the cable until everything feels comfortable.

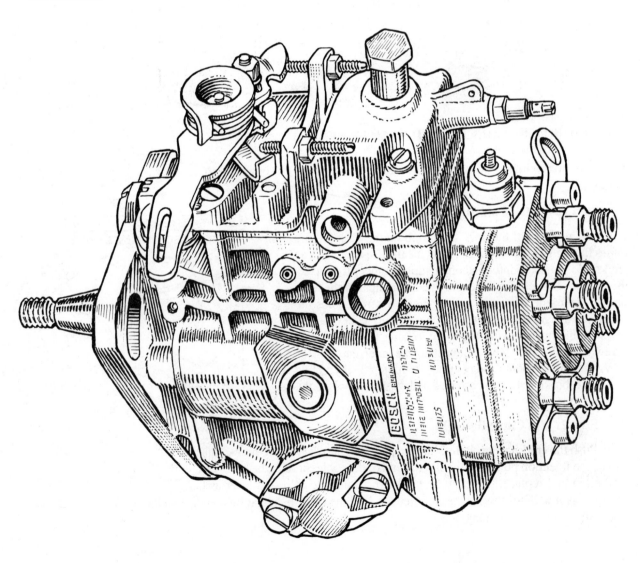

Step 4. (Cont'd.)

Push the injection pump lever as far forward as possible and push the end of the cable through the pivot pin in the end of the lever. Pull the cable tight and tighten the locking screw. Pull the knob inside the car to see if it all works smoothly. Great. Check the locknut on the pump lever after a ride around the block. The cable must be secure.

PROCEDURE 11: CHECK STOP SOLENOID. Phase 1.

Tools and materials: Volt Ohmmeter (VOM) or a test lamp.

Step 1. Check Condition of Stop Solenoid

Turn the VOM to 15 volts DC or test with the test lamp by grounding one wire and touching the other to the positive post of the battery.

The stop solenoid is screwed into the top rear of the injection pump. An electrical wire is attached to it by an 8mm nut. Turn the ignition to ON and touch the positive probe of the VOM or one end of the test light to the nut on the solenoid. Ground the other probe. The light should shine or the meter show 12 volts DC. If so, the stop solenoid is OK. If not, #9 fuse in the relay plate is blown ('79 and on cars don't have a fuse on the stop solenoid) or there's a problem between the solenoid and the relay plate.

Step 2. Check Fuse

Remove the carpet cover from above the driver's knees and check #9 fuse in the relay plate. If it's blown, replace it with an 8 amp fuse.

Step 3. Check Connection

If the fuse is OK, check the connection on the wire at the stop solenoid and replace it if it's worn or broken. Try the VOM or test light again. No go? There's a broken wire somewhere. To find the break, read Chapter 20, Procedure 10. If you can't find it, go to VW or a good electrical shop.

If your test lamp (or VOM) shows there's current to the solenoid, carry on.

Step 4. Check Solenoid

Check that the stop solenoid is screwed in tight.

Ask Friend to switch the ignition on and off a few times as you listen to hear if the solenoid 'clicks' as the key turns. No clickee? Buy a new solenoid and install it. (Chapter 7, Procedure 8, Step 4)

If your solenoid clicks but the engine won't start, check the glow plugs (next Procedure).

PROCEDURE 12: CHECK GLOW PLUGS. Phase 2.

Condition: Car difficult to start, especially on cold mornings.

Tools and materials: Phase 2 tool kit including a VOM, maybe new glow plug relay or new glow plugs.

Remarks: See Procedure 13 if the glow plug light on the dash doesn't work.

Step 1. Check Glow Plugs

Touch the positive probe of your VOM (switched to 15 volts DC) to the electrical connection on #4 glow plug. The glow plugs are just beneath the diesel fuel injectors. Touch the negative probe to a good clean metal ground. The ignition key should be turned to ON; the pre-glow position. If there's juice, the VOM should read 12 volts. No juice? Go to Step 2.

If there's juice, remove the 8mm nuts from the end of each glow plug and pull off the electrical wire (the busbar). Touch the positive probe of your VOM to the positive (+) battery post. Touch the negative probe to each glow plug in turn. If the meter shows 12 volts, the glow plug is OK. No juice means a defective glow plug. Unscrew and replace any defective glow plugs (13mm wrench). Clean out the glow plug hole with a Q-Tip before you screw in a new plug.

Step 2. Check Glow Plug Relay

No juice at the glow plugs? Get out the VOM again and switch it to 15 volts DC.

Let's check the glow plug relay on the firewall, opposite the rear of the cylinder head. Pull the relay out of its socket. Stick one end of your VOM into terminal 30 of the relay *socket*, not the relay itself. There should be current to this terminal at all times. The ignition key doesn't have to be turned to ON. If there's no juice to the terminal, the relay plate inside the car is bad or there's a break in the wire running to terminal 'H' on the relay plate. Get VW or an electrical shop to fix it.

If there's voltage to the relay socket, I'll bet the relay is broken. However, before you rush out and buy a new one, let's test the terminals again.

Step 3. Test Terminals

Check fuse #6 again in the relay plate. If it's blown, replace it with an 8 amp fuse. Turn the ignition key to ON, the pre-glow position. Put the positive probe of your VOM into terminal 86 of the glow plug relay socket plate. Ground the other probe. You should get a reading of 12 volts DC. If you don't, check the fuse again. If you do, touch one probe to terminal 30 and the other to terminal 85. OK? Then the relay is bad. First check it (Procedure 13, Step 2) and if necessary buy a new one from VW and install it. No juice between the two terminals indicates that 85 has a faulty ground wire. Terminal 85 is the ground for the relay.

If 85 is faulty, strip a few millimeters of insulation from the ends of a piece of 1.5mm^2 electrical wire. Push one end into the relay socket behind terminal 85 and secure it with a toothpick or wooden matchstick. Ground the other end on an unpainted metal surface and secure it.

Step 4. Test Terminal 86 Again

Disconnect the battery ground strap (10mm wrench). Switch the VOM to Rx1K. Put the positive probe into terminal 86 and ground the other probe. The needle should swing over to zero Ohms. If not, there's a break in the wire between terminal 86 and terminal D20 in the relay plate. Replace the wire running between terminal 86 and connection 20 in the plug which fits into connection D in back of the relay plate (Chapter 19, Procedure 15). That Procedure shows a different plug and terminal but the method is the same.

If the wire is OK, the relay plate or the ignition switch is bad. Get the relay plate tested by VW or a good electrical repair shop. If it's bad, see Chapter 7, Procedure 6, and check/replace the switch.

If your electrics checked out with flying colors but the car won't start, we'll have to look into the fuel system, Procedure 14.

PROCEDURE 13: GLOW PLUG INDICATOR LIGHT ON DASH DOESN'T WORK. Phase 1.

Condition: No glow light on dash when the knob is pulled.

Tools and materials: Phase 2 tool kit including VOM, new bulb (maybe), Friend.

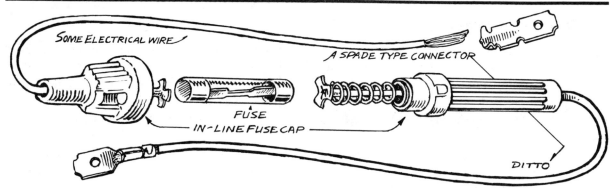

Step 1. Test Bulb

Remove the glow plug relay from it's socket. See Procedure 12, Step 2, if you don't know where it is. Stick one end of your jumper wire into terminal L of the relay plate *socket* (not the relay). Turn the ignition key to ON (the pre-glow position) and touch the other end to a good bare metal ground; the cylinder head is fine if it's clean. Ask Friend if the glow plug warning light stays off. If so, the bulb is blown. Replace the bulb; just feel behind the dash and twist the bulb holder ¼ turn and pull the holder away from the dash. Now turn back to Chapter 8, Procedure 1, Step 6, and check the bulb/holder.

If the bulb glows when you ground terminal L, it's alive and in excellent health and disposition.

Step 2. Check Glow Plug Relay

Disconnect the red/white wire from the coolant temperature sensor on the rear of the cylinder head. Don't let it touch metal. Install the glow plug relay into its lovely little plate and turn the ignition key to ON, the pre-glow position. The warning light should light for 60 seconds or so. Ground the end of the red/white wire to the cylinder head. The light should go out.

If the light didn't come on at all or stayed on when you grounded the red/white wire, the glow plug relay is broken. Buy a new one from VW and install it in the relay plate socket.

If the light came on when you pulled the red/white wire and went out when you grounded it, the coolant temperature sensor is shot. Screw out the old with a crescent wrench and screw in the new. Reconnect the red/white wire.

PROCEDURE 14: CHECK FUEL SYSTEM. Phase 2.

Condition: Car stalls, won't idle, difficult to start, loses power, drinks fuel, blows lotsa smoke.

Tools and materials: Phase 2 tool kit, Friend, maybe new injector or two and four new heat shields.

Remarks: You have fuel in the tank.

Step 2. Bleed Fuel System

The first thing to do if you're having any of the above conditions is to bleed; just like the first physicians used to do. Turn back to Procedure 3 in this Chapter and do Step 5 or 6. If that doesn't help, continue.

Step 2. Check Fuel Lines

If you've been working on the car (or had work done) it's possible the fuel lines are crossed. Let's check. The lines are marked on the rear of the injection pump. Line A goes to injector #1, line B to #3, line C to #4 and line D to #2. Injector #1 is closest to the right fender, at the front of the engine where the V-belts are. Check the line connections carefully for leaks. Is there fuel coming out of them? All OK?

Step 3. Check Fuel Line

Look at the plastic fuel line that goes from the fuel filter to the front of the injection pump. The fittings at both ends and the line itself should be in good condition. The big bolt holding the line to the pump should be tight. Pull the fitting from the other end of the line and look for crud inside the fitting or at the end of the line. If the fuel line is cracked, replace it. Buy a length of hose from VW or an auto parts store. Put a new small hose clamp around the end of the line if you can't get a tight fit on the connections. Run the engine and check for leaks.

It is remotely possible that the fuel lines are plugged or water in the pump or filter has frozen and is blocking fuel flow to the cylinders. First inspect the fuel filter and if it looks as though it hasn't been changed for years, change it (Procedure 3). Now run the following basic injector test.

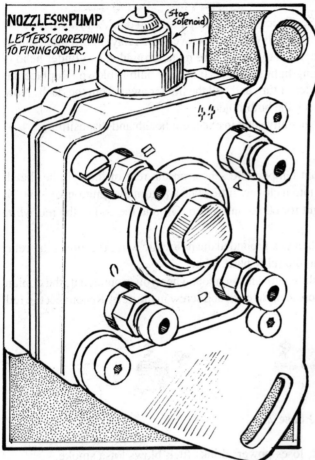

NOZZLES ON PUMP
LETTERS CORRESPOND TO FIRING ORDER.
(Stop Solenoid)

Step 4. Test Fuel Lines and Injectors

Start the engine and adjust the idle screw so the engine runs fairly fast, or have Friend press on the gas pedal a mite. Loosen the 17mm fuel line connection from #1 injector. Fuel will squirt out, so wear safety glasses and keep the fire extinguisher handy. If the engine speed remains the *same* after a fuel line is loosened, the injector is faulty. Make a note of the faulty injector number and continue.

If the engine speed *slows* when the line is loose, the injector is OK. Tighten the line connection and go to injector #2. After checking all four injectors, tighten all the fuel line connections and bleed the air from the lines (Procedure 3). If you think you have a faulty injector, go to Step 5. No injector problem? Re-adjust the idle (Procedure 6) and continue with the end of Step 7—the part about the bubbles—through Step 8.

Step 5. Test Injectors for Diesel Flow

WARNING! When you do this test, put the tip of the injector into a jar. Don't let the injectors spray fuel on your hand. They blast fuel at such a high pressure that the fuel will easily penetrate your skin and cause serious poisoning.

Remove the fuel line from #1 injector (17mm wrench). Unscrew the injector (Crescent wrench or 27mm socket). There's a heat shield at the bottom of the hole in the cylinder head from where you just removed the injector. It's the thickness of two quarters with holes in the middle. Use a screwdriver to fish it out. Loosen fuel line connection A (17mm) on the rear of the injection pump. Move the fuel line slightly and install the injector on the other end of the line. Tighten both 17mm connections.

Ask Friend to turn the ignition key all the way over to start (but not pull the cold start knob) to crank the starter. Hold the injector with your hands well away from the tip. If fuel squirts out of the tip of the injector, it's probably OK. Only a quantity test can tell if the thing is definitely A-1. Test all four injectors in the same way. If no diesel fuel comes out or the injectors leak when the starter stops cranking, go to Step 6.

If the injectors seem OK, buy four new heat shields from VW and go to Step 7.

If you get a goodly amount of fuel from the injectors but the car still won't start, tow it to VW and have them test the injection pump. They'll install a new (or rebuilt) pump to see if the engine runs. The dealers have no way of repairing a faulty pump as yet. They send 'em back to Bosch to be rebuilt. When a new pump is installed, the pump timing has to be set by VW, another job beyond our scope.

Step 6. Have Injectors Checked

Loosen the four fuel line connections (17mm) on the back of the injection pump, then the line connections on the four injectors. When all are free, take the fuel lines out of the car. Remove the little rubber plugs from #1 and #4 injectors and pull off the pieces of hose which connect the injectors together. Use a crescent wrench or a 27mm socket to remove #1 injector. Clean it and label it #1. Remove and clean the other three injectors and lable them #2, #3 and #4 to correspond to the cylinder from which they came. Use a thin screwdriver to fish out the heat shields at the bottom of the injector holes in the cylinder head.

Ask VW to test the injectors for you. Buy replacements if necessary, along with four new heat shields. If they found dirt in any injectors, be safe and buy a new fuel filter and install it (Procedure 3).

Step 7. Replace Injectors

Install a new heat shield in each injector hole. The recess in the shield faces up toward the tip of the injector. Screw in the four injectors and torque them to 7.0 mkg (50 ft lbs). No torque wrench? Get 'em tight.

Install the fuel lines after blowing through them. Then install the hoses and little rubber plugs on #1 and #4 injectors. Now change the fuel filter and bleed the system (Procedure 3).

If your injectors checked out fine but the engine still won't idle properly, remove the return fuel connection on the filter and blow through the line. You should hear bubbles in the tank. If not, reconnect and use gas station air to clear the line.

You heard bubbles? Well, then the injection pump is out of time or faulty. Only VW can fix this problem. Ask them to do a compression check because the engine may have a poorly seating valve.

Step 8. Check Pump Lever and Springs

Check that the lever on top of the injection pump (to which the accelerator cable is attached) is secure on the pump. The 10mm nut holding a U-shaped metal washer over the spring should be tight. Pull the lever back and forth by hand. Does it move easily? Is the spring broken or out of place? It may have slipped off the lever if the top nut is loose.

Remove the nut and U washer, reposition the spring over the little ear on the arm, and install the U washer. Catch the ear over the washer behind the spring before you install the nut.

Check the other spring beneath the pump lever. If the top nut was loose, the spring may have slipped. Look at Peter's diagram and see how the springs and levers should

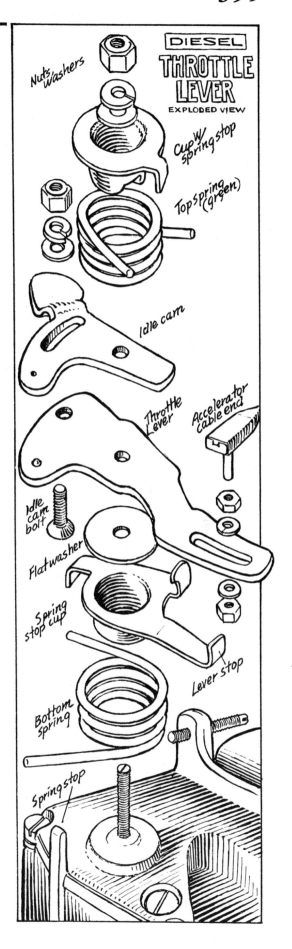

DIESEL THROTTLE LEVER EXPLODED VIEW

Nuts, Washers
Cup w/ Spring stop
Top Spring (green)
Idle cam
Throttle Lever
Accelerator Cable end
Idle cam bolt
Flatwasher
Spring stop cup
Lever stop
Bottom Spring
Spring stop

Step 8. (Cont'd.)

be secured. If either spring is broken, you'll have to order another; VW rarely have them in stock.

If the springs are OK but the lever flops around like a donkey on roller skates, the injection pump shaft has broken. You'll have to take the car to VW to get a new pump installed. Lever and springs OK? Proceed.

If the car still won't run properly, the fuel injection timing is off or the injection pump is bad. Tow the car to VW and tell the service manager what tests you've done. Have them run a compression test. You may have a sticking valve or worn piston rings, especially if there are more than 60,000 miles on the engine. Before you go, check the pump on the engine. If it's cracked, you'll still have to take the car to VW. You need them to do the injection timing once the pump is removed, so they may as well do the whole job.

PROCEDURE 15: CHECK ACCELERATOR CABLE. Phase 1.

Condition: Car won't start (or is difficult to start), accelerator pedal flat to the floor.

Tools and materials: Phase 1 tool kit, maybe a new cable.

Step 1. Check Cable

The cable is held to the injection pump lever by a ball and socket arrangement. The cable sheath is fastened by two 10mm nuts and rubber washers to the pump bracket. Check that the nuts are tight and the cable is free to move in and out of the sheath.

A metal clip on the end of the cable keeps the cable sprocket from popping off the ball on the end of the pump lever. Hold the clip between your finger and thumb and pull the cable off the lever. Ask Friend to depress the accelerator pedal as you pull the other end of the cable. Does the cable move in and out easily? If not, squirt thin oil (WD-40 is great) down the inside of the cable sheath and work the cable in and out again to free it up.

If this doesn't free it, crawl into the driver's compartment and have a look at the way the cable hooks onto the accelerator pedal. There are different methods of attachment. In late models, the cable goes through a plastic bushing. See if the cable or the bushing is in properly. In early models the cable may just hook over the pedal. Check for junk caught behind the pedal.

Step 2. Replace Accelerator Cable

If the cable is difficult to move inside its sheath, one or more strands of the cable may have broken. If so, or if the cable is broken, unhook the cable from the accelerator pedal and push it through the firewall. Remove the rubber grommet in the firewall hole. Go to the engine compartment and remove the 10mm nut closest to the injection pump from the cable sheath. Pull the cable through the hole in the bracket. Don't lose the rubber grommet and the metal clip from the end of the cable. Put 'em in a Baggie. Take the old cable to VW and buy a new one exactly like it.

When you get back home, put the grommet on the new cable (if it doesn't have one) and push the end of the cable through the firewall from the engine side to the driver's side. Hook it onto the accelerator pedal and position the grommet in the firewall hole with a screwdriver.

Unscrew the end nut from the sheath and slip the cable onto the bracket. Put a rubber washer on each side of the bracket and pop the socket on the end of the cable into the ball on the injection pump lever. Install

Step 2. (Cont'd.)

the metal clip. The cable should lie 'naturally' in place without kinks or any strain on the outer sheath. Loosely snug the two 10mm nuts until the cable is secure but not under strain. Tighten the two nuts up against the bracket. Try the accelerator pedal. If the pedal sticks down, the sheath is too tight against the bracket. Loosen the rearmost nut to allow the sheath to move toward the pump a little. Retighten both nuts. Better?

Lisa called me complaining of a sticking accelerator pedal. I told her what to do, but as she was driving in the vicinity of the office she said she'd like to visit. The diesel limped into the parking lot at idle. ''Just made it here,'' she sighed.

I broke out the tool box fully expecting to replace the accelerator cable. With the hood duly lifted and propped, we looked around the engine compartment and noticed a big ball of what looked like seat stuffing and a few leaves. This ball was wedged between the crankcase and the injection pump. No wonder the cable was sticking. I looked a little closer at the ball of junk and asked Lisa how long the car had been parked. She assured me that overnight was the longest the vehicle ever lay idle.

All I can say is that the mice in this part of the world work fast. Fried mice. Really.

Tune Up Your Rabbit Book

Changes and Additions to the 1986 Edition

PROCEDURE 00: HOW TO USE THIS SECTION

Tools and Materials: Pencil or pen.

Remarks: Here's where you find the changes to Procedures, and additions covering fuel injected, carbureted and diesel Rabbits and Sciroccos (1975-1985) and information and Procedures for the 1981 thru 1984 Jettas and Pickups

Step 1: Check the List-All models

Pages 398 to 426 cover changes to all models, including Jetta and Pickup. Read the following pages of 1986 changes and additions with pencil in hand. Check (✓) or otherwise mark any change or addition relevant to your model and year car.

Step 2: Mark the Book-All Models

Now turn back to the page of the change(s) you checked (✓) in Step 1. Star or otherwise mark the place in the text where the new information goes and write the page number of the change from this section.

Step 3: Using the Changes-All Models

Now your book is set up and ready to be used for any Procedure. When you run across a star in the Procedure you're doing, it tells you to come back here to the change and do what it calls for.

For Example:

The change below for p.16 is a description of the electronic ignition systems that became standard equipment for all 1980 and on gasoline Rabbits. If you have 1980 and on non-diesel Rabbit, turn back to page 16 and star or otherwise mark the text after the illustration on that page and write p.398 in the margin. Then in the future when you're working on p.16 you'll know where to turn for this addition.

————————————————— 1986 Changes —————————————————

Page	Model & Year	Location
16	All Gasoline 1980-on	(Insert after illustration)

Electronic Ignition

Since 1980 most gasoline powered vehicles have come equipped with an electronic ignition system. This setup eliminates bothersome points and the need to regularly adjust and replace them.

Here's how it all works. Inside the distributor is a device called a **Hall electromagnetic generator.** When you start the engine the shaft inside the distributor turns a trigger wheel that generates an electrical signal. This signal is amplified by what's called the ignition control unit, and primary current then flows through the coil.

From the coil follow the thin wires which go to the left side of the firewall, ending up at the ignition control unit. OK?

ge	Model & Year	Location

When voltage in the Hall generator rises to a certain point, voltage at the control unit stops, and the primary current is switched off. Now voltage is available at the spark plugs (distributed through the plug wires coming from the top of the distributor cap). Ignition takes place.

Some vehicles (mainly California) have an added gizmo called a **digital idle stabilizer.** This device is located right next to the ignition control unit. Look for it: it's a black box with two thick wires plugged into it. If you don't have this unit, the wires are there, but they're plugged into one another. Mated as it were. How nice.

The idle stabilizer keeps the speed of the engine constant when the air conditioner or radiator fan is on, or when you engage Drive in a car with an automatic transmission. The stabilizer advances the ignition timing when the car speed falls below 940 rpm. It only does this between 600 and 940 rpm. The timing isn't affected when you are trying to start the engine or driving at speed.

Fuel Injection 1981-on   (See *Change* for p.208 below)

A detail illustration of the oxygen sensor system appears with the change for p.208 below, on p.409.

All Gas Models '82 on (Add to the end of Step 2)

On these vehicles the oil pressure and battery/alternator warning lights should wink on/off a coupla times, then they'll stay on. That means the battery is fine (for now) and there's enough oil in the crankcase to safely start the engine.

All Models   (Insert after 1st paragraph, Step 1)

Use SAE 10W-40 detergent oil.

All Models 1982-on   (Combination Wrenches)

Add 18mm to complete your set.

All Models 1982-on   (C.V. Joint Tool)

You require 7mm 6-point star Allen socket.

All Models 1982-on   (Add to Step 4, 1st paragraph)

1982 and on vehicles have an economy light which flashes when it's time to upshift.

Jettas 1982-on   (Add to Step 2, 2nd paragraph)

Includes Jettas

Page	Model & Year	Location

46 All Models (Step 8, 2nd, 3rd, and 4th paragraphs)

The 2nd paragraph should read, "When that time comes, push both the clutch and brake pedals down toward the floor boards at the same time. Depressing the clutch pedal prevents the engine from pulling the car along while the brake system tries to stop the wheels."

The 3rd paragraph should read, "Try to 'squeeze' the pedal rather than stomp on it. You want the tires to retain their grip on the road. Lose grip and you lose direction and . . ."

The 4th paragraph should read, "I've taken my Rabbit onto a state police skidpan (a big flat tarred area covered with a thin layer of mineral oil and water to make it slippery) and done all sorts of fancy sliding tricks. Not only was it lots of fun, but I was pleased to see how easily the car pulled out of the skids. So were the state police; they hate cleaning up."

46 All Models (Step 9, 4th paragraph)

The 4th paragraph should read, "Let the engine idle when you come to a complete stop. Don't rev the engine to impress the bystanders."

50 Jettas (3rd paragraph)

Add Jettas to 3rd paragraph.

51 All Models Pre-1980 (3rd paragraph)

First line of the 3rd paragraph should read "**(Pre-1980)** Beneath the distributor cap . . ."

51 Gas Models '80 and on (Add to end of IGNITION SYSTEM)

These vehicles were fitted with electronic or 'breakerless' ignition systems which eliminated the points and condenser. The distributor, however, looks pretty much the same on the outside as the conventional one in Peter's drawing.

52 Fuel Injection 1981-on

For detail of oxygen sensor system see 1982 *Changes* for page 208 below.

53 All Models (Add to end of ELECTRICAL SYSTEM)

Most of the vehicle's electrical circuits (except those used to actually start the engine or keep it running) are protected from damage by sensitive fuses. These fuses are sensitive to extra electrical loads and 'blow' when pushed to the limit. The fuse box containing both the fuses and a number of electrically operated relays that operate items such as the headlights, windshield wipers, seat-belt buzzer, etc. is located just above the driver's feet.

53 1981 and '82 Pickup trucks and '83 and on vehicles (Add to end of COOLING SYSTEM)

These vehicles are fitted with a separate plastic expansion tank affixed on the inside of the left fender.

All Gas Models 1981-on   (Add to last paragraph)

1981 and on vehicles have an **oxygen sensor** that's screwed into the middle of the exhaust manifold. A black wire attached to it ends up at a plastic pull-apart connector in the wiring harness close to the left fender on the right side of the engine. With the engine cold (so you don't burn yourself) feel for the sensor screwed into the exhaust manifold on the right side of the engine. It's best seen from the left side of the car.

Fuel Injection (Change second paragraph to read)

1980 California and all 1981 and later vehicles (except non-California Pickup Trucks) have an extra pollution control device called the oxygen sensor (or Lambda sensor) screwed into the exhaust manifold on the right of the engine. It works along with a three-way catalytic converter to monitor and control the content of the engine's exhaust gasses.

All Gas Models 1982-on   (Add to 3rd paragraph)

First two sentences of 3rd paragraph should read, ''All carbureted and injected cars have a black **EGR counter box.** Prior to 1982 it's a plastic box fastened behind the left side of the firewall with one speedometer cable in the front running to the transmission.

All Models 1982-on   (Insert after 3rd paragraph)

1982 and on cars have the EGR box stashed behind the instrument panel. You have to remove the panel before you can reset the EGR light. The oxygen sensor light on these late-model vehicles is activated by a gizmo located right next to the EGR box behind the panel. VW gets tricky in its old age.

All Models   (Revise 4th paragraph)

The 4th paragraph should read, ''This anti-pollution device prevents the release of fuel vapor into the outside atmosphere. Check the diagram to see how it works. The activated charcoal filter is located behind the firewall on the left side of the engine compartment or inside the left fender. There's no maintenance to this system other than checking that the hoses and hose clamps are all tight and that the connecting hoses are in good condition.''

All Models 1981-on   (Insert before Procedure 1)

As strange as it may seem, sometimes a poorly fitted ground strap will cause a Rabbit not to start. On 1981 and on vehicles there's quite a few ground straps. So check 'em all before tearing out the fuel injection system.

First check the ground strap at the battery itself. If that's OK, find the strap under the mixture control unit (fuel injection) that fastens to the inside of the left fender. On diesel models the strap is easily visible. Check that the end of the strap is secured to the vehicle body and that the strap isn't broken. Also check the end of the strap where it fastens onto the transmission. All shipshape?

Beginning in 1981 all U.S. made vehicles had a device called a **fusible link** installed between the battery and the wiring harness. This link 'blows' if an electrical excess load is suddenly exerted on the electrical system. If it blows, you won't have any power to anything and the car cannot start. Is that your problem? If so, before you attempt to repair this link, it's important to find out what caused the link to blow in the first place. Usually it's a faulty alternator or voltage regulator. A short in the wiring harness will also cause the fusible link to give up the ghost. When you've found the cause and remedied it, turn to Procedure 12 of this chapter for how to fix the link.

Fuel injected vehicles built before 1981 had a terrible time with the relay plates. One of the wires in the white plug frequently burned out, causing the car to quit in mid-stream or suddenly become impossible to start. My friend Turtle went through four. A simple solution was found by the end of 1981, too late to appease a lot of VW owners. The solution is use of a new wiring harness which fits into the relay plate and bypasses the offending white plug wire. VW will install this kit under a recall program, but if for some reason you don't qualify, don't fret because it's an easy job. Here's how:

PROCEDURE 0: MODIFY RELAY PLATE. Phase 1.

Conditions: Your 1975 through '79 fuel injected vehicle quit.

Tools and materials: Phase 1 Tool kit, new harness called an **EK/EQ+ (V.W. part #171-971-761B).**

Remarks: VW should do this modificaton for you, but if for some reason they won't, here's how. VW also recommends that you do the EK modification which is to weatherseal the hole in the left inner fender through which passes the antenna lead. Seal it with a waterproof sticky compound. 1979 vehicles eligible for this recall are chassis numbers 1793750001 through 1793845899.

Step 1: Disconnect Battery Ground Strap

You can do it.

Step 2: Check New EK/EQ+

It seems that VW supplied some EK/EQ+ harnesses with the wires crossed. To check if you got one, plug the female end of the harness into the male end. It fits only one way. Do the same colored wires meet at both the female and male end? Yes. It's OK. No, then one or more of the wires is wrongly fitted. Pull the ends apart and check the positions. Here's how:

At the male end of the harness match up the little numbers on the back (where the wires come from) against the following list. If one is wrong, simply pull the wire out of the wrong hole and put it into the correct one.

Number	Color of Wire
12	red/black stripe
13	red
15	brown
16	black

Now check the female end and make any changes as needed:

Model & Year   Location

Number	Color of Wire
1	vacant
2	red
3	brown
4	red/black stripe
5	vacant
6	black
7	vacant
8	red/yellow stripe (this *doesn't* attach to the male end)
9	vacant

After checking the EK/EQ+, remove the protective carpet from around the relay plate/fuse box above the driver's knees, then remove the screw holding the relay plate in position. Now pull out the fuel pump relay. It's the last one with the fuse on the end, and it fits into position L on the relay plate. Be sure you've pulled out the correct relay. Next plug the male end of your EK/EQ+ into position L from whence came the old fuel pump relay.

Now look on top of the relay plate and you'll see some wide shallow slots. A couple of relays are mounted atop the relay plate via these slots. Find an empty slot and push the unconnected end of the EK/EQ+ into the slot. Make sure it's in good and tight with the wires facing toward the front of the car. Now plug the old fuel pump relay into the EK/EQ that now sits on top of the relay plate.

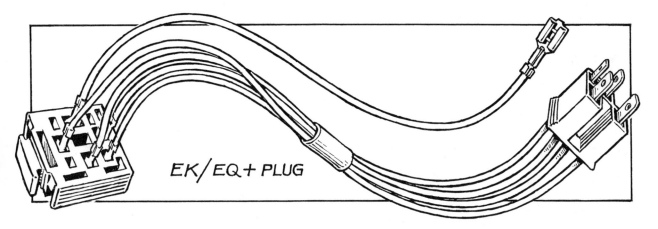

EK/EQ+ PLUG

Look behind the relay plate and find a clear plastic Y which has three wires running to it. One of these wires (usually black with a purple stripe) runs from the Y to position A8 in the rear of the white plastic plug which is pushed into the rear of the relay plate at position A. If you look closely you'll see that the plug probably is burned slightly around that wire. Follow the wire to the clear Y and pull the end of the wire out of the Y. Stick the new red wire with a yellow stripe which is connected to the EK/EQ+ into the plastic Y. Make sure it is properly pushed home. (That's not what you want to be doing with the car later.)

Either pull the old wire out of the white plug or tape up the metal connector on the end of that wire. Put the relay plate and carpet back the way it was. Then reconnect the battery ground strap and your fuel pump/starting problems are over for now. I hope.

Page   Model & Year   Location

57   Most '83 and on Fuel Injected Models (Add to Step 1, 6th paragraph)

These vehicles are fitted with a cheap-and-nasty cable fastening device that uses a metal clip to secure the cable to the bracket. Pull the clip and pop the cable end off the throttle lever on the intake manifold. It's all free.

58   All Fuel Injected Models (Add after second paragraph)

Late model people with the clip-secured cable should pop the end of the cable onto the throttle lever then adjust the cable sheath until it looks and feels right. Secure the cable with the clip. OK?

60   All Models   (Procedure 3, add to Tools and Materials)

Phase 1 tool kit, perhaps a new battery or battery cables/clamps.

60   All Models '82-on   (Procedure 3, add to Remarks)

. . . distributor. 1982 and on check the plastic connectors on the battery cables also.

74   '82 and on (Add to end of Step 5)

If your shifter set-up looks just a little different from Peter's illustration, don't panic. The later models work in exactly the same manner as the earlier versions.

74   All Models   (Add after Step 6.)

PROCEDURE 12: REPAIR FUSIBLE LINK. (Some Models after 1980) Phase 1

Condition: Fusible link blown.

Tools and materials: New fusible link(s), soldering iron, 60% tin 40% lead rosin core solder, crimping tool, butt connectors.

Remarks: If you can't solder, find someone who can.

Step 1. Disconnect Battery

Disconnect both battery cables from the battery; then remove the battery from the car.

Step 2. Remove Windshield Washer Reservoir.

Just unhook it from its little niche.

Step 3. Find Fusible Links

They are right under the place where the washer reservoir hangs. Follow the battery cables until you come to them. You'll immediately see which link is gone.

Step 4. Repair Link

Cut the link out of the wiring harness

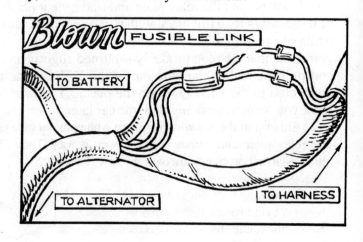

e   Model & Year   Location

after removing the tape from the connections. From the wire left in the harness strip about 13mm (½ in.) of the plastic insulation and, using the butt connectors, install a new fusible link to the wires. Crimp the connectors with the crimping tool.

Now solder the wires inside the butt connectors and make sure the wires are held firmly. When all that has cooled down, wrap the joints with electrical tape.

Step 5. Finish up

While the battery is out you may as well clean the battery posts with a wire brush (safety glasses, please) and rinse off any white stuff with a solution of baking soda and water. Then sluice the battery with plain water, dry it, then reinstall in the car. Hook up the battery cables, rehang the windshield washer reservoir and tidy up.

(Add to beginning of Step 4)

On 1981 Sciroccos and everything else except Jetta, turn to Step 5. On 1981 and on models built in US, you'll need to remove the left speaker grille and the speaker beneath it to get at the instrument bulbs. It's an easy job.

All 1982 Models with power steering   (Add to Procedure 2, After Tools and materials)

Remarks: If you have a 1982 vehicle with power steering, removing the alternator is a bigger hassle than climbing Mt. Everest in a bathing suit and sneakers. I think that if my 1982 alternator went bad, I'd take it to VW to get them to do it. They designed it; let 'em fix it.

All Models   (Add to last line on page)

...bolt if you are replacing the alternator.) Cars built after 1981 should have a rubber plug in the drive belt guard. This keeps grunge off the belt. Remove it with a screwdriver. Then you will be able to slip your 6mm allen wrench through the hole in the drive belt...

All U.S. Models '81-on   (After Step 6)

1981 saw a big change in the electrical system. The terrible relay plate that stopped lots of cars in their treads was eliminated. A new type of American fuse box was substituted. This fuse box has 16 or so pin type fuses pushed into the box next to the relays. It's easy to tell if a fuse has burned out. How? A good fuse has an unbroken wire between the two prongs on the back of the fuse. If the wire isn't continuous, the fuse has blown. A blown fuse (unlike blown glass) is useless, so

Newer type Fuse Panel W/ASSORTED RELAYS

5 Amp.

Blown!

Page   Model & Year   Location

replace it with one of the same amperage. The amperage appears on the front of each fuse so you can't go wrong. The new type fuse box is shown on the previous page.

All cars made in Germany (Scirocco, Jettas and Rabbit convertible) have the old type relay plate. You'll know what you've got.

84   All Fuel Injected Models   (Insert right before Procedure 1)

Excessive oil consumption has plagued early Rabbits. The valve guide seal design was poor, causing the seals to wear and oil to escape into the cylinders.

If you own a '77 through '79 fuel injected vehicle, VW will rectify this situation. Call the Service Manager at VW for an update.

85   All Models, '81-on   (Add to end of Step 1, Paragraph 2)

. . . shock. Check the plastic connectors on vehicles built after 1981. Fusible links OK?

86   All U.S. Models '81-on, and all German-built Models '82-on
(Replaces Step 3, Paragraphs 3 and 4, plus additional paragraphs)

Disconnect the battery ground strap (10mm wrench). The relay plate is just above the driver's knees. There may be a protective carpet hiding it. If so, either take out the small plastic clip holding the center of the carpet in place or remove the two 10mm bolts, then pull the carpet down and out.

Pre 1981 and **cars built in Germany:** To free the relay plate, first remove the Phillips screw from the bottom right side of the plate. Now lift the plate up from the two metal retaining ears. Twist the plate around to expose the colored plastic plugs with all the wires running into them.

1981 and on vehicles (not convertible or Scirocco) have the new type of American relay plate/fuse box. If the oil light is malfunctioning, first check the fuses. If one is blown, replace it with one of the same amperage. If the fuses are OK, disconnect the battery ground strap, remove the fuse box from its retaining ears and check that all the connections are in place and that the plugs in the rear are pushed home. Reconnect the battery ground strap and try the key. Oil light on? Good, replace everything and be on your way.

1982 and on vehicles (not Scirocco or convertible) have what's known as a "dynamic oil pressure system." What that means only der engineers at VW know. I've heard of dynamic personalities, but dynamic oil pressure systems. Really.

Anyway, this system uses an oil pressure relay that's stuck up at the top left part of the relay plate. If your oil light is malfunctioning, maybe the relay is bad. The best way to test it is to borrow a new, good relay from the VW dealer, stick it into your socket and see if the oil pressure light goes on. If it does, your old relay is bad.

To check the oil pressure sensor on **1982 and on models produced in Germany,** do the following test: Turn on the engine and pull the wire off the oil pres-

e   **Model & Year**   **Location**

sure sensor that's found on top of the oil filter flange. Rev the engine to at least 2000 rpm. The oil pressure warning light should flash and a buzzer should sound. Yes? You've got a bad sensor.

If nothing happens, check the oil pressure relay.

If you've got a US produced vehicle, there are two oil pressure sensors; one on the oil filter flange and an extra one screwed into the back of the cylinder head. To check this system, do the above test with the oil filter flange sensor. If nothing happens, reinstall the wire. Next pull the wire from the cylinder head sensor and touch it to ground with the engine on. The dash light should glow continuously. If not, check the relay. That's likely your problem. Reinstall the wires. If the light doesn't work with the borrowed relay, you need to find someone to fix it for you. At the time of this writing I'm still investigating repairs and modifications to this new electrical system, so please bear with me.

U.S. Models '81-on   (end of Step 3)

See change for page 83

(Add to Remarks)

A friend of mine had a 1984 Convertible that made 'funny noises' after the engine had started. I checked the oil level, started the engine and watched the oil pressure gauge. It showed good pressure and the oil light went out on time. The valves continued to 'tick' for about thirty seconds indicating that the oil pump wasn't doing its thing despite what the gauge told me. I watched the gauge and it wavered a while then held steady. I figured the oil pump was on the blink, pulled the pan and discovered that the pump was due for early retirement.

All Models   (Add to end of first paragraph on Synthetic Oils)

. . . the rings won't seat properly. While what I said here is still valid, it seems that a reputable brand-name synthetic oil will reduce internal friction and thus increase gas mileage. The problem of oil contaminants still remains, but I've seen impressive results from extended use of synthetic and 'slippery oils.' The wear on essential engine parts was greatly reduced and the costs of operating the vehicle were lowered. Make up your own mind, but *never* use a synthetic or slippery oil in a newly rebuilt engine.

1   All Models   (Add to procedure 5, before Step 1)

In these days of oil shortages and high priced petroleum products, I have to bow to economics and say extend your oil change period from 3000 miles to 5000. Likewise, if you live in very dusty areas, up the oil change from 1500 miles to 3000 miles.

3   All Models   (Procedure 9, Replace Conditions and add to Tools and materials)

Condition: You've put 300 or 600 miles on a new or rebuilt engine or you've driven 3000 dusty miles or 5000 regular miles.

Tools and materials: Phase 1 tool kit, new oil filter, 3.7 U.S. quarts (3.1 Imperial qts or 3.5 liters) or for 1982-and-on 4.7 U.S. qts) of new oil . . .

Page	Model & Year	Location

114   **All Models pre '80**   **(Replace Procedure 16 head)**

PROCEDURE 16: ADJUST IGNITION TIMING. Phase 1. Regular Distributors (Points)

114   **Gas Engines (Add to Procedure 16, Step 2, second paragraph after fifth sentence)**

1980 vehicles fitted with carburetors have a timing mark at 7.5 degrees BTDC. 1983 and 1984 cars sold in the US, and pickup trucks with manual transmissions sold in California have a mark at 6 degrees BTDC. To make things even more complicated, some 1983 and 1984 US-built Rabbits and pickups have a timing scale etched on the flywheel. Each of the little lines indicates 2 degrees, with the zero showing the position of TDC.

116   **All Models '80-on**   **(Add after end of Step 6)**

PROCEDURE 16A: ADJUST IGNITION TIMING (Electronic Ignition, no Points).

Condition: Tune-up

Tools and materials: Strobe timing light, phase 1 tool kit, tachometer or tach dwell meter and adaptation materials as per instructions.

Remarks: Warm up the engine to operating temperature, idle between 880-1000 rpm.

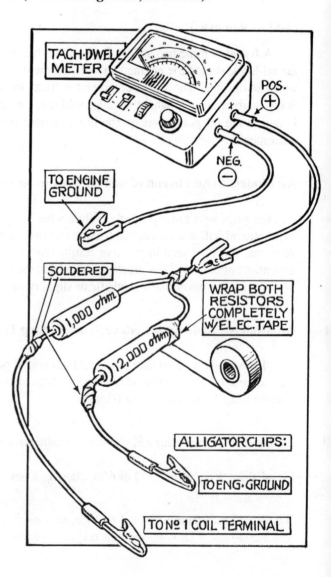

Step 1. Make This Device

Go to Radio Shack or a similar radio supply store and buy one 1000 ohm and one 12,000 ohm resistor along with three small alligator clips and a length of 3mm² (14 or 12 gauge) wire. Now make the gizmo as shown in the diagram.

Step 2. Get Ready

Turn to Procedure 16 and do the first two steps.

Step 3. Hook Up

Clip the alligator lead from the positive side of your tach dwell meter onto terminal #1 on the coil. Now clip the negative lead onto something metal on the engine. Hook up a timing light as explained in Step 3 of Procedure 16.

Step 4. Unhook

If you've got a **digital idle stabilizer** (that's the small black box in the engine compartment up at the firewall on the left, next to the windshield wiper motor). It has two black plastic plugs pushed into it.

Pull them out and connect the two plugs together. You are thus isolating the idle stabilizer. If you don't have a stabilizer, the two plugs should have been connected together at the factory.

If you've got a carbureted engine made after 1980, remove the vacuum line from the distributor and plug it with a pencil.

Step 5. Time's Up

Start the engine, then point the timing light into the hole in the transmission and see if the light illuminates the timing mark. If the engine is timed properly, the timing mark on the flywheel will line up beautifully with the pointer inside the transmission hole. If nothing lines up, turn back to Procedure 16 and adjust the timing as per Step 4, then come back here. Properly timed? Good, turn off the engine and unhook all your equipment.

Step 6. Reconnect

Reattach the vacuum hose to the distributor (carbureted engines) and reinsert the plugs into the idle stabilizer. If you've got an idle stabilizer, when you restart the engine, rev it up to about 2000 rpm, then let your foot off the gas and watch the revs fall back to between 850 and 1000 rpm. If the idle is too low or high, adjust it as per Procedure 18 in this chapter.

(Add before Procedure 19)

PROCEDURE 18A: CHECK DIGITAL IDLE STABILIZER AND IGNITION CONTROL UNIT. Phase 2

Condition: Tune-up, erratic idle.

Tools and Materials: As per above Procedure plus a VOM and a friend.

Remarks: This Procedure is for cars with transistorized ignition and a carburetor as well as California fuel injected cars.

Step 1. What?

These vehicles have a digital idle stabilizer housed on the firewall 'tray' just below the windscreen. This electrical marvel monitors the idle speed and advances the ignition timing if the idle speed falls below the correct level. If your idle is erratic or the engine stops for no reason when the engine is supposed to be idling, try this. First identify the idle stabilizer and the ignition control unit. Simply follow the cables from the ignition distributor and the ignition coil until you find the two components. The control unit has one large multi-connector-type plug and is bolted to an aluminum heat sink. Found it? Break out your VOM.

Step 2. Is It Broken, Dick?

Turn the ignition key off and disconnect the two connectors from the idle stabilizer and plug them to one another, effectively by-passing the stabilizer. Pull the multiple connector from the control unit, switch your VOM to Volts DC and insert the negative probe into the connector's terminal 2 and the positive probe into terminal 4. Turn the ignition on and check the meter. Got about 12 volts showing on the scale? No? There's a problem with the wiring or ignition switch. Yes? Turn off the ignition and plug back the connector into the ignition control unit.

Step 3. Keep Going

Move over to the distributor and disconnect the multiple connector from its side. Turn your attention to the coil and switch the VOM to a low DC Volt scale and hook up the positive probe to terminal 15 on the coil, and the negative probe to terminal 1. Those are the two small terminals on each side of the big center wire running to the distributor.

Get friend to turn the ignition on as you watch the VOM scale. You should get around a 2 volt reading for a second or two, then the voltage should drop to nothing. No? You probably have a bad control unit. You can only be sure if you install a new coil and control unit. Get VW or an electrical shop to check your work, electrical parts are expensive and non-returnable!

If the voltage is fine, continue.

Step 4. Jump To It

Keep the VOM hooked up as per the previous Step. Find a short piece of electrical wire, bare the ends and stick one end into the center terminal of the connector you just pulled off the distributor. Ask friend to turn the ignition on as you ground the other end of the wire onto a clean unpainted metal surface. The the VOM should jump to 2 volts. No? There's a problem with the multiple connector or the wire running to it. Look carefully and find out what's wrong. If the plug and wire is OK, the control unit is shot. Install a new one. If you've got voltage, keep going.

Step 5. Final Test

Turn the ignition off and keep the VOM connected as for the Step above. Plunge the VOM probes into the far left and right terminals on the multiple connector that was connectecd to the distributor. Friend, turn the ignition on yet again. The VOM should read at least 5 volts. No? You've got a break in the wire attached to the multiple connector or a bad pin in the connector. Check carefully. You don't? The control unit has breathed its last. Buy and install a new unit.

When you've found the trouble, hook everything back as it was. Don't forget the idle stabilizer plugs.

117   PROCEDURE 18B: CHECK IDLE AIR STABILIZER SYSTEM. Phase 2

Condition: Erratic Idle.

Tools and Materials: Vise Grips and a VOM

Remarks: This applies only to '83 and on fuel injected vehicles.

Step 1. Find the Components

Lift the hood and look on the end of the intake air distributor (intake manifold as it used to be called) up by the right fender. You have two (or one) intake air bypass valves sitting there minding their own business. These valves allow a small amount of air to bypass the throttle plate and thus increase the engine speed when the idle drops below 750 rpm. The valve is electrically operated by a relay that monitors the engine speed.

Step 2: Test

Warm up the engine then shut it off. Use Vise Grips to clamp shut the thick rubber hose that runs from the upper part of the bypass valve to a T in front of the intake air distributor. Clamp the hose pretty close to the T. If you have a test tachometer connect it and start the engine. Unhook the electrical connection onto the oxygen sensor (see Step 7 page if you don't know what/where it is).

Adjust the brass-colored idle speed screw on the side of the intake air distributor until the tach reads below 750 rpm (use the dash tach if needed). As the idle is lowered the bypass valve should 'tick' once. That means it's open. Take off the Vise Grips and see if the idle increases. If it does, turn the idle screw again until the valve clicks once again. Now it's closed. If it all works OK adjust the idle until it's right and re-hook what you un-hooked.

Step 3: Test Electrics

If the above Step yielded no results then the electrics are suspect. The bypass valve is controlled by a relay bolted onto the steering column brace right next to the fuse box on U.S.-built vehicles and on the

German-built cars the relay is right above the fuse box. Remove the protective panel above the driver's feet to find it. Use a VOM (or test light) switched to Volts DC, start the engine and listen under there to hear if the relay is 'clicking' that's way you'll find the right one. I have never come across a bad relay but there's always a first time. Check that the connector on the bypass valve is pushed home tight and that the wires running to it are in place. Keep the engine running and pull the connector from the relay at terminal 87. Repeat the test as per Step 2 and see if you have voltage below 750 rpm or no voltage above 1100 rpm. If so, the bypass valve is faulty since the relay is doing its thing. If you have no voltage below 750 rpm and voltage above 1100 rpm the relay is shot, or less likely, the wiring to the relay is askew. Check.

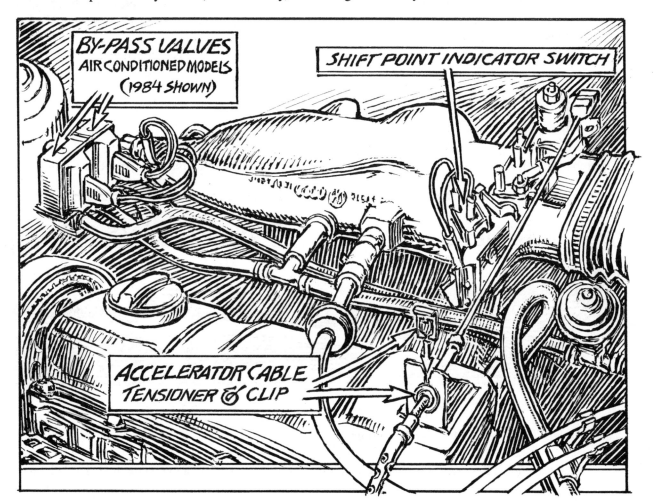

All Models except diesel   (Procedure 20, add new paragraph under Remarks)

If your vehicle has electronic ignition (no points) you must ground the central coil wire before cranking the engine. Failure to do so may damage the electronic gizmos; and replacing them is an expensive proposition. Here's how:

First, don't pull the coil wire out of the coil as indicated in Step 1 for vehicles with points (not electronic ignition). Simply pull the center wire from the distributor cap and ground it against something metal. You can hold the wire in place with an alligator clip, a piece of electrical tape or something of that ilk.

When you've finished the test, remember to reinstall the center wire all the way into the distributor cap.

Page	Model & Year	Location

120   All Fuel Injected Models   (Replace Step 2)

Step 2. Remove Filter. KEEP THOSE SPARKS AND FLAMES AWAY!

Place a clean rag under the filter fuel line connections to mop up dripping gasoline. Loosen and free the front facing 17mm brass colored captive nut which holds the gas line onto the filter. Use a 22mm wrench or adjustable wrench to hold the filter if the nut is tight. Watch out for gas spurting from the gas line when the nut first comes loose. Now remove the 19mm brass nut from the gas line on the rear of the filter. Next loosen the 10mm nut holding the filter into its clamp. Late models have the fuel filter held in a bracket on the end of the mixture control unit. If that's yours, use a screwdriver or a 10mm wrench to loosen the screw holding the filter. In all cases slide the filter out.

'82 and on Sciroccos have a big filter held by a hose clamp. This filter is changed every 60,000 miles.

124   All Models '82 on   (Insert before Remarks)

1982 and on vehicles require a different type of cam follower depresser. It isn't possible to use the old type tool on the new type cam followers. If you're buying a tool, give the parts person the year and chassis number of your car. A sticker on top of the cam cover reminds owners with the new type of cam follower.

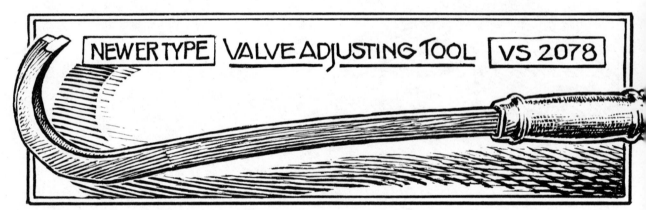

NEWER TYPE VALVE ADJUSTING TOOL   VS 2078

126   All Models '80 on   (Add to end of first paragraph)

. . . nuts in a marked Baggie. 1980 and on vehicles have a different type of mounting method. The belt guard is now secured by a 6mm allen bolt in the cover's face, so you've got to get that out first. After removing the allen bolt, undo the four 10mm bolts securing the cover to the engine. Now you will be able to pull off the protective shield from around the camshaft drive belt sprocket along with the cam cover. When it's time to reinstall the belt guard, don't tighten the allen bolt too much. That'll strip out the bolt and it's a pain to replace.

130   Gas Engines with Breakerless (Transistorized) Ignition   (Add after Step 6)

PROCEDURE 26A: CHECK BREAKERLESS DISTRIBUTOR'S INNARDS. Phase 2

Condition: Tune-up, erratic idle, poor gas mileage, etc.

e   **Model & Year**   **Location**

Tools and Materials: Phase 1 tool kit, a friend and a VOM

Remarks: You did the preceding Procedure to check advance and the general good workings of the distributor I take it?

Step 1. What Is There To Test?

We can test the Hall sending unit also called the impulse coil in some remote areas of the world. First complete Procedure 18A to check that your troubles don't lie elsewhere, then come back here.

Pull the plugs from the digital idle stabilizer (if fitted, see Procedure 18A if you don't know what or where it is) and re-connect the two plugs to one another. Remove the high tension wire from the center of the distributor cap and ground it firmly onto a clean unpainted metal part of the engine. Pull the multiple connector from the control unit (see Procedure 18A again perhaps) and switch your VOM to low Volts DC. Push the positive probe into terminal 6 in the multiple connector and the negative probe into terminal 3.

Step 2. What's Happenin?

Ask your good friend to turn the ignition on as you watch the VOM. Stick a socket and ratchet handle onto the bolt on the crankshaft pulley (usually 17mm). Turn the crankshaft clockwise using the ratchet) and see if the VOM first shows a reading of at least 2 volts, then moves to zero volts as you continue to turn the ratchet handle. If you get such a reading then the Hall sending unit is doing its job properly. If not, buy a new sending unit. It's easily installed. You have to remove the distributor cap, pull off the rotor and dust shield, take off the snap pin, trigger wheel and washers then unscrew the Hall sending unit. Simple.

Step 3. Tidy Up.

Reconnect the high tension wire into the distributor cap and hook up the digital idle stabilizer connections. Better now?

All gas California models '80 on and all Models '81 on   **(Add to bottom of page)**

On 1980 California vehicles, and on almost everything made since 1981, there's another item in the system which works in conjunction with the oxygen sensor that's screwed into the rear of the exhaust manifold. The frequency valve, as it's called, is fitted to the fuel distributor and constantly adjusts the fuel/air mixture. You can hear it humming away when the engine is running. Its operation is controlled by the oxygen sensor and another electronic control unit apparatus. Things are getting quite complicated.

All Models   **(Add to fourth paragraph, 2nd line)**

. . . checking the ground wire, turn to Procedure 17 in this Chapter. If, however, your fuel pump checks out OK . . .

All Fuel Injected Models   **(Add to Step 2 between first and second paragraph)**

See change for page 120

Page   Model & Year   Location

198   1985 All Models: Typical hose layout with A/C

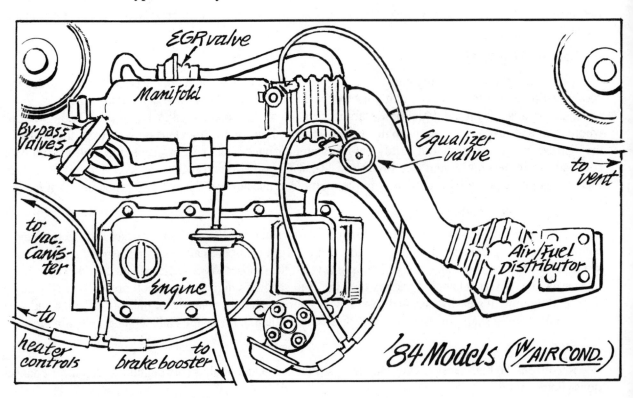

206   **All Models '81 on   (Procedure 7, add to Remarks)**

1981 and on vehicles have all the exhaust pipe flanges sealed with an epoxy substance. Before you try to pull the pieces of the exhaust system apart, heat the joints with a propane torch or the like. **Keep the flame away from gasoline and brake lines, or anything or anybody that can burn, and have a fire extinguisher handy.** Be very careful.

When replacing any exhaust system parts, reseal the pipe joints with something like Mortell Epoxy Sealer®. Your VW dealer will have that or an equivalent.

208   **Gas Models '81 on   (Add at end of page, after Step 7)**

Oxygen Sensor System (All Gas '81 on)

Now this system can cause a lot of strange happenings when any part of it goes on the blink. It can cause hesitation, poor hot starting, excessive fuel consumption, no acceleration and a host of other wierdnesses. Also, it must be working correctly before you can adjust the idle. Let's go through the system.

PROCEDURE 8: CHECK OXYGEN SENSOR SYSTEM. Phase 2

Condition: You name it. See above.

Tools and materials: Phase 1 tool kit, maybe a new oxygen sensor or thermoswitch, a candy or meat thermometer, anti-seize compound.

Remarks: Check all fuses before you begin.

Step 1. Check Thermoswitch Resistance

Run the engine until normal operating temperature has been reached. When it has, turn off the engine, lift and prop the hood and disconnect the wires coming from the thermoswitch on the rear of the cylinder head. The switch is held into the coolant hose by two hose clamps. Use your VOM set at RX1K to test for continuity at the thermoswitch. Nothing? You'll have to wait awhile until the engine cools down. Relax.

Step 2. Drain Coolant. ENGINE MUST BE COOL

Turn to Chapter 17, Procedure 1, Step 3, and do it.

Step 3. Remove Thermoswitch

The electrical connections should already be off the switch so now use a screwdriver to loosen the two hose clamps securing the thermoswitch into the coolant hose. When they're loose, slide the switch free of the hoses.

Step 4. Test Switch

Immerse the switch and your thermometer in a pan of cold water. Heat the water and test the continuity of the switch. When the water is below 20° C (68° F) there should be continuity (0 ohms). when the water temperature gets above 25° C (77° F) there should be no continuity (infinite ohms). If you get irregular readings, replace thermoswitch. And don't forget to turn off the stove!

If the thermoswitch is **OK** (or you need to install a new one) here's how to put things back together.

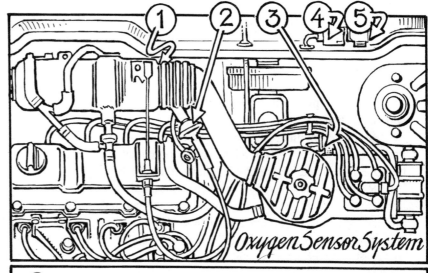

Oxygen Sensor System

(1) Oxygen sensor (hidden by intake manifold. Screws into exhaust manifold—1981 on) (2) Two-way vacuum valve (1981 on) (3) Frequency valve (4) Idle stabilizer (some models) (5) Ignition control unit (1980 on)

Step 5. Install Switch

Simply slide the switch into the two coolant hoses and tighten the hose clamps. Connect the electrical connectors to the two prongs atop the switch.

Step 6. Top Up Coolant

Sounds like the name for a Punk star. Turn to Chapter 17, Procedure 1, Step 10.

Page   Model & Year   Location

Step 7. Keep Going.

If the thermoswitch turned out to be in good shape, we need to investigate the sensor system more closely. You need a dwell meter for this test along with a 1.5 volt battery. Solder 8 in of 3mm^2 (12 or 14 gauge) wire onto each end of the 1.5 volt battery and strip about 13mm (½ in) of insulation from the ends of the wires.

Warm up the engine and bypass the idle stabilizer that's up behind the firewall on the left, close to the wiper motor. You may not have one. If you do, pull the two plugs from the unit and plug them into one another. The unit is thus bypassed. Now see that all the electrical accessories are turned off (lights, radio, etc.)

Look at the big aluminum casting on the right side of the engine (the intake manifold). Find the coldstart injector that's bolted into the end of the intake manifold facing the right fender. Just behind the injector is a small white plastic test plug with a cap covering the innards. Pull off the cap and connect the positive lead from your dwell meter into the plug opposite the blue wire with the white stripe. Ignore the brown wire going to that connector. Ground the negative lead from the dwell meter.

Now find the wire running to the oxygen sensor that's screwed into the rear of the exhaust manifold. The sensor is easiest seen from the left side of the car. It has one single black wire running from it to a pull-apart connection just behind the test plug. Just note its position for now.

Start the engine and let it idle. If you have a fancy dwell meter, adjust it to zero and check that it's switched to the 4 cylinder scale. Disconnect the oxygen sensor at the pull-apart connector and watch the dwell meter. It should read $45^o \pm 2^o$. No matter what the reading, continue this test.

Ground the green wire which runs from the oxygen sensor connector to the control unit hidden behind the dash. The dwell reading should increase to at least 78°. Don't ground the green wire and take your 1.5 volt battery and touch the positive lead to the green wire and ground the other battery wire. The dwell reading should decrease to no more than 18°.

Finally, remove the 1.5 volt battery and reconnect the oxygen sensor to the green wire. The dwell reading should fluctuate.

If you get anything other than the above readings, the oxygen sensor is defective. Simply unscrew the old one and screw in a replacement after coating the threads with anti-seize compound. Wait until the engine is cool because a hot intake manifold will relieve you of flesh.

Reconnect the idle stabilizer when you are finished with the test.

If none of the above tests showed anything unusual, and the sensor system still isn't up to par, perhaps the problem is with the electronic control unit. If you are a mechanical "idiot", this is where I would quit. If you buy one of those expensive control units from VW and the problem still isn't fixed, then, my friend, you own the sucker. There's no refunds on electrical parts, mate! So take the vehicle to VW and ask them to fix it. But if you want to continue, get the VW manual from the library and Xerox the pertinent pages. Then follow them.

231   All U.S.-made Models '82 on   (Add to end of Step 2)

1982 and on U.S. made vehicles have a new type of master cylinder. The switches for the rear brake lights are mounted on a valve on the inner left fender.

The on/off switch which actuates the brake lights is now mounted just above the brake pedal. To test if there's power at this switch, use your VOM (see Chapter 20, Procedure 10). Pull the connectors off the pedal switch and insert the VOM probes into those connectors. Simple enough.

240   Procedure 3 (Add to Remarks)

If you are here to just replace a worn ball joint, there is no need to remove the entire tie rod unless your vehicle is fitted the old non-adjustable tie rods. Just remove the ball joint from the end of the tie rod after freeing the ball joint as described in Step 2. Buy adjustable tie rods if you are here to replace a bent/worn one.

age	Model & Year	Location

41   (Add to the end of Step 3)

People with power steering have a different type of tie rod. The inner housing is permanantly attached to the tie rod so in order to remove the tie rod you must roll back the rubber boot from the end of the steering rack which will bring the inner housing to light. Use a wrench to loosen and remove the tie rod from the steering rack. It's not an easy job since the factory uses Loctite to secure the rod. Once the rod is off, use solvent and a wire brush to shine up the threads on the rack.

43   (Add to the end of Step 7)

Power steering owners installing a new tie rod should remove the ball joint from the end of the rod in order to install a new rubber boot. Next install the ball joint and check the rod's dimension with the dimensions in the chart. Apply Loctite to the threads on the end of the steering rack before you screw on the tie rod, and keep screwing until the rod 'hits bottom.'

46   All models except Pickup truck. (Add to Procedure 7)

Remarks: The shock absorber inside MacPherson strut is easily removed without the use of a spring compressor, so ignore the 'Remarks' on page 246. The strut is removed in its entirety from inside the car then refurbished in the comfort and privacy of your own workshop.

Tools and Materials: Late model struts have a slotted nut on top of the shock that requires special tool – 50-200 to remove. Borrow one, or use Vise Grips like every other mechanic in the world!

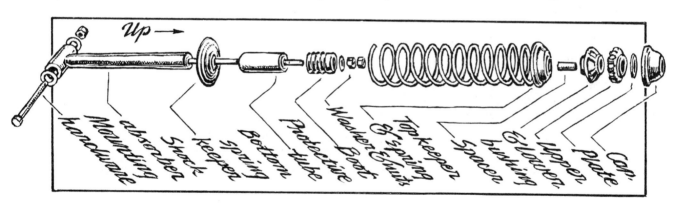

46   All models except Pickup truck (Change last sentence at end of Step 4 to read)

Now remove the strut from the other side of the car in the same manner and lay them both on your workbench.

47   Procedure 7, Step 5 All models except Pickup truck (Add before Step 5 which is now Step 6)

Work on one of the strut assemblies at a time and begin by securing the strut in the vise. Remove the top nut (using the special tool or Vise Grips if needed) from the top of the shock absorber piston. Once the nut is off remove the other lock nut (if fitted) and take the remaining strut components off. Clean everything until it shines and buy replacement shock absorbers and whatever other parts you find you need. Install the shocks and the strut components in the same order as they were removed (check the illustration) and secure the lot with the top nut(s).

Page	Model & Year	Location

247 **Pickup only** (Add after Step 5, before Procedure 8)

PROCEDURE 7A: REPLACE PICKUP REAR SHOCKS. Phase 2

Condition: Rear shocks worn out

Tools and materials: Phase 1 tool kit, new shocks.

Remarks: The little truck uses a conventional method of damping the movement of the rear axle, with the rear suspension consisting of leaf springs and shock absorbers. When you determine that the rear shocks require replacement, also check the two leaf springs very carefully for cracks and breaks.

Step 1. Support Rear Axle

Chock the front wheels, loosen the lug nuts on the rear wheel, then jack up the rear of the truck. Support the vehicle on jack stands or stout blocks. Do both wheels together if you have four jack stands or other stout support.

Now position your jack directly under the axle close to the brake drum. Leave enough room for you to get at the shock mounts. Pump the jack until the shock begins to compress. At this stage stick another jack stand or block under the axle.

Step 2. Remove shock.

Squirt some Liquid Wrench® onto the top and bottom shock retaining bolts. Use a 15mm wrench to remove the bottom bolt, then undo the top bolt and liberate the shock.

Step 3. Install New Shock.

Take a new shock out of its box and pump it up and down a few times. Now clean around the shock mountings under the truck and gather your tools and bolts. Take the new shock and push the top part into position in the top mount. Wiggle it about until it's possible to push the bolt through into the nut. Give the bolt a few turns, then line up the bottom part of the shock with the axle mount.

Push the bolt through the shock, and tighten up the top and bottom bolts to 40Nm (30 ft lbs.)

Put the wheel back on, jack it up and remove the jack stand from under the axle, lower the truck and tighten the lug nuts. If you didn't have enough stout support to do both at once, replace the shock on the other side in exactly the same manner.

247 **Pick-up only** (Insert right before Procedure 8)

PROCEDURE 7B: REPLACE PICK-UP REAR LEAF SPRINGS OR SPRING BUSHINGS

Condition: Springs and/or bushings lost their bounce.
Tools and materials: Phase 1 tool kit, new springs/bushings. **1982 and on** epoxy exhaust sealant.
Remarks: New springs come with new front bushings already installed. You should buy new two-part rear bushings, replace the bushings at both ends of the springs and do both sides!

Step 1. Get Ready.

Chock the front wheels and raise the rear of the truck and support it with jack stands. There is no need to remove the wheels.

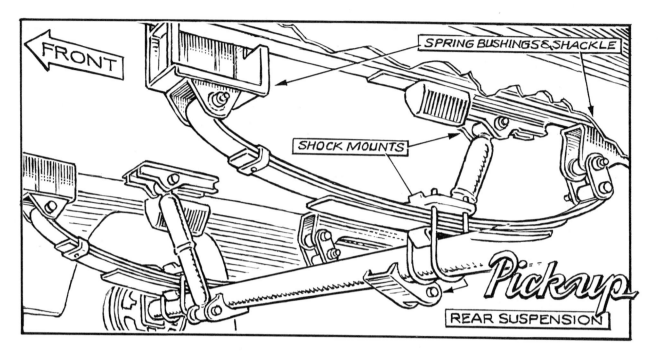

Step 2. Unhook Cable.

Find the parking brake cables and see how they attach to a clamp atop each spring. Remove the 13mm bolt holding the cable clamp, and cut the plastic tie strap securing the cable. It may be missing, so don't go cutting the cable by mistake.

Step 3. Support Axle.

Slide your jack under the axle and pump it up until the shock absorbers begin to compress. Squirt a little Liquid Wrench® onto the bottom bolt holding each shock onto the axle and remove the 15mm bolt. Don't remove the top shock bolts. Do both shocks and push them up out of your way.

Step 4. Remove U-Bolts.

See how the axle is held onto the leaf spring by two U-bolts? Remove the 15mm nuts from the top of the U-bolts, pull the bolts and the metal spring mounting plate off the axle/leaf spring assembly and stash 'em. Now do the same thing to the other side.

Step 5. Remove Exhaust Pipe (Left Spring Removers Only)

Believe it or not, Ripley, the rear part of the exhaust pipe (which includes the muffler) has to be removed in order to take out the bolt securing the front part of the left spring. A rotten drag. Begin by following the exhaust pipe up toward the front of the truck. About half-way along the pipe you'll notice a clamp with a bolt through it. This clamp secures the rear exhaust section to the middle section. **1982 and on:** use a propane torch to heat up the joint. They are sealed with epoxy. **Beware of Fire.** Keep the torch away from gasoline and brake lines. Loosen the bolt and then unhook the rear exhaust section from its mounting hooks on the underbody. Use a screwdriver to lever the rubber exhaust hangers from the hooks. And mind your knuckles. Twist the rear pipe around until it's free from the other section and slide it out from under the car.

Non-U.S. vehicles may have a different exhaust system, in which case you will have to remove the three 13mm bolts which connect the flex part of the exhaust pipe to the header pipe up front. Then unhook the rubber hangers holding the system to the underbody, and slide the pipe out from under the car. Make a note to buy a new gasket which fits between the flex and header pipes.

Step 6. Remove Spring.

The rear part of the spring is fastened to the underbody by a two-part metal shackle. Loosen the 21mm bolt holding the top part of the shackle onto the frame, then remove the lower shackle bolt which passes through the spring. It's the same size.

To remove the spring entirely, carefully take out the front 21mm bolt and thread the spring out from the truck. Now remove the other spring in the same fashion.

Step 7. Install New Bushings (If that's why you're here)

If you've gone through all this torture in order to install replacement bushings into your old springs, now's the time to do it. Hammer out the old one-piece bushing from the front of the spring. Use a drift or a short piece of wooden dowel if the bushing is hard to shift. When it's out, clean out the orifice and press in the new bushing.

The rear bushings are in two parts and easy to remove/install. Do it.

Step 8. Install New Spring

After checking that the two-part rear bushing is in position, slip the spring into place over the axle. A bolt in the center of the spring enables you to line up the spring with the hole in the middle of the axle mount. When the spring lines up properly, push the front part of the spring into the mount and slide in the bolt. Tighten it a few turns. Now line up the rear shackle and spring and push home its bolt.

Step 9. Attach U-Bolts and Shocks.

Position the spring mounting plate and push the U-bolts up through it so the U part of the bolts fits around the axle. Screw on the nuts and torque them to 40 NM (30 ft. lbs.)

Next, pull down the shock absorber and position it in its comfy mount. Install the bottom bolt and torque it to 40 Nm (30 ft. lbs.)

Step 10. Secure Springs.

When you have performed all the above steps on both sides of the suspension, remove the jack stands and lower the vehicle until the springs begin to flex. The wheels will be on the ground. Torque the bolts holding the rear part of the spring to the shackle to 60 Nm (44 ft. lbs.). Remember to do the top and bottom bolts. Now torque the front bolt to 95 Nm (70 ft. lbs.). Do both springs.

Step 11. Finish Off.

If you want more room to work, jack up the truck again and block it well. This step isn't vital, but I like room to breathe. Attach the parking brake cable to its little clamp atop each spring (13mm bolt). Secure the cable to the spring with a plastic telephone cable clamp or some plastic electrical tape.

Reattach the exhaust system if you removed it and hook it to the underbody hooks with new rubber hangers (if you ruined them during removal). Use a new exhaust gasket if you unhooked the pipe from the header (**non-U.S. vehicles**). Tighten the exhaust clamp or three 13mm bolts. That's all folks.

279   All models (Add to Step 6)

The seven little bolts that hold the water pump halves together have a nasty habit of snapping if you try to twist them off. They seem to corrode easily since they live in such a hostile environment. Squirt some

WD-40 (or the like) onto the back of the bolts and have a pint of beer while the squirts do their stuff.

When you come back to work, remove the bolts as if they were made of glass and slooowly twist them out. A bit of rocking back-and-forth helps a lot. If one (or more) refuse to budge, give the rear another squirt then tap the head of the bolt to shock some sense into it. If you do break one even after this dire warning, then once the pump is off, remove the broken bolt with an easy out or get a machine shop to do it for you. Buy new bolts from VW when it's time to bolt the two pump halves back together again.

87   **All '75 to '82 vehicles (Add to end of Step 1)**

If you need to replace the heater control wire (that's the wire that runs from the lower heater control lever in the dash to the heater valve in the upper heater hose near the firewall under the hood), first remove the radio or glove box (see illustration on page 78).

Unhook the old cable from the heater valve by removing the clip that holds the cable housing onto the valve. Use a screwdriver to get the clip off. Now unhook the end of the old cable from the valve. Check that the valve opens and closes properly. If not, buy and install a new valve. Take your new cable and hook the valve-end of the cable to the heater valve then thread the new cable through the firewall and up over the steering column under the dash. Slide the heater control all the way to the left (the off position). Remove the two screws at the bottom of the lever assembly near the edge of the dash; that allows you to wriggle the lever assembly about a bit. Remove the clip that holds the cable housing onto the lever assembly then un-hook the L-shaped end of the old cable from the lever. If you can't get the old cable unhooked easily, cut the wire and just pull it out of there.

Thread the new cable up into position behind the lever assembly and stick the end of the new cable into the hole on the end of the lever. If that seems impossible, unhook the two upper cables from their levers to get more room to twist and shout. Once that lower cable is in place, re-install the other two loose cables and secure them with the clips. Leave about 1/2 in of cable housing sticking out of the clip then move the heater control lever back and forth to check that the heater valve in the engine compartment is opening/closing OK. Adjust the position of the cable in its clip, if needed, then put everything back as it was.

Page   **Model & Year**   **Location**

288   **'80 and on vehicles (Add to Procedure 5)**

These later models have a system of levers and vacuum hoses to open and close the various flaps and controls. The only cable-actuated control is the heater valve located in the heater hose inside the engine compartment. To repair a non-functioning heater, first start the engine and move the upper lever in dash and listen for a 'swish' of vacuum. If there's no sound, check the vacuum reservoir on the underside of the hood. The hose is probably broken or has fallen off. If that's not your trouble, remove the levers and fan knob from the heater controls (they just pull out) and carefully lever out the plastic panel. That action reveals the controls of the heater. Check all the vacuum lines, especially the vacuum distribution valve on the right corner of the heater control assembly. If you patiently follow all the hoses to and from the valve you'll eventually find your problem. I've only seen one broken valve but it's easily removed and replaced.

379   **All Models   (Replace paragraph "Using Jumper Cables")**

Using Jumper Cables:

Keep the Samaritan's engine running and use one jumper cable to connect the positive terminals on the two batteries. Now hook the other cable to the negative terminal on your friend's car but onto a clean metal ground on your car, **not** the negative terminal. Check your work and start your car. As soon as your car's engine bursts into life, take off the jumper cables and thank your helper kindly.

381   **'80 on Diesel only   (Insert just before Procedure 1)**

A number of changes—most of them good—have improved the diesel engine, making it more reliable and quicker to start. Here are a few of the general ones.

The drive belt guard is held on in the same manner as the gasoline engine version, but **1980/81 models** had a phillips screw holding the right side of the guard (closest to the firewall) to the engine. It's murder to get off and on, so, if you have to remove the guard, when you re-install it, replace that screw with a short 10mm bolt. (the same size holding on the rest of the guard). It'll be a lot easier to work with in the future.

The upshift light's electrical connections are mounted on the fuel pump. They're easily disconnected should you need to do so.

Electrical grounding has been improved by the addition of another ground strap from the battery negative cable to the left fender. It's easy to get at from underneath the car.

The CV joints for 1982 and on are attached to the drive shaft by a new type of bolt. See the Phase 2 tool list in Chapter 4.

If you are having starting problems, use a VOM to test each glow plug individually. Sometimes the glow plugs stay on far too long and burn out quickly. If you have your injectors out you can visually check the glow plugs by turning on the ignition, pulling out the glow knob and looking into the hole that held the injectors. Test them with the VOM, as well as with your eye. If you use a cold starting fluid to get old "oil burner" going in the morning, your glow plugs will die an early death.

Here's some great suggestions from William Fetcher. Thanx William.

To check if the glow plugs stay on too long (red glow light on dash stays illuminated), pull out the glow plug relay from the relay plate (It's on the extreme right of the plate). The glow light will go out when the relay is pulled. If you can't get to the dealer for a new relay, next time you want to start the car, plug the relay back in, start the engine, and remove the relay once the engine has fired up. Buy a new one as soon as you have the $$$$.

You can tell if your early model (primer pump on the filter housing) fuel lines are blocked by ice, junk, etc., if the primer knob is sucked into its housing. Buy some new fuel line and change the filter.

Page	Model & Year	Location

The diesel's rubber fuel by-pass lines are a weak point in an otherwise sound design. These rubber tubes collect excess fuel that's been used to lubricate and cool the injectors and return it to the tank. They are prone to cracking and leaking due to heat and age. You can tell when one has let go—you can smell fuel leaking down the hot engine block. Should the radiator cooling fan kick in, there's no mistaking it when a hot, diesel- 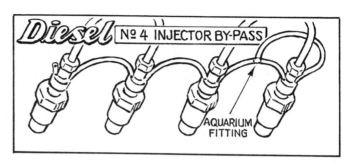 smelling draft hits you as you step out of the car. Keep a length of replacement tubing in the car at all times. You can get it at VW. As for that rubber cap on the unused nipple, #4 injector, the following trick will save trips to the dealer for replacement caps. At a pet store, buy a small T-fitting used to connect air hoses for tropical fish tanks. Fit two lengths of tube to the injector nipples of #4 injector and connect them to your T-fitting. The remaining nipple on the T-fitting will be connected with #3 injector as before. See diagram.

For those of you who live in cold climates I recommend an engine block heater. It fits into the middle freeze plug under the exhaust manifold. Mine is made by GE for VW of Canada.

Once last summer while driving in a heavy downpour, wipers, headlights and heater blower, at one time going full blast, shut off at once. No fuses blown or wires burned out. Pulling back the headlight dimmer switch (on the steering column) would set everything roaring and flashing to life. I got home safely and began tracing the wiring. All the above circuits pass through the ignition switch which apparently couldn't handle the load. Its housing had melted, allowing the contacts to separate—opening the cirucit. Replacement switch about $18.00

VW puts out an excellent pamphlet on the diesel engine called ''Diesel Fuel Injection'' Course # 4.06VW Cat # 420078751 which is an excellent reference sourse.

Finally, if your diesel suddenly quits on you, replace the stop solenoid. That'll fix it every time (I hope).

383   All Diesels Only   Procedure 2, Step 4

Should read Procedure 6.

391   Add to the beginning of Step 1

Lift the hood and look on the engine side of the firewall for a little black plastic box. Lever the box open and check the state of the 50 amp fuse contained therein. If it's broken, the diesel will never start unless you replace the fuse. Buy three and keep two in the glove box. Make sure that the ignition is turned off before you replace the fractured fuse; then, once installed, start the engine. Everything fine and dandy?

Index to Illustrations

A Story...

ONE crisp September morning, the wayward Illustrator was wending his weary way home.

Having been falsely fortified by Kountless Kups of Kourtesy Koffee generously supplied by various airlines and braced again by breathing the brisk morning breeze, he reclaimed the Rabbit at the parking lot and found the road north to Santa Fe.

The sun shook itself free from the mountains and mists, pinking out to a brief golden burst and slowly faded to flat whiteness which flashed off the shoulders of the long, straight, shadowless highway, contrasting gently with the ribbon of black, the hiss of tires, the...ZZZ ZZZZZZZZZZZZZZZZZZZZZZZZZZZZZZZZZZZZZZZZzzzzzzzzzzzzzzzzzzzzzzzzzzzzzzzzzzzzzzzzzzzzzzzzzzzz.

The ear awakens first, alerted perhaps by the crunch of gravel as the right front tire seeks relief from the awful monotony, the hands and elbows swing briefly into action, and the careening car executes a few clever capers, awakening the eyes which look on with some considerable astonishment as the speeding rodent drops off the highway and continues its journey down a rock strewn arroyo. All members attempt to jog the mind into action to deal with this awesome situation but it looks on bemusedly, overwhelmed by the quickly shifting scenery like moving day at the furniture factory. □ □ ◇ ◇ □ □ ⟨·⟨·⟨·

And yet an attempt is made to control the madly careening vehicle. The Illustrator grips the wheel and pretends to drive, but the tires continue to seek each its own path down the rock and rubble; and an earthen embankment, closing off the mouth of the arroyo, is approaching head-on, at a high rate of speed. ☆☆☆

A last moment of grandeur for the badly bruised bunny as it responds at last to the wheel...climbs nimbly up the right bank and clears the obstacle. And here, at the high point of its last graceful arc, momentum is at last overcome. Slowed down by rubble, debris and blown tires, combined with the steep angle of ascent, the battered Rabbit flips at last to play out the remainder of its journey sledding down the (fortunately) sandy gully on its roof and coming to a stop in a shower of brush, sand, and beer cans only when the top edge of the windshield finds a rock large enough to stop it. ★★

Out of the growing silence the radio still plays the same monotonous tune that had helped lull the weary traveler to sleep in the first place. The Illustrator turns this off along with the ignition, in his befuddlement he carefully pockets the key before opening the door, giving his first shaky Thanks and emerging into the beautiful clear morning. ☆☆☆☆☆☆☆☆☆☆☆☆☆☆☆☆☆☆☆☆☆☆☆☆☆☆☆☆☆☆☆☆☆☆

A few things of interest were discovered after this final test drive: ◎ The vulnerable oil pan, the bane of off-road rabbiting suffered nary a dent and lost no oil. It all came out the dipstick hole and oil filler cap. ◎ The vulnerable Illustrator was pleased to discover that his number was not up and that his injuries consisted of; one small scrape on L. side of nose; one bruise on R. shin bone; slight backache and strong smell about him of carbon which persisted for some days. ◎ The bottles fore and aft containing spare water and oil were neither one broken and held their contents. ◎ The Illustrator's spectacles were totalled. (It took him some time to discover he wasn't wearing them). ◎ Top center of the windshield was shattered by encounter with rock, but retained its integrity. No other window was damaged ◎ L. front fender and accordian frame structure collapsed according to VW's consumer protection plan. Right rear panel was similarly damaged and driver's side door took two men and a boy to open it. Other door operated normally. ◎ Hood and hatch both battered but remained closed. ◎ Under-structure—hmmmmmm...looked pretty bad. ◎ The field was liberally strewn with tiny plastic body strips, hubcaps, nut covers, etc. ◎ The roof looked pretty good. ◎ The driver's seat was flattened like a couch with the seatback planted firmly into the rear seat cushion, allowing room for the driver to finish his ride on hands and knees on the Rabbit's ceiling. Two men and a boy were unable to straigten it. ◎ As of last word, the engine and transmission will go into powering a Scirocco. Other parts will go into a platoon of other Rabbits and the old brown chassis shall either be converted into a '76 hatchback chicken coop, or will, in time, become another small bulwark against the relentlessly blowing sands of the high desert. BABZ!Z!☆XMBLAZZMMXXXXBZ END

Index

-G-

- H -

- I -

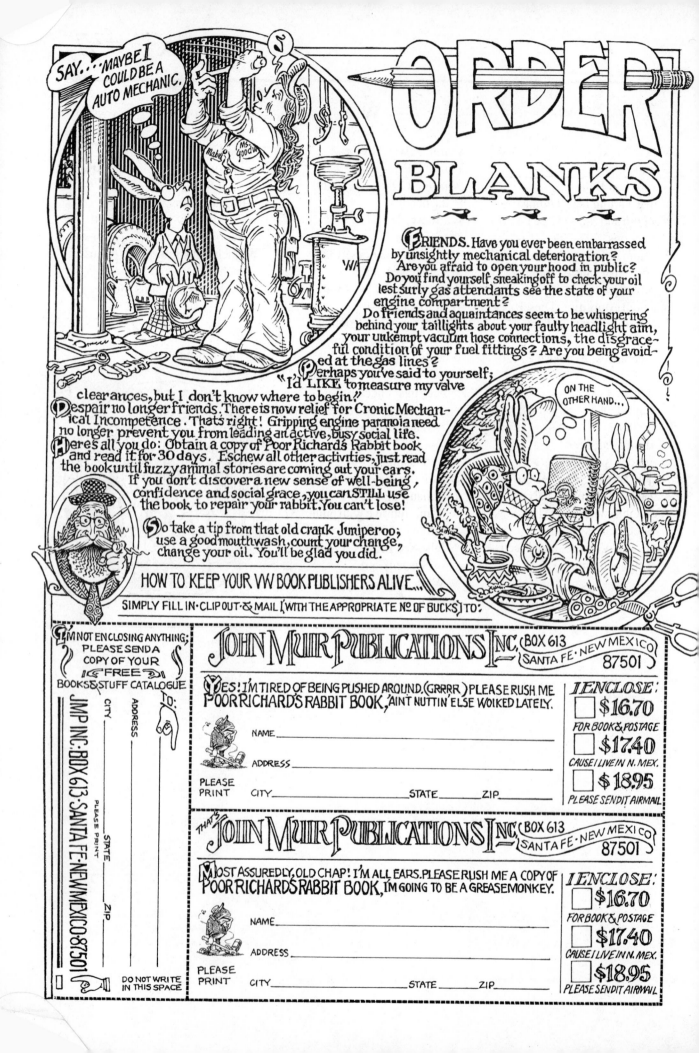

ORDER BLANKS

SAY... MAYBE I COULD BE A AUTO MECHANIC.

FRIENDS. Have you ever been embarrassed by unsightly mechanical deterioration? Are you afraid to open your hood in public? Do you find yourself sneaking off to check your oil lest surly gas attendants see the state of your engine compartment?

Do friends and aquaintances seem to be whispering behind your taillights about your faulty headlight aim, your unkempt vacuum hose connections, the disgraceful condition of your fuel fittings? Are you being avoided at the gas lines?

Perhaps you've said to yourself; "I'd LIKE to measure my valve clearances, but I don't know where to begin."

Despair no longer friends. There is now relief for Cronic Mechanical Incompetence. That's right! Gripping engine paranoia need no longer prevent you from leading an active, busy social life.

Here's all you do: Obtain a copy of Poor Richard's Rabbit book and read it for 30 days. Eschew all other activities, just read the book until fuzzy animal stories are coming out your ears.

If you don't discover a new sense of well-being, confidence and social grace, you can STILL use the book to repair your rabbit. You can't lose!

So take a tip from that old crank Juniperoo; use a good mouthwash, count your change, change your oil. You'll be glad you did.

ON THE OTHER HAND...

HOW TO KEEP YOUR VW BOOK PUBLISHERS ALIVE...

SIMPLY FILL IN · CLIP OUT · & MAIL (WITH THE APPROPRIATE Nº OF BUCKS) TO:

I'M NOT ENCLOSING ANYTHING; PLEASE SEND A COPY OF YOUR FREE BOOKS & STUFF CATALOGUE

TO:
CITY
ADDRESS
JMP INC: BOX 613 · SANTA FE · NEW MEXICO · 87501
PLEASE PRINT
STATE
ZIP
DO NOT WRITE IN THIS SPACE

JOHN MUIR PUBLICATIONS Inc. BOX 613 SANTA FE · NEW MEXICO 87501

YES! I'M TIRED OF BEING PUSHED AROUND. (GRRRR.) PLEASE RUSH ME POOR RICHARD'S RABBIT BOOK, AIN'T NUTTIN' ELSE WOIKED LATELY.

NAME

ADDRESS

PLEASE PRINT   CITY _____ STATE _____ ZIP _____

I ENCLOSE:
☐ $16.70 FOR BOOK & POSTAGE
☐ $17.40 CAUSE I LIVE IN N. MEX.
☐ $18.95 PLEASE SEND IT AIRMAIL

THAT'S JOHN MUIR PUBLICATIONS Inc. BOX 613 SANTA FE · NEW MEXICO 87501

MOST ASSUREDLY, OLD CHAP! I'M ALL EARS. PLEASE RUSH ME A COPY OF POOR RICHARD'S RABBIT BOOK, I'M GOING TO BE A GREASEMONKEY.

NAME

ADDRESS

PLEASE PRINT   CITY _____ STATE _____ ZIP _____

I ENCLOSE:
☐ $16.70 FOR BOOK & POSTAGE
☐ $17.40 CAUSE I LIVE IN N. MEX.
☐ $18.95 PLEASE SEND IT AIRMAIL

Distributor point gap	0.40mm (.016 in)
Distributor point dwell	44°-50° new points 42°-58° wear limit
Idle r.p.m.	850-1000
Ignition timing conventional distributor (points)	3° after TDC at 850 to 1000 rpm with the vacuum hoses connected and the digital idle stabilizer disconnected.
Ignition timing breakerless distributor (no points)	Carburetor engine: 7.5° before TDC at 850 to 1000 rpm; digital idle stabilizer disconnected, vacuum advance hose connected, and vacuum retard hose disconnected and plugged up.
	Fuel injection engine, except Pick-up Truck sold outside California: 3° after TDC at 850 to 1000 rpm; digital idle stabilizer disconnected and plugged up.
	Fuel injection engine for Pick-up Truck sold outside California: 3° after TDC at 850 to 1000 rpm; vacuum hoses connected.
Spark plug type	1975, 1976 Bosch W200T30 Champ N8Y 1977 Bosch W215T30 Champ N7Y 1978, 1979 Bosch W175T30 Champ N8Y Bronze Edition: Bosch W175T30 Champ N6Y
Spark plug type (1980)	Vehicles sold in the US: Champion N-8GY, Bosch WR 7DS, Beru RS-35 Vehicles sold in Canada: Champion N-10Y, Bosch W 8D or W 145 T30, Beru 14-8D or 145/14/3A
Spark plug type (1981 and on)	Vehicles sold in the US (except California): Champion N-8Y, Bosch W 7D or W 175 T30, Beru 14-7D or 175/14/3A Vehicles sold in California: Champion N-8GY, Bosch WR 7DS, Beru RS-35 Vehicles sold in Canada (normal service): Champion N-8Y, Bosch W 7D or W 175 T30, Beru 14-7D or 175/14/3A Vehicles sold in Canada (primarily short trips): Champion N-10Y, Bosch W 8D or W 145 T30, Beru 14-8D or 145/14/3A
Spark plug gap	0.60mm−0.70mm (.024 in—.028 in)
Firing order	1-3-4-2; #1 cylinder at front of engine
Oil capacity with filter change (pre-1981)	3.5 litres (3.7 U.S. qts., 3.2 Imp. qts.)
Oil capacity without filter change (pre-1981)	3.0 litres (3.2 U.S. qts., 2.6 Imp. qts.)
Oil capacity with filter change (1981 and on)	4.5 litres (4.7 U.S. qts., 3.9 Imp. qts.)
Oil capacity without filter change (1981 and on)	4.0 litres (4.2 U.S. qts., 3.5 Imp. qts.)

Note: some 1981 vehicles were fitted with an early model oil pan so the pre-1981 oil capacity specs relate to them. Check the dipstick before you add the final quart!

Valve clearances cold		Intake 0.15mm−0.25mm (.006 in−.010 in) Exhaust 0.35mm−0.45mm (.014 in−.018 in)
Gas engine compression pressure at sea level		$10-13$ kg/cm^2 ($142-184$ psi) Deduct 0.14 kg/cm^2 (2 psi) per 1000 ft of altitude
Maximum difference between adjacent cylinders		3.0 kg/cm^2 (42 psi)
Diesel engine compression pressure at sea level		$28-34$ kg/cm^2 ($398-483$ psi) Deduct 0.14 kg/cm^2 (2 psi) per 1000 ft of altitude
Maximum difference between adjacent cylinders		5 kg/cm^2 (71 psi)
Tire pressures	normal load	1.90kg/cm^2 (27 psi)
	heavy load	Add 0.21 kg/cm^2 (3 psi) to rear tires